HUTCHINSON

LOADS
of LISTS

Helicon Publishing Ltd
3rd Floor
Clarendon House
Shoe Lane
Oxford OX1 2DP
United Kingdom
E-mail: admin@helicon.co.uk
Web site: http//www.helicon.co.uk

First published 2001
Reprinted 2001

ISBN: 1-85986-360-4

British Library Cataloguing in Publication Data
A catalogue record for this book is available from the British Library.

Typeset by TechType, Abingdon, Oxon
Printed and bound in England by
Cox & Wyman, Reading, Berkshire

Contents

The Lists

Art and Literature

Stage and Screen

Music

Science and Technology

Health and the Human Body

Animals, Plants, and the Environment

People, History, and Society

Geography and Transport

Sport, Games, and Leisure

Introduction

Loads of Lists is intended to amuse, excite, and entertain as much as inform the reader. A huge range of subjects is covered, from the serious to the seriously wacky, from the biggest volcanic explosions to the countries that eat the most fish. The selection of subjects is designed to appeal to everyone who is fascinated by the surprising as well as the famous aspects of the world – from remarkable bridges to pop music.

In order to avoid scattering lists on a similar theme throughout the book in a purely alphabetical structure, the lists have been split into sections. This means that all the lists about a similar subject will be found in the same part of the book. The placing of the lists into these thematic sections is intended to help the reader who is interested in a particular subject. However, many lists could have been placed in a number of different sections (for example lists about film soundtracks are in the Music section, but could equally well have been placed in the Stage and Screen section). A full contents list is provided to help readers to find all related lists throughout the book.

The sections in the book are very broad groupings of subject, so, for example, the Art and Literature section includes lists about language and literary mythology, the Stage and Screen section includes dance, theatre, cinema, and television, and the Science and Technology includes architecture, buildings, and Earth sciences. Every list has been given a short, eye-catching title for ease of reference and the lists are arranged in alphabetical order by title within each section.

Although it contains hundreds of facts and figures, researched from the most up to date and reliable sources, *Loads of Lists* is intended to be a book for browsing. It is hoped that part of the enjoyment of the book will come from happening upon the unexpected and that each list will draw the reader on to the next.

Acknowledgements

CONTRIBUTORS

Robin Batchelor-Smith
Julian Beecroft
Peter Blair
Gerry Brisch
John O E Clark
Andrew Colquhoun
Chris Cooper
William Gould
Louise Hutchinson
Carolyn Newton
Emma Pearse
Kath Pilgrem
Bernard Simon

EDITORIAL

EDITORIAL DIRECTOR
Hilary McGlynn

DEPUTY EDITORIAL DIRECTOR
Roger Tritton

PROJECT EDITOR
Fran Alexander

TECHNICAL PROJECT EDITOR
Stuart Brown

PROJECT MANAGING EDITOR
John O E Clark

SCREEN EDITORS
Andrew Bacon
John Barnes
Sarah Jordan
Tracey Kifford
Pete Lewis
Kath Pilgrem
Bernard Simon

EDITORIAL ASSISTANTS
Elizabeth Whiting
Georgina Giraldi

DATABASE AND COMPUTER SYSTEMS
Tracey Auden
Lorraine Cotterell
Claire Lishman
Rachel Margolis

DESIGN AND PRODUCTION

PRODUCTION MANAGER
John Normansell

PRODUCTION CONTROLLER
Stacey Penny

DESIGN AND TYPOGRAPHY
Stephen Strong

Art
and
Literature

African Words
Used in English

banana
banjo
basenji
chimpanzee
cola
guinea
harmattan
hoodoo
impi
juju
kwashiorkor
marimba
mau-mau
mumbo jumbo
nagana
okra
tango
tote
voodoo
yam
zombie

American Indian Words
Used in English

avocado
barbecue
cannibal
canoe
capybara
caribou
cashew
caucus
cayman
chilli
chipmunk
chocolate
cocoa
coyote
coypu
curare
hammock
hickory
hurricane
igloo

ipecacuanha
jaguar
kayak
llama
maize
moccasin
moose
muskeg
musquash
opossum
papaya
papoose
pampas
parka
pemmican
petunia
peyote
piranha
poncho
puma

quetzal
quinine
raccoon
rumba
sequoia
skunk
tamarack
tanager
tapioca
tapir
terrapin
tobacco
toboggan
tomahawk
tomato
totem
toucan
wampum
wapiti
wigwam

American Words
Used in British English

bluff (cliff)
blurb
bobcat
bootlegging
bunkum
caboodle
caucus
commuter
cowhand
freight

gerrymander
gimmick
hobo
jive
know-how
lifestyle
loafers
lunch
maverick
motel

panties
popcorn
prairie
stagecoach
steamboat
stetson
stunt
teenager
tuxedo
Yank

Arabic Words
Used in English

alfalfa	dhow	jihad	mufti	sirocco
arsenal	djellaba	kasbah	mullah	soda
assassin	douane	kismet	muslin	sofa
burnous	elixir	Koran	nadir	sultan
cadi	fakir	lemon	oasis	sultana
camphor	fatwa	lime (fruit)	popinjay	sumac
candy	fez	loofah	pumper	syrup
carafe	gain	lute	quintal	tabby
carat	gazelle	magazine	racket	talisman
caraway	giraffe	marabou	realgar	tamarind
carboy	ghoul	mask	safari	tarboosh
carmine	haik	mattress	saffron	tare
carob	harem	minaret	saker	tariff
checkmate	hazard	mocha	saluki	vizier
cipher	henna	mohair	sash	wadi
cotton	hookah	monsoon	sequin	yashmak
crimson	howdah	mosque	shawl	zenith
cypher	jar	muezzin	sheikh	zero

Art
Early European Art Galleries and Museums

Year	Gallery/museum	Location
1683	Ashmolean Museum	Oxford, England
1734	Capitoline Museum	Rome, Italy
1759	British Museum	London, England
1785	Prado (opened fully 1819)	Madrid, Spain
1793	Louvre	Paris, France
1800	Huis ten Bosch Gallery	The Hague, Netherlands
1824	National Gallery (moved to Trafalgar Square in 1938)	London, England
1830	Gallery of Art	Berlin, Germany
1836	Gallery of Art	Munich, Germany
1852	Hermitage	St Petersburg, Russia

Art

Stolen Paintings

Painter(s)	Title(s)	Scene of crime	Year
Cézanne	*Auvers-sur-Oise*	Ashmolean Museum, Oxford, UK	2000
Picasso	*Bust of a Woman* (Dora Maar)	yacht *Coral Island* at Antibes, France	1999
Rembrandt	*Child with Soap Bubbles*	Draguignan Museum, France	1999
Chagall; Jawlensky; Matisse; Renoir; Valtat	various	Zurich Art Gallery, Switzerland	1997
Titian; Veronese	*Rest on the Flight to Egypt; Personification of Justice*	Longleat House, UK	1995
J M W Turner	*Shade and Darkness; Light and Colour*	Schirn Kunsthalle, Frankfurt, Germany	1994
Picasso; Braque	various	Museum of Modern Art, Stockholm, Sweden	1993
Vermeer; Rembrandt	*The Concert; Storm on the Sea of Galilee*	Gardner Museum, Boston, USA	1990
Bonnard; Boudin; Dufy; Marquet; Renoir; Vuillard	various	Bagnols-sur-Cèze Town Hall, France	1972
Brueghel; Corot; Courbet; Daumier; Delacroix; Gainsborough; Heem; Millet; Penna; Piezzetta; Rubens; Van Gogh	various	Museum of Fine Art, Montreal, Canada	1972
Caravaggio	*Nativity with St Francis and St Lawrence*	Oratorio de San Lorenzo, Italy	1969
Van Gogh – 18 paintings[1]	various	various	various
Van Gogh	*The Painter on His Way to Tarascon*	vanished (possibly looted)	unknown

[1] One painting confiscated by the Nazis in 1937, one stolen in 1989, one possibly stolen in 1944, and one last seen for sale in Paris exhibition at Galerie Schmitt in 1994.

Art
Works of Early Domestic Art

Location	Title	Date
Palatine Hill, Rome	*The House of the Griffin*	100 BC
Prima Porte, Rome	*The Villa Albus*	30 BC
Pompeii	*The House of the Floral Chambers*	1st century BC
Egypt	*The Fayum Memorial Portraits*	1st to 2nd century AD

Artists
'The Eight'

Name	Birthplace	Life dates
Arthur B Davies	Utica, NY	1862–1928
William Glackens	Philadelphia, PA	1870–1938
Robert Henri	Cincinnati, OH	1865–1929
Ernest Lawson	San Francisco, CA	1873–1939
George Luks	Philadelphia, PA	1867–1933
Maurice Prendergast	St John's, NF	1861–1924
Everett Shinn	Philadelphia, PA	1876–1953
John Sloan	Lock Haven, PA	1871–1951

Artists
Interesting Facts

Artist	Life dates	Fact
El Greco	1548–1614	his real name was Domenikos Theotocopoulos
Paul Klee	1879–1940	the Nazis in Germany confiscated 102 of his paintings as being 'degenerate'
Leonardo da Vinci	1459–1519	he wrote 'backwards' (in mirror image)
Michelangelo	1475–1564	his full name was Michelangelo di Lodovico Buonarroti Simoni
Claude Monet	1840–1926	he had to cease painting when he went blind
Rembrandt	1606–1669	his real name was Harmensz Van Rijn
Tintoretto	1518–1594	his *Paradise* is the world's largest oil painting
Titian	1487–1576	he died during an epidemic of bubonic plague
Henri de Toulouse-Lautrec	1864–1901	he was crippled in his teens in two separate accidents that broke both his legs
Vincent van Gogh	1853–1890	he cut off his ear and later shot himself

Authors
Famous Authors and their Pseudonyms

Real name	Pseudonym	Real name	Pseudonym
François-Marie Arouet (1694–1778)	Voltaire	Charles Lamb (1775–1834)	Elia
Eric Blair (1903–1950)	George Orwell	Charles Leland (1825–1903)	Hans Breitmann
Samuel Clemens (1835–1910)	Mark Twain	Hector Munro (1870–1916)	Saki
Charles Dickens (1812–1870)	Boz	Violet Paget (1856–1935)	Vernon Lee
Charles Dodgson (1832–1898)	Lewis Carroll	Alexey Peshkov (1868–1936)	Maxim Gorky
Amandine Dudevant (1804–1876)	George Sand	William Porter (1862–1910)	O Henry
Mary Ann Evans (1819–1880)	George Eliot	Frederick Rolfe (1860–1913)	Baron Corvo
Benjamin Franklin (1706–1790)	Poor Richard		

Baldwin
Principal Works of James Baldwin

Title	Year	Title	Year
Go Tell It on the Mountain	1953	Tell Me How Long the Train's Been Gone	1968
Notes of a Native Son	1955	One Day, When I was Lost	1972
Giovanni's Room	1956	If Beale Street Could Talk	1974
Nobody Knows My Name: More Notes of a Native Son	1961	A Deed from the King of Spain	1974
Another Country	1962	The Devil Finds Work	1976
Blues for Mr Charlie	1964	Just Above My Head	1979
Going to Meet the Man	1965	The Evidence of Things Not Seen: An Essay	1985
The Amen Corner	1965	Jimmy's Blues	1986

Beckett
Principal Works of Samuel Beckett

Dates given are for a work's first appearance in English.

Work	Type	Year	Work	Type	Year
Whoroscope	poetry	1930	Waiting for Godot	play	1955
More Pricks than Kicks	short stories	1934	Malone Dies	novel	1956
Murphy	novel	1938	All That Fall	play	1957
Watt	novel	1953	The Unnameable	novel	1958
Molloy	novel	1955	Krapp's Last Tape	play	1958

Beckett: Principal Works of Samuel Beckett (*continued*)

Work	Type	Year	Work	Type	Year
Endgame	play	1958	*Come and Go*	play	1966
Embers	play	1959	*Breathe*	play	1970
How It Is	novel	1961	*Not I*	play	1972
Happy Days	play	1961	*Footfalls*	play	1976
Play	play	1963	*Stirrings Still*	play	1989

Bellow
Principal Works of Fiction by Saul Bellow

Title	Year	Title	Year
Dangling Man	1944	*Humboldt's Gift*	1975
The Victim	1947	*The Dean's December*	1983
The Adventures of Augie March	1953	*Him with His Foot in His Mouth and Other Short Stories*	1984
Seize the Day	1956		
Henderson the Rain King	1959	*More Die of Heartbreak*	1987
Herzog	1964	*Something to Remember Me By*	1993
Mosby's Memoirs and Other Stories	1968	*The Actual*	1998
Mr Sammler's Planet	1970	*Ravelstein*	2000

Booker Prize Winners

The Booker Prize is the UK's most prestigious literary prize.

Year	Winner	Awarded for
1991	Ben Okri	*The Famished Road*
1992	Barry Unsworth	*Sacred Hunger*
	Michael Ondaatje	*The English Patient*
1993	Roddy Doyle	*Paddy Clarke Ha Ha Ha*
1994	James Kelman	*How Late It Was, How Late*
1995	Pat Barker	*The Ghost Road*
1996	Graham Swift	*Last Orders*
1997	Arundhati Roy	*The God of Small Things*
1998	Ian McEwan	*Amsterdam*
1999	J M Coetzee	*Disgrace*
2000	Margaret Atwood	*The Blind Assassin*

Booker Prize
Winners Adapted for Television or Cinema

Title	Author	Winning year
Heat and Dust (film)	Ruth Prawer Jhabvala	1975
Staying On (TV)	Paul Scott	1977
Schindler's Ark (film) [1]	Thomas Keneally	1982
Hotel du Lac (TV)	Anita Brookner	1984
Oscar and Lucinda (film)	Peter Carey	1988
The Remains of the Day (film)	Kazuo Ishiguro	1989
Possession (film)	A S Byatt	1990
The English Patient (film)	Michael Ondaatje	1992
Paddy Clark Ha Ha Ha (TV)	Roddy Doyle	1993

[1] Now *Schindler's List*.

Books
Countries that Publish Most Books

Country	Number of titles
China	110,300
UK	107,300
Germany	71,500
USA	68,200
Japan	56,200
Spain	46,300
Russian Federation	36,200
Italy	35,200
France (1995)	34,800
South Korea	30,500

Books
Famous Books Written in Prison

Book title	Date	Author and nationality
Le Morte d'Arthur	1470	Thomas Malory (English)
Don Quixote	1597	Miguel de Cervantes (Spanish)
History of the World	1614	Walter Raleigh (English)
Pilgrim's Progress	1678	John Bunyan (English)
Fanny Hill	1750	John Cleland (English)
Ballad of Reading Gaol	1898	Oscar Wilde (Irish)
Mein Kampf	1923	Adolf Hitler (German)
India and the World	1936	Jawaharlal Nehru (Indian)

Books

Highest Prices Paid for Books and Manuscripts at Auction

As of May 2000.

Work	Date of sale	Price (US$)
The Codex Leicester, Leonardo da Vinci's autographed manuscript	11 November 1994	30,802,500
The Rothschild Prayerbook, illuminated manuscript	8 July 1999	13,400,000
The Gospels of Henry the Lion, 12th-century illuminated manuscript	6 December 1983	11,000,920
John James Audubon's *The Birds of America* (1827–38)	10 March 2000	8,800,000
Chaucer's *Canterbury Tales* (printed by William Caxton c.1476)	8 July 1998	7,565,396
The Northumberland Bestiary (c.1250–60)	29 November 1990	5,900,000
The Gutenberg Bible (1455)	22 October 1987	5,390,000
The Cornaro Missal (c.1503)	8 July 1999	4,461,078
autographed manuscript of nine symphonies by Wolfgang Amadeus Mozart (c.1773–74)	22 May 1987	4,316,950
John James Audubon's *The Birds of America* (1827–38) (resold later, see above)	6 June 1989	3,960,000

Books

Major Reprinted Titles

Title	Author	Number of copies
The Bible	various translations	over 6,000,000,000
Little Red Book	Mao Zedong (Mao Tse Tung) (1893–1976)	over 800,000,000
Eclectic Readers (*The McGuffey Readers*)	William Holmes McGuffey (1800–1873)	up to 122,000,000
A Grammatical Institute of the English Language (*Webster's Spelling Book,* or *American Spelling Book*)	Noah Webster (1758–1843)	100,000,000
The Guinness Book of Records	–	79,000,000
A Message to Garcia	Elbert Hubbard (1856–1915)	up to 50,000,000
The World Almanac	–	over 40,000,000
The Common Sense Book of Baby and Child Care	Benjamin Spock (1903–1998)	over 39,200,000
The Valley of the Dolls	Jacqueline Susann (c.1926–1974)	30,000,000
In His Steps: What Would Jesus Do?	Charles Monroe Sheldon (1857–1946)	28,500,000

Books
The Longest in English 1980–2000

Number of pages	Book	Author published	Year
1,492	*Les Miserables*	Victor Hugo	1988 (republished)
1,246	*The Power Broker: Robert Moses and the Fall of New York*	Robert A Caro	1992
1,117	*Truman*	David G Mcullough	2000
1,084	*Atlas Shrugged*	Ayn Rand	1993
1,079	*Infinite Jest: a Novel*	David Foster Wallace	1996
1,071	*The Powers That Be*	David Halberstam	1990
1,064	*Parting the Waters: America in the King Years*	Taylor Branch	1998
1,043	*The Witching Hour*	Anne Rice	1995
981	*Liberty and Sexuality: the Right to Privacy and the Making of Roe v. Wade*	David G Garrow	1994
886	*The Making of the Atomic Bomb*	Richard Rhodes	1993
885	*The Prize: the Epic Quest for Oil, Money and Power*	Daniel Yergin	1993
882	*The Path to Power*	Robert A Caro	1994

Books
World's Best-selling Authors of 2000

Fiction

John Grisham
Jerry B Jenkins and Tim LaHaye
Tom Clancy
Patricia Cornwall
Danielle Steele

Non-fiction

Spencer Johnson
Guinness World Records Ltd
Bill Phillips
Mitch Albom
The Beatles

Celtic Words
Used in English

English	Celtic origin
bin (container)	Celtic (O E binne)
brill (fish)	Cornish brythel
dolmen (tomb)	Cornish tolmen
hog (pig)	Celtic (O E hogg)
menhir (standing stone)	Breton men hir

Censorship
Banned Books and when Ban Was Lifted

Author	Title	Details
James Joyce	*Ulysses* (1922)	banned in the USA until 1933
	The Bible, and the Koran	banned from import in Soviet Union 1926–56
John Locke	*An Essay Concerning Human Understanding* (1790)	on the Papal Index until 1951
D H Lawrence	*Lady Chatterley's Lover* (1928)	not published in its original form in the USA until 1959 and in the UK until 1960
François Voltaire	*Lettres Philosophiques sur les Anglais* (1734)	burned
	Dictionaire Philosophique (1764)	burned and banned in France
Ernest Hemingway	*A Farewell to Arms* (1929)	banned in Italy in 1929
Pierre Abelard	*The Letters of Abelard and Heloise* (12th century)	US customs ban on importation until 1930
Galilei Galileo	*Dialogues on the Two Chief Systems of the World* (1632)	placed on the Papal Index
John Calvin	*Institutes of the Christian Religion* (1536)	this and all his works were on the Papal Index by 1564
Hans Christian Andersen	*Andersen's Fairy Tales* (1835)	banned in Russia 1835–49
Aldous Huxley	*Point Counter Point* (1928)	banned in Ireland in 1930
Salman Rushdie	*The Satanic Verses* (1988)	banned in India until 1999; Iranian government lifted *fatwa* in 1998
Victor Hugo	*Les Miserables* (1862)	on the Papal Index 1864–1959
Copernicus	*De Revolutionibus Orbium Coelestium*	on the Papal Index 1616–1835

Censorship
Infamous Acts of Censorship

Year	Details
399 BC	Socrates condemned to death by Athenian Assembly for corrupting the youth of the city. First recorded incident of censorship.
35 AD	Roman Emperor Caligula attempts to ban *The Odyssey* for its democratic ideals.
1244	*The Talmud* is burned in Paris for blasphemy and immorality.
1497	Works by Ovid, Dante, and Propertius are burned in the 'bonfire of the vanities' in Florence, Italy.
1521	Martin Luther excommunicated by Papal bull and prohibited 'from printing, selling, reading, or quoting his works'. The ban increases the popularity of his works.
1521–26	William Tyndale translates part of The New Testament into English. Printed in Cologne, 6000 copies of the book are smuggled into England, discovered and publicly burned by church authorities. First printed book banned in England.

(continued)

Year	Details
1559	The Roman Catholic Church issues the first edition of the *Index Librorum Prohibitorum/Index of Prohibited Books* of banned and recommended books. Further editions follow until 1966, when the *Index* is itself suppressed.
1597	A scene depicting the monarch being deposed is removed from Shakespeare's *Richard II* on the orders of Queen Elizabeth I.
1633	Pope Urban VIII bans Galileo's *Dialogo sopra i due Massimi Sistemi/Dialogues on the Two Chief Systems of the World* for heresy and breach of good faith.
1660	Friends of John Milton intervene to prevent him hanging after his *Eikonoklastes* is burned for its attack on Catholicism and the divine right of kings.
1778	Louis XVI of France bans *Le Mariage de Figaro/The Marriage of Figaro* by Beaumarchais for six years for immorality. Its author is imprisoned.
1792	English publishers are prosecuted for publishing Thomas Paine's *The Rights of Man*. Its author is indicted for treason.
1873	The US Congress passes the *Federal Obscenity Act*, or *Comstock Law* which outlaws the mailing of materials considered to be indecent or obscene. Among the offending items are works by Chaucer, Balzac, Victor Hugo, Oscar Wilde, and Ernest Hemingway.
1959	The UK Postmaster General bans *Lady Chatterley's Lover* by D H Lawrence from being mailed. He considers the book obscene. The ban is successfully overturned in the law courts.
1988	Salman Rushdie's *The Satanic Verses* is accused of blasphemy against Islam and banned throughout the Muslim world. A death sentence, or *fatwa*, is issued against him and several people associated with the book are killed or injured in attacks by extremists.

Children's Books

Major Children's Books Producers

Country	Number of titles produced in 1996
Brazil	10,000
UK	8,000
USA	5,000
Germany	5,000
South Korea	4,000
Japan	3,000
China	3,000
Iran	3,000
Malaysia	3,000
Spain	2,000

Children's Books

World's Most-translated Children's Authors

Author	Dates
Charles Perrault	1628–1703
Jacob and Wilhelm Grimm	1785–1863 and 1786–1859
Hans Christian Andersen	1805–1875
Charles Dickens	1812–1870
Jules Verne	1828–1905
Mark Twain (Samuel Langhorne Clemens)	1835–1910
Robert Louis Stevenson	1850–1894
Arthur Conan Doyle	1859–1930
Jack London (John Griffith Chaney)	1876–1916
Enid Blyton	1897–1968

Conrad
Principal Works of Joseph Conrad

Title	Year	Title	Year
Almayer's Folly	1895	*The Secret Agent*	1907
An Outcast of the Islands	1896	*The Secret Sharer*	1910
The Nigger of the 'Narcissus'	1897	*Under Western Eyes*	1911
Lord Jim	1900	*Chance*	1913
Heart of Darkness/Youth	1902	*Victory*	1915
Typhoon	1903	*The Rescue*	1920
Nostromo	1904	*The Rover*	1923

Consonants
All-consonant Words

Word	Meaning
brr	expression that it is cold
cwm	natural amphitheatre
hmm	sound expressing doubt or contemplation
hmph	expression of disbelief or contempt
mmm-hmmm	an affirmative response
nth	the last in an infinite series or, the utmost degree
pshw	expression of impatience or contempt
scrnch	word relating to data compression
sh	sound meaning 'be quiet'
tsk	a sound indicating annoyance or impatience
zzz	the sound of a person snoring or, sleep

Coward
Principal Stage Works of Noël Coward

Title	Year
The Young Idea	1922
The Vortex	1924
Fallen Angels	1925
Hay Fever	1925
Private Lives	1930
Cavalcade	1931
Design for Living	1933
Blithe Spirit	1941
Present Laughter	1942
This Happy Breed	1942
Peace in Our Time	1947
Look after Lulu	1959
Suite in Three Keys	1966

CWA Cartier Diamond Dagger Prize Winners

The Crime Writers Association (CWA) awards prizes annually in a number of different categories. Recipients since 1986 of the Diamond Dagger Prize for outstanding contribution to the genre are given below.

Year	Author	Year	Author
2000	Peter Lovesey	1998	Ed McBain
1999	Margaret Yorke	1997	Colin Dexter

(*continued*)

CWA Cartier Diamond Dagger Prize Winners (*continued*)

Year	Author	Year	Author
1996	H R F Keating	1990	Julian Symons
1995	Reginald Hill	1989	Dick Francis
1994	Michael Gilbert	1988	John le Carré
1993	Edith Pargeter (Ellis Peters)	1987	P D James
1992	Leslie Charteris	1986	Eric Ambler
1991	Ruth Rendell		

CWA Macallan Gold Dagger Prize Winners

Recipients since 1980 of the Gold Dagger award for the best crime novel of the year are:

Year	Novel	Author
2000	*Motherless Brooklyn*	Jonathan Lethem
1999	*Small Death in Lisbon*	Robert Wilson
1998	*Sunset Limited*	James Lee Burke
1997	*Black & Blue*	Ian Rankin
1996	*Popcorn*	Ben Elton
1995	*The Mermaids Singing*	Val McDermid
1994	*The Scold's Bridle*	Minette Walters
1993	*Cruel and Unusual*	Patricia Cornwell
1992	*The Way Through the Woods*	Colin Dexter
1991	*King Solomon's Carpet*	Barbara Vine (Ruth Rendell)
1990	*Bones and Silence*	Reginald Hill
1989	*The Wench is Dead*	Colin Dexter
1988	*Ratking*	Michael Dibdin
1987	*A Fatal Inversion*	Barbara Vine (Ruth Rendell)
1986	*Live Flesh*	Ruth Rendell
1985	*Monkey Puzzle*	Paula Gosling
1984	*The Twelfth Juror*	B M Gill
1983	*Accidental Crimes*	John Hutton
1982	*The False Inspector Dew*	Peter Lovesey
1981	*Gorky Park*	Martin Cruz Smith
1980	*The Murder of the Maharajah*	H R F Keating

Cyrillic Alphabet

The Cyrillic alphabet is used for writing Russian and various other Slavic languages.

Letter	Transliteration	Letter	Transliteration	Letter	Transliteration
А а	a	К к	k	Х х	kh
Б б	b	Л л	l	Ц ц	ts
В в	v	М м	m	Ч ч	ch
Г г	g, gh	Н н	n	Ш ш	sh
Д д	d	О о	o	Щ щ	shch
Е е	ye	П п	p	Ъ ъ	hard symbol
Ё ё	yo	Р р	r	Ы ы	y
Ж ж	zh	С с	s	Ь ь	soft (or mute) symbol
З з	z	Т т	t		
И и	i	У у	ou	Э э	e
Й й	i	Ф ф	f	Ю ю	yu
				Я я	ya

Dickens

The Major Works of Charles Dickens

Book title	Well-known characters
A Christmas Carol	Ebenezer Scrooge, Bob Cratchit, Marley's Ghost, Tiny Tim
A Tale of Two Cities	Dr Manette, Charles Darnay, Sydney Carton, Jerry Cruncher, Madame Defarge
Barnaby Rudge	Simon Tappertit (Sim), Miss Miggs, Gashford
Bleak House	John Jarndyce, Esther Summerson, Harold Skimpole, Lady Dedlock, Mrs Jellyby
David Copperfield	David Copperfield, Mr Micawber, Mr Dick, Uriah Heep, Little Em'ly, Betsey Trotwood
Dombey and Son	Dombey, Paul and Florence Dombey, Edith Granger, James Carker, Major Bagstock
Great Expectations	Pip, Estella, Miss Havisham, Joe Gargery, Wemmick, Magwitch
Hard Times	Gradgrind, Tom and Louisa Gradgrind, Josiah Bounderby, Bitzer, Cissy Jupe
Little Dorrit	Amy Dorrit, Flora Finching, Mr Merille
Martin Chuzzlewit	Martin Chuzzlewit (Junior), Mr Pecksniff, Mrs Gamp, Tom Pinch
Nicholas Nickleby	Nicholas Nickleby, Wackford Squeers, Madame Mantalini, Smike, Vincent Crummles
Oliver Twist	Oliver Twist, Fagin, Mr Bumble, The Artful Dodger
Our Mutual Friend	Noddy Boffin, Silas Wegg, Mr Podsnap, Betty Higden, Bradley Headstone, Reginald Wilfer

(continued)

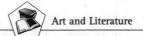 Art and Literature   **15**

Dickens: The Major Works of Charles Dickens (*continued*)

Book title	Well-known characters
The Mystery of Edwin Drood (unfinished)	Rosa Bud, John Jasper
The Old Curiosity Shop	Little Nell, Dick Swiveller, Daniel Quilp
The Pickwick Papers	Mr Pickwick, Sam Weller, Mr Snodgrass, Mr Jingle, Mr and Mrs Bardell

Dutch Words
Used in English

advocaat
beer
beleaguer
blunderbuss
boor
boom
booze
bowsprit
brandy
bulwark
bumpkin
buoy
bush
caboose
cruise
daffodil
decoy
dock
domineer
dotard
drill
easel
etch
exercise
foist
freebooter
frolic

gherkin
gin
golf
groove
hobble
hoist
hose
huckster
hop (plant)
hustle
iceberg
isinglass
keelhaul
kit
knapsack
landscape
loiter
luck
maelstrom
marlin
mart
rack
skate
sketch
skipper
sledge
slim

sloop
slur
smuggle
snap
snatch
snore
snort
snuff
splice
splint
splinter
split
spool
stipple
stoker
tackle
taffrail
tarpon
trigger
uproar
wainscot
wagon
walrus
yacht
yaw
yawl

Eliot
Principal Works of Fiction by George Eliot

Title	Year
Scenes of Clerical Life	1858
Adam Bede	1859
The Mill on the Floss	1860
Silas Marner	1861
Romola	1862–63
Felix Holt the Radical	1866
Middlemarch	1871–72
Daniel Deronda	1874–76
The Impressions of Theophrastus Such	1879

Exhibitions
Most Popular Art Exhibitions Around the World

Source: *The Art Newspaper* **(London and New York)**

Name	Museum and date	Total attendance number
Cézanne to Matisse: Paintings from the Barnes Foundation	Musée d'Orsay, Paris (September 1993–January 1994)	1,500,000
Claude Monet: 1840–1926	Art Institute of Chicago (July–November 1995)	964,895
Van Gogh's Van Goghs	Los Angeles County Museum, Los Angeles (January–May 1999)	821,004
The Origins of Impressionism	Metropolitan Museum of Modern Art, New York (September 1994–January 1995)	794,108
Monet in the 20th Century	Royal Academy, London (January–April 1999)	739,324
Flemish Artists in Rome: 1508–1608	Palais des Beaux-Arts, Brussels (February–May 1995)	675,658
Treasures from Mount Athos	Museum of Byzantine Culture, Thessaloniki (June 1997–April 1998)	675,208
Richard Serra	Bilbao Guggenheim, Bilbao (March–October 1999)	675,071
The Greeks in the West	Palazzo Grassi, Venice (May–December 1996)	600,000
Monet in the 20th Century	Museum of Fine Arts, Boston (September–December 1998)	565,992

Farsi/Persian Words
Used in English

ayatollah	divan	mummy	spinach
azure	jasmine	narg(h)ile/nargilch	sugar
bazaar	jerboa	orange	taffeta
caravan	kiosk	paradise	tiger
cummerbund	lilac	roc	van
dervish	magus	scimitar	

Faulkner
Principal Works of Fiction by William Faulkner

Title	Year	Title	Year
Soldiers' Pay	1926	*The Wild Palms*	1939
Mosquitoes	1927	*The Hamlet*	1940
Sartoris	1929	*Go Down Moses*	1942
The Sound and the Fury	1929	*Intruder in the Dust*	1948
As I Lay Dying	1930	*Collected Stories*	1950
Sanctuary	1931	*Requiem for a Nun*	1951
Light in August	1932	*A Fable*	1954
Pylon	1935	*The Town*	1957
Absalom, Absalom!	1936	*The Mansion*	1959
The Unvanquished	1938	*The Reivers*	1962

Frescoes
Some Early Frescoes

From 5000 BC.

Location	Title/description	Date
Gizeh, Egypt	Egyptian tomb paintings	*c.* 2600 BC
Mari	*Zimmilin's Palace*	*c.* 1700 BC
Thera, Greece	wall-paintings from Knossos and Santorini	*c.* 1500 BC
Thebes	*The Garden of Nebamun*	*c.* 1400 BC
Italy	The Tarquinii tombs (Etruscan)	*c.* 500 BC
Manchuria	*The Liao-Yang Tomb*	*c.* 200 BC

Gaelic Words
Used in English

English	Gaelic origin	English	Gaelic origin
bard (poet)	bàrd	colcannon (potato/cabbage dish)	càl ceannann
bog (marsh)	bogach	claymore (sword)	claidheamh mòr
brogue (shoe)	brog	coracle (boat)	curach
caber (pole)	cabar	corrie (hollow)	coire
cairn (pile of stones)	càrn	drumlin (long mound)	druim
capercaillie (grouse)	capull coille	glen (valley)	gleann
ceilidh (folksong/dance meeting)	ceilidh	gombeen (usuary)	gaimbin

Gaelic Words: Used in English (*continued*)

English	Gaelic origin	English	Gaelic origin
kerfuffle (rumpus)	curfuffle	slogan	sluagh gairm
loch (lake)	loch	sporran (purse)	sporan
mull (promontory)	maol	strath (valley)	strath
pibroch (bagpipe music)	piobaireachd	trousers	triubhas
plaid (cloth)	plaide	twig (understand)	tuig
ptarmigan (arctic bird)	tarmachan	whiskey	uisge beatha
Sassenach (Englishman)	Sussunnach		

German Words
Used in English

blitz	flak	marzipan	quartz	strafewindle
carouse	flatter	meerschaum	roast	veneer
cobalt	frock	nickel	rucksack	waltz
cramp	garden	noodle	sabre	yodel
crush	glockenspiel	paraffin	scale	zeitgeist
dachshund	hamster	plunder	seminar	zigzag
dollar	hinterland	poltergeist	snorkel	zinc
ersatz	kindergarten	poodle	spanner	zither
feldspar	lager	pretzel	spitz	
feud	loafer	protein	stout	

Golding
Principal Works of Fiction by William Golding

Title	Year	Title	Year
Lord of the Flies	1954	*The Scorpion God*	1971
The Inheritors	1955	*Darkness Visible*	1979
Pincher Martin	1956	*Rites of Passage*[1]	1980
Free Fall	1959	*The Paper Men*	1984
The Spire	1964	*Close Quarters*[1]	1987
The Pyramid	1967	*Fire Down Below*[1]	1989

[1] Collectively known as *The Ends of the Earth* (1991).

Grammar
Parts of Speech in English

Part of speech	What it does
adjective	describes a noun or pronoun (e.g. happy)
adverb	modifies a verb (e.g. happily)
article	*a* or *an* (indefinite articles) or *the* (definite article)
conjunction	joins words, phrases, or clauses (e.g. and, but, since, when)
interjection	exclaims an emotion (e.g. Hello, Hey!, Wow!)
noun	names somebody or something (e.g. John, cat, happiness)
preposition	goes before a noun or pronoun and relates it to other parts of a sentence (e.g. down, into, up)
pronoun	stands for a noun (e.g. she, it, his, them)
verb	expresses an action (e.g. cry, hit)

Greek Words
Used in English

acme	hoi polloi
acropolis	ion
amnesia	idiosyncrasy
amnesty	kudos
analgesia	macro-
aphasia	macron
bathos	mega-
chaos	miasma
chimera	micro-
chiton	myth
climax	narcosis
cosmos	nemesis
crisis	pathos
crypt	pentathlon
dilemma	pseudo-
enigma	sepsis
epoch	syntax
ethos	theory
eureka	tmesis
euthanasia	trauma
exegesis	zed
glaucoma	zone

Greene
Principal Works of Fiction by Graham Greene

Title	Year	Title	Year
The Man Within	1929	*The Quiet American*	1955
Stamboul Train	1932	*A Burnt-Out Case*	1961
It's a Battlefield	1934	*The Comedians*	1966
England Made Me	1935	*Travels with My Aunt*	1969
A Gun for Sale	1936	*The Honorary Consul*	1973
Brighton Rock	1938	*The Human Factor*	1978
The Confidential Agent	1939	*Doctor Fischer of Geneva*	1980
The Power and the Glory	1940	*Monsignor Quixote*	1982
The Heart of the Matter	1948	*The Captain and the Enemy*	1989
The End of the Affair	1951		

Hardy

The Major Works of Thomas Hardy

Book title	Well-known characters
Under the Greenwood Tree	Joseph Bowman, Fancy Day, Dick Dewy, Reuben Dewy, William Dewy, Arthur Maybold, Farmer Fred Shiner
Far From the Madding Crowd	William Boldwood, Bathsheba Everdene, Gabriel Oak, Joseph Poorgrass, Fanny Robin, Lyddy Smallbury, Sergeant Francis Troy
The Return of the Native	Christian Cantle, Grandfer Cantle, Diggory Venn, Eustacia Vye, Clym Yeobright, Mrs Yeobright, Thomasin Yeobright, Damon Wildeve
The Trumpet Major	Festus Derriman, Anne Garland, Mrs Garland, Bob Loveday, John Loveday
The Mayor of Casterbridge	Suke Damson, Donald Farfrae, Elizabeth-Jane Henchard, Mrs Henchard, Michael Henchard, Richard Newson, Lucetta Templeman/Le Sueur
The Woodlanders	Felice Charmond, Robert Creedle, Edred Fitzpiers, Grace Melbury, Marty South, Giles Winterbourne
Tess of the d'Urbervilles	Mercy Chant, Angel Clare, Rev James Clare, Dairyman Crick, Car Darch, Izz Huett, Marian, Retty Priddle, Alec d'Urberville, Tess Durbeyfield, John and Joan Durbeyfield
Jude the Obscure	Sue Bridehead, Arabella Donn, Jude Fawley, Little Father Time, Richard Phillotson

Hebrew Words

Used in English

amen
behemoth
cherub
hosanna
jubilee
kibbutz
kosher
leviathan
manna
matzo
rabbi
sabbath
sapphire
Satan
seraph
shekel

Hemingway

Principal Works of Ernest Hemingway

Title	Year
In Our Time	1925
The Torrents of Spring	1926
The Sun Also Rises [1]	1926
Men Without Women	1928
A Farewell to Arms	1929
Death in the Afternoon	1932
Winner Takes Nothing	1933
Green Hills of Africa	1935
To Have and Have Not	1937
The Fifth Column and the First Forty-nine Stories	1938
For Whom the Bell Tolls	1940
Across the River and into the Trees	1950
The Old Man and the Sea	1952

[1] Known in the UK as *Fiesta*.

Hindi Words
Used in English

bandana	jungle
bangle	kedgeree
Blighty	krait
bungalow	kukri
cheetah	loot
chintz	mahout
chit	mina (bird)
chukka	mugger (crocodile)
chukker	punch (drink)
chutney	pundit
coolie	pyjamas
cot	raj
cowrie	sari
dacoit	shampoo
dekko	Sikh
dinghy	sitar
dixie	thug
dungarees	toddy
gavial	tom-tom
guru	topi
gymkhana	veranda
jodhpurs	wallah
juggernaut	

Icons
Most Popular in Art

Icon	Date
Cretan Snake Goddess	c. 1500 BC
The Venus de Milo	2nd century BC
Botticelli's *Venus*	15th century
Michelangelo's *David*	16th century
The Mona Lisa	16th century
The Turin Shroud	Date unknown (c. 17th century)
Frans Hals's *Laughing Cavalier*	1624
Edvard Munch's *Scream*	1893
Andy Warhol's *Marilyn*	1967
Athena Poster: Tennis Girl	1960s/1970s

International Phonetic Alphabet

A	Alpha	H	Hotel	O	Oscar	V	Victor
B	Bravo	I	India	P	Papa	W	Whisky
C	Charlie	J	Juliet	Q	Quebec	X	X-ray
D	Delta	K	Kilo	R	Romeo	Y	Yankee
E	Echo	L	Lima	S	Sierra	Z	Zulu
F	Foxtrot	M	Mike	T	Tango		
G	Golf	N	November	U	Uniform		

Irish Words
Used in English

Irish word	Meaning in the English language	Irish word	Meaning in the English language
abainin (Irish báinín)	white collarless jacket	leprechaun (Irish luchorpán)	('small body') a small and often mischievous supernatural creature
banshee (Irish bean sidhe)	('fairy woman') a supernatural female being who wails under the windows of a house where death is near	poteen (Irish poitín)	('little pot') an alcoholic spirit, illegally brewed from potatoes
blarney	flattering or cajoling talk; to talk in such a way, named after a village near Cork	shamrock (Irish seamróg)	a trifoliate plant
		shillelagh (Irish sail éille)	club
brat (Irish bratt)	child	slob (Irish slab)	stupid person
brock (Irish broc)	badger	smithereens (Irish smidirin)	small fragments
car (Irish carr)	vehicle	spalpeen (Irish spailpin)	itinerant, rascal
colleen (Irish caillín)	girl	Taoiseach	('chieftain') the title of the prime minister of the Republic of Ireland
galore (Irish go léor)	abundance		
kibosh (Irish cie bais)	termination	Tory (Irish tóraighe)	affiliate of what is now the Conservative party

Italian Words
Used in English

arcade	burlesque	citadel	figurine	macaroni
aria	bust	colonel	finale	madrigal
artisan	cameo	concert	florin	malaria
attack	cantata	confetti	fugue	manifesto
balcony	canto	contraband	gazette	mercantile
balloon	caprice	cornice	gelatin	mezzanine
ballot	caress	corridor	ghetto	million
bandit	caricature	dado	imbroglio	miniature
bankrupt	carnival	dilettante	incognito	mountebank
battalion	cartoon	ditto	infantry	moustache
bravo	casino	domino	influenza	musket
brigand	cavalier	ducat	intaglio	muslin
broccoli	cello	diet	lagoon	nepotism
bronze	charlatan	fiasco	lava	opera

(*continued*)

 Art and Literature 23

Italian Words: Used in English (*continued*)

parapet	race (noun)	sequin	stanza	trio
pastel	regatta	serenade	stiletto	trombone
pedantry	replica	sonata	stucco	umbrella
pedestal	risk	sonnet	studio	vendetta
piano	ruffian	soprano	tarantula	viola
picturesque	salami	spaghetti	terracotta	violin
profile	scenario	spinet	tirade	virtuoso
quartet	sentinel	squadron	traffic	vista

James
Principal Works of Fiction by Henry James

Title	Year
Roderick Hudson	1876
The American	1877
The Europeans	1878
Daisy Miller	1879
An International Episode	1879
The Madonna of the Future and Other Tales	1879
Washington Square	1880
The Portrait of a Lady	1881
The Siege of London	1883
The Bostonians	1886
The Princess Casamassima	1886
The Aspern Papers	1888
The Lesson of the Master	1892
The Real Thing and Other Tales	1893
Terminations	1895
Embarrassments	1896
The Spoils of Poynton	1897
What Maisie Knew	1897
The Turn of the Screw	1898
The Awkward Age	1899
The Sacred Fount	1901
The Wings of the Dove	1902
The Ambassadors	1903
The Golden Bowl	1904
The Outcry	1911

Japanese Words
Used in English

Japanese word	Meaning in the English language
futon	a quiltlike bed
geisha	('person of pleasing accomplishments') a woman skilled in the arts of entertaining men with music, dance, and conversation
hara-kiri	('belly-cut') ceremonial suicide by disembowelling, formerly practised by samurai faced with disgrace
kamikaze	a mythical 'divine wind' which destroyed a fleet of invading Mongols; used of Japanese airmen who made suicidal crashes onto enemy targets; now used to imply recklessness
karate	('open hand') a martial art, which injures by striking vital nerve centres in the body with the edge of the open hand or foot, or the elbows and legs
kimono	('silk thing') a long sashed robe with loose sleeves; a similar garment worn in the West
mikado	('exalted door') formerly the title of the emperor
origami	the art of 'folding paper' into decorative shapes
saké/saki	rice wine
samurai	a warrior retainer of a prince or nobleman; a member of the military caste
shōgun	('army leader') hereditary commander of the army; virtual ruler of Japan
sushi	a dish of shaped balls of cold rice with slices of raw fish
tycoon	('great prince') formerly the title of the shōgun; anyone of great power, especially in industry

Languages
Commons Roots of Indo-European Languages

Similarities between three words in selected Indo-European languages contrasted with the differences between them in other non-Indo-European language groups.

Indo-European languages

English	mother	nose	three
French	mère	nez	trois
Spanish	madre	nariz	tres
Italian	madre	naso	tre
German	Mutter	Nase	drei
Dutch	moeder	neus	drie
Greek	meter	rhïs	treis
Russian	mat	nos	tri

Non-Indo-European languages

Finnish	äiti	nenä	kolme
Hungarian	anya	orr	három
Turkish	anne	burun	úç

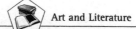

Languages
Greek Alphabet

Letter		Name	Transliteration	Letter		Name	Transliteration
A	α	alpha	a	N	ν	nu	n
B	β	beta	b	Ξ	ξ	xi	x
Γ	γ	gamma	g	O	υ	omicron	o
Δ	δ	delta	d	Π	π	pi	p
E	ε	epsilon	e	P	ρ	rho	r
Z	ζ	zeta	z	Σ	σ	sigma	s
H	η	eta	e	T	τ	tau	t
Θ	θ	theta	th	Υ	υ	upsilon	u
I	ι	iota	i	Φ	б	phi	ph
K	κ	kappa	k	X	χ	chi	ch, kh
Λ	λ	lambda	l	Ψ	ψ	psi	ps
M	μ	mu	m	Ω	ω	omega	o

Languages
Least Widely Spoken Main Languages

Language	Number of speakers (millions)
Afrikaans	10
Belorussian	10
Kurdish	10
Madurese	10
Oromo	10
Greek	11
Czech	12
Malagasy	12
Cebuano	13
Fula	13
Sinhalese	13
Uzbek	13

Languages
Most Popular Languages with Adult UK Learners

Language
French
Spanish
German
Dutch
Italian
Russian
Portuguese
Japanese
Arabic
Mandarin Chinese

Languages
Most Widely Spoken Languages

Language	Number of mother-tongue speakers (millions)
Mandarin Chinese	800
Hindustani	500
English	400
Spanish	400
Arabic	200
Bengali	190
Portuguese	180
Russian	170
Malay-Indonesian	150
Japanese	120

Languages
Most Widely Spoken Official Languages

Language	Number of countries spoken in
English	56
French	32
Arabic	24
Spanish	22
Portuguese	8
Russian	7
German	6
Dutch	3
Chinese	3
Danish	3

Languages
World's Arterial Languages

An arterial language is a language that is spoken by at least 1% of humankind, that is, by at least 60 million in the year 2000. The top 10 arterial languages are given here.

Arterial language	Total speakers (in millions)	Arterial language	Total speakers (in millions)
Standard Chinese (Putonghua)	1,000	Maghribi Arabic + Mashriqi Arabic ('Arabiyya)	250
English	1,000	Bengali (Bangla)	250
Hindi + Urdu	900	Portuguese (Português)	200
Spanish (Español)	450	Malay + Indonesian	160
Russian (Russkiy)	320	Japanese (Nihongo)	130

Latin
Selection of Latin Phrases

Phrase	Meaning
carpe diem	'seize the day'; live for the present
cave canem	beware of the dog
cogito, ergo sum	'I think, therefore I am'
compos mentis	of sound mind
de gustibus non est disputandum	there is no accounting for taste
in vino veritas	in wine (there is) the truth
nil desperandum	never despair
postmortem	'after death'; autopsy
tempus fugit	time flies
terra firma	dry land; solid ground

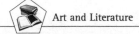

Lawrence

Principal Works of Fiction by D H Lawrence

Title	Year
The White Peacock	1911
The Trespasser	1912
Sons and Lovers	1913
The Prussian Officer	1914
The Rainbow	1915
Women in Love	1920
The Lost Girl	1920
Aaron's Rod	1922
England, My England	1922
Kangaroo	1923
The Ladybird, The Fox, The Captain's Doll	1923
St Mawr/The Princess	1925
The Plumed Serpent	1926
Sun	1926
Lady Chatterley's Lover	1928
The Woman Who Rode Away	1928
The Escaped Cock[1]	1929
Love Among the Haystacks	1930
The Virgin and the Gipsy	1930

[1] Also known as *The Man Who Died*.

Letters

Most Commonly Used Letters in Written English

Letter
E
T
I
O
A
S
N
R

Letters

Silent Letters in Some English Words

Letter	Words
b	aplomb, bdellium, bomb, comb, crumb, debt, doubt, dumb, indebted, jamb, lamb, numb, plumb, plumber, redoubtable, succumb, tomb
c	acquaint, acquire, acquit, ctenoid, ctenophore, indict, victuals
ch	chthonic, fuchshia
d	handkerchief, handsome, sandwich, Wednesday

Letters: Silent Letters in Some English Words (*continued*)

Letter	Words
g	align, apophthegm, assign, campaign, champagne, coign, condign, consign, deign, diaphragm, epergne, feign, foreign, gnat, gnathic, gnarled, gnash, gnat, gnaw, gnome, gnomon, gnosis, Gnostic, gnu, impugn, oppugn, paradigm, phlegm, physiognomy, poignant, reign, repugn, resign, seraglio, sign, sovereign, syntagm
h	aghast, ankh, cirrhosis, dhow, exhaust, exhibit, ghastly, gherkin, ghetto, ghost, ghoul, haemorrhage, heir, heiress, heirloom, honest, honorary, honour, honourable, hour, hourly, khaki, khol, myrrh, posthumous, rhapsody, rhea, rhesus, rhetoric, rheumatism, rhinoceros, rhubarb, rhyme, rhythm, saccharin, and various words beginning with *ch-* and *wh-*
k	knack, knag, knapsack, knar, knave, knead, knee, kneel, knell, knew, knickers, knife, knight, knit, knitting, knob, knock, knockout, knoll, knot, knout, know, knowledge, knuckle, knurl, unknown
l	balm, calm, half, palm, could, salmon, should, would
m	mnemonics
n	autumn, column, condemn, damn, damning, hymn, limn, solemn
p	cupboard, pneumatic, pneumonia, ptarmigan, pterodactyl, Ptolemy, ptomaine, raspberry, receipt, sapphire, and various words beginning with *ps-*
ph	apophthegm, phthalic, phthisis
s	island, isle, debris, prècis, viscount
t	ballet, bustle, crochet, depot, epsistle, glisten, listen, listener, mortgage, nestle, rustle, tsar, whistle, wrestle
th	asthma
u	biscuit, buoy, buoyant, circuit, guarantee, guard, guide, guilt(y), guitar, honour, labour, mould, moult, plague, rogue, savour, smoulder, tongue, vague
w	answer, playwright, sword, who, whole, whore, whose, and various words beginning with *wr-*

Literature

A Dozen Fictional Detectives and their Authors

Detective	Author
Father Brown	G K Chesterton
Sherlock Holmes	Arthur Conan Doyle
Inspector Maigret	George Simenon
Philip Marlowe	Raymond Chandler
Miss Marple	Agatha Christie
Sam Spade	Dashiell Hammett
Inspector Wexford	Ruth Rendell
Inspector Morse	Colin Dexter
Brother Cadfael	Ellis Peters
Aurelio Zen	Michael Dibdin
Dr Kay Scarpetta	Patricia Cornwell
Inspector John Rebus	Ian Rankin

Literature
Shipwrecked Characters

Literary work	Author	Character
Don Juan	Lord Byron	Don Juan
Gulliver's Travels	Jonathon Swift	Lemuel Gulliver
Robinson Crusoe	Daniel Defoe	Robinson Crusoe
Shogun	James Clavell	John Blackthorn
Swiss Family Robinson	Johann Wyss	Robinson family
The Aenead	Virgil	Aeneas
The Coral Island	R M Ballantyne Jack Martin	Ralph Rover Peterkin Gay
The Odyssey	Homer	Odysseus
The Tempest	William Shakespeare	Alonzo Antonio Sebastian Ferdinand Gonzalo, and others

Literature
Ten Literary Late Starters

Name	Life dates	Details
Daniel Defoe	1660–1731	he made his debut in 1701 with *The True-Born Englishman*
George Eliot	1819–80	*Scenes of Clerical Life* (1858) was her first book
Theodor Fontane	1819–98	the writer of *Effi Briest* was almost 60 before finishing his first book
Robert Frost	1874–1963	the great American poet's first collection, *A Boy's Will*, appeared in 1913
William Golding	1911–93	his first novel, the classic *Lord of the Flies*, was published in 1954
Giuseppe di Lampedusa	1900–56	*The Leopard*, widely regarded as one of the 20th century's great novels, was written in the last two years of his life and published posthumously
Penelope Fitzgerald	1916–2000	the writer of the 1979 Booker prizewinner, *Offshore*, published nothing until 1975
Alexander Solzhenitsyn	1918–	he finished his first novel, *One Day in the Life of Ivan Denisovich*, in 1960
José Saramago	1922–	the 1998 Nobel prizewinner started writing poetry in his forties, and published his first novel, *The Manual of Painting and Calligraphy*, in 1976
Anita Brookner	1928–	a distinguished art historian, her first novel, *A Start in Life*, appeared in 1981

Literature

Ten Parisian Emigré Writers

Name	Life dates	Details
Ivan Turgenev	1818–83	a committed Europhile, the Russian writer spent much of his adult life in France, and was well known in Parisian literary circles
W Somerset Maugham	1874–1965	Maugham settled in Paris in 1898, and travelled widely after World War I, a fact reflected in his fiction
Gertrude Stein	1874–1946	the *grande dame* of American modernism lived in France from 1903 until her death. Her Parisian salon attracted many of the great literary and artistic figures of the 1920s
James Joyce	1882–1941	Joyce left Dublin in 1904 for Trieste, Zurich, and eventually Paris, but his literary output is exclusively concerned with Irish life
Henry Miller	1891–1930	Miller lived in Paris from 1930 until the outbreak of war and in 1934 published the autobiographical *Tropic of Cancer* about his promiscuous lifestyle at the time
Joseph Roth	1894–1939	the Austrian novelist moved to Paris in 1926 as foreign correspondent of the *Frankfurter Zeitung*. He lived and wrote his major novels in various Parisian hotels
F Scott Fitzgerald	1896–1940	with his wife Zelda, he travelled back and forth between Europe and America in the late 1920s. His classic novel, *The Great Gatsby,* was written in Paris in 1924–25
Ernest Hemingway	1898–1961	Hemingway's work reflects his own experiences of living and writing in variously: Europe in World War I, Paris in the 20s, Spain during the civil war, Cuba, and Africa
Samuel Beckett	1906–89	he moved to Paris in 1927, served as Joyce's amanuensis, and went on to write all his mature work in French
Milan Kundera	1929–	banned from publication and prohibited from teaching, the Czech novelist left his native land in 1975 and settled in Paris. His recent books have been written in French

Literature

Ten Works of English Literature Set on Islands

Title	Writer	Year
The Tempest	William Shakespeare	1611
Robinson Crusoe	Daniel Defoe	1719
The Coral Island	R M Ballantyne	1858
Treasure Island	Robert Louis Stevenson	1883
The Island of Dr Moreau	H G Wells	1896

(*continued*)

Literature: Ten Works of English Literature Set on Islands
(*continued*)

Title	Writer	Year
Lord of the Flies	William Golding	1954
Pincher Martin	William Golding	1956
Island	Aldous Huxley	1962
Concrete Island	J G Ballard	1994
The Beach	Alex Garland	1997

Literature
The Three Musketeers

Name	Characteristics
Aramis	loyal and ambitious
Athos	gallant and noble
Porthos	strong and womanizing

Lovers
Some Famous Literary Lovers

Romeo and Juliet

Heathcliffe and Cathy

Elizabeth and Darcy

Scarlet and Rhett

Troilus and Cressida

Constance Chatterley and Oliver Mellors

Lancelot and Guinevere

Tristan and Isolde

Humbert Humbert and Lolita

Othello and Desdemona

Anna Karenina and Vronski

Jane Eyre and Mr Rochester

Hero and Leander

Pyramus and Thisbe

Cupid and Psyche

Echo and Narcissus

Paris and Helen

Hector and Andromache

Dido and Aeneas

Malay Words
Used in English

amah	cachou	compound (enclosure)	kampong	orang-utan
amok	caddy (tea)	gecko	kapock	paddy (rice)
bamboo	cassowary	gingham	ketchup	rattan
barbirusa	catechu	gong	kris	sago
batik	cockatoo		launch (boat)	sarong

Mythology
Nymphs

Name	Association	Name	Association
Aegina	Zeus's wife	Eurydice	Orpheus's dryad wife
Amalthea	Zeus's wet nurse	Galatea	sea nymph
Arethusa	water nymph	Glauce	sea nymph, a nereid
Asteria	Hecate's mother	Hyades	seven rain nymphs
Calyce	Endymion's mother	Lodona	river nymph
Calypso	sea nymph	Maia	eldest of the Pleiades
Castalia	nymph of Apollo's spring	Meliae	nymphs of the ash (tree)
Clymene	Phaeton's mother	Merope	Asopos's wife
Clyte	ocean nymph	Minthe	nymph of a river in hell
Cymodoce	sea nymph	Oenone	nymph of Mount Ida
Cyrene	Thessalian nymph	Penelope	Pan's mother
Daphne	mountain nymph	Periboca	Penelope's mother
Echenias	loved by Daphnis	Pleiades	seven sisters of the Hyades
Echo	Roman nymph	Rhodas	mate of Helios (Sun)
Egeria	advisor nymph	Syrinx	Arcadian nymph
Electra	one of the Pleiades, mother of Dardanus	Thetis	chief of the nereids, Achilles' mother
		Thoosa	Polyphemus's mother

Mythology
Seven Against Thebes

In Greek mythology, the seven against Thebes were the seven captains led by Adrastus, king of Argos, who attacked the seven gates of ancient Thebes.

Adrastus	Parthenopaeus
Amphiaraüs	Polynices
Capaneus	Tydeus
Hippomedon	

Mythology
The Four Ancient Greek Winds

Name	Direction
Boreas	north wind
Eurus	east wind
Notus	south wind
Zephyrus	west wind

Mythology
The Nine Muses

Name	Associated art
Calliope	epic poetry and music
Clio	history
Erato	love poetry
Euterpe	lyric poetry and music
Melpomene	tragedy
Polyhymnia	mime and sacred dance
Terpsichore	choral song and dance
Thalia	comedy and pastoral poetry
Urania	astronomy

Mythology
The Rivers of Hades

Name	Description
Styx	river of horror and terror
Acheron	river of woe and mourning
Phlegethon	river of fire streams
Cocytus	river of death laments
Lethe	river of forgetfulness

Mythology
The Three Fates

Name	Meaning of name	Function
Atropos	she who cannot be avoided	severs the thread of life
Clotho	the spinner	spins the thread of life
Lachesis	the measurer	determines the length of the thread of life

Mythology
The Three Furies

Name	Meaning of name
Alecto	the implacable one
Megaera	the jealous one
Tisiphone	the avenger of blood (murder)

Mythology
The Three Judges of the Underworld

Rhadamanthus
Monos
Aeacus

Mythology
The Twelve Labours of Heracles

Labour	Labour
kill the lion of Nemea	overcome the Cretan bull
slay the Hydra of Lerna	capture the mares of Diomedes
capture the Ceryneian hind	fetch the girdle of Hippolyta
trap the Erymanthian boar	steal the cattle of Geryon
clean the Augean stables	collect the golden apples of the Hesperides
drive off the Stymphalean birds	drag Cerberus from the Underworld

Mythology
Types of Nymph

Type	Description	Type	Description
dryad	wood nymph	naiad	water nymph
hamadryad	tree nymph	nereid	sea nymph
houri	nymph of paradise (Muslim)	nixie	water nymph
maelid	apple nymph	oceanid	sea nymph
maenad	orgiastic nymph-like attendant of Dionysus (Bacchus)	oread	mountain nymph
		siren	sea nymph
		undine	water nymph

National Gallery
Most Popular Paintings at the National Gallery, London

Artist	Life dates	Painting
Vincent van Gogh	1853–1890	*Sunflowers* (1888)
Claude Monet	1840–1926	*The Water-lily Pond* (1896)
Vincent van Gogh	1853–1890	*A Cornfield with Cypresses* (1889)
Claude Monet	1840–1926	*The Thames below Westminster* (1871)
Pierre-Auguste Renoir	1841–1919	*The Umbrellas* (1881–86)
Jan van Eyck	c. 1390–1441	*The Arnolfini Portrait* (1434)
Andrea del Verrocchio (follower of)	c. 1435–1488	*Tobias and the Angel* (1470–80)
Georges-Pierre Seurat	1859–1891	*Bathers at Asnières* (c. 1884)
Leonardo da Vinci	1452–1519	*The Virgin and Child with Saints Anne and John the Baptist* (Cartoon; c. 1495)
Vincent van Gogh	1853–1890	*The Chair and the Pipe* (1888)

Nobel Prize
Literature Prize: Recent winners

Year	Winner	Year	Winner
1990	Octavio Paz (Mexico)	1996	Wisława Szymborska (Poland)
1991	Nadine Gordimer (South Africa)	1997	Dario Fo (Italy)
1992	Derek Walcott (Santa Lucia)	1998	José Saramago (Portugal)
1993	Toni Morrison (USA)	1999	Günter Grass (Germany)
1994	Kenzaburō Ōe (Japan)	2000	Gao Xingjian (China)
1995	Seamus Heaney (Ireland)		

Nobel Prize
Literature Prize: UK and Ireland Winners

Year	Winner	Country	Main field of activity
1995	Seamus Heaney	Ireland	poet
1983	William Golding	UK	novelist
1981	Elias Canetti[1]	UK	novelist and philosopher
1969	Samuel Beckett[2]	Ireland	novelist and playwright
1953	Winston Churchill	UK	historian
1950	Bertrand Russell	UK	philosopher
1948	T S Eliot	UK	poet
1932	John Galsworthy	UK	novelist and playwright
1925	George Bernard Shaw	UK	playwright
1923	William Butler Yeats	Ireland	poet
1907	Rudyard Kipling	UK	novelist and poet

[1] Though resident in Britain after 1938, Elias Canetti wrote principally in German.
[2] Resident in France for the whole of his adult life, Samuel Beckett's major works were written in French.

Nobel Prize
Literature Prize: US Winners

Year	Winner	Main field of activity
1993	Toni Morrison	novelist
1980	Czeslaw Milosz[1]	poet
1978	Isaac Bashevis Singer[2]	novelist
1976	Saul Bellow	novelist
1962	John Steinbeck	novelist
1954	Ernest Hemingway	novelist
1949	William Faulkner	novelist
1938	Pearl S Buck	novelist
1936	Eugene O'Neill	playwright
1930	Sinclair Lewis	novelist

[1] Czeslaw Milosz won under dual nationality (Poland/USA) and writes in Polish.
[2] An immigrant to the United States as a young man, Isaac Bashevis Singer wrote in Yiddish.

O'Neill
Principal Stage Works of Eugene O'Neill

Title	Year	Title	Year
Bound East for Cardiff	1916	The Great God Brown	1926
In the Zone	1917	Strange Interlude	1928
The Long Voyage Home	1917	Mourning Becomes Electra	1931
The Moon of the Caribees	1918	Ah, Wilderness!	1933
The Dreamy Kid	1919	Days without End	1934
The Emperor Jones	1920	The Iceman Cometh	1946
Beyond the Horizon	1920	Long Day's Journey into Night [1]	1956
Anna Christie	1921	A Moon for the Misbegotten [1]	1957
The Hairy Ape	1922	A Touch of the Poet [1]	1957
All God's Chillun Got Wings	1924	Hughie [1]	1958
Desire Under the Elms	1924	More Stately Mansions [1]	1962

[1] First performed after the playwright's death.

Orange Prize Winners

The Orange Prize is a UK literary prize open only to women, of any nationality. It was established in 1996.

Year	Winner	Awarded for
1996	Helen Dunmore	A Spell of Winter
1997	Anne Michaels	Fugitive Pieces
1998	Carol Shields	Larry's Party
1999	Suzanne Berne	A Crime in the Neighborhood
2000	Linda Grant	When I Lived in Modern Times

Paintings
Most Expensive Oil Paintings at Auction

Source: Art Sales Index Ltd

As of May 2000.

Work	Artist	Place and date of sale	Price (US$)
Portrait du Dr Gachet	Vincent van Gogh	Christie's, New York, 1990	75,000,000
Au Moulin de la Galette	Pierre-Auguste Renoir	Sotheby's, New York, 1990	71,000,000
Portrait de l'artiste sans barbe	Vincent van Gogh	Christie's, New York, 1998	65,000,000

(continued)

Work	Artist	Place and date of sale	Price (US$)
Rideau, cruchon et compotier	Paul Cézanne	Sotheby's, New York, 1999	55,000,000
Les noces de Pierette	Pablo Picasso	Binoche et Godeau, Paris, 1989	51,672,000
Irises	Vincent van Gogh	Sotheby's, New York, 1987	49,000,000
Femme assise dans un jardin	Pablo Picasso	Sotheby's, New York, 1999	45,000,000
Le Rêve	Pablo Picasso	Christie's, New York, 1997	44,000,000
Self Portrait: Yo Picasso	Pablo Picasso	Christie's, New York, 1989	43,500,000
Nu au fauteuil noir	Pablo Picasso	Christie's, New York, 1999	41,000,000

Paintings

Most Expensive Paintings by Living Artists at Auction

Source: Art Sales Index Ltd

As of May 2000.

Work	Artist	Place and date of sale	Price (US$)
False start	Jasper Johns	Sotheby's, New York, 1988	15,500,000
Rebus	Robert Rauschenberg	Sotheby's, New York, 1991	6,600,000
Large interior, W11	Lucian Freud	Sotheby's, New York, 1998	5,300,000
Untitled	Cy Twombly	Sotheby's, New York, 1990	5,000,000
Tomlinson Court Park	Frank Stella	Sotheby's, New York, 1989	4,600,000

Paintings

Rock and Cave Paintings

Location	Title
Lascaux, France	
Niaux, France	*Deer and Horses*
The Chauvet Caves, The Ardèche, France	*The Rhinoceros*
Altamira, Spain	
Sahara, North Africa	*The Hunters*
Cape York Peninsula, Australia	*The Emu*

Paintings
Some Early Paintings

Artist/date	Title	Location
Cimabue (c. 1280)	*Madonna Enthroned*	Florence
Giotto (1305)	*The Triumph of Death*	Padua
Martini (c. 1315)	*Maestá*	Siena
Gaddi (c. 1330)	*St Eligius*	Madrid
Duccio (1333)	*The Annunciation*	Florence
Pietro Lorenzetti (1342)	*Birth of the Virgin*	Siena
Orcagna (c. 1360)	*St Matthew*	Florence

Paintings
Some Famous Paintings

Excluding 20th-century paintings.

Artist/dates	Title	Location
Paolo Uccello (1397–1475)	*The Rout of San Romano*	National Gallery, London
Sandro Botticelli (1446–1510)	*Primavera*	Uffizi Gallery, Florence
Jan van Eyck (c. 1390–1441)	*The Arnolfini Portrait*	National Gallery, London
Leonardo da Vinci (1452–1519)	*The Mona Lisa*	Louvre, Paris
Diego Velazquez (1599–1660)	*Las Meninas*	The Prado, Madrid
Pieter Bruegel (c. 1530–1569)	*Hunters in the Snow*	National Gallery, Vienna
Albrecht Dürer (1471–1528)	*Self Portrait*	The Prado, Madrid
Johannes Vermeer (1632–1675)	*The Lacemaker*	Louvre, Paris
Frans Hals (c. 1580–1666)	*The Laughing Cavalier*	Wallace Collection, London
John Constable (1776–1837)	*The Haywain*	National Gallery, London
John Landseer (1802–1873)	*The Monarch of the Glen*	Edinburgh
Jean Millet (1814–1875)	*The Gleaners*	Museé d'Orsay, Paris

Palindromes

The word palindrome is of Greek origin. It is a compound word meaning running back again.

aga	bib	dad	dud	eve
alula	bob	deed	eke	ewe
anna	boob	did	ere	eye

(continued)

Palindromes (*continued*)

gag	minim	pep	solos	Able was I ere I saw Elba
gig	mum	pip	tat	
kayak	nan	poop	tenet	Eros saw Bob was sore
keek	noon	pop	tit	
level	non	pup	toot	Madam, I'm Adam
maam	nun	radar	tot	
madam	otto	reviver	tut	Was it a rat I saw?
mam	pap	sees	wow	
marram	peep	sexes		Rats live on no evil star

Pen Names
Of Famous Authors

Author	Pen name
Albert Camus	Louis Neuville
Charles Dickens	Boz
Victor Hugo	Hierro
D H Lawrence	L H Davidson
Sylvia Plath	Victoria Lucas
George Bernard Shaw	Corno di Bassetto
Percy Bysshe Shelley	John Fitzvictor
Alfred Tennyson	Alcibiades
Bronte Sisters	Currer, Ellis, and Acton Bell
Walter Scott	The Aristo of the North

Photography
Top 20th-century Photographers

Name	Life dates
Ansel Adams	1902–1984
Cecil Beaton	1904–1980
Bill Brandt	1904–1983
Henri Cartier-Bresson	1908–
Robert Capa	1913–1954
Yousuf Karsh	1908–
Andre Kertesz	1894–1985
Man Ray	1890–1976
Alfred Steiglitz	1864–1946
Arthur Weegee	1899–1968

Photography
Top Contemporary Photographers

Name	Life dates	Name	Life dates
Diane Arbus	1923–1971	Robert Mapplethorpe	1946–1989
Richard Avedon	1923–	Helmut Newton	1920–
David Bailey	1938–	Norman Parkinson	1913–1990
Horst P Horst	1906–1999	Herb Ritts	1952–
Annie Leibovitz	1949–	Clarence Sinclair Bull	1896–1979

Pinter
Selected Stage Works of Harold Pinter

Title	Year	Title	Year
The Room	1957	*The Homecoming*	1965
The Birthday Party	1957	*No Man's Land*	1975
The Dumb Waiter	1960	*Betrayal*	1978
The Caretaker	1960	*A Kind of Alaska*	1982
A Slight Ache	1961	*One for the Road*	1984
The Collection	1962	*Mountain Language*	1988
The Dwarfs	1963	*Party Time*	1991
The Lover	1963		

Poetry
Les Pléiades

Les Pléiades were a group of 16th-century French poets who borrowed their name from the seven tragic poets of Alexandria.

Name	Life dates
Pierre de Ronsard	1524–1585
Joachim Du Bellay	c. 1522–1560
Remy Belleau	1528–1577
Estienne Jodelle	1532–1573
Pontus de Tyard	c. 1521–1605
Jean Antoine de Baïf	1532–1589
Jean Daurat	c. 1508–1588

Poetry
Poetic Metres

Metre of poetry	What it sounds like
amphibranch	three syllables with stress on the central one
anapest	three syllables with stress on the final one
choriamb	four syllables with two stressed between a pair of unstressed ones
cretic	three syllables with the central one unstressed
dactyl	three syllables with stress on the first one
iambus	two syllables with stress on the second one
Pyrrhic	two unstressed syllables
spondee	two stressed syllables
tribrach	three syllables, all unstressed
trochee	two syllables with stress on the first one

Poetry
UK Poets Laureate

Appointed	Poet Laureate	Appointed	Poet Laureate
1668	John Dryden	1715	Nicholas Rowe
1689	Thomas Shadwell	1718	Laurence Eusden
1692	Nahum Tate	1730	Colley Cibber

(*continued*)

Appointed	Poet Laureate	Appointed	Poet Laureate
1757	William Whitehead	1913	Robert Bridges
1785	Thomas Warton	1930	John Masefield
1790	Henry James Pye	1968	Cecil Day Lewis
1813	Robert Southey	1972	Sir John Betjeman
1843	William Wordsworth	1984	Ted Hughes
1850	Alfred, Lord Tennyson	1999	Andrew Motion
1896	Alfred Austin		

Poetry
US Poets Laureate

Term of appointment	Poet Laureate
1986–87	Robert Penn Warren
1987–88	Richard Wilbur
1988–90	Howard Nemerov
1990–91	Mark Strand
1991–92	Joseph Brodsky
1992–93	Mona Van Duyn
1993–95	Rita Dove
1995–97	Robert Hass
1997–	Robert Pinsky

Portraits
20th-century Personalities with the Most Portraits

Mahatma Gandhi
Adolf Hitler
Che Guevara
John F Kennedy
Winston Churchill
Martin Luther King
Nelson Mandela

Portuguese Words
Used in English

albatross
albino
bantam (originally from Java)
bossa nova
caravel (originally from Java)
caste
cobra
dodo
flamingo
junk (ship)
mandarin
marmalade
pagoda
palaver
port (wine)
tank

Printing
Former Names for Point Sizes

Point size	Former name	Point size	Former name
$3\frac{1}{2}$	gem	9	bourgeois
4	brilliant	10	long primer
		11	small pica
$4\frac{1}{2}$	diamond	12	pica
$4\frac{3}{4}$	pearl	14	English or ruby
$5\frac{1}{2}$	agate	16	columbian
6	nonpareil	18	great primer
$6\frac{1}{2}$	emerald	20	paragon
7	minion	22	double pica
8	brevier	48	canon

Prix Goncourt Winners

Founded in 1903, this French literary award is presented annually in November by the Académie Goncourt for the best French novel of the year.

Year	Winner	Awarded for
1991	Pierre Combescot	*Les Filles du Calvaire*
1992	Patrick Chamoisean	*Texaco*
1993	Amin Maalouf	*Le Rocher de Tanios*
1994	Didier van Cauwelaert	*Un Aller Simple*
1995	Andreï Makine	*Le Testament Français*
1996	Pascale Roze	*Le Chasseur Zéro*
1997	Patrick Rambeau	*La Bataille*
1998	Paule Constant	*Confidence pour confidence*
1999	Jean Echenoz	*Je m'en vais*
2000	Jean-Jacques Schuhl	*Ingrid Caven*

Proverbs

Key Proverbs about Children

Proverb	Meaning
'A burned child dreads the fire'	do not repeat a painful experience
'Boys will be boys'	immature behaviour should not be surprising from immature people
'Children should be seen and not heard'	children should not emphasize their presence by obtrusive behaviour
'Spare the rod and spoil the child'	not reprimanding a child when needed results in an uncontrollable brat
'The child is father of the man'	interpret a child's manner correctly and you will know what sort of adult he or she will become

Proverbs

Key Proverbs about Men

Proverb	Meaning
'A drowning man will clutch at straws'	faced with extreme difficulty, you will take any available chance of salvation
'A man's best friend is his dog'	a dog remains loyal even when friends' affections diminish
'Every man for himself (and the devil take the hindmost)'	concentrate on taking care of yourself and your own interests
'Every man has his price'	given enough inducement, everyone is capable of being bribed
'Give a man enough rope and he will hang himself'	given enough freedom, all people will create their own undoing

(continued)

Proverbs: Key Proverbs about Men (*continued*)

Proverb	Meaning
'Man proposes but God disposes'	you have no real control over your own plans
'Manners maketh man'	a person's reputation is determined by his or her social behaviour
'No man can serve two masters'	you cannot comply equally with two conflicting principles
'One man's meat is another man's poison'	not everybody enjoys the same things
'You can judge a man by the company he keeps'	the type of people someone associates with is an indication of what he or she is like

Public Art

Some Large Works of Public Art

Artist	Title/date(s)	Size	Location
Christo and Jeanne-Claude	*Running Fence* (1972–76)	5.5 m × 39.5 km/ 18 ft × 25 mi	California (now removed)
Christo and Jeanne-Claude	*Wrapped Reichstag* (1995)	length 136 m × width 96 m × height (roof) 32 m × height (tower) 42 m/446 ft × 315 ft × 105 ft × 138 ft	Berlin
Anthony Caro and Norman Foster	*The Millennium Bridge* (1998–2000)	370 m/1,214 ft	The River Thames, London
Antony Gormley	*Quantum Cloud* (1999)	30 m/98 ft	The Millennium Dome, London
Antony Gormley	*The Angel of the North* (1997)	20 m/66 ft	Newcastle upon Tyne, UK
Louise Bourgeois	*Maman (Spider in Progress)* (1999)	12 m/39 ft	Tate Modern, London (temporary exhibit)
Jeff Koons	*Puppy* (1992)	11 m × 5 m × 6 m/ 36 ft × 16 ft × 20 ft	Arolson, Germany (temporary installation)
Judy Chicago	*The Dinner Party* (1974–79)	15 m/49 ft	UCLA, Los Angeles (temporary installation)
Pablo Picasso	*Guernica* (1937)	3.5 m × 7.8 m/ 11 ft × 26 ft	Guggenheim Museum, Bilbao, Spain
Diego Rivera	Murals for the Ministry of Education building (1923–28)	235 fresco panels, approx. 1600 sq m/ 17,200 sq ft	Mexico City
Raoul Dufy	Murals for the 1938 Paris Exhibition	600 m/1,969 ft	Palace of Electricity, Paris

Pulitzer Prizes in Letters
Biography or Autobiography

Year	Winner(s)	Awarded for
1990	Sebastian de Grazia	*Machiavelli in Hell*
1991	Steven Naifeh and Gregory White Smith	*Jackson Pollock: An American Saga*
1992	Lewis B Puller Jr	*Fortunate Son: The Healing of a Vietnam Vet*
1993	David McCullough	*Truman*
1994	David Levering Lewis	*W E B DuBois: Biography of a Race, 1868–1919*
1995	Jean D Hedrick	*Harriet Beecher Stowe: A Life*
1996	Jack Miles	*God: A Biography*
1997	Frank McCourt	*Angela's Ashes*
1998	Katharine Graham	*Personal History*
1999	A Scott Berg	*Lindbergh*
2000	Stacey Schiff	*Vera (Mrs Vladimir Nabokov)*

Pulitzer Prizes in Letters
Drama

Year	Winner	Awarded for
1990	August Wilson	*The Piano Lesson*
1991	Neil Simon	*Lost in Yonkers*
1992	Robert Schenkkan	*The Kentucky Cycle*
1993	Tony Kushner	*Angels in America: Millennium Approaches*
1994	Edward Albee	*Three Tall Women*
1995	Horton Foote	*The Young Man from Atlanta*
1996	Jonathan Larson	*Rent*
1997	no award	
1998	Paula Vogel	*How I Learned to Drive*
1999	Margaret Edson	*Wit*
2000	Donald Margulies	*Dinner with Friends*

Pulitzer Prizes in Letters
Fiction

Year	Winner	Awarded for
1990	Oscar Hijuelos	*The Mambo Kings Play Songs of Love*
1991	John Updike	*Rabbit at Rest*
1992	Jane Smiley	*A Thousand Acres*
1993	Robert Olen Butler	*A Good Scent From a Strange Mountain*
1994	E Annie Proulx	*The Shipping News*
1995	Carol Shields	*The Stone Diaries*
1996	Richard A Ford	*Independence Day*

(continued)

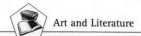

Year	Winner	Awarded for
1997	Steven Millhauser	*Martin Dressler: The Tale of an American Dreamer*
1998	Philip Roth	*American Pastoral*
1999	Michael Cunningham	*The Hours*
2000	Jhumpa Lahiri	*Interpreter of Maladies*

Pulitzer Prizes in Letters
General Non-Fiction

Year	Winner(s)	Awarded for
1990	Dale Maharidge and Michael Williamson	*And Their Children After Them*
1991	Bert Holldobler and Edward O Wilson	*The Ants*
1992	Daniel Yergin	*The Prize: The Epic Quest for Oil, Money and Power*
1993	Garry Wills	*Lincoln at Gettysburg: The Words That Remade America*
1994	David Remick	*Lenin's Tomb: The Last Days of the Soviet Empire*
1995	Jonathan Weiner	*The Beak of the Finch: A Story of Evolution in Our Time*
1996	Tina Rosenberg	*The Haunted Land: Facing Europe's Ghosts After Communism*
1997	Richard Kluger	*Ashes to Ashes: America's Hundred-Year Cigarette War, the Public Health, and the Unabashed Triumph of Philip Morris*
1998	Jared Diamond	*Guns, Germs, and Steel: The Fates of Human Societies*
1999	John McPhee	*Annals of the Former World*
2000	John W Dower	*Embracing Defeat: Japan in the Wake of World War II*

Pulitzer Prizes in Letters
History

Year	Winner(s)	Awarded for
1990	Stanley Karnow	*In Our Image: America's Empire in the Philippines*
1991	Laurel Thatcher Ulrich	*A Midwife's Tale: The Life of Martha Ballard, Based on Her Diary, 1785–1812*
1992	Mark E Neely Jr	*The Fate of Liberty: Abraham Lincoln and Civil Liberties*
1993	Gordon S Wood	*The Radicalism of the American Revolution*
1994	no award	
1995	Doris Kearns Goodwin	*No Ordinary Time: Franklin and Eleanor Roosevelt: The Home Front in World War II*

Pulitzer Prizes in Letters: History (*continued*)

Year	Winner(s)	Awarded for
1996	Alan Taylor	*William Cowper's Town: Power and Persuasion on the Frontier of the Early American Republic*
1997	Jack N Rakove	*Original Meetings: Politics and Ideas in the Making of the Constitution*
1998	Edward J Larson	*Summer for the Gods: The Scopes Trial and America's Continuing Debate Over Science and Religion*
1999	Edwin G Burrows and Mike Wallace	*Gotham: A History of New York City to 1898*
2000	David M Kennedy	*Freedom From Fear: The American People in Depression and War, 1929–1945*

Pulitzer Prizes in Letters
Poetry

Year	Winner	Awarded for
1990	Charles Simic	*The World Doesn't End*
1991	Mona Van Duyn	*Near Changes*
1992	James Tate	*Selected Poems*
1993	Louise Gluck	*The Wild Iris*
1994	Yusef Komunyakaa	*Neon Vernacular*
1995	Philip Levine	*Simple Truth*
1996	Jorie Graham	*The Dream of the Unified Field*
1997	Lisel Mueller	*Alive Together: New and Selected Poems*
1998	Charles Wright	*Black Zodiac*
1999	Mark Strand	*Blizzard of One*
2000	C K Williams	*Repair*

Real Names
Of Famous Authors

Author	Real name
Lewis Carroll	Charles Dodgson
George Eliot	Mary Ann Evans
Ruth Rendell	Barbara Vine
Catherine Sefton	Martin Waddell
Dr Seuss	Theodor Seuss Geisel
Mark Twain	Samuel Langhorne Clemens
Voltaire	Francois Marie Arouet
Oscar Wilde	Fingal O'Flahertie Wills

Russian Words
Used in English

babushka	cosmonaut	karakul	samovar	taiga
balalaika	czar	knout	samoyed	tokamak
beluga	dacha	kulak	shaman	troika
Bolshevik	glasnost	mammoth	soviet	tsar
bortsch	gulag	perestroika	sputnik	tundra
borzoi	intelligentsia	samizdat	steppe	vodka

Sanskrit Words
Used in English

Word	Meaning in the English language
ahimsa	('non-injury') the Hindu, Buddhist, and Jain doctrine of harming no living being; non-violence
avatar	('descent') the manifestation or incarnation of a principle or deity in human or animal form
chakra	('wheel') a mystical circle placed in the hands of images of Hindu gods; in yoga, one of the centres of spiritual power in the human body; the emblem on the flag of the Indian Union
karma	('action') in Hinduism and Buddhism, the total of a person's actions in one incarnation, which determines their fate in the next
mantra	('device') a sacred text used as a prayer or incantation; a sacred word or syllable used for meditation
nirvana	('blowing out') the extinction of individual existence with its desires and passions
Prana	('Ancient') one of a group of sacred verse stories about Hindu gods and heroes
swaraj	('self-rule') in British India, the agitation in favour of self-government
swastika	('mark of well-being') an equal-armed cross with right-angled ends, a symbol of good fortune
Tantra	('loom') one of many Hindu and Buddhist works of a magical or mystical nature

Scandinavian Words
Used in English

English	Origin	English	Origin
atto-	Danish	gauntlet	Swedish
bark (tree)	Norse	geyser	Icelandic
berserk	Norse	krill	Norwegian
femto-	Danish	landrace	Danish
fjord	Norwegian	lemming	Lapp/Norwegian
floe	Norwegian	moped	Swedish

Scandinavian Words: Used in English (*continued*)

English	Origin	English	Origin
mink	Danish	slalom	Norwegian
ombudsman	Swedish	smorgasbord	Swedish
orienteering	Swedish	smørrebrød	Danish
rug	Swedish	troll	Norwegian
sauna	Finnish	tundra	Lapp
ski	Norwegian	tungsten	Swedish

Scott
Principal Works of Fiction by Walter Scott

Title	Year	Title	Year
Waverley	1814	*Quentin Durward*	1823
Guy Mannering	1815	*St Ronan's Well*	1823
The Antiquary	1816	*Redgauntlet*	1824
The Black Dwarf	1816	*The Betrothed*	1825
Old Mortality	1816	*The Talisman*	1825
Rob Roy	1817	*Woodstock*	1826
The Heart of Midlothian	1818	*The Highland Widow*	1827
The Bride of Lammermoor	1819	*The Surgeon's Daughter*	1827
The Legend of Montrose	1819	*The Two Drovers*	1827
The Abbot	1820	*St Valentine's Day: or, The Fair Maid of Perth*	1828
The Monastery	1820	*Anne of Geierstein*	1829
Kenilworth	1821	*Count Robert of Paris*	1829
The Pirate	1821	*Castle Dangerous*	1832
The Fortunes of Nigel	1822		
Peveril of the Peak	1823		

Scottish Words
Used in English

English	Scottish origin
burn (small stream)	burna (Old English)
firth (sea inlet)	fjörthr (Norse)
gruesome (repugnant)	grua (Norse)
raid (surprise attack)	rad (Old English)
wee (very small)	waeg (Old English)
wraith (apparition)	vörthr (Norse)

Sculpture
Most Expensive Sculptures at Auction

Source: Art Sales Index Ltd

As of May 2000.

Work	Artist	Place and date of sale	Price (US$)
Petite danseuse de quatorze ans	Edgar Degas	Sotheby's, New York, 1999	11,250,000
Petite danseuse de quatorze ans (resold later, see above)	Edgar Degas	Sotheby's, New York, 1996	10,800,000
The dancing faun	Adriaen de Vries	Sotheby's, London, 1989	9,796,000
Petite danseuse de quatorze ans (resold later, see above)	Edgar Degas	Christie's, New York, 1988	9,250,000
Petite danseuse de quatorze ans (resold later, see above)	Edgar Degas	Sotheby's, New York, 1988	9,200,000
Nu couche, Aurore	Henri Matisse	Christie's, New York, 1999	8,400,000
La negresse blonde	Constantin Brancusi	Sotheby's, New York, 1990	8,000,000
La muse endormie III	Constantin Brancusi	Christie's, New York, 1989	7,500,000
La forêt - sept figures et une tête	Alberto Giacometti	Sotheby's, New York, 1998	6,800,000
Mlle Pogany II	Constantin Brancusi	Christie's, New York, 1997	6,400,000

SFWA Nebula Award Grand Master

The Science Fiction and Fantasy Writers of America Inc. (SFAW) do not award the title of Grand Master every year.

Year	Writer	Year	Writer
2000	Philip Hosé Farmer	1990	Lester Del Ray
1999	Brian W Aldiss	1988	Ray Bradbury
1998	Hal Clement (Harry Stubbs)	1987	Alfred Bester
1997	Poul Anderson	1986	Isaac Asimov
1996	Jack Vance	1985	Arthur C Clarke
1995	A E Van Vogt	1983	Andre Norton
1994	Damon Knight	1981	Fritz Leiber
1992	Frederik Pohl		

SFWA Nebula Awards Winners

The Science Fiction and Fantasy Writers of America Inc. (SFWA) award prizes annually in a number of different categories

Year	Book	Writer
2000	*Darwin's Radio*	Greg Bear
1999	*Parable of the Talents*	Octavia E Butler
1998	*Forever Peace*	Joe Haldeman
1997	*The Moon and the Sun*	Vonda N McIntyre
1996	*Slow River*	Nicola Griffith
1995	*The Terminal Experiment*[1]	Robert J Sawyer
1994	*Moving Mars*	Greg Bear
1993	*Red Mars*	Kim Stanley Robinson
1992	*Doomsday Book*	Connie Willis
1991	*Stations of the Tide*	Michael Swanswick
1990	*Tehanu: The Last Book of Earthsea*	Ursula K Le Guin
1989	*The Healer's War*	Elizabeth Ann Scarborough
1988	*Falling Free*	Lois McMaster Bujold
1987	*The Falling Woman*	Pat Murphy
1986	*Speaker for the Dead*	Orson Scott Card
1985	*Ender's Game*	Orson Scott Card
1984	*Neuromancer*	William Gibson
1983	*Startide Rising*	David Brin
1982	*No Enemy But Time*	Michael Bishop
1981	*The Claw of the Conciliator*	Gene Wolfe

[1] Serialized as *Hobson's Choice*.

Shakespeare

Characters who Disguise Themselves as the Opposite Sex

Character	Play
Falstaff	*The Merry Wives of Windsor*
Imogen	*Cymbeline*
Julia	*Twelve Gentlemen of Verona*
Portia	*The Merchant of Venice*
Rosalind	*As You Like It*
Viola	*Twelfth Night*

Shakespeare
Chronology of Shakespeare's Plays

First performed	Play	First printed	First performed	Play	First printed
1590–91	Henry VI, Part II	c. 1594	1599–1600	Julius Caesar	1623
1590–91	Henry VI, Part III	c. 1594	1599–1600	As You Like It	1623
1591–92	Henry VI, Part I	1623	1599–1600	Twelfth Night	1623
1592–93	Richard III	1594	1600–01	Hamlet	1603
1592–93	The Comedy of Errors	1623	1600–01	The Merry Wives of Windsor	1602
1592–93	Titus Andronicus	1594			
1593–94	The Taming of the Shrew	1623	1600–01	Troilus and Cressida	1609
			1602–03	All's Well That Ends Well	1623
1594–95	Two Gentlemen of Verona	1623			
			1604–05	Measure for Measure	1623
1594–95	Love's Labour's Lost	c. 1598	1604–05	Othello	1622
1595–96	Romeo and Juliet	1597	1605–06	King Lear	1608
1595–96	Richard II	1597	1605–06	Macbeth	1623
1595–96	A Midsummer Night's Dream	1600	1606–07	Antony and Cleopatra	1623
			1607–08	Coriolanus	1623
1596–97	King John	1623	1607–08	Timon of Athens	1623
1596–97	The Merchant of Venice	1600	1608–09	Pericles	1609
1597–98	Henry IV, Part I	1598	1609–10	Cymbeline	1623
1597–98	Henry IV, Part II	1600	1610–11	The Winter's Tale	1623
1598–99	Much Ado About Nothing	1600	1611–12	The Tempest	1623
			1612–13	Henry VIII	1623
1598–99	Henry V	1600	1612–13	The Two Noble Kinsmen[1]	1634

[1] Shakespeare's authorship of this play is widely disputed by scholars.

Shakespeare
Ghosts in Shakespeare's Plays

Play	Act/scene	Details
Richard III	Act V Scene III	the ghosts of Richard's victims appear before him one after another to announce his coming defeat
Julius Caesar	Act IV Scene III	Caesar's ghost appears to Brutus to predict his death at Philippi
Hamlet	Act I Scenes I, IV and V	the ghost of Hamlet's father appears on the battlements of Elsinore Castle, at first to Horatio and others, then in later scenes to Hamlet, confirming the young prince's suspicions of his mother's and stepfather's treachery
Macbeth	Act III Scene IV	Banquo's ghost appears to Macbeth at a banquet, predicting the ultimate failure of his line
Cymbeline	Act V Scene IV	Cymbeline's father, mother, and brothers appear as ghosts to petition Jupiter for a change in his fortunes

Shakespeare
Selected Shakespeare Plays

Title	First performed/ written (approximate)	Title	First performed/ written (approximate)
A Midsummer Night's Dream	1594–95	Julius Caesar	1599
		As You Like It	1599–1600
Romeo and Juliet	1594–95	Twelfth Night	1600–02
The Merchant of Venice	1596–98	Hamlet	1601–02
		Macbeth	1606
Much Ado About Nothing	1598	The Tempest	1611

Shakespeare
Shakespeare's Plays Set in Italy

First performed	Play	First printed
1592–93	Titus Andronicus	1594
1593–94	The Taming of the Shrew	1623
1594–95	Two Gentlemen of Verona	1623
1595–96	Romeo and Juliet	1597
1596–97	The Merchant of Venice	1600
1598–99	Much Ado About Nothing	1600
1599–1600	Julius Caesar	1623
1602–03	All's Well That Ends Well	1623
1604–05	Othello	1622
1606–07	Antony and Cleopatra	1623
1607–08	Coriolanus	1623
1609–10	Cymbeline	1623
1610–11	The Winter's Tale	1623

Shakespeare
Some Miscellaneous Facts

Miscellaneous	Details
first published work	Venus and Adonis (1593)
first published play	Titus Andronicus (1594)
first play to be filmed	thought to be four scenes from King John in 1899 (a one minute fragment survives)
first filmed adaptation	The Life and Death of King Richard III, shot in 1912 and thought to be the earliest film to exist in complete form

(continued)

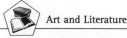

Shakespeare: Some Miscellaneous Facts (*continued*)

Miscellaneous	Details
foreign language translations of the complete works	over 30 langauges
foreign language translations of individual plays and poems	over 80 languages
total number of words written	884,647
total number of lines written	118,406
total number of speeches written	31,959
total number of individual/ different words written	29,066
Shakespeare's London theatres	The Theatre, Curtain, Fortune, Red Bull, The Rose, Swan, Hope, Newington Butts, Blackfrairs
theatres Shakespeare was associated with	The Theatre, Curtain, Rose, Swan, Globe, Blackfriars
the longest written part	Hamlet, with over 1,507 lines
the longest part over several plays	Henry V, with over 1,922 lines
the longest female role	Rosalind in *As You Like It,* with 721 lines
the longest female part over several plays	Queen Margaret, who has 847 lines

Shakespeare
Ten Shakespeare Plays on Film

Play	Director	Year of release
Hamlet	Tony Richardson	1964
Henry V	Laurence Olivier	1944
Julius Caesar	Joseph L Mankiewicz	1953
King Lear	Peter Brook	1970
Macbeth	Roman Polanski	1971
Much Ado About Nothing	Kenneth Branagh	1994
Othello	Orson Welles	1952
Richard III	Richard Loncraine	1996
Romeo and Juliet	Baz Luhrmann	1997
Taming of the Shrew	Franco Zeffirelli	1967

Slang
Cockney Rhyming Slang

What you say	Origin	Meaning
Adam and Eve it		believe it
apples	apples and pears	stairs
arris	Aristotle	'bottle' (courage)
bangers and mash		cash
barnet	Barnet Fair	hair
Bath bun		sun
bees	bees and honey	money
bird	bird lime	time (in prison)
boat	boat race	face
boracic	boracic lint	skint (broke)
bottle	bottle and glass	class
brass tacks		facts
bristols	Bristol cities	titties (breasts)
bull and cow		row (argument)
burnt	burnt cinder	winder (window)
bushel	bushel and peck	neck
butchers	butcher's hook	look
Cain and Abel		table
cherry ripe		pipe
china	china plate	mate
cock and hen		ten (pounds)
conan	Conan Doyle	boil
country cousin		dozen
currant bun		sun
daisy roots		boots
derby kel	Derby Kelly	belly
dickory	dickory dock	clock

What you say	Origin	Meaning
dicky	dicky bird	word
dicky	dicky dirt	shirt
dog	dog and bone	(tele)phone
earwig		eavesdrop
elephants	elephant's trunk	drunk
farmers	Farmer Giles	piles (haemorrhoids)
frog	frog and toad	road
George	George Raft	draught
Germans	German bands	hands
ginger	ginger beer	queer
godfers	God forbids	kids (children)
gold watch		Scotch (drink)
gooses	goose's neck	cheque
Gregory Peck		neck
half-inch		pinch (steal)
jack	Jack Jones	alone (on ones own)
jacks	Jack's alive	five (pounds)
jam-jar		car
jam roll		dole
Jimmy	Jimmy Riddle	piddle
Joanna		piano
Kate and Sidney		steak and kidney
kettle	kettle and hob	fob (watch) or bob (shilling)
Lady Godiva		fiver
loaf	loaf of bread	head
Lord Mayor		swear
Lucy Locket		pocket
minces	mince pies	eyes

(continued)

Slang: Cockney Rhyming Slang (*continued*)

What you say	Origin	Meaning	What you say	Origin	Meaning
mutton	Mutt and Jeff	deaf	sausage	sausage and mash	cash
Nelsons	Nelson Eddys	readies (banknotes)	scarper	Scapa Flow	go (run away)
north and south		mouth	Sexton	Sexton Blake	fake
pen and ink		stink	skin and blister		sister
pig's ear		beer	sky	sky rocket	pocket
plates	plates of meat	feet	snake	snake in the grass	looking glass
porkies	pork pies	lies	square	square and round	pound
pot and pan		old man	Sweeney	Sweeney Todd	Flying Squad
rabbit	rabbit and pork	talk	tea-leaf		thief
rhythm and blues		shoes	tiddlywink		drink
Richard	Richard III	bird	titfer	tit for tat	hat
Rosie	Rosie Lee	tea	tod	Tod Sloan	own
round the houses		trousers	tom	tom-foolery	jewellery
rub-a-dub		pub	Tom and Dick		sick
Ruby	Ruby Murray	curry	trouble	trouble and strife	wife
			twig		understand
			two and eight		state
			whistle	whistle and flute	suit

Spoonerisms

Ten (Allegedly) Genuine Spoonerisms

William Archibald Spooner (1844–1930), after whom the phenomenon of spoonerism is named, was an English academic and cleric who had a tendency to transpose the initial sounds of words.

'I remember your name perfectly, but I just can't think of your face.'

'It moved easily, just like a well-boiled icicle.'

'Kinquering Congs their titles take.'

'Please be good enough to sew me to another sheet.'

'Poor soul; her late husband, a very sad death – eaten by missionaries!'

'To our queer old dean.'

'We all know what it is to have a half-warmed fish within us.'

'Yes, indeed; the Lord is a shoving leopard.'

'You have tasted your worm, you have hissed my mystery lectures, and you must leave by the first town drain.'

'You will find as you grow older that the weight of rages will press harder and harder upon the employer.'

Steinbeck
Principal Works of Fiction by John Steinbeck

Title	Year	Title	Year
Cup of Gold	1929	*The Moon is Down*	1942
The Pastures of Heaven	1932	*Cannery Row*	1945
To a God Unknown	1933	*The Pearl*	1947
Tortilla Flat	1935	*The Wayward Bus*	1947
In Dubious Battle	1936	*East of Eden*	1952
Of Mice and Men	1937	*Sweet Thursday*	1954
The Long Valley	1938	*The Winter of Our Discontent*	1961
The Grapes of Wrath	1939		

Tamil Words
Used in English

catamaran
cheroot
curry (food)
mulligatawny
mung (bean)
pariah
poppadom

Tate Modern
Some Popular Exhibits at the Tate Modern, London

Artist	Exhibit
Bill Viola	*Nantes Triptych* (1992)
Richard Long	*Slate Circle* (1979)
David Hockney	*A Bigger Splash* (1967)
Marcel Duchamp	*Fountain* (1917)
Pierre Bonnard	*The Bath* (1925)
Salvador Dali	*Lobster Telephone* (1936)
Damien Hurst	*Forms Without Life* (1991)
Cornelia Parker	*Cold Dark Matters: An Expanded View* (1991)
Gilbert and George	*Death Hope Life Fear* (1984)
Henri Matisse	*The Snail* (1953)

Trade Names
Dictionary Words that are Still Trade Names

Benzedrine	Freon	Ozalid	Pyrex	Terylene
Biro	Hoover	Pentothal	Scotch tape	Thermos
Cellophane	Jeep	Perrier	Sellotape	Valium
Cinemascope	Levis	Perspex	Spam	Vaseline
Coca Cola	Lysol	Photostat	Tannoy	Velcro
Dacron	Muzak	Plasticine	Tarmac	Xerox
Durex	Novocaine	Polaroid	Technicolor	Y-fronts
Formica	Ouija board	Pullman	Teflon	

Trade Names
Former Trade Names that Are Now Ordinary English Words

aspirin	brilliantine	escalator	linoleum	polythene
autogiro	carborundum	gramophone	melamine	rayon
bakelite	celluloid	gunk (slang)	mimeograph	
barathea	duralumin	heroin	nylon	

Trilogies
Some Famous Literary Trilogies

Author	Book	Author	Book
Leo Tolstoy	*Childhood* (1852) *Boyhood* (1854) *Youth* (1857)	Margaret Drabble	*The Radiant Way* (1987) *A Natural Curiosity* (1989) *The Gates of Ivory* (1991)
William Shakespeare	*Henry VI* (in three parts) (c. 1590)	William Faulkner	*The Hamlet* (1940) *The Town* (1957) *The Mansion* (1959)
J R R Tolkien	*The Fellowship of the Ring* (1954) *The Two Towers* (1954) *Return of the King* (1955)	Emile Zola	*Lourdes* (1894) *Rome* (1896) *Paris* (1898)
Mervyn Peake	*Titus Groan* (1946) *Gormenghast* (1950) *Titus Alone* (1959)	William Golding	*Rites of Passage* (1980) *Close Quarters* (1987) *Fire Down Below* (1989)
Isaac Asimov	*Foundation* (1951) *Foundation and Empire* (1952) *Second Foundation* (1953)	Evelyn Waugh	*Men at Arms* (1952) *Officers and Gentlemen* (1955) *Unconditional Surrender* (1961)
Henry Miller	*Tropic of Cancer* (1934) *Black Spring* (1936) *Tropic of Capricorn* (1938)	Sophocles	*Antigone* (443 BC) *Oedipus the King* (429 BC) *Oedipus at Colonus* (401 BC)

Turkish Words
Used in English

bosh	dervish	kebab	pasha
caftan	dolman	kilim	shagreen
caracal	effendi	kiosk	sherbet
caviare	janissary	macramé	turban
coffee	kaftan	mezé	yogurt

Turner Prize Winners

Year	Winner
1990	no award
1991	Anish Kapoor
1992	Grenville Davey
1993	Rachel Whiteread
1994	Antony Gormley
1995	Damien Hirst
1996	Douglas Gordon
1997	Gillian Wearing
1998	Chris Ofili
1999	Steve McQueen
2000	Wolfgang Tillmans

Urdu Words
Used in English

khaki
nabob
numdah
purdah
pyjamas
sepoy
shawl
tandoor
tandoori

Vowels
All-vowel Words[1]

Word	Meaning
aa	volcanic lava with a rough surface
aie	an Indian or South African nursemaid
ay	ever, always
ea	stream or river
eau	watery perfume
eye	organ of sight
oi	used to attract attention
oo	exclamation
yea	an affirmation or vote of assent
yo-yo	a toy spun along a string

[1] *y* is sometimes classed as a semivowel

Waugh
Principal Works of Fiction by Evelyn Waugh

Title	Year
Decline and Fall	1928
Vile Bodies	1930
Black Mischief	1932
A Handful of Dust	1934
Scoop	1938
Put Out More Flags	1942
Brideshead Revisited	1945
The Loved One	1948
Helena	1950
Men at Arms[1]	1952
Officers and Gentlemen[1]	1955
The Ordeal of Gilbert Pinfold	1957
Unconditional Surrender[1]	1961

[1] Published collectively as the *Sword of Honour* trilogy in 1965.

Welsh Words
Used in English

English	Welsh origin	English	Welsh origin
bug (evil spirit)	bwg	flummery (trifle(s))	llymru
corgi (dog)	cor ci	gull (bird)	gwylan
crag (rocky peak)	creik	penguin (antarctic bird)	pen gwyn
cromlech (stone circle)	crom llech	pikelet (cake)	bara pyglyd
flannel (cloth)	gwlanen	vassal (protected servant)	gwas

Williams
Selected Stage Works of Tennessee Williams

Title	Year	Title	Year
The Glass Menagerie	1944	*Suddenly Last Summer*	1958
A Streetcar Named Desire	1947	*Night of the Iguana*[2]	1959
Summer and Smoke[1]	1947	*The Milk Train Doesn't Stop Here Anymore*	1962
The Rose Tattoo	1951		
Camino Real	1953	*In The Bar of a Tokyo Hotel*	1969
Cat on a Hot Tin Roof	1955	*Vieux Carré*	1977
Sweet Bird of Youth	1956	*Clothes for a Summer Hotel*	1980

[1] Revised 1964 as *The Eccentricities of a Nightingale*.
[2] Revised 1961.

Woolf
Principal Works of Virginia Woolf

Title	Year	Title	Year
The Voyage Out	1915	*A Room of One's Own*	1929
Night and Day	1919	*The Waves*	1931
Jacob's Room	1922	*The Years*	1937
Mrs Dalloway	1925	*Three Guineas*	1938
To the Lighthouse	1927	*Between the Acts*	1941
Orlando	1928		

Words
Back-formed Words

Later back-formation	Original word it was formed from	Later back-formation	Original word it was formed from
automate	automation	diagnose	diagnosis
brindle	brindled	difficult	difficulty
burgle	burglar	eavesdrop	eavesdropper
chamfer	chamfering	edit	editor
cobble	cobbler	escalate	escalator
commuter	commutation	fixate	fixation
craze	crazy	greed	greedy
demote	demotion	grovel	grovelling
devolute	devolution	haze	hazy

Words: Back-formed Words (*continued*)

Later back-formation	Original word it was formed from	Later back-formation	Original word it was formed from
henpeck	henpecked	salve	salvage
kidnap	kidnapper	shoplift	shoplifting
laze	lazy	swindle	swindler
liaise	liaison	teethe	teething
moonlit	moonlight	televise	television
peddle	pedlar		

Words
Killing Words Ending in –cide

Word	Meaning	Word	Meaning
bactericide	drug or chemical that kills bacteria	matricide	killing of one's mother
		parricide	killing of a near relative
fratricide	killing a brother or sister	patricide	killing of one's father
fungicide	drug or chemical that kills fungi and moulds	pesticide	killing of pests
		regicide	killing of a king or queen
genocide	killing of a race or nation	spermicide	drug or chemical that kills sperm
germicide	drug or chemical that kills germs		
		suicide	killing of oneself
homicide	killing of a human being	vermicide	killing of worms
infanticide	killing of one's baby		

Words
Longest Words

Word[1]	Number of letters	Language	Meaning
Nordöstersjökustartilleriflygspaningssimulatoranläggningsmaterielunderhållsuppföljningssystemdiskussionsinläggsförberedelsearbeten	130	Swedish	preparatory work on the contribution to the discussion concerning maintaining the system of support of the material of the aviation survey simulator device within the northeast part of the coast artillery of the Baltic
Donaudampfschiffahrtselektrizitaetenhauptbetriebswerkbauunterbeamtengesellschaft	80	German	the club for subordinate officials of the head office management of Danube Steamboat Electrical Services
Rindfleischetikettierungsüberwachungsaufgabenübertragungsgesetz	63	German	a law pertaining to British beef and so-called 'mad cow disease' (BSE)
Cekoslovakyalilastirabilemediklerimizlerdenmisiniz?	50	Turkish	are you not of that group of people that we were said to be unable to Czechoslovakianize?

(continued)

Words: Longest Words (*continued*)

Word[1]	Number of letters	Language	Meaning
Tkanuh'stasrihsranuh-we'tsraaksahsrakarata-ttsrayeri'	50	Mohawk	the praising of the evil of the liking of the finding of the house is right
Kindercarnavalsoptoc-htvoorbereidingsverk-zaamheden	49	Dutch	preparation activities for a children's carnival procession
Megszentségtelenithet-etlenségeskedéseitekért	44	Hungarian	for your unprofanable actions

[1] Not including scientific words

Words

Most Commonly Used Words in Spoken English

the	I	is
of	to	was
and	in	it
a	you	was

Words

Most Commonly Used Words in Written English

the	a	was
of	for	that
to	in	on
and	is	at

Words

Some New English Words from the 1970s, 1980s, and 1990s

1970s	1980s	1990s
action replay	cashback	alcopop
bulimia	chat line	bad hair day
car bomb	cyberspace	cybercafé
cling film	download	docusoap
environmentalism	ghetto-blaster	DVD
flexitime	gridlock	ethnic cleansing
gentrify	lager lout	gangsta rap
junk food	lap-top	GM
passive smoking	OTT	home page
sell-by date	pear-shaped	jobseeker
speed bump	road rage	puffa jacket
teletext	safe sex	screen saver
user-friendly	shell suit	slacker
	yuppie	World Wide Web

Words
Weapons that Are Named after People

Weapon	Named after	Nationality
Bowie knife	Jim Bowie (1799–1836)	US
Browning automatic	John Browning (1855–1926)	US
Colt revolver	Samuel Colt (1814–62)	US
Congreve rocket	William Congreve (1772–1828)	British
Derringer pistol	Henry Deringer (1786–1868)	US
Gatling gun	Richard Gatling (1818–1903)	US
Kalashnikov rifle	Mikhail Kalashnikov (1919–)	Russian
Lewis gun	Isaac Lewis (1858–1931)	US
Mauser rifle	Peter Mauser (1838–1914)	German
Maxim machine gun	Hiram Maxim (1814–1916)	US
Mills bomb	William Mills (1856–1932)	British
Molotov cocktail	Vyacheslav Molotov (1890–1986)	Russian
Shrapnel shell	Henry Shrapnel (1761–1842)	British
Tommy gun	John Thompson (1860–1940)	US
Winchester rifle	Oliver Winchester (1810–80)	US

Words
Words that Mean what They Sound Like

Initial letter	Words
b	babble, bang, blabber, bubble, burble, buzz
c	cackle, caw, chatter, chirp, chuckle, clang, clatter, click, clink, clunck, coo, crackle, crash, creak, croak, crunch, cuckoo
d	ding, dong, drip, drumming
f	fizz, flutter
g	gabble, gaggle, gargle, gibber, giggle, glug, gobble, grate, growl, grunt, gurgle
h	hiccup, hiss, honk, hum
j	jabber, jangle, jingle, judder
l	lap (verb), lisp
m	meow, mew, miaow, moo, mumble, munch, murmur, mutter
n	neigh
p	patter, ping, pitter-patter, plink, plonk, plop, pom-pom, pop, puff, purr
q	quack
r	ratatat-tat, rattle, rev, roar, rustle
s	screech, sizzle, slither, slosh, slurp, snuffle, splash, splutter, squeak, squish, strum, swash, swish, swoosh
t	thwack, tick, ting, tinkle, toot, twang, tweet, twitter
v	vroom
w	whack, wham, whine, whinny, whir, whistle, whiz, whoop, whoosh, woof
y	yap

Yeats
Major Works by W(illiam) B(utler) Yeats

Poetry	Year
The Wanderings of Oisin	1889
The Celtic Twilight	1893
The Wind Among the Reeds	1899
In the Seven Woods	1904
The Green Helmet	1910
Responsibilities	1914
The Wild Swans at Coole	1917
Michael Robartes and the Dancer	1921
The Tower	1928
The Winding Stair	1933
A Full Moon in March	1935
Last Poems	1939

Plays	Year
The Countess Cathleen	1892
The Land of Heart's Desire	1894
Deirdre	1907
The Death of Cuchulain	1939

Prose	Year
A Vision	1925 and 1937
Autobiographies	1926
Dramatis Personae	1936

Stage
and
Screen

Academic Awards

Year of release	Best Picture	Best Director	Best Actor	Best Actress	Best Supporting Actor	Best Supporting Actress
1990	*Dances With Wolves*	Kevin Costner *Dances With Wolves*	Jeremy Irons *Reversal of Fortune*	Kathy Bates *Misery*	Joe Pesci *GoodFellas*	Whoopi Goldberg *Ghost*
1991	*The Silence of the Lambs*	Jonathan Demme *The Silence of the Lambs*	Anthony Hopkins *The Silence of the Lambs*	Jodie Foster *The Silence of the Lambs*	Jack Palance *City Slickers*	Mercedes Ruehl *The Fisher King*
1992	*Unforgiven*	Clint Eastwood *Unforgiven*	Al Pacino *Scent of a Woman*	Emma Thompson *Howard's End*	Gene Hackman *Unforgiven*	Marisa Tomei *My Cousin Vinny*
1993	*Schindler's List*	Steven Spielberg *Schindler's List*	Tom Hanks *Philadelphia*	Holly Hunter *The Piano*	Tommy Lee Jones *The Fugitive*	Anna Paquin *The Piano*
1994	*Forrest Gump*	Robert Zemeckis *Forrest Gump*	Tom Hanks *Forrest Gump*	Jessica Lange *Blue Sky*	Martin Landau *Ed Wood*	Dianne Wiest *Bullets Over Broadway*
1995	*Braveheart*	Mel Gibson *Braveheart*	Nicolas Cage *Leaving Las Vegas*	Susan Sarandon *Dead Man Walking*	Kevin Spacey *The Usual Suspects*	Mira Sorvino *Mighty Aphrodite*
1996	*The English Patient*	Anthony Minghella *The English Patient*	Geoffrey Rush *Shine*	Frances McDormand *Fargo*	Cuba Gooding Jr *Jerry Maguire*	Juliette Binoche *The English Patient*
1997	*Titanic*	James Cameron *Titanic*	Jack Nicholson *As Good As It Gets*	Helen Hunt *As Good As It Gets*	Robin Williams *Good Will Hunting*	Kim Basinger *L A Confidential*
1998	*Shakespeare in Love*	Steven Spielberg *Saving Private Ryan*	Roberto Benigni *La vita é bella/Life is Beautiful*	Gwyneth Paltrow *Shakespeare in Love*	James Coburn *Affliction*	Judi Dench *Shakespeare in Love*
1999	*American Beauty*	Sam Mendes *American Beauty*	Kevin Spacey *American Beauty*	Hilary Swank *Boys Don't Cry*	Michael Caine *Cider House Rules*	Angelina Jolie *Girl, Interrupted*
2000	*Gladiator*	Steven Soderbergh *Traffic*	Russell Crowe *Gladiator*	Julia Roberts *Erin Brockovich*	Benicio del Toro *Traffic*	Marcia Gay Harden *Pollock*

Action and Adventure Films

Film	Year
Jurassic Park	1993
The Lost World: Jurassic Park	1997
Mission Impossible II	2000
Terminator 2: Judgement Day	1991
Indiana Jones and the Last Crusade	1989
Mission Impossible	1996
Die Hard: With a Vengeance	1995
Indiana Jones and the Temple of Doom	1984
Fight Club	1999
Romancing the Stone	1984

Actors
(Female) Most Prolific Film Actors

Actor (excluding voice-over actors)	Number of films
Bess Flowers	371
Florence Lawrence	275
Mary Pickford	248
Sridevi	248
Ann Doran	237
Mary Gordon	226
Mabel Normand	219
Zasu Pitts	203
Claire McDowell	202
Minerva Urecal	201

Actors
(Female) with Most Academy Award Nominations

Nominations	Actor
12	Katharine Hepburn
	Meryl Streep
10	Bette Davis
8	Geraldine Page
7	Ingrid Bergman
	Jane Fonda
	Greer Garson
6	Deborah Kerr
	Jessica Lange
	Vanessa Redgrave
	Thelma Ritter
	Norma Shearer

Actors
(Male) Most Prolific Film Actors

Actor (excluding voice-over actors)	Number of films
Tom London	464
Bud Osborne	442
Edmund Cobb	419
Irving Bacon	357
George Chesebro	350
Lee Phelps	350
Wade Boteler	341
Raymond Hatton	334
Emmett Vogan	327
Charles King	325

Actors
(Male) with Most Academy Award Nominations

Nominations	Actor	Nominations	Actor
11	Jack Nicholson	7	Richard Burton
10	Laurence Olivier		Dustin Hoffman
9	Spencer Tracey		Peter O'Toole
8	Jack Lemon	6	Robert de Niro
	Paul Newman		
	Al Pacino		

Actors
(Male and Female) Appearing in Most Films in 2000

Number of films	Actor
5 films	Michael Rapaport (*The 6th Day; Small Time Crooks; Lucky Numbers; Men of Honour; Bamboozled*)
4 films	Danny DeVito (*Screwed; The Big Kahuna; The Virgin Suicides; Drowning Mona*)
	Mel Gibson (*The Patriot; What Women Want; Chicken Run* (voice); *Mad Max* (re-release))
	Helen Hunt (*Pay it Forward; Castaway; What Women Want; Dr T and the Women*)
	Greg Kinnear (*What Planet Are You From?; Loser; Nurse Betty; The Gift*)
	Anna Paquin (*X-Men; Almost Famous; All the Rage; Finding Forrester*)
	Charlize Theron (*Legend of Baggar Vance; Men of Honour; The Yards; Reindeer Games*)
3 films	Casey Affleck, Don Cheadle, Matt Damon, Robert de Niro, Vincent D'Onofrio, Phillip Baker Hall, Samuel L Jackson, David Morse, Keanu Reeves, Marlon Wayans, Alfre Woodard

Actors
(Male and Female) Earning Most for a Single Film

Actor	Reported earnings (million US$)	Film	Year
Mike Myers	20	*Spockets*	2000
Adam Sandler	20	*Waterboy*	1998
Jim Carey	20	*Cable Guy*	1996
Demi Moore	12	*Striptease*	1995
Julia Roberts	9	*Mary Reilly*	1996
Whoopi Goldberg	8.5	*Sister Act 2*	1994

Actors
(Female) Highest-earning Film Actors

Carrie Fisher
Julia Roberts
Whoopi Goldberg
Kathy Bates
Sally Field
Glenn Close
Meg Ryan
Drew Barrymore
Demi Moore
Bonnie Hunt

Actors
(Male) Highest-earning Film Actors

Harrison Ford
Tom Hanks
Samuel L Jackson
Robin Williams
Tom Cruise
Bruce Willis
Bill Paxton
Eddie Murphy
Gene Hackman
Tommy Lee Jones

Actors

(Male and Female) Oldest Academy Award Winners

Actor	Age at ceremony	Film	Award	Year (of award)
Jessica Tandy	80	*Driving Miss Daisy*	Best Actress	1989
George Burns	80	*The Sunshine Boys*	Best Supporting Actor	1975
Peggy Ashcroft	77	*A Passage to India*	Best Supporting Actress	1984
Henry Fonda	76	*On Golden Pond*	Best Actor	1981
George Cukor	65	*My Fair Lady*	Best Director	1964
Richard Farnsworth	79	*The Straight Story*	Best Actor (Nominee)	1999
Gloria Stuart	87	*Titanic*	Best Actress (Nominee)	1997

Actors

(Male and Female) With Three or More Academy Awards

Number of awards	Actor
4	Katharine Hepburn
3	Ingrid Bergman
	Jack Nicholson

Actors

(Male and Female) Youngest Academy Award Winners

Actor	Age at ceremony	Awarded for	Year (of award)
Shirley Temple	6	outstanding contribution during the year	1934
Tatum O'Neil	10	Best support in *Paper Moon*	1973
Anna Paquin	11	Best support in *The Piano*	1993
Timothy Hutton	19	Best support in *Ordinary People*	1980
Marlee Matlin	21	Best Actress in *Children of a Lesser God*	1986
Richard Dreyfuss	29	Best Actor in *The Goodbye Girl*	1977
William Friedkin	32	Best Director for *The French Connection*	1971

Advertisements
All-Time Top Ten UK Television

Advertisement	Year	Advertisement	Year
Guinness: Horses and Surfers	1999	Levi Strauss: Launderette	1985
Smash: Martians	1973	R Whites: Secret Lemonade Drinker	1972
Tango: Orange Man	1992		
Electricity Association: Heat (Creature Comforts)	1992	Hamlet: Photo Booth	1986
		Walker's Crisps: Gary Lineker	1993
Boddingtons: Ice Cream	1997	Impulse: Chance Encounter	1998

Animations and Cartoons by Disney

Film	Year
Snow White and the Seven Dwarfs	1937
Fantasia	1940
The Jungle Book	1978
Beauty and the Beast	1991
Aladdin	1992
The Lion King	1994
Toy Story	1995
Pocahontas	1995
Toy Story 2	1999
Tarzan	1999

Animations and Cartoons (Excluding Disney)

Film	Year
A Bug's Life	1998
The Land Before Time	1988
Wallace and Gromit: The Wrong Trousers	1993
A Christmas Story	1983
Antz	1998
Who Framed Roger Rabbit?	1988
Wallace and Gromit: A Close Shave	1995
An American Tail	1986
Chicken Run	2000

Ballet
Oldest Companies

Name	Location	Date started
Royal Danish Ballet	Copenhagen	c. 1560
Stuttgart Ballet	Stuttgart	c. 1609
Royal Swedish Ballet	Stockholm	c. 1638
Maryinski Ballet[1] (Kirov Ballet)	St Petersburg	1738
Bolshoi Ballet	Moscow	1776
Ballet Rambert	London	1926
Stanislavsky Ballet	Moscow	1929
Royal Ballet (Vic-Wells Ballet)[2]	London	1928–31
San Francisco Ballet	San Francisco	1933
New York City Ballet (School of American Ballet)[3]	New York	1934

Ballet: Oldest Companies (*continued*)

[1] The Maryinski developed from the St Petersburg School of this date; renamed the Kirov in 1935, it has now resumed its old name.

[2] The Royal Ballet (now the Birmingham Royal Ballet) arose out of the Vic-Wells Ballet that was founded by de Valois/Ashton in 1928 or 1936; by 1936, this had become the Sadler's Wells Ballet and, by 1956, the Royal Ballet.

[3] Although the School of American Ballet was not strictly a ballet company, the New York City Ballet developed directly from it in 1948.

Ballet
The First European Ballet Companies and Theatres

Name of company	Location	Performances
Royal Danish Ballet	Copenhagen, Denmark	from mid-16th century
Royal Swedish Ballet	Stockholm, Sweden	1638
Dutch Ballet	Amsterdam, Holland	from 1642
Académie Royale de Danse	Paris, France	1661
The Royal Opera House, Covent Garden	London, UK	1732
Teatro di San Carlo	Naples, Italy	1737
Austrian Ballet	Vienna, Austria	from mid-18th century
The Royal Opera House	Berlin, Germany	1742
Teatro alla Scala	Milan, Italy	1778
Munich Theatre Ballet	Munich, Germany	1792

Ballet
Various Dance Steps

Name of step	Description
arabesque	standing on one leg with the other leg stretched out behind
ballon	a floating leap
batterie	leap while beating the calves together
bourrée	small step on the points of the toes
brisé	leap from one leg, beating the legs together and landing on both feet
capriole	leap while beating one leg against the other
chassé	step while sliding the foot with no heel lift
ciseaux	leap with the legs wide apart
entrechat	vertical jump beating the calves together
glissade	slow sliding steps with feet brought together between each step
jeté	leap from one leg to the other
pointes	dancing on the toes

Ballets
Major First Performances

Date	Ballet	Composer	Location
1670	*Le Bourgeois Gentilhomme*	Lully	Chambord, France
1761	*Don Juan*	Gluck	Vienna, Austria
1828	*La Fille mal gardée*	Hérold	Paris, France
1869	*Don Quixote*	Minkus	Moscow, Russia
1870	*Coppélia*	Delibes	Paris, France
1877	*Swan Lake*	Tchaikovsky	Moscow, Russia
1890	*The Sleeping Beauty*	Tchaikovsky	St Petersburg, Russia
1892	*Nutcracker*	Tchaikovsky	St Petersburg, Russia
1905	*The Dying Swan*	Saint-Saëns	St Petersburg, Russia
1938	*Romeo and Juliet*	Prokofiev	Brno, Czech Republic

Biblical Films

Film	Year
Quo Vadis	1951
The Greatest Story Ever Told	1965
King of Kings	1927
The Ten Commandments	1956
Barabbas	1962
Exodus	1960
King David	1985
The Robe	1953

Box Office
Biggest Loss-making Films

Film	Year released	Estimated losses (US$ million)
Cutthroat Island	1995	79
Inchon	1981	49
Santa Claus: The Movie	1985	49
Hudson Hawk	1991	48
The Postman	1997	45
Heaven's Gate	1980	42
Billy Bathgate	1991	34
The Adventures of Baron Munchausen	1988	32
Pirates	1986	30
Ishtar	1987	26

Box Office
Global Grosses

Country	Box office grosses in 1998 (US$ millions)	Country	Box office grosses in 1998 (US$ millions)
USA	6,580	Italy	675
Japan	1,561	Spain	445
France	998	India	430
Germany	914	Australia	419
UK	825	Brazil	380

Box Office
Highest Earning Films in 2000

Film	Director	Stars
Mission Impossible II	John Woo	Tom Cruise, Dougray Scott
Gladiator	Ridley Scott	Russell Crowe, Joaquin Phoenix
The Perfect Storm	Wolfgang Petersen	George Clooney, Mark Wahlberg
X-Men	Bryan Singer	Hugh Jackman, Patrick Stewart
Scary Movie	Keenen Ivory Wayans	Shannon Elizabeth, Regina Hall
Erin Brockovich	Steven Soderbergh	Julia Roberts, David Brisbin
Dinosaur	Eric Leighton, Ralph Zondag	D B Sweeney, Alfre Woodard
Gone in Sixty Seconds	Dominic Sena	Nicolas Cage, Angelina Jolie
What Lies Beneath	Robert Zemeckis	Harrison Ford, Michelle Pfeiffer
The Patriot	Roland Emmerich	Mel Gibson, Heath Ledger

Box Office
High-earning Films in the 1930s

Film	Year	Stars
Hell's Angels	1930	Ben Lyon, James Hall
King Kong	1933	Fay Wray, Robert Armstrong
It Happened One Night	1934	Clark Gable, Claudette Colbert
Mutiny on the Bounty	1935	Charles Laughton, Clark Gable
Modern Times	1936	Charlie Chaplin, Paulette Goddard
Lost Horizon	1937	Ronald Colman, Jane Wyatt
Snow White and the Seven Dwarves	1937	(voices of) Adriana Caselotti, Harry Stockwell
The Adventures of Robin Hood	1938	Errol Flynn, Olivia de Havilland
Gone With the Wind	1939	Clark Gable, Vivien Leigh
The Wizard of Oz	1939	Judy Garland, Ray Bolger

Box Office
High-earning Films in the 1940s

Film	Year	Stars
Fantasia	1940	(voices of) Leopold Stokowski, Deems Taylor
Pinocchio	1940	(voices of) Dickie Jones, Christian Rub
Citizen Kane	1941	Orson Welles, Joseph Cotton
Bambi	1942	(voices of) Donnie Dunagan, Peter Behn
Casablanca	1942	Humphrey Bogart, Ingrid Bergman
The Bells of St Mary's	1945	Bing Crosby, Ingrid Bergman

(*continued*)

Box Office: High-earning Films in the 1940s (*continued*)

Film	Year	Stars
Duel in the Sun	1946	Jennifer Jones, Joseph Cotten
It's a Wonderful Life	1946	James Stewart, Donna Reed
Song of the South	1946	Ruth Warrick, James Baskett
Cinderella	1949	(voices of) Ilene Woods, William Phipps

Box Office
High-earning Films in the 1950s

Film	Year	Stars
The Greatest Show on Earth	1952	James Stewart, Betty Hutton
Peter Pan	1953	(voices of) Bobby Driscoll, Kathryn Beaumont
The Robe	1953	Richard Burton, Jean Simmons
Lady and the Tramp	1955	(voices of) Peggy Lee, Barbara Luddy
Around the World in 80 Days	1956	David Niven, Cantinflas
The Ten Commandments	1956	Charlton Heston, Yul Brynner
The Bridge on the River Kwai	1957	William Holden, Alec Guinness
South Pacific	1958	Rossano Brazzi, Mitzi Gaynor
Ben Hur	1959	Charlton Heston, Jack Hawkins
Sleeping Beauty	1959	(voices of) Mary Costa, Bill Shirley

Box Office
High-earning Films in the 1960s

Film	Year	Stars
One Hundred and One Dalmatians	1961	(voices of) Rod Taylor, Betty Lou Gerson
Cleopatra	1963	Elizabeth Taylor, Richard Burton
Mary Poppins	1964	Julie Andrews, Dick Van Dyke
Doctor Zhivago	1965	Omar Sharif, Julie Christie
The Sound of Music	1965	Julie Andrews, Christopher Plummer
Thunderball	1965	Sean Connery, Claudine Auger
The Graduate	1967	Anne Bancroft, Dustin Hoffman
The Jungle Book	1967	(voices of) Phil Harris I, Sebastian Cabot
You Only Live Twice	1967	Sean Connery, Akiko Wakabayashi
Butch Cassidy and the Sundance Kid	1969	Paul Newman, Robert Redford

Box Office
High-earning Films in the 1970s

Film	Year	Stars
The Godfather	1972	Marlon Brando, Al Pacino
The Exorcist	1973	Ellen Burstyn, Max von Sydow
The Sting	1973	Paul Newman, Robert Redford
Jaws	1975	Roy Scheider, Robert Shaw
Close Encounters of the Third Kind	1977	Richard Dreyfuss, François Truffaut
Saturday Night Fever	1977	John Travolta, Karen Lynn Gorney
Star Wars	1977	Mark Hamill, Harrison Ford
Grease	1978	John Travolta, Olivia Newton-John
Jaws 2	1978	Roy Scheider, Lorraine Gary
National Lampoon's Animal House	1978	Tom Hulce, Stephen Furst

Box Office
High-earning Films in the 1980s

Film	Year	Stars
Star Wars: Episode V – The Empire Strikes Back	1980	Mark Hamill, Harrison Ford
Raiders of the Lost Ark	1981	Harrison Ford, Karen Allen
E. T. the Extra-Terrestrial	1982	Dee Wallace-Stone, Henry Thomas
Star Wars: Episode VI – Return of the Jedi	1983	Mark Hamill, Harrison Ford
Beverley Hills Cop	1984	Eddie Murphy, Judge Reinhold
Ghostbusters	1984	Bill Murray, Dan Aykroyd
Back to the Future	1985	Michael J Fox, Christopher Lloyd
Top Gun	1986	Tom Cruise, Kelly McGillis
Batman	1989	Michael Keaton, Jack Nicholson
Indiana Jones and the Last Crusade	1989	Harrison Ford, Sean Connery

Box Office
High-earning Films in the 1990s

Film	Year	Stars
Jurassic Park	1993	Sam Neill, Laura Dern
The Lion King	1994	(voices of) Rowan Atkinson, Matthew Broderick
Forrest Gump	1994	Tom Hanks, Robin Wright
Independence Day	1996	Will Smith, Bill Pullman
Titanic	1997	Leonardo DiCaprio, Kate Winslet
The Lost World: Jurassic Park	1997	Jeff Goldblum, Julianne Moore
Men in Black	1997	Tommy Lee Jones, Will Smith

(continued)

Film	Year	Stars
Armageddon	1998	Bruce Willis, Billy Bob Thornton
The Sixth Sense	1999	Bruce Willis, Haley Joel Osment
Star Wars: Episode I – The Phantom Menace	1999	Liam Neeson, Ewan McGregor

Box Office
Highest Takings

Film	Year	Receipts (US$)	Director
Titanic	1997	1,835,300,000	James Cameron
Star Wars: Episode I – The Phantom Menace	1999	923,000,000	George Lucas
Jurassic Park	1993	919,700,000	Steven Spielberg
Independence Day	1996	813,100,000	Roland Emmerich
Star Wars	1977	780,000,000	George Lucas
The Lion King	1994	767,700,000	Roger Allers, Rob Mintoff
E.T. the Extra Terrestrial	1982	700,800,000	Steven Spielberg
Forrest Gump	1994	679,400,000	Robert Zemeckis
The Sixth Sense	1999	660,700,000	M Night Shyamalan
The Lost World: Jurassic Park	1997	614,100,000	Steven Spielberg

Box Office
Highest Takings for Children's Films

Film	Year	Receipts (US$)	Director
The Lion King	1994	767,700,000	Roger Allers, Rob Minkoff
E. T. the Extra-Terrestrial	1982	700,800,000	Steven Spielberg
Home Alone	1990	533,700,000	Chris Columbus
Toy Story 2	1999	485,700,000	John Lasseter, Ash Brannon, Lee Unkrich
Aladdin	1992	478,900,000	Ron Clements, John Musker
Tarzan	1999	435,200,000	Chris Buck, Kevin Lima
A Bug's Life	1998	357,900,000	John Lasseter, Andrew Stanton
Toy Story	1995	354,200,000	John Lasseter
Beauty and the Beast	1991	351,800,000	Gary Trousdale, Kirk Wise

Box Office
Recent Loss-making Films

Film	Year	Film	Year
Asterix and Obelix	1999	*The Cable Guy*	1996
Meet Joe Black	1998	*Mary Reilly*	1995
Babe: Pig in the City	1998	*Last Action Hero*	1993
The Peacemaker	1997	*The Bonfire of the Vanities*	1990
Mr Magoo	1997	*Heaven's Gate*	1980

Box Office
High-earning Re-releases

Film	Re-released
Snow White (1938)	1993
Vertigo (1958)	1996
Belle du Jour (1967)	1995
The Godfather (1972)	1997
Star Wars (1977)	1997
Grease (1978)	1998
The Empire Strikes Back (1980)	1997
Return of the Jedi (1983)	1997
Oliver and Company (1988)	1996
The Little Mermaid (1989)	1997

Cable Television
Top Networks in the USA

Network

ESPN
CNN
TNT (Turner Network Television)
TBS
C-SPAN
USA Network
The Discovery Channel
TNN (The Nashville Network)
Lifetime Television (LIFE)
The Family Channel

Celebrities
Famous Film Star Families

Family name	Family members	Family name	Family members
Arquette	Cliff, David, Patricia, Rosanna	Huston	Anjelica, John, Walter
Baldwin	Alec, Daniel, Stephen, William	Marx	Chico, Groucho, Harpo, Zeppo
Barrymore	Drew, Ethel, John, Lionel	McGann	Joe, Mark, Paul, Stephen
Bridges	Beau, Jeff, Lloyd	Sheen/Estevez	Charlie and Martin Sheen, Emelio Estevez
Fonda	Bridget, Henry, Jane, Peter	Redgrave	Corin, Lynne, Michael, Vanessa

Celebrities
Former Occupations of Film Stars

Film star	Former occupation	Film star	Former occupation
Clint Eastwood	swimming instructor	Steve McQueen	lumberjack
Errol Flynn	gold miner	Robert Mitchum	boxer
Harrison Ford	carpenter	Dudley Moore	jazz pianist and television comedian
Greta Garbo	latherer in barber's shop	Michelle Pfeiffer	supermarket cashier
Whoopi Goldberg	mortuary beautician	Oliver Reed	nightclub bouncer
Gene Hackman	radio DJ	Sylvester Stallone	zoo cage sweeper
Burt Lancaster	circus acrobat		

Celebrities
Generations of Film Stars

20th century star(s)	Previous generation	Next generation
Kirk Douglas		Michael Douglas
Jason Robards	Jason Robards, Sr	Jason Robards III
Martin Sheen		Charlie Sheen, Emilio Estevez
Jane Fonda, Peter Fonda	Henry Fonda	Bridget Fonda
Judy Garland/Vincente Minnelli		Liza Minnelli
Tony Curtis/Janet Leigh		Jamie Lee-Curtis
John Huston	Walter Huston	Anjelica Huston
Ingrid Bergman/Roberto Rossellini		Isabella Rossellini
Maureen O'Sullivan		Mia Farrow
Donald Sutherland		Kiefer Sutherland
Debbie Reynolds/Eddie Fisher		Carrie Fisher
Douglas Fairbanks, Jr	Douglas Fairbanks, Sr	

Celebrities
Generations of Stage Stars

20th century star(s)	Previous generation(s)	Next generation
John Gielgud	Frank Gielgud/Kate Terry, Ellen Terry, Gordon Craig	
Michael Redgrave/ Rachel Kempson		Vanessa, Corin & Lynn Redgrave
Vanessa Redgrave/ Tony Richardson	Michael Redgrave/ Rachel Kempson	Natasha & Joely Richardson
Corin Redgrave	Michael Redgrave/ Rachel Kempson	Jemma Redgrave
Edward Woodward		Sarah & Peter Woodward
Alan Badel		Sarah Badel

Celebrities: Generations of Stage Stars (*continued*)

20th century star(s)	Previous generation(s)	Next generation
Alan Howard	Arthur Howard/Jean Compton & Leslie Howard	
Cyril Cusack		Sinead, Sorcha & Niamh Cusack
Raymond Massey/ Adrienne Allen		Daniel & Anna Massey
Nigel Davenport/ Maria Aitken		Laura & Jack Davenport
Maggie Smith/Robert Stephens		Toby Stephens
Timothy West/Prunella Scales		Sam West

Celebrities
Highest Earning in Films

George Lucas
Tom Hanks
Steven Spielberg
Bruce Willis
Julia Roberts

Celebrities
Husbands of Elizabeth Taylor

Name	Occupation
Nicky Hilton	hotel-chain heir
Michael Wilding	actor
Michael Todd	producer
Eddie Fisher	singer
Richard Burton	actor
Richard Burton (re-marriage)	actor
John Warner	US senator (after their marriage)
Larry Fortensky	trucker

Celebrities
Husbands of Zsa Zsa Gabor

Name	Years married
Burhan Belge	1937–41
Conrad Hilton	1942–47
George Sanders	1949–54
Herbert Hutner	1962–66
Joshua S Cosden Jr	1966–67
Jack Ryan	1975–76
Michael O'Hara	1976–82
Felipe De Alba	1982 (not legal – she was not divorced)
Prince Frederick von Anhalt	1986–present

Celebrities
Real Names of the Stars

Star	Real or original name	Star	Real or original name
Alan Alda	Alphonse d'Abruzzo	Judy Garland	Frances Ethel Gumm
Woody Allen	Allen Konigsberg	Whoopi Goldberg	Caren Johnson
Jennifer Aniston	Jennifer Anistonapoulos	Cary Grant	Alexander Archibald Leach
Fred Astair	Fred Austerlitz	Rita Hayworth	Margarita Cansino
Lauren Bacall	Betty Perske	Rock Hudson	Roy Harold Scherer
Brigitte Bardot	Camille Javal	Boris Karloff	William Henry Pratt
Mel Brooks	Melvyn Kaminsky	Ben Kingsley	Krishna Bhanji
Yul Brynner	Taidje Kahn	Marilyn Monroe	Norma Jean Baker
Michael Caine	Maurice Mickelwhite	Demi Moore	Demetria Guynes
Cher	Cherilyn Sarkisian	Ginger Rogers	Virginia McMath
Tom Cruise	Thomas Mapother IV	Omar Sharif	Michael Shalhoub
Doris Day	Doris Von Kappelhoff	John Wayne	Marion Morrison
Kirk Douglas	Issur Danielovitch		

Celebrities
Stars who have (Reportedly) been in Rehab for Substance or Alcohol Abuse

Name	Year	Name	Year
Drew Barrymore	1988	Charlton Heston	2000
Michael Douglas	1992	Matthew Perry	1999 and 1997
Robert Downey Jr	2000	Charlie Sheen	1998
Carrie Fisher	1998	Christian Slater	1997
Edward Furlong	2000	Jean-Claude Van Damme	1996
Melanie Griffith	2000		

Celebrity Separations

Wife or Partner	Husband or Partner	Year of separation
Nicole Kidman	Tom Cruise	2001
Jane Fonda	Ted Turner	2000
Elizabeth Hurley	Hugh Grant	2000
Meg Ryan	Dennis Quaid	2000
Grace Hightower	Robert de Niro	1999
Cindy Crawford	Richard Gere	1995
Madonna	Sean Penn	1989

Celebrity Separations
Divorce Settlements of the Stars

Divorcees	Estimated settlement (million US$)	Occupation of spouse making payment
Neil Diamond, Marcia Diamond	150	singer/actor
Norman Lear, Frances Lear	112	producer
Steven Spielberg, Amy Irving	105	director
Kevin Costner, Cindy Costner	80	actor/director
Michael Douglas, Deandre Douglas	60	actor

Celebrity Weddings

Bride	Groom	Year of wedding
Catherine Zeta Jones	Michael Douglas	2000
Madonna	Guy Ritchie	2000
Jennifer Aniston	Brad Pitt	2000
Victoria Adams	David Beckham	1999
Kate Winslet	Jim Threapleton	1998
Sarah Jessica Parker	Matthew Broderick	1997
Kim Basinger	Alec Baldwin	1993
Cindy Crawford	Richard Gere	1991
Nicole Kidman	Tom Cruise	1990
Janet Jones	Wayne Gretsky	1988
Madonna	Sean Penn	1985
Priscilla Ann Beaulieu	Elvis Presley	1967
Grace Kelly	Prince Rainier of Monaco	1956

Censorship
Famous Banned Films

Film	Director
Agitator (1969)	Dezso Magyar
Driller Killer (1979)	Abel Ferrara
Le Droit Asile (1969)	Jean-Pierre Lajournade
Island of Lost Souls (1932)	Erle C Kenton
Texas Chainsaw Massacre (1974)	Tobe Hooper
Zombie Flesh Eaters (1979)	Lucio Fulci

Christmas Films

Film	Year
A Christmas Carol (and several re-makes)	1908
White Christmas	1954
Santa Claus: The Movie	1985
Scrooged	1988
National Lampoon's Christmas Vacation	1989
The Muppets Christmas Carol	1992
The Nightmare Before Christmas	1993
Miracle on 34th Street	1994
The Santa Clause	1994
Jingle All the Way	1996
How the Grinch Stole Christmas	2000

Cinemas
Countries with Largest Cinema Attendance

Country	Annual attendance (millions)
China	14,428
India	4,300
USA	1,210
Russian Federation	140
France	130
Japan	127
Germany	125
UK	115
Lebanon	99
Spain	95

Cinemas
Countries with Most Cinemas

Country	Number of cinemas
China	40,000
USA	26,586
India	13,448
France	4,365
Germany	3,861
Italy	3,816
Spain	2,090
UK	2,019
Russian Federation	2,016
Japan	1,776

Cinemas
Countries with Most Cinemas Per Person

Country	Number of cinemas (per 1,000 people)
Gibraltar	80.7
San Marino	72.3
Monaco	53.4
Lebanon	35.3
Czech Republic	32.0
Canada	26.0
Iceland	22.4
Norway	21.4

Comedy Films
High-earning

Film	Year released	Director	Film	Year released	Director
Notting Hill	1999	Roger Michell	*Pretty Woman*	1990	Gary Marshall
There's Something About Mary	1998	Bobby Farrelly, Peter Farrelly	*Home Alone*	1990	Chris Columbus
The Mask	1994	Chuck Russell	*Who Framed Roger Rabbit?*	1988	Robert Zemeckis
The Flintstones	1994	Brian Levant	*Crocodile Dundee*	1986	Peter Faiman
Mrs Doubtfire	1993	Chris Columbus	*Beverley Hills Cop*	1984	Martin Best

Costume Epics

Film	Year
Ben Hur	1959
Gladiator	2000
Spartacus	1960
The Last Emperor	1987
Braveheart	1995
Lawrence of Arabia	1962
The Madness of King George	1994
Gandhi	1982
Henry V	1989
A Passage to India	1984

Crime and Gangster Films

Film	Year
The Godfather	1972
The Godfather, Part II	1974
Reservoir Dogs	1992
Pulp Fiction	1994
GoodFellas	1990
LA Confidential	1997
Fargo	1996
The Untouchables	1987
Dirty Harry	1971
The French Connection	1971

Dance
Selected Dances

Dance	Country of origin	Dance	Country of origin
Bolero	Spain	Limbo	West Indies
Bossa nova	Brazil	Mambo	Latin America
Czardas	Hungary	Mazurka	Poland
Fandango	Spain	Polonaise	Poland
Flamenco	Spain	Rumba	Cuba
Habanera	Cuba	Samba	Brazil
Hula	Hawaii	Tarantella	Italy

Disaster Films
High-earning

Film	Year released	Director
The Perfect Storm	2000	Wolfgang Petersen
Armageddon	1998	Michael Bay
Titanic	1997	James Cameron
Volcano	1997	Mick Jackson
Twister	1996	Jan de Bont
Apollo 13	1995	Ron Howard
Outbreak	1995	Wolfgang Petersen
Airport '77	1977	Jerry Jameson
Earthquake	1974	Mark Robson
The Towering Inferno	1974	Irwin Allen

Drama Films

Film	Year
Erin Brockovich	2000
Rain Man	1988
Apollo 13	1995
The Shawshank Redemption	1994
One Flew Over The Cuckoo's Nest	1975
Philadelphia	1993
Citizen Kane	1941
Midnight Cowboy	1969
On the Waterfront	1954
The Piano	1993

Film Casts
Films with Large Casts

Film	Year	Comment
Gandhi	1982	the most extras ever assembled for one scene, 300,000
Kolberg	1945	the last Nazi-made epic
War and Peace	1967	battle scenes used the Red Army as extras
Intolerance	1916	60,000 extras were used
Ben Hur	1959	thousands of extras were required for the chariot race scene
Gone With the Wind	1939	battle scenes required a large cast
Quo Vadis?	1912	an army of extras were employed

Film Directors
With Three or More Best Picture Academy Awards

Director	Film	Year
John Ford – 4 Awards, 1 other nomination	*The Informer*	1935
	The Grapes of Wrath	1940
	How Green was my Valley	1941
	The Quiet Man	1952
Frank Capra – 3 Awards, 3 other nominations	*It Happened One Night*	1934
	Mr Deeds Goes to Town	1936
	You Can't Take it with You	1938
William Wyler – 3 Awards, 9 other nominations	*The Best Years of Our Lives*	1946
	Ben Hur	1959
	Mrs Minever	1942

Film Directors
Working with Most Academy Award-Winning Actors

Academy Award-winning actors	Director	Academy Award-winning actors	Director
14	William Wyler	5	John Ford
9	Elia Kazan	4	John Huston
6	Fred Zinnemann	4	Sidney Lumet
5	George Cukor	4	Martin Scorsese

Film Musicals

Film	Year	Film	Year
Grease	1978	*The Sound of Music*	1964
Saturday Night Fever	1977	*Oliver!*	1968
Amadeus	1984	*Cabaret*	1972
West Side Story	1961	*Singin' in the Rain*	1952
South Pacific	1959	*My Fair Lady*	1964

Film Producers

Most Prolific Producers

Producer	Number of films	Most recent film
Paul Terry	950	*The Reformed Wolf* (1964)
Walt Disney	622	*I'm No Fool with Electricity* (1970)
Max Fleischer	610	*Rudolph the Red-Nosed Reindeer* (1944)
Hal Roach	586	*One Million Years B.C.* (1966) (associate producer)
Walter Lantz	521	*Walter, Woody and the World of Animation* (1982)
Leon Schlesinger	432	*Uncensored Cartoons* (1982)
Charles Mintz	316	*Park Your Baby* (1939)
Tom Daly	311	*Musical Magic: Gilbert and Sullivan in Stratford* (1984)
Jules White	304	*Stop! Look! and Laugh!* (1960) (associate producer)
Friz Freleng	301	*Daffy Duck's Movie: Fantastic Island* (1983)

Film Producers

Producers with Most Academy Awards for Best Picture

Producer	Film	Year
Daryl F Zanuck – 3 Awards	*How Green was my Valley*	1941
	Gentleman's Agreement	1947
	All About Eve	1950
Sam Spiegel – 3 Awards	*On the Waterfront*	1954
	The Bridge on the River Kwai	1957
	Lawrence of Arabia	1962

Film Production

Average Cost

Date	Cost ($ millions)
1941	0.4
1972	1.9
1980	8.5
1988	18.1
1997	54.0

Film Production
Global Film Production in 1998

Country	Number of films
India	693
USA	661
Japan	249
France	182
Germany	119
Italy	92
Hong Kong	91
UK	87
China	80
Spain	65

Film Production
Largest Production Budgets

Film	Year	Budget (US$ million)
Titanic	1997	200
Waterworld	1995	175
Wild Wild West	1999	170
Pearl Harbour	2001	145
Armageddon	1998	140
Lethal Weapon 4	1998	140
Dinosaur	2000	127.5
Batman and Robin	1997	125
Godzilla	1998	125
Mission Impossible 2	2000	125
The Perfect Storm	2000	120
Star Wars: Episode 1 – The Phantom Menace	2000	120

Film Remakes
Most Remakes on the Same Theme

Original film	Year
The Greeks Had a Word for Them	1932

Remakes on same theme	
Ladies in Love	1936
Three Blind Mice	1938
Moon over Miami	1941
Three Little Girls in Blue	1946
How to Marry a Millionaire	1953
Three Coins in the Fountain	1954
The Pleasure Seekers	1964

Film Remakes

Some Famous Examples

Film	Starring	Date of original film
Bedazzled (2000)	Liz Hurley, Brendan Fraser, Frances O'Connor	1967
Ben Hur (1959)	Charlton Heston, Stephen Boyd, Haya Harareet	1926
The Champ (1979)	Jon Voigt, Faye Dunaway, Rick Schroder	1931
Dial M for Murder (1981)	Angie Dickinson, Christopher Plummer	1954
The Fly (1986)	Jeff Goldblum, Geena Davis	1958
The Getaway (1993)	Alec Baldwin, Kim Basinger	1972
Invasion of the Body Snatchers (1978)	Donald Sutherland, Brooke Adams	1956
King Kong (1976)	Jeff Bridges, Charles Grodin, Jessica Lange	1933
Little Women (1994)	Winona Ryder, Claire Danes, Susan Sarandon	1948
Notorious (1992)	John Shea, Jenny Robertson	1946
Scarface (1983)	Al Pacino, Steven Bauer, Michelle Pfeiffer	1932
The 39 Steps (1958)	Kenneth More, Taina Elg	1935

Films

All-time Top 10 Films in the UK

Film	Year	Gross receipts at the UK Box Office (£ million)
Titanic	1998	70.0
The Full Monty	1997	52.2
Star Wars: Episode I – The Phantom Menace	1999	51.0
Jurassic Park	1993	47.9
Toy Story 2	2000	43.4
Independence Day	1996	37.2
Men in Black	1997	35.8
Bridget Jones' Diary	2001	32.2
Gladiator	2000	30.9
Notting Hill	1999	31.0
Chicken Run	2000	29.4
A Bug's Life	1999	29.3

Films

Areas Producing Most Films

Area	Approximate number of films per year
Africa	125
North America	470
South America	130
Asia	2,850
Europe	880
Oceania	20

Films

Expensive Films of Their Day

Date	Film	Cost ($ millions)
1927	*Uncle Tom's Cabin*	1.8
1930	*Hell's Angels*	3.8
1946	*Duel in the Sun*	5.0
1957	*Bridge on the River Kwai*	3.0
1960	*Spartacus*	12.0
1967	*War and Peace*	40.0
1968	*2001: A Space Odyssey*	10.5
1980	*The Blues Brothers*	27.0
1982	*Firefox*	21.0

Films

Films Featuring Animals

Film	Animals featured
The Adventures of Rex and Rinty (1935)	horse, dog
Babe (1995)	pig
Beethoven (1992)	dog
Benji (1974)	dog
Black Beauty (1946)	horse
The Black Stallion (1980)	horse
K9 (1988)	dog
Kes (1969)	bird
Lassie Come Home (1943)	dog
White Fang (1990)	wolf

Films

Films Featuring Robots

Film	Robot featured
Buck Rogers in the 25th Century (1979)	Twiki
The Bang Bang Kid (1967)	The Bang Bang Kid
D.A.R.Y.L (1985)	D.A.R.Y.L
Galalxina (1980)	Galalxina
The Invisible Boy (1957)	Toby
Logan's Run (1977)	REM
Metropolis (1926/1984)	Maria
Robocop (1987)	Murphy (Robocop)
Short Circuit (1986)	Number 5
2001: A Space Odyssey (1968)	Hal

Films

Films with Most Sequels

Series	Details
The Carry Ons	30 sequels from 1958 (*Carry on Sergeant*) to 1992 (*Carry on Columbus*)
Godzilla	20 sequels from 1954 to 1995
Charlie Chan	18 sequels from 1931 to 1949
Fu Manchu	10 sequels from 1929 to 1970
Star Trek	9 sequels from 1979 (*Star Trek: The Motion Picture*) to 1998 (*Star Trek: Insurrection*)
The Kettles	9 sequels from 1949 to 1957
A Nightmare on Elm Street	5 sequels from 1984 to 1989

Films

Major Annual Film Awards

Award	Winner in 2000
The American Academy Awards (The Oscars)	*American Beauty*
The Australian Film Institute Awards	*Two Hands*
The UK BAFTAs	*American Beauty*
The Canadian Film Awards	*Sunshine*
The Cannes Film Festival Awards	*Dancer in the Dark*
The French Academy Awards (The Cesars)	*Venus Beauty*
The Hollywood Foreign Press Association Awards (The Golden Globes)	*American Beauty*
The Venice International Film Awards	*Not One Less*
The Sundance Film Festival (Colorado, USA) – joint winners	*Girl Fight* *You Can Count On Me*
The London Film Critics' Awards (The Alfs)	*American Beauty*
The US National Society of Film Critics Awards – joint winners	*Being John Malkovich* *Topsy-Turvy*

Films

Most Academy Award Nominations

Film	Year	Number of nominations	Final number of awards
Titanic	1997	14	11
All About Eve	1950	14	6
Gone With the Wind	1939	13	8
From Here to Eternity	1953	13	8
Shakespeare in Love	1998	13	7
Forrest Gump	1994	13	6
Mary Poppins	1964	13	5

(continued)

Film	Year	Number of nominations	Final number of awards
Who's Afraid of Virginia Woolf	1966	13	5
Ben Hur	1959	12	11
The English Patient	1996	12	9
On the Waterfront	1954	12	8
My Fair Lady	1964	12	8
Dances With Wolves	1990	12	7
Schindler's List	1993	12	7
Mrs Miniver	1942	12	6
The Song of Bernadette	1943	12	4
A Streetcar Named Desire	1951	12	4
Reds	1981	12	3

Films

Most Academy Awards

Film	Year	Number of awards
Titanic	1997	11
Ben Hur	1959	11
West Side Story	1961	10
The English Patient	1996	9
The Last Emperor	1987	9
Gigi	1958	9
Amadeus	1984	8
Gandhi	1982	8
Cabaret	1972	8
My Fair Lady	1964	8
On the Waterfront	1954	8
From Here to Eternity	1953	8
Gone With the Wind	1939	8

Films

Some of the Longest Films

Film	Year	Producer	Length (minutes)
Die Zweite Heimat	1992	Edgar Reitz	1,632
Heimat	1984	Edgar Reitz	924
War and Peace	1967	Sergei Bondarchuk	507
Greed	1924	Erich von Stroheim	420
Nashville	1975	Robert Altman	360 (uncut)
Napoleon	1927	Abel Gance	378
Little Dorrit	1987	Christine Edzard	357
The Greatest Story Ever Told	1965	George Stevens	260 (uncut)
Cleopatra	1963	Joseph Mankiewicz	243
Once Upon a Time in America	1984	Sergio Leone	227
The Greatest Story Ever Told	1965	George Stevens	225
Gone with the Wind	1939	Victor Fleming	220
Lawrence of Arabia	1962	David Lean	220
Heaven's Gate	1980	Michael Cimino	219
War and Peace	1956	King Vidor	208

Films

Stars of Five or More $100m+ Movies

Number of movies	Film stars
11 movies	Harrison Ford; Tom Hanks
9 movies	Mel Gibson
8 movies	Tom Cruise; Robin Williams; Julia Roberts
7 movies	James Earl Jones; Jim Carrey; Eddie Murphy
6 movies	Samuel L Jackson; Clint Howard; Bruce Willis; Arnold Schwarzenegger; Dustin Hoffman; John Travolta; Dabney Coleman; Gene Hackman
5 movies	Joe Pesci; Michael Gough; John Heard; Jack Nicholson; Glenn Close; Paul Giamatti; Bonnie Hunt; Christopher Lloyd; Rick Moranis; Brian Doyle-Murray; Tim Curry; Danny Glover; Morgan Freeman

Films

The Seven Dwarfs in Disney's Snow White

Bashful
Doc
Dopey
Grumpy
Happy
Sleepy
Sneezy

Films

UK Top 10 Films in 1999

Film	Receipts (£ million)	Film	Receipts (£ million)
Star Wars: Episode I – The Phantom Menace	51.0	The Sixth Sense	24.3
Notting Hill	31.0	Shakespeare in Love	20.4
A Bug's Life	29.3	Tarzan	17.5
The World is Not Enough	28.6	The Mummy	17.4
Austin Powers 2	25.8	The Matrix	17.3

Films

World's All-Time Top 10 Films

Film	Year
Titanic	1997
Star Wars: Episode I – The Phantom Menace	1999
Jurassic Park	1993
Independence Day	1996
Star Wars	1977

(continued)

Film	Year
The Lion King	1994
E.T. the Extra-Terrestrial	1982
Forrest Gump	1994
The Sixth Sense	1999
The Lost World: Jurassic Park	1997

Foreign Language Films
Some Famous Examples

Film	Year	Film	Year
Das blaue Engel	1930	*Jules et Jim*	1961
La grande illusion	1937	*Il gattopardo*	1963
Les enfants du paradis	1945	*Le charme discret de la bourgeoisie*	1972
Ladri di biciclette	1948		
Shichinin no samurai	1954	*Das Boot*	1981
La strada	1954	*Fanny och Alexander*	1982
La dolce vita	1960	*La vita è bella*	1997

Ghost Films
Highest-earning

Film	Year released	Director
The Sixth Sense	1999	M Night Shyamalan
Ghost	1990	Jerry Zucker
Ghostbusters	1984	Ivan Reitman
Casper	1995	Brad Silberling
What Lies Beneath	2000	Robert Zemeckis
Ghostbusters II	1989	Ivan Reitman
Sleepy Hollow	1999	Tim Burton
The Haunting	1999	Robert Wise
Beetlejuice	1988	Tim Burton
The House on Haunted Hill	1999	William Malone

Golden Globe Awards
Winning Films

Year	Motion Picture (Drama)	Male Actor in a Motion Picture (Drama)	Female Actor in a Motion Picture (Drama)	Director
1995	*Sense and Sensibility*	Nicolas Cage *Leaving Las Vegas*	Sharon Stone *Casino*	Mel Gibson *Braveheart*
1996	*The English Patient*	Geoffrey Rush *Shine*	Brenda Blethyn *Secrets and Lies*	Milos Forman *The People vs Larry Flynt*
1997	*Titanic*	Peter Fonda *Ulee's Gold*	Judi Dench *Mrs Brown*	James Cameron *Titanic*
1998	*Saving Private Ryan*	Jim Carrey *The Truman Show*	Cate Blanchett *Elizabeth*	Steven Spielberg *Saving Private Ryan*
1999	*American Beauty*	Denzel Washington *The Hurricane*	Hilary Swank *Boys Don't Cry*	Sam Mendes *American Beauty*

Golden Globe
Recent Awards for Television

Year	Award	Winner
2001	Television Series (Drama)	*The West Wing*
	Actor, Series (Drama)	Martin Sheen *The West Wing*
	Actress, Series (Drama)	Sela Ward *Once and Again*
	Series (Musical or Comedy)	*Sex and the City*
2000	Television Series (Drama)	*The Sopranos*
	Actor, Series (Drama)	James Gandolfini *The Sopranos*
	Actress, Series (Drama)	Edie Falco *The Sopranos*
	Series (Musical or Comedy)	*Sex and the City*
1999	Television Series (Drama)	*The Practice*
	Actor, Series (Drama)	Dylan McDermott *The Practice*
	Actress, Series (Drama)	Keri Russell *Felicity*
	Series (Musical or Comedy)	*Ally McBeal*
1998	Television Series (Drama)	*The X-Files*
	Actor, Series (Drama)	Anthony Edwards *ER*
	Actress, Series (Drama)	Christine Lahti *Chicago Hope*
	Series (Musical or Comedy)	*Ally McBeal*
1997	Television Series (Drama)	*The X-Files*
	Actor, Series (Drama)	David Duchovny *The X-Files*
	Actress, Series (Drama)	Gillian Anderson *The X-Files*
	Series (Musical or Comedy)	*3rd Rock from the Sun*
1996	Television Series (Drama)	*Party of Five*
	Actor, Series (Drama)	David Smits *NYPD Blue*
	Actress, Series (Drama)	Jane Seymour *Dr Quinn, Medicine Woman*
	Series (Musical or Comedy)	*Cybill*
1995	Television Series (Drama)	*The X-Files*
	Actor, Series (Drama)	Dennis Franz *NYPD Blue*
	Actress, Series (Drama)	Clare Danes *My So-called Life*
	Series (Musical or Comedy)	*Mad About You* and *Frasier*

Golden Lion
Recent Winning Films

Year	Golden Lion (Grand Prix) for Best Film	Year	Golden Lion (Grand Prix) for Best Film
1990	*Rosencrantz and Guildenstern are Dead* (UK)	1995	*Cyclo* (France)
1991	*Urga* (Russia)	1996	*Michael Collins* (USA)
1992	*Story of Qiu Ju* (China)	1997	*Hana-bi* (Japan)
1993	*Short Cuts* (USA); *Three Colors Blue* (Poland)	1998	*Cosi ridevano* (Italy)
1994	*Vive l'Amour* (Taiwan); *Before the Rain* (Macedonia)	1999	*Yi Ge Bu Neng Shao/Not One Less* (China)
		2000	*Dayareh/The Circle* (Iran)

Hitchcock
Selected Cameo Appearances by Alfred Hitchcock

Film	Date	Role
The Thirty-Nine Steps	1935	seven minutes after the beginning of the film, walking in the street throwing litter
The Lady Vanishes	1938	in a train station, wearing a black coat and smoking a cigarette, near the end of the film
Suspicion	1941	in a village scene, about 45 minutes after the beginning of the film, posting a letter
Spellbound	1945	about 40 minutes after the beginning of the film, coming out of a hotel elevator smoking a cigarette and carrying a violin case
Rear Window	1954	about 30 minutes after the beginning of the film, winding a clock in the songwriter's apartment
Vertigo	1958	11 minutes after the beginning of the film, in a street scene, carrying a black case
North by Northwest	1959	at the end of the opening credits, missing a bus
Psycho	1960	seen through an office window, standing on the street wearing a cowboy hat
The Birds	1963	at the beginning of the film, walking two dogs out of the pet shop
Torn Curtain	1966	soon after the beginning of the film, sitting in a hotel lobby holding a baby
Frenzy	1972	in the crowd scene by a river, listening to a politician's speech at the beginning of the film

James Bond Films

Film	Year
Doctor No	1962
From Russia with Love	1963
Goldfinger	1964
Thunderball	1965
Casino Royale	1967
You Only Live Twice	1968
Diamonds are Forever	1971
Live and Let Die	1973
The Spy Who Loved Me	1977
For Your Eyes Only	1981
A View to a Kill	1985
The Living Daylights	1987
Licence to Kill	1989
On Her Majesty's Secret Service	1994
GoldenEye	1995
Tomorrow Never Dies	1997
The World is Not Enough	1999

Love Stories
Films of Love Stories

Film	Year
Gone with the Wind	1939
Notting Hill	1999
Shakespeare in Love	1998
The English Patient	1996
Four Weddings and a Funeral	1994
Casablanca	1942
Annie Hall	1979
Love Story	1970
Kramer vs. Kramer	1979
Brief Encounter	1946

Military Films
Highest-earning

Film	Year released	Director
Saving Private Ryan	1998	Steven Spielberg
Top Gun	1986	Tony Scott
The Rock	1996	Michael Bay
Rambo: First Blood Part II	1985	George P Cosmatos
A Few Good Men	1992	Rob Reiner
The Patriot	2000	Roland Emmerich
Platoon	1986	Oliver Stone
An Officer and a Gentleman	1982	Taylor Hackford
Good Morning Vietnam	1987	Barry Levinson
The Hunt for Red October	1990	John McTiernan

Musicals
Andrew Lloyd Webber Shows that Have Been Successful Around the World

Show	Country	City	Show	Country	City
Aspects of Love	Germany	Dresden	*Starlight Express*	Germany	Bochum
	Hungary	Budapest		UK	London
Cats	Germany	Hamburg	*Sunset Boulevard*	USA	national tour
	Hungary	Budapest			
	Japan	Fukuoka	*The Phantom of the Opera*	Canada	Toronto
	UK	London		Germany	Hamburg
	USA	New York national tour		Japan	Tokyo
				UK	London national tour
Jesus Christ Superstar	UK	national tour		USA	New York national tour
Joseph and the Amazing Technicolour Dreamcoat	Germany	Essen	*Whistle Down the Wind*	UK	London
	Hungary	Budapest			
	Slovak Republic	Bratislava			
	UK	national tour			

Musicals
With Famous UK Original Casts

Show title

Cats
Evita
The Phantom of the Opera
Jesus Christ Superstar
Aspects of Love
Les Miserables
The King and I
Oliver!

Musicals
With Famous US Original Casts

Show title

The Sound of Music
West Side Story
My Fair Lady
Hair
Camelot
Oklahoma
The King and I

Palme d'Or
Best Films

Year	Palme d'Or for Best Film	Year	Palme d'Or for Best Film
1990	*Wild at Heart* (USA)	1996	*Secrets and Lies* (UK)
1991	*Barton Fink* (USA)	1997	*The Eel/Unagi* (Japan)
1992	*The Best Intentions* (Sweden)		*The Taste of Cherries* (Iran)
1993	*The Piano* (New Zealand/ Australia)	1998	*Mia Eoniotita Ke Mia Mera/ Eternity and A Day* (Greece)
	Farewell, My Concubine (Hong Kong/China)	1999	*Rosetta* (Belgium)
1994	*Pulp Fiction* (USA)	2000	*Dancer in the Dark* (Denmark)
1995	*Underground* (Bosnia-Herzegovina)		

Plays
Influential Post-war UK Plays

Writer	Life dates	Play	Year
Samuel Beckett	1906–89	*Waiting for Godot*	1955
Eugene Ionesco	1909–94	*The Lesson*	1955
John Osborne	1929–94	*Look Back in Anger*	1956
John Arden	1930–	*Sergeant Musgrave's Dance*	1959
Harold Pinter	1930–	*The Caretaker*	1960
Arnold Wesker	1932–	*Chips with Everything*	1962
Peter Shaffer	1926–	*The Royal Hunt of the Sun*	1964
Tom Stoppard	1937-	*Rozencrantz and Guildenstern are Dead*	1966

Plays
Some of the Earliest Known Western Plays

Writer	Location	Play	Dates
Aeschylus (c. 525–456 BC)	Athens	*The Persians*	c. 472 BC
		Seven Against Thebes	c. 467 BC
Sophocles (c. 496–406 BC)	Athens	*Antigone*	c. 442 BC
		King Oedipus	c. 420 BC
Euripides (c. 485–407 BC)	Athens	*Alcestis*	c. 438 BC
		Medea	c. 431 BC
Aristophanes (c. 447–388 BC)	Athens	*The Birds*	c. 414 BC
		The Frogs	c. 405 BC
Menander (c. 342–290 BC)	Athens	*Dyscolos*	c. 316 BC
		Samia	c. 315 BC
Titus Plautus (c. 254–184 BC)	Rome	*The Braggart Soldier*	c. 200 BC
		The Rope	c. 189 BC
Publius Terence (c. 190–159 BC)	Rome	*Andria*	c. 166 BC
		Hecyra	c. 165 BC
Lucius Seneca (c. 4 BC–65 AD)	Rome	*Medea*	1st century AD
		Phaedra	1st century AD

Radio
Countries with Most Radios

Country	Number of radios (thousands)	Country	Number of radios (thousands)
USA	524,000	India	65,000
China	206,000	Brazil	55,000
Japan	110,000	France	50,000
Russia	90,000	Italy	43,350
UK	65,400	South Korea	42,570

Radio

Recent Sony Radio Award Winners

Award	Winner in 2000
Event Award	*The Open* (BBC Radio 5 Live)
Feature Award	*Out of the Darkness: the Triumph of Nelson Mandela* (BBC Radio 4)
'Music Special' Award	*For Your Ears Only* (BBC Radio 2)
Specialist Music Award	*Worldwide with Gilles Peterson* (BBC Radio 1)
Entertainment Award	*Jon & Andy* (103.2 Power FM)
Comedy Award	*Blue Jam* (BBC Radio 1)
Speech Award	*The Evacuation: the True Story* (BBC Radio 4)
Sports Award	*Super Sunday* (GLR News for GLR)
Drama Award	*Plum's War* (BBC Radio 4)
News Award	*Late Night Live* (BBC Radio 5 Live)
News and Talk Broadcaster Award	Roger Phillips (BBC Radio Merseyside)
Station of the Year (audience up to 500,000)	BBC Radio Foyle
Station of the Year (audience 500,000 to 12 million)	Kiss 100
Station of the Year (UK audience)	Classic FM
Station Sound Award	Classic FM
Breakfast Music Award	*Bam Bam Breakfast* (Kiss 100)
Breakfast News and Talk Award	*The Morning Programme* (BBC Radio Foyle)
Interactive Award	*On the Ball* (BBC Scotland)
Public Service Award	BBC Music Entertainment for BBC Radio 1
Short Form Award	*Woman's Hour* (BBC Radio 4)
Competition Award	*Jon's Australian Experience* (Heart 106.2)
Music Broadcaster Award	Pete Tong (BBC Radio 1)
Music Presentation Award (audience 500,000 to 12 million)	*Bam Bam Breakfast* (Kiss 100)
Music Presentation Award (UK audience)	*Jonathan Ross Show* (BBC Radio 2)

Sci-fi Films

Highest-earning

Film	Year released	Director
Star Wars: Episode I – The Phantom Menace	1999	George Lucas
Jurassic Park	1993	Steven Spielberg
Independence Day	1996	Roland Emmerich
Star Wars	1977	George Lucas
E.T. The Extra-Terrestrial	1982	Steven Spielberg
The Lost World: Jurassic Park	1997	Steven Spielberg
Men in Black	1997	Barry Sonnenfeld
Armageddon	1998	Michael Bay
Star Wars: Episode V – The Empire Strikes Back	1980	Irvin Kershner
Terminator 2: Judgement Day	1991	James Cameron

Sports Films
Recent Films with a Sports Theme

Film	Year	Film	Year
Days of Thunder	1990	*Tin Cup*	1996
Rocky V	1990	*Fever Pitch*	1997
A League of Their Own	1992	*Any Given Sunday*	1999
White Men Can't Jump	1992	*For Love of the Game*	1999
The Fan	1996	*The Hurricane*	1999
Jerry Maguire	1996	*The Match*	1999

Studios
Film Studios with Most Best Picture Academy Awards

Studio	Number of best picture Academy Awards	Founded
Columbia	12	1920 by Harry and Jack Cohn
United Artists	12	1919 by Charlie Chaplin, D W Griffith, Mary Pickford, and Douglas Fairbanks
Paramount	11	1913 by Adolph Zukor
MGM	9	1924 by Nicholas M Schenck
Twentieth Century Fox	7	1913 by William Fox
Universal	6	1912 by Carl Laemmle
Warner Bros	6	1923 by Jack, Sam, Harry, and Albert Warner
Orion	4	1978 by Arthur Krim and Robert Benjamin
Miramax	2	1979 by Harvey and Bob Weinstein
RKO	2	1929 by Joseph P Kennedy and David Sarnoff

Stunts
Some Celebrated Film Stunts

Film	Year	Stunt
Ben Hur	1959	perhaps the most well-known stunt scene, the famous chariot race
Bullitt	1968	record-breaking car chase
Crouching Tiger, Hidden Dragon	2000	martial arts, with perhaps the most mesmerizing and breathtaking sequences yet
The French Connection	1971	car chase
The Fugitive	1993	train and bus smash
The Great Escape	1963	Steve McQueen's 18 m/60 ft motorcycle jump

(continued)

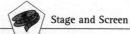 Stage and Screen **99**

Film	Year	Stunt
Jackie Chan – The Armour of God	1987	martial arts
Raiders of the Lost Ark	1981	the five-ton truck sequence, which involved 13 stuntmen performing 50 stunts and took five weeks to shoot
Steamboat Bill Jnr	1928	Buster Keaton stands in the eye of a cyclone as a house wall falls around him

Television Drama
Top UK Original Productions

Drama	Producer	1999	Audience (millions)
Coronation Street	Granada	7 March	19.9
Heartbeat	Yorkshire	28 February	17.0
A Touch of Frost	Yorkshire	21 March	16.8
EastEnders	BBC	7 January	15.7
Emmerdale	Yorkshire	20 January	13.4
Casualty	BBC	13 February	13.1
Lost For Words	Bard Entertainment/Yorkshire	3 January	12.2
Forgotten	LWT	15 February	12.0
Coronation Street	Granada	13 November	12.0
Where the Heart Is	United/Anglia	18 April	11.7

Television
Countries with the Most TV Sets

Country	Number of television sets (per 1,000 population)
USA	850
Canada	715
Japan	705
El Salvador	675
UK	645
Australia	640
Finland	640
France	600
Oman	595
Denmark	585

Television
Emmy Awards For Outstanding Drama Series

Year	Drama series
2000	*The West Wing* (NBC)
1999	*The Practice* (ABC)
1998	*The Practice* (ABC)
1997	*Law & Order* (NBC)
1996	*ER* (NBC)
1995	*NYPD Blue* (ABC)
1994	*Picket Fences* (CBS)
1993	*Picket Fences* (CBS)
1992	*Northern Exposure* (CBS)
1991	*LA Law* (NBC)
1990	*LA Law* (NBC)

Television
Emmy Awards for Outstanding Made for Television Movie

Year	Television movie
2000	*Oprah Winfrey Presents: Tuesdays with Morrie* (ABC)
1999	*A Lesson Before Dying* (HBO)
1998	*Don King: Only in America* (HBO)
1997	*Miss Evers' Boys* (HBO)
1996	*Truman* (HBO)
1995	*Indictment: The McMartin Trial* (HBO)
1994	*And the Band Played On* (HBO)
1993	*Barbarians at the Gate* (HBO)
1992	*Miss Rose White Hallmark Hall of Fame* (NBC)

Television
Top Television Watching Countries

Country	Average daily viewing time (minutes)
USA	255
Spain	240
Japan	<240
Estonia	237
Italy	230
UK	210

Theatre
Film Stars with Recent UK Stage Appearances

Actor	Play	Theatre	Date
Juliette Binoche	*Naked*	Almeida	winter 1998
Julie Christie	*Suzanna Andler*	Chichester	summer 1997
Macaulay Culkin	*Madame Melville*	Vaudeville	autumn 2000
Ralph Fiennes	*Ivanov*	Almeida	spring 1997
Jerry Hall	*The Graduate*	Gielgud	summer 2000
Nicole Kidman	*The Blue Room*	Donmar Warehouse	autumn 1998
Ben Kingsley	*Waiting for Godot*	Old Vic	autumn 1997
Jessica Lange	*A Streetcar Named Desire*	Haymarket	spring 1997
Liam Neeson	*The Judas Kiss*	Playhouse	spring 1998
Kevin Spacey	*The Iceman Cometh*	Almeida	spring 1998
Kathleen Turner	*Tallulah, Our Betters*	Chichester	summer 1997
Kathleen Turner	*The Graduate*	Gielgud	spring 2000

Theatre
Myths and Superstitions

It is thought to be back luck in the theatre to:

whistle in your dressing room
wish an actor good luck
mention the play *Macbeth* by name
wear green, blue, or yellow
use real flowers, drink, or jewellery on
stage

wear peacock feathers
drop a comb or spill a make-up box
use another's mirror
open a new show on a Friday
put up any pictures in your dressing-room

Theatre
Notable Broadway Opening Nights

Show	Opening date	Category
Candide (revival)	29 April 1997	musical
Jekyll and Hyde	28 April 1997	musical
Annie (revival)	26 April 1997	drama
Titanic	23 April 1997	musical
Barrymore	25 March 1997	drama
Play On	20 March 1997	musical
Ivanov	20 November 1996	drama
Chicago	14 November 1996	musical
Rent	29 April 1996	musical
The King and I	11 April 1996	musical

Theatre
Shortest-running Broadway Shows (1996–97)

Show	Opening date	Closing date
Dream	2 April 1997	6 July 1997
An American Daughter	13 April 1997	29 June 1997
Steel Pier	24 April 1997	28 June 1997
God's Heart	6 April 1997	25 May 1997
Play On	20 March 1997	11 May 1997
Present Laughter	18 November 1996	20 April 1997
Big	28 April 1996	13 October 1996
A Delicate Balance	21 April 1996	29 September 1996
Seven Guitars	28 March 1996	8 September 1996
State Fair	27 March 1996	30 June 1996

Theatre
Some Famous Theatrical Families

Family	Location	Period	Number of members
The Drew-Barrymore Family	UK	18th to 20th century	13
The Lupino Family	UK/USA	18th to 20th century	13
The Wallack Family	UK/USA	19th to 20th century	8
The Redgrave-Richardson Family	UK	20th century	7
The Hallam Family	UK/USA	18th to 19th century	7
The Power Family	Ireland/USA	18th to 20th century	5

Thrillers
Famous Film Thrillers

Film	Year	Film	Year
Jaws	1975	*The Silence of the Lambs*	1991
The Fugitive	1993	*Basic Instinct*	1991
Air Force One	1997	*Fatal Attraction*	1987
Ransom	1996	*Witness*	1985
Speed	1994	*Psycho*	1960

Tony (Antoinette Perry) Awards

These annual US theatre awards are presented on the first Sunday in June for the previous theatre season, ending in April.

2000

Best Play	*Copenhagen*
Best Musical	*Contact*
Best Performance by a Leading Actress in a Play	Jennifer Ehle *The Real Thing*
Best Performance by a Leading Actor in a Play	Stephen Dillane *The Real Thing*
Best Performance by a Leading Actress in a Musical	Heather Headley *Aida*
Best Performance by a Leading Actor in a Musical	Brian Stokes Mitchel *Kiss Me, Kate*
Best Director of a Play	Michael Blakemore *Copenhagen*
Best Director of a Musical	Michael Blakemore *Kiss Me, Kate*
Best Book	Richard Nelson *James Joyce's The Dead*
Best Original Score	Elton John (music) and Tim Rice (lyrics) *Aida*
Special Tony Award for a live theatrical event	*Dame Edna: The Royal Tour*
Lifetime Achievement in the Theatre	T Edward Hambleton, founder of the Phoenix Theatre

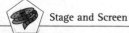

TV Movies
Top US TV Movies

Film	Percent of TV households watching (1998–99)
Noah's Ark, Part 1	20.9
Noah's Ark, Part 2	17.0
The Christmas Wish	16.3
Joan of Arc, Part 1	15.2
Forever Love	15.1
The '60s, Part 1	15.1
The Temptations, Part 1	15.0
Alice in Wonderland	14.8
The Secret Path	14.7
Marriage of Convenience	14.6

US Box Office
Highest Takings

Film	Year	Gross receipts (US$ million)	Film	Year	Gross receipts (US$ million)
Titanic	1997	601	Jurassic Park	1993	356
Star Wars	1977	461	Forrest Gump	1994	329
Star Wars: Episode 1 – The Phantom Menace	1997	431	Independence Day	1996	306
E.T. the Extra-Terrestrial	1982	399	The Sixth Sense	1999	294

US Box Office
Highest Takings for Children's Films

Film	Year	Gross receipts (US$ million)
E.T. the Extra-Terrestrial	1982	399
The Lion King	1994	313
Home Alone	1990	285
How the Grinch Stole Christmas	2000	260
Toy Stoy 2	1999	246
Aladdin	1992	217
Toy Story	1995	192
Snow White and the Seven Dwarfs	1937	189

Vampire Films
Highest-earning

Film	Year released	Director
Interview With the Vampire	1994	Neil Jordan
Bram Stoker's Dracula	1992	Francis Ford Coppola
Blade	1998	Stephen Norrington
From Dusk til Dawn	1996	Robert Rodriguez
Love at First Bite	1979	Stan Dragoti
The Lost Boys	1987	Joel Schumacher
Vampires	1998	John Carpenter
Dracula	1979	John Badham
Fright Night	1985	Tom Holland
Vampire in Brooklyn	1995	Wes Craven

Videos
Most Rented Videos in the USA

In 2000, to November.

Film	Year released	Film	Year released
The Green Mile	1999	*The Thomas Crown Affair*	1999
Deuce Bigalow: Male Gigolo	1999	*Double Jeopardy*	1999
The Sixth Sense	1999	*End of Days*	1999
The Whole Nine Yards	2000	*Erin Brockovich*	2000
The Talented Mr Ripley	1999	*The Hurricane*	1999

Videos
Popular Videos in Early 2001

Video	Video
Me, Myself and Irene (Fox Video)	*Scary Movie* (Dimension)
Gladiator (Dreamworks)	*Chicken Run* (Dreamworks)
The Cell (New Line)	*Erin Brockovich* (Universal)
Hollow Man (Columbia TriStar)	*Gone in 60 Seconds* (Touchstone)
The Virgin Suicides (Paramount)	*Autumn in New York* (MGM)

West End

Longest-running West End Shows

Show	Category	Years	Show	Category	Years
The Mousetrap	whodunnit	48	*Blood Brothers*	musical	12
Cats	musical	19	*Buddy*	musical	11
Starlight Express	musical	16	*Miss Saigon*	musical	11
Les Misérables	musical	15	*The Woman in Black*	thriller	11
The Phantom of the Opera	musical	14	*An Inspector Calls*	play	5

Westerns

Highest-earning

Film	Year released	Director	Film	Year released	Director
Dances With Wolves	1990	Kevin Costner	*Jeremiah Johnson*	1972	Sydney Pollack
Wild Wild West	1999	Barry Sonnenfeld	*How the West Was Won*	1962	Henry Hathaway
Maverick	1994	Richard Donner	*Young Guns*	1988	Christopher Cain
Unforgiven	1992	Clint Eastwood	*Young Guns II*	1990	Geoff Murphy
Butch Cassidy and the Sundance Kid	1969	George Roy Hill	*Pale Rider*	1985	Clint Eastwood

Music

Academy Awards
Best Song Academy Award-winning Singles in the UK

Year	Artist/band	Song
1986	Berlin	'Take My Breath Away'
1984	Stevie Wonder	'I Just Called to Say I Love You'
1983	Irene Cara	'Flashdance ... What a Feeling'
1981	Christopher Cross	'Arthur's Theme'
1980	Irene Cara	'Fame'
1976	Barbra Streisand	'Evergreen'
1971	Isaac Hayes	'Theme From Shaft'
1961	Danny Williams	'Moon River'
1954	Frank Sinatra	'Three Coins in the Fountain'
1953	Doris Day	'Secret Love'

Academy Awards
Winners for Best Song in the 1940s

Year	Song	Film title
1940	'When You Wish Upon a Star'	*Pinocchio*
1941	'The Last Time I Saw Paris'	*Lady Be Good*
1942	'White Christmas'	*Holiday Inn*
1943	'You'll Never Know'	*Hello, Frisco, Hello*
1944	'Swinging on a Star'	*Going My Way*
1945	'It Might as Well be Spring'	*State Fair*
1946	'On the Atchinson, Topeka and the Santa Fe'	*The Harvey Girls*
1947	'Zip-a-dee-doo-dah'	*Song of the South*
1948	'Buttons and Bows'	*The Paleface*
1949	'Baby, it's Cold Outside'	*Neptune's Daughter*

Academy Awards
Winners for Best Song in the 1950s

Year	Song	Film title
1950	'Mona Lisa'	*Captain Carey, USA*
1951	'In the Cool, Cool, Cool of the Evening'	*Here Comes the Groom*
1952	'High Noon (Do Not Forsake Me, Oh My Darlin)'	*High Noon*
1953	'Secret Love'	*Calamity Jane*
1954	'Three Coins in the Fountain'	*Three Coins in the Fountain*
1955	'Love is a Many-Splendored Thing'	*Love is a Many-Splendored Thing*
1956	'Whatever Will be, Will Be'	*The Man Who Knew Too Much*
1957	'All the Way'	*The Joker is Wild*
1958	'Gigi'	*Gigi*
1959	'High Hopes'	*A Hole in the Head*

Academy Awards
Winners for Best Song in the 1960s

Year	Artist	Song	Film title
1960	Don Costa	'Never on Sunday'	*Never on Sunday*
1961		'Moon River'	*Breakfast at Tiffany's*
1962	Henry Mancini	'Days of Wine and Roses'	*Days of Wine and Roses*
1963		'Call Me Irresponsible'	*Papa's Delicate Condition*
1964	Dick Van Dyke	'Chim Chim Cheree'	*Mary Poppins*
1965		'The Shadow of Your Smile'	*The Sandpiper*
1966	Roger Williams	'Born Free'	*Born Free*
1967	Rex Harrison and Cast	'Talk to the Animals'	*Doctor Dolittle*
1968	Noel Harrison	'The Windmills of Your Mind'	*The Thomas Crown Affair*
1969	B J Thomas	'Raindrops Keep Fallin' on My Head'	*Butch Cassidy and the*

Academy Awards
Winners for Best Song in the 1970s

Year		Song	Film title
1970	The Carpenters	'For All We Know'	*Lovers and Other Strangers*
1971	Isaac Hayes	'Theme From Shaft'	*Shaft*
1972	Maureen McGovern	'The Morning After'	*The Poseidon Adventure*
1973	Barbra Streisand	'The Way We Were'	*The Way We Were*
1974	Maureen McGovern	'We May Never Love Like This Again'	*The Towering Inferno*
1975	Keith Carradine	'I'm Easy'	*Nashville*
1976	Barbra Streisand	'Evergreen'	*A Star is Born*
1977	Debby Boone	'You Light Up My Life'	*You Light Up My Life*
1978	Donna Summer	'Last Dance'	*Thank God it's Friday*
1979	Jennifer Warnes	'It Goes Like it Goes'	*Norma Rae*

Academy Awards
Winners for Best Song in the 1980s

Year	Artist	Song	Film title
1980	Irene Cara	'Fame'	*Fame*
1981	Christopher Cross	'Arthur's Theme'	*Arthur*
1982	Joe Cocker and Jennifer Warnes	'Up Where We Belong'	*An Officer and a Gentleman*
1983	Irene Cara	'Flashdance . . . What a Feeling'	*Flashdance*
1984	Stevie Wonder	'I Just Called to Say I Love You'	*The Woman in Red*
1985	Lionel Richie	'Say You, Say Me'	*White Nights*
1986	Berlin	'Take My Breath Away'	*Top Gun*
1987	Bill Medley and Jennifer Warnes	'(I've Had) The Time of My Life'	*Dirty Dancing*
1988	Carly Simon	'Let the River Run'	*Working Girl*
1989	Samuel Wright	'Under the Sea'	*The Little Mermaid*

Academy Awards
Winners for Best Song 1990–2000

Year	Artist	Song	Film title
1990	Madonna	'Sooner or Later (I Always Get My Man)'	*Dick Tracey*
1991	Céline Dion and Peabo Bryson	'Beauty and the Beast'	*Beauty and the Beast*
1992	Regina Bell and Peabo Bryson	'A Whole New World'	*Aladdin*
1993	Bruce Springsteen	'Streets of Philadelphia'	*Philadelphia*
1994	Elton John	'Can You Feel the Love Tonight'	*The Lion King*
1995	Vanessa Williams	'Colours of the Wind'	*Pocahontas*
1996	Madonna	'You Must Love Me'	*Evita*
1997	Céline Dion	'My Heart Will Go On'	*Titanic*
1998	Mariah Carey and Whitney Houston	'When You Believe'	*Prince of Egypt*
1999	Phil Collins	'You'll be in My Heart'	*Tarzan*
2000	Bob Dylan	'Things Have Changed'	*Wonder Boys*

Austrian Composers

Name	Dates	Compositions
Alban Berg	1885–1935	operas, chamber music
Anton Bruckner	1824–1896	symphonies
Franz Joseph Haydn	1732–1809	symphonies, oratorios, chamber music
Gustav Mahler	1860–1911	symphonies
Wolfgang Amadeus Mozart	1756–1791	symphonies, operas, chamber music
Arnold Schoenberg	1874–1951	concertos, vocal, orchestral, chamber music
Franz Schubert	1797–1828	songs, symphonies, chamber music
Johann Strauss II	1825–1899	waltzes, operettas
Anton Webern	1883–1945	chamber, vocal music

Birtwistle

The Operas and Music Theatre of Harrison Birtwistle

Title	Year
Punch and Judy	1968
Down by the Greenwood Side	1969
The Mask of Orpheus	1973–75, 1981–84
Bow Down	1977
Yan Tan Tethera	1986
Gawain	1989–91, rev. 1993–94
The Second Mrs Kong	1994

Brit Award Winners

Performer(s)	Number of awards
Robbie Williams	9
Annie Lennox	8
Michael Jackson	6
Prince	6
U2	6
Phil Collins	5
George Michael	5
Bjork	4
Blur	4
Manic Street Preachers	4
Oasis	4
Spice Girls	4
Dave Stewart	4
Take That	4

Britten
The Operas and Church Parables of Benjamin Britten

Title	Year	Title	Year
Paul Bunyan	1940–41, revised 1974	The Turn of the Screw	1954
		Noye's Fludde	1958
Peter Grimes	1945	A Midsummer Night's Dream	1960
The Rape of Lucretia	1946		
Albert Herring	1947	Curlew River[2]	1964
The Beggar's Opera[1]	1948	The Burning Fiery Furnace[2]	1966
Let's Make an Opera	1949		
Billy Budd	1951, revised 1960	The Prodigal Son[2]	1968
		Owen Wingrave	1971
Gloriana	1953	Death in Venice	1973

[1] New version of Gay's opera.
[2] Church parables.

Celebrities
Wives of Frank Sinatra

Name	Year married
Nancy Barbato	1939
Ava Gardner	1951
Mia Farrow	1966
Barbara Marx	1976

Christmas Songs

Artist	Title
Bing Crosby	'White Christmas'
Bill Haley	'Rocking Around the Christmas Tree'
Elton John	'Step into Christmas'
Greg Lake	'I Believe in Father Christmas'
John Lennon	'Merry Christmas (War is Over)'
Mud	'Lonely this Christmas'
Frank Sinatra	'Have Yourself a Merry Little Christmas'
Slade	'Merry Christmas Everybody'
Wings	'Simply Having a Wonderful Christmas Time'
Wizard	'I Wish it could be Christmas Every Day'

Composers

Name	Dates	Nationality	Compositions
Béla Bartók	1881–1945	Hungarian	operas, concertos, chamber music
Benjamin Britten	1913–1976	English	vocal music, opera
Frédéric Chopin	1810–1849	Polish	piano music
Edward Elgar	1857–1934	English	orchestral music
César Franck	1822–1890	Belgian	symphony, organ works
George Gershwin	1898–1937	US	musicals, operas
Edvard Grieg	1843–1907	Norwegian	concertos, orchestral music
Franz Liszt	1811–1886	Hungarian	piano, orchestral music
Carl Nielsen	1865–1931	Danish	symphonies
Henry Purcell	1659–1695	English	vocal music, opera
Jean Sibelius	1865–1957	Finnish	symphonies, orchestral music

Composers
'Les Six'

Name	Birthplace	Life dates	Name	Birthplace	Life dates
Georges Auric	Lodéve	1899–1983	Francis Poulenc	Paris	1899–1963
Louis Durey	Paris	1888–1979	Germaine	Parc-St-	1892–1983
Arthur Honegger	Le Havre	1892–1955	Tailleferre	Maur	
Darius Milhaud	Aix-en-Provence	1892–1974			

Composers
Most Prolific

Name	Life dates	Name	Life dates
Georg Philipp Telemann	1681–1767	Wolfgang Amadeus Mozart	1756–1791
Johann Sebastian Bach	1685–1750	Richard Strauss	1864–1949
Antonio Vivaldi	1675–1741	Ludwig van Beethoven	1770–1827
Josef Haydn	1732–1809	Johannes Brahms	1833–1897
George Frederick Handel	1685–1759	Guiseppe Verdi	1813–1901

Composers
The 'Mighty Five' Russian Composers

Name	Birthplace	Life dates
Mily Balakirev	Nizhny-Novgorod	1837–1910
Alexander Borodin	St Petersburg	1833–1887
César Cui	Vilnius	1835–1918
Modest Mussorgsky	Karevo	1839–1881
Nikolai Rimsky-Korsakov	Tikhvin	1844–1908

Czech Composers

Name	Dates	Compositions
Antonin Dvořák	1841–1904	symphonies, operas
Leoš Janáček	1854–1928	operas, chamber music
Bedřich Smetana	1824–1884	symphonies, operas

French Composers

Name	Dates	Compositions
Hector Berlioz	1803–1869	operas, symphonies
Pierre Boulez	1925–	instrumental, vocal, orchestral
Claude Debussy	1862–1918	operas, orchestral music
Olivier Messiaen	1908–1992	piano, organ, orchestral music
Maurice Ravel	1875–1937	orchestral, piano, chamber music
Camille Saint-Saëns	1835–1921	symphonies, concertos, operas

German Composers

Name	Dates	Compositions
Johann Sebastian Bach	1685–1750	keyboard choral music, concertos
Ludwig van Beethoven	1770–1827	symphonies, chamber music
Johannes Brahms	1833–1897	symphonies, concertos
Felix Mendelssohn	1809–1847	symphonies, concertos
Robert Schumann	1810–1856	piano, vocal music, concertos
Karlheinz Stockhausen	1928–	electronic, chamber music, music theatre
Richard Strauss	1864–1949	operas, orchestral music
Richard Wagner	1813–1883	operas
Carl Maria von Weber	1786–1826	operas, concertos

Gilbert and Sullivan
The Operettas of Gilbert and Sullivan

Title	Year	Title	Year
Thespis	1871, lost	*Princess Ida*	1883
Trial by Jury	1875	*The Mikado*	1884–85
The Sorcerer	1877	*Ruddigore*	1886
HMS Pinafore	1878	*The Yeomen of the Guard*	1888
The Pirates of Penzance	1879	*The Gondoliers*	1889
Patience	1880–81	*Utopia Limited*	1893
Iolanthe	1882	*The Grand Duke*	1895–96

Glass
The Operatic Works of Philip Glass

Opera	Year	Opera	Year
Einstein on the Beach	1976	*Akhnaten*	1984
Attacca – A Madrigal Opera[1]	1980	*The Civil Wars*	1984
Satyagraha: M. K. Gandhi in South Africa	1980	*The Juniper Tree* (in collaboration with Robert Moran)	1985
The Photographer	1982	*A Descent into Maelstrom*	1986

(continued)

 Music 113

Glass: The Operatic Works of Philip Glass (*continued*)

Opera	Year
The Fall of the House of Usher	1988
The Making of the	1988
Representative for Planet 8	
1,000 Airplanes on the Roof	1988
Hydrogen Jukebox	1990

Opera	Year
The Voyage	1992
Orphée	1993
The White Raven	1993
La belle et la bête	1994

[1] As *The Panther*, 1982; *A Madrigal Opera*, 1985.

Gold Albums
Female Performers with Most in the UK

Female performer	Number
Madonna	24
Diana Ross	17
Barbra Streisand	13
Mariah Carey	11
Donna Summer	11
Céline Dion	10
Kate Bush	9
Cher	9
Whitney Houston	9
Tina Turner	8

Gold Albums
Female Performers with Most in the USA

Female performer	Number
Barbra Streisand	40
Reba McEntire	19
Linda Ronstadt	17
Olivia Newton-John	15
Aretha Franklin	13
Madonna	13
Dolly Parton	13
Gloria Estefan	12
Anne Murray	12
Tanya Tucker	12

Gold Albums
Male Performers with Most in the UK

Male performers	Number
Cliff Richard	24
Elton John	23
Rod Stewart	23
Neil Diamond	18
David Bowie	17
Mike Oldfield	16
Elvis Presley	16
James Last	15
Michael Jackson	15
Paul McCartney	11

Gold Albums
Male Performers with Most in the USA

Male performers	Number
Elvis Presley	81
Neil Diamond	35
Elton John	33
Bob Dylan	31
Kenny Rogers	28
George Strait	27
Frank Sinatra	26
Willie Nelson	23
Hank Williams Jnr	21
Paul McCartney	20
Eric Clapton	20
Barry Manilow	18

Gold Albums
Pop Groups with Most in the UK

Queen
Abba
Status Quo
UB40
Genesis
The Beatles
The Carpenters
The Bee Gees
Roxy Music
Pink Floyd

Gold Albums
Pop Groups with Most in the USA

The Rolling Stones
The Beatles
Chicago
The Bee Gees
Earth Wind and Fire
The Beach Boys
The Carpenters
Kiss
Hall and Oates
Led Zeppelin

Gold and Platinum
US Singles and Albums

Fact	Details
top certified group of the 20th century	The Beatles (106 million)
top solo artists	Garth Brooks (89 million), Elton John, Billy Joel, Barbra Streisand, Elvis Presley
first gold single	Perry Como 'Catch a Falling Star' (1958)
first gold album	Original Cast *Oklahoma!* (1958)
first platinum single	Johnny Taylor 'Disco Lady'
first platinum album	The Eagles *Greatest Hits 1971–75* (This album is now the best-selling album of the 20th century, with over 27 million copies sold, replacing Michael Jackson's *Thriller,* which held the top position from 1984 until 1999.)

Grammy Award Winners

2000 (for releases in 1999)

Category	Winner	Category	Winner
Song of the Year	Itaal Shur and Rob Thomas, songwriters, Santana featuring Rob Thomas 'Smooth'	Rock Album	Santana *Supernatural*
		R&B Album	TLC *Fanmail*
		Rap Album	Eminem *The Slim Shady LP*
Album of the Year	Santana *Supernatural*	Country Album	Dixie Chicks *Fly*
Record of the Year	Santana 'Smooth'	Best Reggae Album	Burning Spear *Calling Rastafari*
New Artist	Christina Aguilera		
Best Dance Recording	Cher 'Believe'	Legend Award	Elton John
Best Pop Album	Sting *Brand New Day*		

Grammy Awards
Performers with Most Classical Grammy Awards

Performer	Number of awards	Performer	Number of awards
Georg Solti	31	Leonard Bernstein	13
Vladimir Horowitz	24	Yo-Yo Ma	13
Pierre Boulez	18	Itzhak Perlman	13
Robert Shaw	16	Leontyne Price	13
John Williams	15	Artur Rubinstein	10

Grammy Awards
Performers with Most Non-classical Grammy Awards in One Year

Year	Performer	Number of awards
2000	Carlos Santana	8
1983	Michael Jackson	8
1965	Roger Miller	6
1976	Stevie Wonder	5
1974	Stevie Wonder	5
1973	Stevie Wonder	5
1961	Henry Mancini	5

Grammy Awards
Performers with Most Non-classical Grammy Awards

Performer	Number of awards
Quincy Jones	26
Stevie Wonder	21
Henry Mancini	20
Aretha Franklin	15
Paul Simon	15
Chet Atkins	14
Sting	14
Ella Fitzgerald	13
Michael Jackson	13
Paul McCartney	13
Ray Charles	12

Grammy Awards
Winners of Best Record and Best Album Awards

Year of release	Best Record	Best Album
1990	Phil Collins 'Another Day in Paradise'	Quincy Jones *Back on the Block*
1991	Natalie Cole, with Nat 'King' Cole 'Unforgettable'	Natalie Cole, with Nat 'King' Cole *Unforgettable*
1992	Eric Clapton 'Tears in Heaven'	Eric Clapton *Unplugged*
1993	Whitney Houston 'I Will Always Love You'	Whitney Houston *The Bodyguard*

Grammy Awards: Winners of Best Record and Best Album Awards (*continued*)

Year of release	Best Record	Best Album
1994	Sheryl Crow 'All I Wanna Do'	Tony Bennett *MTV Unplugged*
1995	Seal 'Kiss from a Rose'	Alanis Morissette *Jagged Little Pill*
1996	Eric Clapton 'Change the World'	Céline Dion *Falling into You*
1997	Shawn Colvin 'Sunny Came Home'	Bob Dylan *Time Out of Mind*
1998	Céline Dion 'My Heart Will Go On'	Lauryn Hill *The Miseducation of Lauryn Hill*
1999	Santana 'Smooth'	Santana *Supernatural*

Heavy Metal
Biggest-selling UK Albums

Artist/band	Album	Year
Led Zeppelin	*Led Zeppelin II*	1969
Def Leppard	*Hysteria*	1987
Guns 'N' Roses	*Use Your Illusion*	1991
Def Leppard	*Adrenalize*	1992
Iron Maiden	*The Number of the Beast*	1982
Black Sabbath	*Paranoid*	1970
Deep Purple	*Fireball*	1971
Deep Purple	*Machine Head*	1972
Iron Maiden	*Seventh Son of a Seventh Son*	1988
Deep Purple	*Deepest Purple*	1980

Heavy Metal
Top UK Singles

Artist/band	Single	Year
Iron Maiden	'Bring Your Daughter to the Slaughter'	1991
Deep Purple	'Black Night'	1970
Def Leppard	'When Love and Hate Collide'	1995
The Stone Roses	'Love Spreads'	1994
Iron Maiden	'Be Quick or be Dead'	1992
Iron Maiden	'Holy Smoke'	1990
Guns 'N' Roses	'Knockin' on Heaven's Door'	1992
Black Sabbath	'Paranoid'	1970
Aerosmith	'I Don't Want to Miss a Thing'	1998
Deep Purple	'Strange Kind of Woman'	1971

Instrumentals
Top UK Singles

Artist/band	Single	Year	Artist/band	Single	Year
Eddie Calvert	'Oh Mein Papa'	1953	B Bumble and the Stingers	'Nut Rocker'	1962
The Shadows	'Wonderful Land'	1962	Fleetwood Mac	'Albatross'	1969
Acker Bilk	'Stranger on the Shore'	1961	Herb Alpert	'Spanish Flea'	1965
The Tornadoes	'Telstar'	1962	Vangelis	'Chariots of Fire'	1981
The Shadows	'Apache'	1960	Mike Oldfield	'Tubular Bells'	1974

Italian Composers

Name	Dates	Compositions
Claudio Monteverdi	1567–1643	operas, vocal music
Giovanni Palestrina	c. 1525–1594	motets, masses
Giacomo Puccini	1858–1924	operas
Gioacchino Rossini	1792–1868	operas
Giuseppe Verdi	1813–1901	operas
Antonio Vivaldi	1678–1741	concertos, chamber music

James Bond Films
Songs

Year	James Bond film	Artist/band	Song
1997	*Tomorrow Never Dies*	Sheryl Crow	'Tomorrow Never Dies'
1995	*Goldeneye*	Tina Turner	'Goldeneye'
1989	*Licence to Kill*	Gladys Knight and the Pips	'Licence to Kill'
1987	*The Living Daylights*	A-Ha	'The Living Daylights'
1985	*A View to a Kill*	Duran Duran	'A View to a Kill'
1981	*For Your Eyes Only*	Sheena Easton	'For Your Eyes Only'
1977	*The Spy Who Loved Me*	Carly Simon	'Nobody Does it Better'
1973	*Live and Let Die*	Paul and Linda McCartney	'Live and Let Die'
1971	*Diamonds are Forever*	Shirley Bassey	'Diamonds are Forever'
1969	*On Her Majesty's Secret Service*	Louis Armstrong	'We Have All the Time in the World'
1968	*You Only Live Twice*	Nancy Sinatra	'You Only Live Twice'
1967	*Casino Royale*	Burt Bacharach	'The Look of Love'
1965	*Thunderball*	Tom Jones	'Thunderball'
1964	*Goldfinger*	Shirley Bassey	'Goldfinger'
1963	*From Russia With Love*	Matt Monro	'From Russia With Love'

Janáček
The Operas of Leoš Janáček

Title	Year
Šárka	1887–88, revised 1918, 1924
The Beginning of a Romance	1891, produced 1894
Jenufa	1894–1903, revised before 1908
Osud/Fate	1903–05, revised 1906–07
The Excursions of Mr Brouček	1908–17
Káta Kabanova	1919–21
The Cunning Little Vixen	1921–23
The Makropoulos Case	1923–25
From the House of the Dead	1927–28

Jazz
Biggest-selling UK Albums

Artist/band	Album	Year
Ball, Barber and Bilk	*Best of Ball, Barber and Bilk*	1962
Frank Sinatra and Count Basie	*Frank Sinatra and Count Basie*	1963
Chris Barber and Acker Bilk	*Best of Barber and Bilk*	1961
Kenny Ball	*Kenny Ball's Golden Hits*	1963
Louis Armstrong	*We Have All the Time in the World*	1994
Duke Ellington	*Nut Cracker Suite*	1961
Louis Armstrong	*Hello Dolly*	1964
Dave Brubeck	*Time Further Out*	1962
Ella Fitzgerald	*Ella Sings Gershwin*	1960

Jazz
Influential Albums

Artist/band	Album	Artist/band	Album
Louis Armstrong	*The Hot Five Recordings*	Benny Goodman	*Live at Carnegie Hall*
Count Basie	*Swinging the Blues*	Billie Holiday	*The Quintessential Billie Holiday*
Bix Beiderbecke	*Singing the Blues*	Charles Mingus	*Pithecanthropus Erectus*
Miles Davis	*Miles Ahead*		
Duke Ellington	*1943 Carnegie Hall Concert*	Thelonius Monk	*Genius of Modern Music*
Ella Fitzgerald	*Pure Ella*	Sonny Rollins	*Saxophone Colossus*
Dizzy Gilespie	*Groovin' High*		

Keyboard Instruments

Instrument	Description
accordion	instrument with metal reeds operated by 'wind' produced by pleated bellows
carillon	set of (tower) bells operated by wires and keys
celeste	set of metal bars with bell-like sound when struck with key-operated hammers
cembalo	harpsichord
clavichord	quiet piano-like instrument with strings struck by metal pins
electric organ	instrument that produces pipe organ-like sounds electronically
harmonium	reed organ worked by foot-operated bellows
harpsichord	piano-like instrument with strings plucked by quill or leather plectrums
spinet	small harpsichord with a triangular shape
synthesizer	instrument that produces a wide range of sounds electronically
virginal	small harpsichord
wurlitzer	electric cinema organ

Mozart

The Operas of Wolfgang Amadeus Mozart

Title	Köchel number	Year	Title	Köchel number	Year
Apollo et Hyacinthus	intermezzo, K38	1767	Idomeneo, Rè di Creta	K366	1780
Bastien und Bastienne	K50	1768	Die Entführung aus dem Serail	K384	1781 –82
Mitridate, Rè di Ponto	K87	1770	L'Oca del Cairo	K422	1783
Ascanio in Alba	K111	1771	Lo sposo deluso	K430	1783
Il sogno di Scipione	K126	1772	Der Schausspieldirektor	K486	1786
Lucio Silla	K135	1772	Le nozze di Figaro	K492	1786
La finta giardiniera	K196	1774	Don Giovanni	K527	1787
Il Rè Pastore	K208	1775	Così fan tutte	K588	1790
Zaide	K344	1780	Die Zauberflöte	K620	1791
Thamos, König in Ägypten	K345, incidental music	1780	La Clemenza di Tito	K621	1791

Music Festivals
Major Annual Music Festivals

Name	Location	Year started	Name	Location	Year started
Aldeburgh	Suffolk, UK	1948	Promenade Concerts	London, UK	1895
Bayreuth	Germany	1872	Salzburg	Austria	1920
Edinburgh	Scotland	1947	Tanglewood	Boston	1937
Glyndebourne	Sussex, UK	1934	Verona	Italy	1913
Lucerne	Switzerland	1938	Zurich	Switzerland	1909
Munich	Germany	1901			

Music
Richest Musicians in the UK

Star	Wealth (£ million)
Paul McCartney	700
Andrew Lloyd Webber	420
Cameron Mackintosh	400
Mick Jagger	150
Elton John	150
Keith Richards	130
David Bowie	120
Phil Collins	103
George Harrison	100
Sting	90

Music
Some Musical Expressions

Expression	Meaning
adagio, adagietto	slow, easy-going
allegro, allegretto	fast, with lightness of action
concerto	the solo (group)
crescendo	gradually louder
dolce, dolcissimo	soft and sweetly
forte	loud
fortissimo	very loud
legato	smoothly
pianissimo	very soft
piano	soft
staccato, staccatissimo	short, very short
subito	sudden, suddenly
voce, voci	voice, voices

Musicals
Longest-running Broadway Shows

Musical	Year	Number of performances
The Fantasticks	1960	still running
Cats	1982	still running
Les Misérables	1987	still running
The Phantom of the Opera	1988	still running
Miss Saigon	1991	still running
Rent	1996	still running
Grease	1972	3,388
Fiddler on the Roof	1964	3,242

(continued)

Musicals: Longest-running Broadway Shows
(*continued*)

Musical	Year	Number of performances
Hello Dolly	1964	2,844
My Fair Lady	1956	2,717
Godspell	1971	2,651
Man of La Mancha	1965	2,328
Oklahoma!	1943	2,248

Musicals
Shortest-running Broadway Shows

Musical	Year	Number of performances	Musical	Year	Number of performances
Anyone Can Whistle	1964	9	*Pickwick*	1965	56
Valmouth	1960	14	*Mack and Mabel*	1974	65
Merrily We Roll Along	1982	16	*Chess*	1988	68
The Rocky Horror Show	1975	45	*Salad Days*	1958	80

Musicians
With Most Academy Award Nominations for Their Music

Musician	Number of Academy Award nominations	First Academy Award nomination	
		Year	Nominated for
Alfred Newman	43	1937	*Prisoner of Zenda*
John Williams	36	1967	*The Valley of the Dolls*
Dimitri Tiomkin	22	1937	*Lost Horizon*
Henry Mancini	17	1954	*The Glenn Miller Story*
Randy Newman	13	1981	*Ragtime*
Marvin Hamlisch	11	1971	*Kotch*
Michel Legrand	11	1964	*Les Parapluies de Cherbourg*
Alan Menkin	11	1990	*The Little Mermaid*
Andre Previn	11	1950	*Three Little Words*
Elmer Bernstein	10	1955	*The Man with the Golden Arm*

Musicians
With Most Academy Awards for Their Music

Musician	Year	Film	Musician	Year	Film
John Barry	1990	*Dances with Wolves*	Henry Mancini	1982	*Victor/Victoria*
	1985	*Out of Africa*		1962	*Days of Wine and Roses*
	1967	*Lion in Winter*		1961	*Breakfast at Tiffany's*
	1966	*Born Free*			
Andre Previn	1964	*My Fair Lady*	Alan Menken	1992	*Aladdin*
	1963	*Irma la Douce*		1991	*Beauty and the Beast*
	1959	*Porgy and Bess*			
	1958	*Gigi*		1989	*The Little Mermaid*
Maurice Jarre	1984	*A Passage to India*	Giorgio Moroder	1986	*Top Gun*
	1965	*Doctor Zhivago*		1983	*Flashdance*
	1962	*Lawrence of Arabia*		1978	*Midnight Express*
Michel Legrand	1983	*Yentl*	John Williams	1982	*E.T. the Extra-Terrestrial*
	1971	*Summer of '42*		1977	*Star Wars*
	1968	*The Thomas Crown Affair*		1975	*Jaws*

Number One Albums
First Performers with Gold Albums in the USA

Artist	Album	Year
Gordon Macrae	*Oklahoma*	1958
Ernie Ford	*Hymns*	1959
Johnny Mathis	*Johnny's Greatest Hits*	1959
Mitch Miller and the Gang	*Sing Along with Mitch*	1959
Rogers and Hammerstein	*South Pacific*	1959
Henry Mancini	*Peter Gun*	1959
Mario Lanzo	*Student Prince*	1960
Pat Boone	*Pat's Greatest Hits*	1960
Elvis Presley	*Elvis*	1960
Kingston Trio	*Kingston Trio*	1960

Number One Albums
Performers with Several Albums Selling Ten Million Copies

Artist/group	Number of albums
The Beatles	5
Garth Brooks	4
The Eagles	?
Whitney Houston	2
Elton John	2
Pink Floyd	2
Bruce Springsteen	2
Van Halen	2

Number One Singles
First Pop Singles to go Straight in at Number One in the UK

Artist/band	Single	Date
Al Martino	'Here in My Heart'	15 November 1952
Elvis Presley	'Jailhouse Rock'	25 January 1958
Lonnie Donegan	'My Old Man's a Dustman'	26 March 1960
Elvis Presley	'It's Now or Never'	5 November 1960
Elvis Presley	'Surrender'	27 May 1961
Cliff Richard	'The Young Ones'	13 January 1962
The Beatles	'I Want to Hold Your Hand'	7 December 1963
The Beatles	'Can't Buy Me Love'	28 March 1964
The Beatles	'A Hard Day's Night'	18 July 1964
The Rolling Stones	'Little Red Rooster'	21 November 1964

Opera
Major First Performances

Date	Opera	Composer	Location
1607	*Orfeo*	Monteverdi	Mantua, Italy
1786	*The Marriage of Figaro*	Mozart	Vienna, Austria
1787	*Don Giovanni*	Mozart	Prague, Czech Republic
1790	*Così fan tutte*	Mozart	Vienna, Austria
1791	*The Magic Flute*	Mozart	Vienna, Austria
1853	*La Traviata*	Verdi	Venice, Italy
1871	*Aida*	Verdi	Cairo, Egypt
1875	*Carmen*	Bizet	Paris, France
1885	*The Mikado*	Sullivan	London, UK
1904	*Madame Butterfly*	Puccini	Milan, Italy

Opera
Major Opera Houses

Name	Location	Number of seats
Teatro San Carlo	Naples, Italy	3,500
The Metropolitan Opera, The Lincoln Centre	New York, USA	3,500
Dallas Opera, The State Fair Park Music School	Dallas, Texas, USA	3,400
Teatro alla Scala	Milan, Italy	3,000
The Philadelphia Opera Company, The Academy	Philadelphia, USA	2,800
The Opera-Bastille	Paris, France	2,700
The Opera	Barcelona, Spain	2,700
Teatro Colon	Buenos Aires, Argentina	2,500
Teatro Costanzi	Rome, Italy	2,300
The Bolshoi	Moscow, Russia	2,200
The Royal Opera House, Covent Garden	London, UK	2,000
Deutsche Oper	Berlin, Germany	1,900

Opera
Selected World Opera Companies

Country	Company	Director
Australia	Opera Australia	Moffatt Oxenbould
Czech Republic	The National Theatre Opera/Národní Divadlo	Josef Prudek
Denmark	The Royal Danish Opera	Elaine Padmore
France	L'Opéra Comique	Pierre Medecin
	Opéra National de Paris-Bastille	Pierre Bergé
Italy	Teatro Alla Scala	Riccardo Muti
	Teatro Municipale Valli	Bruno Borghi
New Zealand	National Opera	Patricia Hurley
Poland	Grand Theatre/National Opera	Jerzy Bojar
	Warsaw Chamber Opera	Stefan Sutowski
USA	Baltimore Opera Company	William Yannuzzi
	Cleveland Opera	David Bamberger
	The Metropolitan Opera	James Levine

Opera
Ten Ground-breaking Operas of the 20th Century

Opera	Composer, year	Details
Pelléas et Mélisande	Debussy, 1902	a seminal musical composition for the 20th century and a stand-alone opera with a unique approach to form, harmony, and vocal declamation

(continued)

Opera: Ten Ground-breaking Operas of the 20th Century
(*continued*)

Opera	Composer, year	Details
Wozzeck	Berg, 1925	an unsettling piece of expressionist theatre, as much for its bracing mixture of tonal and atonal elements and different musical styles as for the pessimism of the drama
Die Dreigroschenoper/ The Threepenny Opera	Weill, 1928	hardly an opera at all. Weill's vernacular music matches Brecht's song lyrics for irony and sophistication. A piece that blurred the line between opera and music theatre
From the House of the Dead	Janáček, 1930	perhaps the most radical of Janáček's extraordinary last operas, with an almost exclusively male cast, a drastically pared-down orchestral texture, and a dramatic sensibility in part dictated by the documentary nature of Dostoevsky's story
A Lady Macbeth of the Mtsensk District	Shostakovich, 1934	a modernist masterpiece that proved too controversial for Stalin, who banned performances of the work and forced its composer to rethink his approach to music
Porgy and Bess	Gershwin, 1935	another piece that blurs a line, in this case between opera and the American musical. Gershwin's genius as a composer of memorable musical numbers finds its fullest dramatic expression in what has been called the most vital of American operas
Curlew River	Britten, 1964	according to its composer not an opera at all, but a parable for church performance. Strongly influenced by the Japanese Nō theatre, Britten simplified his musical language and demanded an ascetic acting style for this essentially religious work
Einstein on the Beach	Glass, 1976	the first minimalist opera, Glass's slowed-down approach to harmony through sustained repetition favours philosophical reflection over narrative
Le Grand Macabre	Ligeti, 1978	a high-modern opera about death that is also funny, Ligeti's only full opera is a surreal farce that quotes liberally from other music
Donnerstag aus Licht/ Thursday from Light	Stockhausen, 1981	the first of a projected seven-opera cycle, one for every day of the week, Stockhausen's grand project dwarfs even Wagner's Ring Cycle in ambition. It has also pioneered the use of electronics in the musical theatre

Opera
Ten Operas Based on Shakespeare

Opera	Composer	Based on
Otello	Rossini	Othello
Der widerspenstigen Zähmung	Goetz	The Taming of the Shrew
Hamlet	Thomas	
Béatrice et Bénédict	Berlioz	Much Ado About Nothing
Falstaff	Verdi	The Merry Wives of Windsor
Macbeth	Bloch	
A Midsummer Night's Dream	Britten	
Antony and Cleopatra	Barber	
The Knot Garden	Tippett	The Tempest
Lear	Reimann	King Lear

Opera
The First Opera Houses

Name	Location	Year
Teatro Tron	Venice, Italy	1637
L'Opéra	Paris, France	1671
Covent Garden	London, UK	1732
Teatro San Carlo	Naples, Italy	1737
The John Street Theater	New York, USA	1767
Teatro alla Scala	Milan, Italy	1778
Théâtre Italian	Paris, France	1783
Teatro La Fenice	Venice, Italy	1792
Staatsoper	Vienna, Austria	1869
Festspielhaus	Bayreuth, Germany	1872

Opera
The First Operas

Name	Composer	Performed	Year
Orfeo	Angelo Poliziano	Mantua	c. 1480
Dafne	Peri	Florence	1598
Euridice	Caccini	Florence	1601
Orfeo	Monteverdi	Mantua	1607
Dafne	Gagliano	Mantua	1608
Dafne	Schütz	Torgau	1627
Landi	Sant 'Alessio	Rome	1632
The Coronation of Poppea	Monteverdi	Venice	1643
Alceste	Lully	Paris	1674
Dido and Aeneas	Purcell	London	1689

Operas
Some Famous Operas

Name	Composer	Year
17th century		
Orfeo	Monteverdi	1607
18th century		
Giulio Cesare/ Julius Caesar	Handel	1724
Così fan Tutte/ All Women Do It	Mozart	1789
19th century		
Fidelio	Beethoven	1805

Name	Composer	Year
Der Fliegende Holländer/The Flying Dutchman	Wagner	1843
La Traviata	Verdi	1854
Carmen	Bizet	1875
La Bohème	Puccini	1896
20th century		
Der Rosenkavalier/ The Rose Cavalier	Strauss	1911
Lulu	Berg	1937
Nixon in China	Adams	1987

Orchestra
Composition of a Typical Western Orchestra

Section	Instruments
strings	violins (two groups), violas, cellos, double basses, harp
woodwind	flutes (including piccolo), clarinets (including piccolo and bass clarinets), oboes (including cor anglais), bassoons (including double bassoon)
brass	horns, trumpets, trombones (including bass trombone), tubas
percussion	timpani, bass drum, side drum, cymbals, triangle, xylophone, celesta, glockenspiel, piano

Orchestras
Selected European Symphony Orchestras

Country	Orchestra	Director/conductor
Austria	Mozarteum Orchester	Hubert Soudant
	Wiener Symphoniker	Rainer Bischof
Czech Republic	Czech Philharmonic Orchestra	Ing Jiri Kovár
	Czech Symphony Orchestra	Jiri Kauders
Denmark	Danish National Radio Symphony Orchestra	Per Erik Veng
	Royal Danish Orchestra	Elaine Padmore
France	Orchestre National de France	Charles Dutoit
	Orchestre Philharmonique de Radio-France	Marek Janowski
Germany	Berlin Philharmonic	Simon Rattle
	Radio-Sinfonie-Orchester Frankfurt	Hugh Wolff
Poland	Warsaw Philharmonic	Kazimierz Kord
Russia	Bolshoi Symphony Orchestra	Mark Ermter
	Russian National Symphony Orchestra	Mikhail Pletnev
	Russian State Philharmonic Orchestra	Valery Poliansky

Percussion Instruments

Instrument	Description
bongos	pair of small drums (from Cuba) hit with the hands
castanets	shell-shaped wooden discs clicked in the hand
Chinese block	hollow wooden block struck with drumsticks
claves	wooden sticks hit together
cymbal	metal plate hit with a drumstick or clashed in pairs
glockenspiel	tuned metal bars struck with a hammer to produce a bell-like sound
kettledrum	tunable bowl-shaped metal drum
maracas	rattle made from seed filled gourd
marimba	type of xylophone played with soft-headed hammers
side drum	shallow two-skinned drum played with wooden sticks
snare drum	side drum with loose wires across the lower skin to produce a rattling sound
tabla	pair of small drums (from India) hit with the hands
tabor	small drum hit with the hand
tambourine	tabor with metal discs in the frame that jingle when it is struck
tenor drum	larger, deeper-pitched side drum
timpani	set of kettledrums
tom-toms	pair of small drums (from Asia) hit with the hands or sticks
tubular bells	hanging cylindrical bells struck with a hammer
vibraphone	set of tuned metal bars with resonators beneath them driven by small electric fans
xylophone	set of tuned wooden bars struck with hard hammers

Platinum Albums
Female Pop Performers with Most in the UK

Female performer	Number
Madonna	38
Céline Dion	23
Tina Turner	21
Whitney Houston	18
Cher	13
Enya	12
Shania Twain	12
Kate Bush	10
Mariah Carey	10
Kylie Minogue	10
Alanis Morissette	10

Platinum Albums
Female Pop Performers with Most in the USA

Female performer	Number
Barbra Streisand	49
Madonna	47
Mariah Carey	45
Whitney Houston	45
Céline Dion	34
Reba McEntire	24
Linda Ronstadt	23
Janet Jackson	19
Sade	19
Shania Twain	19
Gloria Estefan	18

Platinum Albums
Male Pop Performers with Most in the UK

Male performer	Number
Michael Jackson	35
Phil Collins	31
Elton John	31
George Michael	24
Robbie Williams	21
Meat Loaf	18
Chris Rea	14
Cliff Richard	14
Rod Stewart	14
Michael Bolton	13

Platinum Albums
Pop Groups with Most in the UK

Group	Number
Simply Red	39
Queen	35
Oasis	31
U2	25
Dire Straits	23
Fleetwood Mac	23
Spice Girls	23
Abba	21
Boyzone	20
Wet Wet Wet	19

Platinum Albums
Pop Groups with Most in the USA

Group	Number
The Beatles	36
The Rolling Stones	25
AC/DC	19
Alabama	19
Aerosmith	17
Led Zeppelin	14
Pink Floyd	14
U2	13
Van Halen	12
Queen	11

Pop Albums
Top-grossing Performers in the US Album Charts

Artist/band
The Beatles
Garth Brooks
Led Zeppelin
Elvis Presley
The Eagles
Billy Joel
Barbra Streisand
Elton John
Aerosmith
Pink Floyd

Pop Albums
Top UK Albums from the 1950s

Artist/band	Album	Artist/band	Album
Film soundtrack	*South Pacific*	Elvis Presley	*Elvis Presley*
Original cast	*My Fair Lady*	Frank Sinatra	*Come Fly With Me*
The Kingston Trio	*The Kingston Trio at Large*	Original cast	*The King and I*
		Johnny Mathis	*Warm*
Film soundtrack	*Around the World in 80 Days*	Doris Day/Film soundtrack	*Calamity Jane*
Film soundtrack	*Gigi*		

Pop Albums
Top UK Albums from the 1960s

Artist/band	Album	Artist/band	Album
The Beatles	*Please Please Me*	Elvis Presley	*Blue Hawaii*
The Beatles	*Sgt Pepper's Lonely Hearts Club Band*	The Beatles	*A Hard Day's Night*
		Elvis Presley	*GI Blues*
Film soundtrack	*West Side Story*	Cliff Richard	*Summer Holiday*
The Beatles	*With the Beatles*	Film soundtrack	*South Pacific*
Film soundtrack	*The Sound of Music*		

Pop Albums
Top UK Albums from the 1970s

Artist/band	Album	Artist/band	Album
Simon and Garfunkel	*Bridge Over Troubled Water*	Elton John	*Elton John's Greatest Hits*
Bee Gees/Film soundtrack	*Saturday Night Fever*	The Beach Boys	*20 Golden Greats*
		Pink Floyd	*Dark Side of the Moon*
Film soundtrack	*Grease*	Fleetwood Mac	*Rumours*
The Carpenters	*The Singles 1969–73*	Meat Loaf	*Like a Bat Out of Hell*
Abba	*Greatest Hits*		

Pop Albums
Top UK Albums from the 1980s

Artist/band	Album	Artist/band	Album
Queen	*Greatest Hits*	Bob Marley and the Wailers	*Legend*
Dire Straits	*Makin' Movies*	Phil Collins	*Face Value*
U2	*Under a Blood Red Sky*	Madonna	*Like a Virgin*
Michael Jackson	*Thriller*	Michael Jackson	*Bad*
Dire Straits	*Brothers in Arms*	Paul Simon	*Graceland*

Pop Albums
Top UK Albums from the 1990s

Artist/band	Album	Artist/band	Album
Oasis	What's the Story Morning Glory	The Spice Girls	Spice
Meat Loaf	Bat Out of Hell II	Robson and Jerome	Robson and Jerome
Eurythmics	Greatest Hits	Céline Dion	Falling into You
Madonna	The Immaculate Collection	The Verve	Urban Hymns
Simply Red	Stars	Cher	Cher's Greatest Hits

Pop Albums
Top US Albums

Artist/band	Album	Sales (millions)
The Eagles	Greatest Hits 1971–75	27
Michael Jackson	Thriller	26
Pink Floyd	The Wall	23
Led Zeppelin	Led Zeppelin IV	22
Billy Joel	Greatest Hits, Vols. I & II	21
Shania Twain	Come on Over	18
Fleetwood Mac	Rumours	18
The Beatles	The Beatles	18
Whitney Houston/Film Soundtrack	The Bodyguard	17
AC/DC	Back in Black	16

Pop Albums
Top US Albums from the 1950s

Artist/band	Album
Film soundtrack	South Pacific
Harry Belafonte	Calypso
Doris Day/Film soundtrack	Love Me or Leave Me
Original cast/Film soundtrack	My Fair Lady
The Kingston Trio	The Kingston Trio at Large
Original cast	The Music Man
Film soundtrack	Around the World in 80 Days
Film soundtrack	Gigi
Elvis Presley	Elvis Presley
Elvis Presley/Film soundtrack	Loving You

Pop Albums
Top US Albums from the 1960s

Artist/band	Album
Film soundtrack	West Side Story
Elvis Presley/ Film soundtrack	Blue Hawaii
The Monkees	More of the Monkees
Original cast/ Film soundtrack	The Sound of Music
Andy Williams	Days of Wine and Roses
The Beatles	Sgt Pepper's Lonely Hearts Club Band
Film soundtrack	Mary Poppins
Film soundtrack	Exodus
Ray Charles	Modern Sounds in Country and Western Music
The Monkees	The Monkees

Pop Albums
Top US Albums from the 1970s

Artist/band	Album
Fleetwood Mac	Rumours
Bee Gees/ Film soundtrack	Saturday Night Fever
Carole King	Tapestry
Stevie Wonder	Songs in the Key of Life
Film soundtrack	Grease
Peter Frampton	Frampton Comes Alive!
Simon and Garfunkel	Bridge Over Troubled Water
Elton John	Greatest Hits
The Eagles	The Long Run
Janis Joplin	Pearl

Pop Albums
Top US Albums from the 1980s

Artist/band	Album	Artist/band	Album
Michael Jackson	Thriller	Pink Floyd	The Wall
Prince/Film soundtrack	Purple Rain	Whitney Houston	Whitney Houston
Police	Synchronicity	Whitney Houston	Whitney
Men at Work	Business as Usual	Foreigner	'4'
REO Speedwagon	Hi Infidelity	Dire Straits	Brothers in Arms

Pop Charts
First Artists to Have a Number One in the UK Album Chart

Year	Artist	Album
1958	film soundtrack	South Pacific
1960	Freddy Cannon	The Explosive Freddy Cannon
1960	Elvis Presley	Elvis is Back
1960	101 Strings	Down Drury Lane to Memory Lane
1961	George Mitchell Minstrels	Black and White Minstrel Show
1961	Shadows	The Shadows
1961	Cliff Richard	21 Today
1962	Kenny Ball, Chris Barber, Acker Bilk	Best of Ball, Barber and Bilk
1962	film soundtrack	West Side Story
1963	The Beatles	Please Please Me

Pop Charts

First *New Musical Express* Singles Chart

Published in the UK on 14 November 1952.

Number	Artist/band	Single
1	Al Martino	'Here in My Heart'
2	Jo Stafford	'You Belong to Me'
3	Nat King Cole	'Somewhere Along the Way'
4	Bing Crosby	'Isle of Innisfree'
5	Guy Mitchell	'Feet Up'
6	Rosemary Clooney	'Half as Much'
7=	Frankie Laine	'High Noon'
	Vera Lynn	'Forget-me-not'
9=	Doris Day and Frankie Laine	'Sugarbush'
	Ray Martin	'Blue Tango'

Pop Charts

Performers with Most Weeks at Number One in the UK Singles Charts

Elvis Presley
The Beatles
Cliff Richard
Frankie Laine
Abba
Wet Wet Wet
Spice Girls
Madonna
Take That
Queen

Pop Charts

Performers with Most Weeks at Number One in the UK Album Charts

Artist/band	Number of weeks
The Beatles	164
Cast of *South Pacific*/Film soundtrack	115
Cast of *The Sound of Music*/Film soundtrack	70
Abba	50
Elvis Presley	49
Simon and Garfunkel	48
Rolling Stones	44
Cliff Richard	30
Carpenters	29
Elton John	28

Pop Charts

Performers with Most Consecutive Singles Reaching Number One in the UK

The Beatles	7	Take That	4	Jason Donovan	3
Westlife	7	The Shadows	4	Gerry and the Pacemakers	3
Spice Girls	6	Abba	3	Frank Ifield	3
The Rolling Stones	5	All Saints	3	Jive Bunny and the Mastermixers	3
Mario Lanza	4	B*Witched	3	Robson and Jerome	3
Elvis Presley	4	Blondie	3		

Pop Charts
Performers with Most Weeks in the UK Charts in Any One Year

Year	Artist/band
1968	Tom Jones
1970	Simon and Garfunkel
1973	David Bowie
1983	David Bowie
1983	U2
1984	Michael Jackson
1985	Bruce Springsteen
1985	Dire Straits
1986	Dire Straits

Pop Charts
Performers with Most Weeks in the UK Singles Charts

Artist/band	Number of weeks
Elvis Presley	1,168
Cliff Richard	1,142
The Shadows	770
Elton John	566
Diana Ross	560
Madonna	546
Michael Jackson	546
David Bowie	477
Rod Stewart	475
The Beatles	456
Frank Sinatra	440

Pop Charts
Performers with Most Weeks in the US Album Charts

Year	Artist/band	Album
1962	Film soundtrack	*West Side Story*
1982	Michael Jackson	*Thriller*
1958	Film soundtrack	*South Pacific*
1977	Fleetwood Mac	*Rumours*
1978	Bee Gees/Film soundtrack	*Saturday Night Fever*
1984	Prince/Film soundtrack	*Purple Rain*
1961	Elvis Presley/Film soundtrack	*Blue Hawaii*
1976	The Eagles	*Greatest Hits 1971–1975*
1979	Pink Floyd	*The Wall*

Pop Charts
Performers with Most Weeks in the US Singles Charts

Year	Artist/band	Single
1956	Elvis Presley	'Hound Dog'
1955	Perez Prado	'Cherry Pink and Apple Blossom Time'
1955	The McGuire Sisters	'Sincerely'
1956	Guy Mitchell	'Singing the Blues'
1981	Olivia Newton-John	'Physical'
1977	Debby Boone	'You Light Up My Life'
1958	Bobby Darin	'Mack the Knife'
1957	Elvis Presley	'All Shook Up'
1981	Kim Carnes	'Bette Davis Eyes'
1968	The Beatles	'Hey Jude'

Pop Charts
Top UK Singles from the 1950s

Artist/band	Single	Artist/band	Single
Frankie Laine	'I Believe'	Al Martino	'Here in My Heart'
Slim Whitman	'Rose Maria'	Perry Como	'Magic Moments'
David Whitfield	'Cara Mia'	Frankie Laine	'Answer Me'
Doris Day	'Secret Love'	Tennessee Ernie Ford	'Give Me Your Word'
Eddie Calvert	'Oh Mein Papa'		
Paul Anka	'Diana'		

Pop Charts
Top UK Singles from the 1960s

Artist/band	Single	Artist/band	Single
The Shadows	'Wonderful Land'	The Beatles	'From Me to You'
Elvis Presley	'It's Now or Never'	The Everly Brothers	'Cathy's Clown'
The Archies	'Sugar, Sugar'	The Beatles	'Hello Goodbye'
Frank Ifield	'I Remember You'	The Beatles	'She Loves You'
Tom Jones	'Green Green Grass of Home'	Cliff Richard	'The Young Ones'

Pop Charts
Top UK Singles from the 1970s

Artist/band	Single
John Travolta and Olivia Newton-John	'You're the One That I Want'
Paul McCartney and Wings	'Mull of Kintyre'
Queen	'Bohemian Rhapsody'
John Travolta and Olivia Newton-John	'Summer Nights'
Mungo Jerry	'In the Summertime'
Brotherhood of Man	'Save All Your Kisses for Me'
Dave Edmunds	'I Hear You Knocking'
Elvis Presley	'The Wonder of You'
Elton John and Kiki Dee	'Don't Go Breaking My Heart'
Bay City Rollers	'Bye Bye Baby'

Pop Charts
Top UK Singles from the 1980s

Artist/band	Single
Frankie Goes to Hollywood	'Two Tribes'
Stevie Wonder	'I Just Called to Say I Love You'
Black Box	'Ride on Time'
Culture Club	'Karma Chameleon'
Lionel Richie	'Hello'
Frankie Goes to Hollywood	'Relax'
Jennifer Rush	'The Power of Love'
Rick Astley	'Never Gonna Give You Up'
Jive Bunny and the Mastermixers	'Swing the Mood'

Pop Charts
Top UK Singles from the 1990s

Artist/band	Single
Elton John	'Candle in the Wind' (1997)
Bryan Adams	'(Everything I Do) I Do It For You'
Wet Wet Wet	'Love is All Around'
Whitney Houston	'I Will Always Love You'
Shakespear's Sister	'Stay'
Céline Dion	'Think Twice'
Britney Spears	'. . . Baby One More Time'
Cher	'Believe'
Robson Green and Jerome Flynn	'Unchained Melody'
Spice Girls	'Wannabe'

Pop Charts
Top US Singles from the 1950s

Artist/band	Single
Elvis Presley	'Don't be Cruel'
Bill Haley and His Comets	'(We're Gonna) Rock Around the Clock'
Roger Williams	'Autumn Leaves'
Guy Mitchell	'Singing the Blues'
Pat Boone	'Love Letters in the Sand'
Bobby Darin	'Mack the Knife'
The Four Lads	'Moments to Remember'
Elvis Presley	'Heartbreak Hotel'
Nelson Riddle	'Lisbon Antigua'
Jimmy Dorsey	'So Rare'

Pop Charts
Top US Singles from the 1960s

Artist/band	Single
Chubby Checker	'The Twist'
The Beatles	'Hey Jude'
Percy Faith	'Theme From A Summer Place'
Bobby Lewis	'Tossin' and Turnin''
5th Dimension	'Aquarius / Let the Sunshine in'
The Archies	'Sugar, Sugar'
The Beatles	'I Want to Hold Your Hand'
Marvin Gaye	'I Heard it Through the Grapevine'
Elvis Presley	'It's Now or Never'
Jim Reeves	'He'll Have to Go'

Pop Charts
Top US Singles from the 1970s

Artist/band	Single
Debby Boone	'You Light Up My Life'
Bee Gees	'How Deep is Your Love'
Andy Gibb	'I Just Want to be Your Everything'
Chic	'Le Freak'
Andy Gibb	'Shadow Dancing'
Bee Gees	'Staying Alive'
Bee Gees	'Night Fever'
B J Thomas	'Raindrops Keep Fallin' on My Head'
The Emotions	'Best of My Love'
Rod Stewart	'Tonight's the Night (Gonna be Alright)'

Pop Charts
Top US Singles from the 1980s

Artist/band	Single
Olivia Newton-John	'Physical'
Kim Carnes	'Bette Davis Eyes'
Queen	'Another One Bites the Dust'
Police	'Every Breath You Take'
Diana Ross and Lionel Richie	'Endless Love'
Survivor	'Eye of the Tiger'
Irene Cara	'Flashdance . . . What a Feeling'
Paul McCartney and Michael Jackson	'Say, Say, Say'
Blondie	'Call Me'
J Geils Band	'Centrefold'

Pop Groups
First Number One Hits by UK groups in the USA

Year	Group	Single
1962	Tornados	'Telstar'
1964	The Beatles	'I Want To Hold Your Hand'
1964	The Beatles	'She Loves You'
1964	The Beatles	'Can't Buy Me Love'
1964	The Beatles	'Love Me Do'
1964	The Beatles	'A Hard Day's Night'
1964	The Animals	'House of the Rising Sun'
1964	Manfred Mann	'Do Wah Diddy Diddy'

Pop Groups
First Number One Hits by US groups in the UK

Year	Group	Single
1955	Bill Haley and His Comets	'(We're Gonna) Rock Around the Clock'
1956	The Dreamweavers	'It's Almost Tomorrow'
1956	Kay Starr with the Hugo Winterhalter Orchestra	'Rock and Roll Waltz'
1956	The Teenagers featuring Frankie Lymon	'Why do Fools Fall in Love?'
1957	The Crickets	'That'll be the Day'
1958	The Everly Brothers	'All I do is Dream'
1958	The Kalin Twins	'When'
1959	The Platters	'Smoke Gets in Your Eyes'
1961	The Marcels	'Blue Moon'
1962	B Bumble and the Stingers	'Nut Rocker'

Pop Music
Largest Pre-chart Sheet Music Sales

Sheet music	Year	Sheet music	Year
'Music! Music! Music!'	1950	'The Tennesse Waltz'	1951
'My Foolish Heart'	1950	'Mockin' Bird Hill'	1951
'Bewitched'	1950	'Too Young'	1951
'Goodnight Irene'	1950	'Unforgettable'	1952
'I Tawt I Taw a Puddy Cat!'	1951	'My Resistance is Low'	1951

Pop Performers
Oldest to have Number One UK Chart Hits

Year	Performer	Age	Song
1968	Louis Armstrong	67	'What a Wonderful World'
1999	Cliff Richard	59	'Millennium Prayer'
1998	Isaac Hayes	56	'Chocolate Salty Balls'
2000	Brian May (with 5ive)	53	'We Will Rock You'
1998	Cher	52	'I Believe'

Pop Performers
With Most Number One Albums in the UK Chart

Artist/band	Number
The Beatles	14
The Rolling Stones	10
Abba	9
Queen	9
David Bowie	7
Led Zeppelin	7
Genesis	7
Paul McCartney and Wings	7
Cliff Richard	7
Rod Stewart	7

Pop Performers
With Most Number One Singles in the UK Chart

Artist/band	Number	Artist/band	Number
The Beatles	17	The Rolling Stones	8
Elvis Presley	17	Take That	8
Cliff Richard	14	Westlife	8
Madonna	11	Michael Jackson	7
Abba	9	George Michael	7
Spice Girls	9		

Pop Performers
With Most Top 10 Albums in the UK Chart

Artist/band	Number
Elvis Presley	37
Cliff Richard	33
The Rolling Stones	31
Frank Sinatra	29
Bob Dylan	25
David Bowie	22
Elton John	21
The Beatles	20
Iron Maiden	19
Paul McCartney	19

Pop Performers
With Most UK Hit Albums

Elvis Presley
James Last
Frank Sinatra
Cliff Richard
The Rolling Stones
Diana Ross
Bob Dylan
Elton John
Shirley Bassey
David Bowie

Pop Performers
With Top US Unit Sales

Performer(s)	Sales (millions)
The Beatles	152
Led Zeppelin	101
Garth Brooks	100
Elvis Presley	87
Billy Joel	76
Pink Floyd	69
Barbra Streisand	66
Eagles	65
Elton John	63
Madonna	57

Pop Performers
Youngest with Number One UK Chart Hits

Year	Performer	Age	Song
1972	Little Jimmy Osmond	9	'Long Haired Lover From Liverpool'
1956	Frankie Lymon	13	'Why Do Fools Fall in Love'
1972	Donny Osmond	14	'Puppy Love'
1961	Helen Shapiro	14	'You Don't Know'
1998	Billie Piper	15	'Because We Want To'

Youngest male solo artist to have a Number One single and album:

2000	Craig David	18	'Fill me in'/*Born to do it*

Youngest girl group to have a Number One single:

1998	B*Witched	20, 17, 17, 16	'C'est la Vie'

Pop Singles
First Performers with Gold Singles in the USA

Artist	Single	Year
Perry Como	'Catch a Falling Star'	1958
Laurie London	'He's Got the Whole World in His Hands'	1958
Elvis Presley	'Hard Headed Woman'	1958
Perez Prado	'Patricia'	1958
Kingston Trio	'Tom Dooley'	1959
Lawrence Welk	'Calcutta'	1961
Jimmy Dean	'Big Bad John'	1961
The Tokens	'The Lion Sleeps'	1962
Ray Charles	'I Can't Stop Loving You'	1962
Bobby Vinton	'Roses Are Red'	1962

Pop Singles
First Performers with Platinum Singles in the USA

Artist	Single	Year
Johnnie Taylor	'Disco Lady'	1976
The Manhattans	'Kiss and Say Goodbye'	1976
Wild Cherry	'Play That Funky Music'	1976
Rick Dees	'Disco Duck'	1976
Rose Royce	'Car Wash'	1977
Debby Boone	'You Light Up My Life'	1977
Heatwave	'Boogie Nights'	1977
Bee Gees	'Stayin' Alive'	1978
Samantha Sang	'Emotion'	1978
Queen	'We Are The Champions'	1978

Pop Singles
Selling over Five Million Copies

Artist/band	Single	Year
Elton John	'Candle in the Wind'	1997
Band Aid	'Do They Know It's Christmas'	1984–85
Bing Crosby	'White Christmas'	1942
Boney M	'Rivers of Babylon'	1978
Bill Haley and His Comets	'(We're Gonna) Rock Around the Clock'	1954
The Beatles	'Hey Jude'	1968
Whitney Houston	'I Will Always Love You'	1993
Bryan Adams	'(Everything I Do) I Do It For You'	1991
The Beatles	'I Want to Hold Your Hand'	1963
Elvis Presley	'It's Now or Never'	1960

Pop Singles
Spending Longest in the UK Charts

Year	Artist/band	Single	Number of weeks
1961	Englebert Humperdinck	'Release Me'	56
1961	Acker Bilk	'Stranger on the Shore'	55
1984	Frankie Goes to Hollywood	'Relax'	48
1969	Frank Sinatra	'My Way'	42
1978	Boney M	'Rivers of Babylon'	40
1964	Jim Reeves	'I Love You Because'	39
1973	Dawn	'Tie a Yellow Ribbon'	39
1961	Andy Stewart	'A Scottish Soldier'	38
1994	Wet Wet Wet	'Love is All Around'	37
1953	Frankie Laine	'I Believe'	36

Pop Singles
With Most Weeks at Number One in the UK Chart

Year	Artist/band	Single	Number of weeks
1953	Frankie Laine	'I Believe'	18
1991	Bryan Adams	'(Everything I Do) I Do It For You'	16
1994	Wet Wet Wet	'Love is All Around'	15
1975 & 1992	Queen	'Bohemian Rhapsody'	14
1955	Slim Whitman	'Rose Marie'	11
1954	David Whitfield	'Cara Mia'	10
1993–94	Whitney Houston	'I Will Always Love You'	10
1952–53	Al Martino	'Here in My Heart'	9
1954	Eddie Calvert	'Oh Mein Papa'	9
1954	Doris Day	'Secret Love'	9
1957	Paul Anka	'Diana'	9
1978	John Travolta and Olivia Newton John	'You're the One that I Want'	9

Pop Soloists
First UK Solo Performers to have a Number One Hit in the USA

Year	Artist	Single
1958	Laurie London	'He's Got the Whole World in His Hands'
1962	Acker Bilk	'Stranger on the Shore'
1965	Petula Clark	'Downtown'
1967	Lulu	'To Sir With Love'
1970	George Harrison	'My Sweet Lord'
1971	Rod Stewart	'Maggie May'
1972	Gilbert O'Sullivan	'Alone Again (Naturally)'
1972	Elton John	'Crocodile Rock'
1973	George Harrison	'Give Me Love – Give Me Peace on Earth'
1973	Ringo Starr	'Photograph'
1973	Ringo Starr	'You're Sixteen'

Pop Soloists
First US Solo Performers to have a Number One Hit in the UK

Year	Artist	Single
1952	Al Martino	'Here is My Heart'
1952	Jo Stafford	'You Belong to Me'
1952	Kay Starr	'Comes A-long A-love'
1953	Eddie Fisher	'Outside of Heaven'
1953	Perry Como	'Don't Let the Stars Get in Your Eyes'
1953	Guy Mitchell	'She Wears Red Feathers'
1953	Frankie Laine	'I Believe'
1954	Doris Day	'Secret Love'
1954	Johnnie Ray	'Such a Night'
1954	Kitten Kallen	'Little Things Mean a Lot'

Pop Songs
Top UK Singles

Artist/band	Single	Year
Elton John	'Candle in the Wind'	1997
Bryan Adams	'(Everything I Do) I Do It For You'	1991
Wet Wet Wet	'Love is All Around'	1994
Band Aid	'Do They Know It's Christmas'	1984–85
Queen	'Bohemian Rhapsody'	1974, 1991
Paul McCartney and Wings	'Mull of Kintyre'	1977
Frankie Goes to Hollywood	'Two Tribes'	1984
John Travolta and Olivia Newton-John	'You're the One That I Want'	1978
The Beatles	'From Me to You'	1963
The Beatles	'She Loves You'	1963

Pop Stars
Famous Pop Star Deaths

Year	Star	Age	Cause of death
1997	Michael Hutchence	37	suicide
1994	Kurt Cobain	27	suicide
1991	Freddie Mercury	45	AIDS-related illness
1981	Bob Marley	36	cancer
1980	John Lennon	40	shot
1979	Sid Vicious	22	drug overdose
1977	Marc Bolan	30	car crash

(*continued*)

Pop Stars: Famous Pop Star Deaths (*continued*)

Year	Star	Age	Cause of death
1977	Elvis Presley	42	heart attack
1971	Jim Morrison	27	drug overdose
1970	Jimi Hendrix	27	drug overdose
1970	Janis Joplin	27	drug overdose
1969	Brian Jones	26	drowned
1964	Sam Cooke	31	shot
1964	Jim Reeves	40	flight accident
1960	Eddie Cochrane	22	car crash (with Gene Vincent)
1960	Gene Vincent	25	car crash (with Eddie Cochrane)
1959	Buddy Holly	23	flight accident

Puccini
The Operas of Giacomo Puccini

Title	Year
Le Villi	(1 act) 1883, (2 act) 1884
Edgar	(4 act) 1884–88, (3 act) 1892, revised 1901, 1905
Manon Lescaut	1890–92
La Bohème	1894–95
Tosca	1898–99
Madama Butterfly	(2 act) 1901–03, (3 act) 1904, revised 1906
La fanciulla del West	1908–10
La rondine	1914–16
Il trittico (Il tabarro, Suor Angelica, Gianni Schicchi)	1913–18
Turandot	1920–26

Pulitzer Prizes in Music Winners

Year	Winner	Awarded for
1990	Mel Powell	*Duplicates: A Concerto for Two Pianos and Orchestra*
1991	Shulamit Ran	*Symphony*
1992	Wayne Peterson	*The Face of the Night, The Heart of the Dark*
1993	Christopher Rouse	*Trombone Concerto*
1994	Gunther Schuller	*Of Reminiscences and Reflections*
1995	Morton Gould	*Stringmusic*
1996	George Walker	*Lilacs*
1997	Wynton Marsalis	*Blood on the Fields*
1998	Aaron Jay Kernis	*String Quartet No. 2, Musica Instrumentalis*
1999	Melinda Wagner	*Concerto for Flute, Strings, and Percussion*
2000	Lewis Spratlan	*Life is a Dream, Opera in Three Acts: Act II, Concert version*

Punk
Biggest-selling UK Albums

Artist/band	Album	Year
The Sex Pistols	*Never Mind the Bollocks, Here's the Sex Pistols*	1977
Blondie	*Eat to the Beat*	1979
The Jam	*The Gift*	1982
The Clash	*Give 'em Enough Rope*	1978
Elvis Costello and the Attractions	*Armed Forces*	1979
Blondie	*Parallel Lines*	1978
Siouxsie and the Banshees	*Kaleidoscope*	1980
The Undertones	*Hypnotised*	1980
The Sex Pistols	*The Great Rock 'n' Roll Swindle*	1979
The Buzzcocks	*Love Bites*	1978

Punk
Top UK Singles

Artist/band	Single	Year
Blondie	'Heart of Glass'	1979
Jam	'Going Underground'	1980
Jam	'Beat Surrender'	1982
Jam	'Start!'	1982
Jam	'A Town Called Malice'	1982
Elvis Costello	'Oliver's Army'	1979
The Sex Pistols	'God Save the Queen'	1977
Siouxsie and the Banshees	'Hong Kong Garden'	1978
The Undertones	'My Perfect Cousin'	1980
Clash	'London Calling'	1979

Russian Composers

Name	Dates	Compositions
Modest Mussorgsky	1839–1881	operas, orchestral music
Sergei Prokofiev	1891–1953	symphonies, operas, ballets, piano music
Sergei Rachmaninov	1873–1943	symphonies, concertos
Nikolai Rimsky-Korsakov	1844–1908	operas, orchestral music
Dmitri Shostakovich	1906–1975	symphonies, chamber music
Igor Stravinsky	1882–1971	ballets, operas, orchestral, chamber music
Pyotr Tchaikovsky	1840–1893	ballet music, symphonies

Singers
Celebrated Duets

Year	Performers	Song
1956	Bing Crosby and Grace Kelly	'True Love'
1965	Sonny and Cher	'I Got You Babe'
1967	Frank and Nancy Sinatra	'Somethin' Stupid'
1976	Elton John and Kiki Dee	'Don't Go Breaking My Heart'
1978	John Travolta and Olivia Newton-John	'You're the One That I Want'
1982	Paul McCartney and Stevie Wonder	'Ebony and Ivory'
1983	Paul McCartney and Michael Jackson	'The Girl is Mine'
1985	David Bowie and Mick Jagger	'Dancin' in the Street'
1992	George Michael and Elton John	'Don't Let the Sun Go Down on Me'
1995	Robson Green and Jerome Flynn	'Unchained Melody'
1997	Puff Daddy and Faith Evans	'I'll be Missing You'

Singles
First Artists to Sell 2 Million Copies of a Single in the USA

Year	Artist	Single
1985	USA For Africa	'We are the World'
1989	Tone Loc	'Wild Thing'
1990	Madonna	'Vogue'
1991	Color Me Badd	'I Wanna Sex You Up'
1991	Bryan Adams	'(Everything I Do) I Do It For You'
1992	Elvis Presley	'All Shook Up'
1992	Naughty By Nature	'O.P.P.'
1992	Kris Kross	'Jump'
1992	Sir Mix-a-lot	'Baby Got Back'
1992	Whitney Houston	'I Will Always Love You'

Songwriters
Famous Song-writing Partnerships

Year	Song-writers	Song	Performer(s)
1993	Ashford and Simpson	'I'm Every Woman'	Whitney Houston
1984	Steinberg and Kelly	'Like a Virgin'	Madonna
1977	The Gibb Brothers	'How Deep is Your Love'	The Bee Gees
1968	Lennon and McCartney	'Hey Jude'	The Beatles
1969	Jagger and Richards	'Honky Tonk Woman'	The Rolling Stones
1964	Holland, Dozier and Holland	'Baby Love'	The Supremes
1957	Bryant and Bryant	'Bye Bye Love'	The Everley Brothers
1956	Lieber and Stoller	'Hound Dog'	Elvis Presley

Soundtracks
Top UK Film Soundtracks

Film title

South Pacific
The Sound of Music
GI Blues
A Hard Day's Night
Blue Hawaii
Saturday Night Fever
Help!
West Side Story
Grease
Calamity Jane

Soundtracks
Top US Film Soundtracks

Film title

West Side Story
South Pacific
Saturday Night Fever
Purple Rain
Blue Hawaii
Love Me or Leave Me
The Sound of Music
My Fair Lady
Calamity Jane
Grease

Strauss
The Operas of Richard Strauss

Title	Opus No.	Year	Title	Opus No.	Year
Guntram	Op. 25	1894	*Intermezzo*	Op. 72	1924
Feuersnot	Op. 50	1901	*Die ägyptische Helena*	Op. 75	1928
Salome	Op. 54	1905	*Arabella*	Op. 79	1933
Elektra	Op. 58	1909	*Die schweigsame Frau*	Op. 80	1935
Der Rosenkavalier	Op. 59	1911	*Friedenstag*	Op. 81	1938
Ariadne auf Naxos	Op. 60	1912, revised 1916	*Daphne*	Op. 82	1938
			Die Liebe der Danae	Op. 83	1940
Die Frau ohne Schatten	Op. 65	1919	*Capriccio*	Op. 85	1942

String Quartets
Famous String Quartets

Composer	Title of work	Date
Berg	'Lyric Suite'	1925–26
Sibelius	'Voces intimae' Opus 66 in D minor	1908–09
Dvořák	'American' Opus 96 in F	1893
Smetana	'From My Life' No. 1 in E minor	1880
Beethoven	'Grosse Fuge' Opus 135 in F	1826
Schubert	'Death and the Maiden' No. 14 in D minor	1824
Beethoven	'Rasoumovsky' Opus 59/1–3 in F, E minor, and C	1805–06

(continued)

Composer	Title of work	Date
Haydn	'Emperor' Opus 76 No. 3 in C	c. 1799
Haydn	'Seven Last Words' Opus 51	1787
Mozart	'Dissonance' No. 19 in C K465	1785

Stringed Instruments

Instrument	Description
aeolian harp	box with strings sounded by the passage of the wind
balalaika	3-stringed fretted triangular instrument played like a guitar
bouzouki	long-necked flute-like instrument with 3 or 4 pairs of metal strings
cimbalom	large dulcimer
dulcimer	instrument with strings across a soundboard, played with hammers
harp	any of many types of instrument with strings stretched on a basically U-shaped frame and plucked with the fingers
koto	13-string Japanese 'violin' with a box-like body
lute	guitar-like fretted instrument with a half pear-shaped body, many strings, and played with the fingers or a plectrum
lyre	ancient type of harp
mandolin	small round-backed, fretted, lute-like instrument with 4 pairs of strings, played with a plectrum
samisen	3-stringed guitar-like instrument from Japan
sitar	long-necked lute-like Indian instrument with movable frets and a gourd as the main body
ukulele	small 4-stringed guitar from Hawaii, usually strummed
viol	any early bowed violin-like instrument with a fretted fingerboard and usually 6 strings
zither	many-stringed instrument resembling a dulcimer but played by plucking the strings

The Beatles
Albums Spending Longest in the UK Charts

Year	Album	Number of weeks
1967	Sgt Pepper's Lonely Hearts Club Band	148
1969	Abbey Road	81
1970	Let It Be	59
1963	With the Beatles	51
1963	Please Please Me	50
1964	Beatles for Sale	46
1965	Rubber Soul	42
1964	Hard Day's Night	38
1965	Help!	37

The Beatles
Albums Spending Longest in the US Charts

Year	Album
1967	Sgt Pepper's Lonely Hearts Club Band
1964	Hard Day's Night
1969	Abbey Road
1964	Meet the Beatles
1965	Beatles '65
1965	Help!
1968	The Beatles (White Album)
1968	Magical Mystery Tour

The Beatles
First UK Singles

Year	Single
1962	'Love Me Do'
1963	'Please Please Me'
1963	'From Me to You'
1963	'She Loves You'
1963	'I Want to Hold Your Hand'
1964	'Can't Buy Me Love'
1964	'A Hard Day's Night'
1964	'I Feel Fine'
1965	'Ticket to Ride'
1965	'Help!'

The Beatles
Most Valuable Albums

Year	Comment	Album
1963	gold/black label	*Please Please Me*
1968	mint Apple issue	*The Beatles*
1968	export LP	*The Beatles*
1969	export LP	*Yellow Submarine*
1969	export LP	*Abbey Road*
1970	export LP	*Let It Be*
1966	export LP	*Beatles VI*
1966	rare remixed trucks	*Revolver*
1966	export LP	*The Beatles' Second Album*
1970	box set	*Let it Be*

The Beatles
Most Valuable Singles

Year	Comment	Single
1962	demo. single	'Love Me Do'
1963	demo. single	'Please Please Me'
1968	demo. single	'Hey Jude'
1958	Quarrymen single	'That'll Be The Day'
1965	demo. single	'Help!'
1963	demo. single	'She Loves You'
1966	demo. single	'Yellow Submarine'
1968	WWF demo.	'Across the Universe'
1966	demo. single	'Paperback Writer'
1963	orange label	'My Bonnie'

The Beatles
Singles Spending Longest in the UK Charts

Year	Single	Number of weeks	Year	Single	Number of weeks
1963	'She Loves You'	31	1969	'Get Back'	17
1963	'From Me to You'	21	1968	'Hey Jude'	16
1963	'I Want to Hold Your Hand'	21	1964	'Can't Buy Me Love'	14
1962	'Love Me Do'	18	1965	'Help!'	14
1963	'Please Please Me'	18	1966	'Yellow Submarine'	13
			1967	'Penny Lane'	11

The Beatles
Singles Spending Longest in the US Charts

Year	Single
1968	'Hey Jude'
1964	'I Want to Hold Your Hand'
1969	'Get Back'
1964	'She Loves You'
1970	'Let It Be'
1964	'A Hard Day's Night'
1965	'Help!'
1964	'Twist and Shout'
1966	'We Can Work it Out'
1964	'I Feel Fine'
1964	'Can't Buy Me Love'
1965	'Yesterday'

The Beatles
US Album Sales

Album	Sales (millions)
The Beatles	18
The Beatles 1967–70	15
The Beatles 1962–66	14
Abbey Road	11
Sgt Pepper's Lonely Hearts Club Band	11

Tippett
The Operas of Michael Tippett

Opera	Year
The Midsummer Marriage	1946–52
King Priam	1958–61
The Knot Garden	1966–69
The Ice Break	1973–76
New Year	1989

Vaughan Williams
The Operas of Ralph Vaughan Williams

Title	Year
Hugh the Drover	1910–14, revised 1924, 1956
The Shepherds of the Delectable Mountains	1921–22
Sir John in Love	1924–28
Riders to the Sea	1925–32
The Poisoned Kiss	1927–29, revised 1934–37, 1956–57
The Pilgrim's Progress	1925–36, 1944–51

Verdi
The Operas of Giuseppe Verdi

Title	Year	Title	Year
Oberto, Conti di san Bonifacio	1837–38	Ernani	1843
Un giorno di regno	1840	I due Foscari	1843–44
Nabucco	1841	Giovanna D'Arco	1844
I Lombardi alla prima crociata	1842	Alzira	1845
		Attila	1845–46
		Macbeth	1846–47, revised 1865

Verdi: The Operas of Giuseppe Verdi (continued)

Title	Year	Title	Year
I masnadieri	1846–47	*Les Vêpres siciliennes*	1854
Il corsaro	1847–48	*Simon Boccanegra*	1856–57,
La battaglia di Legnano	1848		revised
Luisa Miller	1849		1880–81
Stiffelio	1850	*Un ballo in maschera*	1857–58
Rigoletto	1850–51	*La forza del destino*	1861–62
Il trovatore	1851–52,	*Don Carlos*	1866
	revised 1857	*Aida*	1870
La Traviata	1852–53	*Otello*	1884–86
		Falstaff	1889–92

Videos
Influential Pop Videos

Year	Artist/group	Video	Year	Artist/group	Video
1996	Oasis	'Wonderwall'	1983	Michael Jackson	'Thriller'
1993	Annie Lennox	'Diva'	1981	Ultravox	'Vienna'
1986	Peter Gabriel	'Sledgehammer'	1980	David Bowie	'Ashes to Ashes'
1985	Talking Heads	'Road to Nowhere'	1978	Meatloaf	'Bat Out of Hell'
1984	Madonna	'Like a Virgin'	1975	Queen	'Bohemian Rhapsody'

Vocal Albums
Top UK Vocal Albums

Artist/band	Album	Year
Film soundtrack	*South Pacific*	1958
Film soundtrack	*The Sound of Music*	1960
Simon and Garfunkel	*Bridge Over Troubled Water*	1970
The Beatles	*Sgt Pepper's Lonely Hearts Club Band*	1967
Elvis Presley	*Blue Hawaii*	1961
Queen	*Greatest Hits*	1981
Bee Gees/Film soundtrack	*Saturday Night Fever*	1978
Michael Jackson	*Thriller*	1982
Meat Loaf	*Bat Out of Hell*	1972
Pink Floyd	*Dark Side of the Moon*	1973

Wagner
The Operas and Music Dramas of Richard Wagner

Title	Translation	Year
Die Feen	The Fairies	1833–34
Das Liebesverbot	Forbidden Love	1835–36
Rienzi		1838–40
Der Fliegende Holländer	The Flying Dutchman	1841
Tannhäuser		1843–45, revised 1861
Lohengrin		1846–48
Der Ring des Nibelungen comprising:	The Nibelung's Ring	
Das Rheingold	The Rhine Gold	1853–54
Die Walküre	The Valkyrie	1854–56
Siegfried		1856–57 and 1864–71
Tristan und Isolde		1857–59
Die Meistersinger von Nürnberg	The Mastersingers of Nuremberg	1862–67
Götterdämmerung	Twilight of the Gods	1869–74
Parsifal		1878–82

Wind Instruments

Instrument	Description
bassoon	low-pitched double-reeded instrument with a wooden tube doubled back on itself
bombardon	large tuba
clarinet	single-reeded woodwind instrument with a conical bore
contrabassoon	woodwind instrument pitched an octave below a bassoon
cor anglais	double-reeded woodwind instrument of lower pitch than an oboe
cornet	high-pitched valved brass instrument
euphonium	tenor tuba
fife	high-pitched flute
flageolet	six-holed end-blown flute (tin whistle)
flügelhorn	valved brass instrument with a pitch slightly lower than a trumpet
flute	side-blown cylindrical instrument
french horn	coiled valved brass instrument with a wide bell
harmonica	mouth organ, with double reeds played by sucking or blowing
oboe	double-reeded woodwind instrument with a slightly conical bore
ocarina	egg-shaped clay or metal instrument with finger-holes
panpipes	set of short vertical pipes played by blowing across their tops
piccolo	small high-pitched flute
saxophone	metal single-reeded woodwind instrument
syrinx	panpipes
trombone	brass instrument with a slide and a bore doubled back on itself
tuba	bass valved brass instrument

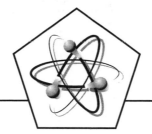

Science
and
Technology

Acidity
Acidity or Alkalinity of Some Common Substances

pH of 7 is neutral, pH below 7 is acid, pH above 7 is alkaline.

Substance	pH
hydrochloric acid	0
digestive juices	0.9
accumulator acid	1.0
ant venom	2.0
lemon juice	2.3
apple juice	3.0
malt vinegar	3.5
soda water	4.0
rainwater	5.6
milk	6.6
pure water	7.0
blood	7.4
seawater	7.5
bicarbonate of soda	8.5
toothpaste	9.8
washing soda	11.5
ammonia solution	12.0
caustic soda	14.0

Acronyms and Abbreviations
Used Online

Acronym/ abbreviation	Meaning
ATM	At The Moment
B4	Before
BTW	By The Way
FAQ	Frequently Asked Question
FWIW	For What It's Worth
FYI	For Your Information
HTH	Hope That Helps
IMO	In My Opinion
IOW	In Other Words
OTOH	On The Other Hand
OTT	Over The Top
TYVM	Thank You Very Much
WYSIWYG	What You See Is What You Get

Alchemy
The Four Elements

Name	Association	Humour
air	blood	sanguine
earth	black bile	melancholic
fire	yellow bile	choleric
water	phlegm	phlegmatic

Alchemy
The Seven Alchemical Metals

Name	Associated heavenly body and deity
copper	Venus
gold	Sun (Apollo)
iron	Mars
lead	Saturn
mercury	Mercury
silver	Moon (Diana)
tin	Jupiter

Alloys

Name	Approximate composition	Uses
brass	10–35% zinc, 65–90% copper	decorative metalwork, plumbing fittings
bronze – coinage	1% zinc, 4% tin, 95% copper	coins
cast iron	2–4% carbon, 96–98% iron	decorative metalwork, engine blocks, industrial machinery
dentist's amalgam	30% copper, 70% mercury	dental fillings
gold – coinage	10% copper, 90% gold	coins
silver – coinage	10% copper, 90% silver	coins
steel – stainless	8–20% nickel, 10–20% chromium, 60–80% iron	kitchen utensils
steel – armour	1–4% nickel, 0.5–2% chromium, 95–98% iron	armour plating

Aluminium
Countries that Consume the Most

Country	Annual consumption (thousand tonnes)
USA	5,410
Japan	2,170
China	1,320
Germany	1,300
Russia	1,190
France	670
Korea, South	560
Italy	550
India	480
UK	480

Aluminium
Countries that Produce the Most

Country	Annual production (thousand tonnes)
Australia	41,730
Guinea	17,040
Jamaica	11,570
Brazil	8,280
China	7,260
India	5,280
Russia	4,000
Suriname	3,200
Venezuela	2,540
Greece	2,170

Animals in Space

Name	Type of animal	Date of launch	Spacecraft
Laika (USSR)	female dog	November 1957	Sputnik II
Mia, Laska, and Benjy (USA)	mice	December 1958	Thor-Able rockets
Gordo (USA)	male monkey	December 1958	Jupiter Missile AM-13
Able and Baker (USA)	female monkeys	May 1959	Jupiter Missile AM-18
Sam (USA)	male monkey	December 1959	Mercury Little Joe 2
Miss Sam (USA)	female monkey	January 1960	Mercury Little Joe 4
Belka and Strelka (USSR)	female dogs	August 1960	Sputnik 5

Architecture
Chicago School

The Chicago School was a 19th-century North American movement that emphasized verticality and developed the skyscraper.

Famous building designed	Architect	Life dates
Wainwright building, St Louis	Louis Sullivan	1856–1924
Home Insurance building, Chicago	William Le Baron Jenney	1832–1907
Monadnock building, Chicago; and	Daniel H Burnham	1846–1912
Reliance building, Chicago	John Welbourn Root	1850–1891

Architecture
Orders of Architecture

Composite
Corinthian
Doric
Ionic
Tuscan

Architecture
Recent Pritzker Architecture Prize Winners

This US premier architecture award is named after Jay A Pritzker, president of the Hyatt Foundation, which sponsors it. The award has been presented annually in April since 1979.

Year	Winner	Nationality
1996	José Rafael Moneo	Spanish
1997	Sverre Fehn	Norwegian
1998	Renzo Piano	Italian
1999	Norman Foster	English
2000	Rem Koolhaas	Dutch

Architecture
Royal Gold Medallists

Year	Winner
1990	Aldo van Eyck
1991	Colin Stansfield Smith
1992	Peter Rice
1993	Giancarlo de Carlo
1994	Michael and Patricia Hopkins
1995	Colin Rowe
1996	Harry Seilder
1997	Tadao Ando
1998	Oscar Neimeyer
1999	Barcelona, its government, its citizens, and design professionals
2000	Frank Gehry

Arms Trade
Leading Suppliers of Conventional Weapons

Supplier	Value of exports in US$ (1994–98)
USA	53,882
Russian Federation	12,260
France	10,585
UK	8,913
Germany	7,211
China	2,826
Netherlands	2,344
Italy	1,742
Ukraine	1,541
Canada	1,394

Artificial Satellites
First to Orbit Earth

Satellite and country	Date of launch	Satellite and country	Date of launch
Sputnik 1 (USSR)	4 October 1957	*Sputnik 3* (USSR)	15 May 1958
Sputnik 2 (USSR)	3 November 1957	*Explorer 4* (USA)	26 July 1958
Explorer 1 (USA)	31 January 1958	*SCORE* (USA)	18 December 1958
Vanguard I (USA)	17 March 1958	*Vanguard II* (USA)	17 February 1959
Explorer 3 (USA)	26 March 1958	*Discoverer I* (USA)	28 February 1959

Artificial Satellites
Most Successful Launches

Launch site	Number of successes (1957–99)	Launch site	Number of successes (1957–99)
Plesetsk, Russia	1,468	Wallops Island, USA	35
Tyuratam (Baikonur), Kazakhstan	1,050	Tanegashima (Osaki), Japan	31
		Xichang, China	25
Cape Canaveral and Kennedy Space Center, USA	609	Jiuquan, China	24
Vandenberg AFB, USA	565	Uchinoura (Kagoshima), Japan	23
Kourou, France	129		

ASCII Codes
Capital Letters A–Z

Character	Binary (base 2)	Decimal (base 10)	Hexadecimal (base 16)	Character	Binary (base 2)	Decimal (base 10)	Hexadecimal (base 16)
A	01000001	65	41	N	01001110	78	4E
B	01000010	66	42	O	01001111	79	4F
C	01000011	67	43	P	01010000	80	50
D	01000100	68	44	Q	01010001	81	51
E	01000101	69	45	R	01010010	82	52
F	01000110	70	46	S	01010011	83	53
G	01000111	71	47	T	01010100	84	54
H	01001000	72	48	U	01010101	85	55
I	01001001	73	49	V	01010110	86	56
J	01001010	74	4A	W	01010111	87	57
K	01001011	75	4B	X	01011000	88	58
L	01001100	76	4C	Y	01011001	89	59
M	01001101	77	4D	Z	01011010	90	5A

ASCII Codes
Numbers 0–9

Character	Binary (base 2)	Decimal (base 10)	Hexadecimal (base 16)	Character	Binary (base 2)	Decimal (base 10)	Hexadecimal (base 16)
0	00110000	48	30	5	00110101	53	35
1	00110001	49	31	6	00110110	54	36
2	00110010	50	32	7	00110111	55	37
3	00110011	51	33	8	00111000	56	38
4	00110100	52	34	9	00111001	57	39

Asteroids
Largest

Name	Diameter (km/mi)	Average distance from Sun (Earth = 1)	Orbital period (years)
Ceres	940/584	2.77	4.6
Pallas	588/365	2.77	4.6
Vesta	576/357	2.36	3.6
Hygeia	430/267	3.13	5.5
Interamnia	338/210	3.06	5.4
Davida	324/201	3.18	5.7

Astronauts
Countries whose Astronauts Have Made the Most Flights

Country	Crewed spaceflights (overall numbers)	Number of flights	
		Men	Women
USA	119	542	63
USSR/Russia/CIS	86	175	5
France	–	11	1
Germany	–	11	0
Canada	–	7	1
Japan	–	5	1
Italy	–	3	0
Switzerland	–	3	0
Bulgaria	–	2	0
UK	–	0	1

Astronauts
First People to Orbit Earth

Name and country	Spacecraft	Date of orbit	Number of orbits
Yuri Gagarin (USSR)	*Vostok 1*	12 April 1961	1
Gherman Titov (USSR)	*Vostok 2*	6–7 August 1961	17
John Glenn (USA)	*Friendship 7*	20 February 1962	3
M Scott Carpenter (USA)	*Aurora 7*	24 May 1962	3
Andriyan Nikolayev (USSR)	*Vostok 3*	11–15 August 1962	64
Pavel Popovich (USSR)	*Vostok 4*	12–15 August 1962	48
Walter M Schirra (USA)	*Sigma 7*	3 October 1962	6
L Gordon Cooper (USA)	*Faith 7*	15–16 May 1963	22
Valery Bykovsky (USSR)	*Vostok 5*	14–19 June 1963	81
Valentina Tereshkova (USSR)	*Vostok 6*	16–19 June 1963	48

Astronauts
First People to Walk on the Moon

All 12 astronauts who visited the Moon are US citizens.

Dates of landing	Name and space mission
20 July 1969	Neil A Armstrong (*Apollo 11*)
	Edwin ('Buzz') Aldrin (*Apollo 11*)
18 November 1969	Charles ('Pete') Conrad Jr (*Apollo 12*)
	Alan Bean (*Apollo 12*)
3 February 1971	Alan B Shepard (*Apollo 14*)
	Edgar Mitchell (*Apollo 14*)
30 July 1971	David R Scott (*Apollo 15*)
	James B Irwin (*Apollo 15*)
20 April 1972	John Young (*Apollo 16*)
	Charles M Duke Jr (*Apollo 16*)
11 December 1972	Eugene Cernan (*Apollo 17*)
	Harrison H Schmitt (*Apollo 17*)

Astronauts
First Women in Space

As of 1 January 2000, 36 women had travelled in orbit around the Earth. They included one each from France, India, Japan, and the UK, two from Canada, and 27 from the USA.

Name and country	Dates of first flight	Spacecraft or mission	Comments
Valentina Tereshkova (USSR)	16–19 June 1963	*Vostok 6*	first woman in space
Svetlana Savitskaya (USSR)	19–27 August 1982	*Soyuz/ Salyut 7*	first woman to walk in space

(*continued*)

 Science and Technology 159

Astronauts: First Women in Space (*continued*)

Name and country	Dates of first flight	Spacecraft or mission	Comments
Sally Ride (USA)	18–24 June 1983	*Challenger*	first US woman in space
Judith Resnik (USA)	30 August–5 September 1984	*Discovery*	
Kathryn Sullivan (USA)	5–13 October 1984	*Challenger*	first US woman to walk in space
Anna Fisher (USA)	8–16 November 1984	*Discovery*	
Rhea Seddon (USA)	12–19 April 1985	*Discovery*	
Shannon Lucid (USA)	17–24 Jun 1985	*Discovery*	in 1996 spent 188 days in space as member of joint Russian–US crew aboard *Mir*, setting US space endurance record
Bonnie Dunbar (USA)	30 October–6 November 1985	*Challenger*	
Mary Cleave (USA)	26 November–3 December 1985	*Atlantis*	

Astronauts
Most Experienced Female Astronauts

Duration (days in space)	Name	Country
222	Shannon Lucid	USA
178	Yelena Kondakova	Russia/CIS
53	Tamara Jernigan	USA
50	Bonnie Dunbar	USA
43	Marsha Ivins	USA
40	Kathryn Thornton	USA
37	Janice Voss	USA
37	Wendy Lawrence	USA
33	Susan Helms	USA
30	Chiaki Mukai	Japan/USA

Astronauts
Most Experienced Male Astronauts

Duration (days in space)	Name	Country
678	Valeri Poliakov	USSR/Russia/CIS
651	Anatoli Solovyov	USSR/Russia/CIS
541	Musa Manarov	USSR/Russia/CIS
488	Aleksandr Viktorenko	USSR/Russia/CIS
483	Sergei Krikalyov	USSR/Russia/CIS
430	Yuri Romanenko	USSR
391	Aleksandr Volkov	USSR/Russia/CIS
387	Vladimir Titov	USSR/Russia/CIS
381	Vasili Tsibliyev	Russia/CIS
375	Yuri Usachyov	Russia/CIS

Astronauts

Number of People Sent into Earth Orbit

As of 1 January 2000, 390 people had made spaceflights involving orbits of the Earth. Among the countries that have sent one person into space as part of a US or Soviet or Russian crew are Austria, Afghanistan, Bulgaria, Cuba, the former Czechoslovakia, Hungary, Mongolia, the Netherlands, Poland, Romania, the present republic of Slovakia, Switzerland, Syria, Ukraine, the UK, and Vietnam. This list includes countries that have sent two or more people into orbit.

Country	Number	Country	Number	Country	Number
USA	235	Canada	8	India	2
USSR/Russia	111	France	8	Italy	2
Germany	10	Japan	5	Kazakhstan	2

Astronauts

Oldest Astronauts

Age	Name	Country
Men		
77	John Glenn	USA
61	Story Musgrave	USA
59	Vance Brand	USA
	Jean-Loup Chretien	France
Women		
53	Shannon Lucid	USA
46	Roberta Bondar	Canada
40	Yelena Kondakova	USSR

Astronauts

Youngest Astronauts

Age	Name	Country
Men		
25	Gherman Titov	Russia
28	Dumitriu Prunariu	Romania
32	Eugene Cernan	USA
Women		
26	Valentina Tereshkova	Russia
27	Helen Sharman	UK
32	Sally Ride	USA

Astronomy

Temperatures in the Universe

Location	Temperature K	Temperature °C	Location	Temperature K	Temperature °C
surface of Pluto	40	−233	surface of Venus	730	457
interstellar clouds	50	−223	sunspot	4,500	4,227
surface of Neptune	60	−213	surface of the Sun	6,000	5,727
surface of Mercury (night)	100	−173	Sun's corona	1,000,000	
surface of Mars (night)	133	−140	centre of the Sun	15,000,000	
surface of Mars (day)	273	0	edge of a black hole	50,000,000	
surface of Mercury (day)	700	427	centre of a nova	5,000,000,000	
			Big Bang fireball	1,000,000,000,000	

Atmosphere

Main Components of the Atmosphere

Component	Percentage by volume	Component	Percentage by volume
nitrogen	78.09	helium	0.0005
oxygen	20.95	methane	0.0003
argon	0.93	krypton	0.0001
carbon dioxide	0.03	nitrous oxide	0.000050
neon	0.002	xenon	0.000009

Authoring Programs for Web Sites

Software	Manufacturer	Description
3D WebMaster	Superscape	interactive 3D authoring tool for creating 3D Web sites
Aesthetic World Visions	Aesthetic Solutions	component-based Virtual Reality authoring tool
Authorware Attain	Macromedia	visual-rich-media authoring tool for online learning
Director	Macromedia	powerful multimedia and Web authoring tool
HoTMetaL	SoftQuad	HTML authoring and publishing tool for Web site development
PageMill	Adobe	easy-to-use Web page creation software
Premiere	Adobe	a powerful tool for professional digital video editing

Beer

Old Beer Measures

Measures are based on the 282 cubic inch beer and ale standard gallon.

Old measurement	Equivalent
1 firkin	9 gallons
1 kilderkin	2 firkins (=18 gallons)
1 barrel	2 kilderkins (=4 firkins/36 gallons)
1 hogshead	1.5 barrels (=54 gallons)
1 puncheon	2 barrels (=72 gallons)
1 butt or pipe	2 hogsheads (=3 barrels/108 gallons)

Binary Number System

In the binary number system numbers can be seen as written under columns based on the number 2. The binary number 1101 corresponds to the decimal number 13.

Binary number system (base 2)

8s	4s	2s	1s
(2^3)	(2^2)	(2^1)	(2^0)
1	1	0	1

Biologists
Some Important Biologists

Name	Life dates	Nationality	Name	Life dates	Nationality
Audubon, John James	1785–1851	French-born American	Lamarck, Jean Baptiste de	1744–1829	French
Baer, Karl Ernst von	1792–1876	Estonian-born German	Leeuwenhoek, Anton van	1632–1723	Dutch
Banks, Joseph	1743–1820	English	Linnaeus, Carolus	1707–1778	Swedish
Bates, Henry Walter	1825–1892	English	Lorenz, Konrad Zaxharias	1903–1989	Austrian
Bateson, William	1861–1926	English	Malpighi, Marcello	1628–1684	Italian
Bilharz, Theodor	1825–1862	German	Mendel, Gregor Johann	1822–1884	Austrian
Borlaug, Norman Ernest	1914–	US	Miller, Stanley Lloyd	1930–	US
Bose, Jagadis Chandra	1858–1937	Indian	Ray, John	1628–1705	English
Brown, Robert	1773–1858	Scottish	Réaumur, René Antoine de	1683–1757	French
Burbank, Luther	1849–1926	US	Sachs, Julius von	1832–1897	German
Camararius, Rudolph Jacob	1665–1721	German	Schleiden, Matthias Jakob	1804–1881	German
Cohen, Stanley H	1922–	US	Schwann, Theodor	1810–1882	German
Cuvier, Georges Léopold	1769–1832	French	Tinbergen, Nikolaas	1907–1988	Dutch-born English
Darwin, Charles Robert	1809–1882	English	Tradescant, John	1570–1633	English
de Vries, Hugo Marie	1848–1935	Dutch	Tull, Jethro	1674–1741	English
Engler, Adolf	1844–1930	German	Wallace, Alfred Russel	1823–1913	Welsh
Frisch, Karl von	1886–1982	Austrian	White, Gilbert	1720–1793	English
Fucjs, Leonhard	1501–1566	German	Wilson, Edmund Beecher	1856–1939	US
Hales, Stephen	1677–1761	English			

Boiling Points
Selected Liquids

Liquid	Boiling point		Liquid	Boiling point	
	°C	°F		°C	°F
Methanol	64.7	148.5	Octane	125.6	258.1
Ethanol	78.2	172.8	Turpentine	156.0	312.8
Benzene	80.1	176.2	Glycerol	290.0	554.0
Water	100.0	212.0	Mercury	356.9	674.4

Bridges
Beautiful Bridges

Bridge	Location	Date
The Rhône Bridge at Avignon	France	from 12th century
Ponte Vecchio	Florence, Italy	14th century
The Rialto Bridge	Venice, Italy	16th century
Tower Bridge	London, England	1862
Brooklyn Bridge	New York, USA	1883
Sydney Harbour Bridge	Sydney, Australia	1932
The Golden Gate Bridge	San Francisco, USA	1937
The Verrazano-Narrows Bridge[1]	New York Bay, USA	1964
The Humber Bridge[2]	The Humber Estuary, England	1981
The Akashi-Kaiko Bridge[3]	Japan	1990

[1] The longest suspension bridge in the USA at 1,298 m/4,259 ft.
[2] The longest suspension bridge in the UK at 1,410 m/4,626 ft.
[3] As of 2001 the longest suspension bridge in the world at just under 2,000 m/6,562 ft.

Bridges
World's Highest Railway Bridges

Bridge	Location	Height (m/ft)
Mala Rijeka Viaduct	Kolasin on Belgrade–Bar line, Yugoslavia	198/650
Vresk	220 km/137 mi from Bandar Shah on Caspian Sea Trans Iranian line	152/499
Fades Viaduct	Clermont-Ferrand–Montluçon line, France	133/436
Khotur	Khotur River near Khoi, Iran	131/430
Victoria Falls	Livingstone, Zambia/Zimbabwe border	128/420
Pfaffenberg–Zwenberg	Mallnitz–Spittal, Austria	120/394
Viaur	Tanus, Rodez–Albi, France	116/380
Garabit Viaduct	Neussargues–Béziers, France	112/367
Müngstner	Mügsten, over River Wupper, Germany	107/351

Bridges
World's Longest Spans

Bridge	Location	Length (m/ft)
Akashi–Kaikyo	Honshu–Awaji Islands, Japan	1,990/6,527
Store Baelt	Zealand–Funen, Denmark	1,624/5,328
Humber Bridge	Kingston-upon-Hull, England	1,410/4,626
Jiangyin	Chang Jiang River, China	1,385/4,544
Tsing Ma	Hong Kong	1,377/4,518
Verrazono Narrows	Brooklyn–Staten Island, New York Harbor (NY), USA	1,298/4,259
Golden Gate	San Francisco (CA), USA	1,280/4,200
Höga Kusten	Veda, Sweden	1,210/3,970
High Coast Bridge	Västernorrland, Sweden	1,210/3,970
Mackinac Straits	Michigan (MI), USA	1,158/3,799

Bridges
World's Most Remarkable Bridges

These bridges involve extraordinary feats of engineering in the construction of a passage for vehicles.

Bridge	Location	Description
Angostura	Cuidad Bolivar, Venezuela	suspension-type bridge; span 712 m/2,336 ft; total length 1,678 m/5,505 ft
Bendorf Bridge	Coblenz, Germany	three-span cement girder bridge; main span 208 m/682 ft; total length 1,030 m/3,380 ft
Gladsville Bridge	Sydney, Australia	the world's longest concrete arch bridge – 305 m/1,000 ft
Humber Bridge	Kingston-upon-Hull, UK	total span 1,410 m/4,626 ft
Ikuchi Bridge	Honshu/Shikoku, Japan	cable-stayed bridge; 490 m/1,607 ft span
Lake Pontchartrain Bridge	New Orleans, USA	the world's longest multiple-span bridge – 38 km/23.6 mi
Oosterscelderbrug	Vlissingen/Rotterdam, the Netherlands	traffic causeway over Zeeland sea arm; total length 19 km/11.8 mi
Rio–Niteroi	Guanabara Bay, Brazil	the world's longest box and plate girder bridge – 14 km/8.7 mi
Tagus River Bridge	Lisbon, Portugal	main span 1,013 m/3,323 ft
Zoo Bridge	Cologne, Germany	steel box girder bridge; main span 259 m/850 ft

Buildings
20th-century Buildings and their Architects

Structure	Location	Architect(s), date
The Fuller (Flatiron) Building	New York, USA	Burnham and Root, 1905
The Bauhaus	Dessai, Germany	Walter Gropius, 1925
The Empire State Building	New York, USA	Shreve, Lamb and Harman, 1929–31
Farnsworth House	Plano, Illinois, USA	M van de Rohe, 1951
Chapel of Notre Dame du Haut	Ronchamp, France	Le Corbusier, 1950–55
The S R Guggenheim Museum	New York, USA	F L Wright, 1956
The Sydney Opera House	Sydney, Australia	J Utzon, 1956–76
The Lloyd's Building	London, England	Richard Rogers, 1978–84
The Louvre Museum Pyramids	Paris, France	I M Pei, 1989–91
Petronas Towers	Kuala Lumpur, Malaysia	C Pelli, 1996
The Millennium Dome	London, England	Richard Rogers, 1999

Buildings
Sacred Structures of the World

Structure	Location	Built
Stonehenge	Wiltshire, England	2200–2300 BC
The Parthenon	Acropolis, Athens, Greece	447 BC
St Sophia	Constantinople (Istanbul), Turkey	4th century AD
Ankor Wat	Cambodia	11th century AD
Chartres Cathedral	Chartres, France	1212–24
St Peter's	Rome, Italy	begun 1506
The Leaning Tower	Pisa, Italy	begun 1174
San Giorgio Maggiore	Venice, Italy	1565–1610 (A Palladio)
St Basil's Cathedral	The Kremlin, Moscow, Russia	14th century
St Paul's Cathedral	London, England	begun 1675
The Taj Mahal	Agra, India	1632–54
The Sagrada Family Church	Barcelona, Spain	begun 1884 (A C Gaudi)

Buildings
Secular Structures

Structure	Location	Built
The Colosseum	Rome, Italy	75 AD
Castle of Krak des Chevaliers	Syria	10th to 11th century
The Palace of the Alhambra	Granada, Spain	10th to 11th century
The Corner Pavilions	The Forbidden City, Beijing, China	15th to 18th century
Machu Picchu	Peru	15th century
The Palace of Versailles	France	1661–87 (André Le Notre)
Palace of Westminister (The Houses of Parliament)	London, England	1836–52 (Charles Barry)
The Eiffel Tower	Paris, France	1884–89 (A G Eiffel)
The CN Tower	Toronto, Canada	1976 (Andrews, Zerafa and Housden)

Buildings
Tallest in Asia

As of March 2000.

Building	City	Height (m/ft)	Storeys
Petronas Tower I	Kuala Lumpur, Malaysia	452/1,483	88
Petronas Tower II	Kuala Lumpur, Malaysia	452/1,483	88
Jin Mao Building	Shanghai, China	420/1,378	88
Central Plaza	Hong Kong, China	374/1,227	78
Bank of China	Hong Kong, China	369/1,210	70

Buildings: Tallest in Asia (*continued*)

Building	City	Height (m/ft)	Storeys
The Centre	Hong Kong, China	350/1,148	73
Emirates Tower 1	Dubai, United Arab Emirates	350/1,148	54
T&C Tower	Kaohsiung, Taiwan	347/1,138	85
Shun Hing Square	Shenzhen, China	325/1,066	69
CITIC Plaza	Guangzhou, China	322/1,056	80

Buildings
Tallest in Australia

As of March 2000.

Building	City	Height (m/ft)	Storeys
Rialto Towers	Melbourne	251/823	61
MLC Centre	Sydney	228/748	65
Governor Philip Tower	Sydney	227/745	54
Central Park Tower	Perth	226/741	52
Bourke Place	Melbourne	224/735	48
BHP Petroleum Plaza	Melbourne	220/722	52
Chifley Tower	Sydney	215/705	50
BankWest Tower	Perth	214/702	52
Melbourne Central	Melbourne	211/692	55
101 Collins Street	Melbourne	195/640	50

Buildings
Tallest in Europe

As of March 2000.

Building	City	Height (m/ft)	Storeys
Commerzbank	Frankfurt, Germany	299/981	63
Messeturm	Frankfurt, Germany	257/843	64
MV Lomonosov State University	Moscow, Russian Federation	239/784	39
1 Canada Square, Canary Wharf	London, England	236/774	56
Palace of Culture and Science	Warsaw, Poland	231/758	42
Tour Maine, Montparnasse	Paris, France	209/686	58
DG Bank	Frankfurt, Germany	208/682	53
Millennium Tower	Vienna, Austria	202/663	50
Currency Stock Exchange	Moscow, Russian Federation	200/656	36
Ukraine Tower	Moscow, Russian Federation	198/650	34
Main Tower	Frankfurt, Germany	198/650	56

Buildings
Tallest in North America

As of March 2000.

Building	City	Height (m/ft)	Storeys
Sears Tower	Chicago (IL)	443/1,453	110
One World Trade Center	New York (NY)	417/1,368	110
Two World Trade Center	New York (NY)	415/1,362	110
Empire State Building	New York (NY)	381/1,250	102
Amoco Building	Chicago (IL)	346/1,135	80
John Hancock Center	Chicago (IL)	344/1,129	100
Chrysler Building	New York (NY)	319/1,047	77
NationsBank Plaza	Atlanta (GA)	312/1,024	55
Library Tower	Los Angeles (CA)	310/1,017	75
AT&T Corporate Center	Chicago (IL)	306/1,004	60

Buildings
Tallest in South America

As of March 2000.

Building	City	Height (m/ft)	Storeys
Parcque Central Torre Officinas I	Caracas, Venezuela	221/725	56
Parcque Central Torre Officinas II	Caracas, Venezuela	221/725	56
Colpatria Tower	Bogotá, Colombia	192/630	50
Coltejer	Medellín, Colombia	175/574	37
Las Americas	Bogotá, Colombia	174/571	47
Ponte Investments Apartments	Johannesburg, South Africa	173/568	54
La Nacional	Bogotá, Colombia	171/561	47
Palacio Zarzur Kogan	São Paulo, Brazil	170/558	50
Edificio Italia	São Paulo, Brazil	165/541	45
Avianca	Bogotá, Colombia	161/528	41

Buildings
World's Tallest Inhabited Buildings

Building	City	Height (m/ft)	Storeys
Petronas Tower 1	Kuala Lumpur, Malaysia	452/1,483	88
Petronas Tower 2	Kuala Lumpur, Malaysia	452/1,483	88
Sears Tower	Chicago (IL), USA	443/1,453	110
Jin Mao Building	Shanghai, China	420/1,378	88
One World Trade Center	New York (NY), USA	417/1,368	110
Two World Trade Center	New York (NY), USA	415/1,362	110
Empire State Building	New York (NY), USA	381/1,250	102
Central Plaza	Hong Kong, China	374/1,227	78
Bank of China	Hong Kong, China	369/1,210	70
The Centre	Hong Kong, China	350/1,148	73

Buildings
World's Tallest Structures

Structure	City	Height (m/ft)
KTHI-TV Mast	Fargo (ND), USA	629/2,063
KSLA-TV Mast	Shreveport (LA), USA	579/1,900
CN Tower	Toronto, Ontario, Canada	553/1,814
Ostankino Tower	Moscow, Russia	537/1,761
WBIR-TV Mast	Knoxville (TN), USA	533/1,749
WTVM and WRBL Television Mast	Columbus (GA), USA	533/1,749
KFVS Television Mast	Cape Girardeau (MO), USA	511/1,677
WPSD-TV Mast	Paducah (KY), USA	499/1,637
WGAN Television Mast	Portland (ME), USA	494/1,621
Oriental Pearl Broadcasting Tower	Shanghai, China	468/1,535

Champagne
Bottle Sizes

Size	Number of standard champagne bottles	Size	Number of standard champagne bottles
Magnum	2	Salmanazar	12
Jeroboam	4	Balthazar	16
Rehoboam	6	Nebuchadnezzar	20
Methuselah	8		

Chemists
Some Important Chemists

Name	Life dates	Nationality	Name	Life dates	Nationality
Arrhenius, Svante August	1859–1927	Swedish	Charles, Jacques Alexandre César	1746–1823	French
Avogadro, Amedeo	1776–1856	Italian	Crookes, William	1832–1919	English
Berzelius, Jöns Jacob	1779–1848	Swedish	Curie, Marie Sklodowska	1867–1934	Polish-born French
Boyle, Robert	1627–1691	Irish	Curie, Pierre	1859–1906	French
Bunsen, Robert Wilhelm	1811–1899	German	Dalton, John	1766–1844	English
Cannizaro, Stanislao	1826–1910	Italian	Davy, Humphry	1778–1829	English
Castner, Hamilton Young	1858–1898	US	Flory, Paul John	1910–1986	US
Cavendish, Henry	1731–1810	English	Gay-Lussac, Joseph-Louis	1778–1850	French
			Gibbs, Josiah Willard	1839–1903	US

(*continued*)

Chemists: Some Important Chemists (*continued*)

Name	Life dates	Nationality	Name	Life dates	Nationality
Glauber, Johann Rudolf	1604–1668	German	Newlands, John Alexander	1836–1898	English
Graham, Thomas	1805–1869	Scottish	Nobel, Alfred Bernhard	1833–1896	Swedish
Haber, Fritz	1868–1934	German	Ostwald, Friedrich Wilhelm	1853–1932	German
Hahn, Otto	1879–1968	German			
Hess, Germain Henri	1802–1850	Swiss-born Russian	Pauling, Linus Carl	1901–1994	US
Hodgkin, Dorothy Crowfoot	1910–1994	English	Perkin, William Henry	1838–1907	English
Kolbe, Adolph Wilhelm	1818–1884	German	Priestley, Joseph	1733–1804	English
Langmuir, Irving	1881–1957	US	Proust, Joseph Louis	1754–1826	French
Lavoisier, Antoine Laurent	1743–1794	French	Rutherford, Daniel	1749–1819	Scottish
Le Chatelier, Henri Louis	1850–1936	French	Scheele, Karl Wilhelm	1742–1786	Swedish
Lewis, Gilbert Newton	1875–1946	US	Soddy, Frederick	1877–1956	English
			van't Hoff, Jacobus Henricus	1852–1911	Dutch
Mendeleev, Dmitri Ivanovich	1834–1907	Russian	Winkler, Clemens Alexander	1838–1904	German
Nernst, Walther Hermann	1864–1941	German	Wöhler, Firedrich	1800–1882	German

Coal
Countries that Produce the Most

Coal in million tonnes oil equivalent (Mtoe).

Country	Production (Mtoe)
China	626
USA	590
India	148
Australia	148
South Africa	118
Russian Federation	105
Poland	76
Germany	61
Canada	41
Ukraine	40

Coal
Countries that Use the Most

Country	Consumption (thousand metric tons)
China	1,129,095
USA	799,412
Russian Federation	315,335
Germany	303,970
India	267,639
Poland	177,805
South Africa	140,231
Ukraine	120,517
Japan	118,900
North Korea	100,950

Coal
Regions that Produce the Most

Coal in million tonnes oil equivalent (Mtoe).

Region	Production (Mtoe)	% of world production	Region	Production (Mtoe)	% of world production
Asia and the Pacific	1,000	44.8	Africa	123	5.5
North America	637	28.5	South and Central America	29	1.3
Europe	261	11.7	Middle East	1	0.04
Countries of the former USSR	181	8.2			

Comets

Name	Orbital period (years)	Comment
Comet Biela	6.6	not seen since 1852
Comet Encke	3.3	very short period; gives rise to Taurid meteors
Comet Giacobini-Zinner	6.5	gives rise to Draconid meteors
Comet Hale-Bopp	1,000	brightest 20th-century comet
Comet Ikeya-Seki	880	a 'sungrazing' comet
Comet Schwassmann-Wachmann	16.1	remains between Jupiter and Saturn
Comet Shoemaker-Levy	2	crashed into Jupiter in 1994
Comet Swift-Tuttle	130	gives rise to Perseid meteors
Comet Tempel-Tuttle	33	gives rise to Leonid meteors
Halley's comet	76	gives rise to Aquarid and Orionid meteors

Comets
Recent Comets

Name	First recorded sighting	Interesting facts
Comet Hyakutake	1996	passed 15 million km from the Earth in 1996; has the longest-known comet tail (550 million km)
Comet Hale-Bopp	1995	produces a surrounding hazy cloud of gas and dust (coma) which was clearly visible with the naked eye in March 1997
Comet Shoemaker-Levy 9	1993	made up of 21 fragments; crashed into Jupiter in July 1994
Comet Austin	1989	passed 32 million km from the Earth in 1990
Comet IRAS-Araki-Alcock	1983	passed only 4.5 million km from the Earth in 1983
Comet Bowell	1980	ejected from Solar System after close encounter with Jupiter
Comet West	1975	nucleus broke into four parts
Comet Kohoutek	1973	observed from space by *Skylab* astronauts

Computer Crashes
Major Computer Crashes

Year	Victim	Event	Time down
1992	London Ambulance Service	despatch and other systems overloaded	several days
1997	Russian space station, Mir	collapse of main computer	briefly
1997	Brussels Stock Exchange	trading system breakdown	3 hours
1997	Network Solutions	millions of e-mails gridlocked because of breakdown in 13 routing centres	briefly
1998	Microsoft	system collapse during Bill Gates's demo of Windows 98	briefly
1998	Gateway	E-com Web site overloaded	24 hours
1999	EBay	online auction system breakdown	24 hours
2000	National Security Agency	glitch in US intelligence computers	3 days
2000	London Stock Exchange	system breakdown stopped trading on last day of tax year	several hours
2000	UK Inland Revenue	bugs found in online self-assessment software	36 hours

Computer Crime
Computer Crimes by Europeans

Hacker's nationality	Hacker's target	Hacker's intention	Year
French	ATT phone records	steal FBI's connection numbers	1994
Russian	AOL and CompuServe	destroy their businesses	1997
Dutch	34 US military sites	sell military information to Iraqis	1997
Czech/Slovak	Central European Web sites	software piracy/subversion	1997
German	US government computers	infiltration	1998
German	academic sites	clogging systems	1998
Serbian	NATO computers	retaliation for bombing	1999
English	international banks	ransoms	1999
German	ICANN (Internet Corporation for Assigned Names and Numbers)	hijacking elections	2000
Welsh	E-commerce sites	credit card fraud	2000

Computer Crime
Computer Crimes in the USA

Hacker's victim	Hacker's target	Hacker's intention	Year
1st National Bank of Chicago	central computers	heist of $70 million	1980s
Citibank	central computers	heist of $10 million	1994
Omega.eng	production systems	sabotage	1996
US and Israeli governments	central computers	curiosity	1996
UN Children's Fund	central computers	'holocaust' threat if famous hacker not released from prison	1998
Microsoft	source code	probably curiosity	2000
Egghead.com	customer database	not known	2000
Western Union	credit/debit card numbers	fraud	2000
NASA	jet propulsion laboratories	curiosity	2000
Bloomberg	HQ computer system	extorting money	2000
Dare.com	central computers	pro-drug graffiti on anti-drug network	2000

Computer
World's Worst Computer Viruses

Virus	Date	Details
Melissa	1999	spread via e-mail to over 100,000 computers around the world. Created by David Smith of New Jersey, USA
Love Bug	May 2000	causes billions of pounds worth of damage worldwide: FBI traced perpetrators to the Philippines
Michelangelo	1992	triggered on 6 March (anniversary of the birth of Italian artist Michelangelo), erasing the hard disks of an estimated 10,000 PCs
Stoned	1987	a boot sector virus written in New Zealand, which installs itself on the hard disk of a computer, continues to infect computers today
CIH or Chernobyl	August 1998	wipes software on BIOS chip and erases hard drive of thousands of PCs
Queeg and Pathogen	1994	two viruses written by 'Black Baron', Christopher Pile, which are difficult to track down because their codes are automatically changed as each new program is infected: cost businesses thousands
Worm.ExploreZip	June 1999	spread as an e-mail attachment, it caused chaos in large firms such as BSkyB, Microsoft and Merrill Lynch
XM.Laroux	July 1996	this was the first working macro virus to infect Microsoft Word for Windows
BubbleBoy or Kak	1999	a Java Script worm, propagated via e-mail
Stages	May 2000	a worm, that spreads via e-mail and creates random file names throughout the local system and available drives

Computers
Common Computer File Extensions

File extension	Type of computer file
AI	Adobe Illustrator vector graphics
ANI	animation (various packages)
ASM	assembly source code
ASP	Active Server Page
AVI	Audio Video Interleaved animation
BAK	backup file
BAS	BASIC source code
BAT	DOS batch file
BMP	Windows bitmap image
C	C source code
CDR	CorelDRAW graphics
CGI	Common Gateway Interface script
COB	COBOL source code
CLP	Windows clipboard
COM	Executable program
CPP	C++ source code
CSV	comma-separated text
CUR	cursor
DAT	data
DIR	Macromedia Director movie
DLL	dynamic link library
DOC	word-processed document
DOT	Microsoft Word document template
DRV	device driver
DTD	Document Type Definition for SGML document
EPS	Encapsulated PostScript
EXE	Executable program
FNT	Windows font
GIF	Graphics Interchange Format bitmap image
H	header file
HLP	help information
HTM(L)	HyperText Markup Language document
ICO	Windows icon
INI	initialization or configuration file

File extension	Type of computer file
JPG	Joint Photographic Experts Group bitmap image
LIB	library file
MAC	MacPaint bitmap graphics
MDB	Access database
MID	MIDI audio
MOV	QuickTime movie
MPG, MPEG	MPEG movie
PAS	Pascal source code
PCX	Paintbrush bitmap image
PIC	bitmap image (various packages)
PL	Perl source code
PNG	Portable Network Graphics bitmap image
PPT	Microsoft PowerPoint presentation
PS	PostScript text/graphics
PUB	Microsoft Publisher page template
RA, RAM	RealAudio sound
RTF	Rich Text Format text
SGM(L)	Standard Generalized Markup Language document
SIT	STUFFIT compressed file for Macintosh
SYS	system file
TAR	compressed file
TGA	Targa bitmap image
TIF(F)	Tagged Image File Format bitmap image
TMP	temporary file
TXT	ASCII text
WAV	Windows sound file
WK3, WK4, WKS	Lotus 1–2–3 spreadsheet
WP, WP5, WPD	WordPerfect document
XLS	Microsoft Excel spreadsheet
XML	eXtensible Markup Language document

Computers

Countries with Most Personal Computers

Country	Number of computers (per 1,000 population)
USA	418
Australia	303
Sweden	298
Denmark	296
Finland	288
Canada	286
UK	250
Netherlands	246
Switzerland	229
Belgium	215

Constellations

Selected Constellations

A constellation is one of the 88 areas into which the sky is divided for the purposes of identifying and naming celestial objects.

Constellation	Popular name
Andromeda	–
Aquarius	Water-bearer
Canis Major	Great Dog
Canis Minor	Little Dog
Cassiopeia	–
Centaurus	Centaur
Corona Australis	Southern Crown
Corona Borealis	Northern Crown
Hercules	–
Libra	Scales
Orion	–
Pegasus	Flying Horse
Ursa Major	Great Bear
Ursa Minor	Little Bear

Copper

Countries that Consume the Most

Country	Annual consumption (thousand tonnes)
USA	2,670
Japan	1,370
Germany	980
China	750
Former USSR	560
France	500
Korea, South	480
Italy	470
Belgium	400
UK	380

Copper

Countries that Produce the Most

Country	Annual production (thousand tonnes)
Chile	2,220
USA	1,800
Canada	620
Former USSR	540
China	430
Australia	420
Zambia	380
Poland	380
Peru	360
Indonesia	330

Cotton Yarn

Old Measures

Old measure	Equivalent	Old measure	Equivalent
1 thread	54 inches (=1.4 metres)	1 hank	7 skeins (=768 metres)
1 skein	80 threads (=110 metres)	1 spindle	18 hanks (=13,826 metres)

Dams
World's Highest

Dam	Location	Height above lowest formation (m/ft)	Dam	Location	Height above lowest formation (m/ft)
Rogun	Tajikistan	335/1,164	Manuel M Torres	Mexico	261/856
Nurek	Tajikistan	300/984			
Grand Dixence	Switzerland	285/935	Tehri	India	261/856
			Avlvaro Obregon	Mexico	260/853
Inguri	Georgia	272/892			
Vajont	Italy	262/860	Mauvoisin	Switzerland	250/820

Database Programs

Software	Manufacturer	Description
Access	Microsoft	desktop relational database which features wizards and macros; included in Microsoft Office Professional for Windows
Approach	Lotus	desktop relational database, easy to learn and includes programming capabilities
Filemaker Pro	FileMaker	versatile and easy-to-use desktop relational database software for Windows or Mac
FoxPro	Microsoft	high-level professional relational database management system for Windows, DOS, or Unix
Oracle	Oracle Software	powerful, scalable relational database management system that includes point-and-click GUI tools that speed and simplify database management
SQL Server	Microsoft	powerful, scalable relational database management system designed specifically for distributed client/server computing

Decimal Number System

In the decimal number system numbers can be seen as written under columns based on the number 10.

Decimal number system (base 10)

1000s	100s	10s	1s
(10^3)	(10^2)	(10^1)	(10^0)
2	5	6	7

Desktop Publishing Programs

Software	Manufacturer	Description
FrameMaker	Adobe	powerful; strong on technical reports and book production
PageMaker	Adobe	powerful professional tool; strong layout and colour capabilities for both printed and online pages
PagePlus	Serif	good value, low-level tool; aimed mainly at marketing and home use
Publisher	Microsoft	low-level for beginners; provides wizards and clip art gallery
QuarkXPress	Quark	industry standard; expert type, layout, colour, and graphics handling

Diamonds

Countries that Produce the Most Gem Diamonds

Country	Production (thousand carats)
Botswana	15,000
Australia	13,405
Russian Federation	11,500
South Africa	4,000
Congo	3,500
Canada	2,000
Namibia	1,995
Angola	1,080
Ghana	650
Liberia	600

Diamonds

Countries that Produce the Most Industrial Diamonds

Country	Production (thousand carats)
Australia	16,380
Congo	14,500
Russian Federation	11,500
South Africa	6,000
Botswana	5,000
China	920
Brazil	600
Liberia	400
Ghana	160
Central African Republic	150
Venezuela	150

Diamonds

Some Valuable Diamonds Sold at Auction

Year	Description	Weight (carats)	Price (US$)
1995	named *Star of the Season*	100.0	16,500,000
1994	rectangular blue diamond	20.17	9,000,000
1997	pear-shaped	37.85	1,994,000
1995	blue diamond	5.38	1,980,000
1997	square-cut	20.21	1,927,000
1997	named *The Rajah Diamond*	26.14	1,824,000
1987	Argyle pink	3.14	1,510,000
1999	deep yellowish green	5.12	1,000,000
1999	vivid green	0.90	663,000

Diamonds

World's Largest Uncut Diamonds

Year found	Name	Where found	Weight (carats)
1905	*Cullinan*	South Africa	3,107.0
1893	*Excelsior*	South Africa	995.0
1972	*Star of Sierra Leone*	Sierra Leone	968.8
1984	*Zale*	Democratic Republic of Congo	890.0
1650	*Great Mogul*	India	787.5
1998	*Millennium Star*	Democratic Republic of Congo	770.0
1945	*Woyie River*	Sierra Leone	770.0
1938	*Presidente Vargas*	Brazil	726.6
1934	*Jonker*	South Africa	726.0
1895	*Reitz*	South Africa	650.8

Discoveries
Selected Major Scientific Discoveries

Discovery	Date	Discoverer
anaesthetic, first use (ether)	1842	Crawford Long
bacteria, first observation	1683	Anton van Leeuwenhock
blood, circulation	1619	William Harvey
DNA	1869	Johann Frederick Miescher
Earth's rotation, demonstration	1851	Léon Foucault
evolution by natural selection	1858	Charles Darwin
gravity, laws	1687	Isaac Newton
motion, laws	1687	Isaac Newton
nuclear fission	1938	Otto Hahn, Fritz Strassman
penicillin	1928	Alexander Fleming
planets, orbiting Sun	1543	Copernicus
radioactivity	1896	Henri Becquerel
relativity, special theory	1905	Albert Einstein
X-rays	1895	Wilhelm Röntgen

Dyes
Properties of Dyes

Dye type	Characteristics
Natural dyes	
cochineal, lac	red dyes made from crushed insects; cochineal is used in food colouring
woad, indigo	blue or purple dye extracted from plants; also made synthetically
madder	red dye extracted from plants; also synthesized
saffron, safflower, annatto	yellow dyes extracted from plants; annatto is used in food colouring
logwood	black dye extracted from wood
Tyrian purple	purple dye extracted from molluscs; used for Roman emperors' togas
Synthetic dyes	
basic dyes (for example, mauveine)	low fastness on most materials (that is, they tend to run and fade), but used for acrylics
acid dyes (for example, napthol green)	used on protein fibres such as wool and silk
direct dyes (for example, Congo red)	cheap and moderately fast
dispersed dyes	used for synthetic fibres that are difficult to dye with direct dyes
developed dyes (for example, azo dyes)	cheap and very fast; used for printed fabrics
fibre-reactive dyes	very fast to wash in and light, medium-priced, and easy to use; wide range of colours

Earth's Crust

Most Common Elements in the Earth's Crust

Element	Average percentage by volume
oxygen	46.6
silicon	27.7
aluminium	8.1
iron	5.0
calcium	3.6
sodium	2.8
potassium	2.6
magnesium	2.1
titanium	0.4
hydrogen	0.1

Earthquakes

Most Destructive Since 1980

Location/year	Magnitude (Richter scale)	Estimated number of deaths
Iran (1990)	7.7	50,000
India (2001)	7.9	30,000
USSR (1988)	6.8	25,000
Turkey (1999)	7.4	14,095
India (1993)	6.3	9,800
Japan (1995)	7.2	5,500
Mexico (1985)	8.1	5,000
Italy (1980)	7.2	4,800
Afghanistan (1998)	6.9	4,000
Afghanistan (1998)	6.1	>3,800
Algeria (1980)	7.7	3,000
Indonesia (1992)	7.5	2,500
Taiwan (1999)	7.6	2,256
Turkey (1992)	6.7	2,000
Russia (1995)	7.6	2,000
Iran (1997)	7.1	>1,700
Philippines (1990)	7.7	1,660
Yemen (1982)	6.0	1,600
India (1991)	6.1	1,500
Turkey (1983)	6.9	1,300
Iran (1997)	N/A	>1,000

Earthquakes

World's Most Destructive

Year	Location	Estimated number of deaths
1556	Shaanxi, China	830,000
1737	Calcutta (now Kolkata), India	300,000
1976	Tangshan, China	255,000
526	Antioch, Turkey	250,000
1138	Aleppo, Syria	230,000
1927	near Xining, China	200,000
856	Damghan, Iran	200,000
1920	Gansu, China	200,000
893	Ardabil, Iran	150,000
1923	Kwanto, Japan	143,000
1730	Hokkaido, Japan	137,000
1290	Chihli, China	100,000
1667	Caucasia, Russia	80,000
1727	Tabriz, Iran	77,000
1908	Messina, Italy	70,000–100,000
1755	Lisbon, Portugal	70,000
1932	Gansu, China	70,000
1868	Ecuador/Colombia	70,000
1970	northern Peru	66,000

Eclipses
Solar and Lunar Eclipses

Date	Type of eclipse	Duration of totality	Region for observation
9 January 2001	lunar total	1 hr 2 min	Africa, Europe, Asia
21 June 2001	solar total	4 min 57 sec	central and southern Africa
14 December 2001	solar annular	3 min 53 sec	Pacific Ocean
10 June 2002	solar annular	0 min 23 sec	Pacific Ocean
4 December 2002	solar total	2 min 4 sec	southern Africa, Indian Ocean, Australia
16 May 2003	lunar total	0 hr 53 min	the Americas, eastern and western Africa
31 May 2003	solar annular	3 min 37 sec	Iceland, Greenland
9 November 2003	lunar total	0 hr 24 min	the Americas, Africa, Europe
23 November 2003	solar total	1 min 57 sec	Antarctica

Electrical Conduction
Most Conductive Materials

Material	Resistivity (Ωcm)
silver	1.6×10^{-8}
copper	1.7×10^{-8}
aluminium	2.6×10^{-8}
iridium	6.0×10^{-8}
platinum	11.0×10^{-8}
mercury	98.0×10^{-8}

Electrical Insulation
Most Insulating Materials

Material	Resistivity (Ωcm)
fused quartz	7.5×10^{17}
sulphur	10^{15}
diamond (pure)	10^{14}
nickel oxide (pure)	10^{13}
glass	$10^{10} - 10^{14}$

Electricity

Countries that Produce the Most

Country	Production (billion kWh)
USA	3,805
China	1,165
Japan	1,035
Russian Federation	825
Canada	560
Germany	550
France	505
India	495
UK	355
Brazil	320

Electricity

Power Consumption by Domestic Appliances

Appliance	Power consumed (kW per hour)
dishwasher	1.0
electric fire (3-bar)	3.0
electric hob	2.5
electric iron	1.0
electric oven	1.3
freezer	5.0
hair dryer	1.5
immersion heater	3.0
light bulb (100 watt)	0.1
microwave oven	1.5
stereo player	0.1
television set	0.2
toaster	1.2
washing machine	0.3
vacuum cleaner	0.8

Elements

Common Elements

Name	Symbol	Atomic number	Melting point (°C)	Name	Symbol	Atomic number	Melting point (°C)
aluminium	Al	13	658	iron	Fe	26	1,525
calcium	Ca	20	851	lead	Pb	82	327
chlorine	Cl	17	−102	mercury	Hg	80	−38.9
gold	Au	79	1,062	nitrogen	N	7	−211
helium	He	2	−272	oxygen	O	8	−227
hydrogen	H	1	−258	silver	Ag	47	960

Elements

Heavy Radioactive Elements

Atomic number	Name	Symbol	Year discovered	Atomic number	Name	Symbol	Year discovered
93	neptunium	Np	1940	99	einsteinium	Es	1952
94	plutonium	Pu	1941	100	fermium	Fm	1953
95	americium	Am	1944	101	mendelevium	Md	1955
96	curium	Cm	1944	102	nobelium	No	1958
97	berkelium	Bk	1949	103	lawrencium	Lr	1961
98	californium	Cf	1950	104	rutherfordium	Rf	1969

(*continued*)

Elements: Heavy Radioactive Elements (*continued*)

Atomic number	Name	Symbol	Year discovered	Atomic number	Name	Symbol	Year discovered
105	dubnium	Db	1970	111	unununium	Uuu	1994
106	seaborgium	Sg	1974	112	ununbium	Uub	1996
107	bohrium	Bh	1976	114	ununquodium	Uuq	1999
108	hassium	Hs	1984	116	ununhexium	Uuh	1999
109	meitnerium	Mt	1982	118	ununoctium	Uuo	1999
110	ununnilium	Uun	1994				

Elements
Highest Density

Element	Density (g/cu cm)
osmium	22.48
iridium	22.40
platinum	21.45
rhenium	20.50
neptunium	20.45
plutonium	19.84
gold	19.32

Elements
Highest Melting Points

This list excludes elements such as carbon that sublime – change directly to a vapour – rather than melt.

Element	Melting point	
	°C	°F
tungsten	3,420	6,188
rhenium	3,180	5,756
osmium	3,054	5,529
tantalum	2,996	5,425
molybdenum	2,617	4,743
niobium	2,468	4,474
iridium	2,410	4,370
ruthenium	2,310	4,190
boron	2,300	4,172
hafnium	2,227	4,041

Elements
Lowest Density

Figures in this table refer only to elements that are solid at ordinary room temperature (20°C).

Element	Density (g/cu cm)
lithium	0.535
potassium	0.856
sodium	0.968
rubidium	1.532
calcium	1.550
magnesium	1.738
phosphorus	1.823
beryllium	1.848
caesium	1.879
sulphur	1.960

Elements
Lowest Melting Points

Non-gaseous elements only.

Element	Melting point	
	°C	°F
mercury	−38.87	−37.97
bromine	−7.25	−18.95
caesium	28.60	83.50
gallium	29.78	85.60
rubidium	38.90	102.00
phosphorus (white)	44.10	111.40
potassium	63.65	146.84
sodium	97.81	208.06
sulphur	112.80	235.00
lithium	180.00	356.00

Elements
Most Recently Discovered Elements

Date	Element (symbol)	Discoverers
1999	ununoctium (Uuo)	team at Berkeley, USA
1999	ununhexium (Uuh)	team at Berkeley, USA
1999	ununquodium (Uuq)	team at Dubnia, Russia
1996	ununbium (Uub)	team at GSI heavy-ion cyclotron, Darmstadt, Germany
1994	ununnilium (Uun)	team at GSI heavy-ion cyclotron, Darmstadt, Germany
	unununium (Uuu)	team at GSI heavy-ion cyclotron, Darmstadt, Germany
1984	hassium (Hs)	Peter Armbruster and co-workers, Darmstadt, Germany
1982	meitnerium (Mt)	Peter Armbruster and co-workers, Darmstadt, Germany
1976	bohrium (Bh)	Georgii Flerov and Yuri Oganessian (confirmed by German scientist Peter Armbruster and co-workers)
1974	seaborgium (Sg)	claimed by Georgii Flerov and co-workers, and independently by Albert Ghiorso and co-workers
1970	dubnium (Db)	claimed by Albert Ghiorso and co-workers (claimed earlier by Soviet workers)
1969	rutherfordium (Rf)	claimed by US scientist Albert Ghiorso and co-workers (claimed earlier by Soviet workers)
1967	dubnium (Db)	claimed by Soviet scientist Georgii Flerov and co-workers (later disputed by US workers)

Emoticons

Emoticon	Interpretation
:-)	happy
:-(	sad
;-)	winking
:-t	cross, angry
:-o	surprised, amazed, shocked
:-D	laughing
;-(	crying
|-|	asleep (bored)
$-)	greedy
>:-)	devilish
0:-)	angelic
8-)	smiling with glasses
:-X	kiss

Energy
Countries that Consume the Most per Person

A British thermal unit (Btu) is a measure of energy.

Country	Energy per person (million Btu)
United Arab Emirates	678
Bahrain	452
Norway	404
Canada	402
Kuwait	359
USA	352
Belgium	253
Netherlands	249
Sweden	244
Australia	241

Energy
Countries that Consume the Most in Total

A British thermal unit (Btu) is a measure of energy.

Country	Total energy (quadrillion Btu)
USA	94
China	37
Russian Federation	27
Japan	21
Germany	14
Canada	12
India	12
France	10
UK	10
Italy	8

Energy
Regions that Consume the Most

(In tonnes of coal equivalent.)

Region and energy source	Consumption (million tonnes)	Per capita (kg)
America, North	3,550	7,900
Asia	3,460	1,010
Europe	3,410	4,700
America, South	370	1,180
Africa	310	430
Oceania	160	5,660

Energy
Regions that Produce the Most

A British thermal unit (Btu) is a measure of energy.

Region	1993 Energy production (quadrillion Btu)
America, North	89
Far East and Oceania	66
Europe, Eastern, and former USSR	64
Middle East	46
Europe, Western	39
Africa	23
America, Central and South	18

Explosions
World's Worst 20th-century Explosions

Location/year	Number of deaths
chemical plant, Bhopal, India (1984)	3,849
ship struck old mine, off Shanghai, China (1948)	>3,000
ship collision, Halifax Harbor, Canada (1917)	1,654
ammunition trucks, Cali, Colombia (1956)	1,100
Salang Tunnel, Afghanistan (1982)	>1,000
harbour, Bombay (now Mumbai), India (1944)	700
freighter loaded with chemicals, Texas City pier, USA (1947)	576
chemicals storage facility, Oppau, Germany (1921)	561
oil pipeline, Cubatao, Brazil (1984)	508
petroleum gas pipeline leak, Ural Mountains, Russia (1989)	>500

Fuel
World Production

Fuels in million tonnes oil equivalent (Mtoe).

Fuel	Production (Mtoe)	% of world production
Oil	3,388	36
Coal	2,211	23
Natural Gas	1,927	20
Renewables/waste	1,063	11
Nuclear	636	7
Hydroelectricity	218	2

Fuels
World Producers of Mineral Fuels

Commodity	Leading producers
coal	China, USA, India
dry natural gas	Russian Federation, USA, Canada
natural gas plant liquids	USA, Saudi Arabia, Canada
petroleum, crude	Saudi Arabia, USA, Russian Federation

Galaxies
Nearest

Name	Constellation	Type	Distance (light-years)
Sagittarius Dwarf	Sagittarius	spheroidal	c. 80,000
Large Magellanic Cloud (LMC)	Dorado/Mensa	irregular	160,000
Small Magellanic Cloud (SMC)	Tucana	irregular	190,000
Ursa Minor Dwarf	Ursa Minor	spheroidal	205,000
Draco Dwarf	Draco	spheroidal	247,000
Sculptor Dwarf	Sculptor	spheroidal	254,000
Sextans Dwarf	Sextans	spheroidal	258,000
Carina Dwarf	Carina	spheroidal	284,000
Fornax Dwarf	Fornax	spheroidal	427,000

Gas
Regions that Produce the Most Natural Gas

Natural gas in million tonnes oil equivalent (Mtoe).

Region	Production (Mtoe)	% of world production
North America	665	32.5
Countries of the former USSR	580	28.3
Europe	247	12.1
Asia and the Pacific	221	10.8
Middle East	163	8.0
Africa	91	4.5
South and Central America	78	3.8
World	2,045	100
OECD	930.5	45.5
EUIS	182.0	8.9

Gas
World Natural Gas Reserves

Region	Trillion cubic m/ cubic ft
Eastern Europe	57/2,012
Middle East	45/1,589
Asia and Australia	10/353
Africa	10/353
North America	9/318
Western Europe	5/177
South and Central America	5/177

Gases
Densities of Some Common Gases

At standard temperature and pressure of 0°C and 1 atmosphere.

Substance	Density (kg per cubic m)
hydrogen	0.09
helium	0.18
methane	0.72
nitrogen	1.25
air	1.30
oxygen	1.43
carbon dioxide	1.98
propane	2.02
isobutane	2.60

Geology
Geological Eras, Periods, and Epochs

Eon	Era	Period	Epoch	Began	Stage of life
Phanerozoic	Cenozoic	Quaternary	Holocene	10,000 years ago	end of last ice age; civilization develops
			Pleistocene	1.64 million years ago	*Homo Sapiens* evolves

Geology: Geological Eras, Periods, and Epochs (*continued*)

Eon	Era	Period	Epoch	Began	Stage of life
		Tertiary	Pliocene	5.2 million years ago	earliest hominids evolve
			Miocene	23.5 million years ago	grasslands spread; hoofed mammals evolve
			Oligocene	35.5 million years ago	first anthropoid apes evolve
			Eocene	56.5 million years ago	predecessors of most modern mammals evolve
			Palaeocene	65 million years ago	mammals flourish
	Mesozoic	Cretaceous		146 million years ago	seed-bearing plants evolve; mass extinction (including dinosaurs) at end of period
		Jurassic		208 million years ago	birds evolve
		Triassic		245 million years ago	early dinosaurs; first mammals; mass plant extinction at end of period
	Palaeozoic	Permian		290 million years ago	mass extinction
		Carboniferous		360 million years ago	reptiles evolve
		Devonian		409 million years ago	amphibians and insects evolve
		Silurian		439 million years ago	land plants and jawed fishes evolve
		Ordovician		510 million years ago	reef-building algae and jawless fish evolve
		Cambrian		570 million years ago	invertebrate animals evolve
Precambrian	Proterozoic			2.5 billion years ago	first biological activity; bacteria and algae
	Archaean			4.6 billion years ago	none

Gold
Countries that Produce the Most Gold

Country	Production (tonnes)
South Africa	468.2
USA	366.1
Australia	312.5
Canada	166.8
Indonesia	146.4
Russian Federation	127.9
Peru	89.6
Uzbekistan	80.9
Ghana	73.7
Papua New Guinea	63.5

Gold
Countries with the Most Gold Reserves

Country	Gold reserves (million troy ounces)
USA	261.6
Germany	119.0
France	102.4
Italy	83.4
Switzerland	83.3
Netherlands	33.8
Japan	24.2
UK	23.0
Portugal	20.1
Spain	19.5

Graphics and Design Programs

Software	Manufacturer	Description
Adobe Illustrator	Adobe	industry standard illustration software
Adobe Photoshop	Adobe	professional standard photo design and production tool
AutoCAD	AutoDesk	industry standard CAD software; powerful 2D drawing and editing tool
ClarisDraw	Claris	integrates painting and image editing effects, advanced text handling, presentation features, and drawing tools
CorelDRAW	Corel	graphics suite that includes applications for page layout and illustration, photo editing and bitmap creation, and 3D modelling and rendering
DesignCAD	ViaGrafix	powerful CAD system that includes solid modelling, true 3D texture mapping, animation, and anti-aliasing
FreeHand	Macromedia	established design tool; create and publish professional layouts, designs, and illustrations for print and the Web
Painter	MetaCreations	comprehensive set of image editing features allowing you to paint like the great masters, collage photographs, or design with mosaic tiles
Paint Shop Pro	JASC	popular, easy-to-use image editing and drawing program; versions available as shareware
Visual Reality	Visual Software	create 3D graphics, 3D animations, and complete 3D VRML worlds

Hexadecimal Number System

Hexadecimal number system (base 16)

In the hexadecimal number system numbers can be seen as written under columns based on the number 16. Since digits up to a value of decimal 15 are permitted, the letters A to F are used to represent digits corresponding to decimal 10 to 15. The hexadecimal number 23BF corresponds to the decimal number 9151.

4096s	256s	16s	1s
(16^3)	(16^2)	(16^1)	(16^0)
2	3	B	F

Hydroelectricity
Countries that Produce the Most

Country	Production (billion kWh)
Canada	329
USA	324
Brazil	289
China	203
Russian Federation	151
Norway	115
Japan	90
India	76
Sweden	73

Hydro-electricity
Countries that Use the Most

Hydroelectricity in million tonnes oil equivalent (Mtoe).

Country	Consumption (Mtoe)
Canada	28.6
USA	26.7
Brazil	25.0
China	17.1
Russian Federation	13.6
Norway	10.0
Japan	9.3
India	7.2
Sweden	6.3
France	5.7

Hydroelectricity
Regions that Produce the Most

Region	Production (billion kWh)	% of world production
North America	678	26.4
Central and South America	523	20.4
Western Europe	520	20.3
Far East and Oceania	516	20.1
Eastern Europe	246	9.6
Africa	63	2.5
Middle East	19	0.7
World	2,565	100

Ice Age
Major Ice Ages

Name	Date (years ago)	Name	Date (years ago)
Pleistocene	1.64 million–10,000	Sturtian	820–770 million
Permo-Carboniferous	330–250 million	Gnejso	940–880 million
Ordovician	440–430 million	Huronian	2,700–1,800 million
Verangian	615–570 million		

Internet Service Providers

As of March 2000.

ISP	Subscription	Free Web space (MB)	Helpline
AOL	monthly subscription	10	free
BT Internet	monthly subscription	10	local rate
Cable & Wireless Lite	free to C&W customers	20	national rate
CompuServe	monthly subscription	10	national rate
Demon	monthly subscription	20	national rate
Freeserve	free	15	50p per minute
LineOne	free	10	50p per minute
Virgin Net	free	10	50p per minute
Which? Online	monthly subscription	5	£1 per minute
WHSmith Online	free	12	national rate

Internet

Common Internet Domain Names

Generic top-level domains		UK domains		Other country domains	
Domain	Meaning	Domain	Meaning	Domain	Meaning
.com	commercial business	.ac.uk	academic	.au	Australia
.edu	academic	.co.uk	commercial business	.ca	Canada
.gov	government	.gov.uk	government	.cn	China
.int	organization established by international treaty	.lea.sch.uk	local education authority	.de	Germany
.mil	military	.ltd.uk	limited company	.fr	France
.net	Internet network	.mod.uk	Ministry of Defence	.jp	Japan
.org	non-commercial business	.net.uk	Internet network	.nl	Netherlands
		.nhs.uk	National Health Service	.us	USA
		.org.uk	non-commercial business		
		.plc.uk	public limited company		

Internet

Countries with Most Internet Hosts

Country	Number of Internet hosts (per 1,000 population)	Country	Number of Internet hosts (per 1,000 population)
USA	151	Australia	48
Finland	112	New Zealand	48
Norway	75	Canada	42
Sweden	58	Netherlands	40
Denmark	54	Switzerland	37

Internet
Number of Hosts

Year	Number of hosts	Year	Number of hosts	Year	Number of hosts
1981	213	1992	992,000	1996	12,881,000
1985	1,961	1993	1,776,000	1997	19,540,000
1990	313,000	1994	3,212,000	1998	36,739,000
1991	535,000	1995	6,642,000	1999	56,218,000

Interplanetary Probes

Name and country	Planet	Year	Details
Mariner 2 (USA)	Venus	1962	scanned with infrared and microwave radiometers
Mariner 4 (USA)	Mars	1965	first close-up photographs of another planet
Venera 3 (USSR)	Venus	1966	crashed onto the surface. The first human-made object to reach another planet
Mariner 5 (USA)	Venus	1967	flew within 40,000 km of the planet
Venera 4 (USSR)	Venus	1967	probed atmosphere; tried to land
Mariners 6 + 7 (USA)	Mars	1967	analysed atmosphere and surface with remote sensors
Venera 5 (USSR)	Venus	1969	probed atmosphere; tried to land
Venera 6 (USSR)	Venus	1969	probed atmosphere; tried to land
Venera 7 (USSR)	Venus	1970	sent probe to surface
Mariner 9 (USA)	Mars	1971	orbited
Mars 2 (USSR)	Mars	1971	orbited
Mars 3 (USSR)	Mars	1971	orbited
Venera 8 (USSR)	Venus	1972	sent probe to surface

Inventions

Invention	Date	Inventor
aeroplane, powered	1903	Orville and Wilbur Wright
bicycle	1839	Kirkpatrick Macmillan
car, petrol-driven	1885	Karl Benz
dynamite	1866	Alfred Nobel
electric light bulb	1879	Thomas Edison
gramophone	1877	Thomas Edison
heart, artificial	1982	Robert Jarvik
hydrogen bomb	1952	US government scientists
paper, first	AD 105	Ts'ai Lun
steam engine	50 BC	Hero of Alexandria
telephone	1876	Alexander Graham Bell
television	1926	John Logie Baird
thermometer	1607	Galileo
word processor	1965	IBM
World Wide Web	1990	Tim Berners-Lee

Jupiter
Major Satellites

Satellite	Diameter (km/mi)	Mean distance from Jupiter (km/mi)
Ganymede	5,262/3,269	1,070,000/664,867
Callisto	4,800/2,983	1,883,000/1,170,042
Io	3,630/2,256	422,000/262,218
Europa	3,138/1,950	671,000/416,940
Amalthea	shape irregular, 270/168 × 170/106 × 150/93	181,000/112,468
Himalia	180/112	11,480,000/7,113,339
Thebe	100/62	222,000/137,944
Elara	80/50	11,737,000/7,293,031
Pasiphae	70/43	23,500,000/14,602,219

Lead
Countries that Consume the Most

Country	Annual consumption (thousand tonnes)
USA	1,370
Germany	350
Japan	340
UK	270
Italy	260
France	250
China	210
Former USSR	200
Korea, South	180
Mexico	160

Lead
Countries that Produce the Most

Country	Annual production (thousand tonnes)
Australia	520
China	380
USA	370
Peru	220
Canada	170
Mexico	160
Kazakhstan	160
Sweden	110
Namibia	90
Morocco	80

Liquids
Densities of Some Common Liquids

Substance	Density (kg per cubic m)
petrol, kerosene	800
olive oil	900
water	1,000
milk	1,030
sea water	1,030
glycerine	1,260
Dead Sea brine	1,800

Mathematical Signs

Symbol	Meaning
$a \rightarrow b$	a implies b
∞	infinity
lim	limiting value
$a \approx b$	a approximately equal to b
$a = b$	a equal to b
$a > b$	a greater than b
$a < b$	a smaller than b

Symbol	Meaning
$a \neq b$	a not equal to b
$a \geq b$	a equal to or greater than b, that is a at least as great as b
$a \leq b$	a equal to or less than b, that is a at most as great as b
+	addition sign, positive
−	subtraction sign, negative

Mathematical Signs (*continued*)

Symbol	Meaning
×	multiplication sign, times
: or ÷ or /	division sign, divided by
a+b=c	a+b, read as 'a plus b', denotes the addition of a and b. The result of the addition, c, is also known as the sum

Symbol	Meaning
a−b=c	a−b, read as 'a minus b', denotes subtraction of b from a. a−b, or c, is the difference. Subtraction is the opposite of addition
π	ratio of the circumference of a circle to its diameter = 3.1415925535

Measurement
Troy Weights

The troy system, used for weighing gold, silver, and gemstones, is thought to have derived its name from the town of Troyes, France, where the system was probably first used at the medieval fairs held in the town.

	Troy weight	Metric equivalent
1 pennyweight	=24 grains	1.555 grams
1 ounce troy	=20 pennyweights (=480 grains)	31.103 grams
1 pound troy	=12 ounces troy (=5,760 grains)	373.242 grams

Measurement
Units Named After People

Unit	Name	Unit	Name
ampere (amp)	André-Marie Ampère	lambert	Johann Lambert
angstrom	Anders Angström	maxwell	James Clerk Maxwell
baud	Jean-Maurice Baudot	mho	Georg Ohm (backwards)
becquerel	Antonie-Henri Becquerel	newton	Isaac Newton
		oersted	Hans Christian Oersted
bel	Alexander Graham Bell	ohm	Georg Ohm
biot	Jean-Baptiste Biot	pascal	Blaise Pascal
Celsius	Anders Celsius	poise	J M Poiseuille
coulomb	Charles de Coulomb	roentgen	Konrad Röntgen
curie	Marie Curie	sabin	Wallace Sabine
debye unit	Peter Debye	siemens	William Siemens
Fahrenheit	Gabriel Fahrenheit	sievert	Rolf Sievert
farad	Michael Faraday	stokes	George Stokes
gauss (pl. gauss)	Karl Gauss	svedberg	Theodor Svedberg
gilbert	William Gilbert	tesla	Nikola Tesla
gray	Louis Gray	torr	Evangelista Torricelli
henry (pl. henrys)	Joseph Henry	volt	Alessandro Volta
hertz (pl. hertz)	Heinrich Hertz	watt	James Watt
joule	James Joule	weber	Wilhelm Weber
kelvin	Lord Kelvin, William Thomson		

Measurement
Meanings of Greek Numerical Prefixes

Prefix meaning	Greek equivalent
half	hemi (e.g. hemisphere)
one	mono (e.g. monogram)
two	di (e.g. dioxide)
three	tri (e.g. tripod)
four	tetra (e.g. tetrarch)
five	penta (e.g. pentangle)
six	hexa (e.g. hexagonal)
seven	hepta (e.g. heptane)
eight	oct(a) (e.g. octagon)
nine	ennea (e.g. enneagon)
ten	deca (e.g. decathlon)
eleven	hendeca (e.g. hendecasyllable)
twelve	dodeca (e.g. dodecagon)
twenty	icosa (e.g. icosahedron)
hundred	hecto (e.g. hectogram)
thousand	kilo (e.g. kilocycle)
many	poly (e.g. polygon)
all	pan (e.g. panacea)

Measurement
Meanings of Latin Numerical Prefixes

Prefix meaning	Latin equivalent
half	semi (e.g. semicircle)
one	uni (e.g. unique)
two	bi (e.g. biennial)
three	ter (e.g. tercentennial)
four	quadri (e.g. quadrilateral)
five	quinque (e.g. quinquereme)
six	sex (e.g. sextant)
seven	sept (e.g. September)
eight	oct(o) (e.g. October)
nine	non (e.g. nonet)
ten	decem (e.g. December)
eleven	undecim
twelve	duodecim (e.g. duodecimal)
twenty	viginti
hundred	centi (e.g. centigrade)
thousand	mill (e.g. millennium)
many	multi (e.g. multiplex)
all	omni (e.g. omnipotent)

Metals
World Producers of Metals

Commodity	Leading producers
aluminium	USA, Russian Federation, Canada
bauxite, gross weight	Australia, Guinea, Brazil
chromite, gross weight	South Africa, Turkey, India
copper, metal content	Chile, USA, Canada
gold, metal content	South Africa, USA, Australia
iron ore, gross weight	China, Brazil, Australia

Commodity	Leading producers
lead, metal content	Australia, China, USA
manganese ore, gross weight	China, South Africa, Ukraine
nickel, metal content	Russian Federation, Canada, New Caledonia (France)
steel, crude	European Union, Japan, China
tin, metal content	China, Indonesia, Peru
zinc, metal	Canada, Australia,

Meteorites
Composition

Type		Composition and structure
siderites (iron meteorites)		iron (more than 90%), nickel (8%), cobalt (0.6%), traces of other elements
stony-iron meteorites		mixtures of iron and stony materials (silicates). Teardrop-shaped stones are embedded in iron or iron droplets are embedded in stone
aerolites (stone meteorites)	chondrites	many tiny millimetre-sized globules called chondrules embedded in a matrix of soft, porous material. Both chondrules and matrix consist mainly of olivine, pyroxene, and feldspar with tiny amounts of metal. Composition similar to that of Earth's crust
	carbonaceous chondrites	similar composition to ordinary chondrites but containing far fewer chondrules. The proportion of such minerals as feldspar is higher than in ordinary chondrites and may reach 15%
	achondrites	similar composition and structure to chondrites but showing a complete absence of chondrules. Almost identical to Earth rocks except for the fusion crust. Some achondrites are breccias, consisting of angular stone fragments held together by softer material

Meteorites
Heaviest

Name and location	Weight (tonnes)	Year found
Hoba West, Grootfontein, Namibia	60	1920
Ahnighito, Greenland	30	–
Bacuberito, Mexico	27	1863
Mbosi, Tanzania	26	1930
Agpalik, Greenland	20	–
Armanty, Mongolia	20	1935 (known in 1917)
Chupaderos, Mexico	14	known for centuries; first mentioned in 1852
Willamette (OR), USA	14	1902
Campo del Cielo, Argentina	13	–
Mundrabilla, Western Australia	12	–

Meteorites

Most Common Elements in Meteorites

Element	Average percentage by volume
Siderites (iron–nickel meteorites)	
iron	91.00
nickel	8.00
cobalt	0.60

Element	Average percentage by volume
Acrolites (stony meteorites)	
oxygen	45.30
iron	18.40
silicon	10.30
magnesium	9.60
sulphur	6.20
carbon	3.70
hydrogen	2.20
calcium	1.06

Meteors

Significant Meteor Showers

Name	Date of shower	Name	Date of shower
Quadrantids	1–6 January	Alpha Capricornids	15 July–25 August
Corona Australids	14–18 March	Iota Aquarids	15 July–25 August
Lyrids	19–25 April	Perseids	25 July–18 August
Eta Aquarids	1–10 May	Orionids	16–27 October
Ophiuchids	17–26 June	Taurids	20 October–30 November
Capricornids	10 July–15 August		
Delta Aquarids	15 July–15 August	Leonids	15–20 November
Piscis Australids	15 July–20 August	Geminids	7–15 December
		Ursids	17–24 December

Minerals

Gems and Semi-precious Stones

Stone	Colour	Hardness	Composition
amethyst	purple or blue-violet	7.0	silica (quartz)
aquamarine	pale blue-green	7.5	beryl
carnelian	red or red-brown	7.0	silica (quartz)
citrine	yellow	7.0	silica (quartz)
diamond	colourless, yellow, green, or black	10.0	carbon
emerald	green	7.5	beryl

Minerals: Gems and Semi-precious Stones (*continued*)

Stone	Colour	Hardness	Composition
lapis lazuli	blue	5.5	lazurite
malachite	green	4.0	copper carbonate
moonstone	silver/blue opalescent	6.0–6.5	alkali feldspar
morganite	pink	7.5	beryl
opal	multicoloured	6.0	silica (amorphous)
pearl	white or black	3.5	calcium carbonate
peridot	olive-green	6.0–7.0	olivine
ruby	red	9.0	corundum
sapphire	blue, green, or yellow	9.0	corundum
topaz	green, blue, or yellow	8.0	complex silicate
tourmaline	dark green or pink	7.5	complex borosilicate
turquoise	blue	6.0	aluminium/copper phosphate
zircon	colourless or pink	6.5–7.5	zirconium silicate

Mining
World's Worst Mining Disasters

Location/year	Cause	Number of deaths
Honkeiko, China (1942)	explosion	1,549
Courrières, France (1906)	explosion	1,110
Omuta, Japan (1963)	explosion	458
Senghenydd, Wales, UK (1913)	fire	440
Coalbrook, South Africa (1960)	explosion	437
Zonguldak, Turkey (1992)	explosion	388
Bihar State, India (1965)	fire	375
Monongah, USA (1907)	explosion	361
Dawson, New Mexico, USA (1935)	explosion	265
Cherry, Illinois, USA (1909)	fire	259
Hillcrest, Alberta, Canada (1914)	explosion	189

Moon
Most Common Elements in the Moon

Element	Average percentage by volume	Element	Average percentage by volume
oxygen	40.00	aluminium	5.60
silicon	19.20	magnesium	4.50
iron	14.30	sodium	0.33
calcium	8.00	potassium	0.14
titanium	5.90	chromium	0.02

Moons
Largest

Planet	Satellite	Diameter (km/mi)	Orbital period (Earth days)
Jupiter	Ganymede	5,270/3,275	7.16
Saturn	Titan	5,150/3,200	15.95
Jupiter	Callisto	4,800/2,983	16.69
Jupiter	Io	3,660/2,274	1.77
Earth	Moon	3,476/2,160	27.32
Jupiter	Europa	3,140/1,951	3.55
Neptune	Triton	2,700/1,678	5.88

Moons
Major Planetary Moons

Planet	Satellite	Planet	Satellite
Earth	Moon		Mimas
Mars	Deimos		Phoebe
	Phobos		Rhea
Jupiter	Amalthea		Tethys
	Callisto		Titan
	Carme	Uranus	Ariel
	Elara		Oberon
	Europa		Titania
	Ganymede		Umbriel
	Himalia	Neptune	Despina
	Io		Galatea
	Lysithea		Larissa
	Pasiphae		Naiad
	Sinope		Nereid
Saturn	Dione		Proteus
	Enceladus		Thalassa
	Hyperion		Triton
	Iapetus	Pluto	Charon

Natural Gas
Countries that Produce the Most

Natural gas in million tonnes oil equivalent (Mtoe).

Country	Production (Mtoe)
Russian Federation	496
USA	489
Canada	144
UK	81
Algeria	66
Indonesia	62
Netherlands	57
Uzbekistan	46
Iran	45
Norway	43

Natural Gas
Countries that Use the Most

Natural gas in million tonnes oil equivalent (Mtoe).

Country	Consumption (Mtoe)
USA	551
Russian Federation	328
UK	80
Germany	72
Canada	63
Japan	63
Ukraine	62
Ireland	52
Iran	47
Uzbekistan	42

Neptune
Major Satellites

Satellite	Diameter (km/mi)	Mean distance from Neptune (km/mi)
Triton	2,700/1,678	355,000/220,587
Proteus	400/249	118,000/73,322
Nereid	340/211	5,513,000/3,425,618
Larissa	190/118	74,000/45,981
Despina	180/112	53,000/32,933
Galatea	150/93	62,000/38,525
Thalassa	80/50	50,000/31,069
Naiad	50/31	48,000/29,826

Nickel
Countries that Consume the Most

Country	Annual consumption (thousand tonnes)
Japan	160
USA	140
Germany	90
Former USSR	60
France	40
Italy	40
UK	40
China	30
Finland	20
Sweden	20

Nickel
Countries that Produce the Most

Country	Annual production (thousand tonnes)	Country	Annual production (thousand tonnes)
Former USSR	240	Dominican Republic	30
Canada	150	Cuba	30
Indonesia	80	China	30
New Caledonia	70	South Africa	30
Australia	70	Colombia	20

Nobel Prize
Chemistry

Year	Winner(s)	Awarded for
1990	Elias James Corey (USA)	new methods of making chemical compounds
1991	Richard Ernst (Switzerland)	nuclear magnetic resonance (NMR) imaging
1992	Rudolph Marcus (USA)	reduction and oxidation reactions
1993	Kary Mullis (USA)	technique for amplifying DNA
	Michael Smith (Canada)	techniques for inserting new genes into DNA
1994	George Olah (USA)	technique for examining hydrocarbon molecules
1995	F Sherwood Rowland (USA), Mario Molina (USA), and Paul Crutzen (Netherlands)	chemical process of the ozone layer
1996	Robert Curl Jr (USA), Harold Kroto (UK), and Richard Smalley (USA)	discovery of fullerenes
1997	John Walker (UK), Paul Boyer (USA), and Jens Skou (Denmark)	study of the enzymes involved in the production of adenosine triphospate (ATP)
1998	Walter Kohn (USA), John Pople (USA)	research into quantum chemistry
1999	Ahmed Zewail (USA)	chemical reactions using femtosecond spectroscopy
2000	Alan J Heeger (USA), Alan G MacDiarmid (New Zealand), and Hideki Shirakawa (Japan)	development of electrically conductive polymers

Nobel Prize
Physics

Year	Winner(s)	Awarded for
1990	Jerome Friedman (USA), Henry Kendall (USA), and Richard Taylor (Canada)	discovery of quarks
1991	Pierre-Gilles de Gennes (France)	work on disordered systems
1992	Georges Charpak (France)	invention of detectors used in high-energy physics
1993	Joseph Taylor (USA) and Russell Hulse (USA)	discovery of first binary pulsar
1994	Clifford Shull (USA) and Bertram Brockhouse (Canada)	development of neutron scattering technique
1995	Frederick Reines (USA)	discovery of the neutrino
	Martin Perl (USA)	discovery of the tau lepton
1996	David Lee (USA), Douglas Osheroff (USA), and Robert Richardson (USA)	discovery of superfluidity in helium-3
1997	Claude Cohen-Tannoudji (France), William Phillips (USA), and Steven Chu (USA)	discovery of a way to slow down atoms using lasers
1998	Robert B Laughlin (USA), Horst L Störmer (USA), and Daniel C Tsui (USA)	discovery of a new form of quantum fluid

Nobel Prize: Physics (*continued*)

Year	Winner(s)	Awarded for
1999	Gerardus 'T Hooft (Netherlands) and Martinus Veltman (Netherlands)	studying the quantum structure of electroweak interactions
2000	Zhores I Alferov (Russia) and Herbert Kroemer (Germany)	development of semiconductor heterostructures
	Jack St Clair Kilby (USA)	co-invention of the integrated circuit

Nobel Prize
Physiology or Medicine

Year	Winner(s)	Awarded for
1990	Joseph Murray (USA) and Donnall Thomas (USA)	work on organ and cell transplants
1991	Erwin Neher (Germany) and Bert Sakmann (Germany)	work on ion channels
1992	Edmond Fischer (USA) and Edwin Krebs (USA)	work on the enzyme responsible for a major biological control mechanism
1993	Phillip Sharp (USA) and Richard Roberts (UK)	discovery of split genes
1994	Alfred Gilman (USA) and Martin Rodbell (USA)	discovery of G-proteins
1995	Edward Lewis (USA), Eric Wieschaus (USA), and Christiane Nüsslein-Volhard (Germany)	discovery of genes which control development
1996	Peter Doherty (Australia) and Rolf Zinkernagel (Switzerland)	discovery of how the immune system recognizes virus-infected cells
1997	Stanley Prusiner (USA)	discoveries that could lead to new treatments for Alzheimer's and Parkinson's diseases
1998	Robert Furchgott (USA), Ferid Murad (USA), and Louis Ignarro (USA)	discovery that nitric oxide (NO) acts as a chemical messenger between cells
1999	Günter Blobel (USA)	transport and localization of proteins in cells
2000	Arvid Carlsson (Sweden), Paul Greegard (USA), and Eric Kandel (USA)	how signals are transmitted between nerve cells

Nonmetallic Minerals
World Producers of Nonmetallic Minerals

Commodity	Leading producers
cement, hydraulic	China, Japan, USA
diamond, gem and industrial	Australia, Russian Federation, Democratic Republic of Congo
nitrogen in ammonia	China, USA, India
phosphate rock	USA, China, Morocco
potash, marketable	Canada, Germany, Belarus
salt	USA, China, Germany
sulphur, elemental basis	USA, Canada, China

Nuclear Energy
Countries that Produce the Most

In gigawatt hours (GWh). A gigawatt is one thousand million watts, and a gigawatt hour means that a power station produces one thousand million watts of electrical power in one hour.

Country	GWh
USA	650,000
France	370,000
Japan	250,000
Germany	154,000
Russia	120,000
Canada	95,000
UK	90,000
Ukraine	75,000
Sweden	61,000
Korea	58,000

Nuclear Power
Countries that Use the Most Electricity Produced by Nuclear Power

Nuclear electricity in million tonnes oil equivalent (Mtoe).

Country	Consumption (Mtoe)	Country	Consumption (Mtoe)
USA	183	UK	26
France	100	South Korea	23
Japan	84	Ukraine	19
Germany	42	Canada	19
Russian Federation	27	Sweden	18

Nuclear Power
Regions that Produce the Most

Region	Production (billion kWh)	% of world production
Western Europe	842	36.3
North America	750	32.4
Far East and Oceania	463	20.0
Eastern Europe and countries of the former USSR	240	10.3
Africa	17	0.6
Central and South America	10	0.4
World	2,322	100
OECD	2,014	86.9

Numbers
Large Numbers

Nomenclature for large numbers varies in different countries: in the UK and Germany numbers have traditionally advanced by increments of a million, whereas in the USA and France numbers advance by increments of a thousand. The US usage is becoming more common in the UK and is now universally used by economists and statisticians.

Number	UK and Germany	
million	1,000,000	1×10^6
billion	1,000,000,000,000	1×10^{12}
trillion	1,000,000,000,000,000,000	1×10^{18}
quadrillion	1,000,000,000,000,000,000,000,000	1×10^{24}

Number	USA and France	
billion	1,000,000,000	1×10^9
trillion	1,000,000,000,000	1×10^{12}
quadrillion	1,000,000,000,000,000	1×10^{15}

Higher numbers

Number	UK	USA
quintillion	1×10^{30}	1×10^{18}
sextillion	1×10^{36}	1×10^{21}
septillion	1×10^{42}	1×10^{24}
octillion	1×10^{48}	1×10^{27}
nonillion	1×10^{54}	1×10^{30}
decillion	1×10^{60}	1×10^{33}
vigintillion	1×10^{120}	1×10^{63}
centillion	1×10^{600}	1×10^{303}

Octal Number System

In the octal number system numbers can be seen as written under columns based on the number 8. The octal number 2164 corresponds to the decimal number 1140.

Octal number system (base 8)

512s	64s	8s	1s
(8^3)	(8^2)	(8^1)	(8^0)
2	1	6	4

Oil
Countries that Produce the Most

Country	Production (million tonnes)	Country	Production (million tonnes)
Saudi Arabia	443	Venezuela	172
USA	368	China	160
Russian Federation	304	Norway	150
Iran	188	UK	133
Mexico	174	Canada	125

Oil
Countries that Use the Most

Country	Consumption (barrels)
USA	4,975
Russian Federation	1,689
Japan	1,534
China	1,012
Germany	746
Georgia	746
UK	626
Saudi Arabia	581
France	571
Italy	558
South Korea	545

Oil
Regions that Produce the Most

Region	Production (million tonnes)	% of world production
Middle East	1,097	31.1
North America	667	19.0
Asia and the Pacific	365	10.4
Countries of the former USSR	361	10.3
Africa	360	10.2
South and Central America	343	9.7
Europe	325	9.3

Oil
World Oil Reserves

Region	Thousand million barrels	Region	Thousand million barrels
Middle East	660	Africa	62
North America	88	Eastern Europe	59
South and Central America	78	Asia and Australia	45
		Western Europe	17

Operating Systems

Operating system	Developer	Interface	Platform
DOS	Microsoft and IBM 1981	command line	PC
OS/2	IBM and Microsoft 1987	command line GUI	PC
Mac OS	Apple 1984	pioneered GUI	Macintosh
Unix/Linux	AT&T, Red Hat, and others late 1960s–2000	command line GUI	from mainframes to PCs
Windows NT/2000	Microsoft 1993–2000	GUI	PC or RISC-based system
Windows 95/98/00	Microsoft 1995–2000	GUI	PC

Paper
International Paper Sizes

Name	Dimensions	
Classic series		
large post	419 × 533 millimetres	$16\frac{1}{2} \times 21$ inches
demy	444 × 572 millimetres	$17\frac{1}{2} \times 22\frac{1}{2}$ inches
medium	457 × 584 millimetres	18×23 inches
royal	508 × 635 millimetres	20×25 inches
double crown	508 × 762 millimetres	20×30 inches
A series (books, magazines, stationery)		
A0	841 × 1,189 millimetres	$33\frac{1}{8} \times 46\frac{3}{4}$ inches
A1	594 × 841 millimetres	$23\frac{3}{8} \times 33\frac{1}{8}$ inches
A2	420 × 594 millimetres	$16\frac{1}{2} \times 23\frac{3}{8}$ inches
A3	297 × 420 millimetres	$11\frac{3}{4} \times 16\frac{1}{2}$ inches

(continued)

Paper: International Paper Sizes (*continued*)

Name	Dimensions	
A4	210 × 297 millimetres	$8\frac{1}{4} \times 11\frac{3}{4}$ inches
A5	148 × 210 millimetres	$5\frac{7}{8} \times 8\frac{1}{4}$ inches

B series (posters, etc)

B0	1,414 × 1,000 millimetres	$55\frac{5}{8} \times 39\frac{3}{8}$ inches
B1	1,000 × 707 millimetres	$39\frac{3}{8} \times 27\frac{7}{8}$ inches
B2	707 × 500 millimetres	$27\frac{7}{8} \times 19\frac{5}{8}$ inches
B3	500 × 353 millimetres	$19\frac{5}{8} \times 13\frac{7}{8}$ inches
B4	353 × 250 millimetres	$13\frac{7}{8} \times 9\frac{7}{8}$ inches
B5	250 × 176 millimetres	$9\frac{7}{8} \times 7$ inches

C series (envelopes)

C4	324 × 229 millimetres	$12\frac{3}{4} \times 9$ inches
C5	229 × 162 millimetres	$9 \times 6\frac{3}{8}$ inches
C6	162 × 114 millimetres	$6\frac{3}{8} \times 4\frac{1}{2}$ inches
DL	220 × 110 millimetres	$8\frac{5}{8} \times 4\frac{3}{8}$ inches

Paper
Quantities

Writing paper

1 quire	24 sheets (now often 25 sheets)
1 ream	20 quires (=480 sheets; now often 500 sheets)
1 bundle	2 reams (=960 sheets; now often 1,000 sheets)

Printing paper

1 printer's ream	516 sheets (now often 500 sheets)
1 bundle	2 reams (=1032 sheets; now often 1,000 sheets)
1 bale	5 bundles (=5160 sheets; now often 5,000 sheets)

Physical Constants

Physical constants, or fundamental constants, are physical quantities that are constant in all circumstances throughout the whole universe.

Constant	Symbol	Value in SI units
acceleration of free fall	g	9.80665 m s^{-2}
Avogadro's constant	N_A	6.0221367×10^{23} mol^{-1}
Boltzmann's constant	k	1.380658×10^{-23} J K^{-1}
elementary charge	e	$1.60217733 \times 10^{-19}$ C
electronic rest mass	m_e	$9.1093897 \times 10^{-31}$ kg
Faraday's constant	F	9.6485309×10^4 C mol^{-1}
gas constant	R	8.314510 J K^{-1} mol^{-1}
gravitational constant	G	6.672×10^{-11} N m^2 kg^{-2}
Loschmidt's number	N_L	2.686763×10^{25} m^{-3}
neutron rest mass	m_n	$1.6749286 \times 10^{-27}$ kg
Planck's constant	h	$6.6260755 \times 10^{-34}$ J s
proton rest mass	m_p	$1.6726231 \times 10^{-27}$ kg
speed of light in a vacuum	c	2.99792458×10^8 m s^{-1}
standard atmosphere	atm	1.01325×10^5 Pa
Stefan–Boltzmann constant	σ	5.67051×10^{-8} W m^{-2} K^{-4}

Physicists

Some Important Physicists

Name	Life dates	Nationality
Ampère, André Marie	1775–1836	French
Becquerel, Antoine Henri	1852–1908	French
Bohr, Niels Hendrik	1885–1962	Danish
Boltzmann, Ludwig Edward	1844–1906	Austrian
Born, Max	1882–1970	German-born English
Bose, Satyendra Nath	1894–1974	Indian
Celsius, Anders	1701–1744	Swedish
Chadwick, Lames	1891–1974	English
Clausius, Rudolf Julius	1822–1888	German
de Broglie, Louis Victor	1892–1987	French
Debye, Peter Joseph	1884–1966	Dutch-born US
Doppler, Christian Johann	1803–1853	Austrian
Einstein, Albert	1879–1955	German-born US
Fahrenheit, Daniel	1686–1736	German
Faraday, Michael	1791–1867	English
Fermi, Enrico	1901–1954	Italian-born US
Feynman, Richard Phillips	1918–1988	US
Fleming, John Ambrose	1849–1945	English
Foucault, Jean Bernard	1819–1868	French
Fresnel, Augustin Jean	1788–1827	French
Geiger, Hans Wilhelm	1882–1945	German
Glaser, Donald Arthur	1926–	US

(*continued*)

Physicists: Some Important Physicists (*continued*)

Name	Life dates	Nationality
Heisenberg, Werner Karl	1901–1976	German
Helmholtz, Hermann von	1821–1894	German
Henry, Joseph	1797–1878	US
Hertz, Heinrich Rudolf	1857–1894	German
Hooke, Robert	1635–1703	English
Joule, James Prescott	1818–1889	English
Kelvin, Lord (William Thomson)	1824–1907	Irish
Kirchhoff, Gustav Robert	1824–1887	German
Lawrence, Ernest Otlando	1901–1958	US
Mach, Ernst	1838–1916	Austrian
Maxwell, James Clerk	1831–1879	Scottish
Michelson, Albert Abraham	1852–1931	US
Morley, Edward William	1838–1923	US
Newton, Isaac	1642–1727	English
Ohm, Georg Simon	1787–1854	German
Pauli, Wolfgang	1900–1958	US-born Swiss
Planck, Max Karl Ernst	1858–1947	German
Poisson, Siméon Denis	1781–1840	French
Rayleigh, Lord (John William Strutt)	1842–1919	Irish
Röntgen, Wilhelm Conrad	1845–1923	German
Rumford, Count (Benjamin Thompson)	1753–1814	US-born English
Rutherford, Ernest	1871–1937	New Zealand-born English
Rydberg, Johannes Robert	1854–1919	Swedish
Schrödinger, Erwin	1887–1961	Austrian
Stokes, George Gabriel	1819–1903	Irish
Thomson, Joseph John	1856–1940	English
van de Graaff, Rovert Jemison	1901–1967	US
van de Waals, Johannes	1837–1923	Dutch
Volta, Alessandro Giuseppe	1745–1827	Italian
Wheatstone, Charles	1802–1875	English
Wilson, Charles Thomson Rees	1869–1959	Scottish
Young, Robert	1773–1829	English

Planets

Planet	Main constituents
Mercury	rock, ferrous
Venus	rock, ferrous
Earth	rock, ferrous
Mars	rock
Jupiter	liquid hydrogen, helium
Saturn	hydrogen, helium
Uranus	ice, hydrogen, helium
Neptune	ice, hydrogen, helium
Pluto	ice, rock

Planets
Day Lengths

Planet	Day length
Venus	243d 0h 27m
Mercury	58d 15h 30m
Pluto	6d 9h 17m
Mars	24h 37m
Earth	23h 56m
Uranus	17h 14m
Neptune	16h 7m
Saturn	10h 14m
Jupiter	9h 51m

Planets
Distances from the Sun

Planet	Mean distance from Sun	
	Million km	Million mi
Mercury	58	36
Venus	108	67
Earth	150	93
Mars	228	142
Jupiter	778	484
Saturn	1,427	887
Uranus	2,871	1,784
Neptune	4,400	2,794
Pluto	5,800	3,600

Planets
In Order of Size

Planet	Equatorial diameter (km/mi)
Jupiter	142,800/88,700
Saturn	120,000/75,000
Uranus	50,800/31,600
Neptune	48,600/30,200
Earth	12,755/7,920
Venus	12,100/7,500
Mars	6,780/4,210
Mercury	4,880/3,030
Pluto	2,300/1,438

Planets
Surface Gravities and Escape Velocities

Planet	Gravity (m/s^2)	Escape velocity (km/s)
Mercury	3.70	4.25
Venus	8.87	10.36
Earth	9.78	11.18
Mars	3.72	5.12
Jupiter	22.88	59.56
Saturn	9.05	35.49
Uranus	7.77	21.30
Neptune	11.00	23.50
Pluto	0.40	1.22

Planets
Surface Temperatures

Planet	Average surface temperature	
	°C	°F
Venus	480	896
Mercury	167	333
Earth	22	72
Mars	−23	−9
Jupiter	−150	−238
Saturn	−180	−292
Uranus	−210	−346
Neptune	−220	−364
Pluto	−230	−382

Planets
Year Lengths

Planet	Year length	Planet	Year length
Pluto	247y 336d 2h 9m	Mars	686d 23h 31m
Neptune	164y 288d 13h 16m	Earth	365d 6h 9m
Uranus	84y 6d 5h 1m	Venus	224d 16h 49m
Saturn	29y 163d 6h 28m	Mercury	87d 23h 15m
Jupiter	11y 315d 5h 11m		

Pollution
Levels of Air Pollution in Selected Cities

'Total suspended particulates' refers to smoke, soot, dust, and liquid droplets from combustion that are in the air. Sulphur dioxide is produced when fossil fuels are burnt. Nitrogen dioxide is emitted by bacteria, fertilizers, motor vehicles, and industrial activities; both these dioxides contribute to acid rain formation.
(N/A = not available.)

City/country	Total suspended particulates (µg per cu m)	Sulphur dioxide (µg per cu m)	Nitrogen dioxide (µg per cu m)
Bangkok, Thailand	223	11	23
Beijing, China	377	90	122
Cairo, Egypt	N/A	69	N/A
Delhi, India	415	24	41
Jakarta, Indonesia	271	N/A	N/A
Kolkata (formerly Calcutta), India	375	49	34
London, UK	N/A	25	77
Los Angeles, USA	N/A	9	74
Manila, Philippines	200	33	N/A
Mexico City, Mexico	279	74	130
Moscow, Russia	100	109	N/A
Mumbai (formerly Bombay), India	240	33	39
New York, USA	N/A	29	79
Osaka, Japan	43	19	63
Rio de Janeiro, Brazil	139	129	N/A
São Paulo, Brazil	86	43	83
Seoul, South Korea	84	44	60
Shanghai, China	246	53	73
Tokyo, Japan	49	18	68

Ports

Distances Between Some Major Ports

From	To	Distance (nautical miles)
Cape Town, South Africa	Melbourne, Australia	7,590
	Singapore	6,456
New York (NY), USA	Cape Town, South Africa	7,804
	Southampton, UK	3,644
Panama, Panama	Jakarta, Indonesia	12,193
Port Said, Egypt	Melbourne, Australia	9,069
	Singapore	5,790
San Francisco (CA), USA	Kolkata (formerly Calcutta), India	10,792
	Colón, Panama	3,778
Vancouver, Canada	Kolkata (formerly Calcutta), India	10,036
	Melbourne, Australia	8,470

Prime Numbers

A prime number is a number that can be divided only by 1 and itself, that is, having no other factors. There is an infinite number of primes.

All the prime numbers between 1 and 1,000

2	3	5	7	11	13	17	19	23	29
31	37	41	43	47	53	59	61	67	71
73	79	83	89	97	101	103	107	109	113
127	131	137	139	149	151	157	163	167	173
179	181	191	193	197	199	211	223	227	229
233	239	241	251	257	263	269	271	277	281
283	293	307	311	313	317	331	337	347	349
353	359	367	373	379	383	389	397	401	409
419	421	431	433	439	443	449	457	461	463
467	479	487	491	499	503	509	521	523	541
547	557	563	569	571	577	587	593	599	601
607	613	617	619	631	641	643	647	653	659
661	673	677	683	691	701	709	719	727	733
739	743	751	757	761	769	773	787	797	809
811	821	823	827	829	839	853	857	859	863
877	881	883	887	907	911	919	929	937	941
947	953	967	971	977	983	991	997		

Quarks

Six Flavours of Quarks

Flavour	Charge	Mass (beV)
bottom	$-\frac{1}{3}$	4.72
charmed	$+\frac{2}{3}$	1.50
down	$-\frac{1}{3}$	0.34
strange	$-\frac{1}{3}$	0.54
top	$+\frac{2}{3}$	175.60
up	$+\frac{2}{3}$	0.38

Reservoirs

World's Largest by Volume

Reservoir	Location	Volume cubic m/ft (million)
Kariba	Zambia/Zimbabwe	180,600/6,377,835
Bratsk	Russian Federation	169,000/5,968,184
High Aswan	Egypt	162,000/5,720,981
Akosombo	Ghana	150,000/5,297,205
Daniel Johnson	Canada	141,851/5,009,426
Xinfeng	China	138,960/4,907,330
Guri	Venezuela	135,000/4,767,485
Bennett W A C	Canada	74,300/2,623,882
Krasnoyarsk	Russian Federation	73,300/2,588,568
Zeya	Russian Federation	68,400/2,415,525

Rocks

Composition of Metamorphic Rocks

Rock	Parent rock	Composition
amphibolite	basalt	biotite, chlorite, garnet, hornblende, etc.
gneiss	mudstones/shales	biotite, hornblende, muscovite, quartz, etc.
hornfels	mudstones/shales	andalusite, biotite, cordierite, corundum
marble	limestone	calcite, dolomite
phyllite	mudstones/shales	mainly micas and quartz
pyroxine	basalt	plagioclase, pyroxine, quartz, spinel
schist	mudstones/shales	biotite, chlorite, garnet, quartz, etc.
slate	mudstones/shales	mainly micas and quartz

Rocks

Composition of Sedimentary Rocks

Rock	Type	Composition
arkose	medium mechanical	silicon dioxide with aluminosilicate
breccia	coarse mechanical	angular rock fragments
chert	siliceous	silicon dioxide
coal	carbonaceous	mostly carbon
conglomerate	coarse mechanical	angular rock fragments
dolomite	calcareous	calcium and magnesium carbonate
flint	siliceous	silicon dioxide
greywacke	medium mechanical	silicon dioxide with aluminosilicate
grit	medium mechanical	silicon dioxide
gypsum	saline	calcium sulphate
ironstone	ferruginous	iron mineral and calcium carbonate
mudstone	fine mechanical	clay minerals
oölitic limestone	calcareous	calcium carbonate
rock phosphate	phosphatic	calcium phosphate
rock salt	saline	sodium chloride
sandstone	medium mechanical	silicon dioxide
shale	fine mechanical	clay minerals
siltstone	fine mechanical	clay minerals with silicon dioxide
tillite	coarse mechanical	rock fragments in shale or slate
travertine	calcareous	calcium carbonate

Rocks

Most Common Elements in Igneous Rocks

The commonest constituent elements given here are for basalt and granite respectively.

Rock type	Typical rocks	Commonest constituent elements and percentages
extrusive	basalt, obsidian, perlite, pumice (derived from volcanic lava)	oxygen (44.6%), silicon (24.9%), aluminium (7.9%), calcium (7.8%), iron (7.7%), magnesium (4.0%)
intrusive	granite, gabbro, peridotite, syenite	oxygen (48.2%), silicon (34.0%), aluminium (7.4%), potassium (4.6%), sodium (2.4%)

Roman Numerals

Roman numeral	Arabic numeral	Roman numeral	Arabic numeral	Roman numeral	Arabic numeral
I	1	IX	9	LX	60
II	2	X	10	XC	90
III	3	XI	11	C	100
IV	4	XIX	19	CC	200
V	5	XX	20	CD	400
VI	6	XXX	30	D	500
VII	7	XL	40	CM	900
VIII	8	L	50	M	1,000

Saturn
Major Satellites

Satellite	Year of discovery	Diameter (km/mi)	Mean distance from Saturn (km/mi)
Titan	1655	5,150/3,200	1,222,000/759,315
Iapetus	1671	1,460/907	3,561,000/2,212,702
Rhea	1672	1,530/950	527,000/327,462
Dione	1684	1,120/696	377,000/234,257
Tethys	1684	1,050/652	295,000/183,304
Enceladus	1789	500/310	238,000/147,886
Mimas	1789	390/242	186,000/115,575
Hyperion	1848	shape irregular 410/255 × 260/162 × 220/137	1,481,000/920,251
Phoebe	1898	220/137	12,950,000/8,046,754

Search Engines
Some Popular Search Engines

Search engine	Web address	Description
AltaVista	http://www.altavista.digital.com	funded by DEC; select word search
Infoseek	http://www.infoseek.com	powerful engine searches whole Web or focuses on 9 major topic sections; provides related sites
Lycos	http://www.lycos.com	extensive index of documents, including by words in title, headings, subheadings and hyperlinks
UK Index	http://www.ukindex.co.uk	database of almost exclusively UK sites with vetted selection
WebCrawler	http://www.webcrawler.com	database created using spider (automated search routine)
Yahoo!	http://www.yahoo.com	search-tree offering constant refinement

Search Engines
Top 20 Terms Searched in 2000

Search terms

Britney Spears
Dragonball (cartoon)
Pokémon
WWF (wrestling)
'N Sync
Pamela Anderson
tattoos
Napster
Jennifer Lopez
Sydney Olympics
NFL (National Football League)
election 2000
Las Vegas
Backstreet Boys
Eminem
Christmas
Final Fantasy (game)
Anna Kournikova
halloween
marijuana

Seawater
Most Common Elements in Seawater

Element	Average percentage by volume
oxygen	85.7000
hydrogen	10.7000
chlorine	1.9000
sodium	1.1000
sulphur	0.0900
calcium	0.0400
potassium	0.0400
bromine	0.0070
carbon	0.0030
strontium	0.0008

Seven Wonders of the Ancient World

Structure	Date
The Pyramid of Khufu (Cheops)	c. 2700 BC
The Hanging Gardens of Babylon	6th century BC
The Statue of Zeus at Olympia	462 BC
The Temple of Diana (Artemis) at Ephesus	4th century BC
The Mausoleum at Halicarnassus	353 BC
The Colossus of Rhodes	c. 280 BC
The Pharos (Lighthouse) of Alexandria	c. 240 BC

SI Units
Base Units

Quantity	SI unit	Symbol	Quantity	SI unit	Symbol
length	metre	m	temperature, thermodynamic	kelvin	K
mass	kilogram	kg			
time	second	s	amount of substance	mole	mol
electric current	ampere	A	luminous intensity	candela	cd

SI Units
Derived Units

Quantity	SI unit	Symbol	Quantity	SI unit	Symbol
absorbed radiation dose	gray	Gy	plane angle	radian	rad
			potential difference	volt	V
electric capacitance	farad	F	power	watt	W
electric charge	coulomb	C	pressure	pascal	Pa
electric conductance	siemens	S	radiation dose equivalent	sievert	Sv
energy or work	joule	J			
force	newton	N	radiation exposure	roentgen	R
frequency	hertz	Hz	radioactivity	becquerel	Bq
illuminance	lux	lx	resistance	ohm	Ω
inductance	henry	H	solid angle	steradian	sr
luminous flux	lumen	lm	sound intensity	decibel	dB
magnetic flux	weber	Wb	temperature	degree Celsius	°C
magnetic flux density	tesla	T			

Software Suites

Package	Manufacturer	Description
ClarisWorks	Claris	includes word processor, spreadsheet, database, and paint and draw programs; flexible and creative document design
Microsoft Works	Microsoft	includes Wizards to help create the required document; pre-installed on many new PCs
Perfect Works	Corel	includes paint and draw packages

Solids

Densities of Some Common Solids

Substance	Density (kg per cubic m)
balsa wood	200
oak	700
butter	900
ice	920
ebony	1,200
sand (dry)	1,600
concrete	2,400
aluminium	2,700
steel	7,800
copper	8,900
lead	11,300
uranium	19,000

Sound

The Decibel Scale

The decibel (dB) scale is used to measure relative sound intensities. One decibel is about the smallest change the human ear can detect.

Decibels	Typical sound
0	threshold of human hearing
10	quiet whisper
20	average whisper
20–50	quiet conversation
40–45	light traffic
50–65	loud conversation
65–70	traffic on busy street
65–90	train
75–80	factory (light/medium work)
90	heavy traffic
90–100	thunder
110–140	jet aircraft at take-off
130	threshold of pain for humans
140–190	space rocket at take-off

Space Flight
Astronauts who Have Made the Most Space Flights and Walks

As of March 2000.

Record	Name (number)	Record	Name (number)
Space flights		women	Bonnie Dunbar (5)
men	Curt Brown (6)		Tamara Jernigan (5)
	Franklin Chang-Díaz (6)		Shannon Lucid (5)
	Story Musgrave (6)		Janice Voss (5)
	Jerry Ross (6)	**Spacewalks**	
	John Young (6)	men	Anatoli Solovyov (14)
		women	Kathryn Thornton (3)

Space Flight
Longest Space Flights

Duration (days)	Name	Country	Spacecraft
Men			
437	Valeri Poliakov	USSR/Russia/CIS	*Soyuz* TM18/*Mir*/TM20
365	Musa Manarov	USSR/Russia/CIS	*Soyuz* TM4/*Mir*/TM6
365	Vladimir Titov	USSR/Russia/CIS	*Soyuz* TM4/*Mir*/TM6
326	Yuri Romanenko	USSR	*Soyuz* TM2/*Mir*/TM3
311	Sergei Krikalyov	USSR/Russia/CIS	*Soyuz* TM12/*Mir*/TM13
240	Valeri Poliakov	USSR/Russia/CIS	*Soyuz* TM6/*Mir*/TM7
237	Vladimir Solovyov	USSR	*Soyuz* T10b/*Salyut 7*/T11
237	Oleg Atkov	USSR	*Soyuz* T10b/*Salyut 7*/T11
237	Leonid Kizim	USSR	*Soyuz* T10b/*Salyut 7*/T11
Women			
188	Shannon Lucid	USA	Space Shuttle *Atlantis* STS 76/*Mir*/STS 79
169	Yelena Kondakova	Russia/CIS	*Soyuz* TM20/*Mir*

Space Flight
Notable Uncrewed Flights

Date	Remarks
Interplanetary missions	
February 1999	launch of US *Stardust* to collect particles from the tail of Comet Wild-2 in January 2004
January 1999	launch of US *Mars Polar Lander* to survey the planet's south pole and search for subsurface water ice
December 1998	launch of US *Mars Climate Orbiter* to survey the surface and climate around Mars's south pole
November 1997	launch of probe to orbit Saturn
December 1995	first craft to enter Jupiter's atmosphere
Satellites	
July 1998	first satellites to be launched from a submarine
April 1990	first optical telescope in orbit, Hubble Space Telescope
December 1988	first commercial TV satellite, Astra 1A
September 1988	first Israeli satellite launch
February 1986	first commercial, remote-sensing craft

Space Flight
World Space Budgets

USA and Russia figures include military space expenditures; European figures do not.

Country	Budget (1996) (US$ million)	Country	Budget (1996) (US$ million)
USA	30,570.0	Russian Federation	700.0
Europe	4,594.7	Canada	272.3
Japan	2,263.7		

Space Flights
Some Recent Space Flights

Launch date	Spacecraft	Remarks
23 July 1999	*Columbia* STS 93	first female command of a space shuttle flight
20 February 1999	*Soyuz* TM29	probably the last mission to *Mir*
4 December 1998	*Endeavour* STS 88	first International Space Station (ISS) assembly mission
29 October 1998	*Discovery* STS 95	included the world's oldest astronaut, at 77 years old
13 August 1998	*Soyuz* TM28	delivered new crew for *Mir* and unsuccessfully attempted to unfurl a foil mirror to reflect sunlight onto Arctic cities during the dark winter months

Launch date	Spacecraft	Remarks
2 June 1998	*Discovery* STS 91	final Shuttle/*Mir* mission
17 April 1998	*Columbia* STS 90	final scheduled *Spacelab* mission, carrying out experiments on the neurological effects of microgravity
29 January 1998	*Soyuz* TM27	new crew for *Mir*
23 January 1998	*Endeavour* STS 89	Shuttle/*Mir* mission 8
26 September 1997	*Atlantis* STS 86	Shuttle/*Mir* mission 7

Space Probes
First Probes to the Moon

Spacecraft and country	Year	Details
Luna 1 [Lunik 1] (USSR)	1959	missed the moon. Entered solar orbit
Pioneer 4 (USA)	1959	flew past the Moon and entered solar orbit
Luna 2 (USSR)	1959	deliberately crashed onto the Moon's surface
Luna 3 (USSR)	1959	flew past the Moon and sent back the first photographs of the far side
Ranger 1 (USA)	1961	failed to leave Earth orbit
Ranger 2 (USA)	1961	failed to leave Earth orbit
Ranger 3 (USA)	1962	lost contact with Earth. Missed the Moon
Ranger 4 (USA)	1962	technical failure. Crashed onto the Moon
Ranger 5 (USA)	1962	lost contact with Earth. Missed the Moon
Luna 4 (USSR)	1963	entered orbit around the Earth–Moon system

Space Shuttle
Recent Missions

Date	Shuttle	Remarks
23 January 1998	*Endeavour* STS 89	eighth shuttle/*Mir* mission
19 November 1997	*Columbia* STS 87	science flight, two spacewalks
26 September 1997	*Atlantis* STS 86	seventh shuttle/*Mir* mission
7 August 1997	*Discovery* STS 85	Earth observation, science mission
1 July 1997	*Columbia* STS 84	reflight of the STS 83 mission; fastest return to space for any space travellers and first complete reflight of an entire crew
15 May 1997	*Atlantis* STS 84	sixth shuttle/*Mir* mission
4 April 1997	*Columbia* STS 83	Microgravity Science Laboratory mission; aborted after fuel cell fault
11 February 1997	*Discovery* STS 82	second mission to service the Hubble Space Telescope
12 January 1997	*Atlantis* STS 81	fifth shuttle/*Mir* mission
19 November 1996	*Columbia* STS 80	longest shuttle mission
16 September 1996	*Atlantis* STS 79	fourth shuttle/*Mir* mission

Spacewalks
Longest

As of March 1999.

Duration	Name(s)	Country	Date
8 hr 29 min	Tom Akers, Rick Hieb, Pierre Thuot	USA	13 May 1992
7 hr 54 min	Jeff Hoffman, Story Musgrave	USA	12 May 1993
7 hr 45 min	Tom Akers, Kathryn Thornton	USA	14 May 1992
7 hr 43 min	Takao Doi, Winston Scott	USA	24 November 1997
7 hr 37 min	Eugene Cernan, Jack Schmitt	USA	12 December 1972
7 hr 37 min	Jim Newman, Jerry Ross	USA	7 December 1998
7 hr 28 min	Gregory Harbaugh, Joe Tanner	USA	14 February 1997

Spacewalks
Most Experienced Spacewalkers

Total duration of spacewalks	Name	Remarks
Men		
68 hr 58 min	Anatoli Solovyov	14 spacewalks
29 hr 44 min	Tom Akers	4 spacewalks
8 hr 22 min	Thomas Reiter	2 spacewalks
Women		
21 hr 15 min	Kathryn Thornton	3 spacewalks
Longest Time on Moon		
3 days 2 hr 59 min	Eugene Cernan, Jack Schmitt	including 22 hr 5 min in three moonwalks

Spreadsheet Programs

Software	Manufacturer	Description
1–2–3	Lotus	long-established and full-featured; able to work with e-mail programs, strong on complex analyses
Excel	Microsoft	powerful and user-friendly; with built-in functions and Wizards
Quattro Pro	Corel	extensive built-in functions; good value; provides visual representation of formulae

Stars

Brightest Stars

Astronomical name	Common name	Distance from Sun (light-years)
Alpha Canis Majoris	Sirius	9
Alpha Carinae	Canopus	1,170
Alpha Centauri	Rigil Kent	4
Alpha Boötis	Arcturus	36
Alpha Lyrae	Vega	26
Alpha Aurigae	Capella	42
Beta Orionis	Rigel	910
Alpha Canis Minoris	Procyon	11
Alpha Eridani	Achernar	85
Alpha Orionis	Betelgeuse	310

Sun

Most Common Elements in the Sun

Element	Average percentage by volume
hydrogen	92.1000
helium	7.8000
oxygen	0.0610
carbon	0.0300
nitrogen	0.0084
neon	0.0076
iron	0.0037
silicon	0.0031
magnesium	0.0024

Telephones

Ownership of Telephones in Selected Countries

Country	Total number of lines (thousands)	Per hundred inhabitants	Country	Total number of lines (thousands)	Per hundred inhabitants
Luxembourg	293	69.2	Singapore	1,778	56.2
Sweden	5,965	67.4	UK	32,829	55.7
USA	179,822	66.1	Australia	9,540	50.9
Canada	19,206	63.5	Japan	63,580	50.3
Germany	46,530	56.7	Argentina	7,132	19.7

Telescopes

Largest Ground-based Telescopes

Name of telescope	Dimensions	Location
Keck I	10 m segmented optical mirror	Mauna Kea, Hawaii
Keck II	10 m segmented optical mirror	Mauna Kea, Hawaii
Columbus	2 × 8.4 m honeycomb-back optical mirrors	to be announced
Gemini Northern	8 m thin meniscus optical mirror	Mauna Kea, Hawaii
Gemini Southern	8 m thin meniscus optical mirror	Cerro Pachon, Chile
Subaru ('Pleiades')	8 m thin meniscus optical mirror	Mauna Kea, Hawaii
Magellan	6.5 m honeycomb-back optical mirror	Las Campanas, Chile
Very Large Telescope (VLT)	4 × 8 m optical array	Cerro Paranal, Chile
Big Optical Array (BOA)	6 × 0.5 m optical array, 70 m max. baseline	Flagstaff, Arizona

(continued)

Telescopes: Largest Ground-based Telescopes (*continued*)

Name of telescope	Dimensions	Location
CHARA Array	7 × 1 m optical array, 400 m max. baseline	to be announced
Millimetre Array (MMA)	40 × 8 m radio array, 3 km max. baseline	to be announced
Very Long Baseline Array (VLBA)	10 × 25 m radio array, 8,000 km max. baseline	from Hawaii to St Croix
Multiple Mirror Telescope Conversion	6.5 m honeycomb-back optical mirror	Tucson, Arizona

Telescopes
Major New Telescopes and Observatories

Observatory/Telescope	Location	Year opened
Gemini 8-Metre Telescopes Project	Mauna Kea (HI), USA; Cerro Pachon, Chile	1999; 2001
European Southern Observatory	La Silla, Chile	1999
Green Bank Telescope	Green Bank, Pocahontas County (WV), USA	1999
Subaru ('Pleiades')	Mauna Kea (HI), USA	1999
Very Large Telescope (VLT)	Cerro Paranal, Chile	1999
Magellan	Las Campanas, Chile	1997
McDonald Observatory	Davis Mountains (TX), USA	1997
Dominion Radio Astrophysical Observatory	Penticton, British Columbia, Canada	1996
Keck II	Mauna Kea (HI), USA	1996
Multiple Mirror Telescope	Mt Hopkins (AZ), USA	1996
Mauna Kea	Mauna Kea (HI), USA	1990 and 1996

Time Zones
Time in US Cities

At 12:00 noon, Eastern Standard Time (EST), the standard time in US cities is as follows:

City	Time	City	Time
Boston (MA)	12:00	Miami (FL)	12:00
Chicago (IL)	11:00	New Orleans (LA)	11:00
Dallas (TX)	11:00	New York (NY)	12:00
Denver (CO)	10:00	San Francisco (CA)	09:00
Los Angeles (CA)	09:00	Washington, DC	12:00

Time Zones
Times in World Cities

The surface of the earth is divided into 24 time zones. Each zone represents 15° of longitude or 1 hour of time. At 12:00 noon, GMT, the standard time elsewhere around the world is as follows:

City	Time	City	Time
Athens, Greece	14:00	New York (NY), USA	07:00
Cape Town, South Africa	14:00	Paris, France	13:00
Delhi, India	17:30	Perth, Australia	20:00
Hong Kong, China	20:00	Rio de Janeiro, Brazil	09:00
London, England	12:00	Sydney, Australia	22:00
Mexico City, Mexico	06:00	Tehran, Iran	15:30
Moscow, Russian Federation	15:00	Tokyo, Japan	21:00

Time Zones
Zones in the USA

Time zone	Hours behind GMT
Atlantic Standard Time	4
Eastern Standard Time	5
Central Standard Time	6
Mountain Standard Time	7
Pacific Standard Time	8
Alaska Standard Time	9
Hawaii/Aleutian Standard Time	10

Tin
Countries that Consume the Most Tin

Country	Annual consumption (thousand tonnes)
USA	35
Japan	30
China	25
Germany	20
Former USSR	15
France	10
Korea, South	10
Netherlands	10
UK	10
Thailand	5

Tin
Countries that Produce the Most Tin

Country	Annual production (thousand tonnes)
China	45
Indonesia	30
Peru	20
Brazil	15
Bolivia	15
Malaysia	5
Australia	5
Former USSR	5
Portugal	5
Thailand	5

Tunnels
World's Longest Railway Tunnels

Tunnel	Location	Length (km/mi)
Seikan	Japan	54/34
Channel Tunnel	UK–France	50/31
Dai-Shimizu	Japan	22/14
Simplon Nos 1 and 2	Switzerland–Italy	20/12
Shin-Kanmon	Japan	19/12
Apennine	Italy	19/12
Rokko	Japan	16/10
Sciliar	Italy	16/10
Haruna	Japan	15/9
Furka	Switzerland	15/9

Tunnels
World's Longest Road Tunnels

Tunnel	Location	Length (km/mi)	Tunnel	Location	Length (km/mi)
Saint Gotthard	Switzerland	16.3/10.1	Gudvangen	Norway	11.4/7.0
Arlberg	Austria	14.0/8.7	Kan-Etsu	Japan	11.0/6.8
Fréjus	France–Italy	12.9/8.0	Gran Sasso	Italy	10.0/6.2
Mont Blanc	France–Italy	11.7/7.3	Seelisberg	Switzerland	9.3/5.8

Universe
Most Common Elements in the Universe

Element	Percentage by volume
hydrogen	87.0
helium	12.0
oxygen	0.06
carbon	0.03
neon	0.02
nitrogen	0.008
silicon	0.003
iron	0.002
sulphur	0.002

Web Sites
Most Popular in the USA

Web site	Visitors in August 2000 (millions)
AOL sites	81
Yahoo!	55
Microsoft sites	54
Excite Network	31
Lycos	30
About The Human Internet	21
Amazon	21
CNET sites	20
eBay	20
Walt Disney sites	20

Web Sites
Most Visited

Web site	Number of visitors (August 2000)	Web site	Number of visitors (August 2000)
msn.com	82,931,000	go.com	23,628,000
aol.com	81,252,000	about.com	19,814,000
yahoo.com	78,806,000	altavista.com	19,522,000
lycos.com	46,836,000	real.com	18,309,000
excite.com	34,323,000	amazon.com	16,015,000

Wind
The Beaufort Wind Scale

The Beaufort scale is a system of recording wind velocity (speed) devised in 1806 by Francis Beaufort. It is a numerical scale ranging from 0 to 12, calm being indicated by 0 and a hurricane by 12.

Force	Description	Features	Air speed (kph/mph)
0	calm	smoke rises vertically; water smooth	0–2/0–1.2
1	light air	smoke shows wind direction; water ruffled	2–5/1.2–3.1
2	light breeze	leaves rustle; wind felt on face	6–11/3.7–6.8
3	gentle breeze	loose paper blows around	12–19/7.4–11.8
4	moderate breeze	branches sway	20–29/12.4–18.0
5	fresh breeze	small trees sway, leaves blown off	30–39/18.6–24.2
6	strong breeze	whistling in telephone wires; sea spray from waves	40–50/24.8–31.0
7	near gale	large trees sway	51–61/31.6–38.0
8	gale	twigs break from trees	62–74/38.5–46.0
9	strong gale	branches break from trees	75–87/46.6–54.1
10	storm	trees uprooted; weak buildings collapse	88–101/55.0–62.8
11	violent storm	widespread damage	102–117/63.4–72.7
12	hurricane	widespread structural damage	above 118/73.3

Wind
Wind Chill Index

To determine wind chill, find the outside air temperature on the top line, then read down the column to the measured wind speed in miles per hour. The point at which the two axes intersect provides the wind chill. A wind chill value of –20°F presents little danger. A wind chill value between –21 and –74°F may cause flesh to freeze within a minute. A wind chill value of –75°F and below may cause flesh to freeze within 30 seconds.

Wind speed (mph)	Wind chill chart Temperature (°F)								
	20	15	10	5	0	–5	–10	–15	–20
0	20	15	10	5	0	–5	–10	–15	–20

(continued)

Wind: Wind Chill Index (*continued*)

Wind speed (mph)	Temperature (°F)								
	20	**15**	**10**	**5**	**0**	**−5**	**−10**	**−15**	**−20**
5	16	11	6	1	−5	−10	−16	−21	−26
10	4	−3	−9	−15	−22	−28	−34	−40	−46
15	5	−12	−19	−25	−32	−39	−45	−52	−59
20	−11	−18	−25	−32	−39	−47	−54	−61	−60
25	−15	−22	−30	−37	−45	−52	−60	−67	−74
30	−18	−26	−33	−41	−49	−56	−64	−72	−79
35	−20	−28	−36	−44	−52	−59	−67	−75	−83
40	−22	−30	−38	−46	−54	−61	−69	−77	−85
45	−23	−31	−39	−47	−55	−63	−71	−79	−87

Word Processing Programs

Software	Manufacturer	Description
TopCopy	Top Level	professional program; provides integration with database and accounts
Word	Microsoft	market leader; powerful and easy to use with sophisticated spell checking
Word Pro	Lotus	formerly Ami Pro; good value program; strong on tabling and charting
WordPerfect	Corel	full-featured, including format and spell checking; customizable interface

Zinc
Countries that Consume the Most Zinc

Country	Annual consumption (thousand tonnes)
USA	1,120
Japan	720
China	610
Germany	530
Italy	340
Former USSR	330
France	300
Korea, South	260
Belgium	230
Australia	220

Zinc
Countries that Produce the Most Zinc

Country	Annual production (thousand tonnes)
Canada	1,010
Australia	940
China	900
Peru	600
USA	510
Mexico	370
Sweden	170
Kazakhstan	250
Korea, North	210
Ireland, Republic of	210

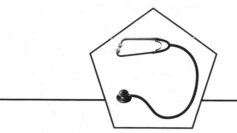

Health
and the
Human Body

Accidents

Worst Countries for Accidental Deaths

Country	Deaths per 100,000 population
Estonia	154
Lithuania	121
South Africa	99
Hungary	74
Latvia	72
Moldova	72
Czech Republic	61
South Korea	60
Romania	57
Slovenia	55

Activities

Energy Requirements for Various Activities

Figures are for a 70-kg adult male; female values are 10% less.

Activity	Energy required (kilojoules per hour)
lying down/sleeping	19
sitting/reading	24
typing/driving a car	29
standing	33
walking	40
cycling	50
digging/rowing	72
riding a horse	84

AIDS

Countries with Most Victims

Country	Percentage of population with HIV/AIDS
Botswana	35.8
Zimbabwe	25.1
Zambia	20.0
South Africa	19.9
Kenya	14.0

AIDS

Life Expectancy of Victims

Country	Disability adjusted life expectancy (years)
Japan	74.5
Australia	73.2
France	73.1
Sweden	73.0
UK	71.7
USA	70.0
Russia	61.3
Sierra Leone	25.9

Alcohol

World's Heaviest Drinkers

Country	Consumption per person per year (litres/pints)	Country	Consumption per person per year (litres/pints)
Luxembourg	12.1/21.3	Austria	9.8/17.2
France	11.3/19.9	Spain	9.5/16.7
Portugal	11.0/19.4	Belgium	9.1/16.0
Germany	10.0/17.6	Ireland	8.9/15.7
Denmark	9.9/17.4	Greece	9.8/15.5

Allergies
Common Allergies

Allergy	Cause	Symptoms/comments
pollen allergy (hay fever)	mainly grass and tree pollen	running eyes and nose, sneezing, nasal congestion, eczema, nettlerash or hives, and asthma
pet allergy	allergens in the pet's saliva, urine, or skin flakes, carried on its fur	symptoms as above
insect bite or sting allergy	proteins in the venom	severe and prolonged swelling at the site of the sting, pain, and – in extreme cases – anaphylactic shock (respiratory difficulties, a rapid fall in blood pressure, and collapse, followed by loss of consciousness and even death)
food allergy	most commonly to proteins in dairy foods, eggs, peanuts, true nuts, wheat and soya products, and shellfish	eczema, urticaria, asthma, itching around the mouth, vomiting, diarrhoea, and – in extreme cases – anaphylactic shock (see above); peanut allergies affect about 0.5% of the UK population
drug allergy	most commonly to the antibiotics penicillin and tetracycline and local anaesthetics	fever, itchy nose, throat or ears, and flushed skin; symptoms of a stronger reaction may include coughing, swelling – especially of the eyes or tongue – and a bluish tint of the skin

Alternative Therapies

Therapy	Description
acupuncture	inserting needles into the skin
Alexander technique	adjusting posture
aromatherapy	using pleasant-smelling oils
chiropractic	manipulating the spine
herbalism	using herbal extracts
homeopathy	using minute doses of drugs or natural substances
moxibustion	burning moxa (mudwort) near the skin
naturopathy	using natural remedies
osteopathy	manipulating bones and joints
reflexology	using foot massage
shiatsu	using finger pressure (sometimes with massage)

Anatomy
Life of Body Cells

Type of cell	Average lifetime
blood platelets	10 days
bone cells	90 days
brain cells	over 90 years
liver cells	40 days
red blood cells	120–130 days
skin cells	30 days
stomach cells	5 days
white blood cells	over 1 year

Barrels
Capacity of Barrels

Name	Quantity (gallons)
pin	4.5
keg	5–10
bushel	8
firkin	9
kilderkin	18
barrel	36
hogshead	54
puncheon	72
pipe	105
butt	110
tun	210

Beer
World's Biggest Drinkers

Country	Amount drunk per person per year (litres/pints)
Czech Republic	155/273
Germany	138/243
Ireland	134/236
Denmark	118/208
Austria	116/206

Blood
Common Disorders of the Blood

Name	Description	Cause
anaemia	not enough red blood cells	lack of iron, haemorrhage, abnormal breakdown of red cells
aplastic anaemia	not enough of all blood cells	damaged bone marrow
haemophilia	excess bleeding	hereditary defect in platelets and clotting mechanism
hypertension	high blood pressure	cardiovascular, endocrine or kidney disease, or unknown
hypotension	low blood pressure	haemorrhage or fluid loss, heart or lung disease, allergies
leukaemia	excess white blood cells	overproduction of cells in bone marrow
megaloblastic anaemia	deformed red blood cells	vitamin deficiency
polycythemia	excess red blood cells	prolonged lack of oxygen
sickle-cell anaemia	distorted red blood cells	hereditary
thrombosis	excessive blood clotting	cardiovascular disease

Blood

Compatibility of Blood Groups

Blood group	Blood groups that can be received by this individual	Blood groups that can receive donations from this individual
A	A, O	A, AB
B	B, O	B, AB
AB	any	AB
O	O	any

Bones

Bones of the Human Body

Part of body	Number of bones
arm	30
leg	30
spine	26
ribs	24
skull	21
pectoral girdle	4
ear	3
breastbone	3
pelvic girdle	2
throat	1

Calories

High-calorie Foods

Food	Calories/joules per 100 grams/3.5 ounces of food
vegetable oil	900/3,768
butter	740/3,098
margarine	730/3,056
walnuts	695/2,909
brazil nuts	620/2,596
almonds	615/2,575
peanuts	570/2,386
plain chocolate	510/2,135
chocolate biscuits (digestive)	505/2,114
biscuits (digestive)	485/2,030

Calories

Low-calorie Foods

Food	Calories/joules per 100 grams/3.5 ounces of food
cabbage (cooked)	11/46
lettuce (raw)	12/50
aubergine (eggplant) (cooked)	14/59
courgettes (zucchini) (cooked)	14/59
green peppers (raw)	14/59
mushrooms (raw)	14/59
tomato (raw)	14/59
turnip (cooked)	14/59
cucumber (raw)	15/63
swede (cooked)	18/75

Carbohydrate

High-carbohydrate Foods

Food	Carbohydrate in grams/ounces per 100 grams/3.5 ounces of food
sugar	100/3.5
white flour	80/2.8
dates	75/2.6
raisins	75/2.6
pasta (uncooked)	70/2.5
porridge	70/2.5
dried apricots	65/2.3
jam	65/2.3
plain chocolate	60/2.1
dried figs	50/1.8

Carbohydrate
Low-carbohydrate Foods

Food with no carbohydrate per 100 grams/ 3.5 ounces

beef steak
ham (no fat) (boiled)
lamb cutlet (grilled)
pork (no fat) (grilled)
poultry, white meat (roast)
prawns (cooked)
salmon (cooked)
shellfish (molluscs)
vegetable oil
white fish (cooked)

Champagne
World's Heaviest Drinkers

USA
UK
Germany
France
Belgium
Italy
Switzerland
Japan
Netherlands

Cheeses

Cheese	Country of origin	Cheese	Country of origin
Bel Paese	Italy	Gouda	Netherlands
Brie	France	Gruyère	Switzerland
Camembert	France	mozzarella	Italy
Danish blue	Denmark	Parmesan	Italy
Dolcelatte	Italy	Port Salut	France
Emmenthal	Switzerland	ricotta	Italy
feta	Greece	Roquefort	France
Gorgonzola	Italy	Tilsit	Germany

Chocolate
Nations Eating the Most

Country	Weight eaten per person per year (kg/lb)
Germany	3.53/7.78
UK	3.27/7.21
France	3.04/6.70
Canada	2.62/5.78
USA	2.46/5.42
Spain	1.77/3.90
Italy	1.59/3.50
Japan	0.99/2.18
Russia	0.81/1.79
Brazil	0.76/1.68

Coffee
World's Biggest Drinkers

Country	Amount drunk per person per year (kg/lb)
Finland	11.7/25.8
Denmark	11.2/24.7
Sweden	10.3/22.7
Netherlands	10.0/22.0
Norway	8.7/19.2
Switzerland	8.6/18.9
Belgium	7.8/17.2
Germany	7.2/15.9
Austria	6.6/14.6
France	5.7/12.6

Contraceptives
Most Reliable

Method	Reliability in practice (%)	Theoretical reliability (%)
female sterilization	99.9	100
male sterilization	99.5	100
injected pill	99.0	99.9
combined pill	99.0	99.99
sequential pill	98.5	99.99
mini-pill	97.6	99.3
interuterine coil (IUD)	96.0	99.0
diaphragm	92.0	97.0
condom	88.0	95.0
rhythm method	70.0	95.0
coitus interruptus	75.0	88.0

Cooking
Loss of Nutrients

Cooking method	Nutrients lost
steaming/pressure cooking	40–70% vitamin C, some vitamin B, and phosphorus
roasting	10–30% thiamin
baking	some vitamins B and C
microwaving	some vitamins B and C
dry heat	20–30% vitamin B

Cooking
Main Methods

Cooking method	Description
Moist heat	
broiling	direct heat over flame
pan broiling	heat through hot dry metal
sautéing	pan broiling with fat
deep frying	food is immersed in hot fat
shallow frying	fat is used to stop sticking
simmering	in pan with water below boiling point
stewing	prolonged simmering
fricaséeing	sauté and stewing
devilling	grilling or frying after coating food
steaming	cooking by steam
pressure cooking	by steam at above 100°C under pressure
Dry heat	
baking	cooked in an oven, often with raising agent added
roasting	cooked in an oven
grilling	direct heat onto food
Microwave	
microwaving	microwaves cause oscillation of food molecules, which produces heat

Death
Commonest Causes by Percentage of World Total

There were 53.9 million deaths from all causes worldwide in 1998.

Cause	% of deaths
cardiovascular diseases	31
infectious diseases	25
cancers	13
injuries	11
respiratory and digestive	9
maternal	5
other	6

Death
Leading Causes by Number of Deaths

ischaemic heart disease
cancers
cerebrovascular disease
acute lower respiratory infection
HIV/AIDS
chronic obstructive pulmonary disease
diarrhoea and dysentery
perinatal diseases
tuberculosis
road traffic accidents
trachae and lung cancers

Diet
Main Dietary Minerals

Mineral	Main dietary sources	Major functions in the body
calcium	milk, cheese, green vegetables, dried legumes	constituent of bones and teeth; essential for nerve transmission, muscle contraction, and blood clotting
fluoride	drinking water, tea, seafoods	helps to keep bones and teeth healthy
iodine	seafoods, dairy products, many vegetables, iodized table salt	essential for healthy growth and development
iron	meat (especially liver), green vegetables, whole grains, eggs	constituent of haemoglobin; involved in energy metabolism

Diet: Main Dietary Minerals (*continued*)

Mineral	Main dietary sources	Major functions in the body
magnesium	whole grains, green vegetables	involved in protein synthesis
potassium	milk, meat, fruits	maintenance of acid–base balance, fluid balance, nerve transmission
zinc	widely distributed in foods	involved in digestion

Diet
Recommended Daily Nutrient Intake

Sex and age		Energy (kcal/kilojoules)	Protein (g/ounces)	Calcium (mg/ounces)	Iron (mg/ounces)
boys	1–8	1,580/6,615	39/1.4	600/0.021	8/0.0003
	9–17	2,600/10,885	65/2.3	670/0.024	12/0.0004
girls	1–8	1,500/6,280	37/1.3	600/0.021	8/0.0003
	9–17	2,120/8,876	52/1.8	670/0.024	12/0.0004
men	18–34	2,920/12,225	73/2.6	500/0.018	10/0.0004
	35–64	2,830/11,849	71/2.5	500/0.018	10/0.0004
	65–74+	2,275/9,525	57/2.0	500/0.018	10/0.0004
women	18–54	2,325/9,734	58/2.0	500/0.018	12/0.0004
	pregnant	2,400/10,048	60/2.1	1,200/0.042	13/0.0005
	55–74+	1,790/7,494	45/1.6	500/0.018	10/0.0004

Diseases and Disorders

Group	Subgroup	Examples
infectious and parasitic diseases	intestinal infectious diseases	cholera, typhoid, amoebiasis
	viral infections characterized by skin lesions	chickenpox, smallpox, measles, rubella,
diseases of the blood	nutritional anaemias	iron deficiency anaemia, vitamin B12 deficiency anaemia
	haemolytic anaemias	thalassaemia, sickle-cell disorder
nutritional and metabolic diseases	diabetes mellitus	insulin-dependent and non-insulin-dependent diabetes
	malnutrition	kwashiorkor, nutritional marasmus
	obesity and other hyperalimentation	obesity, localized adiposity
mental and behavioural disorders	disorders due to substance use	due to use of alcohol, cannabinoids, cocaine, hallucinogens, solvents, tobacco

(*continued*)

Diseases and Disorders (*continued*)

Group	Subgroup	Examples
	schizophrenia and delusional disorders	schizophrenia, delusional disorders, psychotic disorders
	symptoms associated with physiological and physical factors	eating disorders, sleep disorders, sexual dysfunction
diseases of the nervous system	extrapyramidal and movement	Parkinson's disease, dystonia disorders
	degenerative metabolic disorders of the nervous system	Alzheimer's disease
	episodic and paroxysmal disorders	epilepsy, migraine, other headache syndromes, sleep disorders
diseases of the circulatory system	hypertensive diseases	hypertension, hypertensive heart disease, hypertensive renal disease
	other forms of heart disease	acute pericarditis, cardiac arrhythmias, heart failure, cardiac arrest
	diseases of veins and lymph nodes	phlebitis, thrombophlebitis, thrombosis, varicose veins, haemorrhoids
diseases of the respiratory system	influenza and pneumonia	influenza, pneumonia
	chronic lower respiratory diseases	bronchitis (nonacute and nonchronic), emphysema, asthma

Diseases

Cases of Infectious Diseases in Selected Regions

Reported cases of selected diseases during the specified year

Region	AIDS (1996)	Tuberculosis (1996)	Malaria (1995)	Measles (1996)
Africa	15,091	440,189	11,984,132	188,667
Americas	62,722	205,488	946,638	1,585
Europe	17,692	194,698	92,061	139,362
Middle East	752	79,761	415,232	12,918
South East Asia	19,990	1,554,457	5,956,974	88,528
Western Pacific	1,280	832,137	545,327	68,562

Diseases
Fatal Infectious Diseases

Disease	Number of deaths (per year)
Caught from people	
ALR (acute lower respiratory infection)	3,745,000
gonorrhoea	not available
Hansen's disease (leprosy)	2,000
HIV/AIDS	2,300,000
measles	960,000
meningitis (bacterial)	50,000
polio	2,000
soft sore (VD chancroid)	not available
syphilis (VD)	not available
trachoma	not available
tuberculosis (TB)	2,910,000
viral hepatitis (hepatitis B)	605,000
whooping cough (pertussis)	410,000
Caught from animals	
Chagas' disease (trypanosomiasis via blood-sucking bugs)	45,000
breakbone fever (dengue via mosquitoes)	140,000
malaria (via mosquitoes)	2,500,000
leishmaniasis (via sand flies)	80,000
rabies (via dogs)	60,000
river blindness (onchocerciasis via flies)	45,000
sleeping sickness (trypanosomiasis via tsetse flies)	100,000
yellow fever (via mosquitoes)	30,000
Caught from food or water	
amoebiasis (amoebae)	70,000
ascariasis (nematode worms)	60,000
bilharzia (schistosomiasis)	20,000
cholera	10,000
dysentery (and other diarrhoeas)	2,455,000
hookworm disease	65,000
tetanus (neonatal)	275,000
trematode worm disease	10,000
trichuriasis (whipworms)	10,000

Diseases
Newly Recognized Infectious Diseases

Year of recognition	Agent	Disease/comments
1999	Nipah virus	encephalitis cases and deaths caused by the virus have almost exclusively occurred in persons in close contact with pigs

(*continued*)

Year of recognition	Agent	Disease/comments
1997	avian influenza	influenza; can cause Reye syndrome
1996	NvCJD	new variant Creutzfeldt-Jakob disease
1995	human herpes virus 8	associated with Kaposi's sarcoma in AIDS patients
1994	Sabia virus	Brazilian haemorrhagic fever
1993	*Encephalitozoon cuniculi*	disseminated disease
1993	Sin Nombre virus	Hantavirus pulmonary syndrome
1992	*Bartonella henselae*	cat-scratch disease causing flu-like fever; bacillary angiomatosis
1992	*Vibrio cholerae* 0139	new strain associated with epidemic cholera

Drugs
Common Drugs Derived from Plants

Plant	Drug	Use
Amazonian liana	curare	muscle relaxant
coca	cocaine	local anaesthetic
deadly nightshade (belladonna)	atropine	anticholinergic
foxglove	digitoxin, digitalis	cardiotonic
Mexican yam	diosgenin	birth control pill
mint, peppermint	menthol	rubefacient
opium poppy	codeine, morphine	analgesic (codeine is also antitussive)
Pacific yew	taxol	antitumour agent
recured thornapple	scopolamine	sedative
rosy periwinkle	vincristine, vinblastine	antileukaemia
tea, coffee, and kola nuts	caffeine	central nervous system stimulant
yellow cinchona	quinine	antimalarial, antipyretic

Drugs
Commonly Abused Drugs and Their Effects

Drug and class	Description	Effects	
		Short-term	Long-term
amphetamines, stimulant	synthetic drugs that stimulate the nervous system	paranoia, panic, anxiety, insomnia	addiction, mental illness, liver damage, depression
cannabis, hallucinogen	dried leaves or resinous substance produced from the cannabis plant	paranoia, anxiety	forgetfulness, confusion

Drugs: Commonly Abused Drugs and Their Effects (*continued*)

Drug and class	Description	Effects	
		Short-term	**Long-term**
cocaine, stimulant	white powder derived from the coca tree	restlessness, nausea, insomnia	addiction, tolerance, weight loss, nasal damage
Ecstasy, stimulant	tablets of the modified amphetamine MDMA with psychedelic effects	anxiety, panic, depression, kidney failure	brain damage
heroin, analgesic	opiate powder derived from morphine	depression of breathing; risk of overdose	addiction, withdrawal symptoms; risk of infection with HIV from injecting
LSD (lysergic acid diethylamide), hallucinogen	synthetic hallucinogen derived from a fungus; odourless and colourless	anxiety, paranoia, unpleasant hallucinations, impaired judgement	mental illness, depression
magic mushrooms, hallucinogen	psilocybe mushrooms containing chemicals related to mescaline	visual distortion, nausea, vomiting, stomach pains	deaths have been reported
solvents, anaesthetic	aerosols and glues with effects similar to alcohol	confusion, nausea, suffocation, impaired judgement, heart failure	addiction, skin irritation, brain and lung damage

Eating

World's Biggest Eaters

Country	Calories/joules consumed per person per day
Denmark	3,810/15,952
USA	3,700/15,491
Portugal	3,660/15,324
Ireland	3,640/15,240
Greece	3,580/14,989
Belgium	3,545/14,842
Austria	3,540/14,821
France	3,535/14,800
Turkey	3,530/14,779
Italy	3,500/14,654

Epidemics

World's Worst Epidemics

Disease and place	Date	Number killed
Black Death in Eurasia	1347–51	75 million
influenza worldwide	1918–20	21.5 million
AIDS worldwide	1981–	6.5 million
plague in India	1896–1907	5 million
cholera worldwide	1893–94	several million

Eye

Eye Disorders

Medical name	Description	Medical name	Description
ambliopia	double vision	hypometropia	short-sightedness
ametropia	blurred vision	myopia	short-sightedness
astigmatism	distorted vision caused by incorrect lens curvature	nyctalopia	night-blindness
		presbyopia	long-sightedness of old age
diplopia	double vision	protanopsia	red/green colour blindness
hemeralopia	day-blindness		
hemianopia, hemiopia	blindness in half the visual field	xanthopsia	yellow-tinting of vision
hypermetropia	long-sightedness		

Fat

High-fat Foods

Food	Fat in grams per 100 grams/3.5 ounces of food
vegetable oil	100
butter	85
margarine	80
Brazil nuts	65
almonds	55
double cream	50
peanuts	45
potato crisps	40
cheese (Cheddar)	35
plain chocolate	30

Fertility

Countries with Highest Fertility Rates

(Fertility rate is average number of children per woman.)

Country	Fertility rate
Yemen	7.60
Oman	7.20
Niger	7.10
Uganda	7.10
Ethiopia	7.00
Somalia	7.00
Afghanistan	6.90
Maldives	6.80
Angola	6.69
Laos	6.69
Malawi	6.69

Fertility

Countries with Lowest Fertility Rates

(Fertility rate is average number of children per woman.)

Country	Fertility rate	Country	Fertility rate	Country	Fertility rate
Italy	1.19	Russia	1.35	Czech Republic	1.40
Spain	1.22	Greece	1.38	Hungary	1.40
Estonia	1.30	Ukraine	1.38	Latvia	1.40
Germany	1.30	Belarus	1.40	Romania	1.40
Slovenia	1.30	Bosnia-Herzegovina	1.40		

Fibre
High-fibre Foods

Food	Fibre in grams/ounces per 100 grams/3.5 ounces of food
haricot beans (cooked)	25/0.88
dried apricots	24/0.85
dried figs	19/0.67
raw almonds	15/0.53
chick peas (cooked)	15/0.53
raisins	14/0.49
potato crisps (not low-fat)	10/0.35
wholemeal bread	9/0.32
blackcurrants (raw)	9/0.32
Brazil nuts	9/0.32

Fish
World's Biggest Eaters

Country	Weight eaten per person per year (kg/lbs)
Maldives	308/139
Iceland	201/91
Faeroe Islands	191/87
Greenland	181/82
Kiribati	162/73
Japan	154/70
St Helena	154/70
Cook Island	136/62
Seychelles	131/59
Portugal	130/58

Height
Average Height of Young People

Age (years)	Male (cm/ft)	Female (cm/ft)	Age (years)	Male (cm/ft)	Female (cm/ft)
birth	55/1.8	55/1.8	10	136/4.5	136/4.5
2	85/2.8	84/2.8	12	145/4.8	145/4.8
4	100/3.3	98/3.2	14	156/5.1	155/5.1
6	115/3.8	112/3.7	16	170/5.6	161/5.3
8	125/4.1	125/4.1	18	175/5.7	165/5.4

Hormones
Major Hormones

Hormone	Gland	Functions
ACTH	pituitary gland	stimulates production of corticosteroids
ADH	pituitary gland	causes water retention by kidneys
adrenaline	adrenal glands	increases heart rate, breathing and blood flow to muscles; slows digestion and excretion
calcitonin	thyroid gland	regulates blood calcium levels
corticosteroids	adrenal glands	control salt and water levels; regulate use of food products
FSH	pituitary gland	causes maturation of ova in females, sperm production in males
glucagon	pancreas	regulates blood sugar levels
growth hormone	pituitary gland	regulates growth

(continued)

 Health and the Human Body **241**

Hormone	Gland	Functions
insulin	pancreas	regulates blood sugar levels
luteinizing hormone	pituitary gland	ovulation in females, testosterone production in males
oestrogen	ovaries	controls female secondary sexual characteristics
oxytocin	pituitary gland	produces contraction of womb in childbirth
parathormone	parathyroid glands	regulates blood calcium levels
progesterone	ovaries and placenta	prepares and maintains womb in pregnancy
prolactin	pituitary gland	controls milk production
testosterone	testes	controls male secondary sexual characteristics
TSH	pituitary gland	stimulates thyroid to release its hormones
thyroxine	thyroid gland	regulates growth and metabolism

Human Body
Component Statistics

Component	Measurement	Statistic
blood	volume	5 litres/9 pints (man), 4.3 litres/7.6 pints (woman)
red blood cells	number	25,000,000,000
white blood cells	number	25,000,000
nerves	total length	72 kilometres/45 miles (outside brain)
nerve cells	number in brain	10,000,000,000
hairs	number on scalp	2,000,000
skin	total area	1.75 square metres/2.09 square yards
lungs	internal area	70 square metres/84 square yards
taste buds	number on tongue	9,000
ova (eggs)	number at puberty	300,000
sperm	number produced in adult	200,000,000 per day
	number per ejaculation	400,000,000

Human Body
Composition

Chemical element or substance	Body weight (%)
water	60–80
oxygen	65
total solid material	20–40
protein	15–20
carbon	18
hydrogen	10
lipid	3–20
nitrogen	3
calcium	2
carbohydrate	1–15

Ice Cream
Countries Importing Most

France
UK
Germany
The Netherlands
Austria
Japan
Spain
Belgium-Luxembourg
Denmark
Italy

Life Expectancy
Countries with the Highest Female

Country	Life expectancy (years)
Japan	83
Liechtenstein	83
Monaco	83
Sweden	82
Switzerland	82
Australia	81
Belgium	81
Canada	81
France	81
Greece	81

Life Expectancy
Countries with the Highest Male

Country	Life expectancy (years)
Liechtenstein	78
Japan	77
Armenia	76
Costa Rica	76
Cyprus	76
Greece	76
Iceland	76
Sweden	76
Australia	75
Canada	75

Life Expectancy
Countries with the Lowest Female

Country	Life expectancy (years)
Sierra Leone	43
Uganda	44
Malawi	45
Afghanistan	46
Gambia	47
Guinea	47
Guinea-Bissau	47
Zambia	47
Burkina Faso	48
Mozambique	48

Life Expectancy
Countries with the Lowest Male

Country	Life expectancy (years)
Sierra Leone	40
Uganda	42
Guinea-Bissau	44
Malawi	44
Afghanistan	45
Burkina Faso	45
Gambia	45
Mozambique	45
Rwanda	45
Zambia	45

Manias

Type of mania	What you are mad about
bibliomania	books
dipsomania	alcoholic drinks
egomania	yourself
hypomania	anything to a mild extent
kleptomania	stealing
megalomania	your own importance
monomania	a single idea
nymphomania	sex (in females)
pyromania	setting fires
satyriasis	sex (heterosexual, in males)

Meat
World's Biggest Eaters

Country	Weight eaten per person per year (kg/lb)
USA	119/263
Cyprus	112/247
New Zealand	108/238
Australia	105/231
Spain	104/229
Bahamas	103/227
Austria	103/227
The Netherlands	101/223
Denmark	100/220
France	99/218

Medicine
Historical Treatments

Date	Technique	Condition	Where (by whom) pioneered
2600 BC	applying honey	wounds	Egypt
2100 BC	washing, bandaging, making plasters	wounds	Mesopotamia
2100 BC	scraping skull with knife	head diseases	Mesopotamia
400 BC	fresh air, good diet, exercise	helping body to heal itself	Hippocrates, Greece
157 AD	prescribing opposites, e.g. cool liquids and foods for fevers	various	Galen, Greece
6th century	uvula crushing	preventing haemorrhage	Greece
16th century	boiling oil or hot iron rod	wounds	Paracelsus, Germany
18th–19th century	cupping (removing unclean blood)	headaches to gout	universal
until 20th century	bone brush for removing skull dust after trepanning	epilepsy, insanity	universal
until 21st century	leeches	various	universal

Medicine
Major Breakthroughs

Date	Breakthrough	Pioneer	Nationality
1628	identification of blood circulation	William Harvey	English
1773	discovery of laughing gas	Joseph Priestley	English
1796	invention of vaccination	Edward Jenner	English
1816	invention of stethoscope	Rene T H Laennec	French
1846	discovery and first use of ether	Crawford Long, Horace Wells, William Morton, Charles Jackson	US
1864	germ theory of disease	Louis Pasteur	French
1896	invention of psychoanalysis	Sigmund Freud	Austrian
1899	discovery of aspirin	Bayer drug company	German
1928–1941	discovery and development of penicillin	Alexander Fleming, Howard Florey	Scottish, Australian
1960	first oral contraceptive pill	Gregory Pincus	US
1967	first heart transplant	Christiaan Barnard	South African
2000	unravelling of genome	several	international

Medicine
Medical Prefixes

Prefix	Meaning
arthr(o)-	joint
cardi(o)-	heart
cerebr(o)-	brain
dent-	tooth
derm-	skin
gastr(o)-	stomach
haem-	blood
nephr(o)-	kidney
neur(o)-	nerve
oculo/ophthalm(o)-	eye
oro-	mouth
osteo-	bone
ot(o)-	ear
pneumon-	lung

Medicine
Medical Suffixes

Suffix	Meaning
-aemia	condition of blood
-algia	pain
-cele	tumour, swelling
-derm	skin
-ectomy	surgical removal of
-itis	inflammation of
-oma	tumour
-osis	disease, condition
-penia	lack of, deficiency
-plasty	reconstructive surgery
-plegia	paralysis
-scopy	visual examination

Operations
To Remove Parts of the Body

Operation	Part removed	Operation	Part removed
apicectomy	part of a tooth's root	laryngectomy	larynx
appendicectomy	appendix	mastectomy	breast
cystectomy	urinary bladder	orchidectomy	testicle
gastrectomy	all or part of the stomach	pneumonectomy	all or part of the lung
hepatectomy	all or part of the liver	salpingectomy	oviduct (Fallopian tube)
hysterectomy	uterus (womb)	vasectomy	sperm duct (vas deferens)
iridectomy	part of the eye's iris		

Parasites
Human Parasites found in Europeans

Parasite	Disease (clinical name)	Disease (popular name)	Occurrence (per year)
Diphyllobothrium latum	diphyllobothriasis	tapeworm infection	9,000,000
Echinococcus sp. and *granulosis*	hydatidosis	various forms	1,005,000
Strongyloides stercoralis	strongyloidiasis	infection with hookworms and others	almost 2,000,000
Trichinella spiralis	trichinellosis	pork worm	1,500,000
Taenia solium	taeniasis/cysticercosis	tapeworm infection	sporadic
Plasmodium sp.	malaria	malaria	20,000
Giardia lamblia	giardiasis	infection of small intestine	10,000,000

Parasites

Human Parasites found in the USA

Parasite	Disease (clinical name)	Disease (popular name)	Occurrence (per year)
Entamoeba histolytica	amoebiasis	dysentery	2,983 (in 1984)
Balamuthia mandrillaris	amoebic encephalitis	brain inflammation	rare
Strongyloides stercoralis	strongyloidiasis	infection with hookworms and others	less than 1,000,000
Trichinella spiralis	trichinellosis	pork worm	fewer than 40
Taenia solium	taeniasis/cysticercosis	tapeworm infection	1,000
Plasmodium sp. and *falciparum*	malaria	malaria	910
Giardia lamblia	giardiasis	infection of small intestine	141
Cryptosporidium sp.	cryptospiridiosis	enteric disease	1,080 (1999)
Enterobius vermicularis	enterobiasis	worms	50,000,000
Echinococcus sp.	hydatidosis	various forms	7,100
Dirofilaria immitis	pulmonary dirofilariasis	heart/lung worm	118 (since 1961)

Pasta

Types

Name	Type	Name	Type
cannelloni	wide tubes	orzo	rice-grain shaped
conchiglie	cockleshell-shaped	ravioli	small square packets of meat
farfalle	butterfly-shaped		
fettucine	narrow ribbons	rigatoni	short fluted tubes
fusilli	twists or spirals	spaghetti	thin strands
lasagne	flat sheets	spaghettini	thin spaghetti
linguine	thin flat strands	stelline	star-shaped
lumache	snail-shell-shaped	tagliarini	very narrow strips
macaroni	small bent tubes	tagliatelle	narrow strips
manicotti	large tubes	tortellini	small ring-shaped packets of meat
mezzani	medium-sized tubes		
pappardelle	medium-sized strips	vermicelli	very thin strands
penne	short tubes	ziti	large curved tubes

Phobias
Animal Phobias

Fear	Name of phobia	Fear	Name of phobia
animals	zoophobia	insects	entomophobia
bees	apiphobia, melissophobia	lice	pediculophobia
birds	ornithophobia	mice	musophobia
cats	ailurophobia, gatophobia	parasites	parasitophobia
chickens	alektorophobia	snakes	ophidiophobia, ophiophobia
dogs	cynophobia		
fish	ichthyophobia	spiders	arachn(e)ophobia
horses	hippophobia	wasps	spheksophobia

Phobias
Unusual Phobias

Name of phobia	Meaning	Name of phobia	Meaning
arachibutyrophobia	fear of peanut butter sticking to roof of mouth	nebulaphobia	fear of fog
		novercaphobia	fear of stepmother
		oikophobia	fear of home surroundings
belonephobia	fear of pins and needles	panophobia	fear of everything
gymnophobia	fear of nudity	taphephobia	fear of being buried alive
hippopotomonstrosesquippedaliophobia	fear of long words		
		trichopathophobia	fear of hair
koinoniphobia	fear of rooms	venustraphobia	fear of beautiful women
laevophobia	fear of things to the left of the body	zemmiphobia	fear of the great mole rat

Poisons
Common Types of Poisons

Poison type	Poisons
corrosive poisons	hydrochloric acid, nitric acid, sodium hydroxide
systemic poisons	strychnine (rat poison), barbiturates, hydrocyanic acid
poisonous gases	mustard gas, carbon monoxide, chlorine, sulphur dioxide
irritant poisons	antimony, arsenic, cadmium, lead
poisonous foods	Japanese pufferfish, hemlock, amanita toadstools

Poisons

Lethal Doses of Common Poisons

Poison	Lethal dose for a 70-kg adult (grams/ounces)
amanita toadstool	variable; small piece can kill
ammonia	variable; small amount can kill
antihistamines	0.35–3.5/0.01–0.1
arsenic/antimony	0.35–3.5/0.01–0.1
aspirin	3.5–35/0.1–1.2
atropine	less than 0.35/0.01
barbiturates	3.5–35/0.1–1.2
borax	3.5–35/0.1–1.2
carbon monoxide	1.5% in the air
cyanide	less than 0.35/0.01
digitalis	3.5–35/0.1–1.2
glycol	less than 0.35/0.01
iodine	0.35–3.5/0.01–0.1
mercury salts	0.35–3.5/0.01–0.1
nicotine	less than 0.35/0.01
strychnine	less than 0.35/0.01
warfarin	3.5–35/0.1–1.2

Pollution

Indoor Air Pollutants and Human Health

Studies in Denmark and the USA have linked pollutants found in buildings with human symptoms such as dizziness, headaches, and fatigue. This is known as 'sick building syndrome'. New buildings are typically worse than old buildings, due to the release of chemicals from new furnishings, and reduced air exchange due to air conditioning.

Pollutant	Source	Potential threat
1,1,1-trichloroethane	aerosol sprays	dizziness, irregular breathing
asbestos	pipe insulation, ceiling and wall tiles	lung disease, lung cancer
carbon monoxide	faulty or unvented gas and paraffin heaters, wood stoves	headaches, drowsiness, irregular heartbeat; poisonous
formaldehyde	furniture stuffing, panelling, foam insulation	irritation of eyes, throat, skin, and lungs; dizziness
methylene chloride	paint strippers and thinners	nerve disorders, diabetes
styrene	carpets, plastic products	kidney and liver damage
sulphur dioxide	solid fuel heaters	in asthmatics, reduced lung function, chest tightness, and coughing
tetrachloroethylene	dry-cleaning-fluid fumes on clothes and carpets	nerve disorders, liver and kidney damage, cancer threat
tobacco smoke	cigarettes, cigars	lung cancer, respiratory ailments, heart disease

Prescriptions
Meanings and Abbreviations

This table is intended to give general information only. It should not be used to interpret prescriptions. Proper medical advice should be taken from other sources.

Abbreviation	Full form (Latin)	Meaning	Abbreviation	Full form (Latin)	Meaning
b.i.d.	*bis in die*	twice a day	m. et n.	*mane et nocte*	morning and night
b.i.n.	*bis in noctus*	twice a night	noct. maneq.	*nocte maneque*	night and morning
bis	*bis*	twice	omn. bid.	*omnibus bidendis*	every two days
d.d. in d.	*de die in diem*	from day to day	omn. bih.	*omni bihora*	every second hour
dieb. alt.	*diebus alternis*	every other day	omn. hor.	*omni hora*	every hour
dieb. tert.	*diebus tertiis*	every third day	omn. noct.	*omni nocte*	every night
dil.	*dilutus*	dilute(d)	part. aeq.	*partes aequales*	equal parts
e.m.p.	*ex modo prescripto*	as directed	p.o.	*per os*	by mouth
hor. 1 spat.	*horae unius spatio*	one hour's time	p.p.a.	*phiala prius agitata*	first shake the bottle
h.s.	*hora somni*	bedtime	ut. dict.	*ut dictum*	as directed

Protein
High-protein Foods

Food	Protein in grams/ounces per 100 grams/3.5 ounces of food	Food	Protein in grams/ounces per 100 grams/3.5 ounces of food
cheese (Edam)	30/1.06	cheese (Cheddar)	26/0.92
rump steak (grilled)	30/1.06	lamb cutlet (grilled)	25/0.88
pork chop (grilled)	28/0.99	mackerel	25/0.88
canned tuna (in brine)	28/0.99	minced beef	25/0.88
peanuts	26/0.92	turkey (roast)	25/0.88

Road Accidents
Some of the Worst Countries for Road Deaths

Country	Number of deaths per thousand people	Country	Number of deaths per thousand people
South Africa	130	Greece	21
Latvia	36	Poland	18
Portugal	25	USA	15
Russia	24	Spain	15
South Korea	23	France	15

Smoking
Countries with Most Female Smokers

Country	Smokers as % of female population (1997)
Denmark	37.0
Norway	35.5
Czech Republic	31.0
Fiji	30.6
Israel	30.0
Russian Federation	30.0
Canada	29.0
Netherlands	29.0
Poland	29.0
Greece	28.0
Iceland	28.0
Ireland	28.0
Papua New Guinea	28.0

Smoking
Countries with Most Male Smokers

Country	Smokers as % of male population (1997)
Korea, South	68.2
Latvia	67.0
Russian Federation	67.0
Dominican Republic	66.3
Tonga	65.0
Turkey	63.0
China	61.0
Bangladesh	60.0
Fiji	59.3
Japan	59.0

Spirits
Flavours in Spirits and Liqueurs

Drink	Chief flavouring	Drink	Chief flavouring
absinthe	wormwood	kummel	aniseed and cumin
anisette	aniseed/liquorice	maraschino	cherry
Benedictine	various herbs[1]	ouzo	aniseed
calvados	apple	Pernod	aniseed
chartreuse	various herbs[1]	piña colada	coconut and pineapple
Cointreau	orange		
crème de cacao	chocolate	schnapps	caraway seeds
crème-de-menthe	peppermint	slivovitz	plum
curaçao	bitter orange	Southern Comfort	peach
kirsch/kirschwasser	cherry	Tia Maria	coffee

[1]Actual formula is a trade secret.

Sugar
World's Biggest Producers

Country	Metric tons produced per year	Country	Metric tons produced per year
Israel	18,900	Mexico	4,500
Brazil	13,800	Australia	4,400
USA	7,700	Cuba	3,500
China	6,800	South Africa	2,800
Thailand	5,000	Turkey	2,700

Vitamins

Vitamin	Main dietary sources	Established benefit
A	dairy products, egg yolk, liver	aids growth; prevents night blindness; helps keep the skin resistant to infection
B_1	germ and bran of seeds and grains, yeast	essential for carbohydrate metabolism and health of nervous system
B_2	eggs, liver, milk, poultry, broccoli, mushrooms	involved in energy metabolism; protects skin, mouth, eyes, eyelids
B_6	meat, poultry, fish, fruits, nuts, whole grains, leafy vegetables	regulates the central nervous system; helps prevent anaemia, skin lesions, nerve damage
B_{12}	green leafy vegetables, liver, peanuts	helps protect against precancerous cell changes in the uterine cervix
C	citrus fruits, green vegetables, tomatoes, potatoes	prevents scurvy, loss of teeth; aids resistance to some types of virus and bacterial infections
D	liver, fish oil, dairy products, eggs	promotes growth and mineralization of bone
E	vegetable oils, eggs, butter, some cereals, nuts	prevents damage to cell membranes

Vitamins
Chemical Names for Vitamins

Vitamin	Chemical name
A	retinol
A_2	dehydroretinol
B_1	aneurin(e), thiamine[1]
B_2	riboflavin[1]
B_6	pyridoxine[1]
B_{12}	cyanocobalamin[1]
C	ascorbic acid
D_2	calciferol
D_3	cholecalciferol
E	tocopherol
H	biotin
K_1	phylloquinone
K_2	menaquinone
K_3	menadione
P	bioflavonoid, citrin

[1] Biotin, folic acid, and nicotinamide are also B complex vitamins.

Weight
Average Body Weight of Young People

Age (years)	Male (kg/lb)	Female (kg/lb)
birth	3.5/7.7	3.5/7.7
2	12.0/26.5	11.5/25.4
4	15.5/34.2	15.0/33.1
6	21.0/46.3	20.5/45.2
8	26.0/57.3	25.5/56.2
10	31.0/68.3	31.0/68.3
12	37.0/81.6	39.0/86.0
14	48.0/105.8	48.5/106.9
16	55.0/121.3	55.0/121.3
18	64.0/141.1	59.5/131.2

Weight
Healthy Weights for Men and Women

Height (cm/ft)	Men (kg/lb)	Women (kg/lb)
148/4.9		42–54/93–119
152/5.0		44–57/97–126
156/5.1		45–58/99–128
160/5.2	52–65/115–143	48–61/106–134
164/5.4	54–67/119–148	50–64/110–141
168/5.5	56–71/123–157	52–66/115–146
172/5.6	59–74/130–163	55–69/121–152
176/5.8	62–77/137–170	58–72/128–159
180/5.9	65–80/143–176	61–75/134–165
184/6.0	67–84/148–185	
188/6.2	71–88/157–194	
192/6.3	75–93/165–205	

Whisky
World's Biggest Scotch Drinkers

Country	Amount drunk (million bottles)
Spain	145
France	137
USA	117
Japan	60
Germany	34
Venezuela	34
South Korea	34
Greece	32
Australia	30
Thailand	28

Wine
World's Heaviest Wine Drinkers

Country	Consumption per year (litres)
France	63.5
Italy	59.6
Luxembourg	59.3
Portugal	57.7
Argentina	43.6

Animals, Plants,
and the
Environment

Abominable Snowman
Reported Sightings

Year of sighting	By whom	Location
1832	B H Hodson	Himalayas
1921	Col Howard-Bury	Himalayas
1923	Major Alan Cameron	Mt Everest
1925	N A Tombazi	Himalayan lower slopes
1938	Capt D'Auvergne	between Tibet and Nepal
1949	Sherpa Tenzing Norgay	Thyangboche
1951	Eric Shipton and Michael Ward	southwestern slopes of Menlung glacier
1970	Don Whillans	Mt Annapurna
1974	Sherpa girl	near Mt Everest
1986	Reinhold Messner	Himalayas

Agriculture
Annual World Output of Major Food Crops

Crop	Output (thousand tonnes per year)
apples	56,000
bananas	58,500
beans	57,000
cabbages	48,000
carrots	18,500
cocoa	3,000
coconuts	48,000
grapes	57,000
maize	620,000
onions	40,000
oranges	65,500
peas	7,000
pineapples	12,000
potatoes	245,000
rice	548,000
wheat	584,000

Agriculture
Annual World Output of Major Non-food Crops

Crop	Output (thousand tonnes per year)
castor oil beans	1,320
coir (coconut fibre)	655
cotton	19,000
flax	535
hemp	260
hops	120
jute	2,785
natural rubber	6,825
sisal	325
tobacco	7,000

Amphibians
Classification

Order	Number of species	Examples
Apoda	170	caecilians
Anura	4,000	frogs, toads
Urodela	390	axolotl, mudpuppies, newts, salamanders

Animal Noises

Animal noise	Animals	Animal noise	Animals
bark	dog, fox	gobble	turkey
bay	dog, hound	growl	bear, dog, lion, tiger
bell	deer, hound	grunt	pig
bellow	bull, stag	hiss	goose, snake
bleat	calf, lamb, sheep	howl	dog, wolf
boom	bittern	hum	bee
bray	donkey	juck	partridge
buzz	bee, fly	laugh	hyena
cackle	goose, chicken	low	cattle
call	stag	mew	kitten
caw	crow, rook	neigh	horse
chatter	jay, magpie	purr	cat
cheep	chicks	quack	duck
chirp	grasshopper, sparrow	roar	lion, tiger
cluck	chicken	scream	hawk, peafowl, vulture
coo	dove, pigeon	squeak	guinea pig, hare, mouse, pig
croak	frog, raven	squeal	pig
crow	cockerel	whine	dog
cuckoo	cuckoo	whinny	horse
drone	bee	yelp	dog, fox, puppy
gibber	ape, monkey		

Animal Young
Gestation Periods

Animal	Gestation (days)	Animal	Gestation (days)
ass	365	gorilla	257
bear	240	guinea pig	68
beaver	122	horse	330–342
buffalo	270	kangaroo	42
camel	410	lion	108
cat	58–65	moose	240–250
chimpanzee	230	mouse	19
chipmunk	31	pig	112–115
cow	279–292	rabbit	30–35
deer	201	rhinoceros	450
dog	58–70	sheep	144–151
elephant	645	squirrel	30–40
fox	52	tiger	105–113
giraffe	420–450	whale (sperm)	480–500
goat	145–155	zebra	365

Animal Young

Names for Young Animals

Name of young	Animal(s)	Name of young	Animal(s)
calf	cattle, elephant, giraffe, rhinoceros, whale	infant	chimpanzee
		kitten	cat, rabbit, skunk
chick	any bird	lamb	sheep
colt (male)	horse, zebra	leveret	hare
cub	badger, bear, cougar, fox, leopard, lion, seal, skunk, tiger, wolf	nestling	any bird
		owlet	owl
		joey	kangaroo
culch	oyster	kid	antelope, goat
cygnet	swan	parr	salmon
duckling	duck	piglet	pig
eaglet	eagle	poult	domestic fowl
elver	eel	pup	dog, seal
fawn	caribou, deer	puppy	coyote, dog
filly (female)	horse	smolt	salmon
fledgling	any bird	squab	pigeon, rook
foal	horse, zebra	tadpole	frog, toad
fry	fish	whelp	dog, seal, tiger, wolf
gosling	goose	yearling	horse
grig	eel		

Animals

Collective Names

Animal	Collective name	Animal	Collective name
ants	colony, swarm, nest	goldfinches	chirm, charm
badgers	cete	gorillas	band
bees	grist, swarm, hive, nest, colony	horses	pair, team, herd, stable
		hounds	pack, cry, mute
birds	flight, volery, flock	larks	exaltation
cats	clowder, clutter, litter	lions	pride
cattle	drove, herd	monkeys	troop
chicks	brood, clutch	oysters	bed
crows	murder	peafowl	muster, ostentation
deer	herd	piglets	litter
dogs	litter, kennel, pack (wild)	sheep	drove, flock, trip
ducks	brace, team, flock, paddling	swans	bevy, wedge
elephants	herd	termites	colony, nest, swarm
fishes	school, shoal, draught	vipers	nest
geese	flock, gaggle, skein	wolves	pack, rout
goats	tribe, trip, herd		

Animals
Community Names

Name	Animal(s)
army	caterpillars, frogs, toads
badling	ducks
bale	tortoises, turtles
band	gorillas, jays, monkeys
bevy	larks, pheasants, quails, deer, roes
bob	seals
brood	chickens, hens, etc.
busyness	ferrets, skunks
caravan	camels
cast	falcons, hawks
cete	badgers
charm	finches, nightingales
chattering	choughs, starlings
chine	polecats
clamour	rooks
cloud	gnats
colony	ants, gulls, etc.
company	widgeon
congregation	plovers
convocation	eagles
covert	coots
covey	grouse, partridges
desert	lapwings
dole	doves
dopping	sheldrakes
down	hares
drey (or dray)	squirrels
drift	bees
drove	cattle, horses, oxen
dule	doves, turtles
exaltation	larks
fall	woodcock
farrow	piglets
fesnying	ferrets
flight	doves, swallows, etc.
flush	mallards
gaggle	geese (on the ground or in water)
gam	whales
gang	elks
grist	bees
harem	seals
hive	bees
host	sparrows
hover	crows
husk	hares
kindle	kittens
knob	pochards, teal, toads, widgeon
knot	toads
labour	moles
lead	foxes
leap, lepe	leopards
leash	bucks
litter	cubs, kittens, piglets, puppies
mob	kangaroos
murder	crows
murmuration	starlings
muster	peafowl
mustering	storks
mutation	thrushes
ostentation	peafowl
nest	ants, mice, rabbits
nide	geese, pheasants
nye	pheasants
pace	asses, donkeys
paddling	ducks
parcel	deer, penguins
pitying	doves
plump	waterfowl, woodcocks
pod	seals, walruses, whales, whiting
pride	lions, peafowl
raft	coots, teal
rag	colts
richesse	martens
rookery	penguins, rooks, seals
rout	wolves
rush	pochards
school	dolphins, porpoises, whales
sedge, siege	bitterns, cranes, herons
shrewdness	apes
siege	herons
singular	boars
skein	geese (in flight)
skulk	foxes
sleuth, sloth	bears
sord	mallards (on land)
sounder	boars, swine

(continued)

Animals: Community Names (*continued*)

Name	Animal(s)	Name	Animal(s)
spring	teal	troop	antelopes, baboons, kangaroos, monkeys
string	camels, horses		
sute	mallards, wildfowl (on water)	unkindness	ravens
		watch	nightingales
swarm	bees, eels, flies, gnats	wedge	geese (in flight)
team	ducklings, ducks (in flight)	wing	plovers
tribe	goats	wisp	snipe

Animals
Deadly When Eaten

Animal	Location	Animal	Location
shore crab	Philippines	deadly-death pufferfish	tropical Pacific, Indian Ocean, Dead Sea
Asiatic horseshoe crab	southeast Asia		
Greenland shark	Arctic		
moray eel	Indo-Pacific	hawksbill turtle	tropical seas
red snapper	Indo-Pacific	leatherback turtle	temperate and tropical seas
		white whale	Arctic

Animals
Diet in the Wild

Animal	Diet	Quantity eaten (kg/day/ lb/day)
anaconda	can starve for years then swallow whole pig or deer	
armadillo	insects	can eat 40,000 ants in a sitting
bat (vampire)	blood of vertebrates (cows, sheep, horses)	5 spoonfuls
bear (polar)	seal, fish, grass	68–130/150–287
bear (koala)	eucalyptus leaves	0.5–1.0/1.1–2.2
camel	fruit, foliage, grass	27–36/60–79
elephant	fruit, foliage, grass	90–270/198–595
falcon	other birds, carrion	0.1/0.2
hippopotamus	fruit, grass	45/99
lion	other animals	36/79
sealion	fish	20/44
tiger	other animals	20–35/44–77

Animals

Different Genders, Different Names

Name of male	Name of female	Animal(s)	Name of male	Name of female	Animal(s)
billy-goat	nanny-goat	goat	gander	goose	goose
boar	sow	badger, pig	hart	hind	deer
buck	doe	antelope, deer, hare, rabbit	jack	jenny	ass, donkey
			leopard	leopardess	leopard
bull	cow	cattle, elephant, seal, whale	lion	lioness	lion
			peacock	peahen	peafowl
bullock	heifer	calf	ram/tup	ewe	sheep
cob	pen	swan	stag	hind	deer
cock	hen	any bird	stallion	mare	horse, zebra
dog	bitch	dog, otter	tiger	tigress	tiger
dog	vixen	fox	tom	queen	domestic cat
drake	duck	duck			

Animals

Homing Instinct

Distance travelled (km/mi)	Animal
11,260/7,000	Pigeon
8,210/5,100	Albatross
4,910/3,050	Shearwater
2,900/1,800	Dog
2,100/1,300	Salmon
1,170/727	Swallow
1,350/840	Cat
800/500	Starling
160/100	Bear
3/2	Cow

Animals

Lifespans

Animal	Lifespan in years	
	Average in wild	Oldest in captivity
bear	20	35
cat	12	28
chimpanzee	40	45
cow	15	30
dog	12	20
elephant	60	80
fox	7	14
giraffe	25	34
gorilla	35	50
guinea pig	4	8
hippopotamus	45	49
horse	20	46
kangaroo	12	28
lion	15	25
mouse	1	4
pig	10	27
rabbit	5	13
sheep	12	20
tiger	16	26
zebra	15	35

Animals
Longest-Lived Animals

Animal	Longest recorded life span (years)
Marion's tortoise (*Testudo sumerii*)	152
tortoise (*Testudo graeca*)	116
human being (*Homo sapiens*)	113
deep sea clam (*Tindaria callistiformis*)	100
killer whale (*Orcinus orca*)	>90
blue whale (*Balaenoptera musculus*)	90
fin whale (*Balaenoptera physalus*)	90
sturgeon (*Acipenser transmontanus*)	82
freshwater oyster (*Ostrea edulis*)	80
cockatoo (*Cacatua galerita*)	73

Animals
Weighing More than a Tonne

Animal	Weight (tonnes/US tonnes)
blue whale	118/120
fin whale	41/45
right whale	36/40
sperm whale	32/35
grey whale	30/33
humpback whale	24/26
Baird's whale	10/11
African elephant	5/5.5
Indian rhinoceros	4/4.4
elephant seal	3.3/3.6
pilot whale	2.5/2.7
hippopotamus	2.0/2.2
giraffe	1.2/1.3
bison	1.0/1.1

Animals
World's Fastest

For comparison, the speed of a giant tortoise is 0.27 kph/ 0.17 mph. The speed of a three-toed sloth is 0.24 kph/ 0.15 mph. The speed of a garden snail is 0.05 kph/ 0.03 mph.

Animal	Speed		Animal	Speed	
	kph	mph		kph	mph
cheetah	103	64	jackal	56	35
wildebeest	98	61	reindeer	51	32
lion	81	50	giraffe	51	32
elk	72	45	white-tailed deer	48	30
Cape hunting dog	72	45	wart hog	48	30
coyote	69	43	grizzly bear	48	30
horse	69	43	cat (domestic)	48	30
grey fox	68	42	human	45	28
hyena	64	40	elephant	40	25
zebra	64	40	black mamba snake	32	20
greyhound	63	39	squirrel	19	12
whippet	57	35.5	pig (domestic)	18	11
rabbit (domestic)	56	35	chicken	14	9

Birds
Classification of Major Bird Groups

Order	Examples	Order	Examples
Struthioniformes	ostrich	Charadriiformes	wader, gull, auk, oyster-catcher, plover, puffin, tern
Rheiformes	rhea		
Casuariiformes	cassowary, emu		
Apterygiformes	kiwi	Columbiformes	dove, pigeon, sandgrouse
Tinamiformes	tinamou		
Sphenisciformes	penguin	Psittaciformes	parrot, macaw, parakeet
Gaviiformes	loon	Cuculiformes	cuckoo, roadrunner
Podicipediformes	grebe	Strigiformes	owl
Procellariiformes	albatross, petrel, shearwater, storm petrel	Caprimulgiformes	nightjar, oilbird
		Apodiformes	swift, hummingbird
Pelecaniformes	pelican, booby, gannet, frigate bird	Coliiformes	mousebird
		Trogoniformes	trogon
Ciconiiformes	heron, ibis, stork, spoonbill, flamingo	Coraciiformes	kingfisher, hoopoe
		Piciformes	woodpecker, toucan, puffbird
Anseriformes	duck, goose, swan		
Falconiformes	falcon, hawk, eagle, buzzard, vulture	Passeriformes	finch, crow, warbler, sparrow, weaver, jay, lark, blackbird, swallow, mockingbird, wren, thrush
Galliformes	grouse, partridge, pheasant, turkey		
Gruiformes	crane, rail, bustard, coot		

Birds
Incubation Times

Bird	Incubation (days)
chicken	20–22
duck	26–28
finch	11–14
goose	25–28
parrot	17–31
pheasant	24
pigeon	10–18
quail	21–23
swan	33–36
turkey	28

Birds
World's Largest Birds

Bird	Scientific name	Wingspan (m/ft)
wandering albatross	*Diomedea exulans*	3.5/11.5
marabou stork	*Leptoptilos dubius*	3.3/10.8
Andean condor	*Vultur gryphus*	3.2/10.5
white pelican	*Pelicanus onocrotalus*	3.1/10.2
mute swan	*Cygnus olor*	2.3/7.5
crane	*Grus grus*	2.3/7.5
golden eagle	*Aquila chrysaetos*	2.2/7.2
white stork	*Ciconia ciconia*	2.1/6.9
grey heron	*Ardea cinerea*	1.9/6.2

Birds
World's Largest Flightless Birds

Bird	Scientific name	Height (m/ft)
ostrich	*Struthio camelus*	1.75–2.75/5.7–9.0
emu	*Dromaius novaehollandiae*	2.00/6.6
southern cassowary	*Casuarius casuarius*	1.50/4.9
greater rhea	*Rhea americana*	1.50/4.9
emperor penguin	*Aptenodytes patagonica*	1.20/3.9
flightless cormorant	*Phalacrocorax harrisi*	0.90/2.9
kiwi	*Apteryx australis*	0.70/2.3
takahe	*Porphyrio mantelli*	0.63/2.1
weka	*Gallirallus australis*	0.53/1.7

Cats
Breeds of Longhaired Cats

Breed	Coat	Eyes
Persian self black longhair	black	copper or deep orange
Persian self white longhair		
blue-eyed white	white	blue
orange-eyed white	white	copper or deep orange
odd-eyed white	white	one blue, one copper or deep orange
Persian self blue longhair	medium to pale blue	copper or deep orange
Persian red self longhair	deep rich red	copper or deep orange
Persian self cream longhair	pale to medium cream	copper or deep orange
Black smoke longhair	black, with white undercoat	orange or copper
Blue smoke longhair	blue, with white undercoat	orange or copper
Chocolate smoke longhair	chocolate brown, with white undercoat	orange or copper
Lilac smoke longhair	lilac, with white undercoat	orange or copper
Red smoke longhair	red shading to white, with white undercoat	orange or copper
Tortie smoke longhair	black, red, and cream, broken into patches	orange or copper
Blue-cream smoke longhair	blue and cream, intermingled, with white undercoat	orange or copper
Silver tabby longhair	silver, with black markings	green or hazel
Brown tabby longhair	rich tawny sable, with black markings	orange or copper (no green rims)
Red tabby longhair	rich red, with markings of deeper rich red	orange or copper (no green rims)
Chinchilla	white, lightly tipped with black	emerald or blue-green
Pewter longhair	white, with dark tipping	orange or copper, with black rims
Golden Persian	apricot deepening to gold, tipped with seal brown or black	green or blue-green

Cats: Breeds of Longhaired Cats (*continued*)

Breed	Coat	Eyes
Shaded silver	white undercoat, black tipping forming a mantle	emerald or blue-green
Tortoiseshell longhair	black, red, and cream, broken into patches	deep orange or copper
Chocolate tortoiseshell longhair	chocolate, well broken by shades of red	deep orange or copper
Tortoiseshell-and-white longhair	red, cream, black, and white, broken into patches	deep orange or copper
Bi-colour longhair	blue and cream, well intermingled	deep orange or copper
Colourpoint	depending on variety	blue
Birman	depending on variety	deep blue
Auburn Turkish van	chalk white	light amber
Chocolate longhair	medium to dark chocolate brown	copper or deep orange
Norwegian forest	all colours and patterns allowed (except chocolate, lilac, and Siamese pattern)	often copper or deep orange (but all colours allowed)
Lilac longhair	lilac	
Tiffanie	black, blue, chocolate, lilac, red, caramel tortie, or any of the Burmese silver varieties	extensive colour range
Angora	very extensive family; colours vary	colour should be in keeping with the coat colouring
Cameo red series		
shell	sparkling silver	orange or copper (no green rims)
shaded	white, evenly shaded with red	orange or copper (no green rims)
tortie cameo	black, red, and cream, well broken into patches	orange or copper (no green rims)
Cameo cream series		
shell	sparkling silver with cream	orange or copper (no green rims)
shaded	white, evenly shaded with cream	orange or copper (no green rims)
blue cream cameo	blue and cream softly intermingled	orange or copper (no green rims)
Balinese	extensive colour range	bright clear blue
Somali	28 different coats, depending on variety	mainly orange or copper
Maine coon	extensive colour range	extensive colour range
Ragdoll	seal, blue, chocolate, or lilac	extensive colour range
Exotic (shorthair)	extensive colour range	extensive colour range

Cats
British Breeds of Shorthaired Cats

Breed	Coat	Eyes
White shorthairs		
blue-eyed white shorthair	pure white	intense sapphire blue
orange-eyed white shorthair	pure white	gold, orange, or copper (no green rims or flecks)
odd-eyed white shorthair	pure white	one blue, one gold, orange, or copper (no green rims or flecks)
Black shorthair	jet black	gold, orange, or copper
British blue shorthair	light to medium blue	copper, orange, or deep gold
Cream shorthair	pale-toned cream	copper, orange, or deep gold
Shorthaired tabbies		
silver tabby shorthair	clean silver, with black markings	green or hazel
red tabby shorthair	red, with deep red markings	brilliant orange or deep copper
brown tabby shorthair	brilliant copper brown, with black markings	deep gold, copper, or orange
Tortoiseshell shorthair	black, rich red, and pale red, evenly intermingled	brilliant copper or orange
Tortoiseshell-and-white shorthair	black, rich and pale red, and white patches	deep orange or copper
Colourpointed British shorthair	extensive colour range	extensive colour range
Manx	all colours and patterns allowed (except the 'Siamese' pattern)	colour in keeping with coat colouring
Blue-cream shorthair	medium blue and pale cream, evenly intermingled	copper, orange, or deep gold
Spotted shorthair	any colour accepted in the British Breeds	green or hazel (silver cats with black spots) copper, orange, or deep gold (brown cats with black spots) deep orange or copper (all other cats)
Bi-colour shorthair	any colour accepted in the British Breeds	brilliant copper, orange, or deep gold (no green rims)
Smoke British shorthair	silver undercoat; top coat of any recognized self or tortie colour	copper, orange, or deep gold
British tipped shorthair	white undercoat; top coat of any recognized colour	green (cats with black tipping); copper, orange, or deep gold (all other cats)

Cats

Non-British Breeds of Shorthaired Cats

Breed	Coat	Eyes
Russian blue	clear blue	vivid green
Abyssinian		
usual	rich golden brown	amber, hazel, or green
sorrel	lustrous copper red	
blue	blue-grey	
Burmese		
brown	rich warm seal brown	any shade of yellow, from
blue	soft silver grey	chartreuse to amber (golden
chocolate	warm milk chocolate	yellow preferred)
lilac	pale dove-grey	
red	light tangerine	
brown (normal) tortie	mixture of brown and red	
cream	rich cream	
blue tortie (blue cream)	mixture of blue and cream	
chocolate tortie	mixture of chocolate and red	
lilac tortie (lilac cream)	lilac with shades of cream	
Tonkinese	extensive colour range	extensive colour range

Oriental shorthairs

Breed	Coat	Eyes
Havana	rich warm brown	clear, vivid green
Oriental lilac	frosty grey with pinkish tone	clear green
Foreign white	pure white	clear, brilliant blue
Oriental black	jet black	green
Cornish rex	all colours allowed	colour in keeping with coat colouring
Devon rex	all colours allowed	colour in keeping with coat colouring
Korat	any shade of blue, with silver topping	brilliant green (amber acceptable)
Oriental tabby	extensive colour range	extensive colour range
Oriental smoke	any colour recognized for Oriental shorthairs	clear green

Asian group

Breed	Coat	Eyes
Asian self	eight self colours, and five torties	colour in keeping with coat colouring
Burmilla	extensive colour range (standard and silver varieties)	colour in keeping with coat colouring
Asian smoke	as for Asian selfs	colour in keeping with coat colouring
Asian tabbies		
spotted	extensive colour range	any colour
classic		
mackerel		
ticked		

(continued)

Cats: Non-British Breeds of Shorthaired Cats (*continued*)

Breed	Coat	Eyes
Siamese cats		
Seal-point Siamese	cream, with seal brown points	pale green
Blue-point Siamese	glacial white, with blue points	clear vivid blue
Chocolate-point Siamese	ivory, with milk chocolate points	green
Lilac-point Siamese	magnolia-white, with pinkish grey points	vivid blue
Tabby-point Siamese	extensive colour range	extensive colour range
Red-point Siamese	warm white, with reddish gold points	brilliant intense blue
Tortie-point Siamese	extensive colour range	extensive colour range
Cream-point Siamese	creamy white	brilliant intensive blue

Cats
Favourite Cat Names in the USA

Male	Female	Male	Female
Max	Sassy	Charlie	Samantha
Sam	Misty	Oliver	Lucy
Simba	Princess		

Cats
Leading Breeds in the USA

Cat breed	Description
Abyssinian	slender body, short hair in blue, fawn, red, and ruddy colour with darker ticking
American Curl	unusual ears, curled backwards; long hair or short hair
American Shorthair	stocky body, short hair in a wide variety of colours and patterns
American Wirehair	crimped and springy hair, including the whiskers; long hair or short hair
Asian Shorthair	a group of cats of Burmese type with varying colours and patterns
Balinese	semi-longhaired variant of the Siamese; medium length, very silky coat
Bengal	cross between wild Asian Leopard Cats and domestic shorthairs; a large, spotted cat with a short, glossy coat
Birman	stocky body; semi-longhaired with four white feet
Bombay	muscular body with sleek, glossy, black coat and copper eyes
British Shorthair	stocky, sturdy body; typically blue
Burmese	sleek, glossy coat; original colour is sable brown
Chantilly/Tiffany	slender body with silky, semi-long hair; both solid and tabby patterns
Chartreux	sturdy cat with woolly blue coat, brilliant orange eyes, and smiling expression

Cats: Leading Breeds in the USA (*continued*)

Cat breed	Description
Colourpoint Shorthair	long, slender body and long, wedge-shaped head with huge ears
Cornish Rex	racy, slender body; soft, wavy, curly hair, including curly whiskers
Devon Rex	large eyes and ears; soft, short, curly coat
Domestic, household pet	non-pedigreed, resulting in a variety of characteristics
Egyptian Mau	spotted tabby pattern in colours such as bronze spotted, silver spotted, and black smoke
Exotic Shorthair	stocky body with round head, large eyes, and flat face; short, plush coat
Havana Brown	distinctive body and head; warm, chocolate brown colour
Himalayan	stocky body and brilliant blue eyes; longhaired with dark-coloured points
Japanese Bobtail	naturally short tail; typical pattern is the tricolour
Javanese	lynx (tabby) point and tortoiseshell point patterns
Korat	small cat with silvery blue coat, heart-shaped face, and green eyes
LaPerm	distinctive curled coat; either longhaired or shorthaired
Maine Coon Cat	large, rugged-looking cat with heavy coat, bushy tail, tufted ears and toes; brown tabby pattern
Manx	tailless cat, named after the Isle of Man, where it originated; stocky body with a short back and long hind legs
Norwegian Forest Cat	sturdy cat with a heavy coat and almond-shaped eyes
Ocicat	small, wild, spotted cat
Oriental	long, slender body and long, wedge-shaped head with huge ears
Persian	very stocky body and round head with flat face and large eyes; very long coat
Ragdoll	large, semi-longhaired cat with pointed (Siamese) pattern; white markings on the face and feet
Russian Blue	long legs and body, short, silvery blue coat, and bright green eyes
Scottish Fold	distinguished by the ears, which are folded forward and down, and the large round eyes
Selkirk Rex	rounded, stocky body; either longhaired or shorthaired with naturally curly coat
Siamese	long, slender body and long, wedge-shaped head with large ears and bright blue eyes; light-coloured body with seal, blue, chocolate, or lilac colours
Singapura	small cat with large eyes; short coat, in warm beige ticked with brown
Somali	longhaired with soft coat and a bushy tail; ticked tabby pattern
Sphynx	hairless cat covered by a soft down
Tonkinese	medium body with soft coat and aqua eyes; unique 'mink' pattern
Turkish Angora	long-bodied with a silky coat; best known in a solid white colour
Turkish Van	semi-longhaired; white with a coloured head and tail

Cereal Crops
Origins

Crop	Scientific name	Origin
barley	*Hordeum vulgare*	Middle East
maize	*Zea mays*	Central America
millet	*Panicum miliaceum*	temperate regions and tropics
oats	*Avena sativa*	Mediterranean region
rice	*Oryza sativa*	Asia
rye	*Secale cereale*	Mediterranean region
sorghum	*Sorghum vulgare*	Africa and Asia
wheat	*Triticum* spp.	Mediterranean region

Chordates
Classification

Common name	Taxonomic name	Level	Number of species
sea squirts, etc.	Tunicata	subphylum	2,000
lancelets	Cephalochordata	subphylum	14
hags, etc.	Myxini	class	32
lampreys, etc.	Cephalaspidomorphi	class	31
sharks, rays, etc.	Elasmobranchiomorphi	class	630
bony fishes	Osteichthyes	class	18,000
amphibians	Amphibia	class	2,900
reptiles	Reptilia	class	6,300
birds	Aves	class	8,600
mammals	Mammalia	class	4,000
of which:	Prototherians	subclass	6
	Marsupials	subclass	240
	Placentals	subclass	3,800

Classification
Animals and Plants (Taxonomic Groups)

			Taxonomic groups				
Common name	Kingdom	Phylum/ division	Class	Order	Family	Genus	Species
human	Animalia	Chordata	Mammalia	Primates	Hominoidea	*Homo*	*sapiens*
Douglas fir	Plantae	Tracheophyta	Gymnospermae	Coniferales	Pinaceae	*Pseudotsuga*	*douglasii*

Classification
Major Divisions in the Plant Kingdom

Phylum	Translation	Examples
Bryophyta	moss plant	mosses, liverworts, hornworts
Psilophyta	bare, smooth plant	whisk ferns
Lycophyta	wolf-foot plant	club mosses
Sphenophyta	wedge plant	horsetails
Filicinophyta/Pteridophyta	fern plant	ferns
Cycadophyta	palm plant	cycads
Ginkgophyta	silver apricot plant	ginkgo
Coniferophyta	cone-bearing plant	cedar, cypress, juniper, pine, redwood
Gnetophyta	desert cone plant	gnetum, welwitschia, ephedra
Angiospermophyta	little seed case plant	flowering plants

Classification
Major Phyla

The last phylum listed, Chordata, includes all the vertebrates – fish, amphibians, reptiles, birds, and mammals.

Common name of species	Phylum	Number	Common name of species	Phylum	Number
single-celled animals	Protozoa	30,000	lamp shells	Brachiopoda	260
			molluscs	Mollusca	80,000
sponges	Porifera	5,000	peanut worms	Sipunculoidea	250
various parasites	Mesozoa	50	echiurid worms	Echiuroidea	60
corals, jellyfish, etc.	Coelenterata	9,000	segmented worms	Annelida	9,000
comb jellies	Ctenophora	100	tongue worms	Pentastomida	70
flatworms	Platyhelminthes	10,000	water bears	Tardigrada	180
ribbon worms	Nemertina	750	sea spiders	Pycnogonida	500
roundworms	Aschelminthes	17,000	arthropods	Arthropoda	1,000,000
entoprocts	Entoprocta	60	arrow worms	Chaetognatha	50
thorny-headed worms	Acantho-cephala	300	beard-bearers	Pogonophera	80
			echinoderms	Echinodermata	6,000
moss animals	Ectoprocta	4,000	hemichordates	Hemichordata	90
phoronids	Phoronida	15	Chordates	Chordata	43,000

Classification
The Five Kingdoms

Kingdom	Number of species
Monera	>10,000
Protista	>100,000
Fungi	about 100,000
Plantae	>250,000
Animalia	>1,000,000

Climate
Major Climatic Zones

Zone	Location
Polar	Antarctica and Arctic regions of North America and Russia
Boreal	prairies of the USA and parts of Australia, South Africa, and Russia
Temperate	Eastern Asia, New Zealand, northwestern and northeastern USA, southern Chile, and most of Europe
Mediterranean	California, southern Africa and Europe, southwestern Australia, and parts of Chile
Subtropical	most of Australia, Central Asia, the Kalahari, Mexico, and Saharan Africa
Tropical	forests of Africa and the Amazon, parts of Australia, India, Indonesia, Malaysia, and southeastern Asia

Cloning
First Animals to be Cloned

Year	Animals	Notes
1952	frogs	tadpoles died at an early stage
1970	frogs	tadpoles died at an early stage
1981	mice	experiment suspected to be a fake
1984	sheep, cows, goats, pigs, horses	all cloned from embryo cells
1993	humans	destroyed at 32-cell stage
1994	calves	
1995	twin sheep	
1997	sheep (Dolly)	first successful clone from adult cells

Clouds

Different Types

Cloud type	Average height (m/ft)	Description
stratus	1,600/5,249	low parallel sheets
cumulus	2,000/6,562	flat-based and domed
nimbostratus	2,500/8,202	rounded, fluffy rain clouds
altocumulus	3,400/11,155	white clouds in lines
stratocumulus	3,600/11,811	dull grey, sometimes leaden
altostratus	5,200/17,060	extensive grey sheet
cirrocumulus	5,600/18,373	small/large rounded tufts ('mackerel sky')
cirrostratus	7,000/22,966	thin white sheet
cirrus	8,500/22,887	feather wisps ('mares' tails')
cumulonimbus	2,500–11,500/8,202–37,730	rounded rain clouds often reaching great heights

Conservation

Countries with Most Land Preserved for Wildlife

Country	% of land protected	Number of areas protected	Total land protected (sq km/sq mi)
Greenland	45.0	2	982,500/379,345
Venezuela	28.9	100	263,200/101,622
Germany	25.8	504	91,950/35,502
Ecuador	24.1	15	111,150/42,915
Botswana	18.5	9	106,650/41,178
Chile	18.3	66	137,250/52,993
Tanzania	14.8	30	138,900/53,630
Namibia	12.4	12	102,200/39,460
Australia	12.2	892	935,450/361,179
USA	11.1	1,494	1,042,400/402,473

Deforestation

Countries Destroying Greatest Areas of Forest

Country	Area of forest destroyed (ha/acres)	Country	Area of forest destroyed (ha/acres)
Brazil	2,554,000/6,311,072	Venezuela	503,000/1,242,940
Indonesia	1,084,000/2,678,623	Malaysia	400,000/988,422
Congo, Democratic Republic of	740,000/1,828,580	Myanmar	387,000/956,298
		Sudan	353,000/872,282
Bolivia	581,000/1,435,682	Thailand	329,000/812,977
Mexico	508,000/1,255,295		

Deforestation
World Destruction of Tropical Forests

Region	Forest area lost (ha/acres) 1990–95
Africa	18,475,000/45,652,723
Asia	15,275,000/37,745,350
North and Central America	5,185,000/12,812,415
Oceania	+302,000/746,258[1]
South America	23,277,000/57,518,724

[1]This figure represents a gain in forest area.

Dinosaurs
Largest Carnivorous Dinosaurs

Dinosaur	Weight	Length
Gigantosaurus carolinii	8 tonnes/7.8 tons	12 m/39 ft
Carcharodontosaurus saharicus	8.1 tonnes/8.0 tons	13.7 m/45 ft
Tyrannosaurus rex	6.3 tonnes/6.2 tons	12 m/39 ft
Allosaurus	1.80 tonnes/1.78 tons	11 m/36 ft
Megalosaurus	1.0 tonne/0.98 ton	9 m/30 ft
Ceratosaurus	0.5–1.0 tonne/0.49–0.98 ton	4.5–6.0 m/15–20 ft

Dinosaurs
Largest Dinosaurs (by Weight)

Dinosaur	Weight
Agentinasaurus	80–100 tonnes/79–98 tons
Ultrasaurus	more than 80 tonnes/79 tons
Supersaurus vivanae	50–100 tonnes/49–98 tons
Seismosaurus halli	50–100 tonnes/49–98 tons
Brachiosaurus altithorax	45–50 tonnes/44–49 tons
Apatosaurus (brontosaurus)	30–35 tonnes/29–34 tons
Giraffatitan brancai	30 tonnes/29 tons
Diplodocus	10 tonnes/9.8 tons
Iguanodon	5 tonnes/4.9 tons
Ankylosaurus	4 tonnes/3.9 tons

Dinosaurs
Smallest Carnivorous Dinosaurs

Dinosaur	Length	Dinosaur	Length
Compsognathus	60 cm/23 in	Eoraptor	91 cm/36 in
Saltopus	61 cm/24 in	Wannanosaurus	1 m/39 in
Echinodon	61 cm/24 in	Microvenator	1.22 m/48 in
Microceratops	76 cm/30 in	Velociraptor	1.8 m/5.9 ft
Lesothosaurus	91 cm/36 in	Coelophysis	2.74 m/9 ft

Dinosaurs
With the Largest Brains

This list ranks dinosaurs by size of brain, estimated as a percentage of total body size.

Troodon
Dromaeosaurus
Deinonychus
Velociraptor
Utahraptor

Dinosaurs
World's Largest (by Length)

Name	Geological period	Length (m/ft)
Diplodocus	Late Jurassic	27.0/88.6
Brachiosaurus	Late Jurassic/ Early Cretaceous	22.5/73.8
Apatosaurus	Late Jurassic	21.0/68.9
Camarasaurus	Late Jurassic	18.0/59.1
Tyrannosaurus	Late Cretaceous	14.0/45.9
Anatosaurus	Late Cretaceous	13.0/42.7
Edmontosaurus	Late Cretaceous	13.0/42.7
Saltasaurus	Late Cretaceous	12.0/39.4
Opisthacoelicaudia	Late Cretaceous	12.0/39.4
Allosaurus	Late Jurassic	12.0/39.4

Dog Breeds
Gundogs

Height is given at the dog's withers (the highest point of the body, behind the neck). Measurements given are for male dogs, female dogs are usually smaller.

Breed	Country of origin	Height (cm/in)
Barbet	France	45–50/18–20
Braque	France	variety of sizes
Drentse Partridge Dog	Netherlands	55–63/22–25
English Setter	England	65–68.5/26–27
German Shorthaired Pointer	Germany	58.5–63.5/23–25
German Wirehaired Pointer	Germany	61–66/24–26
Gordon Setter	Scotland	66/26
Hungarian Vizsla	Hungary	56–63.5/22–25
Irish Setter	Ireland	no size stipulated
Italian Spinone	France	58–68/23–27
Large Münsterländer	Germany	61/24
Pointer	England	63.5–68.5/25–27
Portuguese Water Dog	Portugal	51–58/20–23
Retriever (Chesapeake Bay)	USA	56–64/22–25
Retriever (Curly Coated and Flat Coated)	origin unknown	63.5–68.5/25–27
Retriever (Golden)	origin uncertain	56–61/22–24
Retriever (Labrador)	Newfoundland	56–57/22–22.5
Spaniel (American Cocker)	USA	38/15
Spaniel (Brittany)	France	48.5–51/19–20
Spaniel (Clumber)	France	48–50/19–19.5
Spaniel (Cocker)	Spain	39–41/15–16
Spaniel (English Springer)	England	51/20
Spaniel (Field)	UK	46/18
Spaniel (Irish Water)	Ireland	56–61/22–24
Spaniel (Sussex)	England	38–40/15–16
Spaniel (Welsh Springer)	Wales	48/19
Weimaraner	Germany	61–69/24–27

Dog Breeds
Hounds

Height is given at the dog's withers (the highest point of the body, behind the neck).
Measurements given are for male dogs, female dogs are usually smaller.

Breed	Country of origin	Height (cm/in)
Afghan Hound	Iran	68–73/27–29
Anglo-Français and Français Hounds	France	variety of sizes
Azawakh	France	60–74/24–29
Balkanski Gonic	Yugoslavia	44–54/17–21
Basenji	central Africa	43/17
Basse Griffon Vendéen	France	38–43/15–17 (grande), 33–38/13–15 (petite)
Basset Hound	France	33–38/13–15
Beagle	UK	33–40.5/13–16
Black and Tan Coonhound	USA	63.5–68.5/25–27
Bloodhound	UK	63.5–68.5/25–27
Bosanski Ostrodlaki Gonic-Barak	Bosnia	46–56/18–22
Borzoi	Russia	73.5/29 upwards
Bracco Italiano	Italy	55–67/22–26
Ceský Foucek	Czech Republic	58–66/23–26
Chart Polski	Poland	68–80/27–31
Dachshund	Germany	12.5–23/5–9
Dachshund (Miniature)	Germany	weight more important than size (5 kg/11 lb preferable)
Deerhound	UK	no less than 76/30
Elkhound	Norway	51/20
Erdélyi Kopó	Hungary	55–65/22–26
Finnish Spitz	Finland	43–51/17–20
Foxhound (English)	England	58/23
Greyhound	ancient (Egyptian) origin	71–76/28–30
Hamiltonstovӓre	Sweden	57/22.5
Harrier	ancient (possibly Greek) origin	46–56/18–22
Hellinikos Ichnilatis	Greece	47–52/18.5–20.5
Ibizan Hound	Spain (Balearic Islands)	59–71/23–28
Irish Wolfhound	Ireland	78.7/31 upwards
Istarski Gonic	Slovenia and Croatia	50–52/19.5–20.5 (Ostrodlaki, wirehaired); 48–50/19–19.5 (Kratkodlaki, smooth)
Kai (Konshu-Tora)	Japan	46–56/18–22
Karelean Bear Dog	Finland	49–60/19–24
Laika, Russko-Evropeiskaia	Russia	48–58/19–23
Laika, Vostochno-Sibirskaia	Russia	51–64/20–25
Laika, Zapadno-Sibirskaia	Russia	51–62/20–24
Ogar Polski	Poland	55–65/22–26
Otterhound	UK	61–69/24–27
Pharaoh Hound	north Africa	56–63/22–25
Planinsky Gonic	Slovenia	45–55/18–22
Rhodesian Ridgeback	South Africa	63–68/25–27
Saluki	north Africa	58–71/23–28
Whippet	England	46/18

Dog Breeds
Terriers

Height is given at the dog's withers (the highest point of the body, behind the neck).
Measurements given are for male dogs, female dogs are usually smaller.

Breed	Country of origin	Height (cm/in)
Airedale Terrier	England	58–61/23–24
Australian Terrier	Australia	25/10
Bedlington Terrier	England	41/16
Black Russian Terrier	Russia	64–72/25–28
Border Terrier	Scotland	33/13
Bull Terrier	England	no size stipulated
Bull Terrier (Miniature)	England	up to 36/14
Cairn Terrier	Scotland	28–30.5/11–12
Dandie Dinmont Terrier	Scotland	20–28/8–11
Fox Terrier	England	N/A
Fox Terrier (Wire-Haired)	N/A	up to 39/15
Glen of Immaal Terrier	Ireland	up to 35.5/14
Irish Terrier	Ireland	48.5/19
Jack Russell Terrier	England	up to 28/11 (smaller size), 28–38/11–15 (larger size)
Kerry Blue Terrier	Ireland	46–48/18–19
Lakeland Terrier	England	up to 36/14
Manchester Terrier	England	41/16
Norfolk Terrier	England	25/10
Norwich Terrier	England	25/10
Scottish Terrier	Scotland	25–28/10–11
Sealyham Terrier	Wales	up to 30/12
Skye Terrier	Scotland	25.5/10
Soft-Coated Wheaten Terrier	Ireland	46–49/18–19
Staffordshire Bull Terrier	England	35.5–40.5/14–16
Welsh Terrier	Wales	up to 38/15
West Highland White Terrier	Scotland	28/11

Dog Breeds
Toys

Height is given at the dog's withers (the highest point of the body, behind the neck).
Measurements given are for male dogs, female dogs are usually smaller.

Breed	Country of origin	Height (cm/in)
Affenpinscher	Germany	24–28/9.5–11
Australian Silky Terrier	Australia	23/9
Bichon Frise	France	23–28/9–11
Cavalier King Charles Spaniel	England	25/10
Chihuahua (Long Coat)	Mexico	weight more important than size (1–2 kg/2–4 lb preferable)
Chihuahua (Smooth Coat)	Mexico	weight more important than size (1–2 kg/2–4 lb preferable)

(*continued*)

Dog Breeds: Toys (*continued*)

Breed	Country of origin	Height (cm/in)
Chinese Crested Dog	China	28–33/11–13
English Toy Terrier (Black and Tan)	England	25–30/10–12
Griffon Bruxellois	Belgium	weight more important than size (2.7–4.5 kg/6–10 lb preferable)
Italian Greyhound	Italy	33–38/13–15
Japanese Chin	Japan	no size stipulated
King Charles Spaniel	England	25/10
Little Lion Dog	Germany	25–33/10–13
Maltese	Malta	up to 25.5/10
Miniature Pinscher	Germany	25.5–30.5/10–12
Papillon	Spain	20–28/8–11
Pekingese	China	18/7
Pomeranian	Arctic Circle	weight more important than size (1.8–2.25 kg/4–5 lb preferable)
Pug	China	weight more important than size (6–8 kg/13–18 lb preferable)
Xoloitzquintli	Mexico	28–30/11–12 (toy), 33–45/13–18 (miniature), 45–55/18–22 (standard)
Yorkshire Terrier	England	18/7

Dog Breeds
Utility Dogs

Height is given at the dog's withers (the highest point of the body, behind the neck). Measurements given are for male dogs, female dogs are usually smaller.

Breed	Country of origin	Height (cm/in)
Boston Terrier	USA	38/15
Bulldog	England	weight more important than size (23–25 kg/51–55 lb preferable)
Chow Chow	China	48.5–56/19–22
Dalmatian	Slovenia and Croatia	58–61/23–24
French Bulldog	France	30/12
Hrvatski Ovcar	Croatia	40–50/16–20
Japanese Akita	Japan	66–71/26–28
Japanese Spitz	Japan	30–40/12–16
Keeshond	Netherlands	45.5/18
Leonberger	Germany	from 76/30
Lhasa Apso	Tibet	25/10
Poodle (Standard)	origin uncertain	38/15
Poodle (Miniature)	origin uncertain	28–38/11–15
Poodle (Toy)	origin uncertain	below 28/11
Schipperke	Belgium	30.5–33/12–13
Schnauzer (Standard)	Germany	48/19
Schnauzer (Miniature)	Germany	35/14

Dog Breeds: Utility Dogs (*continued*)

Breed	Country of origin	Height (cm/in)
Shar-Pei	China	45.5–51/18–20
Shih Tzu	Tibet	up to 26/10
Tibetan Spaniel	Tibet	25.5/10
Tibetan Terrier	Tibet	35–40/14–16

Dog Breeds
Working Dogs

Height is given at the dog's withers (the highest point of the body, behind the neck). Measurements given are for male dogs, female dogs are usually smaller.

Breed	Country of origin	Height (cm/in)
Aïdi	Morocco	52–62/20–24
Ainu	Japan	45–52/18–20
Akbash	Turkey	70–86/27–34
Alaskan Malamute	USA	64–71/25–28
Appenzell Cattle Dog	Switzerland	50–56/20–22
Anatolian Shepherd Dog	Turkey	73.5–78.5/29–31
Australian Cattle Dog	Australia	46–51/18–20
Bauceron	France	63–75/25–30
Bearded Collie	Scotland	53–56/21–22
Belgian Shepherd Dog	Belgium	61–66/24–26
Bergamasco	Italy	54–62/21–24
Berger Picard	France	55–65/22–26
Bernese Mountain Dog	Switzerland	63.5–70/25–28
Border Collie	Scotland	53/21
Bouvier Des Flanders	Belgium	63.5–68.5/25–27
Boxer	Germany	57–63.5/22–25
Briard	France	61–68.5/24–27
Broholmer	Denmark	over 75/30
Bullmastiff	England	63–68/25–27
Collie	Scotland	56–61/22–24
Dobermann	Germany	68.5/27
Estrela Mountain Dog	Portugal	65/26
German Shepherd Dog	Germany	61–66/24–26
Great Dane	Denmark	over 76/30
Hovawart	Germany	61–70/24–28
Hungarian Puli	Hungary	41–46/16–18
Husky (Eskimo Dog)	Russia	58.5–68.5/23–25
Husky (Siberian)	Russia	53–59/21–23
Islenskur Fjárhundur	Iceland	38–48/15–19
Komondor	Hungary	over 63.5/25
Krazski Ovcar	Slovenia and Croatia	52–60/20–24
Lancashire Heeler	England	30.5/12
Maremma Sheepdog	Italy	65–72.5/26–29
Mastiff	UK	over 76/30

(*continued*)

 Animals, Plants, and the Environment   **277**

Breed	Country of origin	Height (cm)
Newfoundland	Newfoundland	71/28
Norwegian Buhund	Norway	up to 45/18
Old English Sheepdog	England	61/24
Ovcharka	Russia	variety of sizes
Pinscher	Germany	43–48.5/17–19
Polski Owczarek Nizinny	Poland	40–52/16–20
Polski Owczarek Podhalański	Poland	62–70/24–28
Pumi	Hungary	35–44/14–17
Pyrenean Mountain Dog	Spain	71/28
Rottweiler	Germany	63.5–68.5/25–27
St Bernard	Switzerland	no maximum height; minimum 70/28
Samoyed	Russia	51–56/20–22
Sarplaninac	Kosovo (Albania)	58–62/23–24
Schnauzer (Giant)	Germany	64–69/25–27
Shetland Sheepdog	Scotland	36/14
Stumpy Tail Cattle Dog	Australia	46–51/18–20
Vastgotaspets (Swedish Vallhund)	Sweden	33–35/13–14
Welsh Corgi (Cardigan)	Wales	30.5/12
Welsh Corgi (Pembroke)	Wales	25–30/10–12

Dogs
Best-in-Show Breeds at Crufts

Year	Breed	Year	Breed
2000	Kerry Blue Terrier	1995	Irish Setter
1999	Irish Setter	1994	Welsh Terrier
1998	Welsh Terrier	1993	Irish Setter
1997	Yorkshire Terrier	1992	Whippet
1996	Cocker Spaniel	1991	Clumber Spaniel

Dogs
Favourite Dog Names in the UK

Male	Female
Ben	Molly
Jack	Millie
Sam	Penny
Murphy	Megan
Max	Holly

Dogs
Favourite Dog Names in the USA

Male	Female
Max	Maggie
Jake	Mollie
Buddy	Lady
Bailey	Sadie
Sam	Lucy

Dogs
Most Popular Breeds in the USA

Breed	Number
Labrador Retriever	149,500
Rottweiler	89,870
German Shepherd	79,080
Golden Retriever	68,990
Beagle	56,950
Poodle	56,800
Dachshund	48,430
Cocker Spaniel	45,300
Yorkshire Terrier	40,220
Pomeranian	39,170
Shih Tzu	38,000
Chihuahua	36,560
Boxer	36,400
Shetland Sheepdog	33,580
Dalmation	32,970
Miniature Schnauzer	31,830
Siberian Husky	25,560
Miniature Pinscher	20,360
Pug	18,400
Doberman Pinscher	17,920

Drugs
Plants that Provide Drugs

Plant	Scientific name	Drug	Used to treat
autumn crocus	*Colchicum autumnale*	cocchicine	cancer
cinchona	*Cinchona calisaya*	quinine	malaria
coca	*Erythroxilon coca*	cocaine	pain (local)
deadly nightshade	*Atropus belladonna*	atropine	muscle spasm, colic
foxglove	*Digitalis purpurea*	digitalin	irregular heartbeat
poppy	*Papaver somniferum*	codeine, morphine	pain, cough
rosy periwinkle	*Vinca* spp.	vincristine	leukaemia
thyme	*Thymus* spp.	thymol	fungal infection
willow	*Salix alba*	salicylate	pain (local)
yew	*Taxus* spp.	taxol	cancer

Ecology
Countries with the Greatest Percentage of Protected Land

'Protected land area' can include marine habitats, such as the Great Barrier Reef Park in Australia, allowing for land area percentages to exceed 100%.

Country	Protected land area (%)	Country	Protected land area (%)
Dominican Republic	173.5	Hong Kong	43.4
Seychelles	111.1	Belize	39.8
Slovakia	75.6	Kiribati	39.0
Venezuela	61.4	Liechtenstein	38.1
Greenland	45.2	Saudi Arabia	34.4

Ecology
Countries with the Greatest Protected Land Area

The number of protected areas in the UK is 515 and the total area protected is
50,001 sq km/19,306 sq mi. This represents 20.4% of the total land area.

Country	Number of protected areas	Protected area (sq km/sq mi)
USA	3,333	1,988,444/767,742
Australia	5,647	1,045,686/403,741
Greenland	2	982,500/379,345
Canada	3,224	953,103/367,995
Saudi Arabia	78	825,620/318,774
China	810	682,407/263,479
Venezuela	194	560,404/216,373
Brazil	582	526,717/203,367
Russian Federation	216	516,688/199,494
Indonesia	1,069	345,118/132,479

Endangered Animals
Animals No Longer Endangered

Common name	Range	Reason removed from endangered list
dove, Palau	West Pacific–Palau Islands	recovered
eagle, bald	North America	recovered
falcon, Arctic peregrine	nests from northern Alaska to Greenland; winters to Central and South America	recovered
fantail, Palau	West Pacific–Palau Islands	recovered
kangaroo, eastern grey	Australia	recovered
kangaroo, red	Australia	recovered
kangaroo, western grey	Australia	recovered
owl, Palau	West Pacific–Palau Islands	recovered
turtle, Indian flap-shelled	India, Pakistan, Bangladesh	better data
whale, grey	North Pacific Ocean–coastal and Bering Sea, formerly North Atlantic Ocean	recovered

Endangered Animals
Animals Threatened by the World Wildlife Trade

Common name	Range	Reason threatened
alligator snapping turtle	North America	used in canned turtle soup, sold as pets
Asian elephant	Asia	poached for ivory and other parts of the body
Beluga sturgeon	Caspian Sea	caviar is a delicacy in many countries

Endangered Animals: Animals Threatened by the World Wildlife Trade (*continued*)

Common name	Range	Reason threatened
black rhino	Africa	hunted for their horns, which are used in oriental medicine
bonobo	Congo, Democratic Republic of	habitat loss, hunted for use in traditional medicine and magic
chimpanzee	Equatorial Africa	habitat loss, hunted for bushmeat, pet trade, and biomedical trade
giant panda	China	destruction of natural habitat, poaching, and demand as zoo animals
green-cheeked parrot	Mexico	hunted and captured for pet trade
hawksbill turtle	tropical seas	the shell is used as tortoiseshell
mako shark	Atlantic, Pacific, and Indian Oceans	shark meat is a delicacy in some countries
tiger	Asia	destruction of jungle; hunted for bones and other parts used in oriental medicine

Endangered Animals
Numbers Endangered Worldwide

Class	Number of extinct species		Number of endangered species	
	Extinct	Only surviving in captivity	Critically endangered	Endangered
mammals	86	3	169	315
birds	104	4	168	235
reptiles	20	1	41	59
amphibians	5	0	18	31
lampreys	1	0	0	1
sharks	0	0	1	7
ray-finned fish	80	11	156	125
lobe-finned fish	0	0	0	1
sea urchins	0	0	0	0
spiders and mites	0	0	0	1
centipedes	0	0	0	0
crustaceans	9	1	54	73
insects	72	1	44	116
aquatic arthropods	0	0	0	0
terrestrial arthropods	3	0	1	3
leeches	0	0	0	0
earthworms	0	0	1	0
bristleworms	0	0	1	0
bivalves	12	0	81	22
snails	216	9	176	190
nematodes	0	0	0	0
flatworms	1	0	0	0
cnidarians	0	0	0	0

Endangered Animals
Mammals Endangered in the USA

Common name	Range
bat, grey	central and southeastern USA
bat, Hawaiian hoary	USA
bat, Indiana	eastern and midwestern USA
bat, lesser (Sanborn's) long-nosed	USA, Mexico, Central America
bat, little Mariana fruit	western Pacific Ocean – USA (Guam)
bat, Mariana fruit	western Pacific Ocean – USA (Guam, Rota, Tinian, Saipan, Agiguan)
bat, Mexican long-nosed	USA, Mexico, Central America
bat, Ozark big-eared	USA
bat, Virginia big-eared	USA
bison, wood	northwestern USA, Canada
caribou, woodland	USA, Canada
deer, Columbian white-tailed	USA
deer, key	USA
ferret, black-footed	western USA, western Canada
fox, northern swift	USA (northern plains), Canada
fox, San Joaquin kit	USA
jaguar	USA, Central and South America
jaguarundi	USA, Mexico
kangaroo rat, Fresno	USA
manatee, West Indian (Florida)	southeastern USA, Caribbean Sea, South America
margay	USA, Central and South America
mountain beaver, Point Arena	USA
mouse, Alabama beach	USA
mouse, Anastasia Island beach	USA
mouse, Choctawahatchee beach	USA
mouse, Key Largo cotton	USA
mouse, Pacific pocket	USA
mouse, Perdido Key beach	USA
mouse, salt marsh harvest	USA
mouse, southeastern beach	USA
ocelot	USA, Central and South America
otter, southern sea	West Coast, USA south – Mexico (Baja California)
panther, Florida	USA
prairie dog, Utah	USA
pronghorn, Sonoran	USA, Mexico
rabbit, Lower Keys	USA
rice rat (silver rice rat)	USA
sea lion, Stellar (northern)	USA, Canada, Russia, North Pacific Ocean
seal, Guadalupe fur	USA
seal, Hawaiian monk	USA
shrew, Dismal Swamp southeastern	USA
squirrel, Carolina northern flying	USA
squirrel, Delmarva Peninsula fox	USA
squirrel, Mount Graham red	USA
squirrel, Virginia northern flying	USA
vole, Amargosa	USA
vole, Florida salt-marsh	USA
vole, Hualapai Mexican	USA
wolf, red	southeastern USA
woodrat, Key Largo	USA

Endangered Animals
Birds Endangered in the USA

Common name	Range
akepa, Hawaii (honeycreeper)	USA
albatross, short-tailed	north Pacific Ocean – Japan, Russia, USA
blackbird, yellow-shouldered	USA
bobwhite, masked (quail)	USA, Mexico (Sonora)
caracara, Audubon's crested	USA south – Panama; Cuba
condor, California	USA, Mexico (Baja California)
coot, Hawaiian	USA
crane, Mississippi sandhill	USA
creeper, Hawaii	USA
crow, white-necked	USA, Dominican Republic, Haiti
curlew, Eskimo	Alaska and northern Canada – Argentina
duck, Hawaiian	USA
eagle, bald	North America south – northern Mexico
eider, spectacled	USA, Russia
falcon, northern aplomado	USA, Mexico, Guatemala
finch, Laysan (honeycreeper)	USA
flycatcher, southwestern willow	USA, Mexico
gnatcatcher, coastal California	USA, Mexico
goose, Aleutian Canada	USA, Japan
goose, Hawaiian	USA
hawk, Hawaiian (io)	USA
hawk, Puerto Rican broad-winged	USA
hawk, Puerto Rican sharp-shinned	USA
honeycreeper, crested (akohekohe)	USA
jay, Florida scrub	USA
kite, Everglade snail	USA, Cuba
megapode, Micronesian (La Perouse's)	west Pacific Ocean – Palau Islands, USA (Mariana Islands)
millerbird, Nihoa (old world warbler)	USA
monarch, Tinian (old world flycatcher)	west Pacific Ocean – USA (Mariana Islands)
moorhen (gallinule), Hawaiian common	USA
moorhen (gallinule), Mariana common	west Pacific Ocean – USA (Guam, Tinian, Saipan, Pagan)
murrelet, marbled	USA, Canada
nightjar, Puerto Rican (whip-poor-will)	USA
nukupu' u (honeycreeper)	USA
o'o, Kauai (o'o a'a) (honeyeater)	USA
o'u (honeycreeper)	USA
owl, Mexican spotted	USA, Mexico
owl, northern spotted	USA, Canada
palila (honeycreeper)	USA
parrot, Puerto Rican	USA
parrotbill, Maui (honeycreeper)	USA
pelican, brown	USA, West Indies, coastal Central and South America
petrel, Hawaiian dark-rumped	USA
pigeon, Puerto Rican plain	USA
plover, piping	USA, Canada, Mexico, Bahamas, West Indies
plover, western snowy	USA, Mexico

(continued)

Endangered Animals: Birds Endangered in the USA (*continued*)

Common name	Range
po' ouli (honeycreeper)	USA
prairie-chicken, Attwater's greater	USA
pygmy-owl, cactus ferruginous	USA, Mexico
rail, California clapper	USA
rail, light-footed clapper	USA, Mexico (Baja California)
rail, Yuma clapper	USA, Mexico
shearwater, Newell's Townsend's (formerly Manx)	USA
shrike, San Clemente loggerhead	USA
sparrow, Cape Sable seaside	USA
sparrow, Florida grasshopper	USA
sparrow, San Clemente sage	USA
stilt, Hawaiian	USA
stork, wood	USA, Mexico, Central and South America
tern, California least	USA, Mexico
tern, least	USA, Greater and Lesser Antilles, Bahamas, Mexico; winters Central America, northern South America
thrush, large Kauai	USA
thrush, small Kauai	USA
towhee, Inyo California	USA
vireo, black-capped	USA, Mexico
vireo, least Bell's	USA, Mexico
warbler (wood), Bachman's	southeastern USA, Cuba
warbler (wood), golden-cheeked	USA, Mexico, Guatemala, Honduras, Nicaragua, Belize
warbler (wood), Kirtland's	USA, Canada, West Indies – Bahama Islands
warbler (Old World), nightingale reed	west Pacific Ocean – USA (Guam, Alamagan, Saipan)
woodpecker, ivory-billed	southcentral and southeastern USA, Cuba
woodpecker, red-cockaded	southcentral and southeastern USA

Endangered Animals
Reptiles Endangered in the USA

alligator, American	southeastern USA
anole, Culebra Island giant	USA
boa, Mona	USA
boa, Virgin Islands tree	US and British Virgin Islands
crocodile, American	USA, Mexico, Caribbean, Central and South America
gecko, Monito	USA
iguana, Mona ground	USA
lizard, blunt-nosed leopard	USA
lizard, Coachella Valley fringe-toed	USA
lizard, island night	USA
lizard, St Croix ground	USA
rattlesnake, New Mexican ridge-nosed	USA, Mexico
skink, bluetail	USA

Endangered Animals: Reptiles Endangered in the USA
(*continued*)

Common name	Range
skink, sand	USA
snake, Atlantic salt-marsh	USA
snake, Concho water	USA
snake, eastern indigo	USA
snake, giant garter	USA
snake, northern copperbelly water	USA
snake, San Francisco garter	USA
tortoise, desert	USA, Mexico
tortoise, gopher	USA
turtle, Alabama redbelly	USA
turtle, flattened musk	USA
turtle, Plymouth redbelly	USA
turtle, ringed map	USA
turtle, yellow-blotched map	USA

Endangered Animals
Amphibians Endangered in the USA

coqui, golden	USA
frog, California red-legged	USA, Mexico
salamander, Barton Springs	USA
salamander, Cheat Mountain	USA
salamander, desert slender	USA
salamander, Red Hills	USA
salamander, San Marcos	USA
salamander, Santa Cruz long-toed	USA
salamander, Shenandoah	USA
salamander, Sonoran tiger	USA, Mexico
salamander, Texas blind	USA
toad, arroyo	USA, Mexico
toad, Houston	USA
toad, Puerto Rican crested	USA, British Virgin Islands

Endangered Animals
World's Endangered Amphibians

Common name	Range
frog, Goliath	Africa
frog, Israel painted	Europe
frog, Panamanian golden	South America
frog, Stephen Island	Australia
salamander, Chinese giant	western China
salamander, Japanese giant	Japan
toad, African viviparous	Africa
toad, Cameroon	Africa
toad, Monte Verde	South America

 Animals, Plants, and the Environment **285**

Endangered Animals
World's Endangered Birds

Common name	Range	Common name	Range
booby, Abbott's	Asia	macaw, glaucous	South America
condor, Andean	South America	macaw, indigo	South America
crane, hooded	Asia	ostrich, Arabian	Asia
crane, Japanese	Asia	ostrich, West African	Africa
crane, whooping	North America	parakeet, gold-shouldered (hooded)	Australia
eagle, harpy	South America		
egret, Chinese	Asia	parakeet, Norfolk Island	Australia
falcon, American peregrine	North America		
		parrot, ground	Australia
hawk, Galapagos	South America	parrot, red-capped	South America
ibis, Japanese crested	Asia	stork, oriental white	Asia
ibis, northern bald	Africa, Asia, Europe	woodpecker, imperial	North America
		woodpecker, Tristam's	Asia

Endangered Animals
World's Endangered Mammals

Common name	Range	Common name	Range
armadillo, giant	South America	monkey, spider	South America
bear, brown	Europe	mouse, Shark Bay	Australia
bear, brown	Asia	orangutan	Asia
bear, Mexican grizzly	North America	panda, giant	Asia
bison, wood	North America	rat-kangaroo, queensland	Australia
bobcat	North America		
camel, Bactrian	Asia	rhinoceros, black	Africa
cat, leopard	Asia	rhinoceros, great Indian	Asia
deer, pampas	South America		
dugong	Africa	seal, Saimaa	Europe
duiker, Jentink's	Africa	sloth, Brazilian three-toed	South America
eland, western giant	Africa		
elephant, African	Africa	tapir, Asian	Asia
elephant, Asian	Asia	tapir, mountain	South America
gazelle, Clark's (Dibatag)	Africa	tiger	Asia
		tiger, Tasmanian (thylacine)	Australia
gorilla	Africa		
kangaroo, Tasmanian forester	Australia	wallaby, banded hare	Australia
		whale, blue	Oceanic
lemurs	Africa	whale, bowhead	Oceanic
leopard	Africa, Asia	whale, finback	Oceanic
leopard, snow	Asia	whale, humpback	Oceanic
manatee, Amazonian	South America	whale, right	Oceanic
manatee, West African	Africa	whale, sperm	Oceanic
monkey, black howler	North America	wombat, hairy-nosed	Australia
monkey, red-backed squirrel	South America	zebra, Grevy's	Africa
		zebra, mountain	Africa

Endangered Animals
World's Endangered Reptiles

Common name	Range	Common name	Range
alligator, Chinese	Asia	monitor, Bengal	Asia
caiman, Apaporis River	South America	monitor, desert	Africa
		monitor, yellow	Asia
crocodile, African dwarf	Africa	python, Indian	Asia
		tartaruga	South America
crocodile, African slender-snouted	Africa	tortoise, Bolson	North America
		tortoise, Galapagos	South America
crocodile, Morelet's	South America	tuatara	Australia
iguana, Barrington land	South America	turtle, aquatic box	North America
lizard, Hierro giant	Europe	turtle, green sea	North America
lizard, Ibiza wall	Europe	viper, Lar Valley	Asia

Extinctions

Animal	Description	Date of extinction
thylacine	largest-known marsupial carnivore of Tasmania, also called the Tasmanian tiger or Tasmanian wolf	1930s
passenger pigeon	bird of North America that may once have been the most numerous bird that ever lived	1914
quagga	species of zebra	1883
Labrador duck	sea duck that lived along the northeast coasts of North America	1875
great auk	large flightless seabird of the north Atlantic	1844
Steller's sea cow	large marine mammal inhabiting cold shallow waters off the Commander islands in the Bering Sea	1768
moa	giant ostrich-like flightless bird of New Zealand	c. 1700
dodo	large flightless bird of Mauritius, related to the pigeon	1681

Fins

Fins	Location
adipose	(single) fleshy fin (on back)
anal	underside at rear (can be more than one in line)
caudal	at tail
dorsal	on back (can be more than one in line)
pectoral	(paired) on sides, to rear of head
pelvic	(paired) on sides, towards rear
ventral	same as anal fin

Fir Trees

Tallest

Common name	Max height (m/ft)	Natural home	Common name	Max height (m/ft)	Natural home
giant fir	91/299	USA	Colorado white fir	37/121	USA
red silver fir	76/249	USA	Grecian fir	30/98	Greece
red fir	61/200	USA	Algerian fir	21/69	Algeria
noble fir	61/200	USA	Forrest's fir	18/59	China
Caucasian fir	61/200	Greece, Asia Minor	balsam fir	12–23/39–75	North America
European silver fir	52/171	Europe	Douglas fir	76/249	North America
Japanese fir	46/151	Japan			

Fish

Classification

Classification of fishes	Number of species
Jawless fishes	
Scaleless fish with round mouths	
lamprey	30
hagfish	30
Jawed fishes	
Cartilaginous fishes	
Sharks and rays	
shark	>200
skate, ray	>300
Rabbitfishes	
chimaera, rabbitfish	20
Bony fishes	
Lobe-finned fishes	
coelacanth	1
Australian lungfish	1
South American and African lungfish	4
Ray-finned fishes	
bichir, reedfish	11
paddlefish, sturgeon	25
Teleostei	
bonefish, tarpon, ladyfish	12
eel	>500
herring, anchovy	390
arapaima, African butterfly fish	7
elephant-trunk fish, featherback	150

Fish: Classification (*continued*)

Classification of fishes	Number of species
salmon, trout, smelt, pike	160
milkfish	15
carp, barb, characin, loach, catfish	6,000
deep-sea lantern fish, Bombay duck	300
toadfish, trout-perch, codfish	853
flying fish, toothcarp, halfbeak	575
stickleback, pipefish, seahorse	150
flatfish, flounder	402
puffer fish, triggerfish, sunfish	250
perch, marlin, mackerel, tuna, swordfish, spiny eel, mullet, barracuda, sea bream	6,500

Fish
World's Rarest

Fish	Family name	Fish	Family name
bluenose sixgill shark	Anchiformes	naked characin	Charachiformes
sand tiger shark	Orectolobiformes	spotted handfish	Lophiiformes
kitefish shark	Squaliformes	anguila ciega	Synbranchiformes
stingray	Myliobatiformes	coelacanth	Coelacanthiformes
bony tail fish	Osteoglossiformes		

Floods
Most Destructive since 1981

A tsunami is an ocean wave generated by vertical movements of the sea floor resulting from earthquakes or volcanic activity.

Event	Location	Number of deaths	Event	Location	Number of deaths
floods	Bangladesh (1991)	150,450	floods	Pakistan (1992)	1,446
floods	Venezuela (1999)	30,000–50,000	floods	China (1994)	1,400
			floods	Afghanistan (1991)	1,367
floods/typhoon	Philippines (1991)	8,890	floods	El Salvador/Guatemala (1982)	>1,300
floods	China (1991)	6,728	floods	Bangladesh (1988)	>1,300
floods	China (1998)	>3,650	floods	India (1998)	>1,300
floods	China (1996)	2,300	floods	China (1995)	1,200
floods	India (1991)	2,024	floods	Malawi (1991)	1,172
floods	Sudan (1991)	2,000	floods	Bangladesh (1987)	>1,000
floods	Somalia (1997)	>1,700	floods	China (1999)	>925
tsunami	Papua New Guinea (1998)	>1,700			

Floods
Worst Floods and Storms in the UK

Year	Location	Event	Details
1703	southwest England	storm	called The Great Storm; 125 people were killed on land and 8,000 at sea
1841	River Till	floods	meltwater burst the banks of the River Till
1897	Tay Bridge	hurricane	the bridge collapsed and a train plunged into the river; 75 people were drowned
1912	Norwich	floods	severe flooding damaged about 3,650 buildings
1920	Louth	storm	115 mm/1.6 in of rain fell in 2.5 hours, causing severe flooding
1927	Glasgow	hurricane	11 people were killed and over 100 injured
1928	London	floods	widespread flooding of the Thames and its tributaries
1950	Berkshire	tornado	wind speed of up to 370 kph/230 mph caused widespread destruction
1952	Lynmouth	floods	rainfall measuring 386 mm/15.2 in in 12 hours caused flooding; 34 people were killed
1952	London	anticyclone	prevented the passage of clean air from clearing fog; 4,000 deaths were caused by the 'smog' that had settled in the air
1957	Hatfield	hurrricane	gale force winds caused damage to 26 houses
1962	Sheffield	hurricane	gusts of up to 154 kph/96 mph caused damage to 100,000 homes
1965	Wisley	tornado	caused destruction 10–30 m/33–100 ft-wide for a distance of 3 km/1.9 mi
1965	Ferrybridge	gusting winds	caused three cooling towers to collapse
1965	Sea Gem oil rig	hurricane	created waves 6 m/20 ft high, and caused oil rig to collapse; nine people died
1967	Mossdale	floods	heavy rains filled the caves, drowning six people inside
1968	Glasgow	hurricane	winds gusting up to 161 kph/100 mph caused damage to over 100,000 homes
1968	River Mole	floods	150–200 mm/6–8 in of rainfall over three days caused the river to burst its banks
1971	Cairngorms	snow blizzard	caused deaths of six members of a school party on a climbing expedition
1987	south England	storm	the worst since 1703, caused widespread damage to tree areas and 17 deaths
1997	Scotland and northwest England	hurricane	damaged many buildings, uprooted thousands of trees, and caused six deaths
1998	eastern and central England	floods	the worst flooding in 50 years, caused five deaths and damage of £500 million
1998	Wales and west England	floods	torrential rain and flooding caused over £100 million damage; four people died
2000	England and Wales	floods	the wettest year since records began caused the worst floods for 40 years

Flowering Plants
Largest Families of Flowering Plants

Family	Number of species	Common name	Family	Number of species	Common name
Compositae	21,000	daisies	Euphorbiaceae	7,750	spurges
Orchidaceae	17,500	orchids	Labiatae	5,600	mint
Leguminosae	16,400	beans	Melastomataceae	4,750	melastoma
Rubiaceae	10,700	madder	Liliaceae	4,550	lilies
Gramineae	7,950	grasses	Scrophulariaceae	4,500	figworts

Forests
Area of World Forests

Continent/region	Forest ecosystems, land area (thousand ha)				
	Closed forests	Mangroves	Tropical forests	Non-tropical forests	Sparse trees and parkland
Africa	2,963,468	3,801	448,197	8,249	69,710
Asia	3,085,414	4,033	210,720	145,101	42,384
Europe	2,260,320	0	0	1,019,178	10,350
Central America	264,835	1,679	71,893	21,293	26
North America	1,838,009	199	443	683,700	148,827
South America	1,752,925	2,929	620,514	39,291	168,216
Oceania	849,135	5,466	53,560	27,088	102,126

Forests
Most Forested Countries

Country	Percentage of total land area	Country	Percentage of total land area
Suriname	95	Cambodia	76
Solomon Islands	91	Finland	76
Papua New Guinea	84	North Korea	74
Guyana	83	Japan	67
Gabon	78	South Korea	66

Gardening
Folklore

Ritual	Traditional meaning
drinking a New Year toast to fruit trees	to encourage good cropping
growing garlic	to cure constipation (not as a food)
knocking iron nails into the bark of fruit trees	to increase their crop
not picking blackberries after 29 September	that is the day the devil spits or stamps on them (Michaelmas)

(continued)

Gardening: Folklore (*continued*)

Ritual	Traditional meaning
not planting on a Sunday	such plants will soon die
picking nettles (for fibres) before May day	to prevent the devil from using them to make his shirts
planting celery among cabbages	to protect the cabbages from caterpillars
planting fruit treets under a full moon	to stimulate abundant cropping
planting in north-south rows	to obtain better cropping
sowing beans and peas two days before a full moon	to increase the rate of germination and cropping
whipping fruit trees	to stimulate them to produce more fruit

Horse
Points

poll	arm	pastern	hind quarters
cheek	breast	hoof	thigh
muzzle	point of the elbow	chest	stifle
chin	brisket	back	buttock
jowl	forearm	belly	gaskin
crest	knee	flank	hamstring
neck	fore cannon	sheath	point of the hock
jugular groove	fetlock	loins	hock joint
withers	coronet	croup	hind cannon
shoulder	chestnut	dock	fetlock
point of shoulder	ergot	hip joint	bulb of heel

Insects
Classification

Classification of Insects	Number of species
Wingless insects	
springtails	2,000
two-pronged bristletails, campodeids, japygids	660
minute insects living in soil	120
three-pronged bristletails, silverfish	600
Winged insects	
Young resemble adults but have externally developing wings	
mayflies	2,000
dragonflies, damselflies	5,000
wingless soil-living insects of North America	12
stoneflies	3,000

Insects: Classification (*continued*)

Classification of Insects	Number of species
Winged insects	
tiny insects living in decaying plants	20
termites	2,000
earwigs	1,500
web-spinners	200
cockroaches, praying mantises	3,700
crickets, grasshoppers, locusts, mantids, cockroaches	24,000
stick insects, leaf insects	2,500
booklice, barklice, psocids	1,600
biting lice, mainly parasitic on birds	2,500
sucking lice, mainly parasitic on mammals	250
true bugs, including shield- and bedbugs, froghoppers, pond skaters, water boatmen	39,500
aphids, cicadas, hoppers, whiteflies	45,000
thrips	5,000

Winged insects	
Young are unlike adults and undergo sudden metamorphosis	
lacewings, alderflies, snakeflies	4,500
scorpion flies	450
butterflies, moths	138,000
caddisflies	7,000
true flies, including bluebottles, mosquitoes, craneflies, midges	150,000
fleas	1,750
bees, wasps, ants, sawflies, chalcids	130,000
beetles, including weevils, ladybirds, glow-worms, woodworms, chafers	250,000

Insects

Insects You Can Eat

Insect	Country
ant	Australia
black tarantula	Thailand
Bogong moth	Australia
desert locust	Algeria
dragonfly	Bali
longhorn beetle larva	Ecuador
redlegged grasshopper	Mexico
silk moth pupa	Japan
termite	Nigeria
wasp larva	Japan
witchety grub (moth larva)	Australia

Invertebrates and Vertebrates
Classification

Name	Examples
Invertebrates	
Porifera	all sponges
Cnidaria	corals, sea anemones, *hydra,* jellyfishes
Ctenophora	sea gooseberries, comb jellies
Platyhelminthes	flatworms, flukes, tapeworms
Nemertina	nemertine worms, ribbon worms
Rotifera	rotifers or wheel animals
Nematoda	roundworms
Ectoprocta	ectoprocts
Mollusca	clams, oysters, snails, slugs, octopuses, squids, cuttlefish
Annelida	ringed worms, including lugworms, earthworms, and leeches
Arthropoda	(subdivided into classes below)
Arachnida	spiders, ticks, scorpions, mites
Branchiopoda	water fleas
Cirripedia	barnacles
Malacostraca	crabs, lobsters, shrimp, woodlice
Diplopoda	millipedes
Chilopoda	centipedes
Insecta	silverfish, dragonflies, mayflies, stoneflies, cockroaches, earwigs, web spinners, termites, booklice, lice, grasshoppers, thrips, lace-wings, scorpion flies, caddis-flies, moths, butterflies, beetles, house flies, fleas, stylopids, ants, bees

Name	Examples
Echinodermata	sea stars, brittle stars, sea urchins, sand dollars, sea cucumbers
Hemichordata	acorn worms, pterobranchs, graptolites
Vertebrates	
Agnatha	(jawless fishes) lampreys, hagfishes
Chondricthyes	(cartilaginous fishes) dogfishes, sharks, rays, skates
Osteichthyes	(bony fishes) sturgeons, eels, herrings, salmon, carps, catfishes, perches, flatfishes including flounder and halibut
Amphibia	caecilians, salamanders, newts, toads, frogs
Reptilia	turtles, tortoises, tuatara, lizards, snakes, crocodiles
Aves	ostriches, rheas, penguins, divers, pelicans, flamingoes, ducks, falcons, pheasants, cranes, gulls, pigeons, parrots, cuckoos, owls, swifts, kingfishers, sparrows
Mammalia	platypus, echidnas, kangaroos, opossums, shrews, bats, rats, anteaters, rabbits, dogs, whales, elephants, manatees, horses, tapirs, camels, pigs, lemurs, monkeys, humans

Loch Ness Monster
Reported Sightings

Number of sightings	Year
17	1933
12	1996
11	1934
9	1966
6	1967
6	1968
5	1997
5	1998
4	1960
4	1969
3	1965
2	1943
1	1871, 1885, 1888, 1895, 1903, 1908, 1923, 1929, 1930, 1932, 1936, 1947, 1954, 1956, 1961–64, 1973, 1979

Mammals
Classification

Classification of Mammals	Number of species
Egg-laying mammals	
echidna, platypus	3
Pouched mammals	
kangaroo, koala, opossum	266
Placental mammals	
rat, mouse, squirrel, porcupine	1,700
all bats	970
shrew, hedgehog, mole	378
cat, dog, weasel, bear	230
lemur, monkey, ape, human	180
pig, deer, cattle, camel, giraffe	145
whale, dolphin	79
rabbit, hare, pika	58
seal, walrus	33
anteater, armadillo, sloth	29
horse, rhinoceros, tapir	16
hyrax	11
pangolin	7
dugong, manatee	4
flying lemur	2
elephant	2
aardvark	1

Mammals
Classification by Order

Order	Number of species	Examples	Order	Number of species	Examples
Monotremata	3	echidnas, duck-billed platypus	Insectivora	378	hedgehog, moles, shrews
Marsupiala	266	kangaroos, koala, opossums, wombats	Lagomorpha	58	hares, pika, rabbits
			Perissodactyla	16	horses, rhinoceroses, tapir
Artiodactyle	145	camels, cattles, deer, giraffe, pigs	Pholidota	7	pangolins
Carnivora	230	bears, cats, dogs, weasels	Pinnipedia	33	seals, sealions, walrus
Cetacea	79	dolphins, whales	Primates	180	apes, human, lemurs, monkeys
Chiroptera	970	bats, flying foxes	Proboscidea	2	elephants
Dermoptera	2	flying lemurs	Rodentia	1,700	rats, mice, porcupine, squirrels
Edentata	29	anteater, armadillos, sloths	Sirenia	3	dugong, manatees
Hyracoida	11	hyraxes	Tubulidentata	1	aardvark

Mammals
Longest Gestation Periods

Mammal	Scientific name	Period (days)	Mammal	Scientific name	Period (days)
African elephant	*Lorodonta africana*	640	Brazilian tapir	*Tapiris terrestris*	390–400
white rhinoceros	*Ceratotherium simum*	485	sei whale	*Baleanoptera borealis*	365
long-finned pilot whale	*Globicephala maleana*	485	common zebra	*Equus burchelli*	365
giraffe	*Giraffa camelopardalis*	400–468	African buffalo	*Synceros caffer*	330
Bactrian camel	*Camelus bactrianus*	370–440	walrus	*Odobenus rosmarus*	330

Mammals
Most Known Species

Family	Typical members	Number of species
Cricetidae	field mice, deer mice, voles, lemmings, muskrats	560
Muridae	Old World rats and mice	450
Soricidae	shrews	291
Vespertilionidae	common bats	290
Sciuridae	squirrels, chipmunks, marmots	250
Pteropodidae	Old World fruit bats, flying foxes	154
Phyllostomatidae	American leaf-nosed bats	120

Family	Typical members	Number of species
Bovidae	cattle, goats, sheep, antelopes, gazelles	110
Molossidae	free-tailed bats	90
Cercopithecidae	Old World monkeys	72

Mammals
Shortest Gestation Periods

Mammal	Scientific name	Period (days)
Eastern barred bandicoot	*Perameles gunii*	11
water opossum	*Chironectes minimus*	14
short-tailed shrew	*Blarina brericauda*	17–21
Northern pocket gopher	*Thomomys talpoides*	18
meadow jumping mouse	*Zapus hudsonius*	18
fat-tailed gerbil	*Pachyuromys duprasi*	19–22
quoll	*Dasyurus viverrinus*	20
dwarf hamster	*Phodopus sungorus*	21
brown rat	*Rattus norvegicus*	21
Western harvest mouse	*Reithrodontonys megalotis*	23

Mammals
That Can Stay Underwater Longest

List excludes whales.

Animal	Latin name	Time underwater (minutes)
harbour seal	*Phoca vitulina*	22
manatee	*Trichechus manatus*	16
hippopotamus	*Hippopotamus amphibius*	15
American muskrat	*Ondatra zibethica*	12
duckbilled platypus	*Ornithorhynchus anatinus*	10
sea otter	*Enhydra lutris*	5
polar bear	*Thalarctos maritimus*	1.5

Mammals
World's Largest Land Mammals

Animal	Scientific name	Weight (tonnes)
African elephant	*Lorodonta africana*	5.90
Asian elephant	*Elephas maximus*	5.40
white rhinoceros	*Ceratotherium simum*	3.50
hippopotamus	*Hippopotamus amphibious*	3.00
American bison	*Bison bison*	1.50
dromedary	*Camelus dromedarius*	0.70
polar bear	*Tharlarctos maritimus*	0.65
brown bear	*Ursus arctos*	0.60
elk, or moose	*Alces alces*	0.55
Galapagos giant tortoise	*Geochelone nigra*	0.50
gorilla	*Gorilla gorilla*	0.35
tiger	*Panthera tigris*	0.30

Mammals
World's Rarest

Mammal	Numbers
black-footed ferret	none known in the wild
kouprey, or Cambodian forest ox	a few dozen
Seychelles sheath-tailed bat	<50
Northern hairy-nosed wombat	<70
Javan rhinoceros	<70
baiji, or Yangtze River dolphin	<100
Vancouver Island marmot	<100
dwarf blue sheep	about 200
Malabar large spotted civet	<250
black-faced Tamarin lion	about 260

Mammals
World's Smallest Mammals

Mammal	Scientific name	Length (cm/in) (excluding tail)
hog-nosed bat	*Craseonycteris thonglongyai*	3.0–3.5/1.2–1.4
pygmy white-tailed shrew	*Suncus etruseus*	3.5–5.0/1.4–2.0
pygmy planigale	*Planigale maculata*	5.0–5.5/2.0–2.2
dwarf hamster	*Phodopus sungorus*	5.0–10.0/2.0–3.9
Western harvest mouse	*Rethrodontomys megalotis*	5.0–14.0/2.0–5.5
long-tailed shrew tenrec	*Microgale longicaudata*	5.0–15.0/2.0–5.9
pygmy glider	*Acrobates pygmaeus*	6.0–8.5/2.4–3.3
Zenker's flying squirrel	*Idiurus zenkeri*	6.0–10.0/2.4–3.9
pale kangaroo mouse	*Mirodipodops pallidus*	6.5–8.0/2.6–3.1
honey possum	*Tarsipes rostratus*	7.0–8.5/2.3–3.3

Milk
Milk from Different Animals

Animal	Protein (g per 100 ml/oz per 3.5 fl oz)	Fat (g per 100 ml/oz per 3.5 fl oz)	Carbohydrate (g per 100 ml/oz per 3.5 fl oz)	Energy (kcal per 100 ml/kj per 3.5 fl oz)
buffalo	4.3/0.15	7.5/0.26	4.5/0.16	105/25
camel	3.7/0.13	4.2/0.15	4.0/0.14	70/17
cow	3.5/0.12	3.5/0.12	5.0/0.18	65/16
ewe	6.5/0.23	7.0/0.25	5.0/0.18	110/26
goat	3.7/0.13	5.0/0.18	4.5/0.16	75/18
human	1.1/0.04	6.2/0.22	7.5/0.26	70/17
mare	1.3/0.05	1.2/0.04	5.5/0.19	30/7
reindeer	10.5/0.37	22.5/0.79	2.5/0.09	250/60

National Parks
Areas of National Parks in the UK

Name	Location	Area (sq km/sq mi)
Lake District	Cumbria	2,290/884
Snowdonia	Gwynedd	2,140/826
Yorkshire Dales	North Yorkshire, Cumbria	1,770/683
Peak District	Derbyshire, Staffordshire, South Yorkshire, Cheshire, West Yorkshire, Greater Manchester	1,440/556
North York Moors	North Yorkshire	1,435/554
Brecon Beacons	Powys, Dyfed, Gwent, Mid Glamorgan	1,350/521
Northumberland	Northumberland	1,050/405
Dartmoor	Devon	955/369
Exmoor	Somerset, Devon	695/268
Pembrokeshire Coast	Dyfed	585/226
Broads	Norfolk, Suffolk	300/116

National Parks
Largest National Parks in the USA

Name	Location	Area (sq km/sq mi)
Wrangell-St Elias	Southeastern Alaska	32,970/12,730
Gates of the Arctic	Northern Alaska	28,550/11,023
Katmai	Southwestern Alaska	17,900/6,911
Denali	Southern Alaska	16,450/6,351
Glacier Bay	Southeastern Alaska	15,700/6,062
Death Valley	California, Nevada	13,650/5,270
Lake Clark	Southern Alaska	9,000/3,475
Yellowstone	Idaho, Montana, Wyoming	8,950/3,456
Kobuk Valley	Northern Alaska	6,900/2,664
Everglades	Southern Florida	5,650/2,181

Oil Spills
World's Worst Oil Spills

Location/year	Ship/oil well name	Size of spill (tonnes)
Sea Island Terminal of The Gulf (1991)	deliberate release of oil by Iraqi troops at end of Gulf War	799,120
Gulf of Mexico (1979)	*Ixtoc 1* oil field	600,000
The Gulf (1983)	*Nowruz* oil field	600,000
off Tobago, West Indies (1979)	*Atlantic Empress* and *Aegean Captain*	370,000
North Sea (1977)	*Ekofisk* oil well	270,000
off Angola (1991)	*ABT Summer*	260,000
off Saldanha Bay, South Africa (1983)	*Castillo de Beliver*	252,000
off Brittany, France (1978)	*Amoco Cadiz*	223,000
Genoa, Italy (1991)	*Haven*	144,000
off Nova Scotia, Canada (1988)	*Odyssey*	132,000

Pets

Most Popular Pets in the UK

budgerigar

cat

dog

goldfish

guinea pig

hamster

marine fish

rabbit

reptiles

tropical fish

Plants

Classification of Carnivorous Plants

Plants that obtain at least some of their nutrition by capturing and digesting prey are called carnivorous plants.

Common name	Trapping mechanism
bladderwort	active trap; shows rapid motion during capture
butterwort	semi-active trap; two-stage trap in which prey is initially caught in sticky fluid
calf's head pitcher plant	passive trap; attracts prey with nectar and then prey drowns in fluid contained within plant
flypaper plant	passive trap; attracts prey with nectar and then prey drowns in fluid contained within plant
sundew	semi-active trap; two-stage trap in which prey is initially caught in sticky fluid
Venus flytrap	active trap; shows rapid motion during capture

Plants

Classification of Plants

Division (phylum)	Examples	Division (phylum)	Examples
Angiospermophyta	all flowering plants	Ginkgophyta	the *Ginkgo*
Bryophyta	hornworts, liverworts, mosses	Gnetophyta	*Welwitschia* and other gnetophytes
Coniferophyta	all conifers	Lycopodophyta	club mosses
Cycadophyta	cycads	Psilophyta	whisk ferns
Filicinophyta	ferns	Sphenophyta	horsetails

Plants

Folklore

Plant	Traditional association
amaryllis	pride and independence
artichoke	aphrodisiac
aster	first approach
buddleia	refinement
candytuft	peace and serenity
chicory	love charm
chrysanthemum	honesty and truth
coriander	long life
daffodil	gallantry
forget-me-not	fidelity
honeysuckle	sweet nature and constancy
hydrangea	boastfulness
ivy	bad luck
lavender	calmness and chastity
lilac	first love
lily of the valley	pureness and unselfishness
marigold	happiness
mistletoe	fertility
narcissus	unrequited love
parsley	female dominance
primrose	sorrow and sadness
rose	true love
rosemary	remembrance
snowdrop	promise of spring (and summer)
sweet pea	tenderness
tomato	aphrodisiac

Plants

Germination Times for Flower Seeds

Flower	Latin name (if different)	Germination time (days)
ageratum		7–11
Californian poppy	Eschscholtzia	5–10
candytuft	Iberis	6–9
Canterbury bells	Campanula	12–15
cosmos		5–15
gaillardia		12–15
helichrysum		5–10
larkspur	Delphinium	15–20
lupin	Lupinus	25–30
marigold	Tagetes	5–8
nicotiana		20–25
petunia		18–20
phlox		20–25
pink	Dianthus	5–8
pot marigold	Calendula	10–12
scabious	Scabiosa	18–20
snapdragon	Antirrhinum	20–25
sweet alyssum		10–13
sweet pea	Lathyrus	15–20
verbena		8–10

Plants

Plants Named After Their Discoverer

Plant	Discoverer	Occupation
aubretia	Claude Aubriet	French flower painter
begonia	Michel Bègon	French science patron and plant collector
bignonia	Abbé Jean-Paul Bignon	French court librarian
bougainvillaea	Louis de Bougainville	French explorer
boysenberry	Rudolph Boysen	US botanist
camellia	Josef Kamel (Camellus)	Moravian missionary and botanist
cattleya	William Cattley	English botanist
cinchona	Countess de Cinchón	Vicereine of Peru
clarkia	William Clark	US explorer
dahlia	Anders Dahl	Swedish botanist

(continued)

Plants: Plants Named After Their Discoverer (*continued*)

Plant	Discoverer	Occupation
deutzia	Jean Deutz	Dutch patron of botany
eschscholtzia	J von Eschscholtz	German botanist
filbert	St Philbert; feast day (22 August) coincides with the ripening of the nuts	
forsythia	William Forsyth	English botanist
fortunella	Robert Fortune	Scottish botanist
freesia	F H T Freese	German physician
fuchsia	Leonard Fuchs	German botanist
gaillardia	Gaillard de Marentonneau	French botanist
gardenia	Alexander Garden	US botanist
garrya	Nicholas Garry	Hudson's Bay Company official
gaultheria	Jean-François Gailtier	Canadian botanist
gazania	Theodore of Gaza	15th-century botanical translator
gentian	Gentius	King of Ilyria 2nd century BC
gloxinia	Benjamin Gloxin	German botanist
godetia	C H Godet	Swiss botanist
greengage	William Gage	English botanist
gunnera	J E Gunnerus	Norwegian botanist
heuchera	J H Heucher	German botanist
hosta	Nicholas Host	Austrian physician
houstonia	William Houston	Scottish botanist
hoya	Thomas Hoy	English gardener
hyacinth	Hyacinthus	mythical Greek youth
kalmia	Peter Kalm	Swedish botanist
kentia	W Kent	Dutch botanist
kniphofia	J H Kniphof	German botanist
kochia	W D J Kock	German botanist
lobelia	Matthias de l'Obel	Flemish botanist
loganberry	James Logan	US judge and horticulurist
macadamia	John Macadam	Australian chemist
magnolia	Pierre Magnol	French botanist
maranta	Bartolomea Maranti	Italian botanist
monarda	N Monardésé	Spanish botanist
montbretia	A Coquebert de Montbret	French botanist
poinsettia	Joel Poinsett	US ambassador
rafflesia	Stamford Raffles	British colonial administrator
sansevieria	Raimondo di Sangro	Prince of San Seviero
shaddock	Captain Shaddock	English sailor in East and West Indies
spreklia	J H von Sprekelsen	German botanist
stapelia	J B Stapel	Dutch botanist
tradescantia	John Tradescant	English botanist
weigela	C E Weigel	German physician
welwitschia	F M Welwitsch	Austrian-born Portuguese botanist
wisteria	Caspar Wistar	US anatomist
zantedeschia	Francesco Zantedeschi	Italian botanist
zinnia	Johann Zinn	German botanist

Plants
Plants with Misleading Place-names

Plant	Origin	Plant	Origin
African marigold	Mexico	Italian poplar	Canada
American wintercress	Mediterranean region	Jersey buttercup	Germany
		Jerusalem artichoke	North America
Bermuda buttercup	Southern Africa	kiwi fruit	China
Chinese yam	Africa	Scotch laburnum	Italy
Florence fennel	Malta	Spanish chestnut	Asia Minor
French bean	tropical America	Swiss chard	France
French marigold	Mexico	Turkish tobacco	Mexico and Texas

Poisonous Plants
Common Poisonous Plants

Common name	Scientific name	Poisonous part
buttercup	*Ranunculus* spp.	all parts
deadly nightshade	*Atropus belladonna*	fruit
elderberry	*Sambucus nigra*	leaves and bark
foxglove	*Digitalis*	leaves
ivy	*Hedera helix*	fruit
lily of the valley	*Convallaria majalis*	leaves and flowers
poison ivy	*Rhus radicans*	flowers and fruit
poison oak	*Rhus toxicodendron*	leaves
poppy	*Papaver* spp.	seed pods
rhubarb	*Rheum rhaponticum*	leaves (not stalks)
yew	*Taxus baccata*	leaves and fruit

Rainbow
Colours of the Rainbow

red	yellow	blue	violet
orange	green	indigo	

Rainfall

In Major Cities of the World from January to March

City	Average monthly rainfall (mm)			City	Average monthly rainfall (mm)		
	Jan	Feb	Mar		Jan	Feb	Mar
Adelaide, Australia	20	18	25	La Paz, Bolivia	114	107	66
Algiers, Algeria	112	84	74	Lhasa, Tibet	0	13	8
Almaty, Kazakhstan	33	23	96	Lima, Peru	3	0	0
Ankara, Turkey	33	31	33	Lisbon, Portugal	111	76	109
Asunción, Paraguay	140	130	109	London, England	54	40	37
Athens, Greece	62	37	37	Los Angeles, USA	79	76	71
Balboa Heights, Panama	25	10	18	Madrid, Spain	39	34	43
Bangkok, Thailand	8	20	86	Manila, Philippines	23	13	18
Barcelona, Spain	31	39	48	Melbourne, Australia	48	46	56
Beijing, China	4	5	8	Mexico City, Mexico	13	5	10
Belfast, Northern Ireland	80	52	50	Milan, Italy	44	60	77
Belgrade, Yugoslavia	47	46	46	Montevideo, Uruguay	74	66	99
Berlin, Germany	46	40	33	Moscow, Russian Federation	39	38	36
Bogotá, Colombia	58	66	102				
Brussels, Belgium	66	61	53	Mumbai (formerly Bombay), India	2.5	2.5	2.5
Bucharest, Romania	48	26	28				
Budapest, Hungary	37	44	38	Nagasaki, Japan	71	84	125
Buenos Aires, Argentina	79	71	109	Nairobi, Kenya	38	64	125
Cairo, Egypt	5	5	5	New York, USA	94	97	91
Cape Town, South Africa	15	8	18	Oslo, Norway	49	35	26
Caracas, Venezuela	23	10	15	Ottawa, Canada	74	56	71
Copenhagen, Denmark	49	39	32	Paris, France	56	46	35
Dakar, Senegal	0	0	0	Prague, Czech Republic	18	18	18
De Bilt, Netherlands	68	53	44	Quito, Ecuador	99	112	142
Delhi, India	23	18	13	Reykjavik, Iceland	89	64	62
Detroit, USA	53	53	64	Rio de Janeiro, Brazil	125	122	130
Djibouti, Djibouti	10	13	25	Riyadh, Saudi Arabia	3	20	23
Dublin, Republic of Ireland	67	55	51	Rome, Italy	71	62	57
				St Petersburg, Russian Federation	35	30	31
Edinburgh, Scotland	57	39	39				
Frankfurt, Germany	58	44	38	Santiago, Chile	3	3	5
Guatemala City, Guatemala	8	3	13	Seoul, South Korea	31	20	38
				Shanghai, China	48	58	84
Havana, Cuba	71	46	46	Singapore, Singapore	252	173	193
Helsinki, Finland	56	42	36	Sofia, Bulgaria	36	28	41
Hong Kong, China	33	46	74	Stockholm, Sweden	43	30	25
Istanbul, Turkey	109	92	72	Sydney, Australia	89	102	127
Jakarta, Indonesia	300	300	211	Tehran, Iran	46	38	46
Jerusalem, Israel	132	132	64	Tokyo, Japan	48	74	107
Johannesburg, South Africa	114	109	89	Toronto, Canada	69	61	66
				Tripoli, Libya	81	46	28
Kabul, Afghanistan	31	36	94	Vancouver, Canada	218	147	127
Karachi, Pakistan	13	10	8	Vienna, Austria	39	44	44
Katmandu, Nepal	15	41	23	Warsaw, Poland	27	32	27
Kiev, Ukraine	46	37	40	Washington, DC, USA	86	76	91
Kinshasa, Democratic Republic of Congo	5	84	178	Wellington, New Zealand	81	81	81
Lagos, Nigeria	28	46	102	Zürich, Switzerland	74	69	64

Rainfall

In Major Cities of the World from April to June

City	Average monthly rainfall (mm)			City	Average monthly rainfall (mm)		
	April	May	June		April	May	June
Adelaide, Australia	46	69	76	La Paz, Bolivia	33	13	8
Algiers, Algeria	41	46	15	Lhasa, Tibet	5	25	64
Almaty, Kazakhstan	102	94	66	Lima, Peru	0	5	5
Ankara, Turkey	33	48	25	Lisbon, Portugal	54	44	16
Asunción, Paraguay	132	117	69	London, England	37	46	45
Athens, Greece	23	23	14	Los Angeles, USA	25	10	3
Balboa Heights, Panama	74	203	213	Madrid, Spain	48	47	27
Bangkok, Thailand	58	198	160	Manila, Philippines	33	130	254
Barcelona, Spain	43	54	37	Melbourne, Australia	58	53	53
Beijing, China	17	35	78	Mexico City, Mexico	20	53	119
Belfast, Northern Ireland	48	52	68	Milan, Italy	94	76	118
Belgrade, Yugoslavia	54	74	96	Montevideo, Uruguay	99	84	81
Berlin, Germany	42	49	65	Moscow, Russian Federation	37	53	58
Bogotá, Colombia	147	114	61				
Brussels, Belgium	60	55	76	Mumbai (formerly Bombay), India	0	18	485
Bucharest, Romania	59	77	121				
Budapest, Hungary	45	72	69	Nagasaki, Japan	185	170	312
Buenos Aires, Argentina	89	76	61	Nairobi, Kenya	211	158	46
Cairo, Egypt	3	3	0	New York, USA	81	81	84
Cape Town, South Africa	48	79	84	Oslo, Norway	43	44	70
Caracas, Venezuela	33	79	102	Ottawa, Canada	69	64	89
Copenhagen, Denmark	38	43	47	Paris, France	42	57	54
Dakar, Senegal	0	0	18	Prague, Czech Republic	27	48	54
De Bilt, Netherlands	49	52	58	Quito, Ecuador	175	137	43
Delhi, India	8	13	74	Reykjavik, Iceland	56	42	42
Detroit, USA	64	84	91	Rio de Janeiro, Brazil	107	79	53
Djibouti, Djibouti	13	5	0	Riyadh, Saudi Arabia	25	10	0
Dublin, Republic of Ireland	45	60	57	Rome, Italy	51	46	37
				St Petersburg, Russian Federation	36	45	50
Edinburgh, Scotland	39	54	47				
Frankfurt, Germany	44	55	73	Santiago, Chile	13	64	84
Guatemala City, Guatemala	31	152	274	Seoul, South Korea	76	81	130
				Shanghai, China	94	94	180
Havana, Cuba	58	119	165	Singapore, Singapore	188	173	173
Helsinki, Finland	44	41	51	Sofia, Bulgaria	61	87	73
Hong Kong, China	137	292	394	Stockholm, Sweden	31	34	45
Istanbul, Turkey	46	38	34	Sydney, Australia	135	127	117
Jakarta, Indonesia	147	114	97	Tehran, Iran	36	13	3
Jerusalem, Israel	28	3	0	Tokyo, Japan	135	147	165
Johannesburg, South Africa	38	25	8	Toronto, Canada	64	74	69
				Tripoli, Libya	10	5	3
Kabul, Afghanistan	102	20	5	Vancouver, Canada	84	71	64
Karachi, Pakistan	3	3	18	Vienna, Austria	45	70	67
Katmandu, Nepal	58	122	246	Warsaw, Poland	37	46	69
Kiev, Ukraine	28	38	35	Washington, DC, USA	84	94	99
Kinshasa, Democratic Republic of Congo	158	137	114	Wellington, New Zealand	97	117	117
				Zürich, Switzerland	76	101	129
Lagos, Nigeria	150	269	460				

Rainfall
In Major Cities of the World from July to September

City	Average monthly rainfall (mm)			City	Average monthly rainfall (mm)		
	July	Aug	Sept		July	Aug	Sept
Adelaide, Australia	66	66	53	La Paz, Bolivia	10	13	28
Algiers, Algeria	0	5	41	Lhasa, Tibet	122	89	66
Almaty, Kazakhstan	36	31	25	Lima, Peru	8	8	8
Ankara, Turkey	15	10	18	Lisbon, Portugal	3	4	33
Asunción, Paraguay	56	38	79	London, England	57	59	49
Athens, Greece	6	7	15	Los Angeles, USA	0	0	5
Balboa Heights, Panama	180	201	208	Madrid, Spain	11	15	32
Bangkok, Thailand	160	175	305	Manila, Philippines	432	422	356
Barcelona, Spain	27	49	76	Melbourne, Australia	48	48	58
Beijing, China	243	141	58	Mexico City, Mexico	170	152	130
Belfast, Northern Ireland	94	77	80	Milan, Italy	64	91	69
Belgrade, Yugoslavia	61	55	50	Montevideo, Uruguay	74	79	76
Berlin, Germany	73	69	48	Moscow, Russian Federation	88	71	58
Bogotá, Colombia	51	56	61				
Brussels, Belgium	95	80	63	Mumbai (formerly Bombay), India	617	340	264
Bucharest, Romania	53	45	45				
Budapest, Hungary	56	47	33	Nagasaki, Japan	257	175	249
Buenos Aires, Argentina	56	61	79	Nairobi, Kenya	15	23	31
Cairo, Egypt	0	0	0	New York, USA	107	109	86
Cape Town, South Africa	89	66	43	Oslo, Norway	82	95	81
Caracas, Venezuela	109	109	107	Ottawa, Canada	86	66	81
Copenhagen, Denmark	71	66	62	Paris, France	59	64	55
Dakar, Senegal	89	254	132	Prague, Czech Republic	68	55	31
De Bilt, Netherlands	77	87	72	Quito, Ecuador	20	31	69
Delhi, India	180	173	117	Reykjavik, Iceland	50	56	67
Detroit, USA	84	69	71	Rio de Janeiro, Brazil	41	43	66
Djibouti, Djibouti	3	8	8	Riyadh, Saudi Arabia	0	0	0
Dublin, Republic of Ireland	70	74	72	Rome, Italy	15	21	63
				St Petersburg, Russian Federation	72	78	64
Edinburgh, Scotland	83	77	57				
Frankfurt, Germany	70	76	57	Santiago, Chile	76	56	31
Guatemala City, Guatemala	203	198	231	Seoul, South Korea	376	267	119
				Shanghai, China	147	142	130
Havana, Cuba	125	135	150	Singapore, Singapore	170	196	178
Helsinki, Finland	68	72	71	Sofia, Bulgaria	68	64	41
Hong Kong, China	381	367	257	Stockholm, Sweden	61	76	60
Istanbul, Turkey	34	30	58	Sydney, Australia	117	76	74
Jakarta, Indonesia	64	43	66	Tehran, Iran	3	3	3
Jerusalem, Israel	0	0	0	Tokyo, Japan	142	152	234
Johannesburg, South Africa	8	8	23	Toronto, Canada	74	69	74
				Tripoli, Libya	0	0	10
Kabul, Afghanistan	3	3	0	Vancouver, Canada	31	43	91
Karachi, Pakistan	81	41	13	Vienna, Austria	84	72	42
Katmandu, Nepal	373	345	155	Warsaw, Poland	96	65	43
Kiev, Ukraine	64	39	36	Washington, DC, USA	112	109	94
Kinshasa, Democratic Republic of Congo	132	165	183	Wellington, New Zealand	137	117	97
Lagos, Nigeria	279	64	140	Zürich, Switzerland	136	124	102

Rainfall

In Major Cities of the World from October to December

City	Average monthly rainfall (mm)			City	Average monthly rainfall (mm)		
	Oct	Nov	Dec		Oct	Nov	Dec
Adelaide, Australia	43	28	25	La Paz, Bolivia	41	48	94
Algiers, Algeria	79	130	137	Lhasa, Tibet	13	3	0
Almaty, Kazakhstan	51	48	33	Lima, Peru	3	3	0
Ankara, Turkey	23	31	48	Lisbon, Portugal	62	93	103
Asunción, Paraguay	140	150	158	London, England	57	64	48
Athens, Greece	51	56	71	Los Angeles, USA	15	31	66
Balboa Heights, Panama	257	259	122	Madrid, Spain	53	47	48
Bangkok, Thailand	206	66	5	Manila, Philippines	193	145	66
Barcelona, Spain	86	52	45	Melbourne, Australia	66	58	58
Beijing, China	16	11	3	Mexico City, Mexico	51	18	8
Belfast, Northern Ireland	83	72	90	Milan, Italy	125	122	77
Belgrade, Yugoslavia	55	61	55	Montevideo, Uruguay	66	74	79
Berlin, Germany	4.9	46	43	Moscow, Russian Federation	45	47	54
Bogotá, Colombia	160	119	66				
Brussels, Belgium	83	75	88	Mumbai (formerly Bombay), India	64	13	2.5
Bucharest, Romania	29	36	27				
Budapest, Hungary	57	70	46	Nagasaki, Japan	114	94	81
Buenos Aires, Argentina	86	84	99	Nairobi, Kenya	53	109	86
Cairo, Egypt	0	3	5	New York, USA	89	76	91
Cape Town, South Africa	31	18	10	Oslo, Norway	74	68	63
Caracas, Venezuela	109	94	46	Ottawa, Canada	74	76	66
Copenhagen, Denmark	59	48	49	Paris, France	50	51	50
Dakar, Senegal	38	3	8	Prague, Czech Republic	33	20	21
De Bilt, Netherlands	72	70	64	Quito, Ecuador	112	97	79
Delhi, India	10	3	10	Reykjavik, Iceland	94	78	79
Detroit, USA	61	61	58	Rio de Janeiro, Brazil	79	104	137
Djibouti, Djibouti	10	23	13	Riyadh, Saudi Arabia	0	0	0
Dublin, Republic of Ireland	70	67	74	Rome, Italy	99	129	93
				St Petersburg, Russian Federation	76	46	40
Edinburgh, Scotland	65	62	57				
Frankfurt, Germany	52	55	54	Santiago, Chile	15	8	5
Guatemala City, Guatemala	173	23	8	Seoul, South Korea	41	46	25
				Shanghai, China	71	51	36
Havana, Cuba	173	79	58	Singapore, Singapore	208	254	257
Helsinki, Finland	73	68	66	Sofia, Bulgaria	65	48	49
Hong Kong, China	114	43	31	Stockholm, Sweden	48	53	48
Istanbul, Turkey	81	103	119	Sydney, Australia	71	74	74
Jakarta, Indonesia	112	142	203	Tehran, Iran	8	20	31
Jerusalem, Israel	13	71	86	Tokyo, Japan	208	97	56
Johannesburg, South Africa	56	107	125	Toronto, Canada	61	71	66
				Tripoli, Libya	41	66	94
Kabul, Afghanistan	15	20	10	Vancouver, Canada	147	211	224
Karachi, Pakistan	0	3	5	Vienna, Austria	56	52	45
Katmandu, Nepal	38	8	3	Warsaw, Poland	38	31	44
Kiev, Ukraine	24	43	52	Washington, DC, USA	74	66	79
Kinshasa, Democratic Republic of Congo	218	198	84	Wellington, New Zealand	102	89	89
Lagos, Nigeria	206	69	25	Zürich, Switzerland	77	73	64

Rainfall
World's Highest Rainfall (Annual Average)

Location	Country	Quantity (mm/in)
Mawsynram	India	12,685/499
Cherrapunji	India	10,990/433
Kukui	Hawaii	9,580/377
Guam	Mariana Islands	9,100/358
Junin	Colombia	8,940/352
Zanderij	Suriname	8,565/337
Novita	Colombia	8,525/336
Agumbe	India	8,085/318
Malaguita	Colombia	8,080/318
Tabubil	Papua New Guinea	8,055/317

Rainfall
World's Highest Rainfall (Monthly Average)

Location	Country	Quantity (mm/in)	Month
Mawsynram	India	3,300/130	June
Cherrapunji	India	2,970/117	July
Hulikal	India	2,825/111	July
Agumbe	India	2,750/108	July
Mahabaleshwar	India	2,570/101	July
Nagar	India	2,485/98	July
Bhagamandala	India	2,225/88	July
Maranahalli	India	2,195/86	July
Gaganbawada	India	2,095/82	July
Kottigehar	India	2,025/80	July

Rainfall
World's Lowest

Location	Country	Annual average quantity (mm/in)
Kharga	Egypt	0.3/0.012
Arica	Chile	0.5/0.020
Wadihalfa	Sudan	0.6/0.024
Iquique	Chile	0.6/0.024
Asyut	Egypt	0.7/0.028
Dakhla	Egypt	0.8/0.031
Tazerbo	Libya	1.0/0.039
Qena	Egypt	1.4/0.055
Pisco	Peru	1.6/0.063
Kufra	Libya	1.6/0.063

Reptiles
Classification

Suborder	Number of species	Examples
Amphisbaenia	160	worm lizards
Crocodilia	23	alligators, caymans, crocodiles, gavial
Cryptodira	220	terrapins, tortoises, turtles
Ophidia	3,000	snakes: anaconda, boa, cobras, pythons, vipers
Pleurodira	70	sideneck turtles
Rhynchocephalia	2	tuatara
Sauria	4,500	lizards: gecko, gila monster, iguanas, skinks

Salmon
Names of Young Salmon

Name	Description	Name	Description
alevin	fry or very young	samlet	young salmon
baggit	just after spawning	smolt	young migrating to the sea
grilse	first return from the sea	sprag	young salmon
kelt	after spawning	sprod	in second year
parr	up to two years old		

Sea Animals
World's Largest Marine Animals

Animal	Scientific name	Weight (tonnes)
blue whale	*Baleana musculus*	120
bow-head whale	*Baleana mysticetus*	100
fin whale	*Baleana phusalus*	80
Southern right whale	*Eubalaena australis*	80
sperm whale	*Physeter macrocephalus*	50
whale shark	*Rhincodon typus*	43
basking shark	*Cetorhinus maximus*	40
grey whale	*Eschrichtius robustus*	35
humpback whale	*Megaptera novaeangliae*	30
Baird's beaked whale	*Berardius bairdii*	15

Sea Creatures
Lethally Venomous

Animal	Location
Portuguese man-o-war	tropical seas
sea wasp	Northern Australia
cone shells	tropical Indo-Pacific region
spotted octopus	Indo-Pacific, Indian Ocean
crown of thorn starfish	Indo-Pacific
long-spined sea urchin	Indo-Pacific
stingray	warm, temperate, and tropical seas
weaverfish	Mediterranean
scorpion fish	temperate and tropical seas
stone fish	Indo-Pacific

Sharks
Unprovoked Attacks by Country

Number of shark attacks 1997–99	Country (deaths)
93	USA (1)
18	South Africa (3)
12	Brazil (4)
8	Australia (2)
5	Bahamas
3	New Zealand
2	Japan (2)
2	Mexico (1)
2	New Guinea (2)
1	Guadaloupe
1	Mozambique (1)
1	Saudi Arabia (1)
1	Djibouti (1)
1	Vanuatu (1)

Sharks
Unprovoked Attacks Worldwide

Number of shark attacks	In decade
20	1900s
24	1910s
60	1920s
100	1930s
105	1940s
202	1950s
320	1960s
175	1970s
275	1980s
525	1990s

Snakes

World's Deadliest Snakes

Name	Scientific name	Where found
inland taipan	*Oxyuranus microlepidotus*	Australia
Australian brown snake	*Pseudonaja textiles*	Australia
Malayan krait	*Bungarus candidus*	Southeast Asia
taipan	*Oxyuranus scutellatus*	Australia
tiger snake	*Notechis scutatus*	Australia
beaked sea snake	*Enhydrina schistose*	South Asian sea
saw-scaled viper	*Echis carinatus*	Middle East/Asia
coral snake	*Micrurus fulvius*	North America
boomslang	*Dispholidus typus*	Africa
death adder	*Aconthopis antarcticus*	Australia

Spices

Origin of Spice Plants

Spice	Scientific name	Origin
allspice	*Pimenta officinalis*	West Indies
black mustard	*Brassica niger*	worldwide except Australasia
cardamom	*Elettaria cardamomum*	Southeastern Asia
cayenne	*Capsicum fructescens*	Africa and America
chilli, paprika	*Capsicum annuum*	America
cinnamon	*Cinnamomum zeylanium*	Sri Lanka
cloves	*Eugenia caryophyllata*	Molucca Islands
coriander	*Coriandrum sativum*	Southern Europe
cumin	*Cuminum cyminum*	Mediterranean region
ginger	*Zingiber officinale*	Southeastern Asia
mace, nutmeg	*Myristica fragrans*	Molucca Islands
pepper	*Piper nigrum*	India
sesame	*Sesamum indicum*	world tropics
turmeric	*Curcuma longa*	Southeastern Asia
white mustard	*Sinapsis alba*	Asia and Europe

Spiders

Deadly Spiders

Spider	Location
black widow	Americas, Africa, Australia, Asia
brown recluse	USA
yellow sac	USA
hobo spider	USA, Europe
scorpions (Centuroides, Tityus, Leirurus)	warm temperate and tropical regions

Storms

Most Destructive since 1995

Event	Location (year)	Number of deaths
hurricane	Central America/Caribbean (1998)	>10,500
cyclone	India (1999)	9,504
typhoon	Vietnam/Thailand (1997)	3,500
cyclone	India (1996)	>1,000
typhoon	Philippines (1998)	>1,000
typhoon	Philippines (1995)	722
hurricane	Caribbean (1998)	602
tornado	Bangladesh (1996)	>600
typhoon	Taiwan (1996)	400
tropical storms	Vietnam (1998)	>265
snowstorms	India (1995)	>200
hurricane/floods	Mexico (1997)	128
cyclone	Bangladesh (1997)	112
storms	France (1999)	88
storms	Brazil (1997)	68
typhoon	India (1999)	66
typhoon	North Korea (1999)	54
hurricane	Panama/El Salvador/Costa Rica (1996)	50
cyclone	Bangladesh (1997)	>47
typhoon	Vietnam/Philippines (1998)	>45

Storms

Names of Atlantic Storms

Atlantic storms (those occurring in the North Atlantic, the Caribbean, and the Gulf of Mexico) that develop into tropical storms or hurricanes are named by the National Hurricane Center, located near Miami, Florida. If a disturbance intensifies into a tropical storm – with rotary circulation and wind speeds above 62 kph/39 mph – the National Hurricane Center gives the storm a name from one of the six lists below. A separate set of names is used each year, beginning with the first name in the set. After the sets have all been used, they are used again.

Six-year list of names allocated to Atlantic storms

2001	2002	2003	2004	2005	2006
Allison	Arthur	Ana	Alex	Arlene	Alberto
Barry	Bertha	Bill	Bonnie	Bret	Beryl
Chantal	Cesar	Claudette	Charley	Cindy	Chris
Dean	Dolly	Danny	Danielle	Dennis	Debby
Erin	Edouard	Erika	Earl	Emily	Ernesto
Felix	Fran	Fabian	Frances	Floyd	Florence
Gabrielle	Gustav	Grace	Georges	Gert	Gordon
Humberto	Hortense	Henri	Hermine	Harvey	Helene
Iris	Isidore	Isabel	Ivan	Irene	Isaac
Jerry	Josephine	Juan	Jeanne	José	Joyce

(continued)

Storms: Names of Atlantic Storms (*continued*)

2001	2002	2003	2004	2005	2006
Karen	Kyle	Kate	Karl	Katrina	Keith
Lorenzo	Lili	Larry	Lisa	Lenny	Leslie
Michelle	Marco	Mindy	Mitch	Maria	Michael
Noel	Nana	Nicholas	Nicole	Nate	Nadine
Olga	Omar	Odette	Otto	Ophelia	Oscar
Pablo	Paloma	Peter	Paula	Philippe	Patty
Rebekah	Rene	Rose	Richard	Rita	Rafael
Sebastien	Sally	Sam	Shary	Stan	Sandy
Tanya	Teddy	Teresa	Tomas	Tammy	Tony
Van	Vicky	Victor	Virginie	Vince	Valerie
Wendy	Wilfred	Wanda	Walter	Wilma	William

Storms
Names of Central Pacific Storms

The naming system of tropical cyclones of the Central Pacific differs from that used for Atlantic and eastern North Pacific storms. In this system, the naming of tropical storms begins with List 1 and continues through the list until all names have been used. The naming then moves to List 2, and so on, through all the lists. Once names in all lists have been exhausted, the procedure begins again with List 1.

Central Pacific tropical cyclone names

List 1	List 2	List 3	List 4	List 1	List 2	List 3	List 4
Akoni	Aka	Alika	Ana	Moke	Mele	Maka	Malia
Ema	Ekeka	Ele	Ela	Nele	Nona	Neki	Niala
Hana	Hali	Huko	Halona	Oka	Oliwa	Oleka	Oko
Io	Iolana	Ioke	Iune	Peke	Paka	Peni	Pali
Keli	Keoni	Kika	Kimo	Uleki	Upana	Ulia	Ulika
Lala	Li	Lana	Loke	Wila	Wene	Wali	Wlaka

Storms
Names of Eastern Pacific Storms

The US National Weather Service is responsible for providing names for eastern Pacific storms that develop into typhoons or hurricanes. The Service gives the storm a name from one of the six lists below. A separate set of names is used each year, beginning with the first name in the set. After the sets have all been used, they are used again. For example, the 2001 set will be used again to name storms in the year 2007.

Six-year list of names allocated to eastern Pacific storms

2001	2002	2003	2004	2005	2006
Adolph	Alma	Andres	Agatha	Adrian	Aletta
Barbara	Boris	Blanca	Blas	Beatriz	Bud
Cosme	Cristina	Carlos	Celia	Calvin	Carlotta

Storms: Names of Eastern Pacific Storms (*continued*)

2001	2002	2003	2004	2005	2006
Dalila	Douglas	Dolores	Darby	Dora	Daniel
Erick	Elida	Enrique	Estelle	Eugene	Emilia
Flossie	Fausto	Felicia	Frank	Fernanda	Fabio
Gil	Genevieve	Guillermo	Georgette	Greg	Gilma
Henriette	Hernan	Hilda	Howard	Hilary	Hector
Ismael	Iselle	Ignacio	Isis	Irwin	Ileana
Juliette	Julio	Jimena	Javier	Jova	John
Kiko	Kenna	Kevin	Kay	Kenneth	Kristy
Lorena	Lowell	Linda	Lester	Lidia	Lane
Manuel	Marie	Marty	Madeline	Max	Miriam
Narda	Norbert	Nora	Newton	Norma	Norman
Octave	Odile	Olaf	Orlene	Otis	Olivia
Priscilla	Polo	Pauline	Paine	Pilar	Paul
Raymond	Rachel	Rick	Roslyn	Ramon	Rosa
Sonia	Simon	Sandra	Seymour	Selma	Sergio
Tico	Trudy	Terry	Tina	Todd	Tara
Velma	Vance	Vivian	Virgil	Veronica	Vincente
Wallis	Winnie	Waldo	Winifred	Wiley	Willa
Xina	Xavier	Xina	Xavier	Xina	Xavier
Zelda	Zeke	Zelda	Zeke	Zelda	Zeke

Temperature
World's Highest (Annual Average)

Location	Country	Annual average temperature (°C/°F)	Location	Country	Annual average temperature (°C/°F)
Mecca	Saudi Arabia	37.9/100.2	Bokoro	Chad	37.3/99.1
			Matam	Senegal	37.3/99.1
Halfa-El-Gedida	Sudan	37.7/99.9	Kassala	Sudan	37.3/99.1
Aroma	Sudan	37.4/99.3	Gao	Mali	37.3/99.1
Hudeiba	Sudan	37.4/99.3	Ati	Chad	37.2/99.1
Atbara	Sudan	37.4/99.3			

Temperature
World's Highest (Monthly Average)

Location	Country	Monthly average temperature (°C/°F)	Month
Sibi	Pakistan	46.0/114.8	June
Amarah	Iran	46.0/114.8	July
Dezful	Iran	46.0/114.8	July
Death Valley	USA	45.7/114.3	July

(*continued*)

Temperature: World's Highest (*continued*)

Location	Country	Monthly average temperature (°C/°F)	Month
Ummalaish	Kuwait	45.4/113.7	July
Alhofuf	Saudi Arabia	45.4/113.7	July
Albusayyah	Iran	45.3/113.5	July
Assalman	Iran	45.2/113.4	July
Abadan	Iran	45.0/113.0	July
Adrar	Algeria	45.0/113.0	July

Temperature
World's Lowest (Annual Average)

Location	Country	Annual average temperature (°C/°F)	Location	Country	Annual average temperature (°C/°F)
Vostok Antarctica	Antarctica	−59.9/−75.8	Byrd Station	Antarctica	−32.4/−26.3
			Little America	Antarctica	−28.3/−18.9
South Pole	Antarctica	−52.3/−62.1	Scott Base	Antarctica	−24.8/−12.6
Mizuho	Antarctica	−36.7/−34.1	Ojmjakon	Russia	−23.3/−9.9
Eismitte	Greenland	−35.1/−31.2	Eureka	Canada	−23.2/−9.7
Northice	Greenland	−34.4/−29.9			

Temperature
World's Lowest (Monthy Average)

Location	Country	Monthly average temperature (°C/°F)	Month
Vostok Antarctica	Antarctica	−71.1/−95.9	July
South Pole	Antarctica	−63.8/−82.5	July
Ojmjakon	Russia	−50.8/−59.4	January
Verhojansk	Russia	−49.8/−57.6	January
Eismitte	Greenland	−47.7/−53.9	February
Northice	Greenland	−47.3/−53.1	March
Ust'-Maja	Russia	−45.0/−49.0	January
Jakutsk	Russia	−44.5/−48.1	January
Mizuho	Antarctica	−43.9/−47.0	August
Olenek	Russia	−42.7/−44.9	January
Byrd Station	Antarctica	−42.5/−44.5	September

Trees
Largest Trees of the USA

Tree species	Height (m/ft)
Douglas fir	100.28/330
coast redwood	95.40/313
giant sequoia	83.82/275
sugar pine	70.71/232
loblolly pine	45.11/148
American elm	26.52/87
sugar maple	26.52/87
white oak	24.08/79
black willow	23.16/75
pinyon pine	21.03/69

Trees
Longest-lived Species in the USA

Common name	Scientific name	Life span/ expectancy (years)
bristlecone pine	*Pinus longaeva*	3,000–4,700
giant sequoia	*Sequoiadendron giganteum*	2,500
redwood	*Sequoia sempervirens*	1,000–3,500
Douglas fir	*Pseudotsuga menziesii*	750
bald cypress	*Taxodium distichum*	600

Trees
World's Oldest Trees

Tree	Scientific name	Age (years)
lime	*Tilia cordata* and *platyphyllos*	6,000
yew	*Taxus baccata*	possibly 5,000
bristlecone pine	*Pinus longaeva*	4,700
baobab	*Andansonia digitata*	4,000
Montezuma cypress	*Taxodium mucronatum*	up to 4,000
Antarctic beech	*Nothofagus moorei*	at least 3,000
redwood	*Sequoia giganteum*	2,700
sweet chestnut	*Castanea sativa*	2,000–4,000
welwitschia	*Welwitschia mirabilis*	over 2,000
kauri	*Agathis australis*	at least 2,000

Water
Countries Predicted to be Short of Water

Region/country	Cubic m/cubic ft of water per person		
	1992	Prediction for 2010	Change (%)
Malawi	1,030/36,374	600/21,189	−42
Sudan	1,130/39,906	710/25,073	−37
Morocco	1,150/40,612	830/29,311	−28
South Africa	1,200/42,378	760/26,839	−37
Oman	1,250/44,143	670/23,661	−46
Somalia	1,390/49,087	830/29,311	−40
Lebanon	1,410/49,794	980/34,648	−30
Niger	1,690/59,682	930/32,843	−45

Weather
Rainfall and Snowfall Records for Selected Locations in the USA

As of April 1997.

Location	Maximum monthly rainfall (mm/in) (mo/yr)	Maximum monthly snowfall (mm/in) (mo/yr)
Atlanta, GA	399/15.72 (11/48)	211/8.3 (1/40)
Boston, MA	434/17.09 (8/55)	1,049/41.3 (2/69)
Chicago, IL	434/17.10 (8/87)	897/35.3 (12/78)
Honolulu, HI	528/20.79 (3/51)	–
JFK Airport, NY	422/17.41 (8/55)	643/25.3 (2/61)
Key West, FL	703/27.67 (11/80)	–
Las Vegas, NV	66/2.59 (8/57)	424/16.7 (1/49)
Memphis, TN	435/17.13 (4/91)	439/17.3 (3/68)
Pittsburgh, PA	281/11.05 (11/85)	1,021/40.2 (1/78)
Salt Lake City, UT	179/7.04 (9/82)	1,064/41.9 (3/77)

Weather
Temperature Records for Selected Locations in the USA

As of April 1997.

Location	High temperature (°C/°F) (mo/yr)	Low temperature (°C/°F) (mo/yr)
Atlanta, GA	41/105 (7/80)	–22/–8 (1/85)
Boston, MA	39/102 (7/77)	–23/–12 (1/57)
Chicago, IL	41/105 (6/88)	–33/–27 (1/85)
Honolulu, HI	34/94 (7/86)	12/53 (2/83)
JFK Airport, NY	40/104 (7/66)	–19/–2 (1/85)
Key West, FL	35/95 (8/57)	5/41 (1/81)
Las Vegas, NV	47/116 (7/85)	–13/8 (1/63)
Memphis, TN	42/108 (7/80)	–25/–13 (12/63)
Pittsburgh, PA	39/103 (7/88)	–28/–18 (1/85)
Salt Lake City, UT	42/107 (7/66)	–34/–30 (2/33)

Weather

UK Weather Records

Record	Location/year	Details
highest temperature	Cheltenham, Gloucestershire (1990)	37.1°C/99°F
lowest temperature	Braemar, Grampian (1895 and 1982)	−27.2°C/−17°F
	Altnaharra, Highland (1995)	−27.2°C/−17°F
greatest temperature range in a single day	Tummel Bridge, Tayside (1978)	from −7°C to 22°C/19–72°F (a range of 29°C/53°F)
highest amount of rainfall in 24 hours	Martinstown, Dorset (1955)	280 mm/11 in
fastest gust of wind (high-level site)	Cairn Gorm station, Highland (1986)	150 knots
fastest gust of wind (low-level site)	Fraserburgh, Aberdeenshire (1989)	123 knots
highest number of days with gale in a year	Lerwick, Shetlands (1949)	86 days
heaviest hailstone	Horsham, Sussex (1958)	141 g/5 oz and 6 cm/2.4 in in diameter
highest amount of sunshine in one month	Eastbourne and Hastings, Sussex (1911)	384 hours
lowest amount of sunshine in one month	Westminster, Greater London (1890)	0 hours

Weather

World Records

Record	Location	Details
highest amount of rainfall in the northern hemisphere in 24 hours	Taiwan	124 cm/49 in
highest amount of rainfall in 24 hours (not induced by the presence of mountains)	India	99 cm/39 in
highest amount of rainfall in 24 hours	La Reunion Island	188 cm/74 in
highest amount of rainfall over 5 days	La Reunion Island	386 cm/152 in
highest amount of rainfall in 12 hours	La Reunion Island	135 cm/53 in
highest amount of rainfall in 20 minutes	Romania	21 cm/8 in
highest yearly number of days of rainfall	Chile	325 days
longest period without rainfall	Chile	14 years
highest yearly average period of thunderstorms	Uganda	242 days per year
highest sustained yearly average period of thunderstorms	Indonesia	322 days per year from 1916–1919

(*continued*)

Animals, Plants, and the Environment   **317**

Weather: World Records (*continued*)

Record	Location	Details
highest yearly average rainfall in Africa	Cameroon	1,029 cm/405 in
lowest yearly average rainfall in Africa	Sudan	3 mm/0.1 in
lowest yearly average rainfall in Asia	South Yemen	5 cm/2 in
highest yearly average rainfall in Europe	Bosnia-Herzegovina	465 cm/183 in
lowest yearly average rainfall in Europe	Russia	16 cm/6 in
highest amount of rainfall in Australia in 24 hours	Queensland	91 cm/36 in
highest yearly average rainfall in Australia	Queensland	864 cm/340 in
lowest yearly average rainfall in Australia	South Australia	10 cm/4 in
highest yearly average rainfall in South America	Colombia	899 cm/354 in
lowest yearly average rainfall in South America	Chile	0.7 mm/0.03 in
highest yearly average rainfall in North America	Canada	650 cm/256 in
lowest yearly average rainfall in North America	Mexico	3 cm/1 in
highest temperature ever recorded in the world	Libya	58°C/136°F
lowest temperature ever recorded in the world	Vostok, Antarctica	−89°C/−128°F
highest yearly average temperature in world	Ethiopia	34°C/93°F
highest yearly average temperature range	Russia	through 63°C/145°F
highest average temperature sustained over a long period	Australia	38°C/100°F for 162 days running
highest temperature in Antarctica	Vanda Station	near 15°C/59°F
lowest temperature in Antarctica	Vostok	−89°C/−128°F
highest temperature in Africa	Libya	58°C/136°F
lowest temperature in Africa	Morocco	−24°C/−11°F
highest temperature in Asia	Israel	54°C/129°F
lowest temperature in Asia	Russia	−68°C/−90°F
highest temperature in Australia	Queensland	53°C/127°F
lowest temperature in Australia	New South Wales	−23°C/−9°F
highest temperature in Europe	Spain	50°C/122°F
lowest temperature in Europe	Russia	−55°C/−67°F
lowest temperature in Greenland	Northice	−66°C/−87°F
highest temperature in North America	Death Valley, USA	57°C/135°F
lowest temperature in North America (excluding Greenland)	Yukon Territory, Canada	−63°C/−81°F
lowest temperature in northern hemisphere	Russia	−68°C/−90°F
highest temperature in South America	Argentina	49°C/120°F
lowest temperature in South America	Argentina	−33°C/−27°F
highest temperature in western hemisphere	Death Valley, USA	57°C/135°F
highest peak wind	Greenland	333 kph/207 mph
highest average wind speed in 24 hours	Antarctica	173 kph/107 mph
highest peak wind gust	USA	372 kph/231 mph
highest monthly average wind speed	Antarctica	104 kph/65 mph

Wildfires
Selected Major US Wildfires since 1977

(Includes fires with over 100,000 acres burned. The data cover land in the US Forest Service system and land under Forest Service protection, and cover fires both in forests and in areas not technically called forests, such as meadows.)

Year	Location	Area (ha/acres)	Year	Location	Area (ha/acres)
1988	Shoshone (WY)	166,750/412,048	1994	Wenatchee (WA)	56,650/139,985
1988	Targhee (ID)	161,900/400,064	1985	Los Padres (CA)	47,750/117,993
			1988	Bridger-Teton (WY)	47,700/117,869
1992	Boise (ID)	71,850/177,545	1994	Payette (ID)	46,800/115,645
1977	Los Padres (CA)	70,400/173,962	1988	Gallatin (MT)	44,100/108,974
1994	Boise (ID)	59,250/146,410	1996	Los Padres (CA)	42,900/106,008

Wind
Winds of the World

Name and type	Where it blows
auster: another term for sirocco	
bise: a cold dry wind	northwards in southern Switzerland in spring
bora: a strong cold wind	from the northeastern coast of the Adriatic in winter
etesian	northwesterly summer wind in the eastern Mediterranean
föhn: warm dry wind	down the northern Alps
ghibli hot: a dry wind	from the south in northern Africa
harmattan: dusty dry wind	on West African coast
khamsin: hot southerly wind	in Egypt during March
kona: stormy southerly wind	in Hawaii
levanter: easterly wind	western Mediterranean in late summer
meltemi: another name for an etesian wind	
mistral: cold dry wind	down the Rhône and other southern French valleys
simoom: hot dusty wind	intermittently in the Arabian desert
sirocco: hot dusty wind	in spring from northern Africa to southern Europe
tramontana: cold dry southerly wind	from the Italian mountains in western Mediterranean
willy-gwilly: duststorm or tropical cyclone	in Australia
zephyr: any gentle breeze	

Wind

World's Windiest Places (Annual Average Speed)

Location	Country	Speed (m per sec/ft per sec)
Sniezka	Poland	12.2/40.0
Fujisan	Japan	11.4/37.4
Vestmannaeyjar	Iceland	11.3/37.1
Mawson	Antarctica	10.7/35.1
Guanaja	Honduras	9.6/31.5
Vf Omu	Romania	9.5/31.2
Puysegur Point	New Zealand	9.3/30.5
Cape St James	Canada	9.0/29.5
Fichtelberg	Germany	8.9/29.2
Grindstone Island	Canada	8.7/28.5

People, History,
and
Society

Abdications

Date	Ruler	Life dates
1567	Mary, Queen of Scots	1542–1587
1815	Napoleon I, Emperor of France	1769–1821
1917	Nicholas II, Tsar of Russia	1868–1918
1918	Wilhelm II, Emperor of Germany	1859–1941
1936	Edward VIII, King of England	1894–1972
1946	Umberto II, King of Italy	1904–1983
1947	Michael, King of Romania	1921–
1948	Wilhelmina, Queen of the Netherlands	1880–1962
1952	Farouk I, King of Egypt	1920–1965
1980	Juliana, Queen of the Netherlands	1909–

Accidents

Worst Industrial Accidents

Place	Date	Number killed
Bhopal, India	1984	4,000
Cali, Columbia	1956	2,700
Honeiko, China	1942	1,549
Courrières, France	1906	1,060
Southern Region, Brazil	1984	934
Icmesa, Italy	1976	760
Oppau, Germany	1921	561
São Paulo, Brazil	1984	508
Ural Mountains, Russian Federation	1989	c. 500
Mexico City, Mexico	1984	452

Address

Forms of Address in the USA

Two dashes indicate first name and surname; one dash indicates surname.

Addressee	Address	Salutation
President of the USA	The President, The White House, Washington, DC 20500	Dear Mr or Madam President
Judge	The Hon. – –	Dear Judge –, or Sir or Madam
Senator, US	The Hon. – –, United States Senate, Washington, DC 20510	Dear Mr or Madam Senator, or Dear Senator –
Speaker of the House	The Hon. Speaker of the House of Representatives, Washington, DC 20515	Dear Mr or Madam Speaker
Governor	The Hon. – –, Governor of (state); in some states: His or Her Excellency – –, the Governor of (state)	Dear Governor –, or Sir or Madam
Mayor	The Hon. – –, Mayor of (city)	Dear Mayor –, or Sir or Madam
Ambassador, US	The Hon. – –, American Ambassador; in Canada or Latin America: The Ambassador of the United States of America	Dear Mr or Madam Ambassador, or Sir or Madam
Pope	His Holiness Pope (name), or His Holiness the Pope	Your Holiness, or Most Holy Father
Archbishop	The Most Reverend – –, Archbishop of (province)	Your Excellency; Eastern Orthodox: Your Eminence

Age
Median Age of World Population

Area	1950	2000	2050
Median age (years)			
Africa	18.7	18.4	30.7
Asia	21.9	26.3	39.3
Europe	29.2	37.5	47.4
Latin America and the Caribbean	20.1	24.5	37.8
North America	29.8	35.9	42.1
Oceania	27.9	31.1	39.3
less developed regions	21.3	24.4	36.7
more developed regions	28.6	37.5	45.6
world total	23.5	26.6	37.8

Air Forces
World's Largest

Country	Personnel
China	420,000
USA	353,600
Russian Federation	184,600
India	150,000
Ukraine	96,000
North Korea	86,000
Germany	73,300
Taiwan	68,000
South Korea	63,000
France	60,500

Aircraft Carriers
Countries with Most

Country	Number of carriers
USA	12
UK	3
Brazil	1
France	1
India	1
Italy	1
Russia	1
Spain	1
Thailand	1

American Civil War
Casualties

Forces	Battle deaths	Other causes[1]	Total war dead	Wounded[2]
Union	110,700	250,152	360,852	275,175
Confederacy	94,000	164,000	258,000	194,026
total	204,700	414,152	618,852	469,201

[1] Includes deaths by disease and deaths of prisoners of war while in custody.
[2] Estimated figures (records incomplete).

American Civil War
Prisoners of War

Forces	Deaths in prisons	Prisoners of war[1]
Union	25,576	284,000
Confederacy	26,246	219,000

[1] Estimated figures (records incomplete).

American Indians
Major Cultural Groups

Region	Cultural group
North America	
Arctic	Inuit, Aleut
Subarctic	Algonquin, Cree, Ottawa
northeast woodlands	Huron, Iroquois, Mohican, Shawnee (Tecumseh)
southeast woodlands	Cherokee, Choctaw, Creek, Hopewell, Natchez, Seminole
Great Plains	Blackfoot, Cheyenne, Comanche, Pawnee, Sioux
northwest coast	Chinook, Tlingit, Tsimshian
Desert West	Apache, Navajo, Pueblo, Hopi, Mojave, Shoshone
Central America	
	Maya, Toltec, Aztec, Mexican
South America	
eastern	Carib, Xingu
central	Guaraní, Miskito
western	Araucanian, Aymara, Chimú, Inca, Jivaro, Quechua

Antipopes
Last

The antipopes were based in Avignon, France and were rivals to the popes who were based in Rome, Italy.

Name	Term	Name	Term
Felix V	1439–49	Alexander V	1409–10
Benedict XIV	1425–30	Benedict XIII	1394–1423
Clement VIII	1423–29	Clement VII	1378–94
John XXIII	1410–15		

Apocalypse
The Four Horsemen of the Apocalypse

Name	Type of horse
death	pale horse
famine	black horse
slaughter	red horse
war	white horse

Argentinian Presidents
Recent

Term	Name	Party
1999–	Fernando de la Rua	Radical Civic Union (UCR)/Alianza
1989–99	Carlos Saúl Menem	Justice Party
1983–89	Raúl Alfonsín	Civic Radical Union
1982–83	Reynaldo Bignone	military
1982	Alfredo Saint-Jean	acting: military
1981–82	Leopoldo Galtieri	military
1981	Roberto Viola	military
1976–81	Jorge Videla	military
1974–76	Maria Estela de Perón	Justice Front of Liberation
1973–74	Juan Perón	Justice Front of Liberation

Armed Forces

Countries with Largest

Country	Percentage of population in armed forces
Korea, North	44
Israel	35
Jordan	27
Syria	21
China (Taiwan)	20
Greece	20
United Arab Emirates	20
Djibouti	19
Iraq	19

Armed Forces

Regions with Greatest Numbers in Armed Forces

Region	Numbers in armed forces (thousands)
East Asia and Australasia	7,160
NATO	3,880
Middle East and North Africa	2,880
Central and South Asia	2,630
non-NATO Europe	1,805
Caribbean, Central, and Latin America	1,300
sub-Saharan Africa	1,270
Russian Federation	1,160
global total	22,085

Armies

World's Largest

Country	Personnel
China	1,700,000
India	1,100,000
North Korea	950,000
South Korea	560,000
Pakistan	550,000
Turkey	495,000
USA	471,000
Iran	450,000
Vietnam	412,000
Iraq	375,000

Armoured Personnel Carriers

Countries with Most

Country	Number of vehicles
USA	17,700
Russian Federation	11,275
Israel	9,900
Ukraine	7,820
China	5,600
Egypt	4,650
Turkey	3,995
France	3,900
UK	3,276
Germany	3,026

Arms Trade
Leading Buyers of Conventional Weapons

Figures given are in millions of US dollars, adjusted to illustrate the arms-buying trends.

Recipient	Arms imports (1994–98)	Recipient	Arms imports (1994–98)
Taiwan	13,311	Greece	4,754
Saudi Arabia	9,748	India	4,149
Turkey	6,615	Japan	4,093
Egypt	5,882	United Arab Emirates	3,267
Korea, South	5,171	Thailand	3,132

Arms Trade
Major Suppliers

Country	Market share	Defence exports (US$)
USA	40–50%	Over 10 billion
Canada, China, France, Germany, Israel, Russian Federation, UK	35–45%	1–10 billion

Arms
Largest Arms-producing Companies

Company/country	Arms sales (US$ million)
Lockheed Martin/USA	18,500
Boeing/USA	14,500
British Aerospace/UK	10,410
General Motors (GM)/USA	7,450
Northrop Grumman/USA	7,210
GEC/UK	6,030
Raytheon/USA	4,600
Thomson/France	4,220
TRW/USA	3,800
General Dynamics/USA	3,650

Assassinations
Famous Assassinations and Attempts

Year	Victim	Details
1997	Gianni Versace, Italian fashion designer	shot dead on the steps of his Miami Beach mansion
1995	Yitzhak Rabin, Israeli prime minister	shot dead following speech at a pro-peace rally in Tel Aviv
1991	Rajiv Gandhi, former Indian prime minister	killed by a bomb during an election campaign
1984	Indira Gandhi, Indian prime minister	murdered by members of her Sikh bodyguard
1981	Pope John Paul II	shot and seriously wounded in St Peter's Square, Rome
1981	Ronald Reagan, US president	shot in the chest and seriously wounded outside the Washington Hilton hotel

Year	Victim	Details
1980	John Lennon, singer and songwriter	shot dead outside his apartment block in New York
1968	Martin Luther King, US black civil rights leader	shot dead on a hotel balcony by James Earl Ray in Memphis (TN)
1965	Malcolm X (Little), US leading representative of the Black Muslims	shot dead at a political rally in New York by followers of rival Black Muslim leader
1963	John F Kennedy, US president	shot dead in a car by rifle fire in Dallas (TX); alleged assassin, Lee Harvey Oswald, was himself shot two days later while under heavy police escort

Australian Prime Ministers

Recent

Term	Name	Party
1996–	John Howard	Liberal–National coalition
1991–96	Paul Keating	Labor
1983–91	Robert Hawke	Labor
1975–83	Malcolm Fraser	Liberal–National coalition
1972–75	Gough Whitlam	Labor
1971–72	William McMahon	Liberal–Country coalition
1968–71	John Gorton	Liberal–Country coalition
1967–68	John McEwen	Liberal–Country coalition
1966–67	Harold Holt	Liberal–Country coalition
1949–66	Robert Menzies	Liberal–Country coalition

Aztec Emperors

Reign	Name
c. 1372–c. 1391	Acamapichtli (chieftain at Tenochtitlán)
c. 1391–c. 1416	Huitzilihuitl (son)
c. 1416–c. 1427	Chimalpopoca (son)
c. 1427–c. 1440	Itzcoatl (son of Acamapichtli)
c. 1440–c. 1468	(Huehue) Motecuhzoma
c. 1468–1481	Axayacatl (grandson of Itzcoatl)
1481–1486	Tizoc (brother)
1486–1502	Ahuitzotl (brother)
1502–20	Motecuhzoma Xocoyotl (son of Axayacatl); known as Montezuma II
1520	Cuitlahuac (brother)
1520–21	Cuauhtemoc (son of Ahuitzotl)

Belgian Monarchs

Leopold of Saxe-Coburg-Gotha was elected the first king of Belgium in 1831.

Reign	Name	Reign	Name
1993–	Albert II	1918–34	Albert I (restored)
1951–93	Baudouin	1914–18	German occupation
1950–51	Leopold III (restored)	1909–14	Albert I
1944–50	Prince Charles (regent)	1865–1909	Leopold II
1940–44	German occupation	1831–65	Leopold I
1934–40	Leopold III		

Belgian Prime Ministers
Recent

Term	Name	Party
1999–	Guy Verhofstadt	(Flemish) Liberal
1992–99	Jean Luc Dehaene	Christian People's Party
1981–92	Wilfried Martens	Christian People's Party
1981	Mark Eyskens	Christian People's Party
1979–81	Wilfried Martens	Christian People's Party
1978–79	Paul van den Boeynants	Christian Social Party
1974–78	Léo Tindemans	Christian Social Party
1972–74	Edmond Leburton	Socialist Party
1968–72	Gaston Eyskens	Christian Social Party
1966–68	Paul van den Boeynants	Christian Social Party

Bible
Books of the New Testament

Name of book	Chapters	Name of book	Chapters	Name of book	Chapters
Matthew	28	Ephesians	6	Hebrews	13
Mark	16	Philippians	4	James	5
Luke	24	Colossians	4	1 Peter	5
John	21	1 Thessalonians	5	2 Peter	3
Acts	28	2 Thessalonians	3	1 John	5
Romans	16	1 Timothy	6	2 John	1
1 Corinthians	16	2 Timothy	4	3 John	1
2 Corinthians	13	Titus	3	Jude	1
Galatians	6	Philemon	1	Revelation	22

Bible
Books of the Old Testament

Name of book	Chapters	Name of book	Chapters	Name of book	Chapters
Genesis	50	2 Chronicles	36	Daniel	12
Exodus	40	Ezra	10	Hosea	14
Leviticus	27	Nehemiah	13	Joel	3
Numbers	36	Esther	10	Amos	9
Deuteronomy	34	Job	42	Obadiah	1
Joshua	24	Psalms	150	Jonah	4
Judges	21	Proverbs	31	Micah	7
Ruth	4	Ecclesiastes	12	Nahum	3
1 Samuel	31	Song of Solomon	8	Habakkuk	3
2 Samuel	24	Isaiah	66	Zephaniah	3
1 Kings	22	Jeremiah	52	Haggai	2
2 Kings	25	Lamentations	5	Zechariah	14
1 Chronicles	29	Ezekiel	48	Malachi	4

Birthdays
Celebrities Born on 25 December

Name	Life dates	Occupation
Annie Lennox	1954–	Scottish pop singer
Anwar el-Sadat	1918–1981	Egyptian president
Barbara Mandrell	1948–	US singer
Jimmy Buffett	1946–	US singer-songwriter
Rod Serling	1924–1975	US scriptwriter
Isaac Newton	1642–1727	English physicist and mathematician
Humphrey Bogart	1899–1957	US film actor
Maurice Utrillo	1883–1955	French painter
Quentin Crisp	1908–1999	English writer and entertainer
Sissy Spacek	1949–	US film actor
(Little) Richard Penniman	1932–	US rock singer and pianist

Birthstones

Month	Stone	Quality
January	garnet	constancy
February	amethyst	sincerity
March	aquamarine, bloodstone	courage
April	diamond	innocence
May	emerald	love
June	alexandrite, pearl	health and purity
July	ruby	contentment
August	peridot, sardonyx	married happiness
September	sapphire	clear thinking
October	opal, tourmaline	hope
November	topaz	fidelity
December	turquoise, zircon	wealth

Birth Flowers

Month	Flower
January	carnation, snowdrop
February	primrose, violet
March	jonquil, violet
April	daisy, sweet pea
May	hawthorn, lily of the valley
June	honeysuckle, rose
July	larkspur, water lily
August	gladiolus, poppy
September	aster, morning glory
October	calendula, cosmos
November	chrysanthemum
December	holly, narcissus, poinsettia

Blindness
Famous People Who Were Born or Became Blind

Person	Life dates	Person	Life dates
Jorge Luis Borges, Argentine poet	1899–1986	Helen Keller, US author and lecturer	1880–1968
Laura Bridgman, US educator	1829–1889	John Milton, English poet	1608–1674
Ray Charles, US jazz musician	1930–	Claude Monet, French Impressionist painter	1840–1926
Marcel Dupré, French classical musician	1886–1971	Joseph Pulitzer, US journalist	1847–1911
Homer, Greek poet	*fl.* 850 BC	James Thurber, US humorist	1894–1961

Bomber Aeroplanes

Countries with Most

Country	Bombers
Russian Federation	910
USA	208
China	120
Iran	6
Iraq	6
Libya	6

Brazilian Presidents

Recent

Term	Name	Party
1995–	Fernando Henrique Cardoso	Social Democratic Party
1992–94	Itamar Franco	National Reconstruction Party
1989–92	Fernando Collor de Mello	National Reconstruction Party
1985–89	José Sarney	Social Democratic Party
1979–85	João Figueiredo	military
1974–79	Ernesto Geisel	military
1969–74	Emilio Medici	military
1967–69	Arthur da Costa e Silva	military
1964–67	Humberto Branco	military
1964	Ranieri Mazzili	independent

Buddhism

Major Southern Festivals

Festival	Description	Date (2001)
New Year Festival	images of the Buddha are bathed in scented water and stupas of sand are built on river banks to be washed away at New Year, symbolizing the clearing away of negative deeds	April
Vesakha	celebrates the Buddha's birth, enlightenment, and passing into nirvana	7 May
Asalha	commemorates the Buddha's first sermon	5 July
Assayuja	celebrates the return of the Buddha from heaven after passing on the teachings to his mother	October
Kattika	commemorates the first Buddhist missionaries who went out to spread the Buddha's teachings	November
Kathina	offerings, especially robes, are presented to the monasteries in elaborate ceremonies	October/ November

Buddhism

The Eightfold Path

right understanding   right speech   right living   right attentiveness
right mindfulness   right action   right effort   right concentration

Calendar
Different Calendars Compared

Jewish	Gregorian	Islamic	Gregorian	Hindu	Gregorian
5758	2 October 1997–20 September 1998	1418	8 May 1997–27 April 1998	1919	22 March 1997–21 March 1998
5759	21 September 1998–10 September 1999	1419	27 April 1998–16 April 1999	1920	22 March 1998–21 March 1999
5760	11 September 1999–29 September 2000	1420	17 April 1999–5 April 2000	1921	22 March 1999–21 March 2000
5761	30 September 2000–17 September 2001	1421	6 April 2000–25 March 2001	1922	22 March 2000–21 March 2001
5762	18 September 2001–6 September 2002	1422	26 March 2001–14 March 2002	1923	22 March 2001–21 March 2002

Calendar
Meanings of the Days of the Week

Day	Meaning	Explanation
Sunday	Sun's day	
Monday	Moon's day	
Tuesday	Tiu's day	Tiu was Saxon god of war
Wednesday	Woden's day	Woden was chief Saxon god
Thursday	Thor's day	Thor was Norse god of thunder
Friday	Frigg's day	Frigg was Norse god of love
Saturday	Saturn's day	Saturn was Roman god of agriculture

Calendars
Months in Different Calendars

The figures in brackets give the number of solar days in each month.

Gregorian	Jewish	Islamic	Hindu
(Basis: sun)	(Basis: combination of solar and lunar cycles)	(Basis: visibility of the new moon)	(Basis: moon)
January (31)	Tishri (September–October) (30)	Muharram (30)	Caitra (March–April) (29 or 30)
February (28 or 29)	Heshvan (October–November) (29 or 30)	Safar (29)	Vaisakha (April–May) (29 or 30)
March (31)	Kislev (November–December) (29 or 30)	Rabi I (30)	Jaistha (May–June) (29 or 30)
April (30)	Tebet (December–January) (29)	Rabi II (29)	Asadha (June–July) (29 or 30)
May (31)	Shebat (January–February) (30)	Jumada I (30)	Dvitiya Asadha (certain leap years)

(continued)

Calendars: Months in Different Calendars (*continued*)

Gregorian (Basis: sun)	Jewish (Basis: combination of solar and lunar cycles)	Islamic (Basis: visibility of the new moon)	Hindu (Basis: moon)
June (30)	Adar (February–March) (29 or 30)	Jumada II (29)	Sravana (July–August) (29 or 30)
July (31)	Adar Sheni (leap years only)	Rajab (30)	Dvitiya Sravana (certain leap years)
August (31)	Nisan (March–April) (29)	Shaban (29)	Bhadrapada (August–September) (29 or 30)
September (30)	Iyar (April–May) (30)	Ramadan (30)	Aswin (September–October) (29 or 30)
October (31)	Sivan (May–June) (30)	Shawwal (29)	Kartik (October–November) (29 or 30)
November (30)	Tammuz (June–July) (29)	Dhu al-Qadah (30)	Agra Hayana (November–December) (29 or 30)
December (31)	Av (July–August) (30)	Dhu al-Hijjah (29 or 30)	Paus (December–January) (29 or 30)
–	Elul (August–September) (29)	–	Magh (January–February) (29 or 30)
–	–	–	Phalgun (February–March) (29 or 30)

Cambridge University
Oldest Colleges

Founded	College	Founded	College	Founded	College
1284	Peterhouse	1496	Jesus	1885	Hughes Hall
1326	Clare	1511	St John's	1896	St Edmund's
1347	Pembroke	1542	Magdalene	1954	New Hall
1348	Gonville and Caius	1546	Trinity	1960	Churchill
1350	Trinity Hall	1584	Emmanuel	1964	Lucy Cavendish
1352	Corpus Christi	1596	Sidney Sussex	1964	Darwin
1441	King's	1695	Homerton	1965	Wolfson
1448	Queens'	1800	Downing	1966	Clare Hall
1448	Christ's	1869	Girton	1966	Fitzwilliam
1473	St Catharine's	1871	Newnham	1977	Robinson
		1882	Selwyn		

Canadian Prime Ministers
Most Recent

In 1867 the British North America Act established the Dominion of Canada.

Term	Name	Party
1993–	Jean Chrétien	Liberal
1993	Kim Campbell	Progressive Conservative
1984–93	Brian Mulroney	Progressive Conservative
1984	John Turner	Liberal
1980–84	Pierre E Trudeau	Liberal
1979–80	Joseph Clark	Progressive Conservative
1968–79	Pierre E Trudeau	Liberal
1963–68	Lester B Pearson	Liberal
1957–63	John G Diefenbaker	Conservative
1948–57	Louis S St Laurent	Liberal

Celebrities
Original Names of Personalities

Adopted/professional name	Original name
Ali, Muhammad	Cassius Marcellus Clay Jr
Bowie, David	David Robert Jones
Boy George	George Alan O'Dowd
Cage, Nicolas	Nicholas Coppola
Cruise, Tom	Thomas Mapother IV
Goldberg, Whoopi	Caryn Johnson
John, Elton	Reginald Kenneth Dwight
Keaton, Michael	Michael Douglas
Michael, George	Georgios Kyriacos Panayiotou
Monroe, Marilyn	Norma Jean Mortenson
Sheen, Charlie	Carlos Irwin Estevez
Starr, Ringo	Richard Starkey
Sting	Gordon Sumner
Turner, Tina	Annie Mae Bullock
Wonder, Stevie	Steveland Judkins Morris

China
Gang of Four

The Gang of Four were a faction that helped direct the Cultural Revolution in Chinese history, and tried to seize power in 1976.

Jiang Qing (widow of Mao Zedong)

Zhang Chunqiao

Wang Hongwen

Yao Wenyuan

Chinese Calendar

Chinese solar term	English translation	Gregorian date	Chinese solar term	English translation	Gregorian date
Li Chun	spring begins	4/5 February	Chun Fen	vernal equinox	20/21 March
Yu Shui	rain water	19/20 February	Qing Ming	clear and bright	4/5 April
			Gu Yu	grain rains	20/21 April
Jing Zhe	insects waken	5/6 March	Li Xia	summer begins	5/6 May

(continued)

Chinese Calendar (*continued*)

Chinese solar term	English translation	Gregorian date	Chinese solar term	English translation	Gregorian date
Xiao Man	grain fills	20/21 May	Han Lu	cold dew	8/9 October
Mang Zhong	grain in ear	5/6 June	Shuang Jiang	frost descends	23/24 October
Xia Zhi	summer solstice	21/22 June	Li Dong	winter begins	7/8 November
Xiao Shu	slight heat	6/7 July	Xiao Xue	little snow	22/23 November
Da Shu	great heat	22/23 July			
Li Qiu	autumn begins	7/8 August	Da Xue	heavy snow	7/8 December
Chu Shu	heat ends	23/24 August	Dong Zhi	winter solstice	22/23 December
Bai Lu	white dew	7/8 September			
Qui Fen	autumn equinox	23/24 September	Xiao Han	little cold	5/6 January
			Da Han	severe cold	20/21 January

Chinese Dynasties

Period	Dynasty	Major events
c. 2205–*c.* 1550 BC	Hsia or Xia	agriculture; use of bronze; first writing
c. 1500–*c.* 1066 BC	Shang or Yin	first major dynasty; first Chinese calendar
c. 1066–*c.* 475 BC	Zhou	developed society using money, iron, and written laws
c. 475–*c.* 221 BC	Warring States period	tendency towards unification; age of Confucius
221–206 BC	Qin	unification after period of Warring States; building of Great Wall begun; roads built
206 BC–AD 220	Han	first centralized and effectively administered empire; introduction of Buddhism
220–265	Wei, Shu, Wu (Three Kingdoms)	division into three parts; prolonged fighting and eventual victory of Wei over Shu and Wu Kingdoms; Confucianism superseded by Buddhism and Taoism
265–316	Tsin	beginning of Hun invasions in the north
317–581	Western Jin (Chin)	Northern and Southern Dynasties
581–618	Sui	reunification; barbarian invasions stopped; Great Wall refortified
618–907	T'ang	centralized government; empire greatly extended; period of excellence in sculpture, painting, and poetry
907–960	Wu Tai (Five Dynasties)	economic depression and loss of territory in northern China, central Asia, and Korea; first use of paper money
960–1279	Song	period of calm and creativity; printing developed; central government restored; northern and western frontiers neglected and Mongol incursions begun

Chinese Dynasties (*continued*)

Period	Dynasty	Major events
1279–1368	Yüan	beginning of Mongol rule in China; Marco Polo visited China; dynasty brought to an end by widespread revolts, centred in Mongolia
1368–1644	Ming	Mongols driven out by native Chinese; Mongolia captured by 2nd Ming emperor; period of architectural development; Beijing flourished as new capital
1644–1912	Qing (Manchu)	China again under non-Chinese rule; trade with the West; culture flourished, but conservatism eventually led to the dynasty's overthrow by nationalistic revolutionaries

Chinese Communist Party Leaders

Although not officially the head of state, the leader of the Communist Party is usually considered to be the most politically influential person in China.

Term	Name
1989–	Jiang Zemin[1]
1987–89	Zhao Ziyang
1981–87	Hu Yaobang
1976–81	Hua Guofeng
1935–76	Mao Zedong

[1] From 1993 Jiang Zemin has also been state president.

Chinese Prime Ministers

In 1949 the Guomindang government was overthrown by the Communists and the People's Republic of China declared.

Term	Name
1998–	Zhu Rongji
1987–98	Li Peng
1980–87	Zhao Ziyang
1976–80	Hua Guofeng
1949–76	Zhou Enlai

Christian Denominations

Denomination	Organization	Characteristics
Anglican	episcopal; the archbishop of Canterbury recognized as 'first among equals' in the various Anglican churches	predominant denomination in the UK; ritual derives from the *Book of Common Prayer*
Baptist	self-governing churches; congregational	only adult Christians, capable of own choice, should be baptized
Catholic	strict hierarchy with the pope as leader	authority of the church regulates every area of life and belief

(*continued*)

Christian Denominations (*continued*)

Denomination	Organization	Characteristics
Lutheran	congregational or episcopal	Bible as the only source of authority
Methodist	superintendent system and conferences	scripture, tradition, and experience are at the core of the church's practices; extensive social involvement
Orthodox	independent and autonomous national churches	emphasis on Christ's resurrection; rich traditions of worship; little social involvement
Pentecostal	a wide range of groups; allows for freedom of organization	emphasis on the personal teachings of the Holy Spirit; charismatic
Presbyterian	government by elders (lay people or ordained ministers)	emphasis on self-control and self-discipline
Calvinist	mostly congregational	belief in predestination; Bible as the only source of authority

Christian Festivals

Festival	Description	Date (2001)
Christmas Day	celebration of the birth of Jesus in Bethlehem	25 December
Epiphany	celebrates the arrival of the three wise men from the east	6 January
Ash Wednesday	Lent recalls the 40 days Jesus spent fasting and praying in the desert	28 February
Palm Sunday	recalls Jesus' entry into Jerusalem during the last week of his life, when he was welcomed by people waving palm fronds	8 April
Good Friday	remembrance of the Crucifixion (the death of Jesus on the cross)	13 April
Easter Sunday	time of rejoicing that recalls the disciples' discovery that Jesus was alive, and that he had been resurrected	15 April
Ascension Day	commemorates the disciples witnessing Jesus being lifted up to heaven 40 days after Easter Day	24 May
Pentecost or Whitsun	celebrates the coming of the Holy Spirit upon the disciples	3 June

Christian Holy Days

Date	Name of holy day
1 January	The naming of Jesus; The Circumcision of Christ; The Solemnity of Mary Mother of God
6 January	Epiphany
25 January	The Conversion of St Paul

Christian Holy Days (*continued*)

Date	Name of holy day
2 February	The Presentation of Christ in the Temple
19 March	St Joseph of Nazareth, Husband of the Blessed Virgin Mary
25 March	The Annunciation of Our Lord to the Blessed Virgin Mary
25 April	St Mark the Evangelist
1 May	St Philip and St James, Apostles
14 May	St Matthias the Apostle
31 May	The Visitation of the Blessed Virgin Mary
11 June	St Barnabas the Apostle
24 June	The Birth of St John the Baptist
29 June	St Peter the Apostle
3 July	St Thomas the Apostle
22 July	St Mary Magdalen
25 July	St James the Apostle
6 August	The Transfiguration of our Lord
24 August	St Bartholomew the Apostle
1 September	New Year (Eastern Orthodox Church)
8 September	The Nativity of the Blessed Virgin Mary
14 September	The Exaltation of the Holy Cross
21 September	St Matthew the Apostle
29 September	St Michael and All Angels (Michaelmas)
18 October	St Luke the Evangelist
28 October	St Simon and St Jude, Apostles
1 November	All Saints
21 November	Presentation of the Blessed Virgin Mary in the Temple
30 November	St Andrew the Apostle
8 December	The Immaculate Conception of the Blessed Virgin Mary
25 December	Christmas
26 December	St Stephen the first Martyr
27 December	St John the Evangelist
28 December	The Holy Innocents

Christianity

Important Dates

Year	Ash Wednesday	Easter Day	Ascension Day	Pentecost (Whit Sunday)	Advent Sunday
2001	28 February	15 April	24 May	3 June	2 December
2002	13 February	31 March	9 May	19 May	1 December
2003	5 March	20 April	29 May	8 June	30 November
2004	25 February	11 April	20 May	30 May	28 November
2005	9 February	27 March	5 May	15 May	27 November
2006	1 March	16 April	25 May	4 June	3 December
2007	21 February	8 April	17 May	27 May	2 December
2008	6 February	23 March	1 May	11 May	30 November
2009	25 February	12 April	21 May	31 May	29 November
2010	17 February	4 April	13 May	23 May	28 November

Christianity
World Adherents

2000 (in millions)

Continent	Anglican	Baptist	Lutheran	Methodist	Orthodox	Pentecostal	Presbyterian
Africa	20.4	9.9	6.7	0.0	29.5	20.5	11.6
Asia	0.5	8.5	5.7	3.0	101.3	14.4	15.3
Europe	25.1	2.9	53.5	1.5	(Asia and Europe combined)	3.6	12.3
North America	4.7	46.8	13.9	12.9	7.9	34.2	8.3
Oceania	5.2	0.5	1.0	0.5	0.5	1.3	0.9
South America	0.2	3.1	1.4	0.5	0.5	45.2	0.8
world total	56.0	71.5	83.1	26.4	140.2	122.4	49.3

Christmas
The Twelve Days

Day	Gift
1	a partridge in a pear tree
2	two turtle doves
3	three french hens
4	four calling birds
5	five gold rings
6	six geese a laying
7	seven swans a swimming
8	eight maids a milking
9	nine ladies dancing
10	ten lords a leaping
11	eleven pipers piping
12	twelve drummers drumming

Cigars
Different Types

Name	What it looks like
cheroot	cigar with ends cut off (may contain chopped tobacco)
cigarillo	thin cigar a little longer than a cigarette
corona	long untapered cigar rounded at the ends
half corona	half the length of a corona with one end cut off
panatella	long thin cigar tapered at the closed end
perfecto	thick cigar tapered at both ends
regalia	large high-quality (Cuban) cigar

Clothing
Types of Boots and Shoes

ankle boots
ballet shoes
ballet slippers
bluchers
boots
bootees
bovver boots
brogues
brogans
brothel creepers
button boots

clodhoppers
clogs
court shoes
cowboy boots
crepe soles
Doc Martin's
dress shoes
espadrilles
evening shoes
flip-flops
galoshes

gumboots
gumshoes
gym shoes
high heels
jackboots
lace-ups
loafers
moccasins
mules
oxfords
overshoes

pattens
platform shoes
plimsolls
pumps
riding boots
running shoes
sabots
sandals
sandshoes
slingbacks
slip-ons

slippers
sneakers
snowshoes
stilettos
thigh boots
top boots
trainers
walking shoes
Wellingtons
waders
wedge heels
winkle-pickers

Clothing
Clothes Named after People

Item of clothing	Person
bloomers	Amelia Bloomer, US feminist
bluchers (shoes)	Gebhard von Blucher, Prussian soldier
bowler hat	John Bowler, British hatmaker
cardigan	James Thomas Brudenell (7th Earl of Cardigan), British soldier and politician
Havelock (headgear)	General Henry Havelock, British soldier who fought in India
knickerbockers	Diedrich Knickerbocker, fictitious Dutch author created by US essayist Irving Washington
leotard	Jules Léotard, French acrobat
mackintosh	Charles Macintosh, Scottish inventor
plimsoll	Samuel Plimsoll, English politician
spencer	John Spencer (Earl Spencer), British nobleman
stetson	John Stetson, US hatmaker
wellingtons (boots)	Arthur Wellesley, Duke of Wellington, British soldier and prime minister

Clothing
Garments and Fabrics Named after Places

Item	Place	Country/Region	Item	Place	Country/Region
astrakhan	Astrakhan	Russian Federation	glengarry	Glengarry	Scotland
			hessian	Hesse	Germany
balaclava	Balaclava	Ukraine	homburg	Homburg	Germany
balbriggan	Balbriggan	Ireland	jeans	Genoa	Italy
calico	Calicut	India	jersey	Jersey	Channel Islands
cambric	Cambrai	France	jodhpurs	Jodhpur	India
cashmere	Kashmir	Indian subcontinent	lawn	Laon	France
			lisle	Lille	France
cretonne	Creton	France	muslin	Mosul	Iraq
damask	Damascus	Syria	nankeen	Nanking	China
denim	de Nîmes	France	panama	Panama	Central America
duffel	Duffel	Belgium	satin	Zaitun	China
dungarees	Dungri	India	tulle	Tulle	France
fez	Fez	Morocco	ulster	Ulster	Northern Ireland

Companies
Most Valuable

Company	Market value in 1999 (US$ million)
General Electric (USA)	540,000
Cisco Systems (USA)	434,000
Intel (USA)	388,000
Microsoft (USA)	347,000
NTT DoCoMo (Japan)	320,000
Vodaphone (UK)	292,000
Exxon Mobil (USA)	278,000
Wal-mart (USA)	262,000
Nokia (Finland)	241,000
Citigroup (USA)	207,000

Companies
Owning the Most US Patents

Company	Patents granted (as of 1996)
International Business Machines Corp	1,867
Canon Kabushiki Kaisha	1,541
Motorola Inc	1,064
NEC Corp	1,043
Hitachi Ltd	963
Mitsubishi Denki Kabushiki Kaisha	934
Toshiba Corp	914
Fujitsu Ltd	869
Sony Corp	855
Matsushita Electric Industrial Co Ltd	841

Countries with Most Public Libraries

Country	Number of libraries
Russian Federation	96,200
UK	24,850
USA	15,900
Ukraine	15,900
Kazakhstan	15,050
Germany	13,050
Poland	9,500
Belarus	9,100
Czech Republic	8,000
Mexico	5,650

Crime
Worst Countries for Violent Crimes

Country
Russian Federation
South Africa
USA
Japan
Spain
Germany
France
UK
Italy
Poland

Danish Monarchs

Reign	Name		Reign	Name
Line of Glücksburg			**House of Oldenburg**	
1972–	Margrethe II		1848–63	Frederick VII
1947–72	Frederick IX			
1912–47	Christian X			
1906–12	Frederick VIII			
1863–1906	Christian IX			

Danish Prime Ministers
Most Recent

Term	Name	Party
1993–	Poul Nyrup Rasmussen	Social Democratic Party
1982–93	Poul Schlüter	Conservative Party
1975–82	Anker Jørgensen	Social Democratic Party
1973–75	Poul Hartling	Liberal Party
1972–73	Anker Jørgensen	Social Democratic Party
1971–72	Jens-Otto Krag	Social Democratic Party
1968–71	Hilmar Baunsgaard	Radical Party
1962–68	Jens-Otto Krag	Social Democratic Party
1960–62	Viggo Kampmann	Social Democratic Party

Days of the Week

English	German	French	Italian	Spanish
Sunday	Sonntag	dimanche	domenica	domingo
Monday	Montag	lundi	lunedì	lunes
Tuesday	Dienstag	mardi	martedì	martes
Wednesday	Mittwoch	mercredi	mercoledì	miércoles
Thursday	Donnerstag	jeudi	giovedì	jueves
Friday	Freitag	vendredi	venerdì	viernes
Saturday	Samstag	samedi	sabato	sábado

Death Penalty
Latest Countries to Abolish

As of 27 April 2000.

Country	Date of abolition
East Timor	1999
Turkmenistan	1999
Ukraine	1999
Azerbaijan	1998
Bulgaria	1998
Canada	1998
Estonia	1998
Lithuania	1998
UK	1998

Debt
Countries with the Highest

Country	Debt (US$ billion)
Brazil	193.6
Mexico	149.7
China	146.7
Korea, South	143.3
Indonesia	136.2
Russian Federation	125.6
Argentina	123.2
India	94.4
Thailand	93.4
Turkey	91.2

Debt
Countries with the Lowest

Country	Foreign Debt (US$ billion)
Slovenia	4.0
Tuvalu	6.0
Kiribati	21.0
Eritrea	46.0
Vanuatu	47.0
St Kitts and Nevis	58.0
Suriname	68.2
Tonga	70.0
Bhutan	87.0
Palau	100.0

Defence Expenditure
Countries with Highest

Country	Total defence budget (1997) (US$ million)
USA	256,788
UK	35,904
France	32,434
Germany	26,500
Italy	17,962
Canada	6,964
Netherlands	6,923
Spain	5,897
Sweden	4,842
Turkey	4,564

Defence Expenditure
NATO Countries

Country	Total spending (1998) (US$ million)	Country	Total spending (1998) (US$ million)
USA	162,938	Turkey	5,932
Germany	28,770	Spain	5,683
UK	21,266	Netherlands	5,376
Italy	19,525	Greece	5,030
Spain	6,683	Canada	4,605

Disarmament
Some Recent Arms Control Agreements

Treaty	Dates	Parties and details
START II Treaty	January 1993	USA and Russian Federation; to limit strategic nuclear weapons by 2003
Comprehensive Test Ban Treaty	September 1996	UK, France, USA, China, India, Pakistan, and the Russian Federation; to ban all explosive nuclear tests
US–Soviet Bilateral Destruction Agreement	June 1990	USA and USSR; to stop producing chemical weapons and reduce stockpiles
Conventional Forces in Europe (CFE) Treaty	November 1990	30 nations; to establish limits on the amount of military machinery in Europe
CFE 1A Treaty	July 1992	30 nations; to establish limits on the number of troops in Europe
Chemical Weapons Convention	January 1993	169 nations; to prohibit the development, acquisition, or use of chemical weapons; existing facilties to be destroyed and routine inspections allowed

Treaty	Dates	Parties and details
Florence Agreement	June 1996	Bosnia-Herzegovina, Bosnian Serb Republic, Croatia, Serbia, and Montenegro; to limit armaments in the Bosnia-Herzegovina conflict
Ottawa Treaty	December 1997	135 countries; to ban the production and use of anti-personnel mines, destroy stockpiles, and clear existing minefields

Divorce
Rates in Selected Countries

Country	Divorces (per thousand people)	
	1987	**1997**
Canada	3.0	2.4
Finland	2.0	2.6
France	1.9	2.1
Germany	2.3	2.1
Greece	0.9	0.9
Italy	0.5	0.6
Japan	1.4	1.7
Spain	0.5	0.8
UK	2.9	2.9
USA	4.8	4.3

Dutch Monarchs
Most Recent

Reign	Name
1980–	Beatrix
1948–80	Juliana
1945–48	Wilhelmina
1940–45	German occupation
1890–1940	Wilhelmina
1849–90	Willem III
1840–49	Willem II
1815–40	Willem I
1813–15	provisional government
1810–13	French annexation

Dutch Prime Ministers
Most Recent

Term	Name	Party
1994–	Wim Kok	Labour Party
1982–94	Rudolphus (Ruud) Lubbers	Christian Democratic Appeal Party
1977–82	Andreas van Agt	Christian Democratic Appeal Party
1973–77	Johannes (Joop) den Uyl	Labour Party
1971–73	Barend Biesheuvel	Anti-Revolutionary Party
1967–71	Petrus de Jong	Catholic Party
1966–67	Jelle Zijlstra	Anti-Revolutionary Party
1965–66	Joseph Cals	Catholic Party
1963–65	Victor Marijnen	Catholic Party
1959–63	Jan de Quay	Catholic Party

Easter
Dates of Easter

Easter is a moveable feast of the Christian church falling on the first Sunday following the full Moon after the vernal equinox (21 March); that is, between 22 March and 25 April.

Year	Easter Day
2001	15 April
2002	31 March
2003	20 April
2004	11 April
2005	27 March
2006	16 April
2007	8 April
2008	23 March
2009	12 April
2010	4 April

Eden
Four Rivers of Eden

Hiddekel (Tigris)
Pishion
Ghion
Euphrates

Education
World Expenditure on Education

Region	Public expenditure on education		
	thousand million US$	% of GNP	per inhabitant (US$)
Africa	29.1	5.9	41
America	481.7	5.3	623
Asia	302.1	3.6	93
Europe	492.6	5.4	982
Oceania	24.5	6.0	878
world total	1,329.9	4.9	252

Egyptian Dynasties
Last

Period	Name	Description
323–30 BC	Ptolemaic Dynasty	Ptolemies
332–323 BC	Alexander the Great	
c. 343–332 BC	thirty-first Dynasty	Persian kings
c. 380–c. 343 BC	thirtieth Dynasty	Sebennytic
c. 399–c. 380 BC	twenty-ninth Dynasty	Mendesian
c. 405–c. 399 BC	twenty-eighth Dynasty	Saite
c. 525–c. 405 BC	twenty-seventh Dynasty	Persian kings
c. 664–c. 525 BC	twenty-sixth Dynasty	Nubian
c. 767–c. 656 BC	twenty-fifth Dynasty	Nubian
c. 740–c. 712 BC	twenty-fourth Dynasty	Saite

Evangelists
Feast Days

Name	Feast day (in UK)	Name	Feast day (in UK)
St Matthew	21 September	St Luke	18 October
St Mark	25 April	St John	27 December

Evangelists

The Four Evangelists

Name	Symbol	Name	Symbol
John	an eagle	Mark	a lion
Luke	an ox	Matthew	an angel (or man)

Fairies

Name	Description
afreet or afrit	powerful evil demon (in Arabia)
brownie	elf that does household chores at night
elf	small, mischievous (male) being
erlking	malevolent German goblin who kidnaps children
fairy	small, clever, playful being, can often do magic
fay	fairy or sprite
genie	wish-fulfilling servant who appears by magic
glaistig	Gaelic fairy or water sprite
gnome	legendary small creature that lives underground
goblin	small, ugly, malevolent creature
gremlin	mischievous imp
hob	hobgoblin or sprite
hobbit	small person living underground (invented by author J R R Tolkien)
hobgoblin	evil or mischievous goblin
imp	small devil or demon, or a mischievous sprite
jinni (plural jinn)	supernatural Muslim spirit in animal or human form
knocker	goblin in mines that indicates rich ore veins
kobold	mischievous household sprite, or spirit that haunts mines (in Germany)
korrigan	fairy that steals children (in Brittany)
leprechaun	treasure-owning mischievous elf (in Ireland)
little people	small supernatural beings (such as elves, pixies, and leprechauns)
nis or nisse	friendly goblin or brownie (in Scandinavia)
nix	unfriendly water sprite
peri	beautiful fairy (in Persia)
phynnodderee	hobgoblin on the Isle of Man
piskie	pixie (in Cornwall)
pixie or pixy	elf or fairy
pooka	hobgoblin (in Ireland)
puck	mischievous or evil spirit
sprite	nimble elfin creature, often associated with water
troll	cave-dwelling supernatural being (may be dwarf or giant)
undine	female water spirit

Famous Last Words

Quotation	Who said it	Life dates
'You as well, Brutus?'	Julius Caesar at his assassination	63 BC–AD 14
'I realize that patriotism is not enough. I must have no hatred or bitterness towards anyone.'	Edith Cavell at her execution by firing squad	1865–1915
'This hand hath offended'	Thomas Cranmer, at the stake, to the hand with which he signed his recantation	1498–1556
'It is not my design to drink or sleep, but my design is to make what haste I can to be gone.'	Oliver Cromwell	1599–1658
'How is the Empire?'	George V of England	1865–1936
'Well, I've had a happy life.'	William Hazlitt	1778–1830
'God will pardon me, it is His trade.'	Heinrich Heine	1797–1856
'Turn up the lights. I don't want to go home in the dark.'	O Henry	1862–1910
'I am about to take my last voyage, a great leap in the dark.'	Thomas Hobbes	1588–1679
'Do not hack me as you did my Lord Russell.'	Duke of Monmouth to his executioner	1649–1685
'I pray you, Master Lieutenant, see me safe up, and for my coming down let me shift for myself.'	Thomas More on mounting the scaffold	1478–1535
'What an artist dies in me!'	Nero	AD 37–68
'Too kind – too kind.'	Florence Nightingale on being handed the Order of Merit	1820–1910
'Die, my dear doctor? That's the last thing I'll do.'	Viscount Palmerston	1784–1865
'I am going in search of a great perhaps.'	François Rabelais	c. 1495–1553
'So the heart be right, it is no matter which way the head lieth.'	Walter Raleigh at his execution	c. 1552–1618
'So little done, so much to do.'	Cecil Rhodes	1772–1826
'For God's sake, look after our people.'	Captain Robert Scott, last journal entry	1846–1932

Fashion

Selected Designers

Name	Dates	Details
Armani, Giorgio	1935–	Italian fashion designer known for understated styles and fine fabrics
Cardin, Pierre	1922–	French pioneering fashion designer who launched menswear and designed ready-to-wear collections
Chanel, Coco (Gabrielle)	1883–1971	French fashion designer and trendsetter who created the 'little black dress'
Dior, Christian	1905–1957	French couturier whose 'New Look' had impact following World War II austerity

Fashion: Selected Designers (*continued*)

Name	Dates	Details
Galliano, John	1960–	visionary English designer working in Paris, currently (since 1996) for the house of Dior, inspired by mythology and historical costume
Gaultier, Jean-Paul	1952–	French fashion designer who is influential in the ready-to-wear market and has designed costumes for US entertainers
Klein, Calvin (Richard)	1942–	US fashion designer who made designer jeans a status symbol
Lauren, Ralph (adopted name of Ralph Lipschitz)	1939–	US fashion designer of the Polo label of menswear
Saint-Laurent, Yves (Henri Donat Mathieu)	1936–	French fashion designer who creates a 'power-dressing' look of classic, stylish city clothes for men and women
Versace, Gianni	1946–1997	Italian designer of provocative clothing using unusual fabric combinations, strong colours, and simple shapes

Fighting Vehicles

Countries with Most

Country	Number of vehicles
Russian Federation	7,590
USA	6,700
China	4,800
Ukraine	3,135
Syria	2,380
Germany	2,253
South Korea	1,770
India	1,700
Poland	1,405
Sweden	1,210

Fires

Worst 20th-century Fires

Place	Date	Number killed
Kwanto, Japan	1923	71,000
San Francisco, USA	1906	c. 3,000
Chonqing, China	1949	1,700
New York City, USA	1904	1,021
Cloquet, USA	1918	1,000
Chicago, USA	1903	602
Boston, USA	1942	491
Mandi Dabwali, India	1995	442
Abadon, Iran	1978	<400
Hoboken, USA	1900	326

French Philosophers

Name	Dates	Representative work
Michel Foucault	1926–1984	*The Order of Things*
Maurice Merleau-Ponty	1908–1961	*The Phenomenology of Perception*
Jean-Paul Sartre	1905–1980	*Being and Nothingness*
Henri Bergson	1859–1941	*Creative Evolution*
Auguste Comte	1798–1857	*Cours de philosophie positive*
Denis Diderot	1713–1784	*D'Alembert's Dream*
Jean-Jacques Rousseau	1712–1778	*The Social Contract*
Blaise Pascal	1623–1662	*Pensées*
René Descartes	1596–1650	*Discourse on Method; Meditations on the First Philosophy*

French Presidents
Most Recent

Term	Name	Party
1995–	Jacques Chirac	Neo-Gaullist Rally for the Republic (RPR)
1981–95	François Mitterand	Socialist
1974–81	Valéry Giscard d'Estaing	Republican/Union of French Democracy
1969–74	Georges Pompidou	Gaullist
1959–69	General Charles de Gaulle	Gaullist

French Prime Ministers
Most Recent

Term	Name	Party
1997–	Lionel Jospin	Socialist
1995–97	Alain Juppé	Neo-Gaullist RPR
1993–95	Edouard Balladur	Neo-Gaullist RPR
1992–93	Pierre Bérégovoy	Socialist
1991–92	Edith Cresson	Socialist

French Revolutionary Calendar

Revolutionary month	Meaning	Time period
Vendémiaire	vintage	22 September–21 October
Brumaire	fog	22 October–20 November
Frimaire	frost	21 November–20 December
Nivôse	snow	21 December–19 January
Pluviôse	rain	20 January–18 February
Ventôse	wind	19 February–20 March
Germinal	budding	21 March–19 April
Floréal	flowers	20 April–19 May
Prairial	meadows	20 May–18 June
Messidor	harvest	19 June–18 July
Thermidor	heat	19 July–17 August
Fructidor	fruit	18 August–16 September
Sanculottides festival		17 September–21 September

French Rulers
1913–58

In 1958 the Algerian crisis caused the collapse of the Fourth Republic, and the establishment of a new constitution for the Fifth Republic.

Date of accession	Ruler
1954	René Coty (President)
1947	Vincent Auriol (President)
1944	provisional government
1940	Philippe Pétain (Vichy government)
1932	Albert Le Brun (President)
1931	Paul Doumer (President)
1924	Gaston Doumergue (President)
1920	Alexandre Millerand (President)
1920	Paul Deschanel (President)
1913	Raymond Poincaré (President)

German Philosophers

Name	Dates	Representative work
Hans-Georg Gadamer	1900–	*Truth and Method*
Martin Heidegger	1889–1976	*Being and Time*
Edmund Husserl	1859–1938	*Logical Investigations*
Friedrich Nietzsche	1844–1900	*Thus Spake Zarathustra*
Wilhelm Dilthey	1833–1911	*The Rise of Hermeneutics*
Karl Marx	1818–1883	*Economic and Philosophical Manuscripts*
Arthur Schopenhauer	1788–1860	*The World as Will and Idea*
Friedrich Schelling	1775–1854	*System of Transcendental Idealism*
Georg Hegel	1770–1831	*The Phenomenology of Spirit*
Johann Fichte	1762–1814	*The Science of Knowledge*
Immanuel Kant	1724–1804	*The Critique of Pure Reason*
Gottfried Leibniz	1646–1716	*The Monadology*
Nicholas of Cusa	1401–1464	*De Docta Ignorantia*

German Political Leaders

In 1949 the US, French, and British zones of occupation established after World War II became the Federal Republic of Germany, and the Soviet zone became the German Democratic Republic. The official reunification of the countries, with Helmut Kohl as chancellor, took place in 1990.

Term	Name	Party
Federal Republic of Germany		
Chancellors		
1982–90	Helmut Kohl	Christian Democrat
1974–82	Helmut Schmidt	Social Democrat
1969–74	Willy Brandt	Social Democrat
1966–69	Kurt Kiesinger	Christian Democrat
1963–66	Ludwig Erhard	Christian Democrat
1949–63	Konrad Adenauer	Christian Democrat

Term	Name	Party
Democratic Republic		
Prime Ministers		
1990–91	Lothar de Maizière	
1989–90	Hans Modrow	
Communist Party leaders		
1989	Egon Krenz	
1971–89	Erich Honecker	
1960–71	Walter Ulbricht	
1949–60	Wilhelm Pieck	
Germany		
Chancellors		
1998–	Gerhard Schroeder	Social Democrat
1990–98	Helmut Kohl	Christian Democrat

Ghosts

Name	Description	Name	Description
apparition	appearance of a ghostly figure	manes	ghost of somebody who is dead
banshee	female spirit that wails to signal imminent death	phantasm	phantom
		phantom	spectre or apparition
bogy or bogey	mischievous or evil spirit	poltergeist	spirit that causes noises and things to be moved about
cacodemon	evil spirit or devil		
demon	evil spirit or devil	revenant	ghost (that returns from the dead)
devil	evil spirit (the Devil of theology has a capital letter)		
		shade	ghost (literary)
Doppelgänger	ghostly duplicate	spectre	phantom or ghost
duppy	Caribbean ghost or spirit	spirit	immaterial being that never had a body; the soul of a dead person
eidolon	apparition or phantom		
fetch	apparition of a living person		
fiend	evil spirit, demon, or devil	spook	ghost (informal)
ghoul	malevolent spirit	taisch	Scottish type of wraith
imp	small demon or devil	visitant	supernatural being
larva	ghost or malevolent spirit (Roman)	wraith	apparition of a living person that appears just before his or her death
lemures	evil spirits of the dead (Roman)		
		zombie	spirit that reanimates a dead person

Giants

Giant	Description	Giant	Description
Aegeon	another name for Briareus	Goliath	Philistine giant killed by David (Old Testament)
Antaeus	African giant killed by Hercules		
		Jotuns	race of Norse giants
Atlas	Titan who held the skies on his shoulders	Magog	giant who, with Gog, founded Britain
Briareus	100-armed 50-headed giant who helped against the Titans	Orion	hunting giant of Greek mythology
		Pantagruel	gigantic prince (son of Gargantua) in Rabelais's work
Brontes	blacksmith member of the Cyclops		
Cacus	three-headed robber giant who vomited flames	Polythemus	one of the Cyclops who captured Odysseus
Cormoran	Cornish giant killed by Jack the Giant Killer	Titans	six giant sons (Crius, Cronos/Kronos, Coeus, Hyperion, Iapetus, and Oceanus) and six giant daughters (Mnemosyne, Phoebe, Rhea, Tethys, Theia, and Themis) of the Greek deities Uranus and Gaia
Cottus	100-armed giant, brother of Briareus		
Cyclops	race of one-eyed giants		
Enceladus	100-armed giant		
Ephialtes	giant son of Poseidon		
Gargantua	giant king known for his eating capacity	Ymir	forefather of the giants in Norse mythology
Gog	giant who, with Magog, founded Britain		

Greek and Roman Gods

Greek god	Concern or province	Roman equivalent	Greek god	Concern or province	Roman equivalent
Aphrodite	love	Venus	Hera	queen of the gods	Juno
Apollo	Sun/music/ prophecy	Apollo	Hermes	messenger of the gods	Mercury
Ares	war	Mars	Hestia	hearth/home	Vesta
Artemis	Moon/hunting	Diana	Kronos	time	Saturn
Athena	wisdom/battle	Minerva	Nike	victory	Victoria
Demeter	agriculture	Ceres	Persephone	queen of the underworld	Prosperina
Dionysus	wine	Bacchus			
Eilythia	birth	Lucina	Pluto	king of the underworld	Dis (or Orcus)
Eos	dawn	Aurora			
the Erinyes	deliverers of justice	the Furies	Poseidon	ocean	Neptune
			Tyche	luck	Fortuna
Eros	erotic love	Cupid	Zeus	king of the gods	Jupiter
Hephaestus	metalcraft/fire	Vulcan			

Greek Philosophers

Name	Dates	Representative work	Name	Dates	Representative work
Plotinus	AD 205–270	*Enneads*	Socrates	469–399 BC	–
Epicurus	341–270 BC	fragments	Plato	428–347 BC	*Republic; Phaedo*
Aristotle	384–322 BC	*Nichomachean Ethics; Metaphysics*	Parmenides	c. 510–c. 450 BC	fragments
			Heraclitus	c. 544–483 BC	*On Nature*

Gunpowder Plot
Conspirators

Name	Life dates	Name	Life dates
Guy Fawkes	1570–1606	Thomas Bates	unknown–1606
Robert Catesby	1573–1605	Christopher Wright	1570–1605
Thomas Wintour	c. 1567–1606	Robert Wintour	c. 1565–1606
Thomas Percy	c. 1563–1605	John Grant	unknown–1606
John Wright	1568–1605	Ambrose Rookwood	c. 1578–1606
Robert Keyes	c. 1563–1606	Francis Tresham	c. 1567–1605
Everard Digby	1578–1606		

Henry VIII
His Six Wives

Name	Nationality	Life dates	Fate
Catherine of Aragon	Spanish	1485–1536	divorced
Anne Boleyn	English	c. 1507–1536	beheaded
Jane Seymour	English	1509–1537	died
Anne of Cleves	German	1515–1557	divorced
Catherine Howard	English	c. 1525–1542	beheaded
Catherine Parr	English	1512–1548	survived

Heraldry
Colours

Heraldic term	Colour	Heraldic term	Colour
argent	silver[1]	purpure	purple
azure	blue	sable	black
gules	red	vert	green
or	gold[1]		

[1] Known as a metal (not a colour).

Heraldry
Postures of Beasts

Posture	Meaning	Posture	Meaning
caboched	full face only, with no neck	rampant	standing on the hind legs
couchant	lying down with the head raised	rampant combattant	two animals rampant facing each other
counter-passant	two beasts moving in opposite directions	rampant endorsed	two animals rampant standing back to back
cowarded	with the tail between the legs	rampant gardant	rampant, but facing the observer
displayed	with wings and claws outspread (of birds)	rampant regardant	rampant, but facing the rear
dormant	lying down with the head down	regardant	facing the rear
gardant	full-faced (whole beast)	salient	jumping (usually of a small animal)
naiant	swimming (of fish)	sejant	seated
passant	walking	statant	standing still
passant gardant	walking, but facing the observer	trippant	running
passant regardant	walking, but facing the rear	volant	flying

Hindu Calendar

Hindu month	Number of days	Gregorian equivalent	Hindu month	Number of days	Gregorian equivalent
Chaitra	29 or 30	March–April	Asvina	29 or 30	September–October
Vaisakha	29 or 30	April–May	Karttika	29 or 30	October–November
Jyaistha	29 or 30	May–June	Margasirsa	29 or 30	November–December
Asadha	29 or 30	June–July	Pausa	29 or 30	December–January
Sravana	29 or 30	July–August	Magha	29 or 30	January–February
Bhadrapada	29 or 30	August–September	Phalguna	29 or 30	February–March

Hindu Calendar

Gregorian Year Equivalents

Years in the Hindu calendar are calculated from AD 78, the beginning of the Saka Era (SE).

Hindu year (SE)	Gregorian equivalent
1922	22 March 2000–21 March 2001
1923	22 March 2001–21 March 2002
1924	22 March 2002–21 March 2003

Hinduism

Major Festivals

Festival	Description	Date (2001)
Mahashivaratri	honours Shiva, his wife Parvati, and their child Ganesh	21 February
Sarasvati Puja	honours Sarasvati, the patron of the arts and learning	29 January
Holi	remembers the stories of Krishna and Prahalad	9 March
Rama Naumi	celebrates the birthday of the god Rama	2 April
Ratha Yatra	a statue of Vishnu is pulled through the streets where lamps, flowers, and other offerings are laid in his path	23 June
Raksha Bandhan	sisters tie rakhis, silk threads decorated with flowers, onto their brothers' wrists as a symbol of protection	3 August
Janamashtarni	celebrates the birth of Krishna	12 August
Navaratri Dusshera	different manifestations of the goddess Durga are honoured over nine nights	26 October
Diwali	accounts are settled at this time and worship is given to Lakshmi, goddess of wealth and good fortune	14 November

Holidays
International Festivals and Holidays

Name	Date(s)	Where celebrated
ANZAC Day	25 April	Australia and New Zealand
Ash Wednesday	7th Wednesday before Easter	Christian countries
Bairam	end of Ramadan and 70 days later	Muslim countries
Bastille day	14 July	France
Canada Day	1 July	Canada
Columbus Day	12 October	USA
Day of the Vow	16 December	South Africa
Fasching	31 December to Ash Wednesday	Austria and Germany
Feast of Lanterns	July	Japan
Feast of Lights	December	Jewish communities
Halloween	31 October	Christian countries
Independence Day	4 July	USA
Labor Day	1st Monday in September	Canada and USA
Mardi Gras	last day before Lent	Mainly Latin America
Muharram	July or August	Muslim countries
Pesach	March or April	Jewish communities
Ramadan	March and April	Muslim countries
Rosh Hashanah	late September or early October	Jewish communities
St John's Eve	23 June	Portugal
Shrove Tuesday	last day before Lent	Christian countries
Tet	January or February	Vietnam
Thanksgiving Day	4th Thursday in November	USA
Waitangi Day	6 February	New Zealand
Walpurgisnacht	May Day Eve	Germany
Yom Kippur	September or October	Jewish communities

Holy Roman Emperors
The Earliest

Reign	Name	Reign	Name
800–14	Charlemagne (Charles the Great)	891–94	Guido of Spoleto
814–40	Louis the Pious	892–98	Lambert of Spoleto (co-emperor)
840–55	Lothair I	896–901	Arnulf (rival)
855–75	Louis II	901–05	Louis III of Provence
875–77	Charles (II) the Bald	905–24	Berengar
881–87	Charles (III) the Fat		

House of Habsburg
1804–1918

Reign	Name
Emperors of Austria-Hungary	
1916–18	Charles (Karl Franz Josef)
1848–1916	Franz Josef
Emperors of Austria	
1835–48	Ferdinand I
1804–35	Francis (Franz) I (of Austria) and II (as Holy Roman Emperor until 1806)

Illiteracy
World's Worst Rates

As of 2000.

Country	Illiterate population (%)
Niger	84.3
Burkina Faso	77.0
Afghanistan	63.7
Sierra Leone	63.7
Gambia	63.5
Guinea-Bissau	63.2
Senegal	62.7
Benin	62.5
Ethiopia	61.3
Mauritania	60.1

Illiteracy
World Adult Female Illiteracy

Region	Percentage
Southern Asia	63
Eastern Asia/Pacific	73
sub-Saharan Africa	61
Middle East and North Africa	64
Latin America/Caribbean	55
developed countries	62
world	64

Illiteracy
World Adult Male Illiteracy

Region	Percentage
Southern Asia	37
Eastern Asia/Pacific	27
sub-Saharan Africa	39
Middle East and North Africa	36
Latin America/Caribbean	45
developed countries	38
world	36

Inca Emperors

Reign	Name	Reign	Name
c. 1200–1400	Capac Yupanqui	1528–32	Huascar
	Inca Roca	1532–33	Atahualpa
	Yahuar Huacadc	1533	Topa Hualpa
until 1438	Viracocha Inca	1533–45	Manco Inca
1438–71	Pachacuti	1545–60	Sayri Tupac
1471–93	Topa Inca	1560–71	Titu Cusi Yupanqui
1493–1528	Huayna Capac	1571–72	Tupac Amaru

Indian Dynasties

Reign (approximate dates)	Major Indian dynasties
7th–4th centuries BC	Saisunaga Dynasty (Magadhan ascendancy, northern India)
4th century BC	Nandas
4th–2nd centuries BC	Mauryan Empire (India, except the area south of Karnataka)

(*continued*)

People, History, and Society **355**

Indian Dynasties (*continued*)

Reign (approximate dates)	Major Indian dynasties
2nd–1st centuries BC	Shungas (Ganges Valley and part of central India)
2nd–1st centuries BC	Indo-Greeks (northwest India)
73–28 BC	Kanvas (northern India)
1st century BC–3rd century AD	Satavahanas (north Deccan)
1st century BC–3rd century AD	Shakas (western India)
1st century BC–3rd century AD	Kushanas (northern India and Central Asia)
4th–6th centuries	Guptas (northern India)
5th–6th centuries	Hunas (northwest India and Central Asia)
6th–7th centuries	Maukharis
6th–7th centuries	Later Guptas of Magadha
7th century	Harsha
300–888	Pallavas (Tamil Nadu)
556–757	Chalukyas of Vatapi (west and central Deccan)
7th–10th centuries	Pandyas of Madurai (Tamil Nadu)
630–970	Eastern Chalukyas of Vengi (Andhra Pradesh)
750–1100	Palas (Bengal and Bihar)
753–973	Rashtrakutras (west and central Deccan)
773–1019	Pratiharas (west India and upper Ganges Valley)
850–1278	Cholas of Thanjavur (Tamil Nadu)
900–1203	Chandellas (Bundelkhand)
950–1195	Kalachuris of Tripuri (Madhya Pradesh)
973–1192	Chahamanis (east Rajasthan)
973–1189	Chalukyas of Kalyani (west and central Deccan)
974–1238	Chaulukyas (Gujarat)
974–1060	Gahadavalas (Qanauj)
1110–1327	Hoysalas of Dvarasamudra (central and south Deccan)
1118–1199	Senas (Bengal)
1190–1294	Yadavas of Devagiri (north Deccan)
1197–1323	Kakatiyas of Warangal (Andhra Pradesh)
1206–1526	Sultans of Delhi
1336–1576	Sultans of Bengal
1346–1589	Sultans of Kashmir
1391–1583	Sultans of Gujarat
1394–1479	Sharqi Sultans of Jaunpur
1401–1531	Sultans of Malva
1347–1527	Bahmanid Sultans of the Deccan and their successors
1484–1572	Imadshahis of Berar
1490–1595	Nizamshahis of Ahmadnagar
1492–1609	Baridishahis of Bidar
1489–1686	Adilshahis of Bijapur
1512–1687	Qutbshahis of Golconda
1370–1601	Faruqi Sultans of Khandesh
1216–1327	Pandyas of Madurai (Tamil Nadu)
1336–1646	Rulers of Vijayanagar Empire
1674–1707	Chatrapati Bhonsles
1526–1858	Mogul Emperors
1526–1707	Great Moguls
1707–1858	Lesser Moguls

Indian Leaders
Last Indian Dynasties and Rulers

Reign	Name
1837–58	Bahadur Shah II (Abul al-Zafar Muhammad Sirajuddin; banished)
1806–37	Akbar Shah II (Muhiyuddin)
1760–1806	Shah Alam II (Jalaluddin Ali Jauhar; deposed briefly in 1788)
1760	Shah Jahan III
1754–60	Alamgir II (Muhammad Azizuddin)
1748–54	Ahmad Shah Bahadur (Abu al-Nasir Muhammad)
1719–48	Muhammad Shah (Nasiruddin)
1719	Nikusiyar
1719	Rafi ud-Daula Shah Jahan II
1719	Rafi ud-Darayat (Shamsuddin)

Indian Prime Ministers

Term	Name	Party
1998–	Atal Behari Vajpayee	Bharatiya Janata Party
1997–98	Inder Kumar Gujral	Janata Dal
1996–97	H D Deve Gowda	Janata Dal
1996	Atal Behari Vajpayee	Bharatiya Janata Party
1991–96	P V Narasimha Rao	Congress (I)
1990–91	Chandra Shekhar	Janata Dal (Socialist)
1989–90	Viswanath Pratap Singh	Janata Dal
1984–89	Rajiv Gandhi	Congress (I)
1980–84	Indira Gandhi	Congress (I)
1979–80	Charan Singh	Janata/Lok Dal

Inflation
Countries with Highest Rate

Country	Inflation rate (%)	Year
Angola	1,200.0	1998
Somalia	363.0	1995
Afghanistan	240.0	1996
Iraq	140.0	1998
Belarus	127.0	1998
Turkey	83.1	1998
Congo, Democratic Republic of	65.0	1998
Romania	59.0	1998
Laos	55.0	1998
Myanmar	51.0	1998

Inflation
Countries with Lowest Rate

Country	Inflation rate (%)	Year
Mozambique	–1.3	1998
Brunei	–0.5	1998
Uganda	0	1998
Switzerland	0.1	1998
Liechtenstein	0.5	1997
Panama	0.6	1998
Dominica	0.7	1998
Andorra	0.8	1998
Bahrain	0.8	1998
Belize	0.8	1997

Initials
Famous People Known by their Initials

Person	Forenames	Dates	Description
J J Thompson	Joseph John	1856–1940	English physicist
A E Houseman	Alfred Edward	1859–1936	English poet
J M Barrie	James Matthew	1860–1937	English author
H G Wells	Herbert George	1866–1946	English author
J C Penny	James Cash	1875–1971	US retailer
W C Fields	William Claude	1880–1946	US actor
D H Lawrence	David Herbert	1885–1930	English author
T E Lawrence	Thomas Edward	1888–1935	British soldier and author
T S Eliot	Thomas Stearns	1888–1965	US-born poet and playwright
J R R Tolkien	John Ronald Reuel	1892–1973	English author
J D Salinger	Jerome David	1919–	US author
P D James	Phyllis Dorothy	1920–	English author

Insults
Famous National Insults

Quotation	Who said it
'America ... where laws and customs alike are based on the dreams of spinsters.'	Bertrand Russell (1872–1970)
'Canada is useful only to provide me with furs.'	Madame de Pompadour (1721–1764)
'The English have no exalted sentiments: they can all be bought.'	Napoleon Bonaparte (1769–1821)
'France is a country where the money falls apart in your hands and you can't tear the toilet paper.'	Billy Wilder (1906–)
'How much disgruntled heaviness, lameness, dampness, how much beer is there in German intelligence.'	Friedrich Nietzsche (1844–1900)
'Many people die of thirst but the Irish are born with one.'	Spike Milligan (1918–)
'They spell it *Vinci* and pronounce it *Vinchy;* foreigners always spell better than they pronounce.'	Mark Twain (1835–1910)
'Poor Mexico, so far from God and so near to the United States!'	Porfirio Diaz (1830–1915)
'There are few virtues which the Poles do not possess and there are few errors they have ever avoided.'	Winston Churchill (1874–1965)
'I have been trying all my life to like Scotchmen, and am obligated to desist from the experiment in despair.'	Charles Lamb (1775–1834)
'I look upon Switzerland as an inferior sort of Scotland.'	Sidney Smith (1771–1845)
'The land of my fathers (Wales). My fathers can have it.'	Dylan Thomas (1914–53)

Insults

Some Famous Insults

Who said it	What was said	About whom
Henry VIII, King of England	'You have sent me a Flanders mare.'	Anne of Cleves, his future queen
Thomas Macaulay, English author	'Anne ... when in good humour, was meekly stupid, and when in bad humour, was sulkily stupid.'	Queen Anne of England
Howard Dietz, US critic	'A day away from Tallulah is like a month in the country.'	Tallulah Bankhead, US actress
Alan Bennet, English playwright	'... giving Clive Barnes his CBE for services to the theatre is like giving Goering the DFC for services to the RAF.'	Clive Barnes, US critic
Samuel Butler, English author	'It was very good of God to let Carlyle and Mrs Carlyle marry one another and so make two people miserable instead of four.'	Thomas Carlyle, Scottish essayist
Denis Healey, British politician	'(His comments are) like being savaged by a dead sheep.'	Geoffrey Howe, British politician
Georges Clemceau, French prime minister	'The only time he ever put up a fight in his life was when we asked for his resignation.'	Marshall Joffre, French soldier
Ronald Regan, US president	'Bobby Kennedy is so concerned about poverty because he didn't have any when he was a kid.'	Robert Kennedy, US politician
Franklin D Roosevelt, US president	'Never underestimate a man who overestimates himself.'	Douglas Macarthur, US soldier
Norman Cousins, US author	'Nixon's motto was if two wrongs don't make a right, try three.'	Richard Nixon, US president
David Lloyd George, British prime minister	'When they circumcised Herbert Samuel they threw away the wrong bit.'	Herbert Samuel, British politician
Oscar Wilde, Irish author	'He hasn't an enemy in the world and none of his friends like him.'	George Bernard Shaw, Irish playwright
Margot Asquith, British writer and wit	'Lord Birkenhead is very clever but sometimes his brains go to his head.'	F E Smith, British statesman
Muriel Spark, Scottish author	'I used to think it a pity that her mother rather than she had not thought of birth control.'	Marie Stopes, Scottish social worker
W C Fields, US actor and comedian	'A plumber's idea of Cleopatra.'	Mae West, US actor

Ireland

Kings and Queens

445–452	Niall of the Nine Hostages (king of Tara; traditional ancestor of claimants to the high kingship)
452–463	Lóegaire (son)
463–482	Ailill Molt (grandnephew of Niall)
482–507	Lugaid (son of Lóegaire)
507–534	Muirchertach I (great-grandson of Niall)
534–544	Tuathal Máelgarb (great-grandson of Niall)
544–565	Diarmait I (great-grandson of Niall)
565–566	Domnall Ilchelgach (brother; co-regent)
566–569	Ainmire (fourth in descent from Niall)
569–572	Bétán I (son of Muirchertach I)
569–572	Eochaid (son of Domnall Ilchelgach; co-regent)
572–586	Báetán II (fourth in descent from Niall)
586–598	Áed (son of Ainmire)
598–604	Áed Sláine (son of Diarmait I)
598–604	Colmán Rímid (son of Báetán I; co-regent)
604–612	Áed Uaridnach (son of Domnall Ilchelgach)
612–615	Máel Cobo (son of Áed)
615–628	Suibne Menn (grandnephew of Muirchertach I)
628–642	Domnall (son of Áed)
642–654	Conall Cáel (son of Máel Cobo)
642–658	Cellach (brother; co-regent)
658–665	Diarmait II (son of Áed Sláine)
658–665	Blathmac (brother; co-regent)
665–671	Sechnussach (son)
671–675	Cennfáelad (brother)
675–695	Fínsnechta Fledach (grandson of Áed Sláine)
695–704	Loingsech (grandson of Domnall)
704–710	Congal Cennmagair (grandson of Domnall)
710–722	Fergal (great-grandson of Áed Uaridnach)
722–724	Fogartach (great-grandson of Diarmait II)
724–728	Cináed (fourth in descent from Áed Sláine)
728–734	Flaithbertach (son of Loingsech; deposed, died 765)
734–743	Áed allán (son of Fergal)
743–763	Domnall Midi (seventh in descent from Diarmait I)
763–770	Niall Frossach (son of Fergal; abdicated, died 778)
770–797	Donnchad Midi (son of Domnall Midi)
797–819	Áed Oirdnide (son of Niall Frossach)
819–833	Conchobar (son of Donnchad Midi)
833–846	Niall Caille (son of Áed Oirdnide)
846–862	Máel Sechnaill I (nephew of Conchobar)
862–879	Áed Findliath (son of Niall Caille)
879–916	Flann Sinna (son of Máel Sechnaill)
916–919	Niall Glúndub (son of Áed Findliath)
919–944	Donnchad Donn (son of Flann Sinna)
944–956	Congalach Cnogba (tenth in descent from Áed Sláine)
956–980	Domnall ua Néill (grandson of Niall Glúndub)
980–1002	Máel Sechnaill II (grandson of Donnchad Donn; deposed)
1002–1014	Brian Bóruma (Dál Cais; king of Munster)
1014–1022	Máel Sechnaill II (restored; interregnum 1022–72)
1072–1086	Tairrdelbach I (grandson of Brian Bóruma; king of Munster)
1086–1119	Muirchertach II (son)
1119–1121	Domnall ua Lochlainn (fourth in descent from Domnall ua Néill?; king of Ailech)
1121–1156	Tairrdelbach II (Ua Conchobair; king of Connacht)
1156–1166	Muirchertach III (grandson of Domnall ua Lochlainn)
1166–1186	Ruaidrí (son of Tairrdelbach II; deposed, died 1198; regional kingships under English domination)

Irish Prime Ministers

Term	Name	Party
1997–	Patrick 'Bertie' Ahern	Fianna Fáil
1994–97	John Bruton	Fine Gael
1992–94	Albert Reynolds	Fianna Fáil
1987–92	Charles Haughey	Fianna Fáil
1982–87	Garrett Fitzgerald	Fine Gael
1982	Charles Haughey	Fianna Fáil
1981–82	Garrett Fitzgerald	Fine Gael
1979–81	Charles Haughey	Fianna Fáil
1977–79	Jack Lynch	Fianna Fáil
1973–77	Liam Cosgrave	Fine Gael

Islam

Five Pillars of Islam

repeating the creed
daily prayer or salat
giving alms
fasting during the month of Ramadan
the hajj, or pilgrimage to Mecca, once in a lifetime

Islam

Major Festivals

Festival	Description	Date (2001)
festival of Ashura	festival commemorating the escape of the Israelites from Egypt, and the day Noah's ark touched ground after the flood	4 April
Ramadan	a month of fasting when adult Muslims refrain from drinking, eating, and smoking from dawn until dusk	17 November
the Night of Power–Lailat ul Qadr	during the last ten days of Ramadan many Muslims spend time praying in the mosque since prayers made on the Night of Power are said to be 'better than a thousand months'	3 December
Eid ul-Fitr	important time of communal prayer and celebration when special foods and gifts are shared	16 December
pilgrimage to Mecca	in the Five Pillars of Islam, this is the most important time, but only those who have sufficient finances and are physically able are expected to make the journey	4–9 March
Eid-ul-Adha	the willingness of the prophet Ibrahim to sacrifice his son Ishmael is remembered	6 March
birthday of the Prophet Muhammad (Milad-un-Nabi)	the scale of celebrations varies according to country, but includes processions, speeches, and prayers	24 May

Islamic Calendar

Month	Number of days	Month	Number of days
Muharram	30	Rajab	30
Safar	29	Sha'ban	29
Rabi I	30	Ramadan	30
Rabi II	29	Shawwal	29
Jumada I	30	Dhu al-Qadah	30
Jumada II	29	Dhu al-Hijjah	29 (30 in a leap year)

Islamic Calendar
Gregorian Year Equivalents

AH=Anno Hegirae, the first year of the Muslim calendar, when the prophet Muhammad travelled from Mecca to Medina.

Islamic year (AH)	Gregorian equivalent
1421	6 April 2000–24 March 2001
1422	26 March 2001–14 March 2002
1423	15 March 2002–3 March 2003

Israeli Prime Ministers

Term	Name	Party
2001–	Ariel Sharon	Likud
1999–2001	Ehud Barak	Labour
1996–99	Binyamin Netanyahu	Likud
1995–96	Shimon Peres	Labour
1992–95	Yitzhak Rabin	Labour
1986–92	Yitzhak Shamir	Likud
1984–86	Shimon Peres	Labour
1983–84	Yitzhak Shamir	Likud
1977–83	Menachem Begin	Likud
1974–77	Yitzhak Rabin	Labour
1969–74	Golda Meir	Labour

Italian Kings

In 1861 Victor Emmanuel II, King of Sardinia, was proclaimed the first king of a united Italy in Turin.

Reign	Name
1946	Umberto II (abdicated)
1900–46	Victor Emmanuel III
1878–1900	Umberto I
1861–78	Victor Emmanuel II

Italian Prime Ministers

Term	Name	Party
2001–	Silvio Berlusconi	House of Liberty coalition
2000–01	Giuliano Amato	Democrats of the Left
1998–2000	Massimo D'Alema	Democrats of the Left
1996–98	Romano Prodi	Olive Tree Alliance
1995–96	Lamberto Dini	independent
1994–95	Silvio Berlusconi	Freedom Alliance
1993–94	Carlo Azeglio Ciampi	Christian Democratic Party
1992–93	Giuliano Amato	Socialist Party
1989–92	Giulio Andreotti	Christian Democratic Party
1988–89	Ciriaco de Mita	Christian Democratic Party
1987–88	Giovanni Goria	Christian Democratic Party

Japanese Emperors

Japanese chronology does not always match the emperor's reign dates. Rather, it is marked by occurrences, such as significant political events, military gains, and natural disasters. A date in brackets indicates the date of enthronement, when it is later than the date of accession.

Reign dates	Name	Reign dates	Name
1989–	Heisei (Akihito)	1780–1817	Kōkaku
1926–89 (1928)	Showa (Hirohito)	1771–79	Go-Momozono
1912–26 (1915)	Taisho (Yoshihito)	1762–71 (1763)	Go-Sakuramachi (empress)
1867–1912 (1868)	Meiji (Mutsuhito)		
1846–67 (1847)	Kōmei	1747–62	Momozono
1817–46	Ninkō		

Japanese Prime Ministers

Term	Name	Party
2000–	Yoshiro Mori	LDP
1998–2000	Keizo Obuchi	LDP
1996–98	Ryutaro Hashimoto	LDP
1994–96	Tomiichi Murayama	Social Democratic Party of Japan (SDPJ)-led coalition
1994	Tsutoma Hata	Shinseito-led coalition
1993–94	Morohiro Hosokawa	Japan New Party (JNP)-led coalition
1991–93	Kiichi Miyazawa	LDP
1989–91	Toshiki Kaifu	LDP
1989	Sōsuke Uno	LDP
1987–89	Noboru Takeshita	LDP

Jewish Calendar

Jewish month	Number of days	Gregorian equivalent
Tishri	30	September–October
Heshvan	29 or 30	October–November
Kislev	29 or 30	November–December
Tebet	29	December–January
Shebat	30	January–February
Adar	29 or 30	February–March
Nisan	30	March–April
Iyar	29	April–May
Sivan	30	May–June
Tammuuz	29	June–July
Ab	30	July–August
Elul	29	August–September

Jewish Calendar
Gregorian Year Equivalents

The Jewish New Year (Rosh Hashanah) – 1 Tishri – falls between 5 September and 5 October in the Gregorian or Western calendar.

Jewish year	Gregorian equivalent
5761	30 September 2000– 17 September 2001
5762	18 September 2001– 6 September 2002
5763	7 September 2002– 26 September 2003
5764	27 September 2003– 15 September 2004
5765	16 September 2004– 3 October 2005

Judaism
Major Festivals

Festival	Description	Date (2001)
Rosh Hashanah	Jewish New Year, a ten-day period of repentance leading up to Yom Kippur	18–19 September
Yom Kippur	Day of Atonement, a time when Jews seek forgiveness of those who have been wronged; also the major fast of the year	27 September
Succoth	Feast of Tabernacles, commemorates the journey of the Israelites to the Promised Land	2–3 October
Simhat Torah	end of Succoth and the end of the annual reading of the Torah	10 October

(continued)

 People, History, and Society **363**

Judaism: Major Festivals (*continued*)

Festival	Description	Date (2001)
Hanukkah	commemorates the rededication of the Temple in Jerusalem in the 2nd century BC	10–17 December
Purim	celebration of the story of Esther who saved her people from destruction at the hands of Haman	9 March
Pesach	Passover, celebrating God's deliverance of the Israelites from captivity in Egypt	8 15 April
Shavuot	also known as the Pentecost, this is a thanksgiving for the gift of Torah to Moses on Mount Sinai	28–29 May
Tishah B'Av	recalls the disasters that have befallen the Jewish people, including the events of the Holocaust	9 August

Kenyan Presidents
From 1963

In 1963 Kenya achieved independence from the UK as a self-governing dominion. It became a republic within the Commonwealth in 1964.

Term	Name	Party
1978–	Daniel arap Moi	KANU
1963–78	Jomo Kenyatta	Kenya African National Union (KANU)

Kidnapping
Ransoms Demanded in Famous Kidnappings

Ransom (US$)	Victim	Kidnapper(s)	Country	Year
18.5 million	Sidney J Reso	Arthur and Jackie Seale	USA	1992
16.0 million	not known	Thomas Drach	Germany	1998
12.5 million	Guissepe Soffiantini	not known	Italy	1997
2.3 million	Samuel Bronfman	Mel Byrne and Pat Lynch	USA	1975
650,000	Charles Geschke	Jack Sayeh and Albukhari	USA	1992
600,000	Bobby Greenlease	Carl Hall and Bonnie Heady	USA	1953
500,000	Adolph Coors, III	Joseph Corbett, Jr	USA	1960
500,000	Barbara Mackle	Gary Krist and Ruth Eisemann Schier	USA	1968
200,000	George Weyerhaeus	Harmon Metz Waley and William Dainard	USA	1935
50,000	Charles Augustus Lindbergh, Jr	Bruno Hauptmann	USA	1932
50,000	Charles Sherman Ross	John Henry Seadlund	USA	1937
48,000	4 French tourists	Sheikh Shaya Bakhtan	Yemen	1998
15,000	Rev Michel Gigord	armed men	Philippines	1986
2,000	Peter Weinberger	Angelo la Marca	USA	1956

Korean War
Casualties

(N/A = not available.)

Country	Killed	Wounded	Total casualties
China	N/A	N/A	900,000[1]
North Korea	520,000[1]	500,000[1]	1,020,000[1]
Republic of Korea (South Korea)	415,004	897,032	1,312,836
USA	33,686	103,284	136,970
UK	746	2,533	3,279
Turkey	741	2,068	2,809
Australia	339	1,216	1,555
Canada	312	1,212	1,524
France	262	1,008	1,270
Thailand	129	1,139	1,268
Netherlands	120	645	765
Greece	192	543	735
Ethiopia	121	536	657
Colombia	163	448	611
Philippines	122	299	421
Belgium	101	336	437
New Zealand	23	79	102
Luxembourg	2	13	15

[1]Estimated.

Korean War
Prisoners of War

Country	Prisoners
North Korea	83,227
China	21,374
Republic of Korea (South Korea)	8,197
USA	7,245
UK	977
Turkey	243
Philippines	41
Canada	32
Colombia	28
Australia	26
France	12
South Africa	9
Greece	3
Netherlands	3
Belgium	1
New Zealand	1

Left-handedness
Famous Left-handed People

In addition, there have been five left-handed presidents of the USA: George Bush, Bill Clinton, Gerald Ford, James Garfield, and Harry S Truman.

Person	Life dates
C P E Bach, German composer	1714–1788
Charlie Chaplin, English actor	1889–1977
Jimmy Connors, US tennis player	1952–
King George II of England	1683–1760
Leonardo da Vinci, Italian artist	1452–1519
Harpo Marx, US comedian	1888–1964
Paul McCartney, English musician	1942–
Michelangelo, Italian artist	1475–1564
Cole Porter, US composer	1891–1964
Tiberius, Roman Emperor	42 BC–AD 37

Les Philosophes

Les Philosophes were the leading intellectuals of pre-revolutionary 18th-century France, including:

Name	Life dates
Denis Diderot	1713–1784
Jean-Jacques Rousseau	1712–1778
Voltaire (pen-name of François Marie Arouet)	1694–1778
Baron Montesquieu	1689–1755
Claude Adrien Helvetius	1715–1771
Marquis de Condorcet	1743–1794

Libraries

Library	Date founded
Alexandrian Library, Alexandria, Egypt	c. 300 BC
Vatican Library, Rome, Italy	4th century
Bibliothèque nationale, Paris, France (Bibliothèque du Roi until 1795)	15th century
Bodleian Library, Oxford, England	1602
British Library, London, England	1759
Library of Congress, Washington, DC, USA	1800
The New York Public Library, New York City, USA	1895

Literacy
Literacy Levels in Developed Countries

Country	% of adults with low literacy
Poland	44
Ireland, Republic of	24
UK	23
USA	22
New Zealand	20
Switzerland (German)	19
Australia	17
Belgium	17
Canada	17
Switzerland (French)	17
Germany	12
Netherlands	10
Sweden	7

Lovers
Some Famous Historical Lovers

Antony and Cleopatra
Napoleon and Josephine
Queen Victoria and Albert
Edward and Mrs Simpson
Bonnie and Clyde
Shah Jahan and Mumtaz Mahal
Horatio Nelson and Lady Emma Hamilton
Heloise and Abelard
Charles Stewart Parnell and Kitty O'Shea
Peter the Great and Catherine I of Russia
Nell Gwyn and Charles II
Adolf Hitler and Eva Braun
Madame de Pompadour and Louis XV
Edward VII and Lillie Langtry
Catherine (II) the Great and Grigory Potemkin

Marriage
Some Famous People Who Never Married

Person	Dates	Description
Joan of Arc	c. 1412–1431	French martyr and saint
Elizabeth I	1533–1603	Queen of England
Isaac Newton	1641–1727	English mathematician and physicist

Marriage: Some Famous People Who Never Married (*continued*)

Person	Dates	Description
Immanuel Kant	1724–1804	German philosopher
Ludwig van Beethoven	1770–1827	German composer
Jane Austen	1775–1817	English author
Frédéric Chopin	1810–1849	French composer
Florence Nightingale	1820–1910	English nurse
George Bernard Shaw	1856–1950	Irish playwright
J Edgar Hoover	1895–1972	head of the FBI

Marriage
Rates in Selected Countries

Country	Marriages (per thousand people) 1987	1997
Canada	6.9	5.2
Finland	5.3	4.6
France	4.8	4.9
Germany	6.7	5.1
Greece	6.6	6.0
Italy	5.4	4.8
Japan	5.7	6.4
Spain	5.6	4.8
UK	7.0	5.4
USA	9.9	8.9

Marriage
Who and How Many Partners?

Type of marriage	Partner(s)
bigamy	illegal marriage to two people
endogamy	marriage within ones' clan/tribe
exogamy	marriage outside ones' clan/tribe
monogamy	marriage to one person
polyandry	having more than one legal husband
polygamy	marriage to many people
polygyny	having more than one legal wife

Mass Murderers
Numbers of Victims

Name of murderer	Number of victims	Country	Year
Countess Elizabet Bathory-Nadasdy	600	Hungary	early 1600s
Andrew Kehoe	45	USA	1927
James Huberty	21	USA	1984
Thomas Hamilton	17	UK	1996
Michael Ryan	16	UK	1987
Patrick Henry	14	USA	1986
Shuko Asahara	11	Japan	1995
Mark Barton	9	USA	1999
Bryan Uyesugi	7	Hawaii	1999
Alexi	6	France	1998
Masumi Hayashi	4	Japan	1998
Frederick Williams	4	USA	2000

Mexican Presidents
From 1946

In 1946 the National Revolutionary Party was renamed the Institutional Revolutionary Party (PRI). Their 71-year rule was ended in 2000 by an election victory for Vicente Fox of the National Action Party (PAN).

Term	Name	Party	Term	Name	Party
2000–	Vicente Fox	PAN	1970–76	Luís Echeverría Alvarez	PRI
1994–2000	Ernesto Zedillo Ponce de Léon	PRI	1964–70	Gustavo Díaz Ordaz	PRI
			1958–64	Adolfo López Mateos	PRI
1988–94	Carlos Salinas de Gortari	PRI	1952–58	Adolfo Ruiz Cortines	PRI
1982–88	Miguel de la Madrid Hurtado	PRI	1946–52	Miguel Alemán Valdés	PRI
1976–82	José López Portillo y Pacheco	PRI			

Military Helicopters
Countries with Most

Country	Army helicopters	Air force helicopters	Total helicopters
USA	5,039	229	5,268
Russian Federation	2,108	0	2,108
Ukraine	455	304	759
Iran	663	46	709
Germany	592	102	694
France	494	89	583
Iraq	500	0	500
Italy	361	101	462
UK	269	173	442
Japan	440	0	440

Mistresses
Some Famous Historical Mistresses

Name	Mistress to:
Delilah	Samson
Clara Petacci	Mussolini
Nell Gwyn	Charles II
Madame de Pompadour	Louis V of France
Marcia	Commodus
Lady Hamilton	Admiral Nelson
Katherine Swinford	John of Gaunt
Lillie Langtry	Edward VII
Dorothea Jordan	William IV
Cleopatra	Julius Caesar
Alice Perrers	Edward III
Jeanne Hébuleme	Amedeo Modigliani

Monarchs
Longest Reigning

Name	Country	Reign	Years
King Mihti	Arakan (Myanmar)	c. 1279–1374	95
Pharaoh Phiops (Pepi) II	Egypt (Neferkare)	c. 2269–2175 BC	94
King Louis XIV	France	1643–1715	72
Prince Johannes II	Liechtenstein	1858–1929	71
King Harald I	Norway	c. 870–940	70
Emperor Franz Josef	Austria	1848–1916	68
Queen Victoria	Great Britain	1837–1901	63
Emperor Hirohito (Showa)	Japan	1926–89	62
Emperor Kangxi	China	1661–1722	61
Emperor Qianlong	China	1735–96	60

Money
Selected World Currencies

Country	Currency	Country	Currency
Afghanistan	afgháni	Israel	shekel
Algeria	Algerian dinar	Italy	lira
Andorra	French franc and Spanish peseta	Jamaica	Jamaican dollar
		Japan	yen
Angola	kwanza	Jordan	Jordanian dinar
Antigua and Barbuda	East Caribbean dollar	Kenya	Kenya shilling
Argentina	peso	Korea, North and South	won
Australia	Australian dollar		
Austria	schilling	Kuwait	Kuwaiti dinar
Bahamas	Bahamian dollar	Lebanon	Lebanese pound
Bahrain	Bahraini dinar	Libya	Libyan dinar
Bangladesh	taka	Liechtenstein	Swiss franc
Barbados	Barbados dollar	Luxembourg	Luxembourg franc
Belgium	Belgian franc	Malaysia	ringgit
Belize	Belize dollar	Malta	Maltese lira
Bolivia	boliviano	Mauritius	Mauritian rupee
Brazil	real	Mexico	Mexican peso
Bulgaria	lev	Morocco	dirham (DH)
Canada	Canadian dollar	Mozambique	metical
Chile	Chilean peso	Netherlands	guilder
China	yuan	New Zealand	New Zealand dollar
Colombia	Colombian peso	Nicaragua	cordoba
Cuba	Cuban peso	Nigeria	naira
Cyprus	Cyprus pound and Turkish lira	Norway	Norwegian krone
		Oman	Omani rial
Czech Republic	koruna (based on Czechoslovak koruna)	Pakistan	Pakistan rupee
		Panama	balboa
		Papua New Guinea	kina
Denmark	Danish krone	Paraguay	guaraní
Dominican Republic	Dominican Republic peso	Peru	nuevo sol
		Philippines	peso
Egypt	Egyptian pound	Poland	zloty
Ethiopia	Ethiopian birr	Portugal	escudo
Finland	markka	Romania	leu
France	franc	Russian Federation	rouble
Gambia	dalasi	St Lucia	East Caribbean dollar
Germany	Deutschmark	Saudi Arabia	rial
Ghana	cedi	Seychelles	Seychelles rupee
Greece	drachma	Singapore	Singapore dollar
Hungary	forint	South Africa	rand
Iceland	krona	Spain	peseta
India	rupee	Sri Lanka	Sri Lankan rupee
Indonesia	rupiah	Sudan	Sudanese dinar
Iran	rial	Sweden	Swedish krona
Iraq	Iraqi dinar	Switzerland	Swiss franc
Ireland, Republic of	Irish pound (punt Eireannach)	Syria	Syrian pound

(continued)

 People, History, and Society **369**

Money: World Currencies (*continued*)

Country	Currency	Country	Currency
Tanzania	Tanzanian shilling	UK	pound sterling (£)
Thailand	baht	USA	US dollar
Trinidad and Tobago	Trinidad and Tobago dollar	Venezuela	bolívar
		Vietnam	dong
Tunisia	Tunisian dinar	Yugoslavia	new Yugoslav dinar
Turkey	Turkish lira	Zambia	Zambian kwacha
Uganda	Uganda new shilling	Zimbabwe	Zimbabwe dollar
United Arab Emirates	UAE dirham		

Months of the Year

Month	Derivation of name	Number of days
January	Janus, Roman god of doorways and beginnings	31
February	Februa, Roman festival of purification	28 (29 in a leap year)
March	Mars, Roman god of war	31
April	Latin *aperire,* to open	30
May	Maia, Roman goddess of spring	31
June	Juno, Roman goddess of marriage	30
July	Julius Caesar, Roman general and dictator	31
August	Augustus Caesar, Roman emperor	31
September	Latin *septem,* seven; the seventh month of the earliest Roman calendar	30
October	Latin *octo,* eight; the eighth month of the earliest Roman calendar	31
November	Latin *novem,* nine; the ninth month of the earliest Roman calendar	30
December	Latin *decem,* ten; the tenth month of the earliest Roman calendar	31

Murder

Cities with Highest Murder Rates

Washington, DC
Pretoria
Moscow
Amsterdam
Belfast
Warsaw
Copenhagen
Berlin
Prague
Madrid

Murder

European Serial Killers

Number of deaths	Name of murderer(s) or era	Nickname/description	Year arrested
52	Andrei Chikatilo	Russian cannibal and mutilator	1992
27	Fritz Haarmann	The Butcher of Hannover	1924
19	John George Haigh	The Acid bath murderer	1949
15	Fred and Rose West	buried murdered girls in their garden	1994
14	Dr Harold Shipman	British GP who murdered patients	2000
14	Dennis Nilsen	mutilated and destroyed victims' bodies	1983
13	Peter Sutcliffe	The Yorkshire Ripper	1981
11	Henri Landru	murdered for money	1919
9+	Peter Kurten	The Vampire of Dusseldorf	1931
6	Ian Brady and Myra Hindley	The Moors murderers	1966
5	1880s	Jack the Ripper	not caught
4	John Christie	murderer who inspired the film *10 Rillington Place*	1953

Murder

US Serial Killers

Number of deaths	Name of murderer(s) or era	Nickname/description	Year arrested
2–200	Henry Lee Lucas	ex-drifter who made many false confessions	1982
50	1980s	The Green River killer	not caught
36	Ted Bundy	educated psychopath who murdered pretty girls	1975
30+	John Wayne Gacy	The Killer Clown	1980
29	Wayne Williams	Atlanta child murders case	1981
20+	Richard Ramirez	raped, tortured, and mutilated his victims	1985
16	Ken Bianchi and Angelo Buono	The Hillside Stranglers	1981
13	1960s	The Boston Strangler	not caught
12	Jeffrey Dahmer	mutilated and cannibalized his victims	1953
12	1930s	The Kingsbury Run Murders	not caught
11	Charles Ng	former marine who mutilated his victims	1985
11	Arthur Shawcross	The Genessee River Killer	1990
10	Richard Speck	murdered student nurses	1966
8	Edmund Kemper	murdered hitchhikers and his mother	1973
7	1960s	Zodiac	not caught
7	Charles Manson and others	cult leader who organized murders	1969
6	David Berkowitz	The Son of Sam	1977
5	Danny Rolling	The Gainseville Ripper	1990
4	Paul Bernardo and Karla Homolka	murdered young girls	1993
4	Albert Fish	sadist and cannibal	1992
3	Harvey Murray Glatman	1st signature killer	1985

Mythical Beasts

Beast	Description
amphisbaena	poisonous snake with a head at each end; it could move forwards or backwards
basilisk	snake with poisonous breath; sometimes called cockatrice
centaur	creature with a man's head, arms, and torso, and the body and legs of a horse
Cerberus	dog with three heads (at the gate of Hades)
chimera or chimaera	fire-breathing creature with a lion's head, goat's body, and snake's tail
cockatrice	creature with a cock's head, birds' wings, and a dragon's tail; sometimes called basilisk
cynocephalus	any dog-headed creature
dragon	winged crocodile with a snake's tail
echidna	creature that is half woman and half snake
Fafnir	German dragon that guarded the gold of the Nibelung
faun	man with a goat's ears, horns, tail, and hind legs
fung-hwang	Chinese phoenix, also called fum
garuda	Indian winged creature half eagle, half man, ridden by Vishnu
griffin, griffon or gryphon	winged creature with an eagle's head and a lion's body
harpy	winged creature, part woman, part bird
hippogriff	creature with an eagle's head, claws, and wings and a horse's body (a cross between a griffin and a mare)
hydra	many-headed water snake
kraken	huge sea monster said to live off the Norwegian coast
lamia	creature with a woman's head and a snake's body
manticore	man-eating creature with a spiny lion's body, scorpion's tail, and human head
marlet	footless bird (in heraldry)
mermaid	creature that is half woman (the upper half) and half fish
Minotaur	man with a bull's head
oannes	creature (a god in Babylon) with a human head and feet on a fish's body
orthos	two-headed dog
Pegasus	winged horse
phoenix	Arabian bird that sets itself on fire and rises from the ashes every 500 years
roc	enormous white Arabian bird with a powerful beak and talons
salamander	reptile or other creature that lived in fire
satyr	man with budding horns, goatlike ears, and the hindquarters of a goat
sphinx	(Egyptian) creature with a lion's body and a man's (Pharaoh's) head
sphinx	(Greek) creature with a woman's head, dog's (or lion's) body, bird's wings, and a snake's tail
typhon	100-headed monster, one of the whirlwinds
unicorn	creature with the head and body of a white horse and a single spiralled horn, sometimes depicted with a lion's tail
wyvern or wivern	two-legged winged dragon with a barbed snake's tail

Names
Most Popular Boys' Names in the UK

Name	Name
Jack	Matthew
Thomas	Samuel
James	Joseph
Joshua	Callum
Daniel	William

Names
Most Popular Girls' Names in the UK

Name	Name
Chloe	Charlotte
Emily	Lauren
Megan	Jessica
Olivia	Rebecca
Sophie	Hannah

National Days

Country	National day
Australia	26 January
Canada	1 July
France	14 July
Germany	3 October
Greece	25 March
Ireland	17 March
Italy	2 June
Spain	12 October
UK	1 March, 17 March, 23 April, 30 November
USA	4 July

Naval Aircraft
Countries with Most

Country	Number of fixed-wing aircraft	Number of helicopters
USA	1,456	543
China	507	37
Russian Federation	244	107
Japan	80	80
Thailand	67	–
France	52	–
Germany	50	40
India	37	–
UK	34	120
Taiwan	31	–

Navies
World's Largest

Country	Number of ships[1]
USA	114
China	60
Japan	55
South Korea	39
France	34
Russia	34
Taiwan	33
UK	31
Italy	29
India	25

[1] Includes cruisers, destroyers and frigates.

Navies
World's Largest by Personnel

Country	Personnel
USA	370,700
China	220,000
Russian Federation	171,500
Thailand	68,000
Taiwan	62,000
South Korea	60,000
Turkey	54,600
India	53,000
France	49,490
Brazil	48,600

New Zealand Prime Ministers

Term	Name	Party
1999–	Helen Clark	Labour
1997–99	Jenny Shipley	National
1990–97	Jim Bolger	National
1990	Michael Moore	Labour
1989–90	Geoffrey Palmer	Labour
1984–89	David Lange	Labour
1975–84	Robert Muldoon	National
1974–75	Wallace Rowling	Labour
1972–74	Norman Kirk	Labour
1972	John Marshall	National

News Agencies

International News Agencies

Country	Agency	Abbreviation	Headquarters
Argentina	Agence Los Diarios	ALD	Buenos Aires
	Noticias Argentinas	NA	Buenos Aires
Australia	Australian Associated Press	AAP	Sydney
	Australian United Press	AUP	Melbourne
Brazil	Agencia Meridional	AM	Rio de Janeiro
	Agencia Nacional	AN	Brasilia
Canada	Canadian Press	CP	Toronto
China	China News Service	CNS	Beijing
	Xinhua		Beijing
France	Agence France Presse	AFP	Paris
	Agence Parisienne de Presse	APP	Paris
	Presse Services	PS	Paris
Germany	Allgemeiner Deutscher Nachrichtendienst	ADN	Berlin
	Deutsche Presse Agentur	DPA	Hamburg
India	Press Trust of India	PTI	Mumbai (formerly Bombay)
	United News of India	UNI	New Delhi
Indonesia	Indonesian National News Agency	ANTARA	Jakarta
Iran	Islamic Republic News Agency	IRNA	Tehran
Italy	Agenzia Nazionale Stampa Associate	ANSA	Rome
	Inter Press Service	IPS	Rome
Japan	Jiji Tsushin-Sha	JIJI	Tokyo
	Kyodo Tsushin		Tokyo
Russia	Agentstvo Pechati Novosti	NOVOSTI	Moscow
	Information Telegraph Agency of Russia	ITAR-TASS	Moscow
Saudi Arabia	Saudi Press Agency	SPA	Riyadh
South Africa	South African Press Association	SAPA	Johannesburg
South Korea	Yonhap (United) Press Agency	YONHAP	Seoul
Spain	Agencia EFE		Madrid
	Logos Agencia de Informacion	LAI	Madrid

Country	Agency	Abbreviation	Headquarters
UK	Exchange and Telegraph Company	EXTEL	London
	Press Association	PA	London
	Reuters		London
USA	Associated Press	AP	New York
	United Press International	UPI	New York

Newspapers

Countries with Most Daily Papers

Country	Number of daily papers
USA	1,520
Brazil	380
Germany	375
Mexico	295
Russia	285
Pakistan	264
Argentina	181
Greece	156
Japan	122
France	117

Newspapers

Dailies with Largest Circulation

Paper	Daily circulation
Yomiuri Shimbun (Japan)	10,224,000
Asahi Shimbun (Japan)	8,321,000
Sichuan Ribao (China)	8,000,000
Bild-Zeitung (Germany)	5,674,000
Mainichi Shimbun (Japan)	3,979,000
The Sun (UK)	3,687,000
Chunicki Shimbun (Japan)	3,075,000
Nihon Keizai Shimbun (Japan)	2,828,000
Gongren Ribao (China)	2,500,000
Daily Mail (UK)	2,364,000

Nigerian Leaders

Nigeria achieved independence from the UK in 1960, and became a federal republic within the Commonwealth in 1963.

Term	Name	Party
Presidents[1]		
1999–	Olusegun Obasanjo	People's Democratic Party
1998–99	Abdusalam Abubakar	military
1993–98	Sani Abacha	military
1993	Ernest Shonekan	independent
1985–93	Ibrahim Babangida	military
1983–85	Mohammed Buhari	military
1979–83	Shehu Shagari	National Party of Nigeria
1976–79	Olusegun Obasanjo	military
1975–76	Murtala Mohammed	military
1966–75	Yakubu Gowon	military

[1] Heads of state from January 1966 until October 1979 and from December 1983 did not officially use the title of president.

Nobel Prize
Economics

Year	Winner(s)	Awarded for
1990	Harry Markowitz (USA), Merton Miller (USA), and William Sharpe (USA)	theories on managing investment and finances
1991	Ronald Coase (USA)	work on value and social problems of companies
1992	Gary Becker (USA)	linking economic theory to aspects of human behaviour
1993	Robert Fogel (USA) and Douglass North (USA)	new method of studying economic history (cliometrics)
1994	John Nash (USA), John Harsanyi (USA), and Reinhard Selten (Germany)	work on game theory
1995	Robert Lucas (USA)	developing the rational expectations school
1996	James Mirrlees (UK) and William Vickrey (USA)	economic theory of incentives
1997	Robert Merton (USA) and Myron Scholes (USA)	new method of determining the value of derivatives
1998	Amartya Sen (India)	research into the causes of famines
1999	Robert A Mundell (Canada)	study of monetary and fiscal policy under different exchange rate regimes
2000	James J Heckman (USA)	methods for analyzing selective samples
	Daniel L Mcfadden (USA)	methods for analyzing discrete choice

Nobel Prize
Peace

Year	Winner(s)	Awarded for
1990	Mikhail Gorbachev (USSR)	helping to end the Cold War
1991	Aung San Suu Kyi (Myanmar)	nonviolent campaign for democracy
1992	Rigoberta Menchú (Guatemala)	campaign for indigenous people
1993	Nelson Mandela (South Africa) and Frederik Willem de Klerk (South Africa)	dismantling apartheid
1994	Yassir Arafat (Palestine), Yitzhak Rabin (Israel), and Shimon Peres (Israel)	Palestinian self-rule
1995	Joseph Rotblat (UK) and the Pugwash Conferences on Science and World Affairs	campaign against nuclear weapons
1996	Carlos Filipe Ximenes Belo (Timorese) and José Ramos-Horta (Timorese)	peaceful solution to the conflict in East Timor
1997	Jody Williams (USA) and the International Campaign to Ban Landmines (ICBL)	campaign for ban of anti-personnel mines
1998	John Hume (UK) and David Trimble (UK)	work towards a peaceful solution to the conflict in Northern Ireland
1999	Médecins sans Frontières/Doctors Without Borders (headquarters in Brussels, founded in France)	assistance to victims of wars and disasters
2000	Kim Dae Jung	democracy and human rights in South Korea, and peace with North Korea

Norwegian Monarchs

In 1905 Norway's union with Sweden was dissolved and Norway achieved independence.

Reign	Name
1991–	Harald V
1957–91	Olaf V
1945–57	Haakon VII (restored)
1940–45	German occupation
1905–40	Haakon VII (exiled)

Norwegian Prime Ministers

Recent

Term	Name	Party
2000–	Jens Stoltenberg	Labour Party
1997–2000	Kjell Magne Bondevik	Christian People's Party
1996–97	Thorbjoern Jagland	Labour Party
1990–96	Gro Harlem Brundtland	Labour Party
1989–90	Jan Syse	Conservative Party
1986–89	Gro Harlem Brundtland	Labour Party
1981–86	Kaare Willoch	Conservative Party
1981	Gro Harlem Brundtland	Labour Party
1976–81	Odvar Nordli	Labour Party
1973–76	Trygve Bratteli	Labour Party

Nuclear Arsenals

Country	Nuclear arsenal	
	Systems	Warheads
USA	1,074	7,416
Russian Federation	1,230	6,170
France	160	484
China	275	395
UK	127	225
Israel	100	100
India	60	60
Pakistan	15	15

Nuclear Missiles

Countries with Most

Country	Number of missiles
Russian Federation	1,280
USA	982
China	330+
France	64
UK	58

Nursery Rhymes

Magpie Nursery Rhyme

Number of magpies	Stands for	Alternatively
1	sorrow	sorrow
2	joy	mirth
3	a girl	a wedding
4	a boy	a birth
5	silver	silver
6	gold	gold
7	a secret never to be told	a secret not to be told
8		heaven
9		hell
10		the devil's own sel'

Nursery Rhymes

Monday's Child

Day born	Child is
Monday	fair of face
Tuesday	full of grace
Wednesday	full of woe
Thursday	far to go
Friday	loving and giving
Saturday	works hard for its living
Sunday	fair and wise (or bonnie and blythe) and good and gay

 People, History, and Society **377**

One Eyed People
Famous People with Only One Eye

Person	Dates	Description
John Milton	1608–1674	English poet
Horatio Nelson	1758–1805	English admiral
Guglielmo Marconi	1874–1937	Italian inventor
James Thurber	1894–1961	US humourist
John Ford	1895–1973	US film director
Joe Davis	1901–1978	English snooker player
Rex Harrison	1908–1990	English actor
Eric Hosking	1909–1990	English photographer
Moshe Dayan	1915–1981	Israeli general
Gordon Banks	1937–	English footballer

Ottoman Emperors
From 1774

Reign	Name
1918–22	Mehmed VI
1909–18	Mehmed V
1876–1909	Abdulhamid II
1876	Murad V
1861–76	Abdulaziz
1839–61	Abdulmecid
1808–39	Mahmud II
1807–08	Mustafa IV
1789–1807	Selim III
1774–89	Abdulhamid I

Oxford University
Colleges

Founded	College	Founded	College
1249	University	1740	Hertford
1263–68	Balliol	1870	Keble
1264	Merton	1878	Lady Margaret Hall
c. 1278	St Edmund Hall	1879	Somerville
1314	Exeter	1886	St Hugh's
1326	Oriel	1893	St Anne's
1340	The Queen's	1893	St Hilda's
1379	New	1929	St Peter's
1427	Lincoln	1953	St Anthony's
1438	All Souls	1958	Nuffield
1458	Magdalen	1962	Linacre
1509	Brasenose	1963	St Catherine's
1517	Corpus Christi	1965	St Cross
1546	Christ Church	1979	Green
1554–55	Trinity	1981	Wolfson
1555	St John's	1984	Templeton
1571	Jesus	1990	Kellogg
1612	Wadham	1995	Mansfield
1624	Pembroke	1996	Manchester
1714	Worcester		

Parents
Famous People whose Parents Never Married One Another

Person	Dates	Description
William I (the Conqueror)	1028–1087	King of England
Leonardo da Vinci	1452–1519	Italian painter
Richard Wagner	1813–1883	German composer
Alexandre Dumas	1824–1895	French author
Ramsay MacDonald	1866–1937	British politician
T E Lawrence	1888–1935	British soldier and author
Juan Péron	1895–1974	Argentine politician
Willy Brandt	1913–1992	German politician
Alec Guinness	1914–2000	English actor
Sophia Loren	1934–	Italian actor

Peacekeeping
United Nations Operations

Source: UN Department of Public Information

Operation	Established	Budget (US$ millions)
Mission in Kosovo	1999	456.4
Transitional Administration in East Timor	1999	386.3
Mission of Observers in Sierra Leone	1999	200.0
Mission in Bosnia-Herzegovina	1995	168.2
Observer Mission in Angola	1997	140.8
Preventive Deployment Force, Macedonia	1995	47.9
Organization Mission in the Democratic Republic of Congo	1999	41.0
Mission in the Central African Republic	1998	29.1
Civilian Police Support Group, Croatia	1998	17.6
Civilian Police Mission in Haiti	1997	14.0

Philosophers
Miscellaneous Nationalities

Name	Dates	Nationality	Representative work
Willard Quine	1908–	US	*Word and Object*
Charles Peirce	1839–1914	US	*How to Make our Ideas Clear*
Ludwig Wittgenstein	1889–1951	Austrian	*Tractatus Logico-Philosophicus; Philosophical Investigations*
Søren Kierkegaard	1813–1855	Danish	*Concept of Dread*
Benedict Spinoza	1632–1677	Dutch	*Ethics*
Georg Lukács	1885–1971	Hungarian	*History and Class Consciousness*

(continued)

Name	Dates	Nationality	Representative work
Giambattista Vico	1668–1744	Italian	*The New Science*
Giordano Bruno	1548–1600	Italian	*De la Causa, Principio e Uno*
Thomas Aquinas	c. 1225–1274	Italian	*Summa Theologica*
Augustine	354–430	North African	*Confessions; City of God*
Lucretius	c. 99–55 BC	Roman	*On the Nature of Things*

Polish Political Leaders
Recent

Term	Name	Party
Presidents		
1995–	Aleksander Kwaśniewski	Democratic Left Alliance
1990–95	Lech Wałesa	Solidarity/independent
1989–90	Wojciech Jaruzelski	

Communist Party leaders[1]

Term	Name	Term	Name
1981–89	Wojciech Jaruzelski	1956	Edward Ochab
1980–81	Stanisław Kania	1948–56	Bolesław Bierut
1970–80	Edward Gierek	1945–48	Władysław Gomułka
1956–70	Władysław Gomułka		

[1] From 1945 to 1990 the political leaders were the Communist Party leaders.

Pollution
Effect of Air Pollutants

Air pollution is harmful not only to living creatures, but also to the materials around them. Damage to buildings in the USA from acid deposition alone is estimated at US$5 billion annually.

Material	Effects	Pollutants responsible
ceramics and glass	surface erosion	particulates
metals	corrosion, tarnishing, loss of strength	sulphur dioxide, sulphuric acid, nitric acid, particulates
paints	surface erosion, discoloration, soiling	sulphur dioxide, ozone, particulates
paper	embrittlement, discoloration	sulphur dioxide
rubber	cracking, loss of strength	ozone
stone and concrete	surface erosion, discoloration, soiling	sulphur dioxide, sulphuric acid, nitric acid, particulates
wood	discoloration, loss of strength, more prone to fungal diseases	sulphur dioxide, ozone

Pollution

Major Air Pollutants

Air pollution is contamination of the atmosphere caused by the discharge, accidental or deliberate, of a wide range of toxic airborne substances.

Pollutant	Sources	Effects
sulphur dioxide (SO_2)	oil, coal combustion in power stations	acid rain formed, which damages plants, trees, buildings, and lakes
oxides of nitrogen (NO, NO_2)	high-temperature combustion in cars, and to some extent power stations	acid rain formed
lead compounds	from leaded petrol used by cars	nerve poison
carbon dioxide (CO_2)	oil, coal, petrol, diesel combustion	greenhouse effect
carbon monoxide (CO)	limited combustion of oil, coal, petrol, diesel fuels	poisonous, leads to photochemical smog in some areas
nuclear waste	nuclear power plants, nuclear weapon testing, war	radioactivity, contamination of locality, cancers, mutations, death
ozone (O_3)	complex chemical reactions in the presence of sunlight	greenhouse effect, acid rain by-product
particulates (PM_{10}, 'smog')	vehicle exhausts, power generation, combustion processes	respiratory effects, acid rain
volatile organic compounds (VOC)	industrial processes, vehicle emissions, petrol evaporation	greenhouse effect, ozone production

Popes

Most Recent

Name	Date reign began
John Paul II	1978
John Paul I	1978
Paul VI	1963
John XXIII	1958
Pius XII	1939
Pius XI	1922
Benedict XV	1914
St Pius X	1903
Leo XIII	1878
Pius IX	1846

Population

Countries with Fewer Women Than Men

Country/territory	Women per 100 men
United Arab Emirates	52
Qatar	55
Bahrain	75
Saudi Arabia	81
Oman	90
Libya	92
Maldives	92
Pakistan	92
French Polynesia	93
Guam	93

Population

Countries with Highest Population Densities

Country	Population per sq km/ per 0.4 sq mi
Monaco	16,074
Singapore	5,662
Vatican City State	2,500
Malta	1,206
Maldives	933
Bahrain	882
Bangladesh	881
Taiwan	685
Barbados	625
Mauritius	616

Population

Countries with Largest Indigenous Populations

Country	Indigenous population	
	Number (millions)	% of total population
Papua New Guinea	3.0	77
Bolivia	5.6	70
Guatemala	4.6	47
Peru	9.0	40
Ecuador	3.8	38
Myanmar	14.0	33
Laos	1.3	30
Mexico	10.9	12
New Zealand	0.4	12
Chile	1.2	9
Philippines	6.0	9
India	63.0	7
Malaysia	0.8	4
Canada	0.9	4
Australia	0.4	2

Population

Countries with Lowest Population Densities

Country	Population per sq km/ per 0.4 sq mi
Australia	2
Mongolia	2
Namibia	2
Botswana	3
Canada	3
Iceland	3
Libya	3
Mauritania	3
Suriname	3
Gabon	4
Guyana	4

Population

Countries with More Women Than Men

Country/territory	Women per 100 men
Cape Verde	112
Estonia	112
Russian Federation	110
Barbados	108
Botswana	108
Cambodia	108
Hungary	108
Portugal	108
Austria	106
Central African Republic	106
Germany	106
Italy	106

Population

Countries with Oldest Populations

Country	% of population aged 60 or over
Greece	24
Italy	24
Germany	23
Japan	23
Belgium	22
Spain	22
Sweden	22
Bulgaria	21
Portugal	21
Ukraine	21
UK	21

Population

Countries with the Fastest-Growing Populations

1995–2000

Country	Average population growth rate %
Liberia	8.2
Rwanda	7.7
Somalia	4.2
Eritrea	3.8
Yemen	3.7
Saudi Arabia	3.4
Oman	3.3
Angola	3.2
Niger	3.2
Kuwait	3.1

Population

Countries with the Slowest-Growing Populations

1995–2000

Country	Average population growth rate %
Latvia	−1.5
Estonia	−1.2
Georgia	−1.1
Bulgaria	−0.7
Albania	−0.4
Hungary	−0.4
Kazakhstan	−0.4
Romania	−0.4
Ukraine	−0.4
Armenia	−0.3
Belarus	−0.3
Lithuania	−0.3

Population

Countries with Youngest Populations

Country	% of population aged under 15
Uganda	50
Marshall Islands	49
Angola	48
Congo, Democratic Republic of	48
Niger	48
São Tomé and Príncipe	48
Somalia	48
Yemen	48
Burkina Faso	47
Burundi	47
Malawi	47
Zambia	47

Population

Greatest Contributors to World Population Growth

Data from 1995–2000.

Country	Increase in population (in thousands)	Percentage of world population increase
India	15,999	20.6
China	11,408	14.7
Pakistan	4,048	5.2
Indonesia	2,929	3.8
Nigeria	2,511	3.2
USA	2,267	2.9
Brazil	2,154	2.8
Bangladesh	2,108	2.7
Mexico	1,547	2.0
Philippines	1,522	2.0
total	46,494	59.8
world total	77,738	100

Population

Growth in World Population

Year	Estimated world population
2000 BC	100,000,000
1000	120,000,000
AD 1	180,000,000
1000	275,000,000
1250	375,000,000
1500	420,000,000
1750	750,000,000
1800	900,000,000
1850	1,260,000,000
1900	1,620,000,000
1950	2,500,000,000
1960	3,050,000,000
1970	3,700,000,000
1980	4,450,000,000
1990	5,245,000,000
2000	6,100,000,000

Population

Regional Population Growth

Region	Average annual growth rate 1950–94 (%)	% increase		
		1950–94	1994–2050	1950–2050
Africa	2.62	217	202	858
Asia	2.01	143	69	311
Europe	0.64	32	–7	24
Latin America and the Caribbean	2.38	186	77	406
North America	1.27	75	34	134
Oceania	1.74	123	64	265

Population
World Population Milestones

World population reached:		World population may reach:	
Number	**Year**	**Number**	**Year**
1 billion	1804	7 billion	2013 (14 years later)
2 billion	1927 (123 years later)	8 billion	2028 (15 years later)
3 billion	1960 (33 years later)	9 billion	2054 (26 years later)
4 billion	1974 (14 years later)		
5 billion	1987 (13 years later)		
6 billion	1999 (12 years later)		

Population
World Urban Population Growth

Main region/continent	Country	Number of additional people living in town, or cities 1990–2000 (millions)
world		679.7
developing countries		592.3
Africa		116.6
	Algeria	6.6
	Côte d'Ivoire	3.1
	Egypt	7.0
	Kenya	5.4
	Nigeria	25.7
	Congo, Democratic Republic of	5.3
Latin America		71.1
	Bolivia	1.5
	Brazil	28.7
	Mexico	18.4
	Peru	4.6
Asia		395.7
	Bangladesh	14.4
	China	149.5
	India	74.8
	Indonesia	26.4
	Pakistan	20.8
	Philippines	10.5
	Thailand	5.6
developed countries		87.5
	Australia	2.2
	USA	25.2
	Europe	28.0
	Japan	5.8

Post Offices
Countries with the Most

Country	Number of post offices	Country	Number of post offices
India	152,382	Germany	22,043
China	52,969	UK	19,702
USA	51,193	France	17,040
Russian Federation	48,061	Ukraine	15,230
Japan	24,680	Iran	13,720

Postage Stamps
Most Valuable

Where issued	Date of issue	Name/value and condition of stamp	Value (US$)
Sweden	1857	3 skilling banco yellow	2,000,000[1]
Mauritius	1847	1d Post Office Mauritius (unused)	1,000,000[1]
British Guiana	1856	1 cent (sold at auction in 1980)	935,000[2]
USA	1868	1 cent Z grill (sold at auction in 1988)	935,000[2]
Hawaiian Islands	1851	2 cent missionary	660,000 (unused); 200,000 (used)
Mauritius	1847	1d and 2d Post Office Mauritius (used)	500,000[1]
USA	1918	inverted Jenny (unused)	150,000[1]
Canada	1851	12 pence Victoria on laid paper (unused)	80,000[1]
British Guiana	1851	2 cent cottonreel (used)	70,000[1]
Western Australia	1854	4d inverted swan (used)	60,000[1]

[1] Estimated value.

[2] The two sales represent the highest amount paid for a postage stamp at auction. They are probably now worth greatly in excess of that figure.

Postage
Countries that Send Most International Mail

Country	Number of letters sent per year	Country	Number of letters sent per year
UK	967,611,000	Spain	173,952,000
USA	644,430,000	Mexico	173,316,000
France	526,462,000	Australia	165,100,000
Saudi Arabia	347,696,000	India	139,270,000
Belgium	193,794,000	Hong Kong	136,622,000

Postage
Countries that Send the Most Mail Per Person

Country	Number of letters per person per year	Country	Number of letters per person per year
Sweden	962	France	436
Russian Federation	700	Austria	420
USA	662	Luxembourg	400
Switzerland	614	Tongo	400
Norway	500		

Poverty
World's Poorest Countries

Country	GDP (US$ million)	Country	GDP (US$ million)
Micronesia	213	Palau	145
Guinea–Bissau	206	Marshall Islands	97
Comoros	196	Kiribati	76
Samoa	194	São Tomé and Príncipe	44
Tonga	180	Tuvalu	8

Presidential Medal of Freedom

The highest civilian award in the USA, the Presidential Medal of Freedom, was established in 1963 by President John F Kennedy to continue and expand presidential recognition of meritorious service granted since 1945 as the Medal of Freedom. Kennedy selected the first recipients, but was assassinated before he could make the presentations; they were made by President Johnson.

2000

James Edward Burke, former chairman of Johnson and Johnson and chairman of the Partnership for a Drug-Free America

John Chafee, senator for Rhode Island who championed environmental legislation and the expansion of health care (posthumous award)

Wesley Clarke, retired army general who was supreme allied commander of NATO during the conflict in Kosovo

William Crowe, retired admiral and former chairman of the Joint Chiefs of Staff

Marian Wright Edelman, president of the Children's Defense Fund and the first black woman admitted to the Mississippi bar

John Kenneth Galbraith, leading economist, advisor to presidents Kennedy and Johnson, and former US ambassador to India

George Higgins, Papal Chamberlain and adjunct lecturer at Catholic University who campaigned for fifty years to ensure worker justice

(*continued*)

Presidential Medal of Freedom (*continued*)

Jesse Jackson, Democratic politician, cleric, and campaigner for minority rights

Mildred 'Millie' Jeffrey, women's labour and Democratic party activist, and the first woman to direct a department of the United Auto Workers (car industry trade union)

Mathilde Krim, founder of the AIDS Medical Foundation and an early leader in the search for a cure for AIDS

George McGovern, US representative to the United Nations' Food and Agriculture Organization and former senator

Daniel Patrick Moynihan, senator for New York since 1977 and strong supporter of Social Security

Cruz Reynoso, a private lawyer and teacher of law, who serves as vice chairman of the US Commission on Civil Rights

Gardner Taylor, cleric, author, and early civil rights supporter, who led his New York City church to great prestige among the black churches of the US

Simon Wiesenthal, Nazi concentration camp survivor who has devoted his life to fighting bigotry and anti-Semitism

Primary Education
Countries with the Highest Enrolment

Cape Verde
Malawi
Namibia
Fiji Islands
Maldives
Portugal
Ecuador
Brazil
China
Peru
Belize
Myanmar

Primary Education
Countries with the Lowest Enrolment

Niger
Djibouti
Burkina Faso
Ethiopia
Afghanistan
Mali
Sierra Leone
Burundi
Guinea
Sudan
Eritrea
Haiti
Central African Republic

Prison

Countries with Highest Prison Populations

Country
USA
Russian Federation
South Africa
Germany
UK
Poland
France
Japan
Italy
Spain

Pubs

Most Popular Pub Names in the UK

Name	Number of pubs
The Crown	1,106
The Red Lion	659
The Swan	603
The Bull	557
The Royal Oak	557
The King's Head	503
The George	447
The Plough	432
The White Hart	370
The Coach and Horses	168

Refugees

Numbers of Refugees in the World

Region	Number of refugees	Total number of persons of concern to the United Nations
Africa	3,523,250	6,250,540
Asia	4,781,750	7,308,860
Europe	2,608,380	7,285,800
Latin America and the Caribbean	61,200	90,170
North America	636,300	1,241,930
Oceania	64,500	80,040
total	11,675,380	22,257,340

Religion

Clerical Titles and Functions

Title	Function
acolyte	attends/assists a priest
abbess	head of convent
abbot	head of abbey of monks
archbishop	highest-ranking bishop
archdeacon	ranking just below a bishop
beadle	parish official who kept order
bishop	head of a diocese
canon	member of cathedral chapter, or the Augustinian or Premonstratensian Canons (monks)
cantor	leader of services in a synagogue

(continued)

Religion: Clerical Titles and Functions (*continued*)

cardinal	member of the Sacred College, papal deputies
chaplain	attached to institutional chapel or armed services
church-warden	parish priest's assistant in secular matters
confessor	priest who hears confessions
curate	parish priest's assistant in religious matters
deacon	lay official assisting minister, or minister ranking below a priest
deaconess	female deacon
dean	head of a chapter of canons, a cathedral administrator, or a cardinal bishop heading a college of cardinals
elder	lay officer with an administrative or pastoral role
Father	title used for Christian priests
friar	member of a mendicant religious order
lord provost	provost of one of the major Scottish burghs, minister of Nonconformist church
moderator	minister who presides over assemblies of the Presbyterian Church
Monsignor	title of senior Roman Catholic clergy
nuncio	diplomatic representative of the pope
padre	chaplain to the armed services
parson	parish priest (who held benefices)
pastor	priest or clergyman in charge of congregation
patriarch	bishop of principal see in Eastern Orthodox Church, or title of the Pope
precentor	cleric who conducts cathedral's choral services
prelate	any high-ranking church dignitary
priest	somebody ordained into the church, or a minister of any religion
primate	an archbishop
prior	head of religious community, or deputy head of abbey or monastery
provost	head of cathedral chapter, abbot's deputy, or senior dignitary of cathedral foundation
rabbi	teacher, congregation leader, or minister of synagogue
rector	parish priest (who formerly received tithes), or cleric in charge of religious establishment or parish
sexton	caretaker of church and grounds
succentor	precentor's deputy
superintendent	cleric who oversees clergy in some Nonconformist churches
thurifer	carries the censer
verger	church official who acts as caretaker, or carries a bishop's or dean's rod of office
vicar	parish priest (who formerly received a stipend, not tithes), an assistant to a rector at communion, or a bishop or priest representing the pope

Religion
Followers of Major Faiths

In 2000.

Christianity	2,015,000,000
Islam	1,215,000,000
Hinduism	786,000,000
Buddhism	362,000,000
Judaism	18,000,000
Sikhism	16,000,000
Confucianism	5,000,000
Baha'ism	4,000,000
Jainism	3,000,000
Shinto	3,000,000

Rocket Systems
Countries with Most

Country	Number of systems
Russian Federation	2,606
China	2,500
North Korea	2,500
Iran	1,273
USA	840
Vietnam	710
Egypt	650
Ukraine	630
Iran	500
Syria	480

Roman Emperors
Earliest

Reign	Name
27 BC–AD 14	Augustus
14–37	Tiberius I
37–41	Caligula (Gaius Caesar)
41–54	Claudius I
54–68	Nero
68–69	Galba
69	Otho
69	Vitellius
69–79	Vespasian
79–81	Titus

Roman Emperors
The Last

The empire was frequently split from AD 305, and was divided for the last time between the sons of Theodosius (I) the Great in 395.

Reign	Name
379–395	Theodosius (I) the Great
375–392	Valentinian II
375–383	Gratian
364–375	Valentinian I
361–363	Julian the Apostate
337–350	Constans I
337–361	Constantius
305–337	Constantine I
293–311	Galerius
293–306	Constantius I

Rome
The Seven Hills of Rome

Name	Meaning
Aventine	from Aventius, Latin king buried there
Caelian	from Caelius Vibenna, Etruscan ally of Rome
Capitoline	from *caput,* meaning head or top
Esquiline	from *excolere,* to cultivate, because of its gardens
Palatine	from Pales, god of herds and shepherds
Quirinal	from Cures, town from which the Sabines came to Rome
Viminal	from *vimina,* meaning willows, which grew there

Royal Family
Living Members of the UK Royal Family

Name	Date of birth	Relationship to monarch	Name	Date of birth	Relationship to monarch
Elizabeth II	1926	queen	Edward	1964	son
Elizabeth Bowes-Lyon	1900	mother	Peter	1977	grandson
			Zara	1981	granddaughter
Philip of Greece	1921	husband	William	1982	grandson
Margaret Rose	1930	sister	Harry	1984	grandson
Charles	1948	son (heir)	Beatrice	1988	granddaughter
Anne	1950	daughter	Eugenie	1990	granddaughter
Andrew	1960	son			

Royal Family
The Succession to the UK Throne

Order of succession	Relationship
The Prince of Wales	eldest son of Her Majesty the Queen
Prince William of Wales	eldest son of the Prince of Wales
Prince Henry of Wales	second son of the Prince of Wales
The Duke of York	second son of Her Majesty the Queen
Princess Beatrice of York	eldest daughter of the Duke of York
Princess Eugenie of York	second daughter of the Duke of York
Prince Edward	third son of Her Majesty the Queen
The Princess Royal	only daughter, second child, of Her Majesty the Queen
Peter Phillips	only son, eldest child, of the Princess Royal
Zara Phillips	only daughter of the Princess Royal

Russian Tsars
Last

Reign	Name
1894–1917	Nicholas II (abdicated)
1881–94	Alexander III
1855–81	Alexander II
1825–55	Nicholas I
1801–25	Alexander I
1796–1801	Paul
1762–96	Catherine (II) the Great
1762	Peter III
1741–62	Elizabeth
1740–41	Ivan VI

Saints
Selected Patron Saints and their Feast Days

Saint	Protector of	Feast day
Agnes	girls	21 January
Andrew	fishermen	30 November
Bartholomew	plasterers	24 August
Catherine of Alexandria	philosophers, preachers, students	25 November
Christopher	travellers	25 July
David	poets	29 December
Francis of Assisi	animals, merchants	4 October
George	soldiers	23 April
Joan of Arc	soldiers	30 May
Luke	artists, butchers, doctors, glassworkers, sculptors, surgeons	18 October
Matthew	accountants, bookkeepers, tax collectors, bankers	21 September
Michael	grocers, police officers	29 September
Peter	fishermen	29 June
Valentine	lovers	14 February

Scandals
Famous Political Scandals

Scandal	Date	Country
The Dreyfus Affair	1890s	France
The Teapot Dome Scandal	1920s	USA
The Profumo–Keeler Affair	1963	UK
The Watergate Scandal	1972–75	USA
The Whitewater Scandal	1994–95	USA
The Cash for Questions Scandal	1997–99	UK
The Clinton–Lewinsky Affair	1998–99	USA

School
World Primary Attendance

Region	%	Region	%
sub-Saharan Africa	57	former USSR and Baltics	94
South Asia	68	Latin America and Caribbean	92
Middle East and North Africa	81	East Asia and Pacific	96

School
World's Largest Class Sizes

Country	Number of pupils per teacher
Central African Republic	77
Congo, Republic of the	70
Mali	70
Bangladesh	63
Burundi	63
Chad	63
Malawi	62
Senegal	59
Afghanistan	58
Mozambique	58
Rwanda	58

School
World's Smallest Class Sizes

Country	Pupils per teacher
San Marino	5
Qatar	9
Denmark	10
Hungary	11
Italy	11
Austria	12
Belgium	12
Bermuda	12
Cuba	12
Sweden	12

Schools
Countries with Most Pupils in Secondary Schools

Country	Number of pupils
China	71,883,000
India	68,872,000
USA	21,474,000
Indonesia	14,210,000
Russia	13,732,000
Japan	9,900,000
Iran	8,776,000
Germany	8,382,000
Mexico	7,914,000
Egypt	6,727,000

Scottish Monarchs
The Last

The crowns of Scotland and England were unified in 1603.

Reign	Name
1567–1625	James VI[1]
1542–67	Mary
1513–42	James V
1488–1513	James IV
1460–88	James III
1437–60	James II
1406–37	James I
1390–1406	Robert III
1371–90	Robert II
1329–71	David II

[1] After the union of crowns in 1603, he became James I of England.

Secondary Education
Countries with the Highest Enrolment

Country	Enrolment (%)	Country	Enrolment (%)
Australia	153	Finland	118
Belgium	146	Ireland, Republic of	118
Sweden	140	Norway	118
Netherlands	132	New Zealand	113
UK	129	France	111
Denmark	121	Portugal	111
Spain	120		

Secondary Education

Countries with the Lowest Enrolment

Countries with less than 14% enrolment.

Country	Enrolment (%)
Tanzania	6
Burundi	7
Mozambique	7
Niger	7
Burkina Faso	8
Central African Republic	10
Chad	10
Rwanda	11
Ethiopia	12
Uganda	12
Guinea	13
Madagascar	13
Mali	13

Self-Propelled Artillery

Countries with Most

Country	Number of vehicles
Russian Federation	4,705
North Korea	4,400
USA	2,500
South Korea	1,530
Ukraine	1,305
China	1,200
Israel	1,100
Turkey	821
Poland	634
Germany	580

Sikh Gurus

Name	Born	Dates as Guru
Guru Nanak Dev	1469	1499–1539
Guru Angad Dev	1504	1539–52
Guru Amar Das	1479	1552–74
Guru Ram Das	1534	1574–81
Guru Arjan Dev	1563	1581–1606
Guru Hargobind	1595	1606–44
Guru Har Rai	1630	1644–61
Guru Harkrishan	1656	1661–64
Guru Tegh Bahadur	1621	1664–75
Guru Gobind Singh	1666	1675–1708

Sikhism

Major Festivals

Festival	Description	Date (2001)
Baisakhi	commemorates the founding of the Order of the Khalsa in 1699	13 April
Martyrdom of the Guru Arjan Dev	time when Sikhs remember those who have suffered for their faith	June
Diwali	commemorates the release from prison of Guru Hargobind	25 October
Guru Nanak's Birthday	honours Guru Gobind Singh the founder of the Khalsa	November
Hola Mohalla	falls at the same time as the Hindu festival of Holi	17 March

Sins

Seven Deadly Sins

anger
avarice
envy
gluttony
lust
pride
sloth

South African Presidents

Recent

Term	Name
1999–	Thabo Mbeki
1994–99	Nelson Mandela
1989–94	F W de Klerk
1984–89	Pieter Botha

South African Prime Ministers

Recent

The post of prime minister was abolished in 1984 and combined with that of president.

Term	Name
1978–84	Pieter Botha
1966–78	Balthazar Johannes Vorster
1958–66	Hendrik Verwoerd
1954–58	J Strijdon
1948–54	Daniel Malan
1939–48	Jan Smuts

Soviet and Russian Presidents

Recent

Term	Name
Russian Federation	
2000–	Vladimir Putin
1999–2000	Vladimir Putin (acting)
1991–99	Boris Yeltsin
USSR	
1988–91	Mikhail Gorbachev
1985–88	Andrei Gromyko
1985	Valery Kuznetsov (acting)
1984–85	Konstantin Chernenko
1984	Valery Kuznetsov (acting)
1983–84	Yuri Andropov
1982–83	Valery Kuznetsov (acting)

Spanish Monarchs

Most Recent

Reign	Name	Reign	Name
1975–	Juan Carlos I	1868–70	provisional government
1886–1931	Alfonso XIII (deposed)	1833–68	Isabel II
1874–86	Alfonso XII	1813–33	Ferdinand VII (restored)
1873–74	first republic	1808–13	Joseph Napoleon
1870–73	Amadeus I (abdicated)	1808	Ferdinand VII (deposed)

Spanish Prime Ministers
Recent

Term	Name	Party
1996–	José Maria Aznar	Popular Party
1982–96	Felipe González Márquez	Socialist Workers' Party
1981–82	Leopoldo Calvo-Sotelo y Bustelo	Union of the Democratic Centre
1976–81	Adolfo Suárez González	Union of the Democratic Centre
1974–76	Carlos Arias Navarro	National Movement
1973–74	Torcuato Fernández Miranda	National Movement
1973	Luis Carrero Blanco	National Movement
1939–73	Francisco Franco Bahamonde	National Movement
1937–39	Juan Negrin	Socialist Party
1936–37	Francisco Largo Caballero	Socialist Party

Stock Market
Major Crashes

Year	Main location	Value down by (%)	Year	Main location	Value down by (%)
1637[1]	Holland	100	1997–2000	South Korea	56
1929	New York[2]	25.0	1997–2000	Malaysia	65
1987	New York	22.6	1997–2000	Philippines	58
1990	Japan	50	1999	Thailand	74

[1] Tulip prices fell dramatically in what may be regarded as a one-product stockmarket crash.
[2] The collapse started in USA and spread worldwide.

Strike Aircraft
Countries with Most

Country	Fighters/strike aircraft
China	3,000
Russian Federation	2,700
USA	2,529
Ukraine	911
India	774
North Korea	621
Syria	589
Egypt	580
Taiwan	570
South Korea	555

Submarines
Countries with Most

Country	Number of submarines[1]
Russian Federation	120
USA	99
China	70
North Korea	40
India	18
France	17
Germany	17
Japan	16
Turkey	16
UK	14

[1] Includes strategic (nuclear weapons carrying) and tactical submarines.

Suicides

Famous Suicides

Name	Year	Circumstances
Kurt Cobain	1994	US rock singer who killed himself with a shotgun
Judy Garland	1969	US film star who took a drug overdose
Brian Epstein	1967	English manager of the Beatles who took a drug overdose
Marilyn Monroe	1962	US film actor who died after an overdose of barbiturates; conspiracy theorists believe she was murdered
Adolf Hitler	1945	German dictator who killed himself as the final Soviet offensive across the Oder River closed in on the centre of Berlin
Virginia Woolf	1941	English novelist who drowned herself after a nervous collapse
Emily Davison	1913	English suffragette who threw herself under the king's horse in the 1913 Derby as a political statement
Vincent Van Gogh	1890	Dutch painter who shot himself at the site of his last painting *Cornfields with Flight of Crows*

Surface-to-Surface Missiles

Countries with Most

Country	Number of missiles
Libya	526
Russian Federation	446
Syria	278
Ukraine	276
Pakistan	122
Belarus	96
Sweden	96
Japan	90
North Korea	90
Bulgaria	72

Swedish Monarchs

Recent

Period	Name
1973–	Carl XVI Gustaf
1950–73	Gustaf VI Adolf
1907–50	Gustaf V
1872–1907	Oscar II
1859–72	Carl XV
1844–59	Oscar I
1818–44	Carl XIV Johan
1809–18	Carl XIII
1792–1809	Gustaf IV Adolf
1771–92	Gustaf III

Swedish Prime Ministers

Recent

Term	Name	Party
1996–	Göran Persson	Social Democratic Labour Party
1994–96	Ingvar Carlsson	Social Democratic Labour Party
1991–94	Carl Bildt	Moderate Party
1986–91	Ingvar Carlsson	Social Democratic Labour Party
1982–86	Olof Palme	Social Democratic Labour Party
1979–82	Thorbjörn Fälldin	Centre Party
1978–79	Ola Ullsten	Liberal Party
1976–78	Thorbjörn Fälldin	Centre Party
1969–76	Olof Palme	Social Democratic Labour Party
1946–69	Tage Erlander	Social Democratic Labour Party

Tanks
Countries with Most

Country	Number of tanks
Russian Federation	21,950
USA	8,303
China	7,060
Syria	4,850
Turkey	4,205
Egypt	3,960
Israel	3,900
Ukraine	3,895
North Korea	3,500
India	3,414

Teachers
Countries with Most Women Primary Teachers

Country	Women teachers in primary schools (%)
Hungary	94
Czech Republic	93
Italy	93
UK	90
Argentina	89
Philippines	89
USA	86
Austria	83
Sweden	83
Germany	81

Teachers
World's Teachers' Highest Salaries

Country	Minimum starting salary (US$)	Country	Minimum starting salary (US$)
Lower secondary level		**Upper secondary level**	
Switzerland	38,100	Switzerland	45,739
Germany	30,933	Germany	32,992
Netherlands	24,555	Spain	28,464
Spain	24,543	Denmark	26,061
Korea	23,960	Belgium	25,228
Ireland, Republic of	23,809	Netherlands	24,764
USA	23,581	Korea	23,960
Denmark	23,269	USA	23,815
France	22,125	Ireland, Republic of	23,809
Belgium	20,386	France	22,125

Templeton Foundation Prize
For Progress in Religion

Year	Winner
1990	Baba Amte, India, and Professor Charles Birch, Sydney, Australia
1991	The Rt. Hon. Lord Jakobovits, Chief Rabbi of Great Britain and the Commonwealth
1992	Dr Kyung-Chik Han, founder of Seoul's Young Nak Presbyterian Church
1993	Charles W Colson, founder of Prison Fellowship, Virginia
1994	Michael Novak, scholar at the American Enterprise Institute, Washington, DC

(*continued*)

Templeton Foundation Prize: For Progress in Religion
(*continued*)

Year	Winner
1995	Dr Paul Davies, professor, University of Adelaide, Australia
1996	Bill Bright, founder of Campus Crusade for Christ, international evangelical ministry
1997	Pandurang Shastri Athavale, Indian spiritual leader
1998	Sir Sigmund Sternberg, Chairman of the Executive Committee of the International Council of Christians and Jews (ICCA)
1999	Ian Barbour, physicist and theologian, advocate for ethics in technology
2000	Freeman Dyson, physicist and author

Ten Commandments

Commandment	
1	to have no other gods besides Jehovah
2	to make no idols
3	mot to misuse the name of God
4	to keep the sabbath holy
5	to honour one's parents
6	not to commit murder
7	not to commit adultery
8	not to commit theft
9	not to give false evidence
10	not to be covetous

Tertiary Education
Countries with the Highest Enrolment

Country	Enrolment (%)
Canada	90
USA	81
Australia	80
Finland	74
Korea, South	68
New Zealand	63
Norway	62
Belgium	56
UK	52
France	51
Spain	51
Sweden	50

Tertiary Education
Countries with the Lowest Enrolment

Country	Enrolment (%)	Country	Enrolment (%)
Djibouti	0.3	Tanzania	0.6
Mozambique	0.5	Angola	0.7
Chad	0.6	Burundi	0.8
Comoros	0.6	Ethiopia	0.8
Malawi	0.6	Burkina Faso	0.9
Rwanda	0.6		

Time

Different Years

Name	Meaning
academic year	school or university year
civil year	365 days (366 in leap year)
calendar year	same as civil year
astronomical year	period between two successive vernal equinoxes (365.242 days)
fiscal (or financial) year	12-month period used in accounting
lunar year	12 lunar months (354.256 days)
Marian year	year originally beginning on 25 March; 11 days added after the 1752 calendar reform made it run from 5 April
regnal year	year dated from the year of a monarch's succession
sabbatical year	every seventh year, during which university staff were allowed (unpaid) leave of absence
school year	12-month period, in the UK beginning in September, during which pupils generally remain in the same class
sidereal year	time taken for earth to make one orbit round the sun (365.257 days)
solar year	same as astronomical year
tropical year	same as astronomical year

Time

Names of Anniversaries

Term	Meaning	Alternative
annual	occurring once a year/every year, lasting for a year	yearly
biannual	ocurring twice a year	twice-yearly
biennial	occurring every 2 years, lasting 2 years	two-yearly
quadrennial	4th anniversary, occurring every 4 years, lasting 4 years, four-yearly, quadrennium period of 4 years	tetrad
quinquennial	5th anniversary, occurring every 5 years, lasting 5 years, five-yearly quinquennium, period of 5 years	pentad
decennial	10th anniversary, occurring every 10 years, lasting 10 years, ten-yearly decennium, period of 10 years	decade
centenary	100th anniversary, to do with a period of 100 years (US centennial), centenary, centennial occurring every 100 years, lasting for 100 years centennial, century period of 100 years	century
sesqui-	every 150 years, relating to centennial 150 years	150-yearly
bicentenary	200th anniversary, occurring every 200 years, lasting 200 years (US bicentennial)	200-yearly
tricentenary	300th anniversary, occurring every 300 years, lasting 300 years (US tercentennial)	300-yearly
millenarian	to do with 1000 years or chiliad period of 1000 years	millennium

Towed Artillery
Countries with Most

Country	Number of systems
China	12,000
Russian Federation	10,065
India	4,885
South Korea	4,200
North Korea	3,000
Vietnam	2,300
Iran	1,950
Iraq	1,900
Pakistan	1,744
Syria	1,540

Transport Aircraft
Countries with Most

Country	Transport aircraft
USA	1,102
China	425
North Korea	300
Russian Federation	280
Spain	214
India	203
France	188
Germany	177
Syria	135
Ukraine	123

UK Kings and Queens
Most Recent

Reign	Name	Relationship
1952–	Elizabeth II	daughter of George VI
1936–52	George VI	son of George V
1936	Edward VIII	son of George V
1910–36	George V	son of Edward VII
1901–10	Edward VII	son of Victoria
1837–1901	Victoria	daughter of Edward (son of George III)
1830–37	William IV	son of George III
1820–30	George IV (regent 1811–20)	son of George III
1760–1820	George III	son of Frederick (son of George II)
1727–60	George II	son of George I
1714–27	George I	son of Sophia (granddaughter of James I)

UK Philosophers

Name	Dates	Representative work
Bertrand Russell	1872–1970	*Principia Mathematica*
John Stuart Mill	1806–1873	*Utilitarianism*
David Hume	1711–1776	*A Treatise of Human Nature*
George Berkeley	1685–1753	*A Treatise Concerning the Principles of Human Knowledge*
John Locke	1632–1704	*Essay Concerning Human Understanding*
Thomas Hobbes	1588–1679	*Leviathan*
Francis Bacon	1561–1626	*Novum Organum; The Advancement of Learning*
William of Occam	c. 1285–1349	*Commentary of the Sentences*
Duns Scotus	c. 1266–1308	*Opus Oxoniense*

UK Prime Ministers

Term	Name	Party
1721–42	Robert Walpole[1]	Whig
1742–43	Spencer Compton, Earl of Wilmington	Whig
1743–54	Henry Pelham	Whig
1754–56	Thomas Pelham-Holles, 1st Duke of Newcastle	Whig
1756–57	William Cavendish, 4th Duke of Devonshire	Whig
1757–62	Thomas Pelham-Holles, 1st Duke of Newcastle	Whig
1762–63	John Stuart, 3rd Earl of Bute	Tory
1763–65	George Grenville	Whig
1765–66	Charles Watson Wentworth, 2nd Marquess of Rockingham	Whig
1766–68	William Pitt, 1st Earl of Chatham	Tory
1768–70	Augustus Henry Fitzroy, 3rd Duke of Grafton	Whig
1770–82	Frederick North, Lord North[2]	Tory
1782	Charles Watson Wentworth, 2nd Marquess of Rockingham	Whig
1782–83	William Petty-Fitzmaurice, 2nd Earl of Shelburne[3]	Whig
1783	William Henry Cavendish-Bentinck, 3rd Duke of Portland	Whig
1783–1801	William Pitt, The Younger	Tory
1801–04	Henry Addington	Tory
1804–06	William Pitt, The Younger	Tory
1806–07	William Wyndham Grenville, 1st Baron Grenville	Whig
1807–09	William Henry Cavendish-Bentinck, 3rd Duke of Portland	Whig
1809–12	Spencer Perceval	Tory
1812–27	Robert Banks Jenkinson, 2nd Earl of Liverpool	Tory
1827	George Canning	Tory
1827–28	Frederick John Robinson, 1st Viscount Goderich	Tory
1828–30	Arthur Wellesley, 1st Duke of Wellington	Tory
1830–34	Charles Grey, 2nd Earl Grey	Whig
1834	William Lamb, 2nd Viscount Melbourne	Whig
1834	Arthur Wellesley, 1st Duke of Wellington	Tory
1834–35	Sir Robert Peel, 2nd Baronet	Tory
1835–41	William Lamb, 2nd Viscount Melbourne	Whig
1841–46	Sir Robert Peel, 2nd Baronet	Conservative
1846–52	John Russell, Lord Russell	Whig-Liberal
1852	Edward Geoffrey Stanley, 14th Earl of Derby	Conservative
1852–55	George Hamilton-Gordon, 4th Earl of Aberdeen	Peelite
1855–58	Henry John Temple, 3rd Viscount Palmerston	Liberal
1858–59	Edward Geoffrey Stanley, 14th Earl of Derby	Conservative
1859–65	Henry John Temple, 3rd Viscount Palmerston	Liberal
1865–66	John Russell, 1st Earl Russell	Liberal
1866–68	Edward Geoffrey Stanley, 14th Earl of Derby	Conservative
1868	Benjamin Disraeli	Conservative
1868–74	William Ewart Gladstone	Liberal
1874–80	Benjamin Disraeli[4]	Conservative

[1] From 1725, Sir Robert Walpole.
[2] From 1790, 2nd Earl of Guilford.
[3] From 1784, 1st Marquess of Lansdowne.
[4] From 1876, Earl of Beaconsfield.

(continued)

UK Prime Ministers (*continued*)

Term	Name	Party
1880–85	William Ewart Gladstone	Liberal
1885–86	Robert Cecil, 3rd Marquess of Salisbury	Conservative
1886	William Ewart Gladstone	Liberal
1886–92	Robert Cecil, 3rd Marquess of Salisbury	Conservative
1892–94	William Ewart Gladstone	Liberal
1894–95	Archibald Philip Primrose, 5th Earl of Rosebery	Liberal
1895–1902	Robert Cecil, 3rd Marquess of Salisbury	Conservative
1902–05	Arthur James Balfour	Conservative
1905–08	Sir Henry Campbell-Bannerman	Liberal
1908–16	Herbert Henry Asquith	Liberal
1916–22	David Lloyd George	Liberal
1922–23	Bonar Law	Conservative
1923–24	Stanley Baldwin	Conservative
1924	Ramsay Macdonald	Labour
1924–29	Stanley Baldwin	Conservative
1929–35	Ramsay Macdonald	Labour
1935–37	Stanley Baldwin	Conservative
1937–40	Neville Chamberlain	Conservative
1940–45	Winston Churchill	Conservative
1945–51	Clement Attlee	Labour
1951–55	Winston Churchill[5]	Conservative
1955–57	Sir Anthony Eden	Conservative
1957–63	Harold Macmillan	Conservative
1963–64	Sir Alec Douglas-Home	Conservative
1964–70	Harold Wilson	Labour
1970–74	Edward Heath	Conservative
1974–76	Harold Wilson	Labour
1976–79	James Callaghan	Labour
1979–90	Margaret Thatcher	Conservative
1990–97	John Major	Conservative
1997–	Tony Blair	Labour

[5] From 1953, Sir Winston Churchill.

Unemployment
Worldwide at October 2000

Country	Percentage	Trend	Country	Percentage	Trend
Argentina	14.7	down	Hong Kong	4.6	down
Australia	6.6	up	Japan	4.8	up
Brazil	6.8	down	Mexico	2.0	steady
Canada	6.9	steady	UK	3.6	steady
France	9.4	down	USA	4.0	up
Germany[1]	8.9	steady			

[1] 7.4% steady in the former West, 17.4% up marginally in the former East.

United Nations
Secretaries-General

Term	Secretary general	Nationality
1946–53	Trygve Lie	Norwegian
1953–61	Dag Hammarskjöld	Swedish
1961–71	U Thant	Burmese
1972–81	Kurt Waldheim	Austrian
1982–92	Javier Pérez de Cuéllar	Peruvian
1992–96	Boutros Boutros-Ghali	Egyptian
1997–	Kofi Annan	Ghanaian

United Nations
Security Council Membership

Permanent members

USA
UK
France
China
Russia

Rotating members

from January 1994	from January 1995	from January 1996
Argentina	Botswana	Chile
Brazil	Germany	Egypt
Czech Republic	Honduras	Guinea-Bissau
Djibouti	Indonesia	Poland
New Zealand	Italy	South Korea
Nigeria		
Oman		
Pakistan		
Rwanda		
Spain		

United Nations
Specialized Organizations

Abbreviation	Full title
FAO	Food and Agriculture Organization
IBRO	International Bank for Reconstruction and Development
ICAO	International Civil Aviation Organization
IDA	International Development Association

(continued)

United Nations: Specialized Organizations (*continued*)

IFAD	International Fund for Agricultural Development
IFC	International Finance Corporation
ILO	International Labour Organization
IMCO	Inter-Governmental Maritime Consultative Organization
IMF	International Monetary Fund
ITU	International Telecommunications Union
UNESCO	United Nations Educational, Scientific, and Cultural Organization
UPU	Universal Postal Union
WHO	World Health Organization
WIPO	World Intellectual Property Organization
WMO	World Meteorological Organization

Universities
Countries with Most University Students

Country	Number of students
USA	14,262,000
China	6,075,000
India	6,060,000
Russia	4,458,000
Japan	3,918,000
South Korea	2,542,000
Indonesia	2,303,000
Germany	2,132,000
France	2,062,000
Philippines	2,022,000

Universities
Countries with Highest Proportion of University Students

Country	Number of students per 100,000 population
Korea	6,100
Canada	5,900
Australia	5,700
USA	5,300
New Zealand	4,500
Finland	4,400
Spain	4,300
Norway	4,200
Ireland	3,700
Israel	3,600

Universities
Oldest in the USA

University	Year established	University	Year established
Harvard	1636	Colombia	1754
William and Mary College	1693	Rutgers	1766
Yale	1701	Dartmouth	1769
Pennsylvania	1741	Brown	1771
Princeton	1746	Cornell	1865

Universities
World's Oldest Universities

University	Founded
Salerno, Italy	1150
Oxford, UK	1160
Bologna, Italy	late 11th century
Cambridge, UK	1209
Montpellier, France	1220
Toulouse, France	1229
Salamanca, Spain	c. 1230
Sorbonne, France	1253

US Administration
Recent Speakers of the House of Representatives

Speaker	Party	State	Term of office
Dennis Hastert	Republican	Illinois	1999–
Newt Gingrich	Republican	Georgia	1995–99
Thomas S Foley	Democrat	Washington	1989–95
James C Wright Jr	Democrat	Texas	1987–89
Thomas P O'Neill Jr	Democrat	Massachusetts	1977–87
Carl Albert	Democrat	Oklahoma	1971–77
John W McCormack	Democrat	Massachusetts	1962–71
Sam T Rayburn	Democrat	Texas	1955–61
Joseph W Martin Jr	Republican	Massachusetts	1953–55
Sam T Rayburn	Democrat	Texas	1949–53
Joseph W Martin Jr	Republican	Massachusetts	1947–49
Sam T Rayburn	Democrat	Texas	1940–47
William B Bankhead	Democrat	Alabama	1936–40
Joseph W Byrns	Democrat	Tennessee	1935–36

US Presidents
Most Recent

Year elected/took office	President	Party
2000	George W Bush	Republican
1992, 1996	Bill Clinton	Democrat
1988	George Bush	Republican
1980, 1984	Ronald Reagan	Republican
1976	James Earl Carter	Democrat
1974	Gerald R Ford	Republican
1968, 1972	Richard M Nixon	Republican
1963, 1964	Lyndon B Johnson	Democrat
1960	John F Kennedy	Democrat
1952, 1956	Dwight D Eisenhower	Republican
1945, 1948	Harry S Truman	Democrat

Veterans
Veteran Population of the USA

Period of service	Total veteran population (in thousands)	Period of service	Total veteran population (in thousands)
all veterans	25,881	Korean War	4,396
wartime veterans	19,897	World War II	7,066
Gulf War service[1]	1,658	World War I	10
Vietnam era	8,248	peacetime veterans	5,984

[1] As of June 1997, the Gulf War service period had not ended; thus, there is no post-Gulf War peacetime service accounting period.

Vietnam War
Casualties

Armed force casualties	Battle deaths	Total deaths	Wounded	Total
US Army	30,914	38,189	96,802	134,991
US Navy	1,631	2,559	4,178	6,737
US Marine Corps	13,082	14,836	51,392	66,228
US Air Force	1,739	2,583	931	3,514
total US forces	47,366	58,167	153,303	211,470
South Vietnamese forces (ARVN)	223,748	223,748	1,169,763	1,393,511
North Vietnamese Army (NVA)/ Viet Cong (VC)[1]	1,100,000	1,100,000	600,000	1,700,000

[1] According to an Agence France Presse press release of 4 April 1995, the Vietnamese government announced that the population of North Vietnam had suffered 2,000,000 casualties, in addition to approximately 2,000,000 civilian casualties in South Vietnam.

Vietnam War
Prisoners of War

Forces	Prisoners
US forces	766
North Vietnamese Army (NVA)/Viet Cong (VC)	26,000
South Vietnamese forces (ARVN)	N/A[1]

[1] Figures are unavailable for South Vietnamese prisoners of war. After the war the government in Hanoi took control of the whole of North and South Vietnam.

Virtues

The Seven Virtues

prudence
temperance
fortitude
justice
faith
hope
hove

Vishnu

The 10 Major Incarnations of Vishnu

Matsya	Parashurama
Kurma	Rama
Varaha	Krishna
Narasimha	Buddha
Vamana	Kalki

War

Major Wars

Date	Name	Combatants
1250 BC	Trojan War	Mycenaeans and Trojans
431–404 BC	Peloponnesian War	Athens and Sparta
264–146 BC	Three Punic Wars	Carthage and Rome
1096–1204	Four Crusades	Christians and Saracens
1337–1453	Hundred Years' War	England and France
1455–85	Wars of the Roses	Houses of Lancaster and York
1618–48	Thirty Years' War	Catholic League against Denmark, France, and Sweden
1642–48	English Civil War	Cavaliers and Roundheads
1700	Great Northern War	Sweden against Denmark, Holland, Poland, and Russia
1701–13	War of Spanish Succession	Bavaria, France, and Spain against Austrian Empire, England, and Holland
1756–63	Seven Years' War	Britain and Prussia against Austria, France, and Russia
1775–83	American Revolutionary War	American colonies against Britain
1793–1815	Napoleonic Wars	France against Austria, Britain, Prussia, Russia, and Sweden
1846–48	Mexican–American War	Mexico and the US
1854–56	Crimean War	Russia against Britain, France, and Turkey
1861–65	US Civil War	Confederates and Unionists
1870	Franco-Prussian War	France and Prussia
1899–1902	Boer War	Britain and Boers (Dutch)
1905	Russo-Japanese War	Russia and Japan
1914–18	World War I	Austria-Hungary and Germany against Britain, France, Russia, and others
1918–21	Russian Civil War	Bolshevics and White Russians
1936–39	Spanish Civil War	Nationalists and Republicans
1939–45	World War II	Germany, Italy, and Japan against the UK, France, USA, USSR, and others
1967	Six Days' War	Arab states and Israel
1950–53	Korean War	North and South Korea

(continued)

Date	Name	Combatants
1964–73	Vietnam War	North and South Vietnam (with the USA)
1982	Falklands War	Argentina and the UK
1991	Gulf War	Iraq against the UK, France, and the USA
1991–96	Yugoslav Civil War	component nations of former Yugoslavia

Warfare

Highest Casualties in Armed Conflicts Since 1945

Country	Conflict	Year	Deaths
Korea	Korean War	1950–53	3,000,000
Vietnam	South Vietnam/USA/North Vietnam	1965–75	2,000,000
Afghanistan	USSR in civil war	1978–92	1,500,000
Angola	civil war: South Africa and Cuba intervene	1975–91	1,500,000
Cambodia	Pol Pot massacre	1975–78	1,000,000
Nigeria	Biafrans/government	1967–70	1,000,000
China	government executions	1950–51	1,000,000
	Kuomintang/communists	1946–50	1,000,000
India	Muslim/Hindu	1946–48	800,000
Vietnam	independence	1945–54	600,000

Wealth

World's Richest Countries

Country	GDP (US$ million)	Country	GDP (US$ million)
USA	8,210,600	Italy	1,171,000
Japan	3,783,100	China	961,000
Germany	2,142,000	Brazil	778,300
France	1,432,900	Canada	598,800
UK	1,357,400	Spain	551,900

Weapons
Major Arsenals

As of January 1999.

Weapon type	Country and weapon strength					
	USA	France	Germany	Russian Federation	UK	Iraq
armoured personnel carriers	17,800	3,820	3,306	3,337	3,016	2,000
main battle tanks	8,087	1,207	3,136	15,500	542	2,200
combat aircraft	4,565	592	503	4,295	495	316
helicopters	6,323	657	765	3,492	537	500
tactical submarines	57	8	14	44	12	0
destroyers	54	4	2	17	11	0
aircraft carriers	12	1	0	1	3	0

Wedding Anniversaries

Anniversary	Material	Anniversary	Material	Anniversary	Material
1st	paper	10th	tin, aluminium	35th	coral, jade
2nd	cotton	11th	steel	40th	ruby
3rd	leather	12th	silk	45th	sapphire
4th	linen	13th	lace	50th	gold
5th	wood	14th	ivory	55th	emerald
6th	iron	15th	crystal	60th	diamond
7th	copper, wool	20th	china	70th	platinum
8th	bronze	25th	silver		
9th	pottery, china	30th	pearl		

Welsh Monarchs
The Last

From 1282 Wales ceased to be a separate political entity.

Reign	Name
1246–82	Llywellyn ap Gruffydd ap Llywellyn
1240–46	Dafydd ap Llywellyn
1240–1194	Llywelyn Fawr
1170–94	Dafydd ab Owain Gwynedd
1137–70	Owain Gwynedd
1081–1137	Gruffydd ap Cynan ab Iago
1075–81	Trahaern ap Caradog
1063–75	Bleddyn ap Cynfyn
1039–63	Gruffydd ap Llywelyn ap Seisyll
1023–39	Iago ab Idwal ap Meurig

White House Staff
Administration of George W Bush

Office	Incumbent
Chief of Staff	Andrew Card
Press Secretary	Ari Fleischer
Counselor to the President	Karen Hughes
General Counsel to the President	Alberto R Gonzales
Assistant to the President and Deputy Chief of Staff for Policy	Joshua Bolton
Assistant to the President and Director of Legislative Affairs	Nicholas Calio
Assistant to the President for Domestic Policy	Margaret La Montagne
National Drug Control Policy	Acting Director, Edward H Jurith
Office of Science and Technology Policy	Acting Director, Rosina Bierbaum
Ambassador to the United Nations	John Negroponte
US Trade Representative	Robert B Zoellick
Office of Management and Budget	Director, Mitch Daniels

Workers
Countries with the Most Female Workers

Norway	Switzerland
Denmark	Canada
Sweden	UK
Finland	Portugal
USA	New Zealand

Workers
Number of Hours Worked in Selected Countries

Country	Average annual hours worked per person in employment		
	1973	1983	1993
Australia	N/A	1,852	1,874
Canada	1,867	1,731	1,718
France	1,904	1,711	1,639
Western Germany	1,868	1,724	1,584
Japan	2,201	2,095	1,905
Norway	1,712	1,485	1,434
Spain	N/A	1,912	1,815
Sweden	1,557	1,453	1,501
UK	1,929	1,719	1,715
USA	1,924	1,882	1,946

Workers
Trades Union Membership in the UK

Union	Number of members
Unison	1,272,330
TGWU (Transport and General Workers Union)	881,625
AEEEU (Amalgamated Engineering and Electrical Union)	717,875
GMB	712,010
MSF (Manufacturing, Science, Finance)	416,000
USDAW (Union of Shop, Distributive and Allied Workers)	303,060
CWU (Communications Workers Union)	287,730
PCS (Public and Commercial Services Union)	254,350
GPMU (Graphical, Paper and Media Union)	203,230
NUT (National Union of Teachers)	194,260

Workers
UK Unemployment

Region	% unemployed
Merseyside	10.6
Northeast England	8.3
Northern Ireland	7.8
London	7.4
Scotland	6.9
Wales	6.7
Yorkshire and Humberside	6.3
West Midlands	6.0
Northwest England	5.8
East Midlands	5.0
Southwest England	4.4
Southeast England	4.0

Workers
World's Largest Working Populations

Country	Number of workers (millions)
China	706
India	c. 400
USA	133
Indonesia	88
Brazil	70
Japan	65
Russian Federation	60
Bangladesh	55
Nigeria	43
Pakistan	39
Mexico	39

World Defence
Countries with the Most Conscripts Serving in the Armed Forces in 1999

Country	Conscripts	Country	Conscripts
China	1,000,000	South Korea	159,000
Turkey	528,000	Eritrea	150,000
Russian Federation	330,000	Germany	128,400
Egypt	322,000	Poland	111,950
Iran	220,000	Italy	111,800

World Defence

Highest Defence Budgets as a Percentage of GDP

Country	% of GDP
Eritrea	44.4
Angola	16.5
Saudi Arabia	15.5
Qatar	15.4
Afghanistan	14.9
North Korea	14.3
Federal Republic of Yugoslavia (Serbia and Montenegro)	12.4
Kuwait	11.1
Oman	10.9
Maldives	9.6

World Defence

Lowest Defence Budgets as a Percentage of GDP

Country	% of GDP
Barbados	0.5
Moldova	0.5
Costa Rica	0.6
Antigua and Barbuda	0.6
Bahamas	0.7
Austria	0.8
Jamaica	0.8
Luxembourg	0.8
Madagascar	0.8
Malta	0.8
Nepal	0.8

World Leaders

During World War I

Country	Name	Position (dates held)
USA	Woodrow Wilson	president (1912–20)
Japan	Yoshihito Taisho	emperor (1912–26)
Belgium	Albert I	monarch (1909–14 and 1918–34)
	Charles de Broqueville	prime minister (1911–18)
UK	George V	monarch (1910–36)
	Herbert Henry Asquith	prime minister (1908–16)
	David Lloyd George	prime minister (1916–22)
France	Raymond Poincaré	president (1913–24)
	Georges Clemenceau	prime minister (1917–20)
Italy	Victor Emmanuel III	monarch (1900–46)
	Antonio Salandra	prime minister (1914–16)
	Paulo Boselli	prime minister (1916–17)
	Vittorio Orlando	prime minister (1917–19)
Russia	Nicholas II	tsar (1894–1917)
	Vladimir Ilyich Lenin	head of state (1917–22)
Spain	Alphonso XIII	monarch (1886–1931)
	Antonio Maura	prime minister (1917–23)
Austria-Hungary	Franz Joseph	emperor (1848–1916)
	Karl	emperor (1916–18)
Turkey	Muhammad V	sultan (1909–18)

World Leaders
During World War II

Country	Name	Position (dates held)
USA	Franklin D Roosevelt	president (1933–45)
France	Albert Lebrun	president (1932–40)
	Phillipe Pétain	prime minister (1940–45)[1]
Germany	Adolf Hilter	chancellor and Führer (1934–45)
UK	George VI	monarch (1936–52)
	Neville Chamberlain	prime minister (1937–40)
	Winston Churchill	prime minister (1940–45)
Italy	Victor Emmanuel III	monarch (1900–46)
	Benito Mussolini	prime minister (1922–43)
	Pietro Badoglio	prime minister (1943–44)
Spain	F Franco Bahamonde	chief of state (1939–75)
USSR	Joseph Stalin	general secretary (1922–53)
	Mikhail Kalinin	president (1922–46)
Japan	Hirohito	emperor (1926–1989)
	Abe Nobuyuki	prime minister (1939–40)
	Yonai Mitsumasa	prime minister (1940)
	Konoe Fumimaro	prime minister (1940–41)
	Tojo Hideki	prime minister (1941–44)
	Koiso Kuniaki	prime minister (1944–45)
China	Lin Sen	president (1931–43)
	Chiang Kai-Shek	president (1943–49) and prime minister (1939–45)
Belgium	Leopold III	monarch (1934–51)
	Hubert Pierlot	prime minister (1939–45)
Australia	Robert Menzies	prime minister (1939–41)
	John Curtin	prime minister (1941–45)
New Zealand	Michael Savage	prime minister (1935–40)
	Peter Fraser	prime minister (1940–49)
Austria	Arthur Seyss-Inquart	chancellor (1938–45)
Hungary	Miklós von Horthy	regent (1920–45)

[1] Combined presidential powers with this office.

World Leaders
Longest Serving

Name	Country	Term(s)	Years
Jiang Jie Shi (Chiang Kai-shek)	China and Taiwan	1928–75	47
Kim II Sung	North Korea	1948–94	46
Ibrahim Didi	Maldives	1883–1925	42
Enver Hoxha	Albania	1954–85	40
Fidel Castro Ruz	Cuba	1959–	42
Francisco Franco Bahamonde	Spain	1939–75	36

(continued)

Name	Country	Term(s)	Years
Antonio de Oliveira Salazar	Portugal	1932–68	36
Marshal Tito	Yugoslavia	1943–80	36
Todor Zhivkov	Bulgaria	1954–89	35
Alfredo Stroessner	Paraguay	1954–89	35
Omar Bongo	Gabon	1967–	35

World War I
Countries that Became Independent 1914–18

Country	Power(s) that ruled in 1914
Armenia	Ottoman Empire
Austria	Austria-Hungary
Azerbaijan	Ottoman Empire and Russian Empire
Czechoslovakia	Austria-Hungary
Estonia	Russian Empire
Finland	Russian Empire
Georgia	Russian Empire
Hungary	Austria-Hungary
Latvia	Russian Empire
Lithuania	Russian Empire
North Yemen	Ottoman Empire
Poland	Austria-Hungary, Russian Empire, and Germany
Ukraine	Russian Empire
Yugoslavia (known as the Kingdom of Serbs, Croats and Slovenes until 1929)	Russian Empire

World War I
Military Casualties

Country	Wounded	Country	Wounded
Germany	4,234,000	Italy	947,000
Russia	4,950,000	Turkey	>400,000
France	2,675,000–4,266,000	Romania	120,000
Austria-Hungary	3,620,000	Serbia	133,250
British Empire	2,090,250	USA	204,000

World War I
Military Fatalities

The final number of deaths due to the war will never be known, since record-keeping in the midst of a battle can never be relied upon, and even records conscientiously kept can be easily destroyed or lost in a subsequent action. The best available figures, collated from a variety of authoritative sources, are as follows:

Country	Dead	Missing
Australia	58,150	–
Austria-Hungary	922,000	855,300
Belgium	102,000	–
Britain	658,700	359,150
Canada	56,500	–
France	1,359,000	361,650
Germany	1,600,000	103,000
India	43,200	5,900
Italy	465,550	–
New Zealand	16,150	–
Russia	1,700,000	–
Turkey	250,000	–
USA	58,500	14,300
total	7,289,750	1,699,300

World War I
Military Strengths of Countries

Country	Number of military divisions at the Front										
	1914		1915	1916		1917		1918			
	Aug	Dec	May	Feb	Aug	July	Oct	Mar	July	Oct	Nov
Belgium	6	6	6	6	6	6	6	12	12	12	12
Britain	20	67	77	79	81	87	87	85	85	85	85
France	74	74	81	99	102	116	116	114	114	114	114
Greece						3	3	4	7	10	10
Italy			36	38	47	59	66	53	56	58	58
Portugal						1	1	2			
Romania					21	15					
Russia	108	108	112	136	142	288	202				
Serbia	12	12	12	6	6	6	6	6	6	6	6
USA							3	5	25	32	42
Allied total	220	267	324	364	405	521	505	281	305	324	329
Austria	49	57	64	60	70	80	78	78	72	74	66
Bulgaria				12	12	12	12	12	12		
Germany	94	117	149	159	169	232	234	234	235	214	210
Turkey		37	38	52	53	45	45	41	37	37	17
Central Powers total	143	212	248	283	304	369	369	365	356	325	278

World War I
Most Prisoners of War

Country	Prisoners of war[1]	Country	Prisoners of war[1]
Russia	2,500,000	Turkey	>200,000
Austria-Hungary	2,200,000	British Empire	191,750
Germany	1,073,500	Serbia	153,000
Italy	530,000	Romania	80,000
France	446,250	Belgium	67,750

[1] Figures have been the subject of controversy over the years. The figures in this table have been compiled from a number of official and unofficial sources.

World War I
US Casualties

Cause of wound	Wounded but survived	Died of wounds	Total
air attacks	170	30	200
artillery (fragments)	18,260	1,780	20,040
artillery (shrapnel)	31,800	1,985	33,785
bayonets	370	5	375
gas	69,330	1,220	70,550
grenades	825	55	880
machine gun	67,410	7,475	74,885
pistol shot	230	15	245
rifle fire	19,460	960	20,420
swords	10	5	15
miscellaneous	2,535	165	2,700

World War II
Merchant Shipping Losses

Source: US Department of Defense

(Ships over 200 tonnes.)

Country	Number of ships
UK	3,194
Japan	2,346
other Allied	1,467
neutral	902
USA	866

World War II
Military Casualties (Wounded)

Country	Wounded
USSR	5,000,000
Germany	N/A
China	1,762,000
Japan	N/A
USA	671,750
Austria	N/A
Poland	530,000
Yugoslavia	425,000
UK	277,000
France	390,000

World War II
Military Casualties (War Dead)

Country	Dead	Country	Dead
Australia	29,400	Italy	226,900
Canada	39,300	Japan	1,740,000
China	1,400,000	New Zealand	12,200
Finland	79,000	Poland	110,800
France	205,700	South Africa	8,700
Germany	3,300,000	UK	305,800
Greece	18,300	USA	292,100
Hungary	136,000	USSR (military and civilian)	6,115,000
India	36,100	total	14,055,300

World War II
Naval Losses

Country	Number of ships lost	Country	Number of ships lost
Germany	672	USSR	102
Japan	433	Netherlands	40
Italy	300	Norway	40
UK	296	Greece	22
USA	157	Others	36
France	129		

World War II
Naval Losses

Figures in brackets indicate vessels scuttled.

Country	Type of vessel						Total
	Aircraft carriers	Battleships	Cruisers	Destroyers	Escorts	Submarines	All vessels
UK	8	5	33	120	71	77	314
USA	11	2	10	71	10	53	157
USSR	–	1	3	33	–	c. 100	137
Germany	–	9 (3)	7 (3)	44 (6)	–	785 (238)	845 (250)
Italy	–	1	11	84	–	84	180
Japan	19	8	37	134	–	130	328

World War II
Worst Military Aircraft Losses

Country	Number of aircraft lost
Germany	95,000
USA	59,295
Japan	49,485
UK	33,090
Australia	7,160
Italy	4,000
Canada	2,390
France	2,100
New Zealand	685
India	525

Years in the Chinese Zodiac

Dates (2000–10)	Animal
5 February 2000–23 January 2001	dragon
24 January 2001–11 February 2002	snake
12 February 2002–31 January 2003	horse
1 February 2003–21 January 2004	goat
22 January 2004–8 February 2005	monkey
9 February 2005–28 January 2006	cockerel
29 January 2006–17 February 2007	dog
18 February 2000–6 February 2008	pig
7 February 2008–25 January 2009	rat
26 January 2009–9 February 2010	ox

Zodiac
Signs of the Zodiac

Sign	Element	Symbol	Dates
Aries	fire	ram	21 March–20 April
Taurus	earth	bull	20 April–21 May
Gemini	air	twins	21 May–21 June
Cancer	water	crab	21 June–23 July
Leo	fire	lion	23 July–23 August
Virgo	earth	virgin	23 August–23 September
Libra	air	balance	23 September–23 October
Scorpio	water	scorpion	23 October–22 November
Sagittarius	fire	archer	22 November–22 December
Capricorn	earth	goat	22 December–20 January
Aquarius	air	water bearer	20 January–19 February
Pisces	water	fishes	19 February–21 March

Geography
and
Transport

Air Disasters
Fatal Air Disasters

Year	Fatal accidents	Passenger deaths	Death rate (per million passenger kilometres flown)	Year	Fatal accidents	Passenger deaths	Death rate (per million passenger kilometres flown)
1999	20	492	2	1994	28	941	4
1998	20	905	3	1993	35	940	5
1997	27	930	4	1992	29	1,097	6
1996	23	1,135	5	1991	30	653	4
1995	26	710	3	1990	25	495	3

Air Disasters
Recent Air Disasters

Only disasters in which ten or more persons have died are listed. As of July 2000.

Date	Aircraft	Location	Details	Fatalities
25 July 2000	Air France Concorde	near Paris, France	caught fire on take-off from Charles de Gaulle airport, Paris, and crashed into a hotel near the airport	113
17 July 2000	Alliance Air 737-200	near Patna, India	during second approach to Patna airport, crashed into a residential area about 2 km from the airport	51
8 July 2000	Aerocaribe BAe Jetstream 32	Villaharmosa, Mexico	crashed in bad weather about 30 minutes after take-off	19
19 April 2000	Air Philippines 737-200	near Davao, Philippines	crashed on Samal Island during second approach to Davao's airport	131
31 January 2000	Alaska Airlines MD83	near Pt Mugu (CA), USA	crashed into Pacific ocean	88
30 January 2000	Kenya Airways A310-300	near Abidjan, Ivory Coast	aircraft crashed into Atlantic Ocean shortly after take-off	170
10 January 2000	Crossair Saab 340	near Zurich, Switzerland	crashed shortly after take-off	10
24 December 1999	Cubana Yak42	near Valencia, Venezuela	aircraft struck high ground on approach to Valencia	22
21 December 1999	Cubana DC10-30	Guatemala City, Guatemala	aircraft overran wet runway and came to rest in a residential neighbourhood near the airport	26
11 December 1999	SATA ATP	Azores, Portugal	crashed on Sao Jorge island	35

Air Disasters
World's Worst Accidents

As of July 2000.

Date	Aircraft	Location	Details	Fatalities
March 1977	Dutch Boeing 747 and US Boeing 747	Tenerife, Canary Islands, Spain	collision on runway	583
August 1985	Japanese Boeing 747	Mount Ogura, Japan	crashed into mountain	520
November 1996	Saudi Arabian Boeing 747-100 and Kazakh Ilyushin IL-76	Charkhi Dadri, India	mid-air collision	349
March 1974	Turkish DC10	Bois d'Ermenonville, near Paris, France	crashed	346
June 1985	Indian Boeing 747	Atlantic Ocean, south of Ireland	crashed	329
August 1980	Saudi Arabian Tristar	Riyadh, Saudi Arabia	burned after emergency landing	301
July 1988	Iranian A300 Airbus	The Gulf	shot down by US Navy warship *Vincennes*	290
May 1979	US DC10	O'Hare International Airport, Chicago (IL), USA	crashed after take-off	275
December 1988	US Boeing 747	Lockerbie, Scotland	exploded and crashed	270
September 1983	South Korean Boeing 747	near Sakhalin Island, Okhokst Sea	shot down after violating Soviet airspace	269

Air Disasters
Worst Aircraft Collisions

Place	Aircraft involved	Date	Number killed
Tenerife, Canary Islands	Two Boeing 747s	1977	582
New Delhi, India	Boeing 747 and Ilyushin-76	1996	349
Zagreb, Yugoslavia	BA Trident and charter DC-9	1976	176
Morioka, Japan	Boeing 727 and F-86 fighter	1971	162
San Diego, USA	Pacific Southwest plane and Cessna	1978	144
New York City, USA	United DC-8 and Transworld Super Constellation	1960	134
Tehran, Iran	Airliner and military jet	1993	132
Painted Desert, USA	United Airlines DC-7 and TWA Super Constellation	1956	128

Aircraft
First Flights by Non-propeller Powered Aircraft

Year	Aircraft	Engine	Nationality
1939	Heinkel He 176	Rocket	German
1939	Heinkel He 178	Jet	German
1940	Caproni-Campini N-1	Jet	Italian
1940	DFS 194	Rocket	German
1941	Gloster E28	Jet	English
1941	Heinkel He 280V-1	Jet	German
1941	Messerschmitt Me 163	Rocket	German
1942	Bell XP-59A	Jet	US

Airlines
Largest Domestic

Airline	Number of passengers in 1998
Delta Air Lines	98,000,000
United Airlines	76,000,000
American Airlines	64,000,000
US Airways	54,000,000
Northwest Airlines	48,000,000

Airlines
Largest International

Airline	Number of passengers in 1998
British Airways	30,315,000
Lufthansa	27,287,000
Air France	20,743,000
American Airlines	17,397,000
KLM	15,322,000

Airports
With Most Passengers

Airport	Number of passengers in 1999 (millions)
Atlanta	77.9
Chicago O'Hare	72.6
Los Angeles International	63.9
London Heathrow	62.3
Dallas Fort Worth	60.0
Tokyo Honeda	54.3
Frankfurt	45.9
Paris Charles de Gaulle	43.6
San Francisco	40.4
Denver	38.0

Airports
World's Busiest

Airport	Number of take-offs and landings 1997	Airport	Number of take-offs and landings 1997
Chicago O'Hare, Illinois, USA	883,760	Detroit, Michigan, USA	541,220
Dallas Fort Worth, Texas, USA	851,190	Miami, Florida, USA	533,080
Atlanta, Georgia, USA	794,620	Oakland, California, USA	519,500
Los Angeles, California, USA	781,490	Phoenix, Arizona, USA	518,900
Sydney Bankstown, Australia	620,960	St Louis, Missouri, USA	516,890

Airships
Worst Airship Accidents

Place	Airship	Date	Number killed
off East Coast, USA	*Akron* (US)	1933	73
Beauvais, France	*R101* (UK)	1930	47
Hull, UK	*R38* (UK)	1921	44
Lakehurst, USA	*Hindenburg* (German)	1937	36
Caldwell, USA	*Shenandoah* (US)	1925	14

Area of Countries
World's Largest

Independent countries, members of the United Nations.

Country	Area (sq km/sq mi)
Russian Federation	17,075,500/6,592,885
Canada	9,971,000/3,849,823
China	9,597,000/3,705,421
USA	9,363,500/3,615,266
Brazil	8,547,500/3,300,207
Australia	7,741,000/2,988,816
India	3,287,500/1,269,310
Argentina	2,780,500/1,073,557
Kazakhstan	2,725,000/1,052,128
Algeria	2,382,000/919,695

Area of Countries
World's Smallest

Independent countries, members of the United Nations or observers there.

Country	Area (sq km/sq mi)
Holy See (Vatican City)	0.5/0.2
Monaco	2/0.8
Nauru	21/8
Tuvalu	26/10
San Marino	60/23
Liechtenstein	160/62
Marshall Islands	181/70
Saint Kitts and Nevis	269/104
Maldives	300/116
Malta	320/124

Australia
Areas of States and Territories

State/Territory	Area (sq km/sq mi)
Australian Antarctic Territory	6,044,000/2,333,600
Western Australia	2,525,500/975,101
Queensland	1,727,200/666,875
Northern Territory	1,346,200/519,771
South Australia	984,400/380,079
New South Wales	801,600/309,499
Victoria	227,600/87,877
Tasmania	67,800/26,178
Australian Capital Territory	2,400/927
Christmas Island	150/60

Australia
Capitals of States and Territories

Capital	State
Adelaide	South Australia
Brisbane	Queensland
Hobart	Tasmania
Melbourne	Victoria
Perth	Western Australia
Sydney	New South Wales
	Territory
Canberra	Australian Capital Territory
Darwin	Northern Territory

Australia

Population of States and Territories

State/Territory	Population
New South Wales	6,341,600
Victoria	4,660,900
Queensland	3,456,300
Western Australia	1,831,400
South Australia	1,487,300
Tasmania	471,900
Australian Capital Territory	308,400
Northern Territory	190,000
Christmas Island	2,500
Australian Antarctic Territory	uninhabited

Aviation

Distances Flown per Country

Country	Passenger km (millions)/mi (millions) flown in 1997
USA	261,741/162,638
UK	129,725/80,607
Japan	84,098/52,256
Germany	79,338/49,298
Netherlands	66,124/41,088
Singapore	55,459/34,461
France	54,823/34,065
South Korea	50,485/31,370
Australia	47,771/29,684
Canada	40,928/25,431

Aviation

First Atlantic Air Crossings

Date	Aircraft	People aboard (nationality)
16-27 May 1919	NC-4 (flying boat)	Lt Com Albert Read (USA)
		Lt Walter Hinton (USA)
		Lt Elmer F Stone (USA)
		Lt James L Breese (USA)
		Chief Eugene S Rhoads (USA)
		Ens Herbert C Rodd (USA)
14-15 June 1919	Vickers Vimy	John Alcock (UK)
		Arthur Whitten Brown (UK)
2-6 July 1919	R-34 (airship)	George Scott and crew (UK) plus William Ballantyne, the first transatlantic aerial stowaway
12-15 October 1924	Z-R3 (airship)	Dr Hugo Eckener and crew (Germany) plus three US observers
23 January-5 February 1926	Dornier Flying Boat	Ramon Franco and crew (Spain)
13-24 February 1927	Savaoia-Marchetti SS	Francesco De Pindedo and crew (Spain)
20-21 May 1927	Ryan Monoplane	Charles Lindbergh (USA)

Aviation

First Transatlantic Flights

Record	Pilot	Nationality	Date
first transatlantic flight	Albert C Read	US	16–27 May 1919
first non-stop transatlantic flight	John Alcock (pilot), Arthur Whitten Brown (navigator)	English	15 June 1919
first solo non-stop transatlantic	Charles Lindbergh	US	21 May 1927
first east–west transatlantic crossing	Hermann Koehl, James Fitzmaurice	German, Irish	13 April 1928
first woman to fly solo across the Atlantic	Amelia Earhart	US	21 May 1932
first east–west transatlantic solo	James A Mollison	Scottish	18 August 1932
first non-stop transatlantic jet flight	David C Schilling	US	22 September 1950

Aviation
Notable Firsts

Date	Flight	Pilot(s)
15 October 1783	first crewed balloon flight	Pilatre de Rozier
17 December 1903	first heavier than air (aeroplane) flight	Orville Wright
14–15 June 1919	first non-stop transatlantic flight	John Alcock and Arthur Brown
20–21 May 1927	first solo transatlantic flight	Charles Lindbergh
12 April 1961	first space flight	Yuri Gagarin
20 July 1969	first Moon landing	Neil Armstrong and Buzz Aldrin
12–17 August 1978	first transatlantic balloon flight	Maxie Anderson, Ben Abruzzo, Larry Newman
9–12 October 1981	first non-stop transcontinental balloon flight	Fred Gorell and John Shucraft
15–18 September 1984	first solo transatlantic balloon flight	Joe W Kittinger
14–23 December 1986	first non-stop unrefuelled global flight; *Voyager*	Dick Rutan and Jeanna Yeager

Aviation
Selected Enshrinees of the US National Hall of Fame

Pioneer	Year of induction	Pioneer	Year of induction
Armstrong, Harry George	1998	Lear Sr, William P	1978
Armstrong, Neil A	1979	Lindbergh, Charles A	1967
Bell, Alexander Graham	1965	Lockheed, Allan H	1986
Boeing, William E	1966	Lovell, James Arthur, Jr	1998
Cessna, Clyde V	1978	Neumann, Gerhard	1986
Dargue, Herbert	1997	Pitcairn, Harold F	1995
Douglas, Donald W	1969	Rickenbacker, Edward V	1965
Earhart (Putnam), Amelia	1968	Sikorsky, Igor I	1968
Fokker, Anthony H G	1980	Slayton, Donald Kent (Deke)	1996
Ford, Henry	1984	Spaatz, Carl A	1967
Glenn Jr, John H	1976	Wright, Orville	1962
Guggenheim, Harry F	1971	Wright, Wilbur	1962

Balloon Flights

Date	Name of balloonist	Achievement
1782	Joseph Michel and Jacques Etienne Montgolfier	first crewless balloon flight
1783	Jean François Pilâtre de Rozier, Marquis François Laurent D'Arlandes	first crewed free flight in a hot air balloon
1785	Jean François Pilâtre de Rozier; Jean-Pierre Blanchard, John Jeffries	first balloon flights across the English Channel

(*continued*)

Balloon Flights (*continued*)

Date	Name of balloonist	Achievement
1960	Joe W Kittinger	highest parachute jump from a balloon (from 31,333 m/102,799 ft); Kittinger broke the sound barrier with his body
1978	Maxie Anderson, Ben Abruzzo, Larry Newman	first transatlantic balloon flight
1984	Joe W Kittinger	first solo transatlantic balloon flight (5,689 km/3535 mi)
1987	Per Lindstrand, Richard Branson	first hot air balloon to cross the Atlantic (4,490 km/2790 mi in 33 hr); largest flown hot air balloon to date (65,090 cubic metres/2,298,634 cubic feet)
1988	Per Lindstrand	hot air high altitude record (19,812 m/65,000 ft); solo world record
1995	Steve Fossett	first solo transpacific balloon flight; distance record of 8,748 km/5436 mi
1997	Steve Fossett	new distance and endurance records: over 16,093 km/10,000 mi in 6 days, 2 hr, 54 min
1998	Andy Nelson, Wim Verstraeten, Bertrand Piccard	longest ever continuous flight without refuelling
1999	Brian Jones, Bertrand Piccard	first non-stop balloon flight around the world
2000	David Hempleman-Adams	first solo flight across the Arctic Ocean

Borders
Countries with Longest Land Borders

Many countries, ranging in size from Australia to tiny island nations, have no land borders – that is, they have no neighbouring countries.

Country	Length of border (km/mi)
China	22,143/13,759
Russia	19,917/12,376
Brazil	14,691/9,129
India	14,103/8,763
USA	12,248/7,611
Kazakhstan	12,012/7,464
Democratic Republic of the Congo	10,744/6,676
Argentina	9,665/6,006
Canada	8,893/5,526
Mongolia	8,114/5,042
Sudan	7,687/4,776
Mali	7,243/4,501

Borders
Countries with Shortest Land Borders

Country	Length of border (km/mi)
Vatican City	3.2/2.0
Monaco	4.4/2.7
San Marino	39/24
Qatar	60/37
Denmark	68/42
Liechtenstein	76/47
Andorra	125/78
South Korea	238/148
Haiti (shared border)	275/171
Dominican Republic (shared border)	275/171

Canada
Area of Provinces

Province	% of total area	Area (sq km/sq mi) Land	Freshwater	Total
Nunavut	21.0	1,936,110/747,536	157,080/60,653	2,093,190/808,185
Quebec	15.4	1,365,130/527,079	176,930/68,313	1,542,060/595,393
Northwest Territories	13.5	1,183,080/456,789	163,020/62,942	1,346,100/519,732
Ontario	10.8	917,740/354,341	158,650/61,255	1,076,390/415,597
British Columbia	9.5	925,190/357,218	19,550/7,548	944,740/364,766
Alberta	6.6	642,320/248,001	19,530/7,541	661,850/255,542
Saskatchewan	6.5	591,670/228,445	59,370/22,923	651,040/251,368
Manitoba	6.5	553,560/213,731	94,240/36,386	647,800/250,117
Yukon	4.8	474,390/183,163	8,050/3,108	482,440/186,271
Newfoundland	4.1	373,870/144,352	31,340/12,100	405,210/156,452
New Brunswick	0.7	71,450/27,587	1,460/564	72,910/28,151
Nova Scotia	0.6	53,340/20,595	1,950/753	55,290/21,348
Prince Edward Island	0.1	5,660/2,185	0	5,660/2,185
Canada, total	100.0	9,093,510/3,511,022	891,170/344,083	9,984,680/3,855,105

Canada
Capitals of Provinces and Territories

Capital	Province
Charlottetown	Prince Edward Island
Edmonton	Alberta
Fredericton	New Brunswick
Halifax	Nova Scotia
Iqaluit	Nunavut (semi-autonomous region)
Québec	Québec
Regina	Saskatchewan
St John's	Newfoundland
Toronto	Ontario
Victoria	British Columbia
Whitehorse	Yukon Territory
Winnipeg	Manitoba
Yellowknife	Northwest Territories

Canada
Population of Provinces and Territories

Province/territory	Population
Ontario	10,753,600
Québec	7,138,800
British Columbia	3,724,500
Alberta	2,696,800
Manitoba	1,113,900
Saskatchewan	990,200
Nova Scotia	909,300
New Brunswick	738,100
Newfoundland	551,800
Prince Edward Island	134,600
Northwest Territories	40,400
Yukon Territory	30,800
Nunavut (semi-autonomous region)	24,000

Canals
Some Famous Canals and Waterways

Name	Country	Opened
St Lawrence	Canada	1959
Volga-Don	Russian Federation, Belarus, Ukraine	1952
Grand Canal	China	485 BC–AD 1972
Erie	USA	1825
Baltic–White Sea	Russian Federation	1933
Bridgewater Canal	UK	1761
Suez	Egypt	1869
Kiel	Germany	1895
Panama	Panama (US zone)	1914
Manchester Ship Canal	UK	1894

Canals
World's Longest

Canal	Route	Length (km/mi)
Karakum Canal, Turkmenistan	Caspian Sea inland	1,100/684
New York State Barge Canal (Erie Canal), USA	Lake Erie to Hudson River	875/544
Volga-Baltic, Russia	River Volga to Baltic Sea	850/528
Rajasthan Canal, India	River Indus (Punjab) to Myajlan	650/404
St Lawrence Seaway, Canada–USA	Montreal to Lake Ontario	305/190
Main-Danube Canal, Germany	Main River (Bamberg) to Danube River	170/106
Suez Canal, Egypt	Mediterranean Sea to Red Sea	160/99
Albert Canal, Belgium	River Meuse (Maes) to River Scheld	130/81
Volga-Don, Russia	River Volga to Black Sea	100/62
Kiel Canal, Germany	North Sea to Baltic Sea	100/62

Capitals
Capital Cities of the World

Capital city	Country	Capital city	Country
Abu Dhabi	United Arab Emirates	Ankara	Turkey
Abuja	Nigeria	Antananarivo	Madagascar
Accra	Ghana	Apia	Samoa
Addis Ababa	Ethiopia	Ashgabat	Turkmenistan
Al Manamah	Bahrain	Asmara	Eritrea
Algiers	Algeria	Astana	Kazakhstan
Amman	Jordan	Asunción	Paraguay
Amsterdam	Netherlands, The	Athens	Greece
Andorra la Vella	Andorra	Baghdad	Iraq

Capitals: Capital Cities of the World (*continued*)

Capital city	Country	Capital city	Country
Bairiki	Kiribati	Dushanbe	Tajikistan
Baku	Azerbaijan	Fongafale	Tuvalu
Bamako	Mali	Freetown	Sierra Leone
Bandar Seri Begawan	Brunei	Gaborone	Botswana
Bangkok	Thailand	Georgetown	Guyana
Bangui	Central African Republic	Guatemala City	Guatemala
		Hanoi	Vietnam
Banjul	Gambia, The	Harare	Zimbabwe
Basseterre	St Kitts and Nevis	Havana	Cuba
Beijing	China	Helsinki	Finland
Beirut	Lebanon	Honiara	Solomon Islands
Belgrade	Yugoslavia	Islamabad	Pakistan
Belmopan	Belize	Jakarta	Indonesia
Berlin	Germany	Jerusalem	Israel
Bern	Switzerland	Kabul	Afghanistan
Bishkek	Kyrgyzstan	Kampala	Uganda
Bissau	Guinea-Bissau	Kathmandu	Nepal
Bogotá	Colombia	Khartoum	Sudan
Brasília	Brazil	Kiev	Ukraine
Bratislava	Slovak Republic	Kigali	Rwanda
Brazzaville	Congo, Republic of	Kingston	Jamaica
Bridgetown	Barbados	Kingstown	St Vincent and the Grenadines
Brussels	Belgium		
Bucharest	Romania	Kinshasa	Congo, Democratic Republic of
Budapest	Hungary		
Buenos Aires	Argentina	Koror	Palau
Bujumbura	Burundi	Kuala Lumpur	Malaysia
Cairo	Egypt	Kuwait	Kuwait
Canberra	Australia	La Paz (seat of government), Sucre (legal capital and seat of judiciary)	Bolivia
Cape Town (legislative), Pretoria (administrative), Bloemfontein (judicial)	South Africa		
		Libreville	Gabon
Caracas	Venezuela	Lilongwe	Malawi
Castries	St Lucia	Lima	Peru
Chişinău	Moldova	Lisbon	Portugal
Colombo	Sri Lanka	Ljubljana	Slovenia
Conakry	Guinea	Lomé	Togo
Copenhagen	Denmark	London	United Kingdom
Dakar	Senegal	Luanda	Angola
Dalap-Uliga-Darrit	Marshall Islands	Lusaka	Zambia
Damascus	Syria	Luxembourg	Luxembourg
Dhaka	Bangladesh	Madrid	Spain
Djibouti	Djibouti	Malabo	Equatorial Guinea
Dodoma	Tanzania	Malé	Maldives
Doha	Qatar	Managua	Nicaragua
Dublin	Ireland, Republic of	Manila	Philippines
		Maputo	Mozambique

(*continued*)

Capitals: Capital Cities of the World (*continued*)

Capital city	Country	Capital city	Country
Maseru	Lesotho	São Tomé	São Tomé and Príncipe
Mbabane	Swaziland		
Mexico City	Mexico	San José	Costa Rica
Minsk	Belarus	San Marino	San Marino
Mogadishu	Somalia	San Salvador	El Salvador
Monrovia	Liberia	San'a	Yemen
Montevideo	Uruguay	Santiago	Chile
Moroni	Comoros	Santo Domingo	Dominican Republic
Moscow	Russian Federation	Sarajevo	Bosnia-Herzegovina
Muscat	Oman	Seoul	South Korea
Nairobi	Kenya	Singapore City	Singapore
Nassau	Bahamas	Skopje	Macedonia
Ndjamena	Chad	Sofia	Bulgaria
New Delhi	India	St George's	Grenada
Niamey	Niger	St John's	Antigua and Barbuda
Nicosia	Cyprus	Stockholm	Sweden
no capital	Monaco	Suva	Fiji Islands
no capital	Vatican City State	Taipei	Taiwan
Nouakchott	Mauritania	Tallinn	Estonia
Nuku'alofa	Tonga	Tashkent	Uzbekistan
Oslo	Norway	Tbilisi	Georgia
Ottawa	Canada	Tegucigalpa	Honduras
Ouagadougou	Burkina Faso	Tehran	Iran
Palikir	Micronesia, Federated States of	Thimphu	Bhutan
		Tirana	Albania
Panamá	Panama	Tokyo	Japan
Paramaribo	Suriname	Tripoli	Libya
Paris	France	Tunis	Tunisia
Phnom Penh	Cambodia	Ulaanbaatar	Mongolia
Port Louis	Mauritius	Vaduz	Liechtenstein
Port Moresby	Papua New Guinea	Valletta	Malta
Port-au-Prince	Haiti	Victoria	Seychelles
Port-of-Spain	Trinidad and Tobago	Vienna	Austria
Port-Vila	Vanuatu	Vientiane	Laos
Porto-Novo (official), Cotonou (de facto)	Benin	Vilnius	Lithuania
		Warsaw	Poland
Prague	Czech Republic	Washington, DC	United States of America
Praia	Cape Verde		
Pyongyang	North Korea	Wellington	New Zealand
Quito	Ecuador	Windhoek	Namibia
Rabat	Morocco	Yamoussoukro	Côte d'Ivoire
Reykjavik	Iceland	Yangon	Myanmar
Riga	Latvia	Yaoundé	Cameroon
Riyadh	Saudi Arabia	Yaren (de facto)	Nauru
Rome	Italy	Yerevan	Armenia
Roseau	Dominica	Zagreb	Croatia

Cars

Commercial Motor Vehicle Ownership

Country	Commercial vehicle ownership in 1998
USA	78,750,000
Japan	20,918,800
Former Soviet Union	8,595,000
France	5,500,000
China	5,200,000
Saudi Arabia	4,375,000
Thailand	4,075,500
Mexico	3,820,000
Canada	3,714,500
Spain	3,561,600

Cars

Commercial Motor Vehicle Production

Country	Commercial vehicle production in 1998
USA	6,487,900
Japan	1,994,000
Brazil	1,342,800
Canada	1,088,600
Spain	609,700
China	573,600[1]
Mexico	457,200
South Korea	382,800
Germany	378,700
France	341,100

[1] 1997 estimate.

Cars

Fastest

Model	Top speed	
	km/h	mph
McLaren F1	372	231
Lambourghini Diablo 6.0 GT	341	212
Aston Martin Le Mans	322+	200+
Ferrari Marranello	320	199
Porsche 911 Turbo	304	189
Ferrari 456 MGT	299	186
Ferrari F355 Spider	298	185
Aston Martin DB7 Vantage	298	185
Ferrari 360 Modena	296	184
Chevrolet Corvette Coupe	282	175

Cars

Most Powerful

Model	Brake horsepower (bhp)
McLaren F1	627
Aston Martin DB7 Vantage	600
Lambourghini Diablo 6.0 GT	575
Aston Martin Le Mans	550
Ferrari 550 Marranello	485
Porsche 911 Turbo	450
Ferrari 456 GT	434
Bentley Continental T	420
Bentley Azure Continental	420
Aston Martin Vantage	420

Cars

Named after People

Car	Person	Life dates	Nationality
Austin	Herbert Austin	1866–1941	English
Chevrolet	Louis Chevrolet	1879–1941	US
Chrysler	Walter Chrysler	1875–1940	US
Citröen	André-Gustav Citröen	1878–1935	French
Daimler	Gottfried Daimler	1834–1900	German

(continued)

Cars: Named after People (*continued*)

Car	Person	Life dates	Nationality
Ferrari	Enzo Ferrari	1898–1988	Italian
Ford	Henry Ford	1863–1947	US
Honda	Soichiro Honda	1906–1992	Japanese
Opel	Fritz von Opel	1899–1971	German
Porsche	Ferdinand Porsche	1875–1951	German
Rolls-Royce	Charles Rolls	1877–1910	British
	Henry Royce	1863–1933	British
Toyota	Kiichiro Toyoda	1894–1952	Japanese

Cars
Production

Country	Car production
Japan	8,055,800
USA	5,547,100
Germany	5,348,100
France	2,582,300
Spain	2,216,400
UK	1,748,300
South Korea	1,576,800
Canada	1,481,100
Italy	1,402,400

Cars
With the Largest Engines

Model	Engine size (cc)
Bentley Arnage – Red Label	6,750
McLaren F1	6,064
Mercedes Benz SL60 AMG	5,956
Bristol Blenheim 2	5,900
Mercedes Benz CL600	5,786
Chevrolet Camaro Z28 Coupe	5,700
Chevrolet Corvette Coupe	5,666
Ferrari 500 Marranello	5,474
Mercedes Benz E55 AMG	5,439
Aston Martin Vantage	5,395

Carts and Carriages

Vehicle	Description
akka	small, two-wheeled carriage (in India)
barouche	four-wheeled carriage with a pair of inward-facing seats and a folding hood over the rear seats
berlin	covered, four-wheeled, two-seater carriage
brake	open, four-wheeled carriage (also break); also a strong, heavy cart with only a driver's seat, used for breaking horses to harness
britzka	long, four-wheeled carriage with two rear-facing seats at the front and a folding hood over the rear, forward-facing seats
brougham	one-horse, four-wheeled, two- or four-seater closed carriage with a raised, open driver's seat
buckboard	open, four-wheeled carriage with a seat on springy boards, situated between the axles
buggy	light, one-horse, two- or four-wheeled carriage
cab	light carriage for public hire
cabriolet	small, one-horse, two-wheeled, two-seater carriage with a folding hood
calash	low, small-wheeled carriage with a folding top

Carts and Carriages (*continued*)

Vehicle	Description
Cape cart	two-wheeled carriage, often with a hood
cariole or carriole	small, open, two-wheeled carriage, usually for one, or a covered light cart
caroche	16th century ceremonial carriage
carryall	light, one-horse, four-wheeled carriage for four passengers
chaise	light, open, two-wheeled carriage for one or two people
chariot	two-wheeled vehicle used in warfare by the ancients, or a light, four-wheeled ceremonial carriage
clarence	closed, four-wheeled carriage with a glass front, for two or more people
coach	large, four-wheeled, closed carriage, also called coach-and-four
Conestoga wagon	large, heavy, covered wagon (in the USA)
coupé	four-wheeled carriage with a seat for two inside and one outside for the driver
covered wagon	large, wagon with an arched canvas top
curricle	two-horse (abreast), two-wheeled open carriage
diligence or dilly	four-wheeled public stagecoach (originally in France)
dogcart	light, one-horse, two-wheeled carriage with side-facing, back-to-back seats (and originally a box section for carrying dogs)
drag	long, generally four-horse, open sporting coach with seats inside and out
dray	strong, heavily wheeled, low cart without sides
droshky	low, four-wheeled, open carriage (in the Russian Federation)
equipage	horse-drawn carriage with (liveried) attendants
fiacre	small, four-wheeled carriage, usually with a folding top; a French hackney cab
fly	light, one-horse hackney carriage (built for speed)
fourgon	long, covered wagon (for luggage or supplies)
four-in-hand	carriage drawn by four horses, but with only one driver (also called tally-ho)
gharry or gharri	carriage for hire (in India)
gig	light, one-horse, two-wheeled carriage without a hood
growler	four-wheeled hansom cab
hackney	carriage for hire
hansom (cab)	one-horse, two-wheeled carriage with a fixed hood and raised driver's seat behind
haywain	large, farm wagon or cart for carrying hay (also haycart)
herdic	small, low, two- or four-wheeled carriage with side seats and a rear entrance
jaunty	low, light, two-wheeled open cart with side-facing seats back-to-back (in Ireland); also jaunting car
karrozzin	horse-drawn cab (in Malta)
kibitka	covered sledge or wagon (in the Russian Federation)

(*continued*)

Carts and Carriages (*continued*)

Vehicle	Description
kuruma	Japanese rickshaw
landau	four-wheeled carriage with a pair of folding hoods, which meet over the seats, that can be both open, one open or both closed
landaulet(te)	small landau with seats on only one side and only the rear half of the hood openable
oxcart	farm cart drawn by an ox or oxen
phaeton	light, one- or (usually) two-horse, open, four-wheeled, one- or two-seater carriage, often with no sides to the front seat(s)
post chaise	closed, four-wheeled coach for rapidly carrying passengers and mail
prairie schooner	another name for a covered wagon
pung	horse-drawn sleigh with a boxlike body (in Canada and the USA)
quadriga	two-wheeled chariot drawn by four horses abreast (in ancient Greece and Rome)
randem	carriage drawn by a team of three horses
ratha	horse- or bullock-drawn, four-wheeled carriage (in India)
rickshaw	small, human-drawn, two-wheeled carriage
rig	carriage or wagon and its horse or horses (in the USA and Canada)
rockaway	four-wheeled carriage with two seats and a hard top (in the USA)
sociable	four-wheeled, open carriage with two side-seats facing inwards
spider phaeton	light, four-wheeled carriage with large thin wheels and a high body
stagecoach	large post chaise on a regular route
stanhope	light, open, two- or four-wheeled carriage for one person
sulky	light, one-horse carriage for one person, often without coachwork
surrey	light, four-wheeled carriage with two or four seats
tandem	two-wheeled carriage drawn by two horses harnessed one behind the other
tarantass	large, four-wheeled, covered carriage with no springs (in the Russian Federation)
tilbury	light, open, two-wheeled carriage for two people
tonga	light, two-wheeled cart for four people (in India)
trap	general term for any light, two-wheeled carriage
trishaw	see rickshaw
troika	carriage or sleigh drawn by three horses abreast (in the Russian Federation)
tumbrel or tumbril	back-tipping, two-wheeled farm cart
victoria	low, light, four-wheeled, two-seater carriage with a folding hood and a raised driver's seat at the front
vis-à-vis	light carriage for two people, with seats facing each other
volante	two-wheeled carriage (in Cuba and formerly in Spain)
wagon or waggon	horse-drawn, four-wheeled cart for heavy loads
wagonette	light, four-wheeled carriage with two lengthwise, inward-facing seats and a crosswise driver's seat
wain	farm cart (see haywain)

Caves

World's Deepest Caves

Name	Location	Depth (m/ft)
Jean Bernard	French Antarctica	1,495/4,905
Snezhnaya	Caucasus	1,340/4,396
Puertas de Illamina	Spain	1,340/4,396
Pierre-Saint-Martin	French Antarctica	1,320/4,331
Sistema Huautla	Mexico	1,240/4,068
Berger	French Antarctica	1,200/3,937
Vqerdi	Spain	1,195/3,920
Dachstein-Mammuthöhle	Austria	1,175/3,855
Zitu	Spain	1,140/3,740
Badolona	Spain	1,130/3,707

China

Capitals of Provinces

Capital	Province
Changchun	Jilin
Changsha	Hunan
Chengdu	Sichuan
Fuzhou	Fujian
Guangzhou	Guangdong
Guiyang	Guizhou
Haikou	Hainan
Hangzhou	Zhejiang
Harbin	Heilongjiang
Hefei	Anhui
Jinan	Shandong
Kumming	Yunnan
Lanzhou	Gansu
Nanchang	Jiangxi
Nanjing	Jiangsu
Shenyang	Liaoning
Shijiazhuang	Hebei
Taiyuan	Shanxi
Wuhan	Hubei
Xi'an	Shaanxi
Xining	Qinghai
Zhengzhou	Henan

China

Population of Provinces

Province	Population (millions)	Province	Population (millions)	Province	Population (millions)
Sichuan	111.0	Hubei	56.5	Fujian	31.5
Henan	89.5	Zhejiang	42.7	Shanxi	30.1
Shandong	86.4	Liaoning	40.4	Jilin	25.6
Jiangsu	69.7	Jiangxi	39.7	Gansu	23.5
Guangdong	66.1	Yunnan	38.8	Hainan	7.0
Hebei	63.3	Heilongjiang	36.4	Qinghai	4.7
Hunan	63.1	Shaanxi	34.4		
Anhui	59.0	Guizhou	34.1		

China

Area of Provinces

Province	Alternative transliteration/English name	Area	
		sq km	sq mi
Qinghai	Tsinghai	721,000	278,378
Sichuan	Szechwan	569,000	219,691
Gansu	Kansu	530,000	204,633

(continued)

China: Area of Provinces *(continued)*

Province	Alternative transliteration/English name	Area sq km	sq mi
Heilongjiang	Heilungkiang	463,600	178,996
Yunnan	–	436,200	168,417
Guangdong	Kwantung	231,400	89,343
Hunan	–	210,500	81,274
Hebei	Hopei	202,700	78,262
Shaanxi	Shensi	195,800	75,598
Hubei	Hupei	187,500	72,394
Jilin	Kirin	187,000	72,201
Guizhou	Kweichow	174,000	67,181
Henan	Honan	167,000	64,479
Jiangxi	Kiangsi	164,800	63,629
Shanxi	Shansi	157,100	60,656
Shandong	Shantung	153,300	59,189
Liaoning	–	151,000	58,301
Anhui	Anhwei	139,900	54,015
Fujian	Fukien	123,100	47,528
Jiangsu	Kiangsu	102,200	39,459
Zhejiang	Chekiang	101,800	39,305
Hainan	–	34,000	13,127

Circumnavigation

First of the World

Type of craft	Record	Expedition leader	Nationality	Name of craft	Date completed trip
ship	first to sail round the world	Ferdinand Magellan (died en route and was succeeded as captain by Sebastian del Cano)	Portuguese	*Vittoria*	6 September 1522
	first solo	Joshua Slocum	Canadian	*Spray*	27 June 1898
plane	first to fly round the world	Lowell Smith, Leslie P Arnold	US	*Chicago, New Orleans*	28 September 1924
	first to fly non-stop round the globe	James Gallagher	US	*Lucky Lady II* (B-50 Superfortress)	2 March 1949
	first to fly non-stop round the globe without refuelling	Richard Rutan, Jeana Yeager	US	*Voyager* (custom built)	23 December 1986
	first solo	Wiley Post	US	*Winnie Mae* (Lockheed Vega)	1933
	first solo woman	Jerri Mock	US	*Spirit of Columbus* (Cessna 180)	17 April 1964

Circumnavigation: First of the World (*continued*)

Type of craft	Record	Expedition leader	Nationality	Name of craft	Date completed trip
helicopter	first circumnavigation	H Ross Perot Jr, Jay Coburn	US	*Spirit of Texas* (Bell 206L-1 Long Ranger II)	30 September 1982
	first solo	Dick Smith	Australian	*Australian Explorer* (Bell 206 Long Ranger III)	22 July 1983
	first solo woman	Jennifer Murray	English	*Robinson R44*	6 September 2000
microlight	first solo	Colin Bodill	English	*Mainair Blade 912S*	6 September 2000

Cities
Altitude of Major Cities in the Northern Hemisphere

City	Altitude (m/ft)	City	Altitude (m/ft)
Algiers, Algeria	59/194	Havana, Cuba	24/79
Almaty, Kazakhstan	775/2,543	Helsinki, Finland	46/151
Amsterdam, Netherlands	3/10	Hong Kong, China	33/108
Ankara, Turkey	862/2,828	Istanbul, Turkey	114/374
Athens, Greece	92/302	Jerusalem, Israel	762/2,500
Bangkok, Thailand	0	Kabul, Afghanistan	1,827/5,994
Barcelona, Spain	93/305	Karachi, Pakistan	4/13
Beijing, China	183/600	Kiev, Ukraine	179/587
Belfast, Northern Ireland	67/220	Lagos, Nigeria	3/10
Belgrade, Yugoslavia	132/433	Lhasa, Tibet	3,685/12,090
Berlin, Germany	34/112	Lisbon, Portugal	77/253
Bogotá, Colombia	2,640/8,661	London, England	75/246
Brussels, Belgium	100/328	Los Angeles (CA), USA	104/341
Bucharest, Romania	92/302	Madrid, Spain	660/2,165
Budapest, Hungary	139/456	Manila, Philippines	14/46
Cairo, Egypt	116/381	Melbourne, Australia	35/115
Caracas, Venezuela	1,042/3,419	Mexico City, Mexico	2,239/7,346
Copenhagen, Denmark	9/30	Montevideo, Uruguay	22/72
Dakar, Senegal	40/131	Moscow, Russian Federation	120/394
Delhi, India	218/715	Mumbai (formerly Bombay), India	8/26
Detroit (MI), USA	178/584	
Djibouti, Djibouti	7/23	Nairobi, Kenya	1,820/5,971
Dublin, Republic of Ireland	47/154	New Delhi, India	235/771
Edinburgh, Scotland	134/440	New York (NY), USA	17/56
Frankfurt, Germany	103/338	Oslo, Norway	94/308
Guatemala City, Guatemala	1,480/4,856	Ottawa, Canada	56/184

(*continued*)

City	Altitude (m/ft)	City	Altitude (m/ft)
Panamá, Panama	0	Stockholm, Sweden	44/144
Paris, France	92/302	Tehran, Iran	1,110/3,642
Prague, Czech Republic	262/860	Tokyo, Japan	9/30
Reykjavik, Iceland	18/59	Toronto, Canada	91/299
Rome, Italy	29/95	Tripoli, Libya	0
St Petersburg, Russian Federation	4/13	Vancouver, Canada	43/141
		Vienna, Austria	203/666
Seoul, South Korea	10/33	Warsaw, Poland	110/361
Shanghai, China	7/23	Washington, DC, USA	8/26
Singapore	10/33	Zurich, Switzerland	493/1,617
Sofia, Bulgaria	550/1,804		

Cities
Altitude of Major Cities in the Southern Hemisphere

City	Altitude (m/ft)
Adelaide, Australia	43/141
Asunción, Paraguay	139/456
Buenos Aires, Argentina	0
Cape Town, South Africa	17/56
Jakarta, Indonesia	8/27
Johannesburg, South Africa	1,750/5,741
Katmandu, Nepal	1,372/4,501
Kinshasa, Democratic Republic of Congo	322/1,056
La Paz, Bolivia	3,658/12,001
Lima, Peru	120/394
Mecca, Saudi Arabia	2,000/6,562
Milan, Italy	121/397
Nagasaki, Japan	133/436
Quito, Ecuador	2,811/9,222
Rio de Janeiro, Brazil	9/30
Santiago, Chile	1,500/4,921
Sydney, Australia	8/26
Wellington, New Zealand	0

Cities
Cities with Largest Populations

City	Population (millions)	City	Population (millions)
Tokyo, Japan	28.0	Shanghai, China	14.2
Mexico City, Mexico	18.1	Lagos, Nigeria	13.5
Mumbai, India	18.0	Los Angeles, USA	13.1
São Paulo, Brazil	17.7	Kolkata (formerly Calcutta), India	12.9
New York, USA	16.6	Buenos Aires, Argentina	12.4

Cities
Growth of the World's Largest Cities

1975		1995		2015	
City	Population (millions)	City	Population (millions)	City	Population (millions)
Tokyo, Japan	19.77	Tokyo, Japan	26.95	Tokyo, Japan	28.90
New York, USA	15.88	Mexico City, Mexico	16.56	Mumbai, India	26.20
Shanghai, China	11.44	São Paulo, Brazil	16.53	Lagos, Nigeria	24.60
Mexico City, Mexico	11.24	New York, USA	16.33	São Paulo, Brazil	20.30
São Paulo, Brazil	10.05	Mumbai, India	15.14	Dhaka, Bangladesh	19.50
Osaka, Japan	9.84	Shanghai,	13.58	Karachi, Pakistan	19.40
Buenos Aires, Argentina	9.14	Los Angeles, USA	12.47	Mexico City, Mexico	19.20
Los Angeles, USA	8.93	Kolkata (formerly Calcutta), India	11.92	Shanghai, China	18.00
Paris, France	8.88	Buenos Aires, Argentina	11.80	New York, USA	17.60
Beijing, China	8.55	Seoul, South Korea	11.61	Kolkata (formerly Calcutta), India	17.30

Cities

Latitude and Longitude of Major Cities in the Northern Hemisphere

City	Latitude		Longitude	
	°	′	°	′
Algiers, Algeria	36	50 N	03	00 E
Almaty, Kazakhstan	43	16 N	76	53 E
Amsterdam, Netherlands	52	22 N	04	53 E
Ankara, Turkey	39	55 N	32	55 E
Athens, Greece	37	58 N	23	43 E
Bangkok, Thailand	13	45 N	100	31 E
Barcelona, Spain	41	23 N	02	09 E
Beijing, China	39	56 N	116	24 E
Belfast, Northern Ireland	54	37 N	05	56 W
Belgrade, Yugoslavia	44	52 N	20	32 E
Berlin, Germany	52	31 N	13	25 E
Bogotá, Colombia	04	32 N	74	05 W
Brussels, Belgium	50	52 N	04	22 E
Bucharest, Romania	44	25 N	26	07 E
Budapest, Hungary	47	30 N	19	05 E
Cairo, Egypt	30	03 N	31	15 E
Caracas, Venezuela	10	28 N	67	02 W
Copenhagen, Denmark	55	40 N	12	34 E
Dakar, Senegal	14	40 N	17	28 W
Delhi, India	28	35 N	77	12 E
Detroit (MI), USA	42	19 N	83	02 W
Djibouti, Djibouti	11	30 N	43	03 E
Dublin, Republic of Ireland	53	20 N	06	15 W
Edinburgh, Scotland	55	55 N	03	10 W
Frankfurt, Germany	50	07 N	08	41 E
Guatemala City, Guatemala	14	37 N	90	31 W
Havana, Cuba	23	08 N	82	23 W
Helsinki, Finland	60	10 N	25	00 E
Hong Kong, China	22	18 N	114	10 E
Istanbul, Turkey	41	06 N	29	03 E
Jerusalem, Israel	31	46 N	35	14 E
Kabul, Afghanistan	34	30 N	69	13 E
Karachi, Pakistan	24	48 N	66	59 E
Kiev, Ukraine	50	26 N	30	31 E
Lagos, Nigeria	06	27 N	03	24 E

Cities: Latitude and Longitude of Major Cities in the Northern Hemisphere (*continued*)

City	Latitude		Longitude	
	°	'	°	'
Lhasa, Tibet	29	40 N	91	07 E
Lisbon, Portugal	38	44 N	09	09 W
London, England	51	32 N	00	05 W
Los Angeles (CA), USA	34	03 N	118	14 W
Madrid, Spain	40	26 N	03	42 W
Manila, Philippines	14	35 N	120	57 E
Melbourne, Australia	37	47 N	144	58 E
Mexico City, Mexico	19	24 N	99	09 W
Montevideo, Uruguay	34	53 N	56	10 W
Moscow, Russian Federation	55	45 N	37	35 E
Mumbai (formerly Bombay), India	18	58 N	72	50 E
Nairobi, Kenya	01	25 N	36	55 E
New Delhi, India	28	36 N	77	12 E
New York (NY), USA	40	45 N	73	59 W
Oslo, Norway	59	57 N	10	42 E
Ottawa, Canada	45	26 N	75	41 W
Panamá, Panama	08	58 N	79	32 W
Paris, France	48	52 N	02	20 E
Prague, Czech Republic	50	05 N	14	26 E
Reykjavik, Iceland	64	04 N	21	58 W
Rome, Italy	41	53 N	12	30 E
St Petersburg, Russian Federation	59	56 N	30	18 E
Seoul, South Korea	37	34 N	127	00 E
Shanghai, China	31	10 N	121	28 E
Singapore	01	14 N	103	55 E
Sofia, Bulgaria	42	40 N	23	20 E
Stockholm, Sweden	59	17 N	18	03 E
Tehran, Iran	35	40 N	51	26 E
Tokyo, Japan	35	42 N	139	46 E
Toronto, Canada	43	39 N	79	23 W
Tripoli, Libya	32	54 N	13	11 E
Vancouver, Canada	49	18 N	123	04 W
Vienna, Austria	48	14 N	16	20 E
Warsaw, Poland	52	15 N	21	00 E
Washington, DC, USA	38	53 N	77	00 W
Zurich, Switzerland	47	21 N	08	31 E

Cities

Latitude and Longitude of Major Cities in the Southern Hemisphere

City	Latitude		Longitude	
	°	'	°	'
Adelaide, Australia	34	55 S	138	36 E
Asunción, Paraguay	25	15 S	57	40 W
Buenos Aires, Argentina	34	36 S	58	28 W
Cape Town, South Africa	33	55 S	18	22 E
Jakarta, Indonesia	06	10 S	106	48 E
Johannesburg, South Africa	26	12 S	28	05 E
Katmandu, Nepal	27	43 S	85	19 E
Kinshasa, Democratic Republic of Congo	04	18 S	15	17 E
La Paz, Bolivia	16	27 S	68	22 W
Lima, Peru	12	00 S	77	02 W
Mecca, Saudi Arabia	21	27 S	39	49 E
Milan, Italy	45	27 S	09	10 E
Nagasaki, Japan	32	48 S	129	57 E
Quito, Ecuador	0	13 S	78	30 W
Rio de Janeiro, Brazil	22	43 S	43	13 W
Santiago, Chile	33	27 S	70	40 W
Sydney, Australia	33	53 S	151	12 E
Wellington, New Zealand	41	18 S	174	47 E

Coastlines

Countries with the Longest Coastlines

Country	Continent
Russian Federation	Eurasia
Canada	North America
Australia	Australasia
Greenland	North America
Chile	South America
USA	North America
China	Asia
India	Asia
Mexico	North America
Argentina	South America

Continents

Most Populated

Continent	Population (millions)
Asia	3,736
Africa	762
Europe	582
South and Central America	498
North America	300
Australasia	22
Antarctica	virtually uninhabited

Continents

Sizes

Continent	Area (thousands of sq km/sq mi)	% of world land area
Africa	30,293/11,696	20.3
Antarctica	13,975/5,396	9.2
Asia	44,493/17,179	29.6
Europe	10,245/3,956	6.7
North America	24,454/9,442	16.2
Oceania	8,945/3,454	6.0
South America	17,838/6,887	12.0

Countries of the World

Country	Capital city	Country	Capital city
Afghanistan	Kabul	Brunei	Bandar Seri Begawan
Albania	Tirana		
Algeria	Algiers	Bulgaria	Sofia
Andorra	Andorra la Vella	Burkina Faso	Ouagadougou
		Burundi	Bujumbura
Angola	Luanda	Cambodia	Phnom Penh
Antigua and Barbuda	St John's	Cameroon	Yaoundé
Argentina	Buenos Aires	Canada	Ottawa
Armenia	Yerevan	Cape Verde	Praia
Australia	Canberra	Central African Republic	Bangui
Austria	Vienna	Chad	Ndjamena
Azerbaijan	Baku	Chile	Santiago
Bahamas	Nassau	China	Beijing
Bahrain	Al Manamah	Colombia	Bogotá
Bangladesh	Dhaka	Comoros	Moroni
Barbados	Bridgetown	Congo, Republic of	Brazzaville
Belarus	Minsk	Congo, Democratic Republic of	Kinshasa
Belgium	Brussels		
Belize	Belmopan	Costa Rica	San José
Benin	Porto-Novo (official), Cotonou (de facto)	Côte d'Ivoire	Yamoussoukro
		Croatia	Zagreb
		Cuba	Havana
		Cyprus	Nicosia
Bhutan	Thimphu	Czech Republic	Prague
Bolivia	La Paz (seat of government), Sucre (legal capital and seat of judiciary)	Denmark	Copenhagen
		Djibouti	Djibouti
		Dominica	Roseau
		Dominican Republic	Santo Domingo
Bosnia-Herzegovina	Sarajevo	Ecuador	Quito
Botswana	Gaborone	Egypt	Cairo
Brazil	Brasília		

(continued)

Countries of the World (*continued*)

Country	Capital city	Country	Capital city
El Salvador	San Salvador	Luxembourg	Luxembourg
Equatorial Guinea	Malabo	Macedonia	Skopje
Eritrea	Asmara	Madagascar	Antananarivo
Estonia	Tallinn	Maldives	Malé
Ethiopia	Addis Ababa	Mali	Bamako
Fiji Islands	Suva	Malta	Valletta
Finland	Helsinki	Malawi	Lilongwe
France	Paris	Malaysia	Kuala Lumpur
Gabon	Libreville	Marshall Islands	Dalap-Uliga-Darrit
Gambia, The	Banjul		
Georgia	Tbilisi	Mauritania	Nouakchott
Germany	Berlin	Mauritius	Port Louis
Ghana	Accra	Mexico	Mexico City
Greece	Athens	Micronesia, Federated States of	Palikir
Grenada	St George's		
Guatemala	Guatemala City	Moldova	Chişinašu
Guinea	Conakry	Monaco	no capital
Guinea-Bissau	Bissau	Mongolia	Ulaanbaatar
Guyana	Georgetown	Morocco	Rabat
Haiti	Port-au-Prince	Mozambique	Maputo
Honduras	Tegucigalpa	Myanmar	Yangon
Hungary	Budapest	Namibia	Windhoek
Iceland	Reykjavik	Nauru	Yaren (de facto)
India	New Delhi	Nepal	Kathmandu
Indonesia	Jakarta	Netherlands, The	Amsterdam
Iran	Tehran	New Zealand	Wellington
Iraq	Baghdad	Nicaragua	Managua
Ireland, Republic of	Dublin	Nigeria	Abuja
Israel	Jerusalem	Niger	Niamey
Italy	Rome	Norway	Oslo
Jamaica	Kingston	Oman	Muscat
Japan	Tokyo	Pakistan	Islamabad
Jordan	Amman	Palau	Koror
Kazakhstan	Astana	Panama	Panamá
Kenya	Nairobi	Papua New Guinea	Port Moresby
Kiribati	Bairiki	Paraguay	Asunción
North Korea	Pyongyang	Peru	Lima
South Korea	Seoul	Philippines	Manila
Kuwait	Kuwait	Poland	Warsaw
Kyrgyzstan	Bishkek	Portugal	Lisbon
Laos	Vientiane	Qatar	Doha
Latvia	Riga	Romania	Bucharest
Lebanon	Beirut	Russian Federation	Moscow
Lesotho	Maseru	Rwanda	Kigali
Liberia	Monrovia	Samoa	Apia
Libya	Tripoli	San Marino	San Marino
Liechtenstein	Vaduz	São Tomé and Príncipe	São Tomé
Lithuania	Vilnius	Saudi Arabia	Riyadh

Countries of the World (*continued*)

Country	Capital city	Country	Capital city
Senegal	Dakar	Taiwan	Taipei
Seychelles	Victoria	Tajikistan	Dushanbe
Sierra Leone	Freetown	Tanzania	Dodoma
Singapore	Singapore City	Thailand	Bangkok
Slovenia	Ljubljana	Togo	Lomé
Solomon Islands	Honiara	Tonga	Nuku'alofa
Somalia	Mogadishu	Trinidad and Tobago	Port-of-Spain
South Africa	Cape Town (legislative), Pretoria (administrative), Bloemfontein (judicial)	Tunisia	Tunis
		Turkey	Ankara
		Turkmenistan	Ashgabat
		Tuvalu	Fongafale
		United Arab Emirates	Abu Dhabi
Spain	Madrid	Uganda	Kampala
Slovak Republic	Bratislava	United Kingdom	London
Sri Lanka	Sri Jayaward-enepura Kotte	Ukraine	Kiev
		Uruguay	Montevideo
St Kitts and Nevis	Basseterre	United States of America	Washington, DC
St Lucia	Castries		
St Vincent and the Grenadines	Kingstown	Uzbekistan	Tashkent
		Vanuatu	Port-Vila
Sudan	Khartoum	Vatican City State	no capital
Suriname	Paramaribo	Venezuela	Caracas
Swaziland	Mbabane	Vietnam	Hanoi
Sweden	Stockholm	Yemen	San'a
Switzerland	Bern	Yugoslavia	Belgrade
Syria	Damascus	Zambia	Lusaka

Countries
World's Largest Projected Populations

Country	Projected population in 2050 (millions)	% of world population
India	1,529	17.16
China	1,478	16.58
USA	349	3.91
Pakistan	346	3.88
Indonesia	312	3.50
Nigeria	244	2.73
Brazil	244	2.73
Bangladesh	213	2.39
Ethiopia	170	1.90
Congo, Democratic Republic of	160	1.79

Countries

World's Smallest Countries (by population)

Country	Population
Vatican City State	1,000
Tuvalu	11,000
Nauru	11,200
Palau	19,000
San Marino	25,000
Liechtenstein	32,000
Monaco	32,000
St Kitts and Nevis	42,000
Marshall Islands	62,000
Andorra	66,000

Craters

Some Large Craters Formed by Meteorites

Location	Diameter (km/ml)
Chicxulub, Mexico	200/125
Sudbury, Canada	140/87
Vredefort, South Africa	140/87
Manson Impact Structure, USA	24/15
Bosumtui, Ghana	10/6.2
Deep Bay, Canada	8/5
New Quebec, Canada	3.2/2
Roter Kamm, Namibia	2.1/1.3
Lonar Crater, India	1.8/1.1
Barringer Crater, USA	1.2/0.7

Cruise Ships

World's Largest

Year	Name	Nationality	Number of passengers
1996	*Carnival Destiny*	Italian	3,360
1999	*Carnival Triumph*	Italian	3,360
2000	*Carnival Victory*	Italian	3,360
2001	*Golden Princess*	Italian	2,758
1992	*Majesty of the Seas*	French	2,744
1991	*Monarch of the Seas*	French	2,744
1998	*Grand Princess*	Italian	2,600
1997	*Rhapsody of the Seas*	French	2,435
1998	*Vision of the Seas*	French	2,435
1988	*Sovereign of the Seas*	French	2,276

Deep-sea Trenches

The World's Deepest

Name	Location	Depth (m/ft)
Mariana Trench	western Pacific	11,034/36,201
Tonga-Kermadec Trench[1]	southern Pacific	10,882/35,702
Kuril-Kamchatka Trench	western Pacific	10,542/34,587
Philippine Trench	western Pacific	10,539/34,577
Idzu-Bonin Trench	western Pacific	9,810/32,185
Puerto Rico Trench	western Atlantic	9,220/30,249
New Hebrides Trench	southern Pacific	9,165/30,069
Solomon Trench[2]	southern Pacific	9,140/29,987
Yap Trench	western Pacific	8,527/27,976
Japan Trench	western Pacific	8,412/27,598

[1] The Kermadec Trench is sometimes considered a separate feature with a depth of 10,047 m./32,963 ft
[2] Also called New Britain Trench.

Depressions
World's Deepest Continental Depressions

Depression	Location	Maximum depth below sea level (m/ft)
Dead Sea	Israel/Jordan	400/1,312
Turfan Depression	Xinjiang, China	154/505
Lake Assal	Djibouti	153/502
Qattâra Depression	Egypt	133/436
Poloustrov Mangyshlak	Kazakhstan	131/430
Danakil Depression	Ethiopia	120/394
Death Valley	California, USA	86/282
Salton Sink	California, USA	71/233
Zapadnyy Chink Ustyurta	Kazakhstan	70/230
Priaspiyskaya Nizmennost	Russian Federation/Kazakhstan	67/220

Deserts
World's Largest Deserts

Desert	Location	Area (sq km/sq mi)
Sahara	northern Africa	9,065,000/3,500,000
Gobi	Mongolia/northeastern China	1,295,000/500,000
Patagonian	Argentina	673,000/260,000
Rub al-Khali	southern Arabian peninsula	647,500/250,000
Kalahari	southwestern Africa	582,800/225,000
Chihuahuan	Mexico/southwestern USA	362,600/140,000
Taklimakan	northern China	362,600/140,000
Great Sandy	northwestern Australia	338,500/131,000
Great Victoria	southwestern Australia	338,500/131,000
Kyzyl Kum	Uzbekistan/Kazakhstan	259,000/100,000
Thar	India/Pakistan	219,000/85,000
Sonoran	Mexico/southwestern USA	181,300/70,000
Simpson	Australia	103,600/40,000
Mojave	southwestern USA	65,000/25,000

Earthquakes
The Mercalli Scale

The Mercalli scale is a measure of the intensity of an earthquake. It differs from the Richter scale, which measures magnitude. It is named after the Italian seismologist Giuseppe Mercalli.

Intensity value	Description
I	not felt except by a very few under exceptional conditions
II	felt only by a few persons at rest, especially on upper floors of buildings

(continued)

Earthquakes: The Mercalli Scale (*continued*)

Intensity value	Description
III	felt quite noticeably by persons indoors, especially on upper floors of buildings; many people do not recognize it as an earthquake; standing motor cars may rock slightly
IV	felt indoors by many, outdoors by a few persons during the day; at night, some awakened; dishes, windows, doors disturbed; walls make cracking sound; standing motor cars rock noticeably
V	felt by nearly everyone; many awakened; some dishes, windows broken; unstable objects overturned; pendulum clocks may stop
VI	felt by all; some heavy furniture moved; a few instances of fallen plaster; damage slight
VII	damage negligible in buildings of good design and construction; slight to moderate in well-built ordinary structures; considerable damage in poorly built or badly designed structures; some chimneys broken
VIII	damage slight in specially designed structures; considerable damage in ordinary substantial buildings with partial collapse; damage great in poorly built structures; fall of chimneys, factory stacks, columns, monuments, walls; heavy furniture overturned
IX	damage considerable even in specially designed structures; damage great in substantial buildings, with partial collapse; buildings shifted off foundations
X	some well-built wooden structures destroyed; most masonry and frame structures with foundations destroyed; rails bent
XI	few, if any (masonry) structures remain standing; bridges destroyed; rails bent greatly
XII	damage total; lines of sight and level are distorted; objects thrown into the air

Earthquakes
The Richter Scale

The Richter scale is based on measurement of seismic waves, and is used to determine the magnitude of an earthquake at its epicentre. The Richter scale is named after US seismologist Charles Richter.

Magnitude	Relative amount of energy released	Examples	Year
1	1		
2	31		
3	960		
4	30,000	Carlisle, England (4.7)	1979
5	920,000	Wrexham, Wales (5.1)	1990
6	29,000,000	San Fernando, USA (6.5)	1971
7	890,000,000	Izmit, Turkey (7.4)	1999
8	28,000,000,000	Tangshan, China (8.0)	1976
9	850,000,000,000	Prince William Sound, USA (9.2)	1964

Elevations
World's Highest Elevations

Continent	Highest elevation	Height (m/ft)
Africa	Kilimanjaro, Tanzania	5,895/19,341
Antarctica	Vinson Massif	5,140/16,864
Asia	Everest, China–Nepal	8,848/29,029
Europe	Elbrus, Russian Federation	5,642/18,511
North America	McKinley, USA	6,194/20,322
Oceania	Jaya, New Guinea	5,030/16,503
South America	Cerro Aconcagua, Argentina	6,960/22,835

Exploration
Discoverers of the Americas

Explorer	Nationality	Expedition date	Area
Leif Ericsson (according to the Sagas)	Viking	1000	North America
Christopher Columbus	Portuguese	1492	West Indies (North America)
Pedro Alvarez Cabral	Portuguese	1500	Brazil
Vasco Nunez de Balboa	Spain	1513	Pacific Ocean
Hernando Cortéz	Spanish	1519	Mexico
Alvar Nuallez Cabeza de Vaca	Spanish	1527	First crossing of North America by a European
Francisco Pizzarro	Spanish	1532	Peru
Hernando De Soto	Spanish	1539	Florida
Francisco de Orellana	Spanish	1541	Amazon
Juan Rodriguez Cabrillo	Spanish or Portuguese (uncertain)	1542	Californian coast

Exploration
Key Discoveries by Europeans

Date	Place	Discoverer	Nationality
c. 900	Greenland	Eric the Red	Norwegian
995	Labrador	Leif Ericsson	Norwegian
1432	Azores	Gonzalo Cabral	Portuguese
1445	Cape Verde	Dinas Diaz	Portuguese
1455	Cape Verde Islands	Alvise da Cadamosto	Italian
1488	Cape of Good Hope	Bartholomeu Dias	Portuguese
1492	West Indies	Christopher Columbus	Italian
1497	Natal	Vasco da Gama	Portuguese
1497	Newfoundland	John Cabot	Italian

Date	Place	Discoverer	Nationality
1500	Brazil	Pedro Cabral	Portuguese
1516	River Plate	Juan de Solis	Spanish
1520	Tierra del Fuego	Ferdinand Magellan	Portuguese
1563	Fernandez Islands	Juan Fernández	Spanish
1576	Baffin Island	Martin Frobisher	English
1596	Spitzbergen	Willem Barents	Dutch
1728	Alaska	Vitus Bering	Danish
1769	New Zealand	James Cook	English
1789	Mackenzie River	Alexander Mackenzie	Scottish
1795	River Niger	Mungo Park	Scottish
1851	River Zambezi	David Livingstone	Scottish

Germany
Capitals of States

Capital	State
Bremen	Bremen
Dresden	Sachsen
Düsseldorf	Nordrhein-Westfalen
Erfurt	Thüringen
Hamburg	Hamburg
Hannover	Niedersachsen
Kiel	Schleswig-Holstein
Magdeburg	Sachsen-Anhalt
Mainz	Rheinland-Pfalz
Munich	Bayern
Potsdam	Brandenburg
Saarbrücken	Saarland
Schwerin	Mecklenburg-Vorpommern
Stuttgart	Baden-Württemberg
Wiesbaden	Hessen
Berlin	Berlin

Germany
Population of States

State	Population
Nordrhein-Westfalen	17,759,300
Bayern	11,863,300
Baden-Württemberg	10,233,900
Niedersachsen	7,648,000
Hessen	5,967,300
Sachsen	4,607,700
Berlin	3,475,400
Rheinland-Pfalz	3,025,900
Sachsen-Anhalt	2,777,900
Schleswig-Holstein	2,694,900
Brandenburg	2,537,700
Thüringen	2,532,800
Mecklenburg-Vorpommern	1,843,500
Hamburg	1,702,900
Saarland	1,084,500
Bremen	683,100

Glaciers

Some Long Glaciers

Name	Location	Length (km/mi)
Lambert-Fisher Ice Passage	Antarctica	402/250
North Island, Novaya Zemlya	Russia	419/260
Bering Glacier	Alaska	204/127
Beardmore Glacier	Antarctica	200/125
Petermanns Glacier	Greenland	200/125
Malaspina Glacier	Alaska	193/120
Fedchenko Glacier	Aral Sea	77/48
Colombia Glacier	Alaska	64/40
Inylchek Glacier	Kyrgyzstan	60/37
Upsala Glacier	Argentina	50/31

India

Capitals of States and Union Territories

Capital	State	Capital	State
Agartala	Tripura	Mumbai	Maharashtra
Aizawl	Mizoram	Panaji	Goa
Bangalore	Karnataka	Patna	Bihar
Bhopal	Madhya Pradesh	Raipur	Chattisgarh
Bhubaneshwar	Orissa	Ranchi	Jharkhand
Chandigarh	Haryana	Shillong	Meghalaya
Chandigarh	Punjab	Shimla	Himachal Pradesh
Chennai	Tamil Nadu	Srinagar	Jammu and Kashmir
Dehra Dun	Uttranchal	Thiruvanaanthapuram	Kerala
Dispur	Assam		
Gandhinagar	Gujarat	**Capital**	**Union Territory**
Gangtok	Sikkim	Chandigarh	Chandigarh
Hyderabad	Andhra Pradesh	Daman	Daman and Diu
Imphal	Manipur	Delhi	Delhi
Itanagar	Arunachal Pradesh	Kavaratti	Lakshadweep
Jaipur	Rajasthan	Pondicherry	Pondicherry
Kohima	Nagaland	Port Blair	Andaman and Nicobar Islands
Kolkata	West Bengal		
Lucknow	Uttar Pradesh	Silvassa	Dadra and Nagar Haveli

India

Populations of States and Union Territories

State	Population	State	Population
Uttar Pradesh	164,346,000	Andhra Pradesh	81,293,000
Maharashtra	97,663,000	Bihar	77,633,000
West Bengal	83,438,000	Madhya Pradesh	64,920,000

(continued)

India: Populations of States and Union Territories (*continued*)

State	Population	State	Population
Tamil Nadu	64,158,000	Meghalaya	2,324,000
Rajasthan	56,728,000	Nagaland	1,817,000
Karnataka	54,907,000	Goa	1,364,000
Gujarat	50,612,000	Arunachal Pradesh	1,163,000
Orissa	37,557,000	Mizoram	976,000
Kerala	33,462,000	Sikkim	516,000
Jharkhand	27,894,000		
Assam	27,428,000	**Union Territory**	**Population**
Punjab	24,475,000	Delhi	13,660,000
Haryana	20,821,000	Pondicherry	1,052,000
Chattisgarh	17,852,000	Chandigarh	976,000
Jammu and Kashmir	9,763,000	Andaman and Nicobar Islands	381,000
Uttranchal	8,115,000	Dadra and Nagar Haveli	186,000
Himachal Pradesh	6,235,000	Daman and Diu	133,000
Tripura	3,631,000	Lakshadweep	65,000
Manipur	2,373,000		

Ireland, Republic of
Area of Provinces

Province	Area (sq km/sq mi)	Province	Area (sq km/sq mi)
Munster	24,100/9,305	Ulster (part of)	8,000/3,089
Leinster	19,600/7,568	Republic of Ireland[1]	70,300/27,143
Connacht	17,100/6,602		

[1] Total area including inland water.

Ireland, Republic of
County Towns

County town	County	County town	County
Carlow	Carlow	Limerick	Limerick
Carrick-on-Shannon	Leitrim	Longford	Longford
		Monaghan	Monaghan
Castlebar	Mayo	Mullingar	Westmeath
Cavan	Cavan	Naas	Kildare
Clonmel	Tipperary North Riding	Navan	Meath
	Tipperary South Riding	Portlaoise	Laoighis
Cork	Cork	Roscommon	Roscommon
Dublin	Dublin	Sligo	Sligo
Dundalk	Louth	Tralee	Kerry
Ennis	Clare	Tullamore	Offaly
Galway	Galway	Waterford	Waterford
Kilkenny	Kilkenny	Wexford	Wexford
Lifford	Donegal	Wicklow	Wicklow

Ireland, Republic of
Population of Counties

County	Population	County	Population
Dublin	1,025,000	Clare	91,000
Cork	410,000	Tipperary South Riding	75,000
Galway	180,000	Kilkenny	74,000
Limerick	162,000	Westmeath	62,000
Donegal	128,000	Tipperary North Riding	58,000
Kildare	123,000	Offaly	58,000
Kerry	122,000	Sligo	55,000
Mayo	111,000	Cavan	53,000
Meath	105,000	Roscommon	52,000
Wexford	102,000	Laoighis	52,000
Wicklow	97,000	Monaghan	51,000
Waterford	92,000	Carlow	41,000
Louth	91,000	Longford	30,000
		Leitrim	25,000

Islands
Major Island Groups

Name and ownership	Location	Number of islands
Indonesia (Republic of Indonesia)	Pacific Ocean	13,700
Philippines (Republic of Philippines)	Pacific Ocean	7,100
Bahamas (UK)	Atlantic Ocean	700
Caroline Islands (USA)	Pacific Ocean	680
Andaman Islands (India)	Bay of Bengal	300
Desolation Islands (France)	Indian Ocean	300
Cyclades (Greece)	Aegean Sea	220
Bismarck Archipelago (Papua New Guinea)	Pacific Ocean	200
Falkland Islands (UK)	Atlantic Ocean	200
Zemlya Frantsa-Iosifa (Russia)	Arctic Ocean	165
Queen Charlotte Islands (Canada)	Pacific Ocean	150
Scilly Isles (UK)	Atlantic Ocean	150
Seychelles (Republic of Seychelles)	Indian Ocean	115
Shetland Isles (UK)	North Sea	100

Islands
World's Largest

Island	Location	Area (sq km/sq mi)
Greenland	northern Atlantic	2,175,600/840,000
New Guinea	southwestern Pacific	800,000/308,882
Borneo	southwestern Pacific	744,100/287,300
Madagascar	Indian Ocean	587,050/226,660

(continued)

Islands: World's Largest (*continued*)

Island	Location	Area (sq km/sq mi)
Baffin	Canadian Arctic	507,450/195,930
Sumatra	Indian Ocean	424,750/164,000
Honshu	northwestern Pacific	230,950/89,170
Great Britain	northern Atlantic	218,100/84,210
Victoria	Canadian Arctic	217,200/83,860
Ellesmere	Canadian Arctic	196,150/75,735
Sulawesi	Indian Ocean	189,200/73,050
South Island, New Zealand	southwestern Pacific	149,900/57,880
Java	Indian Ocean	126,600/48,880
North Island, New Zealand	southwestern Pacific	114,650/44,270
Cuba	Caribbean Sea	110,850/42,800
Newfoundland	northwestern Atlantic	108,850/42,030
Luzon	western Pacific	104,700/40,425
Iceland	northern Atlantic	103,000/39,770

Italy

Capitals of Regions

Capital	Region
Ancona	Marche
Aosta	Valle d'Aosta
Bari	Puglia
Bologna	Emilia-Romagna
Bolzano	Trentino-Alto Adige
Cagliari	Sardegna
Campobasso	Molise
Catanzaro	Calabria
Florence	Toscana
Genoa	Liguria
L'Aquila	Abruzzi
Milan	Lombardia
Naples	Campania
Palermo	Sicily
Perugia	Umbria
Potenza	Basilicata
Rome	Lazio
Trieste	Friuli-Venezia Giulia
Turin	Piedmonte
Venice	Veneto

Italy

Population of Regions

Region	Population
Lombardia	8,882,000
Campania	5,669,000
Lazio	5,162,000
Sicily	4,998,000
Veneto	4,395,000
Piedmonte	4,304,000
Puglia	4,050,000
Emilia-Romagna	3,920,000
Toscana	3,529,000
Calabria	2,075,000
Liguria	1,669,000
Sardegna	1,652,000
Marche	1,434,000
Abruzzi	1,256,000
Friuli-Venezia Giulia	1,195,000
Trentino-Alto Adige	897,000
Umbria	815,000
Basilicata	611,000
Molise	331,000
Valle d'Aosta	117,000

Lakes
World's Largest Lakes

Lake	Location	Area (sq km/ sq mi)
Caspian Sea	Azerbaijan/Russian Federation/Kazakhstan/ Turkmenistan/Iran	370,990/143,240
Superior	USA/Canada	82,070/31,687
Victoria	Tanzania/Kenya/Uganda	69,465/26,821
Aral Sea	Kazakhstan/Uzbekistan	64,500/24,904
Huron	USA/Canada	59,550/22,992
Michigan	USA	57,735/22,292
Tanganyika	Tanzania/Democratic Republic of Congo/Zambia/Burundi	32,880/12,695
Baikal	Russian Federation	31,500/12,162
Great Bear	Canada	31,315/12,091
Malawi (or Nyasa)	Malawi/Tanzania/Mozambique	28,865/11,145

Land-locked Countries
Largest

Country	Area (sq km/sq mi)	Country	Area (sq km/sq mi)
Democratic Republic of the Congo	2,344,885/905,365	Bolivia	1,098,581/424,164
		Zambia	752,614/290,586
Mongolia	1,566,500/604,829	Afghanistan	652,090/251,773
Chad	1,284,000/495,755	Botswana	581,730/224,607
Mali	1,248,574/482,164	Paraguay	406,752/157,048
Niger	1,186,408/458,075		

Landslides
World's Worst 20th-century Landslides and Avalanches

Place	Date	Number killed
landslide in China	1920	100,000
landslide in Yungay, Peru	1970	25,000
avalanche in Italian Alps	1916	10,000
avalanche at Huaraz, Peru	1941	7,000
avalanche at Nevada Huascaran, Peru	1962	3,500
landslide at Medellin, Colombia	1987	685
avalanche at Chungar, Peru	1971	600
landslide at Grand Riviere du Nord, Haiti	1963	500
landslide at Rio de Janiero, Brazil	1966	280
avalanche at Blons, Austria	1954	125

Motoring
Countries Where Cars Drive on the Left

Country	Country	Country
Anguilla	Ireland (Republic of)	St Vincent
Antigua	Jamaica	Seychelles
Australia	Japan	Singapore
Bahamas	Kenya	Solomon Islands
Bangladesh	Kiribati	Somalia
Barbados	Lesotho	South Africa
Bermuda	Malaysia	Sri Lanka
Bhutan	Malawi	Surinam
Botswana	Malta	Swaziland
Brunei	Mauritius	Tanzania
Cook Islands	Montserrat	Thailand
Cyprus	Mozambique	Tonga
Dominica	Namibia	Trinidad and Tobago
Falkland Islands	Nepal	Tuvalu
Fiji Islands	New Zealand	Uganda
Grenada	Norfolk Island	UK (including Guernsey, Jersey, and the Isle of Man)
Guyana	Pakistan	Virgin Islands (British)
Hong Kong	Papua New Guinea	Zambia
India	St Christopher-Nevis	Zimbabwe
Indonesia	St Lucia	

Mountain Ranges
World's Longest Mountain Ranges

Range	Location	Length (km/mi)
Andes	South America	8,000/5,000
Rockies	North America	4,800/3,000
Great Dividing Range	Australia	3,700/2,340
Transantarctic Mountains	Antarctica	3,500/2,175
Himalayas	Asia	2,500/1,550
Appalachians	North America	2,400/1,500
Urals	Asia	2,100/1,305
Altai Mountains	Asia	2,000/1,200
Zagros Mountains	Asia	1,600/1,000
Carpathian Mountains	Europe	1,450/900

Mountains
World's Highest

Region	Mountain	Location	Height (m/ft)
Africa	Kilimanjaro	Tanzania	5,895/19,341
	Kenya	Kenya	5,199/17,057
	Ngaliema	Democratic Republic of Congo/ Uganda	5,110/16,765
Alpine Europe	Mont Blanc	France/Italy	4,807/15,771
	Monte Rosa	Switzerland	4,634/15,204
	Dom	Switzerland	4,545/14,911
Antarctica	Vinson Massif		5,140/16,864
	Tyree		4,965/16,289
	Shinn		4,800/15,748
Asia	Everest	China/Nepal	8,848/29,029
	K2	Kashmir/Jammu	8,611/28,251
	Kangchenjunga	India/Nepal	8,598/28,209
Australia	Kosciusko	New South Wales	2,230/7,316
Carpathians	Gerlachvka	Slovak Republic	2,655/8,711
	Moldoveanu	Romania	2,544/8,346
	Negoiu	Romania	2,535/8,317
Caucasia	Elbrus, West Peak	Russian Federation	5,642/18,511
	Dykh Tau	Russian Federation/Georgia	5,203/17,070
	Shkhara	Russian Federation/Georgia	5,201/17,064
New Zealand	Cook	west coast, South Island	3,754/12,316
North and Central America	McKinley	Alaska, USA	6,194/20,322
	Logan, Yukon	Canada	6,050/19,849
	Citlaltépetl	Mexico	5,610/18,406
Oceania	Jaya	Papua New Guinea	5,030/16,503
	Daam	Papua New Guinea	4,922/16,148
	Oost Carstensz	Papua New Guinea	4,840/15,879
Polynesia	Mauna Kea	Hawaii, USA	4,205/13,796
	Mauna Loa	Hawaii, USA	4,170/13,681
Pyrenees	Pico de Aneto	Spain	3,404/11,168
	Pico de Posets	Spain	3,371/11,060
	Monte Perdido	Spain	3,348/10,984
Scandinavia	Glittertind	Norway	2,472/8,110
	Galdhøpiggen	Norway	2,469/8,100
	Skagastolstindane	Norway	2,405/7,890
South America	Cerro Aconcagua	Argentina	6,960/22,835
	Ojos del Salado	Argentina/Chile	6,908/22,664
	Bonete	Argentina	6,872/22,546

North Pole
First to Reach the North Pole

Record	Expedition leader or craft	Nationality	Date arrived
first overland (disputed)	Robert Peary	American	6 April 1909
first overland (confirmed) by snowmobile	Ralph S Plaisted	American	18 April 1968
first overland by dog team	Wally Herbert	British	6 April 1969
first to fly over the pole in a plane (disputed)	Richard E Byrd Umberto Nobile	American Italian	9 May 1926 12 May 1926
first submarine to cross under the polar ice-cap	William Anderson (captain of *USS Nautilus*)	American	3 August 1958
first submarine to surface at the pole	James F Calvert (captain of *USS Skate*)	American	February 1959
first surface ship to arrive at the pole	*Arktika*	USSR	17 August 1977
first woman to pilot a balloon over the pole	Debbie Harding	American	20 April 1998
first helicopter flight to the pole	Dick Smith	Australian	April 1987

Oceans and Seas
World's Largest

Ocean/sea	Area (sq km/sq mi)	Average depth (m/ft)
Pacific Ocean	166,242,000/64,186,369	3,940/12,927
Atlantic Ocean	86,557,000/33,419,831	3,575/11,729
Indian Ocean	73,429,000/28,351,084	3,840/12,598
Arctic Ocean	13,224,000/5,105,813	1,040/3,412
South China Sea	2,975,000/1,148,653	1,465/4,806
Caribbean Sea	2,754,000/1,063,325	2,575/8,448
Mediterranean Sea	2,510,000/969,116	1,500/4,921
Bering Sea	2,261,000/872,977	1,490/4,888
Sea of Okhotsk	1,580,000/610,041	975/3,199
Gulf of Mexico	1,544,000/596,142	1,615/5,299

Place Names
Cities that Once Had Other Names

Current name	Former name	Country
Beijing	Peking	China
Chicago	Fort Dearborn	United States
Colón	Aspinwall	Panama
Ho Chi Minh City	Saigon	Vietnam
Istanbul	Constantinople	Turkey
Jakarta	Batavia	Indonesia
Mexico City	Tenochtitlán	Mexico
New York	New Amsterdam	United States
Oslo	Christiania	Norway
St Petersburg	Leningrad	Russia
Santa Domingo	Ciudad Trujillo	Dominican Republic
Tokyo	Ido	Japan
Toronto	Fort Rouillé	Canada
Volgograd	Stalingrad	Russia

Place Names
Countries That Once Had Other Names

Current name	Former name	Current name	Former name
Bangladesh	East Pakistan	Mongolia	People's Republic of Mongolia
Belize	British Honduras		
Benin	Dahomey	Myanmar	Burma
Botswana	Bechuanaland	Namibia	South West Africa
Burkina Faso	Upper Volta	Slovak Republic	Czechoslovakia (with Czech Rupublic)
Cambodia	Kampuchea		
Cameroon	Kamerun	Sri Lanka	Ceylon
Central African Republic	Central African Empire	Suriname	Dutch Guiana
		Taiwan	Formosa
Congo, Democratic Republic of	Zaire	Tuvalu	Ellice Islands
		Russia	Russian Soviet Federal Socialist Republic
Czech Republic	Czechoslovakia (with Slovak Republic)		
		Rwanda	Ruanda
Djibouti	French Territory of the Afars and Issas	Tanzania	Tanganyika
		Thailand	Siam
Dominican Republic	Hispaniola (with Haiti)	Togo	Togoland
Ethiopia	Abyssinia	United Arab Emirates	Federation of Arab Emirates (with Bahrain and Qatar)
Ghana	Gold Coast		
Guinea-Bissau	Portuguese Guinea		
Haiti	Hispaniola (with Dominican Republic)	Vanuatu	New Hebrides
		Yugoslavia	Kingdom of the Serbs, Croats, and Slovenes
Indonesia	Dutch East Indies		
Iran	Persia	Zambia	Northern Rhodesia
Kiribati	part of the Gilbert and Ellice Islands	Zimbabwe	Southern Rhodesia

Place Names

Longest

Place name[1]	Number of letters	Country	Explanation
Krungthep Mahanakhon Bovorn Ratanakosin Mahintharayutthaya Mahadilokpop Noparatratchathani Burirom Udomratchanivetmahasathan Amornpiman Avatarnsathit Sakkathattiyavisnukarmprasit	167	Thailand	An expanded version of the Thai name of Bangkok. It gives a potted history of the city. The shortened version means 'City of Angels'.
Taumatawhakatangihangakoauauotamateaturipukakapikimaungahoronukupokaiwhenuakitanatahu	85	New Zealand	The unofficial name in Maori of a hill in southern Hawkes Bay, North Island. It was named in celebration of a Maori chief called Tamatea, who was so powerful that he could metaphorically eat mountains.
Gorsafawddach'idraigodanheddogleddollonpenrhynareurdraethceredigion	67	UK	A railway station name invented by the Fairbourne Steam Railway of Barmouth, Gwynedd, North Wales, as a publicity stunt. It means 'The Mawddach station and its dragon teeth at the northern Penrhyn road on the golden beach of Cardigan Bay'. Although the name consists of 67 letters, the 'll' should be just 'l', making the linguistically correct name only 66 letters long.
Cape St George-Petit Jardin-Grand Jardin-De-Grau-Marches Point-Loretto	59		The name of a community in Newfoundland, Canada.
Llanfairpwllgwyngyllgogerychwyrndrobwllllantysiliogogogoch	58	UK	A picturesque expansion of Llanfairpwllgwyngyll, the official name of a village in southeast Anglesey, North Wales. John Evans, a local poet who wrote under the bardic name of Y Bardd Cocos, concocted the name as a joke in the 19th century. It means 'The church of St Mary by the pool of the white hazel near to the rapid whirlpool of the red cave of the church of St Tysilio'.
El Pueblo de Nuestra Señora la Reina de los Angeles de la Porciuncula	57	USA	The longest place name in the USA. It is the full Spanish name for the city of Los Angeles, and is a combination of the names given by 18th-century Franciscan priests to the river and chapel which formed the basis of the original settlement.

Place Names: Longest (*continued*)

Place name[1]	Number of letters	Country	Explanation
Cours d'eau du Cordon des Terres des Sixième et Septième Rangs	51		The name of a river in Quebec.
Chargoggagoggmanchauggagogg-chaubunagungamaugg	45	USA	A fanciful extension of Chaubunagungamaug, the real Indian name of a lake in Massachusetts, near the town of Webster. The original, unexpanded name meant 'neutral fishing ground'. The longer name was coined in the 1920s by Larry Daly, the editor of the *Webster Times*. It is usually listed on maps as 'Lake Webster'.
Villa Real de la Santa Fe de San Francisco de Asis	40	USA	The full Spanish name for Santa Fe, New Mexico. The name means 'Royal city of the holy faith of St Francis of Assisi'.
Meallan Liath Coire Mhic Dhubhghaill	32	UK	The longest name in Scotland. It is a hill located just north of Aultanrynie, Highland. The name means 'The grey hill of McDoughal's cauldron'.
Sutton-under-Whitestonecliffe	27		This small Yorkshire town has the longest place-name in England.
Nunathloogagamiutbingoi	23		An eskimo name given to a series of dunes in Alaska.

[1] Includes multi-word and hyphenated names

Population
Countries with Largest Percentage of World Population

Country	% of world population	Country	% of world population
China	21.31	Pakistan	2.54
India	16.69	Russian Federation	2.45
USA	4.62	Bangladesh	2.12
Indonesia	3.10	Japan	2.12
Brazil	2.81	Nigeria	1.82

Ports
Busiest in the UK

Source: *Maritime Statistics 1998* © Crown Copyright 1999

Rank	Port	Traffic	
		tonnes (thousands)	% of total UK ports
1	London	57,310	10.1
2	Tees and Hartlepool	51,455	9.1
3	Grimsby and Immingham	48,390	8.5
4	Forth	44,400	7.8
5	Southampton	34,260	6.0
6	Sullom Voe	31,110	5.5
7	Liverpool	30,360	5.3
8	Felixstowe	30,025	5.3
9	Milford Haven	28,785	5.1
10	Dover	17,690	3.1

Ports
Busiest in the USA

Port	Total tons 1995	Port	Total tons 1995
South Louisiana, Port of (LA)	204,482,600	New Orleans (LA)	76,984,000
Houston (TX)	135,231,300	Plaquemine, Port of (LA)	72,897,300
New York (NY and NJ)	119,341,600	Corpus Christi (TX)	70,456,000
Baton Rouge (LA)	83,612,800	Long Beach (CA)	53,227,500
Valdez (AK)	80,955,100	Tampa (FL)	51,911,300

Rail Disasters
Recent Rail Disasters

Date	Location	Fatalities
5 October 1999	Ladbroke Grove, London, England	31
3 June 1998	Eschede, Germany	98
20 August 1995	Firozabad, India	>300
22 September 1994	Tolunda, Angola	>300
8 March 1994	Durban, South Africa	63
14 May 1991	Shigaraki, Japan	42
4 January 1990	Sindh Province, Pakistan	>210
4 June 1989	Chelyabinsk, former USSR	>600
15 January 1989	Maizdi Khan, Bangladesh	>110
12 December 1988	Clapham, London, England	34
19 February 1983	Empalme, Mexico	100

Rail Disasters
World's Worst

Date	Location	Fatalities
6 June 1981	Bihar, India	>800
4 June 1989	Chelyabinsk, former USSR	>600
12 December 1917	Modane, France	>540
2 March 1944	near Salerno, Italy	521
16 January 1944	Leon Province, Spain	>500
22 September 1994	Tolunda, Angola	>300
20 August 1995	Firozabad, India	>300
3 April 1955	Guadalajara, Mexico	300
29 September 1957	Montgomery, Pakistan	>250
4 February 1970	Buenos Aires, Argentina	236

Railways
Busiest Rail Networks

Country	Rail passenger km (millions)/mi (millions)
India	379,897/236,057
China	354,825/220,478
Japan	301,510/187,350
Russian Federation	168,700/104,825
Germany	62,632/38,918
France	61,830/38,419
Egypt	55,638/34,572
Italy	50,300/31,255
Ukraine	49,938/31,030
South Korea	30,073/18,686

Railways
World's Major Systems

Railway system	Year of first railway	Route measure (km/mi)
USA	1830	261,124/162,255
Russia	1837	86,300/53,624
Canada	1836	63,549/39,488
India	1853	61,976/38,510
China	1880	c. 54,000/c. 33,550
Germany	1835	41,039/25,500
Australia	1854	38,803/24,111
France	1832	34,680/21,549
Argentina	1857	c. 34,500/c. 21,437
Poland	1845	27,137/16,862

Rivers
World's Largest by Volume

River	Volume discharged (cubic km per year/cubic mi per year)
Amazon	6,300/1,511
Congo–Zaire	1,250/300
Orinoco	1,100/264
Ganges/ Brahmaputra	970/233
Yangtze	900/216
Mississippi–Missouri	580/139
Yenisei	560/134
Lena	515/124
Mekong	470/113
Parana–La Plata	470/113

Rivers

World's Longest Rivers

River	Location	Approximate length (km/mi)
Nile	Africa	6,695/4,160
Amazon	South America	6,570/4,082
Chang Jiang (Yangtze)	China	6,300/3,915
Mississippi–Missouri–Red Rock	USA	6,020/3,741
Huang He (Yellow River)	China	5,464/3,395
Ob–Irtysh	China/Kazakhstan/Russian Federation	5,410/3,362
Amur–Shilka	Asia	4,416/2,744
Lena	Russian Federation	4,400/2,734
Congo	Africa	4,374/2,718
Mackenzie–Peace–Finlay	Canada	4,241/2,635
Mekong	Asia	4,180/2,597
Niger	Africa	4,100/2,548
Yenisei	Russian Federation	4,100/2,548
Paraná	Brazil	3,943/2,450
Mississippi	USA	3,779/2,348
Murray–Darling	Australia	3,751/2,331
Missouri	USA	3,726/2,315
Volga	Russian Federation	3,685/2,290
Madeira	Brazil	3,241/2,014
Purus	Brazil	3,211/1,995

Road Disasters

Worst Countries for Road Accident Deaths

Country	Number of deaths	Country	Number of deaths
India	74,204	France	8,487
USA	41,345	Germany	7,749
Thailand	17,176	Poland	6,730
South Korea	10,402	Italy	6,724
Japan	10,372	Spain	6,319

Sailing Ships

Vessel	Description
barque	three or more masts, square-rigged except for fore-and-aft rig on the aftermast (mizzen)
barquentine	like a barque but square-rigged on only the foremast (the rest were fore-and-aft rigged)
brig	two masts, square-rigged on both
brigantine	two masts, square-rigged on the foremast and fore-and-aft mainsail with square topsails on the mainmast

Sailing Ships (*continued*)

Vessel	Description
caique	Mediterranean vessel with spritsails and a square sail on the foremast and jib(s)on the other(s)
caravel	two- or three-masted vessel with lateen rig (triangular sails)
carrack	Mediterranean galleon
catamaran	twin-hulled vessel with a single mast
catboat	single-masted vessel with a large sail (and often a gaff)
clipper	fast sailing vessel (often a barque)
cog	vessel with single square sail
cutter	single-masted vessel with the mast further back than on a sloop
dhow	one- or two-masted Arab vessel with a lateen rig
dinghy	small sailing craft
dromon	large, fast Byzantine war galley
felucca	Mediterranean lateen-rigged vessel
fluit	late 16th-century square-rigged Dutch merchantman
frigate	medium-sized 18th–19th-century square-rigged British warship
galiot (also small fast Mediterranean galley, or coastal galliot)	cargo-carrying European ketch
galleass(e)	three-masted lateen-rigged 16th-century Mediterranean galley
galleon	large, three-masted (or more) sailing vessel, square-rigged on the fore and main and lateen-rigged on the other mast(s)
galley	vessel with a (square) sail but powered principally, and always manoeuvred, by oars
hermaphrodite	two-masted vessel, square-rigged on the brig foremast and fore-and-aft rigged on the aftermast (a brigantine)
jagt	small, single-masted vessel, usually with square sails
junk	Chinese vessel with squarish sails supported by horizontal bamboo battens
ketch	two-masted vessel (tall mainmast and smaller mizzen forward of the stern), generally with fore-and-aft rig on both
longship	narrow (Viking) vessel with a single square sail and oars
lugger	small vessel with a four-sided lugsail
man-of-war	any warship
merchantman	any merchant vessel
nuggar	cargo-carrying Egyptian sailing vessel (on the River Nile)
packet	fast vessel for carrying mail
pink	vessel with overhanging transom
polacre	three-masted Mediterranean sailing vessel
privateer	privately-owned, armed merchantman whose master held a licence (Letter of Marque) to attack enemy shipping
razee	warship with upper gundeck(s) removed
sabot	small Australian sailing boat
schooner	at least two-masted vessel with all lower sails fore-and-aft rigged
shallop	(formerly) two-masted, gaff-rigged vessel; now a light rowing boat
ship	three masts, square-rigged on all masts (perhaps with lower fore-and-aft sail on the mizzen)
ship of the major warship variety	two or more gun decks (and up to 74 guns by the 19th century)

(*continued*)

Sailing Ships (*continued*)

Vessel	Description
skipjack	US sloop
sloop	single-masted vessel with fore-and-aft rig
snow	two-masted, square-rigged vessel
smack	(usually) sloop-rigged coastal vessel
tartan	single-masted usually lateen-rigged Mediterranean vessel
windjammer	large merchant sailing vessel
xebec	three-masted Mediterranean vessel with square and lateen sails
yacht	sailing vessel built for pleasure use
yawl	two-masted vessel (tall mainmast and smaller mizzen right at the stern) rigged fore-and-aft on both

Shipping
Largest Merchant Fleets of the World

For comparison, the UK fleet is ranked 35.

Country of registry	Total number of ships	Number of container ships	Number of cruise/ passenger ships	Number of tankers	Number of bulk carriers	Number of roll– on/roll– off ships	Other
Panama	4,456	469	51	971	1,293	68	1,604
Liberia	1,632	170	40	691	456	12	263
Russian Federation	1,472	25	7	273	113	11	1,043
China	1,465	96	34	244	332	14	745
Cyprus	1,436	121	15	173	488	20	619
Malta	1,305	45	7	349	371	39	494
Bahamas	1,029	53	60	241	151	37	487
Singapore	877	162	1	386	129	5	194
Saint Vincent	782	30	5	96	135	38	478
Greece	741	44	19	257	318	16	87

Shipping Disasters
Recent Shipping Accidents

Date	Vessel	Location	Fatalities
September 2000	*Express Samina*, ferry	struck rocks off the island of Paros in the Aegean Sea	>60
May 1996	*Bukoba*, ferry	sank in Lake Victoria, Uganda, Kenya, and Tanzania	500
September 1994	*Estonia*, ferry	sank in the Baltic Sea when water entered bow door	1,049
October 1993	*West Sea Ferry*, ferry	capsized during storm in the Yellow Sea near South Korea	285
February 1993	*Neptune*, ferry	capsized off Port-au-Prince, Haiti	>500

Shipping Disasters: Recent Shipping Accidents (*continued*)

Date	Vessel	Location	Fatalities
December 1991	*Salem Express,* ferry	rammed coral reef off Egyptian coast	462
April 1991	Car ferry and oil tanker	collided outside Livorno harbour, Italy	140
September 1989	Romanian pleasure boat and barge	collided on the River Danube	161
August 1989	*Bowbelle,* British barge, and *Marchioness,* British pleasure cruiser	collided on the River Thames, UK	56
August 1988	Indian ferry	capsized on the River Ganges, India	>400
December 1987	*Dona Paz,* Philippine ferry, and *Victor,* oil tanker	collided in the Tablas Strait, Philippines	3,000
March 1987	*Herald of Free Enterprise,* British ferry	capsized off Zeebrugge, Belgium, after water entered the bow door	188

Shipping Disasters
World's Worst Shipping Accidents

Date	Vessel	Location	Fatalities
September 1622	at least 12 ships of the Tierra Firme Armada and the New Spain Fleet	wrecked by hurricane in the Florida Keys	thousands
September 1776	100 merchant vessels	wrecked by hurricane at Point Bay, Martinique	around 6,000
November 1949	Chinese army evacuation ship	exploded and sank off South Manchuria	6,000
October 1780	seven Dutch ships	wrecked by hurricane at St Eustatius, Lesser Antilles	around 5,000
February 1916	*Provence,* French cruiser	sank in the Mediterranean sea	3,100
December 1987	*Dona Paz,* Philippine ferry, and *Victor,* oil tanker	collided in the Tablas Strait, Philippines	3,000
September 1954	*Toyo Maru,* Japanese ferry	sank in Tsugaru Strait, Japan	2,750
August 1711	eight English transports	wrecked in storm at Egg Island, Labrador	around 2,000
April 1912	*Titanic,* British steamer	sank after hitting iceberg in the North Atlantic	1,517
April 1865	*Sultana,* US side-wheeled steamer	exploded and burned near Memphis, Tennessee	>1,500

Shipping Disasters
Worst Accidents Involving Merchant Ships

Vessel	Nationality	Date	Fatalities	Vessel	Nationality	Date	Fatalities
Wilhelm Gustloff	German	1945	>7,500	Cap Arcona	German	1945	5,000
				Lancastria	British	1940	3,000
Goya	German	1945	>6,500	Steuben	German	1945	3,000

South Pole
First to Reach the South Pole

Record	Expedition leader	Nationality	Date arrived
first overland	Roald Amundsen	Norwegian	14 December 1911
	Robert F Scott	English	18 January 1912
first to fly over the pole in a plane	Richard Byrd	US	28 November 1929
first to land a plane at the pole	Conrad Shinn	US	31 October 1956
first to cross the Antarctic	Vivian Fuchs	English	2 March 1958
first to cross the Antarctic solo	Borge Ousland	Norwegian	18 January 1997
first unmechanized passage across the Antarctic	Will Steger	US (team from many nations)	3 March 1990
first aerial crossing of the continent	Lincoln Ellsworth, Herbert Hollick-Kenyon	US, Canadian	5 December 1935

Submarine Disasters
Worst Accidents

Towards the end of the war in the Pacific in World War II, the Japanese navy lost five large submarines, each with a crew of 100 or more.

Vessel	Nationality	Date	Number killed
Le Surcouf	French	1942	130
Thresher	US	1963	129
Kursk	Russian	2000	118
Thetis	British	1943	99
Dakar	Israeli	1968	69
Komsomolets	Russian	1989	42

Underground Rail Disasters
World's Worst

Country	Place	Date	Number killed
Italy	Salerno	1944	521
Azerbaijan	Baku	1995	300
Austria	Kaprun	2000	155
France	Paris	1903	>100
USA	Brooklyn	1918	92
England	Moorgate, London	1975	43
England	King's Cross, London	1987	30

Underground Railways
Longest Networks

City	Length (km/mi)
London	408/254
New York City	398/247
Moscow	244/152
Tokyo[1]	237/147
Seoul	218/135
Paris	206/128
Mexico City	178/111
Berlin	136/85
Osaka	106/66
Hamburg	95/59
St Petersburg	92/57
Nagoya	77/48

[1] There are two underground railway systems in Tokyo.

Underground Railways
World's First

City	Opened	Length (km/mi)	Journeys per year (millions)
London	1863	408/254	775
New York City	1867	398/247	1,060
Paris	1900	206/128	1,191

USA
Area of States (including the District of Columbia)

State	Area (sq km/sq mi)	State	Area (sq km/sq mi)
Alaska	1,477,250/570,369	New Mexico	314,350/121,371
Texas	678,350/261,912	Arizona	294,350/113,649
California	403,950/155,966	Nevada	284,400/109,807
Montana	380,850/147,047	Colorado	268,650/103,726

(continued)

USA: Area of States (including the District of Columbia)
(*continued*)

State	Area (sq km/sq mi)	State	Area (sq km/sq mi)
Wyoming	251,500/97,105	Mississippi	121,500/46,911
Oregon	248,650/96,004	Pennsylvania	116,100/44,826
Idaho	214,300/82,742	Louisiana	112,850/43,572
Utah	212,800/82,163	Tennessee	106,750/41,216
Kansas	211,900/81,815	Ohio	106,050/40,946
Minnesota	206,200/79,614	Kentucky	102,900/39,730
South Dakota	199,750/77,123	Virginia	102,550/39,595
Nebraska	196,600/75,907	Indiana	92,900/35,869
North Dakota	178,700/68,996	Maine	79,950/30,869
Missouri	178,450/68,890	South Carolina	78,000/30,116
Oklahoma	177,900/68,688	West Virginia	62,400/24,093
Washington	172,450/66,583	Maryland	25,300/9,768
Georgia	150,000/57,915	Vermont	23,950/9,247
Michigan	147,150/56,815	New Hampshire	23,250/8,977
Iowa	144,700/55,869	Massachusetts	20,300/7,838
Illinois	144,000/55,599	New Jersey	19,200/7,413
Wisconsin	140,650/54,305	Hawaii	16,650/6,429
Florida	139,850/53,996	Connecticut	12,550/4,846
Arkansas	134,850/52,066	Delaware	5,050/1,950
Alabama	131,450/50,753	Rhode Island	2,700/1,042
North Carolina	126,200/48,726	Washington DC	150/579
New York	122,300/47,220		

USA
Capitals of States

Capital	State	Capital	State
Albany	New York	Des Moines	Iowa
Annapolis	Maryland	Dover	Delaware
Atlanta	Georgia	Frankfort	Kentucky
Augusta	Maine	Harrisburg	Pennsylvania
Austin	Texas	Hartford	Connecticut
Baton Rouge	Louisiana	Helena	Montana
Bismarck	North Dakota	Honolulu	Hawaii
Boise	Idaho	Indianapolis	Indiana
Boston	Massachusetts	Jackson	Mississippi
Carson City	Nevada	Jefferson City	Missouri
Charleston	West Virginia	Juneau	Alaska
Cheyenne	Wyoming	Lansing	Michigan
Columbia	South Carolina	Lincoln	Nebraska
Columbus	Ohio	Little Rock	Arkansas
Concord	New Hampshire	Madison	Wisconsin
Denver	Colorado	Montgomery	Alabama

USA: Capitals of States (*continued*)

Capital	State	Capital	State
Montpelier	Vermont	Salem	Oregon
Nashville	Tennessee	Salt Lake City	Utah
Oklahoma City	Oklahoma	Santa Fe	New Mexico
Olympia	Washington	Springfield	Illinois
Phoenix	Arizona	St Paul	Minnesota
Pierre	South Dakota	Tallahassee	Florida
Providence	Rhode Island	Topeka	Kansas
Raleigh	North Carolina	Trenton	New Jersey
Richmond	Virginia	Washington	District of Columbia (Federal District)
Sacramento	California		

USA
Date of Joining the Union

State	Joined the union	State	Joined the union
Delaware	1787	Arkansas	1836
New Jersey	1787	Michigan	1837
Pennsylvania	1787	Florida	1845
Connecticut	1788	Texas	1845
Georgia	1788	Iowa	1846
Maryland	1788	Wisconsin	1848
Massachusetts	1788	California	1850
New Hampshire	1788	Minnesota	1858
New York	1788	Oregon	1859
South Carolina	1788	Kansas	1861
Virginia	1788	West Virginia	1863
North Carolina	1789	Nevada	1864
Rhode Island	1790	Nebraska	1867
District of Columbia (Federal District)	established by Act of Congress 1790–91	Colorado	1876
		Montana	1889
Vermont	1791	North Dakota	1889
Kentucky	1792	South Dakota	1889
Louisiana	1792	Washington	1889
Tennessee	1796	Idaho	1890
Ohio	1803	Wyoming	1890
Maine	1812	Utah	1896
Indiana	1816	Oklahoma	1907
Mississippi	1817	Arizona	1912
Illinois	1818	New Mexico	1912
Alabama	1819	Alaska	1959
Missouri	1821	Hawaii	1959

USA

Nicknames and Abbreviations of States

State	Nickname(s)	Abbreviation
Alabama	Heart of Dixie/Camellia State	AL
Alaska	Mainland State/The Last Frontier	AK
Arizona	Grand Canyon State/Apache State	AZ
Arkansas	Bear State/Land of Opportunity	AR
California	Golden State	CA
Colorado	Centennial State	CO
Connecticut	Constitution State/Nutmeg State	CT
Delaware	First State/Diamond State	DE
Florida	Sunshine State/Everglade State	FL
Georgia	Empire State of the South/Peach State	GA
Hawaii	Aloha State	HI
Idaho	Gem State	ID
Illinois	Inland Empire/Prairie State/Land of Lincoln	IL
Indiana	Hoosier State	IN
Iowa	Hawkeye State/Corn State	IA
Kansas	Sunflower State/Jayhawker State	KS
Kentucky	Bluegrass State	KY
Louisiana	Pelican State/Sugar State/Creole State	LA
Maine	Pine Tree State	ME
Maryland	Old Line State/Free State	MD
Massachusetts	Bay State/Old Colony	MA
Michigan	Great Lakes State/Wolverine State	MI
Minnesota	North Star State/Gopher State	MN
Mississippi	Magnolia State	MS
Missouri	Show Me State/Bullion State	MO
Montana	Treasure State/Big Sky Country	MT
Nebraska	Cornhusker State/Beef State	NE
Nevada	Sagebrush State/Silver State/Battleborn State	NV
New Hampshire	Granite State	NH
New Jersey	Garden State	NJ
New Mexico	Land of Enchantment/Sunshine State	NM
New York	Empire State	NY
North Carolina	Tar Heel State/Old North State	NC
North Dakota	Peace Garden State	ND
Ohio	Buckeye State	OH
Oklahoma	Sooner State	OK
Oregon	Beaver State/Sunset State	OR
Pennsylvania	Keystone State	PA
Rhode Island	Little Rhody/Ocean State	RI
South Carolina	Palmetto State	SC
South Dakota	Coyote State/Mount Rushmore State	SD
Tennessee	Volunteer State	TN
Texas	Lone Star State	TX
Utah	Beehive State/Mormon State	UT
Vermont	Green Mountain State	VT
Virginia	Old Dominion State/Mother of Presidents	VA

USA: Nicknames and Abbreviations of States (*continued*)

State	Nickname(s)	Abbreviation
Washington	Evergreen State/Chinook State	WA
West Virginia	Mountain State/Panhandle State	WV
Wisconsin	Badger State/America's Dairyland	WI
Wyoming	Equality State	WY
District of Columbia (Federal District)	–	DC

USA
States with Highest Population

State	Population	State	Population
California	32,667,000	Utah	2,100,000
Texas	19,760,000	Nevada	1,747,000
Washington	5,689,000	New Mexico	1,737,000
Missouri	5,439,000	Nebraska	1,663,000
Minnesota	4,725,000	Idaho	1,229,000
Arizona	4,669,000	Montana	880,000
Colorado	3,971,000	South Dakota	738,000
Oklahoma	3,347,000	North Dakota	638,000
Oregon	3,282,000	Alaska	614,000
Kansas	2,629,000	Wyoming	481,000

Volcanoes
Most Destructive 20th-Century Eruptions

Volcano	Location	Year	Estimated number of deaths
Pelée	Martinique	1902	28,000
Nevado del Ruiz	Colombia	1985	23,000
Kelut	Java, Indonesia	1919	5,500
Lamington	Papua New Guinea	1951	3,000
El Chichon	Mexico	1982	1,880
Lake Nyos	Cameroon	1986	1,700
Taal	Philippines	1911	1,400
Santa María	Guatemala	1902	1,000
Pinatubo	Luzon, Philippines	1991	639
Vulcan	Papua New Guinea	1937	500
Mayon	Philippines	1993	70
St Helens	USA	1980	57
Unzen	Japan	1991	39
Merapi	Java, Indonesia	1998	38
Soufriere	Montserrat	1997	23
Loki	Iceland	1996	0

Volcanoes

World Volcanic Activity 1999–2000

As of 3 April 2000.

Region	Volcano	Height (m/ft)	Location	Year of last eruption or activity
Africa	Cameroon	4,096/13,438	isolated mountain, Cameroon	1999
	Nyamuragira	3,056/10,026	Democratic Republic of Congo	2000
Asia	Mayon	2,462/8,077	Luzon, Philippines	2000
	Krakatoa	818/2,684	Sumatra, Indonesia	1999
	Taal	300/984	Philippines	1999
Atlantic Ocean	Hekla	1,491/4,892	Iceland	2000
Caribbean	Soufrière Hills/ Chances Peak	968/3,176	Montserrat	2000
Central America	Fuego	3,835/12,582	Sierra Madre, Guatemala	1999
	Pacaya	2,543/8,343	Sierra Madre, Guatemala	2000
Europe	Kliuchevskoi	4,750/15,584	Kamchatka Peninsula, Russia	1999
	Etna	3,236/10,617	Sicily, Italy	2000
	Bezymianny	2,882/9,455	Kamchatka Peninsula, Russia	2000
Indian Ocean	Piton de la Fournaise	1,823/5,981	Réunion Island, France	2000
mid-Pacific	Kilauea	1,247/4,091	Hawaii, USA	2000
North America	Popocatépetl	5,452/17,887	Altiplano de México, Mexico	2000
	Colima	4,268/14,003	Altiplano de México, Mexico	1999
	Shishaldin	2,861/9,386	Aleutian Islands, USA	2000
Oceania	Ruapehu	2,796/9,173	New Zealand	1999
	White Island	328/1,076	New Zealand	2000

Volcanoes
World's Most Destructive Pre-20th-Century Eruptions

Volcano	Location/year	Estimated number of deaths
Santorini	Greece (1470 BC)	unknown; explosion four times more powerful than Krakatoa
Krakatoa	Indonesia (1883)	36,000
Etna	Sicily, Italy (1669)	20,000
Vesuvius	Italy (AD 79)	16,000
Unzen	Japan (1792)	14,500
Kelut	Java, Indonesia (1586)	10,000
Tambora	Sumbawa, Indonesia (1815)	10,000
Laki	Iceland (1783)	9,350
Vesuvius	Italy (1631)	4,000
Papandayan	Java, Indonesia (1772)	3,000

Waterfalls
Largest By Volume of Flow

(Alternative or former names are given in parentheses.)

Falls	River	Mean annual flow (cubic m per sec/ cubic ft per sec)
Boyoma (Stanley)	Lualaba	17,000/600,350
Khône	Mekong	12,000/423,776
Niagara (including Horseshoe, Canadian, and American Falls)	Niagara	6,000/211,888
Paulo Afonso	São Francisco	2,800/98,881
Cataratas del Iguazú	Iguazú	1,700/60,035
Patos-Maribondo	Rio Grande, Brazil	1,500/52,972
Victoria	Zambezi	1,100/38,846
Churchill (Grand)	Churchill	975/34,432
Kaieteur (Koituok)	Potaro	660/23,308

Waterfalls

World's Highest Waterfalls

Waterfall	Location	Total drop (m/ft)
Angel Falls	Venezuela	980/3,215
Yosemite Falls	USA	740/2,428
Mardalsfossen–South	Norway	655/2,149
Tugela Falls	South Africa	615/2,018
Cuquenan	Venezuela	610/2,001
Sutherland	New Zealand	580/1,903
Great Karamang River Falls	Guyana	490/1,608
Ribbon Fall, Yosemite	USA	490/1,608
Mardalsfossen–North	Norway	470/1,542
Della Falls	Canada	440/1,444

Sport, Games,
and
Leisure

Aerobatics
World Championships (Men)

Year	Recent winners
1980	Leo Loudenslager (USA)
1982	Victor Smolin (USSR)
1984	Petr Jirmus (Czechoslovakia)
1986	Petr Jirmus (Czechoslovakia)
1988	Henry Haigh (USA)
1990	Claude Bessiere (France)
1992	(competition abandoned due to adverse weather)
1994	Xavier de Lapparent (France)
1996	Victor Chmal (Russia)
1998	Patrick Paris (France)
2000	Eric Vazeille (France)

Aerobatics
World Championships (Women)

This competition is for the Royal Aero Club Trophy.

Year	Recent winners
1986	Liubov Nemkova (USSR)
1988	Catherine Maunoury (France)
1990	Natalya Sergeeva (USSR)
1992	(competition abandoned due to adverse weather)
1994	Christine Genin (France)
1996	Svetlana Kapanina (Russia)
1998	Svetlana Kapanina (Russia)
2000	Catherine Maunoury (France)

Alpine Skiing
World Champions 2001

The 2001 championships were held at St Anton am Arlberg, Austria 28 January–10 February

Category	Name	Country
Men		
downhill	Hannes Trinkl	Austria
slalom	Mario Matt	Austria
giant slalom	Michael Von Greunigen	Switzerland
super giant slalom	Daron Rahlves	USA
combination	Kjetil Andre Aamodt	Norway
Women		
downhill	Michaela Dorfmeister	Austria
slalom	Anja Paerson	Sweden
giant slalom	Sonja Nef	Switzerland
super giant slalom	Ravine Cavagnoud	France
combination	Martina Ertl	Germany

Alpine Skiing
World Cup Winners 2000-2001

Category	Name	Country
Men		
downhill	Hermann Maier	Austria
slalom	Benjamin Raich	Austria
giant slalom	Hermann Maier	Austria
super giant slalom	Hermann Maier	Austria
overall	Hermann Maier	Austria

Alpine Skiing: World Cup Winners 2000-2001 (*continued*)

Category	Name	Country
Women		
downhill	Isolde Kostner	Italy
slalom	Janica Kostelic	Croatia
giant slalom	Sonja Nef	Switzerland
super giant slalom	Ravine Cavagnoud	France
overall	Janica Kostelic	Croatia

Amateur Sports
Most Hazardous

Sport	Deaths (per million hours played)
air sports	800
climbing	800
water sports	70
horse riding	30
rugby	16
boxing	5

American Football
Largest Stadiums in the NFL

Stadium	Location	Capacity
Pontiac Silverdome	Detroit	80,368
FedExField	Washington	80,116
Giants Stadium	New York	79,469
Arrowhead Stadium	Kansas	79,409
Mile High Stadium	Denver	76,098
Ralph Wilson Stadium	Buffalo	75,339
Pro Player Stadium	Miami	74,916
Sun Devil Stadium	Tucson	73,273
Ericsson Stadium	Charlotte	73,258
Cleveland Browns Stadium	Cleveland	73,200

American Football
Leading Passers During a National Football League (NFL) Career

Name	Total yards passed (as of 2000)
Dan Marino	61,361
John Elway	51,475
Warren Moon	49,247
Fran Tarkenton	47,003
Dan Fouts	43,040
Joe Montana	40,551
Johnny Unitas	40,239
Dave Krieg	38,151
Boomer Esiason	37,920
Jim Kelly	35,467

American Football
Leading Scorers by Career Points

Name	Total points (as of 2000)
Gary Anderson	2,059
George Blanda	2,002
Morten Andersen	1,934
Norm Johnson	1,736
Nick Lowery	1,711
Jan Stenerud	1,699
Eddie Murray	1,549
Pat Leahy	1,470
Jim Turner	1,439
Al Del Greco	1,568

American Football

Leading Scorers by NFL Career Touchdowns (to end of 2000 season)

Name	Touchdowns
Jerry Rice	187
Emmitt Smith	156
Marcus Allen	145
Jim Brown	126
Walter Payton	125
Cris Carter	124
John Riggins	116
Lenny Moore	113
Barry Sanders	109
Don Hutson	105

American Football

Leading Scorers by Points Scored in One Season

Name	Team	Season	Points
Paul Hornung	Green Bay Packers	1960	176
Gary Anderson	Minnesota Vikings	1998	164
Mark Moseley	Washington Redskins	1983	161
Gino Cappelletti	Boston Patriots	1964	155
Emmitt Smith	Dallas Cowboys	1995	150
Chip Lohmiller	Washington Redskins	1991	149
Gino Cappelletti	Boston Patriots	1961	147
Paul Hornung	Green Bay Packers	1961	146
John Kasay	Carolina Panthers	1996	145
Jim Turner	New York Jets	1968	145
Mike Vanderjagt	Indianapolis Colts	1999	145

American Football

Leading Scorers by Touchdowns Scored in One NFL Season

Name	Team	Season	Touch-downs
Emmitt Smith	Dallas Cowboys	1995	25
John Riggins	Washington Redskins	1983	24
O J Simpson	Buffalo Bills	1975	23
Jerry Rice	San Francisco 49ers	1987	23
Terrell Davis	Denver Broncos	1998	23

(A number of players have scored 22 touchdowns in one season.)

American Football

Most Successful Coaches

Coach	Games won (as of 1999)
Don Shula	347
George Halas	324
Tom Landry	270
Earl Lambeau	229
Chuck Noll	209
Chuck Knox	193
Dan Reeves	181
Paul Brown	170
Bud Grant	168
Marv Levy	154

American Football

Most Successful Teams by Super Bowl Wins

Wins	Team	Years
5	Dallas Cowboys	1972, 1978, 1993, 1994, 1996
5	San Francisco 49ers	1982, 1985, 1989, 1990, 1995
4	Pittsburgh Steelers	1975, 1976, 1979, 1980
3	Green Bay Packers	1967, 1968, 1997
3	Oakland Raiders/ LA Raiders	1977, 1981, 1984
3	Washington Redskins	1983, 1988, 1992
2	Miami Dolphins	1973, 1974
2	New York Giants	1987, 1991
2	Denver Broncos	1998, 1999
1	New York Jets	1969
1	Kansas City Chiefs	1970
1	Baltimore Colts	1971
1	Chicago Bears	1986
1	St Louis Rams	2000
1	Baltimore Ravens	2001

American Football

Recent Super Bowl Results

Super Bowl	Year	Result
XXXV	2001	Baltimore Ravens 34, New York Giants 7
XXXIV	2000	St Louis Rams 23, Tennessee Titans 16
XXXIII	1999	Denver Broncos 34, Atlanta Falcons 19
XXXII	1998	Denver Broncos 31, Green Bay Packers 24
XXXI	1997	Green Bay Packers 35, New England Patriots 21
XXX	1996	Dallas Cowboys 27, Pittsburgh Steelers 17
XXIX	1995	San Francisco 49ers 49, San Diego 26
XXVIII	1994	Dallas Cowboys 30, Buffalo Bills 13
XXVII	1993	Dallas Cowboys 52, Buffalo Bills 17
XXVI	1992	Washington Redskins 37, Buffalo Bills 24
XXV	1991	New York Giants 20, Buffalo Bills 19

American Football

World Bowl Winners

Year	Winners	Losers	Score
2000	Rhein Fire	Scottish Claymores	13–10
1999	Frankfurt Galaxy	Barcelona Dragons	38–24
1998	Rhein Fire	Frankfurt Galaxy	34–10
1997	Barcelona Dragons	Rhein Fire	38–24
1996	Scottish Claymores	Frankfurt Galaxy	32–27
1995	Frankfurt Galaxy	Amsterdam Admirals	26–22

Athletics

First Athletes to Run 4-Minute Miles

Date	Athlete (country)	Location	Time (min:sec)
May 1954	Roger Bannister (UK)	Oxford, UK	3:59.4
June 1954	John Landy (Australia)	Turku, Finland	3:57.9
May 1955	Lazlo Tabori (Hungary)	London, UK	3:59.0

(continued)

Date	Athlete (country)	Location	Time (min:sec)
May 1955	Chris Chataway (UK)	London, UK	3:59.8

Svetlana Masterkova of the Russian Federation is the fastest female athlete over this distance. Her record time of 4 minutes 12.56 seconds was set in August 1996 at Zürich, Switzerland.

Athletics
Male World Champions 1999 – Field Events

Event	Name	Country
high jump	Vyacheslav Voronin	Russia
pole vault	Maksim Tarakov	Russia
long jump	Iván Pedroso	Cuba
triple jump	Charles Michael Friedek	Germany
shot	C J Hunter	USA
discus	Anthony Washington	USA
hammer	Karsten Kobs	Germany
javelin	Aki Parviainen	Finland
decathlon	Tomas Dvorak	Czech Republic

Athletics
Male World Champions 1999 – Track Events

Event	Name	Country
100 m	Maurice Greene	USA
200 m	Maurice Greene	USA
400 m	Michael Johnson	USA
800 m	Wilson Kipketer	Denmark
1,500 m	Hicham El Guerrouj	Morocco
5,000 m	Salah Hissou	Morocco
10,000 m	Haile Gebrselassie	Ethiopia
marathon	Abel Anton	Spain
3,000 m steeplechase	Christopher Koskei	Kenya
110 m hurdles	Colin Jackson	Great Britain
400 m hurdles	Fabrizio Mori	Italy
4 × 100 m relay		USA
4 × 400 m relay		USA
20 km walk	Ilya Markov	Russia
50 km walk	German Skurygin	Russia

Athletics

Men's Individual Cross-Country World Champions

This championship is run over 12 km/7.5 mi.

Year	Name	Country
2001	Mohammed Mourhit	Belgium
2000	Mohammed Mourhit	Belgium
1999	Paul Tergat	Kenya
1998	Paul Tergat	Kenya
1997	Paul Tergat	Kenya
1996	Paul Tergat	Kenya
1995	Paul Tergat	Kenya
1994	William Sigei	Kenya
1993	William Sigei	Kenya
1992	John Ngugi	Kenya

Athletics

Team Cross-Country World Champions

Year	Men's team	Women's team
2001	Kenya	Kenya
2000	Kenya	Ethiopia
1999	Kenya	France
1998	Kenya	Kenya
1997	Kenya	Kenya
1996	Kenya	Kenya
1995	Kenya	Kenya

Athletics

Women's Individual Cross-Country World Champions

This championship is run over 12 km/7.5 mi.

Year	Name	Country
2001	Paula Radcliffe	UK
2000	Derartu Tulu	Ethiopia
1999	Jackline Maranga	Kenya
1998	Sonia O'Sullivan	Ireland, Republic of
1997	Derartu Tulu	Ethiopia
1996	Gete Wami	Ethiopia
1995	Derartu Tulu	Ethiopia
1994	Helen Chepngeno	Kenya
1993	Albertina Dias	Portugal
1992	Lynn Jennings	USA

Australian Football

Recent League Champions

Year	Team
2000	Essendon
1999	Kangaroos
1998	Adelaide
1997	Adelaide
1996	North Melbourne
1995	Carlton Blues
1994	West Coast
1993	Essendon
1992	West Coast
1991	Hawthorn

Baseball

Leading Run Scorers Over Career

Player	Runs	Player	Runs	Player	Runs
Ty Cobb	2,245	Pete Rose	2,165	Tris Speaker	1,882
Rickey Henderson	2,178	Willie Mays	2,062	Mel Ott	1,859
Hank Aaron	2,174	Stan Musial	1,949	Frank Robinson	1,829
Babe Ruth	2,174	Lou Gehrig	1,888	Eddie Collins	1,820

Baseball

World Series

Year	Winner	Loser	Score
2000	New York Yankees	New York Mets	4–2
1999	New York Yankees	Atlanta Braves	4–0
1998	New York Yankees	San Diego Padres	4–0
1997	Florida Marlins	Cleveland Indians	4–3
1996	New York Yankees	Atlanta Braves	4–2
1995	Atlanta Braves	Cleveland Indians	4–2
1994	no World Series (players' strike)		
1993	Toronto Blue Jays	Philadelphia Phillies	4–2
1992	Toronto Blue Jays	Atlanta Braves	4–2
1991	Minnesota Twins	Atlanta Braves	4–3

Basketball

Female World Champions

Year	Country
1998	USA
1994	Brazil
1990	USA
1986	USA
1983	USSR
1979	USA
1975	USSR
1971	USSR
1967	USSR
1964	USSR

Basketball

Leading Scorers by Percentage of Free Throws (in a Single Season)

Player (season)	Percentage
Calvin Murphy (1981)	95.8
Mahmoud Abdul-Rauf (1994)	95.6
Jeff Hornacek (2000)	95.0
Mark Price (1993)	94.8
Rick Barry (1979)	94.7
Ernie DiGregorio (1977)	94.5
Chris Mullin (1998)	93.9
Spud Webb (1995)	93.4
Bill Sharman	93.2
Larry Bird	93.0

Basketball

Leading Scorers in the NBA

Player	Career points to end of December 2000
Kareem Abdul-Jabbar	38,387
Karl Malone	31,443
Wilt Chamberlain	31,419
Michael Jordan	29,277
Moses Malone	27,409
Elvin Hayes	27,313
Oscar Robertson	26,710
Dominique Wilkins	26,668
John Havlicek	26,395
Hakeem Olajuwon	26,101
Alex English	25,613
Jerry West	25,192

Basketball

Leading Scorers in the NBA (by percentage of career field goal attempts scored)

Name	Percentage scored [1]	Name	Percentage scored [1]
Artis Gilmore	59.9	Jeff Ruland	56.4
Mark West	58.0	Kareem Abdul-Jabbar	55.9
Shaquille O'Neal	57.7	Kevin McHale	55.4
Steve Johnson	57.2	Bobby Jones	55.0
Darryl Dawkins	57.2	Buck Williams	54.9
James Donaldson	57.1	Otis Thorpe	54.7

[1] To end of 1999–2000 season.

Basketball

Leading Scorers in the NBA by Number of Career Field Goals

Name	Total field goals[1]
Kareem Abdul-Jabbar	15,837
Wilt Chamberlain	12,681
Karl Malone	11,435
Elvin Hayes	10,976
Michael Jordan	10,962
Alex English	10,659
John Havlicek	10,513
Hakeem Olajuwon	10,272
Dominique Wilkins	9,963
Robert Parish	9,614
Oscar Robertson	9,508
Moses Malone	9,435

[1] To end of 1999–2000 season.

Basketball

Male World Champions

Year	Country
1998	Yugoslavia
1994	USA
1990	Yugoslavia
1986	USA
1982	USSR
1978	Yugoslavia
1974	USSR
1970	Yugoslavia
1967	USSR
1963	Brazil

Basketball

Men's Olympic Gold Medallists

An Olympic event since 1948.

Country	Year	Country	Year	Country	Year
USA	1948–68	Yugoslavia	1980	USA	1992
USSR	1972	USA	1984	USA	1996
USA	1976	USSR	1988	USA	2000

Basketball
National Association Champions

Year	Winner	Runner up	Series
2000	Los Angeles Lakers	Indiana Pacers	4–2
1999	San Antonio Spurs	New York Knicks	4–1
1998	Chicago Bulls	Utah Jazz	4–2
1997	Chicago Bulls	Utah Jazz	4–2
1996	Chicago Bulls	Seattle SuperSonics	4–2
1995	Houston Rockets	Orlando Magic	4–0
1994	Houston Rockets	New York Knicks	4–3
1993	Chicago Bulls	Phoenix Suns	4–2
1992	Chicago Bulls	Portland Trail Blazers	4–2
1991	Chicago Bulls	Los Angeles Lakers	4–1

Basketball
Teams in the Women's National Basketball Association (WNBA)

The WNBA, comprising eight teams, was inaugurated in June 1997. Since then, a further eight teams have joined the WNBA; these teams are followed by the season of their incorporation. The WNBA title has been won on all four occasions (1997, 1998, 1999, 2000) by the Houston Comets.

Eastern conference

Charlotte Sting
Cleveland Rockers
Detroit Shock (1998)
Indiana Fever (2000)
Miami Sol (2000)
New York Liberty
Orlando Miracle (1999)
Washington Mystics (1998)

Western conference

Houston Comets
Los Angeles Sparks
Minnesota Lynx (1999)
Phoenix Mercury
Portland Fire (2000)
Sacramento Monarchs
Seattle Storm (2000)
Utah Starzz

Basketball
Teams with Most National Basketball Association (NBA) Titles

Titles	Team	Years	Titles	Team	Years
16	Boston Celtics	1956–86	2	Philadelphia 76ers	1966–83
7	Los Angeles Lakers	1971–2000	2	New York Knicks	1969–73
6	Chicago Bulls	1990–98	2	Detroit Pistons	1988–90
5	Minnesota Lakers	1948–54	2	Houston Rockets	1993–95
2	Philadelphia Warriors	1946–56			

Basketball

Top 10 Coaches in the First 50 Years of the NBA

Selected by balloting media members who cover the NBA, as part of the 'NBA at 50' celebration during the 1996–97 season. Collectively, these coaches have garnered approximately 7500 regular season wins, 30 NBA titles, and 13 NBA Coach of the Year Awards (first awarded 1962–63).

Coach	Wins	Losses	% won
Red Auerbach	938	479	66.2
Chuck Daly	605	420	59.0
Bill Fitch	944	1,106	46.0
Red Holzman	696	604	53.5
Phil Jackson	545	193	73.8
John Kundla	423	302	58.3
Don Nelson	867	679	57.5
Jack Ramsay	864	783	52.5
Pat Riley	914	387	70.3
Lenny Wilkens	1120	908	52.6

Basketball

Women's Olympic Gold Medallists

An Olympic event since 1948.

Country	Year
USSR	1976
USSR	1980
USA	1984
USA	1988
unified team (CIS)	1992
USA	1996
USA	2000

Board Games

Game	Game	Game
Scrabble	Snakes and Ladders	Twister
Cluedo	The Game of Life	Trivial Pursuit
Sorry	Chess	
Monopoly	Risk	

Boxing

Current World Champions

WBA = World Boxing Association; WBC = World Boxing Council; IBF = International Boxing Federation.

Weight	WBA	WBC	IBF
heavyweight	John Ruiz (Puerto Rico)	Hasim Rahman (USA)	Hasim Rahman (USA)
cruiserweight	Virgil Hill (USA)	Juan Carlos Gomez (Cuba)	Vasily Jirov (Kazakhstan)
light heavyweight	Roy Jones Jr (USA)	Roy Jones Jr (USA)	Roy Jones Jr (USA)
super middleweight	Byron Mitchell (USA)	Dave Hilton (UK)	Sven Ottke (Germany)
middleweight	William Joppy (USA)	Bernard Hopkins (USA)	Bernard Hopkins (USA)

(continued)

Boxing: Current World Champions (*continued*)

Weight	WBA	WBC	IBF
super welterweight	Konstantin Tszyu (Australia)	Konstantin Tszyu (Australia)	Zabdiel Judah (USA)
welterweight	Andrew Lewis (Guyana)	Shane Mosley (USA)	vacant
lightweight	Takanori Hatakeyama (Japan)	Juan Luis Castillo (Mexico)	Paul Spadafora (USA)
featherweight	Derrick Gainer (USA)	Erik Morales (Mexico)	Frankie Toledo (USA)
bantamweight	Pauli Ayala (USA)	Veerapol Sahaprom (Thailand)	Tim Austin (USA)
flyweight	Eric Morel (USA)	Pongsaklek Wonjongkam (Thailand)	Irene Pacheco (Columbia)
strawweight	Chana Porpaoin (Thailand)	Jose Antonio Aguirre (Mexico)	vacant

Boxing

World Heavyweight Champions

Present weight limit: over 86.2 kg/190 lb. Fighters are US nationals unless otherwise stated.

WBA champions		WBC champions		IBF champions	
Year	Name	Year	Name	Year	Name
2001–	John Ruiz (Puerto Rico)	2001–	Hasim Rahman	2001–	Hasim Rahman
2000-2001	Evander Holyfield	1997-2001	Lennox Lewis (UK)	1999-2001	Lennox Lewis (UK)
1999-2000	Lennox Lewis (UK)	1996	Mike Tyson	1997-99	Evander Holyfield
1996-99	Evander Holyfield	1995-96	Frank Bruno (UK)	1996	Michael Moorer
1995-99	Bruce Seldon	1994-95	Oliver McCall	1994-95	George Foreman
1996	Mike Tyson	1992-94	Lennox Lewis (UK)	1994	Michael Moorer
1994-95	George Foreman	1992	Riddick Bowe	1993-94	Evander Holyfield
1994	Michael Moorer	1990-92	Evander Holyfield	1992-93	Riddick Bowe
1993-94	Evander Holyfield	1990	James 'Buster' Douglas	1990-92	Evander Holyfield
1992-93	Riddick Bowe	1986-90	Mike Tyson	1990	James 'Buster' Douglas
1990-92	Evander Holyfield	1986	Trevor Berbick (Canada)	1987-90	Mike Tyson
1990	James 'Buster' Douglas				
1987-90	Mike Tyson				

Chess

Recent Male World FIDE Champions

Year	Player	Nationality
1963	Tigran Petrosian	USSR
1969	Boris Spassky	USSR
1972	Bobby Fischer	USA
1975	Anatoly Karpov	USSR
1985	Gary Kasparov	USSR/Azerbaijan
1993	Anatoly Karpov	Russia
1998	Anatoly Karpov	Russia
1999	Alexander Khalifman	Russia
2000	Vishwanathan Anand	India

Chess

Recent Female World FIDE Champions

Year	Player	Nationality
1962	Nona Gaprindashvili	USSR
1978	Maya Chiburdanidze	USSR
1991	Xie Jun	China
1996	Zsuzsu Polgar	Hungary
1997	Harriet Hunt	UK
1998	Judit Polgar	Hungary
1999	Xie Jun	China
2000	Xie Jun	China

Collectors

Collector	What is collected
antiquarian	old objects
bibliophile	fine books
deltiologist	postcards
exlibrist	book plates (illustrations)
numismatist	coins and medals
philatelist	postage stamps
pillumenist	matchbox labels
tegestologist	beer mats

Computer Games

Computer game	Manufacturer
Buggy Boy	Amiga
Birds of Prey	Amiga
Star Wars	Spectrum
Stunt Car Racer	Amiga
Network Q RAC Rally Championship	PC
Arkanoid	Amiga
Pinball Dreams	Gameboy
Civilisation	PC
Lemmings	PC, Eidos
Tomb Raider	PC, Psygnosis
FIFA Soccer	PC, EA Sports
Myst	Cyan

Cricket

Highest Individual Run-making Average in a Test Career

Batsman	Average runs (per wicket lost)	Batsman	Average runs (per wicket lost)
D G Bradman (Australia)	99.94	E D Weekes (West Indies)	58.61
R G Pollock (South Africa)	60.97	W R Hammond (England)	58.45
G A Headley (West Indies)	60.83	G S Sobers (West Indies)	57.78
H Sutcliffe (England)	60.73	S R Tendulkar (India)	56.94
E Paynter (England)	59.23	J B Hobbs (England)	56.94
K F Barrington (England)	58.67	C L Walcott (West Indies)	56.68

Cricket
Most Test Centuries in a Career

Batsman	Test centuries	Batsman	Test centuries
S M Gavaskar (India)	34	I V A Richards (West Indies)	24
D G Bradman (Australia)	29	Javed Miandad (Pakistan)	23
A R Border (Australia)	27	G Boycott (England)	22
G S Sobers (West Indies)	26	M C Cowdrey (England)	22
S R Tendulkar (India)	25	W R Hammond (England)	22
S R Waugh (Australia)	25	M Azharuddin (India)	22
G S Chappell (Australia)	24		

Cricket
Most Test Wickets Taken by a Bowler in a Career

Wickets	Test	Player	Career years
519	132	C A Walsh (West Indies)	1984–2001
434	131	N Kapil Dev (India)	1978–94
431	86	R J Hadlee (New Zealand)	1973–90
409	100	Wasim Akram (Pakistan)	1985–2000
405	98	C E L Ambrose (West Indies)	1988–2000
383	102	I T Botham (England)	1977–92
376	81	M D Marshall (West Indies)	1978–91
376	87	S K Warne (Australia)	1992–2001
362	88	Imran Khan (Pakistan)	1971–92
355	70	D K Lillee (Australia)	1971–84

Cricket
Oldest Cricketers to Play for England in a Test Match

Age		Player	Opponents, venue	Year
Years	Days			
52	165	W Rhodes	West Indies, Kingston	1929–30
50	320	W G Grace	Australia, Nottingham	1899
50	303	G Gunn	West Indies, Kingston	1929–30
49	139	J Southerton	Australia, Melbourne	1876–77
47	249	J B Hobbs	Australia, The Oval	1930
47	87	F E Woolley	Australia, The Oval	1934
46	202	H Strudwick	Australia, The Oval	1926
46	41	E H Hendren	West Indies, Kingston	1934–35
45	245	G O B Allen	West Indies, Kingston	1947–48
45	215	P Holmes	India, Lord's	1932
45	140	D B Close	West Indies, Manchester	1976

Cricket
Oldest Cricketers to Play in a Test Match

Age		Player (country)	Opponents, venue	Year
Years	Days			
52	165	W Rhodes (England)	West Indies, Kingston	1929–30
50	327	H Ironmonger (Australia)	England, Sydney	1932–33
50	320	W G Grace (England)	Australia, Nottingham	1899
50	303	G Gunn (England)	West Indies, Kingston	1929–30
49	139	J Southerton (England)	Australia, Melbourne	1876–77
47	302	Miran Bux (Pakistan)	India, Peshawar	1954–55
47	249	J B Hobbs (England)	Australia, The Oval	1930
47	87	F E Woolley (England)	Australia, The Oval	1934
46	309	D D Blackie (Australia)	England, Adelaide	1928–29
46	206	A W Nourse (South Africa)	England, The Oval	1924
46	202	H Strudwick (England)	Australia, The Oval	1926
46	41	E H Hendren (England)	West Indies, Kingston	1934–35

Cricket
World Cup Winners

This competition was first held in 1975.

Year	Winner	Runner–up	Location	Year	Winner	Runner–up	Location
1999	Australia	Pakistan	UK	1987	Australia	England	India
1996	Sri Lanka	Australia	India, Pakistan, and Sri Lanka	1983	India	West Indies	UK
				1979	West Indies	England	UK
				1975	West Indies	Australia	UK
1992	Pakistan	England	Australia				

Cycling
Tour de France Winners

Year	Name	Country
2000	Lance Armstrong	USA
1999	Lance Armstrong	USA
1998	Marco Pantani	Italy
1997	Jan Ullrich	Germany
1996	Bjarne Riis	Denmark
1995	Miguel Induráin	Spain
1994	Miguel Induráin	Spain
1993	Miguel Induráin	Spain
1992	Miguel Induráin	Spain
1991	Miguel Induráin	Spain

Dice
Chances

Chances with two dice and a single throw.

Total count	Odds against
2	35 to 1
3	17 to 1
4	11 to 1
5	8 to 1
6	31 to 5
7	5 to 1
8	31 to 5
9	8 to 1
10	11 to 1
11	17 to 1
12	35 to 1

Games

Numbers Involved in Various Games

Item	Number
balls used in billiards	3
balls used in pool (including cue ball)	16
balls used in snooker (including cue ball)	22
bowls each player uses in flat and crown green bowls (excluding the jack)	4
cards in a Tarot pack	78
chess pieces each player has to begin with	16
counters each backgammon player has to begin with	15
dominoes (tiles) in a set	28
draughtsmen (checkers) each player has to begin with	12
games in a rubber of bridge	3
hoops on a croquet court	12
playing cards in a pack	52
'points' on a backgammon board	24
squares on a chessboard	64
squares on a Scrabble® board	225
skittles in the traditional game	9
suits in a normal pack of cards	4

Games

Top-Selling US Games (2000)

Game	Manufacturer
Harry Potter Mystery At Hogwarts Board Game	Mattel
Harry Potter Trivia Game	Mattel
Cranium	Cranium
Pass the Pigs	Milton Bradley
Monopoly Pokémon Edition	Hasbro
Wise and Otherwise	Wise and Otherwise
Simpsons Clue	USAopoly
Monopoly the .com Edition	Parker Brothers
Who Wants to be a Millionaire? Board Game	Pressman Toy
Who Wants to be a Millionaire? Junior Board Game	Pressman Toy

Golf
Famous Courses

Course	Location
Augusta National	Georgia, USA
Baltusrol	New Jersey, USA
The Belfry	Warwickshire, England
Carnoustie	Angus, Scotland
Kiawah Island	Hawaii, USA
Muirfield	East Lothian, Scotland
Royal St George's	Sandwich, Kent, England
St Andrews Old Course	Fife, Scotland
Turnberry	Ayrshire, Scotland
Valderrama	Cadiz, Spain

Golf
Highest Earners

In 2000, as of 30 November.

Golfer (country)	Total winnings (US$ millions)
Tiger Woods (USA)	9.19
Phil Mickelson (USA)	4.75
Ernie Els (South Africa)	3.47
Hal Sutton (USA)	3.06
Vijay Singh (Fiji)	2.57
Mike Weir (Canada)	2.55
David Duval (USA)	2.46
Jesper Parnevik (Sweden)	2.41
Davis Love III (USA)	2.34
Stewart Cink (USA)	2.17
Kirk Triplett (USA)	2.10
Tom Lehman (USA)	2.09

Golf
Highest-Earning Women Golfers

In 2000, as of 30 November.

Golfer (country)	Total winnings (US$ millions)
Karrie Webb (Australia)	1.88
Annika Sörenstam (Sweden)	1.40
Meg Mallon (USA)	1.15
Juli Inkster (USA)	0.98
Lorie Kane (Canada)	0.93
Pat Hurst (USA)	0.84
Mi Hyun Kim (South Korea)	0.83
Dottie Pepper (USA)	0.79
Rosie Jones (USA)	0.64
Michele Redman (USA)	0.59
Laura Davies (UK)	0.56
Pak Se-ri (South Korea)	0.55

Golf
Highest-Earning Women Golfers in a Career

In 2000, as of 30 November.

Golfer (country)	Total winnings (US$ millions)
Betsy King (USA)	6.83
Annika Sörenstam (Sweden)	6.20
Karrie Webb (Australia)	6.16
Juli Inkster (USA)	6.06
Beth Daniel (USA)	6.02
Dottie Pepper (USA)	5.88
Pat Bradley (USA)	5.74
Patty Sheehan (USA)	5.50
Meg Mallon (USA)	5.47
Nancy Lopez (USA)	5.30
Laura Davies (UK)	5.20
Rosie Jones (USA)	4.90

Golf
Lowest Winning Four-round Scores in the British Open

Score	Player (country)	Venue	Year
267	Greg Norman (Australia)	Sandwich	1993
268	Tom Watson (USA)	Turnberry	1977
268	Nick Price (Zimbabwe)	Turnberry	1994
270	Nick Faldo (UK)	St Andrews	1990
271	Tom Watson (USA)	Muirfield	1980
271	Tom Lehman (USA)	Lytham	1996
272	Ian Baker-Finch	Royal Birkdale	1991
272	Nick Faldo (UK)	Muirfield	1992
272	Justin Leonard	Royal Troon	1997

Golf
Lowest Winning Four-round Scores in the US Masters

Score	Player (country)	Year	Score	Player (country)	Year
270	Tiger Woods (USA)	1997	275	Severiano Ballesteros (Spain)	1980
271	Raymond Floyd (USA)	1976	275	Fred Couples (USA)	1992
271	Jack Nicklaus (USA)	1965	276	Nick Faldo (UK)	1996
272	Claude Harmon (USA)	1948	276	Jack Nicklaus (USA)	1975
274	Ben Crenshaw (USA)	1995	276	Arnold Palmer (USA)	1964
274	Ben Hogan (USA)	1953	276	Tom Watson (USA)	1977

Golf
Lowest Winning Four-round Scores in the US Open

Score	Player (country)	Venue	Year
272	Jack Nicklaus (USA)	Baltusrol	1980
272	Lee Janzen (USA)	Baltusrol	1993
272	Tiger Woods (USA)	Pebble Beach	2000
273	David Graham (Australia)	Merion	1981
275	Jack Nicklaus (USA)	Baltusrol	1967
275	Lee Trevino (USA)	Oak Hill	1968
276	Ben Hogan (USA)	Riviera	1948
276	Fuzzy Zoeller (USA)	Winged Foot	1984
276	Ernie Els (South Africa)	Congressional	1997
277	Jerry Pate (USA)	Atlanta	1976
277	Scott Simpson (USA)	Olympic Club	1987

Golf

Lowest Winning Four-round Scores in the US PGA Championship

Score	Player (country)	Venue, year	Score	Player (country)	Venue, year
267	Steve Elkington (Australia)	Riviera, 1995	272	Raymond Floyd (USA)	Southern Hills, 1982
269	Davis Love III (USA)	Winged Foot, 1997	272	David Graham (Australia)	Oakland Hills, 1979
269	Nick Price (Zimbabwe)	Southern Hills, 1994	272	Jeff Sluman (USA)	Oaktree, 1988
271	B Nichols (USA)	Columbus, 1964	273	Larry Nelson (USA)	Atlanta, 1981
271	Vijay Singh (Fiji)	Sahalee, 1998	273	Lee Trevino (USA)	Shoal Creek, 1984
272	Paul Azinger (USA)	Inverness (Toledo), 1993			

Golf

Ryder Cup Winners

Year	Winner	Score	Location
1999	USA	14.5–13.5	The Country Club, Brookline (MA), USA
1997	Europe	14.5–13.5	Valderrama, Andalucia, Spain
1995	Europe	14.5–13.5	Oak Hill CC (NY), USA
1993	USA	15–13	The Belfry, Sutton Coldfield, UK
1991	USA	14.5–13.5	Ocean Course (SC), USA
1989	tie	14–14	The Belfry, Sutton Coldfield, UK
1987	Europe	15–13	Muirfield Village GC (OH), USA
1985	Europe	16.5–11.5	The Belfry, Sutton Coldfield, UK
1983	USA	14.5–13.5	PGA National GC (FL), USA
1981	USA	18.5–9.5	Walton Heath, Surrey, UK

Golf

US Masters Winners

Year	Name	Country	Score	Year	Name	Country	Score
2001	Tiger Woods	USA	272	1996	Nick Faldo	UK	276
2000	Vijay Singh	Fiji	278	1995	Ben Crenshaw	USA	274
1999	José-Maria Olazábal	Spain	279	1994	José-Maria Olazábal	Spain	279
1998	Mark O'Meara	USA	279	1993	Bernhard Langer	Germany	277
1997	Tiger Woods	USA	270	1992	Fred Couples	USA	275

Golf
US Open Winners (Women)

Players are of US nationality unless otherwise stated

Year	Winner	Score	Year	Winner	Score
2000	Karrie Webb (Australia)	202	1995	Annika Sorenstam (Sweden)	278
1999	Juli Inkster	272	1994	Patty Sheehan	277
1998	Se Ri Pak (South Korea)	290	1993	Lauri Merten	280
1997	Alison Nicholas (UK)	274	1992	Patty Sheehan[1]	280
1996	Annika Sorenstam (Sweden)	272	1991	Meg Mallon	283

[1] Winner after a playoff.

Golf
Winners of Highest Number of Majors During Career (to end 2000)

The majors are: the British Open, the US Open, the US Masters, and the US PGA Championship.

Golfer (country)	Titles	Golfer (country)	Titles
Jack Nicklaus (USA)	18	Gene Sarazen (USA)	7
Walter Hagen (USA)	11	Sam Snead (USA)	7
Ben Hogan (USA)	9	Harry Vardon (UK)	7
Gary Player (South Africa)	9	Nick Faldo (UK)	6
Tom Watson (USA)	8	Lee Trevino (USA)	6
Bobby Jones (USA)	7	Tiger Woods (USA)	6
Arnold Palmer (USA)	7		

Golf
Winners of Highest Number of Women's Majors During Career since 1983

From 1983 the women's majors were: the US Women's Open, the US LPGA Championship, the du Maurier Classic, and the Nabisco Dinah Shore Championship. In 2001 the Weetabix Women's British Open replaced the du Maurier Classic.

Player (country)	Titles	Player (country)	Titles
Juli Inkster (USA)	6	Pat Bradley (USA)	3
Betsy King (USA)	6	Laura Davies (UK)	3
Patty Sheehan (USA)	6	Annika Sorenstam (Sweden)	3
Amy Alcott (USA)	3	Karrie Webb (Australia)	3

Golf
Winners of the Dinah Shore Women's Tournament

From 2000, this tournament was known as the Nabisco championship.

Year	Golfer	Year	Golfer
1988	Amy Alcott (USA)	1995	Nanci Bowen (USA)
1989	Juli Inkster (USA)	1996	Patti Sheehan (USA)
1990	Betsy King (USA)	1997	Betsy King (USA)
1991	Amy Alcott (USA)	1998	Pat Hurst (USA)
1992	Dottie Mochrie (USA)	1999	Dottie Pepper (USA)
1993	Helen Alfredsson (Sweden)	2000	Karrie Webb (Australia)
1994	Donna Andrews (USA)		

Golf
Winners of US Ladies PGA Championship

Year	Winner	Country
2000	Juli Inkster	USA
1999	Juli Inkster	USA
1998	Se Ri Pak	South Korea
1997	Chris Johnson	USA
1996	Laura Davies	UK
1995	Kelley Robbins	USA
1994	Laura Davies	UK
1993	Patty Sheehan	USA
1992	Betsy King	USA
1991	Meg Mallon	USA
1990	Beth Daniel	USA
1989	Nancy Lopez	USA
1988	Sherri Turner	USA

Golf
World Golf Ranking (Men)

As of April 2001.

Player (country)

Tiger Woods (USA)
Phil Mickelson (USA)
Ernie Els (South Africa)
Lee Westwood (England)
Colin Montgomerie (Scotland)
Vijay Singh (Fiji)
David Duval (USA)
Davis Love III (USA)
Hal Sutton (USA)
Darren Clarke (Northern Ireland)
Jesper Parnevik (Sweden)
Jim Furyk (USA)

Golf
World Golf Ranking (Women)

As of April 2001.

Player	Country	Player	Country
Karrie Webb	Australia	Mi Hyun Kim	South Korea
Annika Sorenstam	Sweden	Laura Davies	England
Juli Inkster	USA	Dottie Pepper	USA
Lorie Kane	Canada	Yuri Fudoh	Japan
Sophie Gustafson	Sweden	Pat Hurst	USA
Se Ri Pak	South Korea		

Gymnastics
World Champions 1999

Category	Name	Country
Men		
individual all-round	Nikolai Krukov	Russia
floor	Alexei Nemov	Russia
pommel horse	Alexei Nemov	Russia
rings	Dong Zhen	China
vault	Li Xiaoping	China
parallel bars	Lee Joo-hyung	South Korea
horizontal bar	Jesus Carballo	Spain
team	China	
Women		
individual all-round	Maria Olaru	Romania
beam	Ling Jie	China
vault	Elena Zamolodchikova	Russia
asymmetric bars	Svetlana Khorkina	Russia
floor	Andreea Raducan	Romania
team	Romania	

Gymnastics
World Overall Individual Champions

Year	Name	Country	Year	Name	Country
Men			**Women**		
1999	Nikolai Krukov	Russia	1999	Maria Olaru	Romania
1997	Ivan Ivankov	Belarus	1997	Svetlana Khorkina	Russia
1995	Li Xiaoshuang	China	1995	Lilia Pôdkopaeva	Ukraine
1993	Vitaly Scherbo	Belarus	1993	Shannon Miller	USA
1991	Gregori Misutin	USSR	1991	Kim Zmeskal	USA
1989	Igor Korobichensky	USSR	1989	Svetlana Boginskaya	USSR

Hockey
Most Olympic Gold Medals (Men)

Wins	Country	Years	Wins	Country	Years
8	India	1928, 1932, 1936, 1948, 1952, 1956, 1964, 1980	2	Holland	1996, 2000
			1	West Germany	1972
			1	New Zealand	1976
3	Pakistan	1960, 1968, 1984	1	Great Britain	1988
2	England	1908, 1920	1	Germany	1992

Hockey
Winners of Olympic Gold Medals (Women)

Hockey became an Olympic sport for women in 1980.

Year	Country
1980	Zimbabwe
1984	Netherlands
1988	Australia
1992	Spain
1996	Australia
2000	Australia

Hockey
World Cup (Men)

Year	Country
1998	Netherlands
1994	Pakistan
1990	Netherlands
1986	Australia
1982	Pakistan
1978	Pakistan
1975	India
1973	Netherlands
1971	Pakistan

Horse Racing
Cheltenham Gold Cup Winners

Year	Horse	Jockey
2000	Looks Like Trouble	Richard Johnson
1999	See More Business	Mick Fitzgerald
1998	Cool Dawn	Andrew Thornton
1997	Mr Mulligan	Tony McCoy
1996	Imperial Call	Conor O'Dwyer
1995	Master Oats	Norman Williamson
1994	The Fellow	Adam Kondrat
1993	Jodami	Mark Dwyer
1992	Cool Ground	Adrian Maguire
1991	Garrison Savannah	Mark Pitman

Horse Racing
Epsom Derby Winners

Year	Horse	Jockey
2000	Sinndar	Johnny Murtagh
1999	Oath	Kieren Fallon
1998	High Rise	Olivier Peslier
1997	Benny the Dip	Willie Ryan
1996	Shaamit	Michael Hills
1995	Lammtarra	Walter Swinburn
1994	Erhaab	Willie Carson
1993	Commander in Chief	Michael Kinane
1992	Dr Devious	John Reid
1991	Generous	Alan Munro

Horse Racing
Grand National Winners

Year	Horse	Jockey
2001	Red Marauder	Richard Guest
2000	Papillon	Ruby Walsh
1999	Bobbyjo	Paul Carberry
1998	Earth Summit	Carl Llewellyn
1997	Lord Gyllene	Tony Dobbin
1996	Rough Quest	Mick Fitzgerald
1995	Royal Athlete	Jason Titley
1994	Miinnehoma	Richard Dunwoody
1993	race void after false start	
1992	Party Politics	Carl Llewellyn

Horse Racing
Jockeys with Most Wins in One Flat Racing Season

Wins	Jockey	Year
269	Gordon Richards	1947
261	Gordon Richards	1949
259	Gordon Richards	1933
246	Fred Archer	1885
241	Fred Archer	1884
232	Fred Archer	1883
231	Gordon Richards	1952
229	Fred Archer	1878
227	Gordon Richards	1951
224	Gordon Richards	1948

Horse Racing
Jockeys with Most Wins in the English Classics

The English Classics are: the St Leger, The Oaks, the 1000 Guineas, the Epsom Derby, and the 2000 Guineas.

Wins	Jockey	Years	Wins	Jockey	Years
30	Lester Piggott	1954–92	16	George Fordham	1859–83
27	Frank Buckle	1792–1827	15	Joe Childs	1912–33
24	Jem Robinson	1817–48	14	Frank Butler	1843–53
21	Fred Archer	1874–86	14	Steve Donoghue	1915–37
19	Bill Scott	1821–46	14	Charlie Elliott	1923–49
19	Jack Watts	1883–97	14	Gordon Richards	1930–53
17	Willie Carson	1972–94	14	Pat Eddery	1975–97
16	John Barham Day	1826–41			

Horse Racing
Most Successful Jockeys in the Grand National

Wins	Jockey	Years
5	George Stevens	1856–70
4	Tom Olliver	1838–53
3	Tommy Pickernell	1860–75
3	Tommy Beasley	1880–89
3	Arthur Nightingall	1890–1901
3	Ernie Piggott	1912–19
3	Jack Anthony	1911–20
3	Brian Fletcher	1968–74
2	Alec Goodman	1852–66
2	John Page	1867–72
2	John Richardson	1873–74
2	Ted Wilson	1884–85
2	Percy Woodland	1903–13
2	Arthur Thompson	1948–52
2	Bryan Marshall	1953–54
2	Fred Winter	1957–62
2	Richard Dunwoody	1986–94
2	Carl Llewellyn	1992–98
2	Pat Taaffe	1955–70

Ice Hockey
Countries with Most World Championship Wins (Men)

Wins	Country	Years
22	USSR	1954–90
21	Canada	1920–97
6	Czechoslovakia	1947–85
6	Sweden	1953–98
6	Czech Republic	1996–2000
2	USA	1933–60
1	Great Britain	1936
1	Russia	1993
1	Finland	1995

Ice Hockey

Most Wins of the National Hockey League Stanley Cup

Wins	Club	Years
24	Montreal Canadiens	1916–93
13	Toronto Maple Leafs[1]	1918–67
9	Detroit Red Wings	1936–98
6	Ottawa Senators	1909–27
5	Boston Bruins	1929–72
5	Edmonton Oilers	1984–90
4	Montreal Victorias	1895–98
4	Montreal Wanderers	1906–10
4	New York Islanders	1980–83
4	New York Rangers	1928–94
3	Montreal AAA	1893–1902
3	Ottawa Silver Seven	1903–05
3	Chicago Black Hawks	1934–61

[1] As Toronto Arenas in 1918, and as Toronto St Patricks in 1922.

Ice Hockey

Players with Most Career Goals in the National Hockey League (NHL)

Goals[1]	Player	Years
894	Wayne Gretzky	1979–99
801	Gordie Howe	1946–71
731	Marcel Dionne	1971–89
717	Phil Esposito	1963–81
613	Mario Lemieux	1984–97
610	Mark Messier	1979–99
596	Jari Kurri	1980–97
592	Steve Yzerman	1983–99
560	Guy Lafleur	1971–92
556	John Bucyk	1955–78

[1] To end of 1998–99 season.

Ice Hockey

Players with Most Career Points in the National Hockey League (NHL)

Points[1]	Player	Years
2857	Wayne Gretzky	1979–99
1850	Gordie Howe	1946–71
1771	Marcel Dionne	1971–89
1660	Mark Messier	1979–99
1590	Phil Esposito	1963–81
1494	Mario Lemieux	1984–97
1487	Paul Coffey	1980–99
1486	Ron Francis	1981–99
1483	Steve Yzerman	1983–98
1468	Ray Bourque	1979–99
1467	Stan Mitika	1958–80
1425	Bryan Trottier	1975–94

[1] To end of 1998–99 season

Ice Hockey

Stanley Cup Winners

Year	Team
2000	New Jersey Devils
1999	Dallas Stars
1998	Detroit Red Wings
1997	Detroit Red Wings
1996	Colorado Avalanche
1995	New Jersey Devils
1994	New York Rangers
1993	Montreal Canadiens
1992	Pittsburgh Penguins
1991	Pittsburgh Penguins

Ice Hockey
World Champions

Year	Country
2000	Czech Republic
1999	Czech Republic
1998	Sweden
1997	Canada
1996	Czech Republic
1995	Finland
1994	Canada
1993	Russia
1992	Sweden
1991	Sweden

Ice Skating
World Champions (Dance)

Skaters	Country	Year
Sergei Ponomarenko and Marina Klimova	USSR	1989
Sergei Ponomarenko and Marina Klimova	USSR	1990
Isabelle and Paul Duchesnay	France	1991
Sergei Ponomarenko and Marina Klimova	CIS	1992
Alesandr Zhulin and Maia Usova	Russia	1993
Yevgeni Platov and Oksana Gritschuk	Russia	1994
Yevgeni Platov and Oksana Gritschuk	Russia	1995
Yevgeni Platov and Oksana Gritschuk	Russia	1996
Yevgeni Platov and Oksana Gritschuk	Russia	1997
Anjekia Krylova and Oleg Ovsyannikov	Russia	1998
Anjekia Krylova and Oleg Ovsyannikov	Russia	1999
Marina Anissina and Gwendal Peizera	France	2000
Barbara Fusar Poli and Maurizio Margaglio	Italy	2001

Ice Skating
World Champions (Men)

Skater	Country	Year	Skater	Country	Year
Brian Boitano	USA	1988	Elvis Stojko	Canada	1995
Kurt Browning	Canada	1989	Todd Eldredge	USA	1996
Kurt Browning	Canada	1990	Elvis Stojko	Canada	1997
Kurt Browning	Canada	1991	Alexei Yagudin	Russia	1998
Viktor Petrenko	CIS	1992	Alexei Yagudin	Russia	1999
Kurt Browning	Canada	1993	Alexei Yagudin	Russia	2000
Elvis Stojko	Canada	1994	Evgeni Plushenko	Russia	2001

Ice Skating
World Champions (Pairs)

Skaters	Country	Year
Sergei Grinkov and Yekaterina Gordeyeva	USSR	1989
Sergei Grinkov and Yekaterina Gordeyeva	USSR	1990
Artur Dmtriev and Natalya Mishkutienok	USSR	1991
Artur Dmtriev and Natalya Mishkutienok	USSR	1992
Lloyd Eisler and Isabelle Brasseur	Canada	1993
Vadim Naumov and Evgenia Shiskova	Russia	1994

Ice Skating: World Champions (Pairs) (*continued*)

Skaters	Country	Year
Rene Novotny and Radka Kovarikova	Czech Republic	1995
Andrei Bushkov and Marina Eltsova	Russia	1996
Ingo Steuer and Mandy Woetzel	Germany	1997
Elena Berezhnaya and Anton Sikharulidze	Russia	1998
Elena Berezhnaya and Anton Sikharulidze	Russia	1999
Maria Petrova and Alexei Tikhonov	Russia	2000
Jamie Sale and David Pelletier	Canada	2001

Ice Skating
World Champions (Women)

Skater	Country	Year
Midori Ito	Japan	1989
Jill Trenary	USA	1990
Kristi Yamaguchi	USA	1991
Kristi Yamaguchi	USA	1992
Oksana Baiul	Ukraine	1993
Yuka Sato	Japan	1994
Lu Chen	China	1995
Michelle Kwan	USA	1996
Tara Lipinski	USA	1997
Michelle Kwan	USA	1998
Maria Butyrskaya	Russia	1999
Michelle Kwan	USA	2000
Michelle Kwan	USA	2001

Lacrosse
World Championships for Men

Winning country	Year
USA	1967
USA	1974
Canada	1978
USA	1982
USA	1986
USA	1990
USA	1994
USA	1998

Lacrosse
World Championships for Women

The women's World Championship has been known as the World Cup since 1982.

Winning country	Year	Winning country	Year
Great Britain	1969	Australia	1986
USA	1974	USA	1990
Canada	1978	USA	1993
USA	1982	USA	1997

Martial Arts

Name	Description
judo	object is to use minimum force to unbalance an opponent and hold on the ground
jujitsu	traditional method of unarmed self-defence
aikido	system of self-defence similar to judo
karate	traditional method of unarmed combat that uses hands, elbows, feet, and legs to chop, kick, and 'smash' an opponent
kendo	stylized form of fencing using bamboo staves (instead of swords)
kung fu	Chinese martial art that combines elements of judo and karate
ninjitsu	martial art that combines stealth and camouflage
shintaido	non-aggressive physical exercise
sumo	traditional Japanese wrestling
tae kwon do	Korean form of karate

Motor Racing
Formula 1 Drivers' World Championship Winners

Year	Name	Country	Car
2000	Michael Schumacher	Germany	Ferrari
1999	Mika Hakkinen	Finland	McLaren-Mercedes
1998	Mika Hakkinen	Finland	McLaren-Mercedes
1997	Jacques Villeneuve	Canada	Williams-Renault
1996	Damon Hill	UK	Williams-Renault
1995	Michael Schumacher	Germany	Benetton-Renault
1994	Michael Schumacher	Germany	Benetton-Ford
1993	Alain Prost	France	Williams-Renault
1992	Nigel Mansell	UK	Williams-Renault
1991	Ayrton Senna	Brazil	McLaren-Honda

Motor Racing
Most Successful Drivers by Number of Grand Prix Wins

Wins	Driver (country)	Years	Wins	Driver (country)	Years
51	Alain Prost (France)	1980–93	25	Niki Lauda (Austria)	1971–85
44	Michael Schumacher (Germany)	1991–2000	24	Juan Manuel Fangio (Argentina)	1950–58
41	Ayrton Senna (Brazil)	1985–94	23	Nelson Piquet (Brazil)	1978–91
31	Nigel Mansell (UK)	1980–95	22	Damon Hill (UK)	1992–99
27	Jackie Stewart (UK)	1965–73	18	Mika Hakkinen (Finland)	1997–2000
25	Jim Clark (UK)	1960–68	16	Stirling Moss (UK)	1951–61

Motor Racing

Most Successful Drivers by Number of Formula 1 World Titles

Titles	Driver (country)	Titles	Driver (country)
5	Juan Manuel Fangio (Argentina)	3	Michael Schumacher (Germany)
4	Alain Prost (France)	2	Alberto Ascari (Italy)
3	Jack Brabham (Australia)	2	Graham Hill (UK)
3	Jackie Stewart (UK)	2	Jim Clark (UK)
3	Niki Lauda (Austria)	2	Emerson Fittipaldi (Brazil)
3	Nelson Piquet (Brazil)	2	Mika Hakkinen (Finland)
3	Ayrton Senna (Brazil)		

Motor Racing

Most Successful Formula 1 Constructors by Number of Grand Prix Wins

Wins	Constructor	Years
135	Ferrari	1951–2000
130	McLaren	1968–2000
103	Williams	1979–2000
79	Lotus	1960–87
35	Brabham	1964–85
27	Benetton	1986–2000
23	Tyrrell	1971–83
17	BRM	1959–72
16	Cooper	1958–67
15	Renault	1979–83

Motor Racing

Most Successful Formula 1 Constructors by Number of World Titles

Titles	Constructor	Years
10	Ferrari	1961–2000
9	Williams	1980–97
8	McLaren	1974–98
7	Lotus	1963–78
2	Cooper	1959–60
2	Brabham	1966–67
1	Vanwall	1958
1	BRM	1962
1	Matra	1969
1	Tyrrell	1971
1	Benetton	1995

Motor Racing

RAC Rally Winners

Year	Name	Country	Car
2000	Richard Burns	UK	Subaru Impreza
1999	Richard Burns	UK	Subaru Impreza
1998	Richard Burns	UK	Mitsubishi Lancer
1997	Colin McRae	UK	Subaru Impreza
1996	Armin Schwarz	Germany	Toyota Celica
1995	Colin McRae	UK	Subaru Impreza
1994	Colin McRae	UK	Subaru Impreza
1993	Juha Kankkunen	Finland	Lancia Delta
1992	Carlos Sainz	Spain	Toyota Celica
1991	Juha Kankkunen	Finland	Lancia Delta

Motor Racing
Recent Land Speed Record Holders

Driver	Car	Date	Speed kph (mph)
Andy Green	Thrust SSC	15 October 1997	1,227.99 (763.04)
Richard Noble	Thrust 2	4 October 1983	1,013.47 (633.47)
Gary Gabelich	Blue Flame	23 October 1970	995.85 (622.41)
Craig Breedlove	Spirit of America – Sonic 1	15 November 1965	960.96 (600.60)
Art Arfons	Green Monster	7 November 1965	922.48 (576.55)
Craig Breedlove	Spirit of America – Sonic 1	2 November 1965	893.40 (555.13)
Art Arfons	Green Monster	27 October 1964	858.73 (536.71)
Craig Breedlove	Spirit of America	15 October 1964	842.04 (526.28)
Craig Breedlove	Spirit of America	13 October 1964	749.95 (468.72)
Art Arfons	Green Monster	5 October 1964	698.81 (434.22)

Motor Racing
Recent Winners of Le Mans 24-hour Race

Year	Team members (nationality)
1991	Volker Weidler (Germany), Johnny Herbert (UK), and Bertrand Gachot (Belgium)
1992	Derek Warwick (UK), Mark Blundell (UK), and Yannick Dalmas (France)
1993	Geoff Brabham (Australia), Christophe Bouchet (France), and Eric Helary (France)
1994	Yannick Dalmas (France), Hurley Haywood (USA), and Mauro Baldi (Italy)
1995	Yannick Dalmas (France), J J Lehto (Finland), and Masanori Sekiya (Japan)
1996	Manuel Reuter (Germany), Davy Jones (USA), and Alexander Würz (Austria)
1997	Michele Alboreto (Italy), Stefan Johansson (Sweden), and Tom Kristensen (Denmark)
1998	Allan McNish (UK), Laurent Aiello (France), and Stephane Ortelli (France)
1999	Pierluigi Martini (Italy), Joachim Winkelhock (Germany), and Yannick Dalmas (France)
2000	F Biela (Holland), Tom Kristensen (Denmark), and E Pirro (Italy)

Motor Racing

Recent Winners of the Daytona 500

Year	Winner
1991	Ernie Irvan (USA)
1992	Davey Allison (USA)
1993	Dale Jarrett (USA)
1994	Sterling Marlin (USA)
1995	Sterling Marlin (USA)
1996	Dale Jarrett (USA)
1997	Jeff Gordon (USA)
1998	Dale Earnhardt (USA)
1999	Jeff Gordon (USA)
2000	Dale Jarrett (USA)

Motor Racing

Recent Winners of the Indianapolis 500

Year	Winner
1991	Rick Mears (USA)
1992	Al Unser, Jr (USA)
1993	Emerson Fittipaldi (Brazil)
1994	Al Unser, Jr (USA)
1995	Jacques Villeneuve (Canada)
1996	Buddy Lazier (USA)
1997	Arie Luyendyk (Holland)
1998	Eddie Cheever (USA)
1999	Kenny Brack (USA)
2000	Juan Montoya (Colombia)

Motorcycling

500 cc World Road Racing Champions

Year	Name	Country	Manufacturer
2000	Kenny Roberts	USA	Suzuki
1999	Alex Criville	Spain	Honda
1998	Michael Doohan	Australia	Honda
1997	Michael Doohan	Australia	Honda
1996	Michael Doohan	Australia	Honda
1995	Michael Doohan	Australia	Honda
1994	Michael Doohan	Australia	Honda
1993	Kevin Schwantz	USA	Suzuki
1992	Wayne Rainey	USA	Yamaha
1991	Wayne Rainey	USA	Yamaha

Motorcycling

Isle of Man Tourist Trophy Senior TT

Year	Name	Country	Manufacturer
2000	David Jefferies	UK	Yamaha
1999	David Jefferies	UK	Yamaha
1998	Ian Simpson	UK	Honda
1997	Phillip McCallen	UK	Honda
1996	Phillip McCallen	UK	Honda
1995	Joey Dunlop	UK	Honda
1994	Steve Hislop	UK	Honda
1993	Joey Dunlop	UK	Honda
1992	Steve Hislop	UK	Norton
1991	Steve Hislop	UK	Honda

Motorcycling
Land Speed Records

Year	Motorcycle	Rider	Speed (kph/mph)
1990	Harley-Davidson	Dave Campos	518.5/322.2
1978	Kawasaki	Donald Vesco	512.7/318.6
1978	Kawasaki	Donald Vesco	507.7/315.4
1975	Yamaha	Donald Vesco	487.5/302.9
1974	Yamaha	Donald Vesco	453.4/281.7
1970	Harley-Davidson	Calvin Rayborn	426.5/265.5
1970	Harley-Davidson	Calvin Rayborn	410.4/255.4

Motorcycling
World Champions 2000

Category	Name	Country	Manufacturer
Road Racing			
125 cc	Roberto Locatelli	Italy	Aprilia
250 cc	Olivier Jacque	France	Yamaha
500 cc	Kenny Roberts Jr	USA	Honda
superbike	Colin Edwards	USA	Ducati
endurance	Warwick Nowland and Peter Linden	Australia and Sweden	Suzuki
sidecar (World Cup)	Steve Webster and David James	UK	Suzuki
Motocross			
125 cc	Grant Langston	South Africa	KTM
250 cc	Frédéric Bolley	France	Honda
500 cc	Joel Smets	Belgium	KTM
sidecar	Kristers Sergis and Artis Rasmanis	Latvia	BSU
trials	Doug Lampkin	UK	Beta

Motorcycling
World Superbike Champions

Year	Name	Country	Manufacturer	Year	Name	Country	Manufacturer
2000	Colin Edwards	USA	Honda	1994	Carl Fogarty	UK	Ducati
1999	Carl Fogarty	UK	Ducati	1993	Scott Russell	USA	Kawasaki
1998	Carl Fogarty	UK	Ducati	1992	Doug Polen	USA	Ducati
1997	John Kocinski	USA	Honda	1991	Doug Polen	USA	Ducati
1996	Troy Corser	Australia	Ducati	1990	Raymond Roche	France	Ducati
1995	Carl Fogarty	UK	Ducati				

Mountaineering
First to Climb Everest

Ascent record	Expedition leader/s	Nationality	Date reached summit	Route
first conquest	Edmund Hillary, Tenzing Norgay	New Zealander/ Nepalese	29 May 1953	South-East Ridge
youngest person (17)	Shambu Tamang	Nepalese	5 May 1973	
first woman	Junko Tabei	Japanese	16 May 1975	South-East Ridge
first without bottled oxygen	Peter Habeler, Reinhold Messner	Austrian/ Italian	8 May 1978	South-East Ridge
first winter ascent	Krzysztof Wielicki, Leszek Cichy	Polish	17 February 1980	South-East Ridge
first solo	Reinhold Messner	Italian	20 August 1980	North Col and North Face
first married couple to reach summit together	Andrej and Marija Stremfelj	Slovenian	7 October 1990	
first ascent by a disabled climber	Tom Whittaker	American	27 May 1998	

Mountaineering
Highest Mountains in the World and their First Ascents

Mountain	Location	Height (m/ft)	Expedition nationality/year
Everest	China/Nepal	8,848/29,029	British (1953)
K2	Kashmir/Jammu	8,611/28,251	Italian (1954)
Kangchenjunga	India/Nepal	8,598/28,209	British (1955)
Lhotse	China/Nepal	8,511/27,923	Swiss (1956)
Yalung Kang (formerly Kangchenjunga West Peak)	India/Nepal	8,502/27,894	Japanese (1973)
Kangchenjunga South Peak	India/Nepal	8,488/27,848	Polish (1978)
Makalu I	China/Nepal	8,481/27,825	French (1955)
Kangchenjunga Middle Peak	India/Nepal	8,475/27,805	Polish (1973)
Lhotse Shar	China/Nepal	8,383/27,503	Austrian (1970)
Dhaulagiri	Nepal	8,172/26,811	Swiss (1960)

Pokémon

Scarcity Value of Pokémon Cards

Name of card	Price at December 2000 (US$)	Name of card	Price at December 2000 (US$)
Charizard	59.99	Poliwrath	14.00
Might of Oaks	50.00	Clefairy	14.00
Blastoise	25.00	Nidoking	14.00
Raichu	20.00	Machamp	12.50
Zapdos	20.00	Gyarados	12.00
Alakazam	16.00	Mewto	12.00
Chansey	16.00	Hitmonchan	10.00

Poker

Winning Hands

Hand	Number possible	Odds against
royal flush	4	649,739 to 1
straight flush	36	72,192 to 1
four of a kind	624	4,164 to 1
full house	3,744	693 to 1
flush	5,108	508 to 1
straight	10,200	254 to 1
three of a kind	54,912	46 to 1
two pairs	123,552	20 to 1
one pair	1,098,240	1.37 to 1
high card	1,302,540	1 to 1

Rowing

The Boat Race

This race was first held in 1829. It is rowed annually by crews from Oxford and Cambridge Universities, between Putney and Mortlake on the River Thames. Cambridge currently lead Oxford by 77 wins to 69.

Year	Team
2001	Cambridge
2000	Oxford
1999	Cambridge
1998	Cambridge
1997	Cambridge
1996	Cambridge
1995	Cambridge
1994	Cambridge
1993	Cambridge
1992	Oxford

Rugby League

Challenge Cup Winners

Year	Team	Year	Team
2001	St Helens	1996	St Helens
2000	Bradford Bulls	1995	Wigan
1999	Leeds Rhinos	1994	Wigan
1998	Sheffield Eagles	1993	Wigan
1997	St Helens	1992	Wigan

Rugby Union
Highest Scores in International Matches (1993–2000)

Score	Winners	Opponents	Year	Score	Winners	Opponents	Year
164–13	Hong Kong	Singapore	1994	110–0	England	Netherlands	1998
145–17	New Zealand	Japan	1995	106–8	England	USA	2000
134–6	Japan	Taiwan	1998	104–8	Italy	Czech Republic	1994
130–10	Zimbabwe	Botswana	1996				
114–12	Hong Kong	Taiwan	1996	104–7	Russia	Denmark	2000
114–3	Brazil	Argentina	1993	103–9	Argentina	Paraguay	1995
112–5	South Korea	Malaysia	1996				

Rugby Union
World Cup Winners

This competition, for the William Webb Ellis Trophy, was first held in 1987.

Year	Winner	Runner-up	Score	Location
1999	Australia	France	35–12	Cardiff
1995	South Africa	New Zealand	15–12	Johannesburg
1991	Australia	England	12–6	Twickenham
1987	New Zealand	France	29–7	Melbourne

Rugby Union
World Rankings 2000

At the end of November 2000. Based on results of matches in the World Cup, the Five (and Six) Nations, and the Tri-Nations

Rank	Country
1	Australia
2	South Africa
3	New Zealand
4	England
5	France
6	Wales
7	Ireland
8	Scotland
9	Argentina
10	Samoa

Scrabble®
High Scoring Words

Word	Meaning	Score (all letters laid at once)
QUARTZY	containing/resembling quartz	$28 + 50[1] = 78$
SQUEEZY	able to be squeezed	$28 + 50 = 78$
BEZIQUE	card game	$27 + 50 = 77$
CAZIQUE	Native American chief	$27 + 50 = 77$
JUKEBOX	coin-operated record player	$27 + 50 = 77$
TZADDIQ	Hasidic leader in Judaism	$27 + 50 = 77$
SQUAWKY	making squawk-like sounds	$26 + 50 = 76$
ZOOTAXY	scientific animal classification	$26 + 50 = 76$
QUETZAL	Central American bird	$25 + 50 = 75$
SQUEEZE	grip tightly	$25 + 50 = 75$
SQUIFFY	slightly drunk	$25 + 50 = 75$
ZYMURGY	chemistry of fermentation	$25 + 50 = 75$

[1] 50-point bonus for using all 7 letters; all words in *The Chambers Dictionary*.

Show Jumping
World Champions

Year	Name	Country	Year	Name	Country
1990	Rodrigo Pessoa	Brazil	1986	Gail Greenhough	Canada
1994	Franke Sloothaak	Germany	1902	Norbert Koof	West Germany
1990	Eric Navet	France			

Soccer
FA Challenge Cup Winners

Year	Winners	Runners-up	Score
2001	Liverpool	Arsenal	2–1
2000	Chelsea	Aston Villa	1–0
1999	Manchester United	Newcastle United	2–0
1998	Arsenal	Newcastle United	2–0
1997	Chelsea	Middlesborough	2–0
1996	Manchester United	Liverpool	1–0
1995	Everton	Manchester United	1–0
1994	Manchester United	Chelsea	4–0
1993	Arsenal	Sheffield Wednesday	1–1[1]
replay	Arsenal	Sheffield Wednesday	2–1[1]
1992	Liverpool	Sunderland	2–0

[1] After extra time.

Soccer
FA Cup – Most Appearances by a Club in the Final

Finals	Club
15	Manchester United
13	Arsenal
13	Newcastle
12	Everton
11	Liverpool
10	Aston Villa
10	West Bromwich Albion
9	Tottenham Hotspur
8	Blackburn Rovers
8	Manchester City
8	Wolverhampton Wanderers
7	Bolton Wanderers
7	Preston North End

Soccer
FA Cup – Most Wins

Wins	Club
10	Manchester United
8	Tottenham Hotspur
7	Arsenal
7	Aston Villa
6	Blackburn Rovers
6	Newcastle United
5	Everton
5	Liverpool
5	Wanderers
5	West Bromwich Albion
4	Bolton Wanderers
4	Manchester City
4	Sheffield United
4	Wolverhampton Wanderers

Soccer
FIFA World Player of the Year

Year	Player	Team	Country of origin
2000	Zinedine Zidane	Juventus	France
1999	Rivaldo	Barcelona	Brazil
1998	Zinedine Zidane	Juventus	France
1997	Ronaldo	Inter Milan	Brazil
1996	Ronaldo	Barcelona	Brazil
1995	George Weah	AC Milan	Liberia
1994	Romario	Barcelona	Brazil
1993	Roberto Baggio	Juventus	Italy
1992	Marco Van Basten	AC Milan	Netherlands
1991	Lothar Matthäus	Inter Milan	Germany

Soccer
Most Expensive Transfer Fees

Fee (£million)	Player	From	To	Year
37.0	Luis Figo	Barcelona	Real Madrid	2000
35.5	Hernan Crespo	Parma	Lazio	2000
32	Christian Vieri	Lazio	Internazionale	1999
23.5	Nicolas Anelka	Arsenal	Real Madrid	1999
22	Denilson	Sao Paulo	Real Betis	1998
22	Gabriel Batistuta	Fiorentina	AS Roma	2000
20.29	Nicolas Anelka	Real Madrid	Paris St Germain	2000
19.0	Ruud Van Nistelrooy	PSV Eindhoven	Manchester United	2001
19.0	Christian Vieri	Atletico Madrid	Lazio	1998
18.0	Marco Amoroso	Udinese	Parma	1999
18.0	Rio Ferdinand	West Ham	Leeds United	2000
18.0	Ronaldo	Barcelona	Inter Milan	1997

Soccer
Most World Cup Wins

Wins	Country	Years
4	Brazil	1958, 1962, 1970, 1994
3	Germany[1]	1954, 1974, 1990
3	Italy	1934, 1938, 1982
2	Argentina	1978, 1986
2	Uruguay	1930, 1950
1	England	1966
1	France	1998

[1] Includes West Germany.

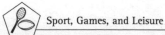

Soccer

UEFA Cup Winners

Year	Team	Country
2000	Galatasaray	Turkey
1999	Parma	Italy
1998	Inter Milan	Italy
1997	Schalke	Germany
1996	Bayern Munich	Germany
1995	Parma	Italy
1994	Inter Milan	Italy
1993	Juventus	Italy
1992	Ajax	Netherlands
1991	Inter Milan	Italy

Soccer

World Cup – Most Goals Scored by a Player in a Single Tournament

Goals	Player (country)	Year
13	Just Fontaine (France)	1958
11	Sándor Kocsis (Hungary)	1954
10	Gerd Müller (West Germany)	1970
9	Eusebio (Portugal)	1966
8	Leonidas da Silva (Brazil)	1938
8	Guillermo Stabile (Argentina)	1930
6	Mario Kempes (Argentina)	1978
6	Gary Lineker (England)	1986
6	Paolo Rosi (Italy)	1982
6	Oleg Salenko (Russia)	1994
6	Salvatore Schillaci (Italy)	1990
6	Hristo Stoichkov (Bulgaria)	1994
6	Davor Suker (Croatia)	1998

Soccer

World Cup – Most Goals Scored by a Player in the Final Stages

Goals	Player (country)	Years	Goals	Player (country)	Years
14	Gerd Müller (West Germany)	1970–74	9	Gabriel Batistuta (Argentina)	1994–98
13	Just Fontaine (France)	1958	9	Leónidas da Silva (Brazil)	1934–38
12	Pelé (Brazil)	1958–70	9	Ademir Marques de Menezes (Brazil)	1950
11	Jürgen Klinsman (Germany)	1990–98	9	Eusebio (Portugal)	1966
11	Sandor Kocsis (Hungary)	1954	9	Jairzhino (Brazil)	1970–74
10	Teófilo Cubillas (Peru)	1970–78	9	Paolo Rossi (Italy)	1978–82
10	Grzegorz Lato (Poland)	1974–82	9	Karl-Heinz Rummenigge (West Germany)	1978–86
10	Gary Lineker (England)	1986–90	9	Uwe Seeler (West Germany)	1958–70
10	Helmut Rhan (West Germany)	1954–58	9	Vavá (Brazil)	1958–62
9	Roberto Baggio (Italy)	1990–98			

Soccer
World Cup – Most Match Appearances by a Player in the Final Stages (1930–98)

Matches	Player (country)
25	Lothar Matthäus (Germany)
21	Diego Maradona (Argentina)
21	Uwe Seeler (Germany)
21	Wladislav Zmuda (Poland)
20	Grzegorz Lato (Poland)
19	Paolo Maldini (Italy)
19	Wolfgang Overath (Germany)
19	Karl-Heinz Rummenigge (Germany)
19	Berti Vogts (Germany)
18	Franz Beckenbauer (Germany)
18	Thomas Berthold (Germany)
18	Antonio Cabrini (Italy)
18	Carlos Dunga (Brazil)
18	Mario Kempes (Argentina)
18	Pierre Littbarski (Germany)
18	Sepp Maier (Germany)
18	Gaetano Scirea (Italy)
18	Claudio Taffarel (Brazil)

Soccer
World Cup – Most Players Sent Off per Country (1930–98)

Red cards	Country
8	Argentina
8	Brazil
6	Cameroon
6	Uruguay
5	Germany[1]
5	Hungary
4	Czechoslovakia
4	Holland
4	Italy
4	Mexico
3	Bulgaria
3	Denmark
3	France
3	USSR

[1] Germany includes the West Germany team, 1950–90.

Soccer
World Cup – Most Tournament Appearances by a Nation in the Final Stages

Tournaments	Country	Tournaments	Country
16	Brazil	10	Spain
14	Germany[1]	9	Hungary
14	Italy	9	Sweden
12	Argentina	9	Uruguay
10	Belgium	8	Russia[2]
10	England	8	Yugoslavia
10	France		

[1] Germany includes appearances by West Germany, 1950–90.

[2] Russia includes appearances by the USSR, 1958–90.

Soccer

World Cup – Most Tournament Appearances by a Player in the Final Stages (1930–98)

Tournaments	Player (country)	Years
5	Antonio Carbajal (Mexico)	1950, 1954, 1958, 1962, 1966
5	Lothar Matthäus (Germany)	1982, 1986, 1990, 1994, 1998
4	Giuseppe Bergomi (Italy)	1982, 1986, 1990, 1998
4	Diego Maradona (Argentina)	1982, 1986, 1990, 1994
4	Pelé (Brazil)	1958, 1962, 1966, 1970
4	Gianni Rivera (Italy)	1962, 1966, 1970, 1974
4	Pedro Rocha (Uruguay)	1962, 1966, 1970, 1974
4	Djalma Santos (Brazil)	1954, 1958, 1962, 1966
4	Karl-Heinz Schnellinger (West Germany)	1958, 1962, 1966, 1970
4	Enzo Scifo (Belgium)	1986, 1990, 1994, 1998
4	Uwe Seeler (West Germany)	1958, 1962, 1966, 1970
4	Frankie van der Elst (Belgium)	1986, 1990, 1994, 1998
4	Wladislav Zmuda (Poland)	1974, 1978, 1982, 1986
4	Andoni Zubizarreta (Spain)	1986, 1990, 1994, 1998

Speed Skating

Olympic Gold Medallists, 1,000 m (Men)

Skater	Country	Year	Skater	Country	Year
Peter Mueller	USA	1976	Olaf Zinke	Germany	1992
Eric Heiden	USA	1980	Dan Jansen	USA	1994
Gaetan Boucher	Canada	1984	Ids Postma	Netherlands	1998
Nikolay Gulyayev	USSR	1988			

Speed Skating

Olympic Gold Medallists, 1,000 m (Women)

Skater	Country	Year
Klara Guseva	USSR	1960
Lidiya Skoblikova	USSR	1964
Carolina Geijssen	Netherlands	1968
Monika Pflug	FRG	1972
Tatyana Averina	USSR	1976
Natalya Petruseva	USSR	1980
Karin Enke	GDR	1984
Christa Rothenburger	GDR	1988
Bonnie Blair	USA	1992
Bonnie Blair	USA	1994
Marianne Timmer	Netherlands	1998

Speed Skating
Olympic Gold Medallists, 1,500 m (Men)

Skater	Country	Year
Roald Aas/Yevgeniy Grischin	Norway/ USSR	1960
Ants Antson	USSR	1964
Cornelis Verkerk	Netherlands	1968
Ard Schenk	Netherlands	1972
Jan Egil Storholt	Norway	1976
Eric Heiden	USA	1980
Gaetan Boucher	Canada	1984
André Hoffmann	GDR	1988
Johann Olav Koss	Norway	1992
Johann Olav Koss	Norway	1994
Ådne Søndrål	Norway	1998

Speed Skating
Olympic Gold Medallists, 1,500 m (Women)

Skater	Country	Year
Lidiya Skoblikova	USSR	1960
Lidiya Skoblikova	USSR	1964
Kaija Mustonen	Finland	1968
Dianne Holum	USA	1972
Galina Stepanskaya	USSR	1976
Annie Borckink	Netherlands	1980
Karin Enke	GDR	1984
Yvonne van Gennip	Netherlands	1988
Jacqueline Börner	Germany	1992
Emese Hunyady	Austria	1994
Marianne Timmer	Netherlands	1998

Speed Skating
Olympic Gold Medallists, 10,000 m (Men)

Skater	Country	Year
Knut Johannesen	Norway	1960
Jonny Nilsson	Sweden	1964
Johnny Höglin	Sweden	1968
Ard Schenk	Netherlands	1972
Piet Kleine	Netherlands	1976
Eric Heiden	USA	1980
Igor Malkov	USSR	1984
Tomas Gustafsson	Sweden	1988
Bart Veldkamp	Netherlands	1992
Johann Olav Koss	Norway	1994
Gianni Romme	Netherlands	1998

Speed Skating
Olympic Gold Medallists, 3,000 m (Women)

Skater	Country	Year
Lidiya Skoblikova	USSR	1960
Lidiya Skoblikova	USSR	1964
Johanna Schut	Netherlands	1968
Christina Baas-Kaiser	Netherlands	1972
Tatyana Averina	USSR	1976
Bjö Eva Jensen	Norway	1980
Andrea Schöne	GDR	1984
Yvonne van Gennip	Netherlands	1988
Gunda Niemann	Germany	1992
Svetlana Bazhanova	Russia	1994
Gunda Niemann-Stirnemann	Germany	1998

Speed Skating
Olympic Gold Medallists, 5,000 m (Men)

Skater	Country	Year	Skater	Country	Year
Viktor Kositschkin	USSR	1960	Tomas Gustafsson	Sweden	1984
Knut Johannesen	Norway	1964	Tomas Gustafsson	Sweden	1988
Anton Maier	Norway	1968	Geir Karlstad	Norway	1992
Ard Schenk	Netherlands	1972	Johann Olav Koss	Norway	1994
Sten Stensen	Norway	1976	Gianni Romme	Netherlands	1998
Eric Heiden	USA	1980			

Speed Skating
Olympic Gold Medallists, 5,000 m (Women)

Skater	Country	Year	Skater	Country	Year
Yvonne van Gennip	Netherlands	1988	Claudia Pechstein	Germany	1994
Gunda Niemann	Germany	1992	Claudia Pechstein	Germany	1998

Speed Skating
Olympic Gold Medallists, 500 m (Men)

Skater	Country	Year
Yevgeniy Grischin	USSR	1960
Terry McDermott	USA	1964
Erhard Keller	FRG	1968
Erhard Keller	FRG	1972
Yevgeniy Kulikov	USSR	1976
Eric Heiden	USA	1980
Sergey Fokichev	USSR	1984
Uwe-Jens Mey	GDR	1988
Uwe-Jens Mey	Germany	1992
Aleksandr Golubev	Russia	1994
Hiroyasu Shimizu	Japan	1998

Speed Skating
Olympic Gold Medallists, 500 m (Women)

Skater	Country	Year
Helga Hasse	GDR	1960
Lidiya Skoblikova	USSR	1964
Lyudmila Titova	USSR	1968
Anne Henning	USA	1972
Sheila Young	USA	1976
Karin Enke	GDR	1980
Christa Rothenburger	GDR	1984
Bonnie Blair	USA	1988
Bonnie Blair	USA	1992
Bonnie Blair	USA	1994
Catriona LeMay-Doan	Canada	1998

Speedway
World Champions

Year	Name	Country
2000	Mark Loram	UK
1999	Tony Rickardsson	Sweden
1998	Tony Rickardsson	Sweden
1997	Greg Hancock	USA
1996	Billy Hamill	USA
1995	Hans Nielsen	Denmark
1994	Tony Rickardsson	Sweden
1993	Sam Ermolenko	USA
1992	Gary Havelock	England
1991	Jan Pedersen	Denmark

Sports Injuries
Most Common Injuries

Injury	Percentage of all sports injuries
muscle strains	32
bruising	30
join or ligament strain	29
bleeding	16
head injuries	10

Most common sites of injuries	Percentage
ankle	32
knee	30
finger	15

Sportspeople
Top-earning

Name	Sport
Michael Schumacher (Germany)	motor racing
Tiger Woods (USA)	golf
Mike Tyson (USA)	boxing
Michael Jordan (USA)	basketball
Grant Hill (USA)	basketball

Top earning sportswomen include Steffi Graf and Martina Navratilova, both of whom have earned over $20 million. Top female tennis stars tend to earn $200,000 to $600,000 per year. Top female golfers Karrie Webb and Betsy King have total career earnings of over $6 million and athlete Marion Jones earned over $7 million in 1998. Top long-distance runners like Gabriella Szabo and Marie-Jose Perec earn up to $1 million per year.

Summer Olympics
Leading Medal-winning Countries

Country	Gold	Silver	Bronze	Total
USA	872	659	581	2,112
USSR/CIS[1]	485	395	354	1,234
UK	188	243	232	663
France	189	195	216	600
Germany[2]	165	198	210	573
Italy	179	144	155	478
Sweden	138	157	176	471
Hungary	150	134	158	442
GDR	153	130	127	410
Australia	103	110	139	352
Japan	98	97	103	298

[1] Not including Russia, which at the Summer Olympics of 1996 and 2000 won 58 gold, 53 silver, and 47 bronze medals – a total of 158 medals.

[2] Germany 1896–64 and 1992–98 (not including West Germany and East Germany).

Summer Olympics
Leading Medal-winning Countries at the 2000 Sydney Olympics

Country	Gold	Silver	Bronze	Total
USA	39	25	33	97
Russia	32	28	28	88
China	28	16	15	59
Australia	16	25	17	58
Germany	14	17	26	57
France	13	14	11	38
Italy	13	8	13	34
Netherlands	12	9	4	25
Cuba	11	11	7	29
UK	11	10	7	28

Summer Olympics
Leading Medal-winning Men

The totals listed include all medals, gold, silver, and bronze.

Medals	Athlete (country)	Sport	Years
15	Nikolai Andrianov (USSR)	gymnastics	1972–80
13	Edoardo Mangiarotti (Italy)	fencing	1936–60
13	Takashi Ono (Japan)	gymnastics	1952–64
13	Boris Shakhlin (USSR)	gymnastics	1956–64
12	Sawao Kato (Japan)	gymnastics	1968–76
12	Paavo Nurmi (Finland)	athletics	1920–28
11	Matt Biondi (USA)	swimming	1984–92
11	Viktor Chukarin (USSR)	gymnastics	1952–56
11	Carl Osburn (USA)	shooting	1912–24
11	Mark Spitz (USA)	swimming	1968–72

Summer Olympics
Leading Medal-winning Women

The totals listed include all medals, gold, silver, and bronze.

Medals	Athlete (country)	Sport	Years
18	Larissa Latynina (USSR)	gymnastics	1956–64
11	Vera Cáslavská (Czechoslovakia)	gymnastics	1960–68
10	Polina Astakhova (USSR)	gymnastics	1956–64
10	Agnes Keleti (Hungary)	gymnastics	1952–56
9	Shirley Babashoff (USA)	swimming	1972–76
9	Nadia Comaneci (Romania)	gymnastics	1976–80
9	Kornelia Ender (GDR)	swimming	1972–76
9	Dawn Fraser (Australia)	swimming	1956–64
9	Margit Korondi (Hungary)	gymnastics	1952–56
9	Sofia Muratova (USSR)	gymnastics	1956–60
9	Ludmila Turischeva (USSR)	gymnastics	1968–76

Summer Olympics
Venues of the Games

Year	Olympiad	Venue	Year	Olympiad	Venue
2004	XXVIII	Athens, Greece	1984	XXIII	Los Angeles, USA
2000	XXVII	Sydney, Australia	1980	XXII	Moscow, USSR
1996	XXVI	Atlanta, USA	1976	XXI	Montreal, Canada
1992	XXV	Barcelona, Spain	1972	XX	Munich, West Germany
1988	XXIV	Seoul, South Korea	1968	XIX	Mexico City, Mexico

Survival
Tips for Escaping from Quicksand

always carry a stout pole in places where you may come across quicksand
if you start to sink, lay the pole on the surface
flop on your back on top of the pole
wait a couple of minutes for an equilibrium to be achieved
you should find that you have stopped sinking
work the pole under your hips, at a right angle to your spine
with your hips supported, slowly pull out each leg
you should be able to float on the surface, because you are more buoyant in quicksand than water
move slowly
make the shortest route to firmer ground

Survival
Tips for Fighting a Mountain Lion

do not run (this will cause the animal to pay greater attention) – hold your ground
try to make yourself appear larger (to discourage it from attacking) by opening your jacket wide
wave your arms
shout
do not crouch
pick up small children (they are at greater risk and this will make you appear larger)
back away slowly or wait until the animal leaves
if it attacks, fight back, aiming especially around the eyes and mouth
do not curl up and play dead
protect your neck and throat (this is where the mountain lion tends to attack)

Survival
Tips for Surviving a Fall Through Ice

do not panic
try to get your arms on to the ice
kick as hard as you can to push yourself on to the ice
do not stand: roll to safety
if you cannot get out of the water, try to remain calm
be prepared for your strength and mobility to decrease progressively
do not swim, you will lose heat faster
act slowly and deliberately to conserve heat
keep your upper body above water as far as possible
call for help

Survival
Tips for Surviving an Avalanche

yell
let go of ski poles
get out of your pack (to make yourself lighter)
push upwards using swimming motions, to stay near the surface of the snow
if you are near the surface, try to stick out an arm or leg
if you are in over your head try to maintain an air pocket by punching in front of your face using your hands
take a deep breath and hold it (this expands your chest so you can breathe after the snow sets)
stay calm to conserve energy
only yell when rescuers are nearby, to preserve air
keep your breathing steady

Survival
Tips for Surviving when a Parachute Fails to Open

signal to a companion whose parachute has not yet opened
wave and point to your parachute, to show it has malfunctioned
when your companion reaches you, link arms
prepare for the single parachute to open by hooking your arms into your companion's harness or straps
open the parachute (your added weight means the sudden shock may dislocate or break your arms)
your companion should steer the canopy while holding on to you with one arm
try to steer the canopy for the least abrupt landing, to minimize injuries
head for water if it is nearby

Survival
Tips for Surviving when Adrift at Sea

stay on the boat for as long as possible, even if it is disabled, then get into the life raft
take as much fresh water as you can
take canned foods that are packed in water
drink water as needed: half a gallon per day should be sufficient if you have limited your activity
do not drink sea water
if you are in a cold environment, keep warm
put on dry clothes and stay out of the water
find food if you can, for example by fishing
try to reach land but do not exhaust yourself
if you see a plane or boat, try to signal to it using radio, flares, or by flashing a mirror

Swimming and Diving
World Champions 1998 (Men)

Event	Athlete	Country
50 m freestyle	Bill Pilczuk	USA
100 m freestyle	Alexander Popov	Russia
200 m freestyle	Michael Klim	Australia
400 m freestyle	Ian Thorpe	Australia
1500 m freestyle	Grant Hackett	Australia
100 m backstroke	Lenny Krayzelburg	USA
200 m backstroke	Lenny Krayzelburg	USA
100 m breaststroke	Frederik Deburghgraeve	Belgium
200 m breaststroke	Kurt Grote	USA
100 m butterfly	Michael Klim	Australia
200 m butterfly	Denis Sylantyev	Ukraine
200 m individual medley	Marcel Wouda	Netherlands
400 m individual medley	Tom Dolan	USA
4 × 100 m freestyle medley		USA
4 × 200 m freestyle medley		Australia
4 × 100 m medley relay		Australia
springboard diving	Zhuocheng Yu	China
highboard diving	Dmitri Sautin	Russia

Swimming and Diving
World Champions 1998 (Women)

Event	Athlete	Country
50 m freestyle	Amy Van Dyken	USA
100 m freestyle	Jenny Thompson	USA
200 m freestyle	Claudia Poll	Costa Rica
400 m freestyle	Chen Yan	China
800 m freestyle	Brooke Bennett	USA
100 m backstroke	Lea Maurier	USA
200 m backstroke	Roxanna Maracineanu	France
100 m breaststroke	Kristy Kowal	USA
200 m breaststroke	Agnes Kovacs	Hungary
100 m butterfly	Jenny Thompson	USA
200 m butterfly	Susie O'Neill	Australia
200 m individual medley	Wu Yanyan	China
400 m individual medley	Chen Yan	China
4 × 100 m freestyle relay		USA
4 × 200 m freestyle relay		Germany
4 × 100 m medley relay		USA
springboard diving	Irina Lashko	Russia
highboard diving	Oleana Zhupyna	Ukraine
synchronized swimming solo	Olga Sedakova	Russia
synchronized swimming duet		Russia
synchronized swimming team		Russia

Swimming
First to Swim the English Channel

Record	Swimmer	Nationality	Date	Time taken
first person	Matthew Webb	English	25 August 1875	21 hours 45 minutes
first woman	Gertrude Ederle	American	6 August 1926	14 hours 31 minutes
fastest person	Chad Hundeby	American	1994	7 hours 17 minutes
fastest woman	Penny Lee Dean	American	1978	7 hours 40 minutes
most crossings (39)	Alison Streeter	English	–	–
most crossings by a man (31)	Mike Read	English	–	–

Swimming
World Records (Men)

As of 23 September 2000.

Category	Name	Country
50 m freestyle	Aleksandr Popov	Russia
100 m freestyle	Pierre van der Hoogenband	Netherlands
200 m freestyle	Pierre van der Hoogenband	Netherlands
400 m freestyle	Ian Thorpe	Australia
800 m freestyle	Kieran Perkins	Australia
1,500 m freestyle	Kieran Perkins	Australia
50 m backstroke	Lenny Krayzelburg	USA
100 m backstroke	Lenny Krayzelburg	USA
200 m backstroke	Lenny Krayzelburg	USA
100 m breaststroke	Roman Sloudnov	Russia
200 m breaststroke	Mike Barrowman	USA
50 m butterfly	George Huegill	Australia
100 m butterfly	Michael Klim	Australia
200 m butterfly	Tom Malchow	USA
200 m individual medley	Jani Sievinen	Finland
400 m individual medley	Tom Dolan	USA
4 × 100 m freestyle relay		Australia
4 × 200 m freestyle relay		Australia
4 × 100 m medley relay		USA

Swimming
World Records (Women)

As of 23 September 2000.

Category	Name	Country
50 m freestyle	Inge de Bruijn	Netherlands
100 m freestyle	Inge de Bruijn	Netherlands
200 m freestyle	Franziska Van Almsick	Germany
400 m freestyle	Janet Evans	USA
800 m freestyle	Janet Evans	USA
1,500 m freestyle	Janet Evans	USA
50 m backstroke	Sandra Voker	Germany
100 m backstroke	Cihong He	China
200 m backstroke	Kristina Egerszegi	Hungary
50 m breaststroke	Penelope Heyns	South Africa
100 m breaststroke	Penelope Heyns	South Africa
200 m breaststroke	Penelope Heyns	South Africa
50 m butterfly	Inge de Bruijn	Netherlands
100 m butterfly	Inge de Bruijn	Netherlands
200 m butterfly	Inge de Bruijn	Netherlands
200 m individual medley	Yanyan Wu	China
400 m individual medley	Yana Klochkova	Ukraine
4 × 100 m freestyle relay		USA
4 × 200 m freestyle relay		East Germany
4 × 100 m medley relay		USA

Table Tennis
Most Corbillon Cup Winners

Wins	Country	Year(s)
12	China	1965–97
8	Japan	1952–71
5	Romania	1950–56
3	Czechoslovakia	1935–38
2	Germany	1933–39
2	USA	1937–49
2	England	1947–48
1	South Korea	1973
1	Korea (unified team)	1991
1	USSR	1969

Table Tennis
Most Wins in the Swaythling Cup

Wins	Country	Year(s)
12	Hungary	1926–79
12	China	1961–97
7	Japan	1954–69
6	Czechoslovakia	1932–51
4	Sweden	1973–93
1	Australia	1936
1	USA	1937
1	England	1953

Table Tennis

World Champions and Winners of the Corbillon Cup for Women's Teams

Year	Winner
1981	China
1983	China
1985	China
1987	China
1989	China
1991	Korea (unified team)
1993	China
1995	China
1997	China
1999	no competition

Table Tennis

World Championship Doubles (Men)

Winners	Country	Year
Cia Zhenhua and Li Zhenshi	China	1981
Dragutin Surbek and Zoran Kalinic	Yugoslavia	1983
Mikael Applegren and Ulf Carlsson	Sweden	1985
Chen Longcan and Wei Quinguang	China	1987
Jaerg Rosskopf and Stefen Fetzner	FRG	1989
Peter Karlsson and Tomas von Scheele	Sweden	1991
Wang Tao and Lu Lin	China	1993
Wang Tao and Lu Lin	China	1995
Liu Guoliang and Kong Linghui	China	1997
Liu Guoliang and Kong Linghui	China	1999

Table Tennis

World Championship Doubles (Women)

Winners	Country	Year
Zhang Deying and Cao Yanhua	China	1981
Shen Jianping and Dai Lili	China	1983
Dai Lili and Geng Lijuan	China	1985
Yang Young-Ja and Hyun Jung-Hwa	South Korea	1987
Qiao Hong and Deng Yaping	China	1989
Chen Zhie and Gao Jun	China	1991
Liu Wei and Qiao Yunping	China	1993
Qiao Hong and Deng Yaping	China	1995
Deng Yaping and Yang Ying Liu	China	1997
Li Ju and Wang Nan	China	1999

Table Tennis

World Championship Mixed Doubles

Winners	Country	Year
Xie Saike and Huang Junqun	China	1981
Guo Yuehua and Ni Xialian	China	1983
Cai Zhenua and Cao Yanhua	China	1985
Hui Jun and Geng Lijuan	China	1987
Yoo Nam-Kyu and Hyun Jung-Hwa	South Korea	1989
Wang Tao and Liu Wei	China	1991
Wang Tao and Liu Wei	China	1993

Table Tennis: World Championship Mixed Doubles (*continued*)

Winners	Country	Year
Wang Tao and Liu Wei	China	1995
Wu Na and Liu Guoliang	China	1997
Xhang Yingying and Ma Lin	China	1999

Table Tennis
World Championship Singles (Men)

Winner	Country	Year
Guo Yuehua	China	1981
Guo Yuehua	China	1983
Jiang Jialiang	China	1985
Jiang Jialiang	China	1987
Jan Ove-Waldner	Sweden	1989
Jorgen Persson	Sweden	1991
Jean-Philippe Gatien	France	1993
Kong Linghui	China	1995
Jan Ove-Waldner	Sweden	1997
Liu Guoliang	China	1999

Table Tennis
World Championship Singles (Women)

Winner	Country	Year
Tong Ling	China	1981
Cao Yanhua	China	1983
Cao Yanhua	China	1985
He Zhili	China	1987
Qiao Hong	China	1989
Deng Yaping	China	1991
Hyun Jung-Hwa	South Korea	1993
Deng Yaping	China	1995
Deng Yaping	China	1997
Wang Nan	China	1999

Tarot Cards
Selected Cards and their Meanings

Card	Meaning
Fool	beginning, spontaneity, apparent folly, faith
Magician	action, conscious awareness, concentration, power
High Priestess	nonaction, unconscious awareness, potential, mystery
Empress	mothering, abundance, senses, nature
Emperor	fathering, structure, authority, regulation
Hierophant	education, belief systems, conformity, group identification
Lovers	relationship, sexuality, personal beliefs, values
Chariot	victory, will, self-assertion, hard control
Strength	strength, patience, compassion, soft control
Hermit	introspection, searching, guidance, solitude
Wheel of Fortune	destiny, turning point, movement, personal vision
Justice	justice, responsibility, decision, cause and effect
Hanged Man	letting go, reversal, suspension, sacrifice
Death	ending, transition, elimination, inexorable forces
Temperance	temperance, balance, health, combination

(*continued*)

Tarot Cards: Selected Cards and their Meanings (*continued*)

Card	Meaning
Devil	bondage, materialism, hopelessness, ignorance
Tower	sudden change, release, downfall, revelation
Star	hope, inspiration, generosity, serenity
Moon	fear, illusion, imagination, bewilderment
Sun	enlightenment, greatness, vitality, assurance
Judgement	judgement, rebirth, inner calling, absolution
World	integration, accomplishment, involvement, fulfillment
Ace of Wands	creative force, enthusiasm, confidence, courage
Ace of Cups	emotional force, intuition, intimacy, love
Ace of Swords	mental force, truth, justice, fortitude
Ace of Pentacles	material force, prosperity, practicality, trust

Team Sports
Numbers of Players per Side

Game/sport	Number on each team
American football	11
Australian rules football	18
bandy	11
baseball	9
basketball	5
Canadian football	12
canoe polo	5
cricket	11
field hockey	11
Gaelic football	15
hurling	15
ice hockey	6
korfball	12
lacrosse	10 (men) or 12 (women)
netball	7
polo	4
roller hockey	5
rounders	9
rugby union	15
shinty	12
soccer	11
softball	9
team handball	7
volleyball	6
water polo	7

Ten-pin Bowling
World Championship (Men)

Year	Player (country)
1963	Les Zikes (USA)
1967	David Pond (UK)
1971	Ed Luther (USA)
1975	Bud Stewart (USA)
1979	Ollie Ongtawco (Philippines)
1983	Armado Marino (Colombia)
1987	Rolland Patrick (France)
1991	Ma Ying-chei (Taiwan)
1995	Marc Doi (Canada)
1999	Gery Verbuggen (Belgium)

Ten-pin Bowling

World Championship (Women)

Year	Player (country)
1963	Helen Shablis (USA)
1967	Helen Weston (USA)
1971	Ashie Gonzales (Puerto Rico)
1975	Annedore Haefker (FRG)
1979	Lita de la Rosa (Philippines)
1983	Lena Sulkanen (Sweden)
1987	Edda Piccini (Italy)
1991	Martina Beckel (Germany)
1995	Debby Ship (Canada)
1999	Kelly Kulick (USA)

Tennis

Davis Cup Winners

Year	Winner	Runner-up	Score
2000	Spain	Australia	3–1
1999	Australia	France	3–2
1998	Sweden	Italy	4–1
1997	Sweden	USA	5–0
1996	France	Sweden	3–2
1995	USA	Russia	3–2
1994	Sweden	Russia	4–1
1993	Germany	Australia	4–1
1992	USA	Switzerland	3–1
1991	France	USA	3–1

Tennis

Female Olympic Gold Medallists

Tennis was reintroduced as a medal sport in 1988 after an absence of 64 years.

Year	Name	Country	Year	Name	Country
Singles			**Doubles**		
2000	Venus Williams	USA	2000	Venus Williams and Serena Williams	USA
1996	Lindsay Davenport	USA	1996	Gigi Fernandez and Mary Joe Fernandez	USA
1992	Jennifer Capriati	USA	1992	Gigi Fernandez and Mary Joe Fernandez	USA
1988	Steffi Graf	West Germany	1988	Pam Shriver and Zina Garrison	USA

Tennis

Male Olympic Gold Medallists

Tennis was reintroduced as a medal sport in 1988 after an absence of 64 years.

Year	Name	Country	Year	Name	Country
Singles			**Doubles**		
2000	Yevgeny Kafelnikov	Russia	2000	Daniel Nestor and Sebastien Lareau	Canada
1996	Andre Agassi	USA	1996	Todd Woodbridge and Mark Woodforde	Australia
1992	Marc Rosset	Switzerland	1992	Boris Becker and Michael Stich	Germany
1988	Miloslav Mecir	Czechoslovakia	1988	Ken Flack and Robert Seguso	USA

Tennis

Most Successful Davis Cup Countries

Wins	Country	Period (years)
31	USA	1900–95
21	Australia	1939–99
8	France	1927–96
7	Sweden	1975–98
6	Australasia	1907–19
5	British Isles	1903–12
4	Great Britain	1933–36
3	Germany	1988–93
1	Czechoslovakia	1980
1	Italy	1976
1	South Africa	1974
1	Spain	2000

Tennis

Official ATP Men's World Rankings at November 2000

Rank	Player (country)
1	Marat Safin (Russia)
2	Gustavo Kuerten (Brazil)
3	Pete Sampras (USA)
4	Magnus Norman (Sweden)
5	Yevgeny Kafelnikov (Russia)
6	Lleyton Hewitt (Australia)
7	Alex Corretja (Spain)
8	Andre Agassi (USA)
9	Thomas Enqvist (Sweden)
10	Tim Henman (UK)
11	Mark Philippoussis (Australia)
12	Juan Carlos Ferrero (Spain)

Tennis

Official WTA Women's World Rankings at November 2000

Rank	Player (country)	Rank	Player (country)
1	Martina Hingis (Switzerland)	7	Mary Pierce (France)
2	Lindsay Davenport (USA)	8	Anna Kournikova (Russia)
3	Venus Williams (USA)	9	Arantxa Sanchez-Vicario (Spain)
4	Monica Seles (USA)	10	Nathalie Tauziat (France)
5	Conchita Martinez (Spain)	11	Amanda Coetzer (South Africa)
6	Serena Williams (USA)	12	Elena Dementieva (Russia)

Tennis

US Open Champions

Year	Men	Women
2000	Marat Safin (Russia)	Venus Williams (USA)
1999	Andre Agassi (USA)	Serena Williams (USA)
1998	Patrick Rafter (Australia)	Lindsay Davenport (USA)
1997	Patrick Rafter (Australia)	Martina Hingis (Switzerland)
1996	Pete Sampras (USA)	Steffi Graf (Germany)
1995	Pete Sampras (USA)	Steffi Graf (Germany)
1994	Andre Agassi (USA)	Arantxa Sanchez Vicario (Spain)
1993	Pete Sampras (USA)	Steffi Graf (Germany)
1992	Stefan Edberg (Sweden)	Monica Seles (Yugoslavia)
1991	Stefan Edberg (Sweden)	Monica Seles (Yugoslavia)

Tennis
Wimbledon Championships Men's Doubles Recent Winners

Year	Winners
1988	Ken Flach and Robert Seguso (USA)
1989	John Fitzgerald (Australia) and Anders Jarryd (Sweden)
1990	Rick Leach and Jim Pugh (USA)
1991	John Fitzgerald (Australia) and Anders Jarryd (Sweden)
1992	John McEnroe (USA) and Michael Stich (Germany)
1993	Todd Woodbridge and Mark Woodforde (Australia)
1994	Todd Woodbridge and Mark Woodforde (Australia)
1995	Todd Woodbridge and Mark Woodforde (Australia)
1996	Todd Woodbridge and Mark Woodforde (Australia)
1997	Todd Woodbridge and Mark Woodforde (Australia)
1998	Jacco Eltingh and Paul Haarhuis (Holland)
1999	Mahesh Bhupathi and Leander Paes (India)
2000	Todd Woodbridge and Mark Woodforde (Australia)

Tennis
Wimbledon Championships Men's Singles Champions

Year	Name	Country	Year	Name	Country
2000	Pete Sampras	USA	1995	Pete Sampras	USA
1999	Pete Sampras	USA	1994	Pete Sampras	USA
1998	Pete Sampras	USA	1993	Pete Sampras	USA
1997	Pete Sampras	USA	1992	Andre Agassi	USA
1996	Richard Krajicek	Netherlands	1991	Michael Stich	Germany

Tennis
Wimbledon Championships Mixed Doubles Recent Winners

Year	Winners
1988	Zina Garrison and Sherwood Stewart (USA)
1989	Jana Novotna (Czechoslovakia) and Jim Pugh (USA)
1990	Zina Garrison and Rick Leach (USA)
1991	Elizabeth Smylie and John Fitzgerald (Australia)
1992	Larissa Savchenko-Neiland (Latvia) and Cyril Suk (Czechoslovakia)
1993	Martina Navratilova (USA) and Mark Woodforde (Australia)
1994	Helena Sukova (Czech Republic) and Todd Woodbridge (Australia)
1995	Martina Navratilova (USA) and Jonathan Stark (USA)
1996	Helena Sukova and Cyril Suk (Czech Republic)
1997	Helena Sukova and Cyril Suk (Czech Republic)
1998	Serena Williams (USA) and Max Mirnyi (Belarus)
1999	Lisa Raymond (USA) and Leander Paes (India)
2000	Kimberley Po and Donald Johnson (USA)

Tennis

Wimbledon Championships Women's Doubles Recent Winners

Year	Winners
1988	Steffi Graf (FRG) and Gabriela Sabatini (Argentina)
1989	Jana Novotna and Helena Sukova (Czechoslovakia)
1990	Jana Novotna and Helena Sukova (Czechoslovakia)
1991	Natalya Zvereva and Larissa Savchenko (USSR)
1992	Gigi Fernandez (USA) and Natalya Zvereva (CIS)
1993	Gigi Fernandez (USA) and Natalya Zvereva (CIS)
1994	Gigi Fernandez (USA) and Natalya Zvereva (CIS)
1995	Arantxa Sanchez Vicario (Spain) and Jana Novotna (Czech Republic)
1996	Helena Sukova (Czech Republic) and Martina Hingis (Switzerland)
1997	Gigi Fernandez (USA) and Natalya Zvereva (Belarus)
1998	Jana Novotna (Czech Republic) and Martina Hingis (Switzerland)
1999	Lindsay Davenport and Corina Morariu (USA)
2000	Venus and Serena Williams (USA)

Tennis

Wimbledon Championships Women's Singles Champions

Year	Name	Country
2000	Venus Williams	USA
1999	Lindsay Davenport	USA
1998	Jana Novotna	Czech Republic
1997	Martina Hingis	Switzerland
1996	Steffi Graf	Germany
1995	Steffi Graf	Germany
1994	Conchita Martinez	Spain
1993	Steffi Graf	Germany
1992	Steffi Graf	Germany
1991	Steffi Graf	Germany

Tennis

Winners of Most Grand Slam Men's Singles Titles

As of November 2000. The Grand Slam tournaments are: the Australian Open, the French Open, Wimbledon, and the US Open.

Titles	Player (country)
13	Pete Sampras (USA)
12	Roy Emerson (Australia)
11	Björn Borg (Sweden)
11	Rod Laver (Australia)
10	Bill Tilden (USA)
8	Jimmy Connors (USA)
8	Max Decugis (France)
8	Ivan Lendl (Czechoslovakia)
8	Fred Perry (UK)
8	Ken Rosewall (Australia)
7	Henri Cochet (France)
7	René Lacoste (France)
7	William Larned (USA)
7	John McEnroe (USA)
7	John Newcombe (Australia)
7	William Renshaw (UK)
7	Richard Sears (USA)
7	Mats Wilander (Sweden)

Tennis
Winners of Most Grand Slam Titles

As of November 2000. The Grand Slam tournaments are: the Australian Open, the French Open, Wimbledon, and the US Open. The totals given here include singles, doubles, and mixed doubles titles.

Titles	Player (country)
66	Margaret Court (Australia)
56	Martina Navratilova (Czechoslovakia/USA)
39	Billie Jean King (USA)
37	Margaret Du Pont (USA)
35	Louis Brough (USA)
35	Doris Hart (USA)
31	Helen Wills-Moody (USA)
28	Roy Emerson (Australia)
26	Elizabeth Ryan (USA)
25	John Newcombe (Australia)

Tennis
Winners of Most Grand Slam Women's Singles Titles

As of November 2000. The Grand Slam tournaments are: the Australian Open, the French Open, Wimbledon, and the US Open.

Titles	Player (country)
24	Margaret Court (Australia)
22	Steffi Graf (Germany)
19	Helen Wills-Moody (USA)
18	Chris Evert-Lloyd (USA)
18	Martina Navratilova (USA)
12	Billie Jean King (USA)
12	Suzanne Lenglen (France)
9	Maureen Connolly (USA)
9	Monica Seles (USA)
8	Molla Mallory (USA)

Tennis
Winners of the Singles Grand Slam

The Grand Slam tournaments are: the Australian Open, the French Open, Wimbledon, and the US Open. The Grand Slam is achieved when all four titles are held simultaneously; more strictly defined, the Grand Slam is the achievement of all four titles within a calendar year. The latter is indicated where a single year is given.

Grand Slams	Player (country)	Years
3	Margaret Court (Australia)	1969–70, 1970, 1970–71
3	Steffi Graf (West Germany/Germany)	1988, 1988–89, 1993–94
2	Donald Budge (USA)	1937–38, 1938
2	Maureen Connolly (USA)	1952–53, 1953
2	Rod Laver (Australia)	1962, 1969
1	Martina Navratilova (USA)	1983–84

Tourism
Highest Spending Countries

Country	Total expenditure (US$ millions)	Country	Total expenditure (US$ millions)
Germany	47,304	Italy	12,366
USA	44,825	Netherlands	11,050
Japan	36,737	Austria	9,500
UK	24,625	Canada	9,484
France	16,038	Taiwan	8,595

 Sport, Games, and Leisure **535**

Tourism
Most Popular Tourist Destinations

Country	Money earned from tourism (US$ millions)	Country	Money earned from tourism (US$ millions)
USA	75,100	Germany	16,400
Italy	30,000	Austria	12,400
France	28,000	China	12,100
Spain	27,200	Australia	9,300
UK	20,600	Hong Kong	9,200

Tourism
Vaccinations for Travellers

Always seek advice from a qualified medical practitioner before travelling.

Disease	Vaccination and timing
cholera	2 shots 1–4 weeks before departure
hepatitis A	1 shot just before departure, or 2 shots 2 months before departure, followed by 3rd shot 6–12 months later
hepatitis B	2 shots before departure, with 3rd shot 4 months later
malaria	no vaccination available; tablets from 1 week before to 4 weeks after travel
polio	3–4 doses of oral vaccine, or 3–4 shots of vaccine up to 7 months before departure
rabies	3-dose series of shots, 5 weeks before departure
tetanus	2 shots 1 month apart, then 3rd shot 6 months later
typhoid	1–2 shots 4–6 weeks apart; or 1 shot; or 4 oral doses on alternate days; all 5–7 weeks before departure
yellow fever	1 shot at least 10 days before departure

Tourism
World's Major Destinations

Country	Number of arrivals in 1999 (thousands)
France	71,400
Spain	51,960
USA	46,985
Italy	35,840
China	27,050
UK	25,740
Mexico	20,215
Canada	19,555
Poland	17,940
Germany	17,095

Toys
Top US Toys

Toy	Manufacturer
yo-yo	various
crayons	Crayola
Barbie	Mattel
Lionel trains	Lionel
Play-Doh	Hasbro
Erector set	Irwin
frisbee	Wham-O
Lincoln Logs	K'Nex
slinky	James Industries Inc
Hot Wheels	Mattel

Winter Olympics
Leading Medal-winning Countries

Country	Gold	Silver	Bronze	Total	Country	Gold	Silver	Bronze	Total
Norway	83	87	69	239	Sweden	39	28	35	102
USSR[1]	87	63	62	212	Switzerland	29	31	32	92
USA	59	59	41	159	Canada	25	25	29	79
Austria	39	53	53	145	Italy	27	27	23	77
Finland	38	49	48	135	Netherlands	19	23	19	61
Germany[2]	66	38	32	116	France	18	17	26	61
GDR	39	36	35	110					

[1] Includes unified team of 1992.

[2] Does not include medals won by the FRG between 1968 and 1988 (39 in total), or those won by the GDR (listed separately).

Winter Olympics
Leading Medal-winning Men

The totals listed include all medals, gold, silver, and bronze.

Medals	Athlete (country)	Sport	Years
12	Bjørn Dæhlie (Norway)	Nordic skiing	1992–98
9	Sixten Jernberg (Sweden)	Nordic skiing	1956–64
7	Ivar Ballangrud (Norway)	speed skating	1928–36
7	Veikko Hakulinen (Finland)	Nordic skiing	1952–60
7	Eero Mäntyranta (Finland)	Nordic skiing	1960–68
7	Bogdan Musiol (GDR/Germany)	bobsledding	1980–92
7	Vladimir Smirnov (USSR/Unified Team/Kazakhstan)	Nordic skiing	1988–98
7	Clas Thunberg (Finland)	speed skating	1924–28

Winter Olympics
Leading Medal-winning Women

The totals listed include all medals, gold, silver, and bronze.

Medals	Athlete (country)	Sport	Years
10	Raisa Smetanina (USSR/Unified Team)	Nordic skiing	1976–92
9	Lyubov Yegorova (Unified Team/Russia)	Nordic skiing	1992–94
8	Marja-Liisa Hämäläinen-Kirvesniemi (Finland)	Nordic skiing	1980–98
8	Karin Kania-Enke (GDR)	speed skating	1980–88
8	Galina Kulakova (USSR)	Nordic skiing	1968–76
8	Gunda Niemann-Stirnemann (GDR/Germany)	speed skating	1992–98
7	Manuela Di Centa (Italy)	Nordic skiing	1988–98
7	Larissa Lazutina (Unified Team/Russia)	Nordic skiing	1992–98
7	Andrea Mitscherlich-Schöne-Ehrlich (GDR)	speed skating	1976–88
7	Yelena Valbe (Unified Team/Russia)	Nordic skiing	1992–98

Winter Olympics
Venues

Year	Venue	Year	Venue
1924	Chamonix, France	1972	Sapporo, Japan
1928	St Moritz, Switzerland	1976	Innsbruck, Austria
1932	Lake Placid (NY), USA	1980	Lake Placid (NY), USA
1936	Garmisch-Partenkirchen, Germany	1984	Sarajevo, Yugoslavia
1948	St Moritz, Switzerland	1988	Calgary, Alberta, Canada
1952	Oslo, Norway	1992	Albertville, France
1956	Cortina d'Ampezzo, Italy	1994	Lillehammer, Norway
1960	Squaw Valley (CA), USA	1998	Nagano, Japan
1964	Innsbruck, Austria	2002	Salt Lake City (UT), USA
1968	Grenoble, France	2006	Turin, Italy

Wrestling
Freestyle Wrestling World Championships

The World Championships are not held in Olympic years, the Olympic champion being deemed that year's world champion. The over 130 kg weight category was formerly over 100 kg.

Year	Wrestler (country)
1988	David Gobedzhishvilli (USSR)
1989	Ali Reiza Soleimani (Iran)
1990	David Gobedzhishvilli (USSR)
1991	Andreas Schroder (Germany)
1992	Bruce Baumgartner (USA)
1993	Bruce Baumgartner (USA)
1994	Mahmut Demir (Turkey)
1995	Bruce Baumgartner (USA)
1996	Mahmut Demir (Turkey)
1997	Zekeriya Güglü (Turkey)
1998	Alexis Rodriguez (Cuba)
1999	Stephen Neal (USA)
2000	David Moussoulbes (Russia)

Wrestling
Graeco-Roman Wrestling World Championships

The World Championships are not held in Olympic years, the Olympic champion being deemed that year's world champion. The over 130 kg weight category was formerly over 100 kg.

Year	Wrestler (country)
1988	Aleksandr Karelin (USSR)
1989	Aleksandr Karelin (USSR)
1990	Aleksandr Karelin (USSR)
1991	Aleksandr Karelin (USSR)
1992	Aleksandr Karelin (CIS)
1993	Aleksandr Karelin (Russia)
1994	Aleksandr Karelin (Russia)
1995	Aleksandr Karelin (Russia)
1996	Aleksandr Karelin (Russia)
1997	Aleksandr Karelin (Russia)
1998	Aleksandr Karelin (Russia)
1999	Aleksandr Karelin (Russia)
2000	Rulon Gardner (USA)

Wrestling

Winners of World and Olympic Titles

Titles	Wrestler	Style	Year(s)
12	Aleksandr Karelin (USSR/Russia)	Graeco-Roman	1988–99
10	Aleksandr Medved (USSR)	freestyle	1962–72
8	Sergey Beloglazov (USSR)	freestyle	1980–88
8	Arsen Fadzeyev (USSR)	freestyle	1983–92
8	Valentin Jordanov (Bulgaria)	freestyle	1983–96
7	Valeriy Rezantsev (USSR)	Graeco-Roman	1970–76
7	Makharbek Khadartsev (USSR)	freestyle	1986–92
6	Abdollah Movahed (Iran)	freestyle	1965–70
6	Levan Tediashvili (USSR)	freestyle	1971–76
6	Nikolay Ba Iboshin (USSR)	Graeco-Roman	1973–79
6	Soslan Andiyev (USSR)	freestyle	1973–80
6	John Smith (USA)	freestyle	1987–92
6	Leri Khabelov (USSR)	freestyle	1985–93

Yachting

Admiral's Cup Winners

Year	Country
1999	Netherlands
1997	USA
1995	Italy
1993	Germany
1991	France
1989	UK
1987	New Zealand
1985	West Germany
1983	West Germany
1981	UK

Yachting

America's Cup Winners

The yachts are from the USA unless otherwise stated.

Year	Winning yacht	Series	Challenger
2000	*NZL 60* (New Zealand)	5–0	*Luna Rossa* (Italy)
1995	*Black Magic* (New Zealand)	5–0	*Young America*
1992	*America*	4–1	*Il Moro di Venezia* (Italy)
1988	*Stars & Stripes*	2–0	*New Zealand* (New Zealand)
1987	*Stars & Stripes*	4–0	*Kookaburra III* (Australia)
1983	*Australia II* (Australia)	4–3	*Liberty*
1980	*Freedom*	4–1	*Australia* (Australia)
1977	*Courageous*	4–0	*Australia* (Australia)
1974	*Courageous*	4–0	*Southern Cross* (Australia)
1970	*Intrepid*	4–1	*Gretel II* (Australia)